T0366793

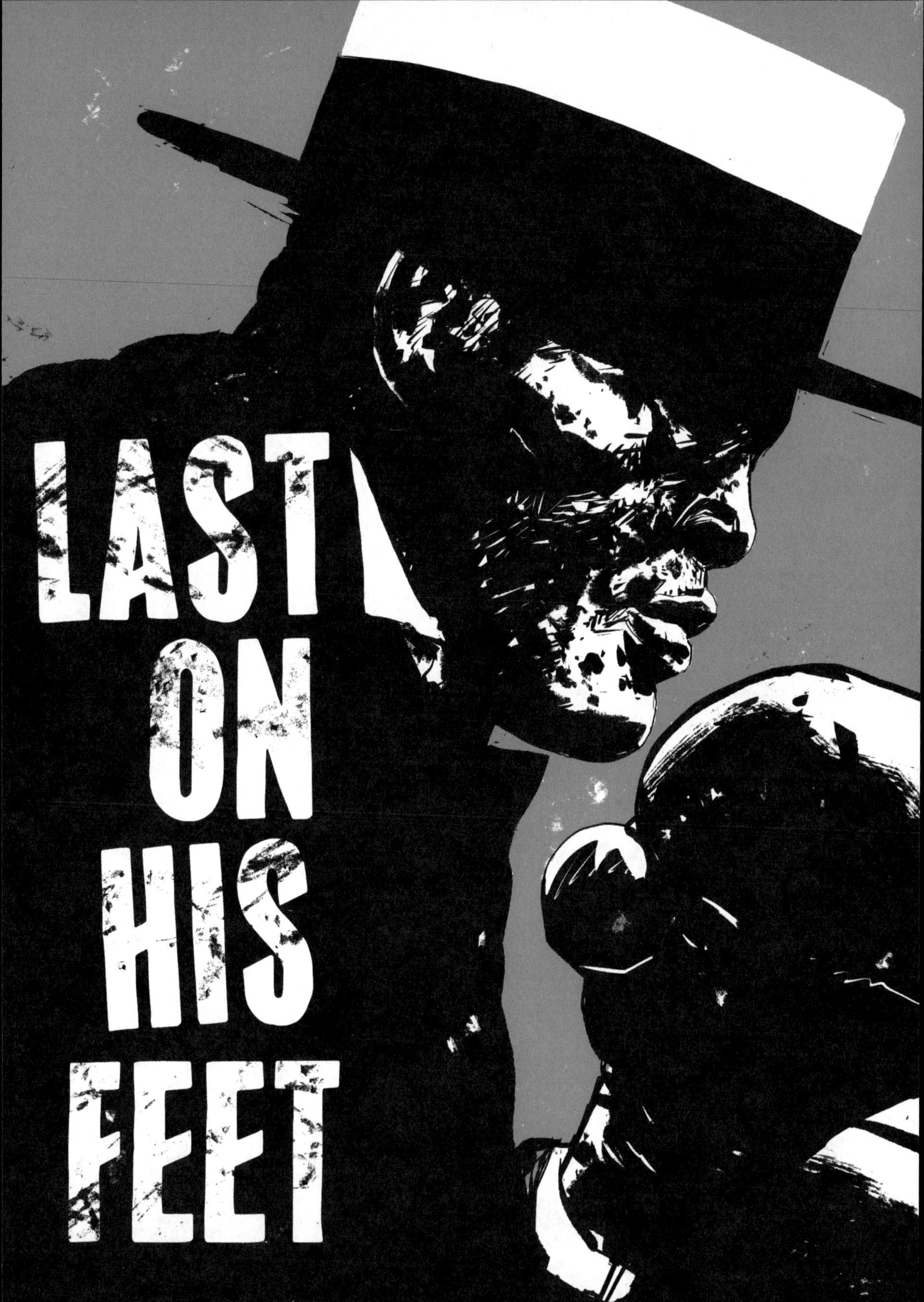
LAST
ON
HIS
FEET

ALSO BY YOUSSEF DAOUDI

Monk! Thelonious, Pannonica, and the Friendship
Behind a Musical Revolution

ALSO BY ADRIAN MATEJKA

Somebody Else Sold the World

Standing on the Verge & Maggot Brain

Map to the Stars

The Big Smoke

Mixology

The Devil's Garden

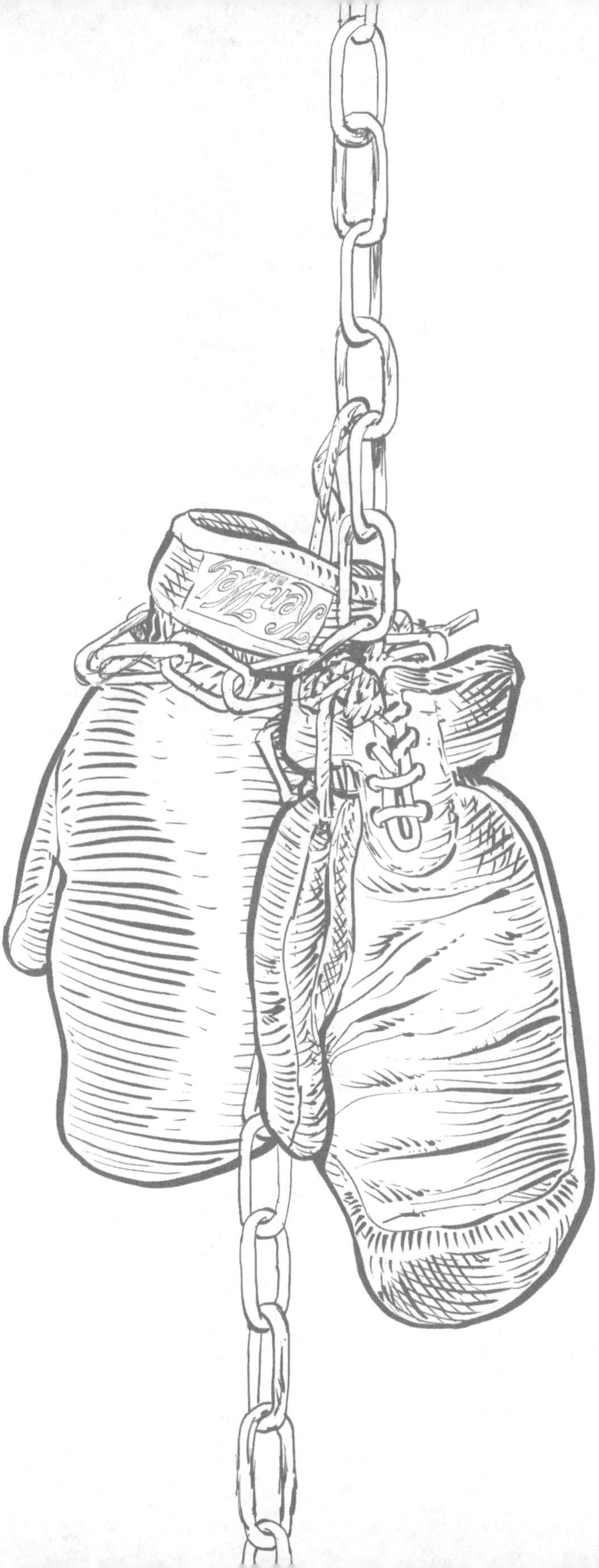
Ken-Wel
BRAND

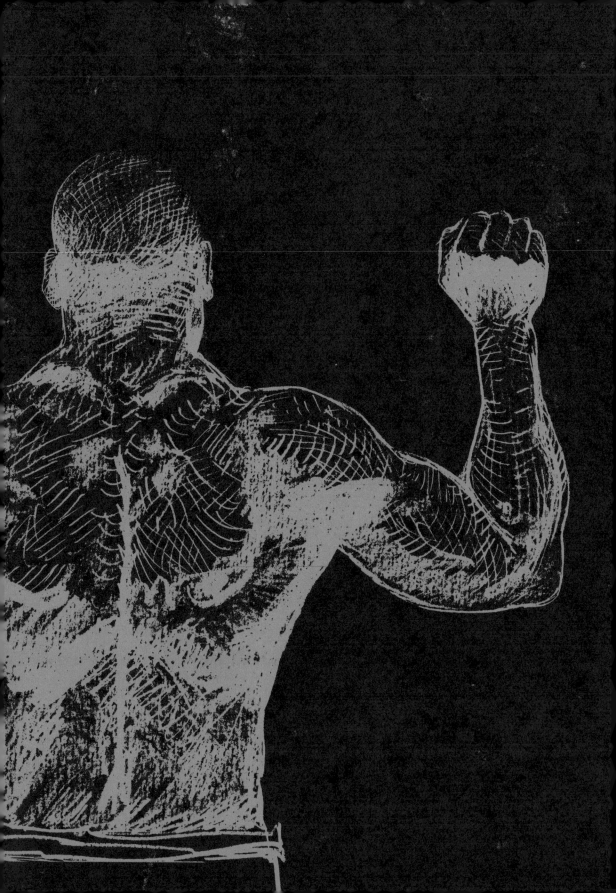

Art by
YOUSSEF DAOUDI

Poetics by
ADRIAN MATEJKA

LAST ON HIS FEET

Jack Johnson and the
Battle of the Century

Liveright Publishing Corporation

A Division of W. W. Norton & Company
Celebrating a Century of Independent Publishing

For information about permission to reproduce selections from this book,
write to Permissions, Liveright Publishing Corporation, a division of
W. W. Norton & Company, Inc., 500 Fifth Avenue, New York, NY 10110

For information about special discounts for bulk purchases, please contact
W. W. Norton Special Sales at specialsales@wwnorton.com or 800-233-4830

Manufacturing by Versa Press
Production manager: Anna Oler

ISBN 978-1-63149-558-8

Liveright Publishing Corporation
500 Fifth Avenue, New York, N.Y. 10110
www.wwnorton.com

W. W. Norton & Company Ltd.
15 Carlisle Street, London W1D 3BS

1 2 3 4 5 6 7 8 9 0

AUTHORS' NOTE

While this graphic novel is based on real events and includes
interpretations of documented incidents and conversations,
as well as other archival materials, please note that some
minor changes to locations and dates have been made for
narrative continuity. It is not our intention to disrespect the
histories in these pages. Rather, we wanted to make this
vital American story more available to
twenty-first-century audiences.

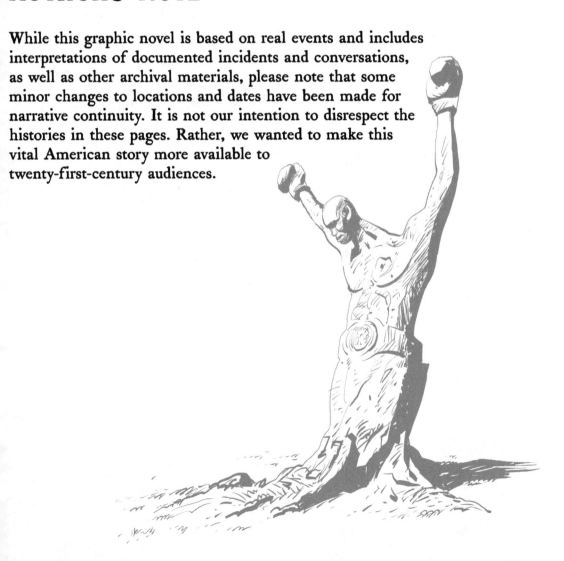

RENO
THE BIGGEST LITTLE
CITY ON THE MAP

MEN HAVE BEEN LOCKED IN COMBAT SINCE BEFORE THERE WAS MONEY IN IT.

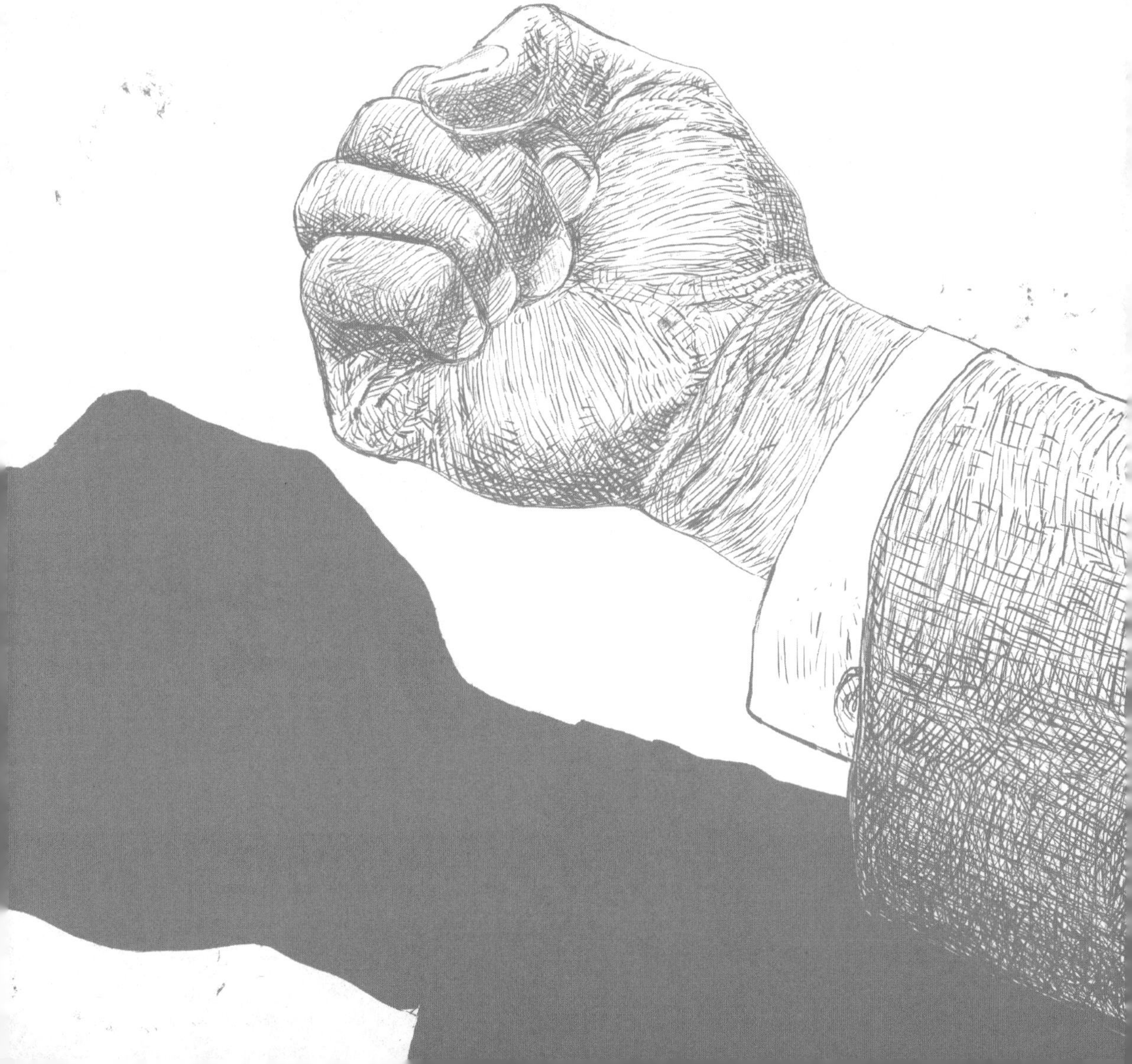

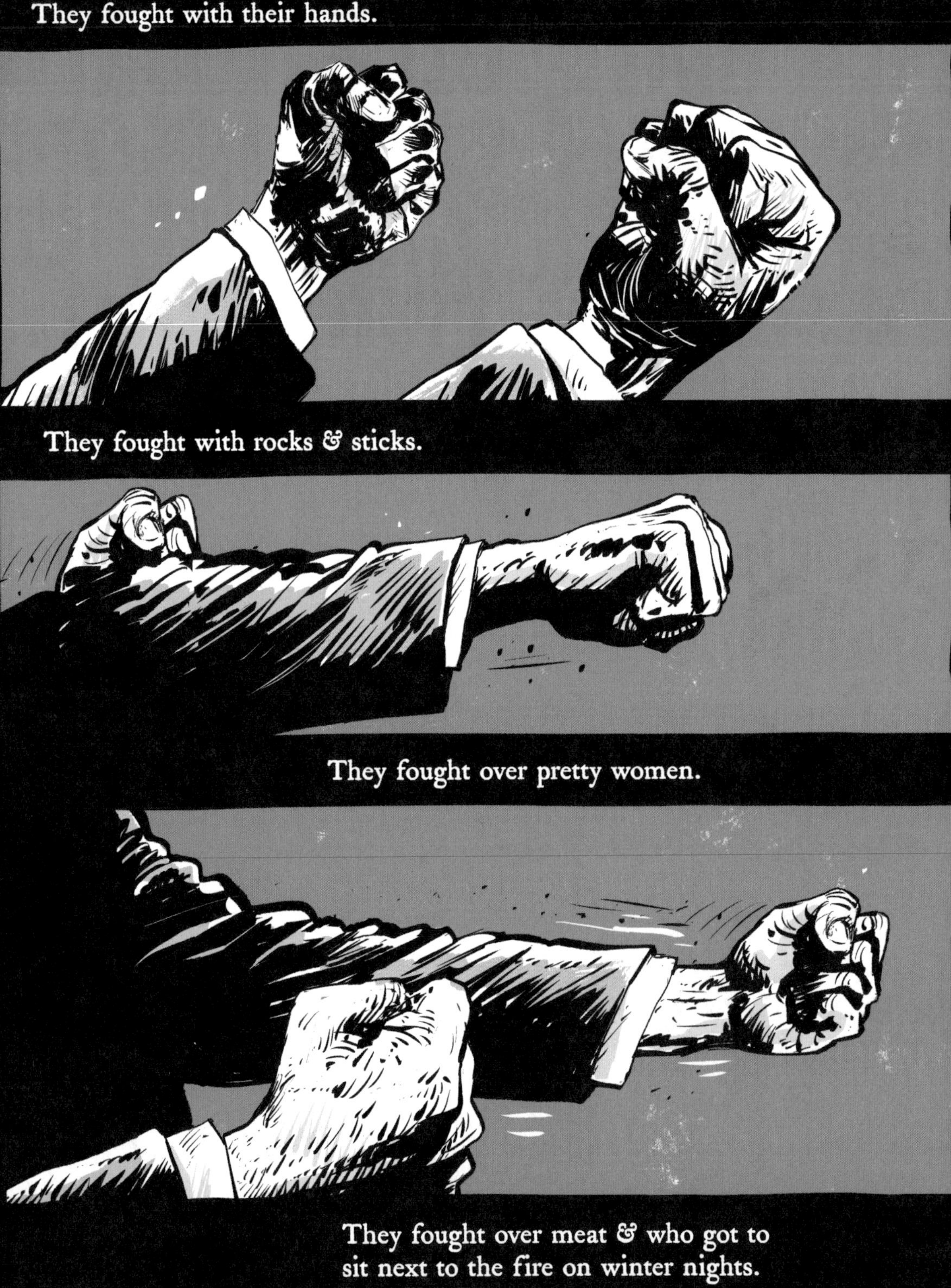
They fought with their hands.
They fought with rocks & sticks.
They fought over pretty women.
They fought over meat & who got to sit next to the fire on winter nights.

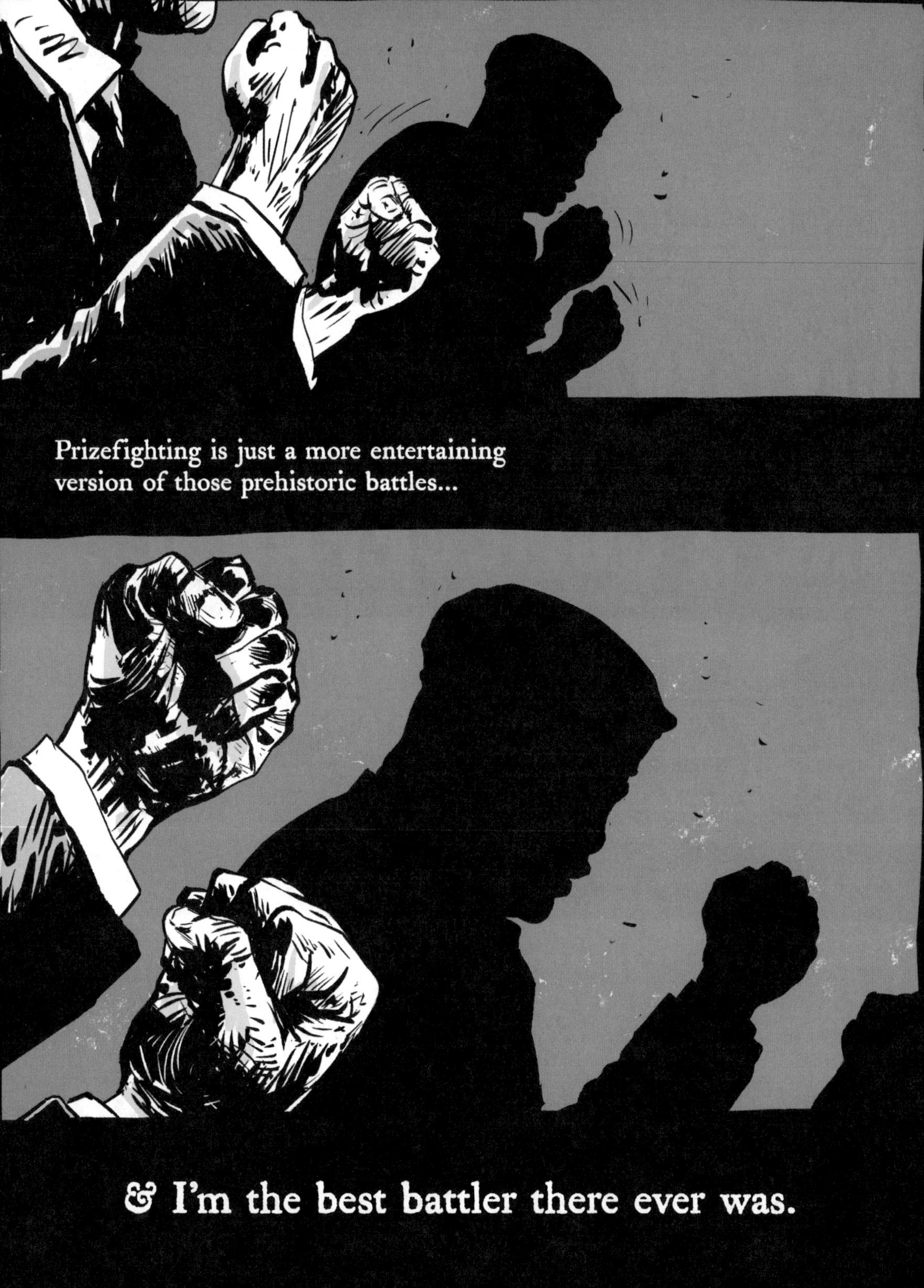
Prizefighting is just a more entertaining version of those prehistoric battles...
& I'm the best battler there ever was.

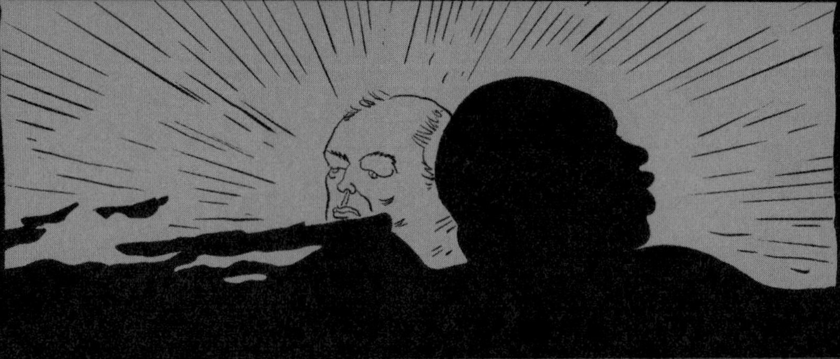

JULY 4TH, 1910, DAWN CAME LIKE A COMEUPPANCE...

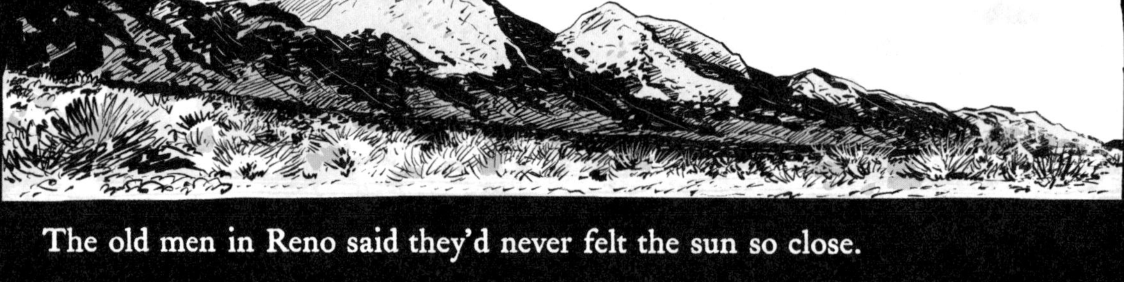

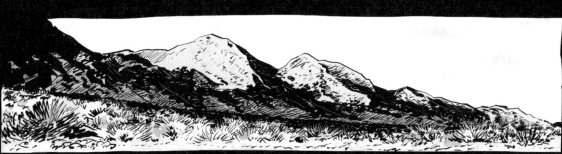

The old men in Reno said they'd never felt the sun so close.

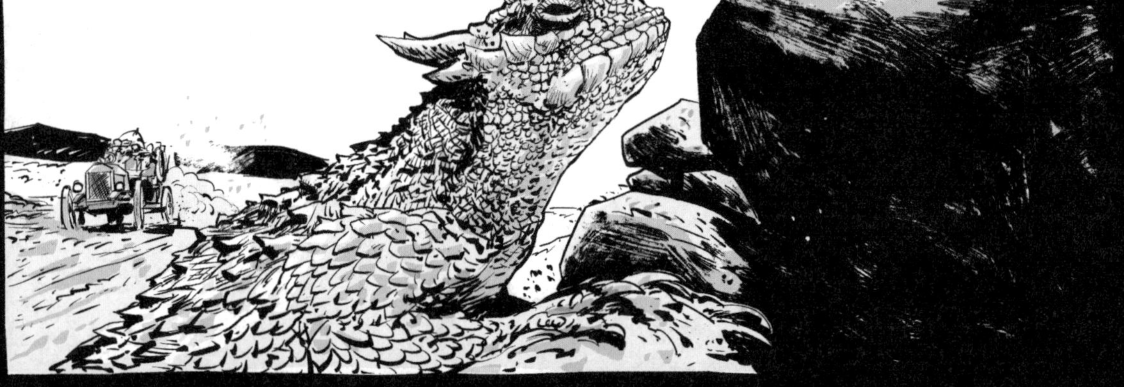

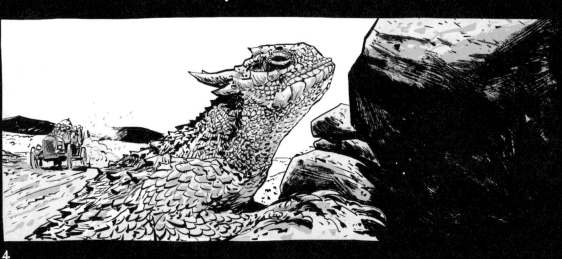

It was the kind of hot that makes water disappear from your glass like magic & boils sweat on the forehead. Eggs fried without a fire.

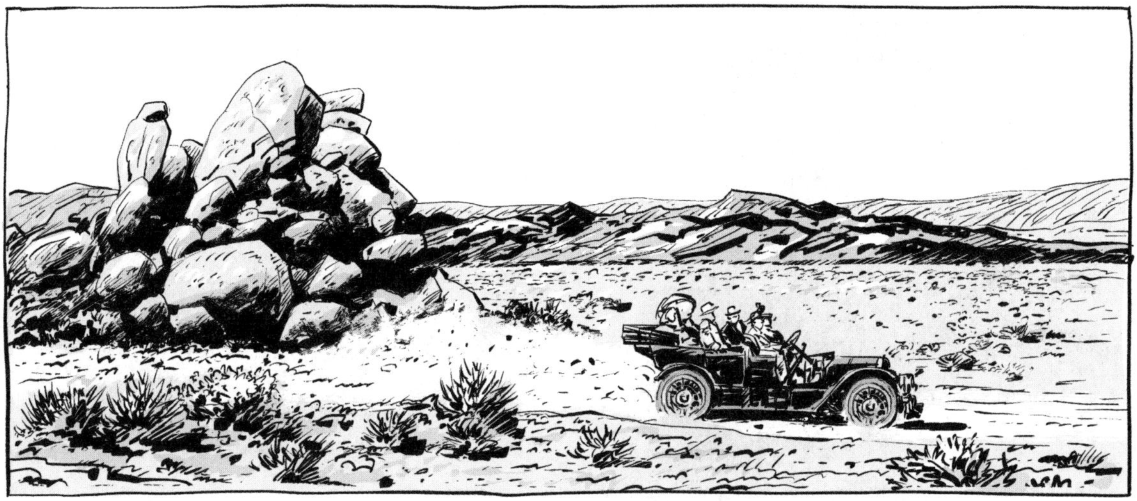

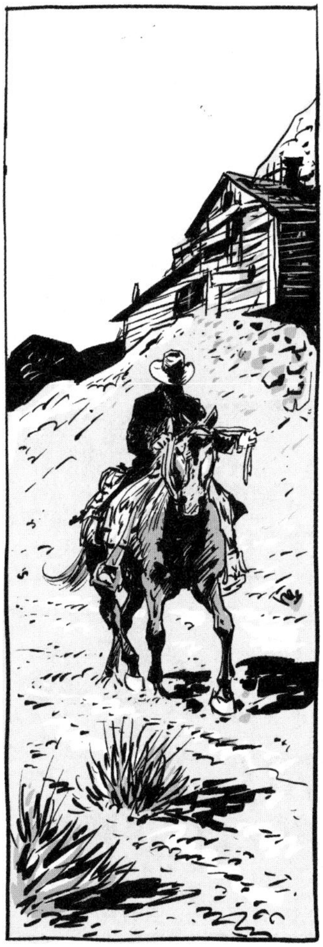

One man's cigar lit on its own.

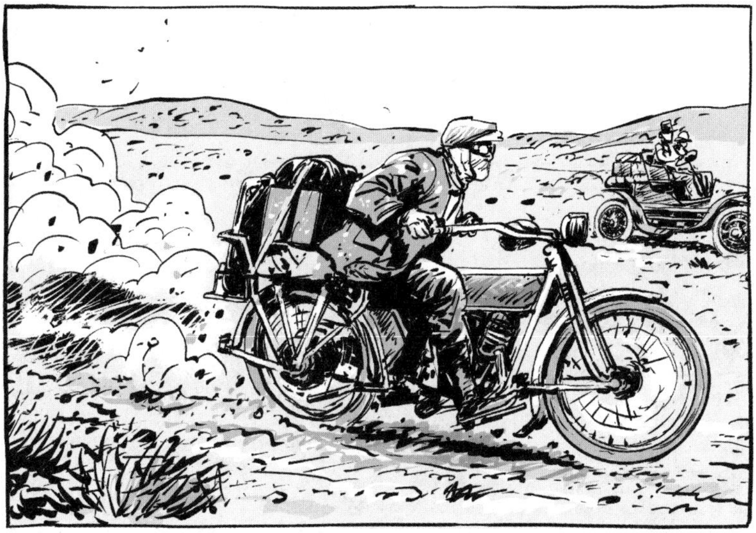

That didn't stop the 20,000 spectators who came in automobiles, on horseback & by horse-drawn wagon.

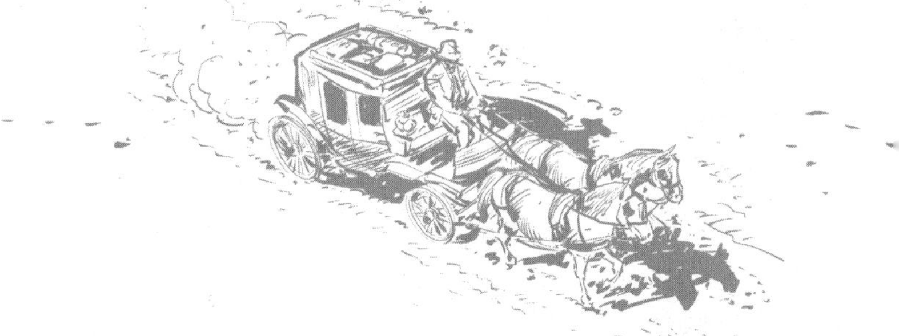

Trains ran from all parts of the country every 30 minutes.

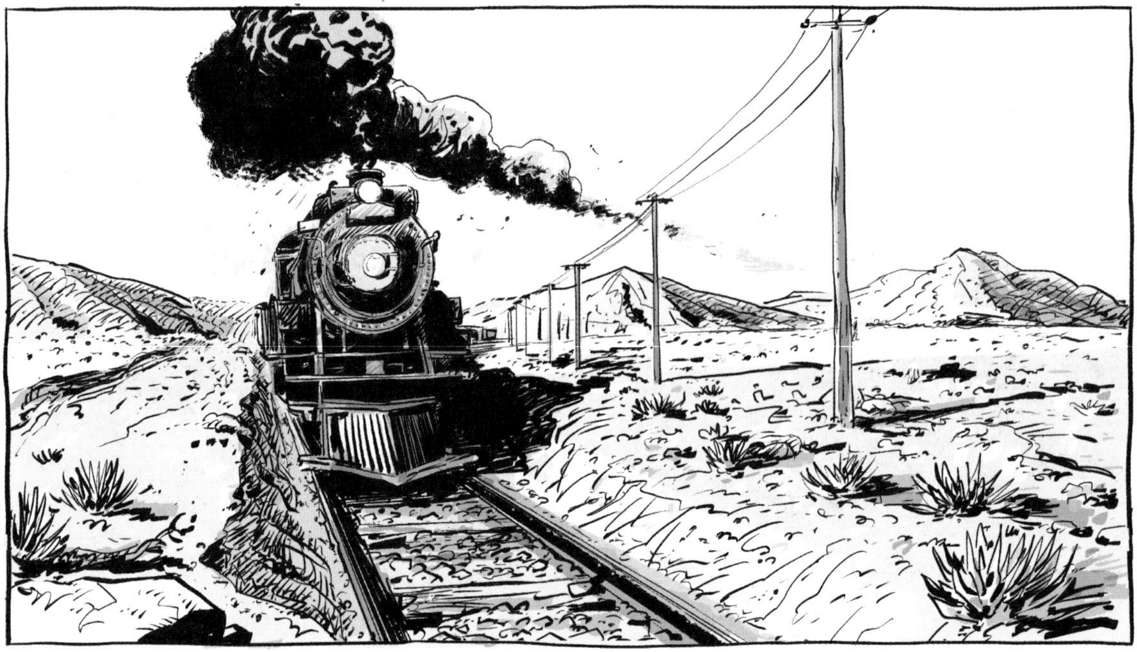

When there wasn't any more room to squeeze inside, fans rode the tops of the trains.

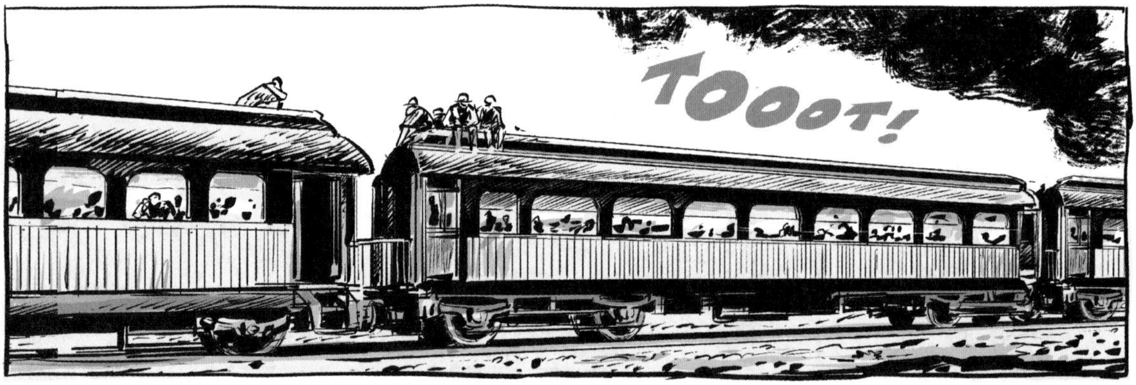

TOOOT!

Better to tie yourself to a locomotive than miss the Battle of the Century.

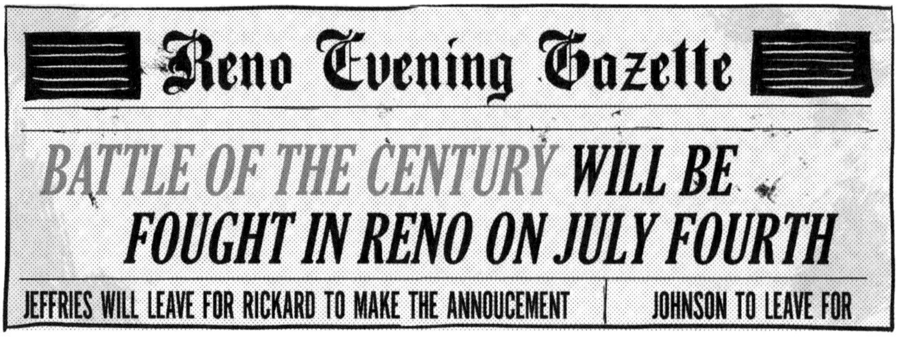
Reno Evening Gazette

BATTLE OF THE CENTURY WILL BE FOUGHT IN RENO ON JULY FOURTH

JEFFRIES WILL LEAVE FOR RICKARD TO MAKE THE ANNOUCEMENT | JOHNSON TO LEAVE FOR

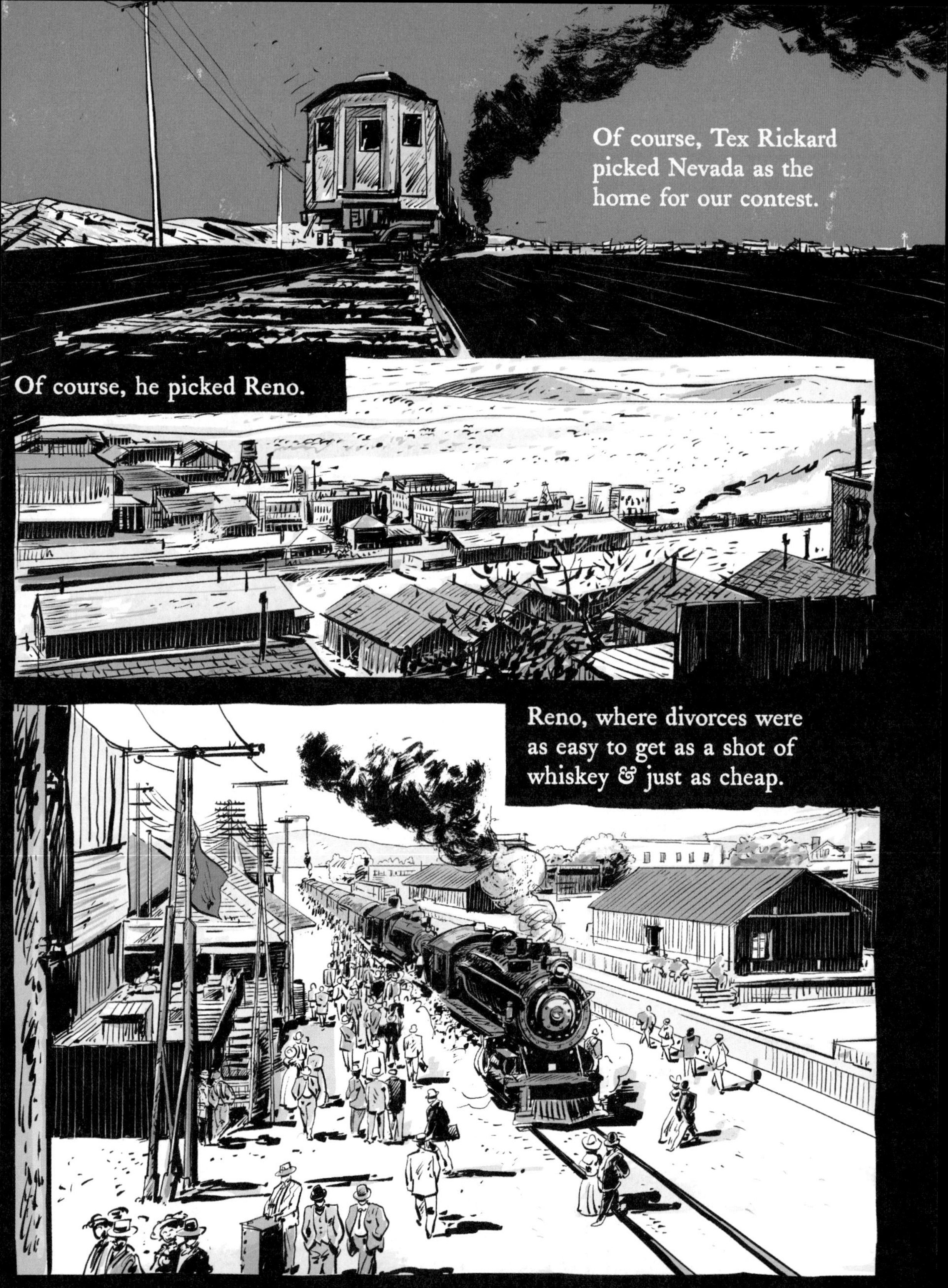
Of course, Tex Rickard picked Nevada as the home for our contest.
Of course, he picked Reno.
Reno, where divorces were as easy to get as a shot of whiskey & just as cheap.

Gamblers, sports, prostitutes & fight fans filled the streets & came with all the cash they could carry.

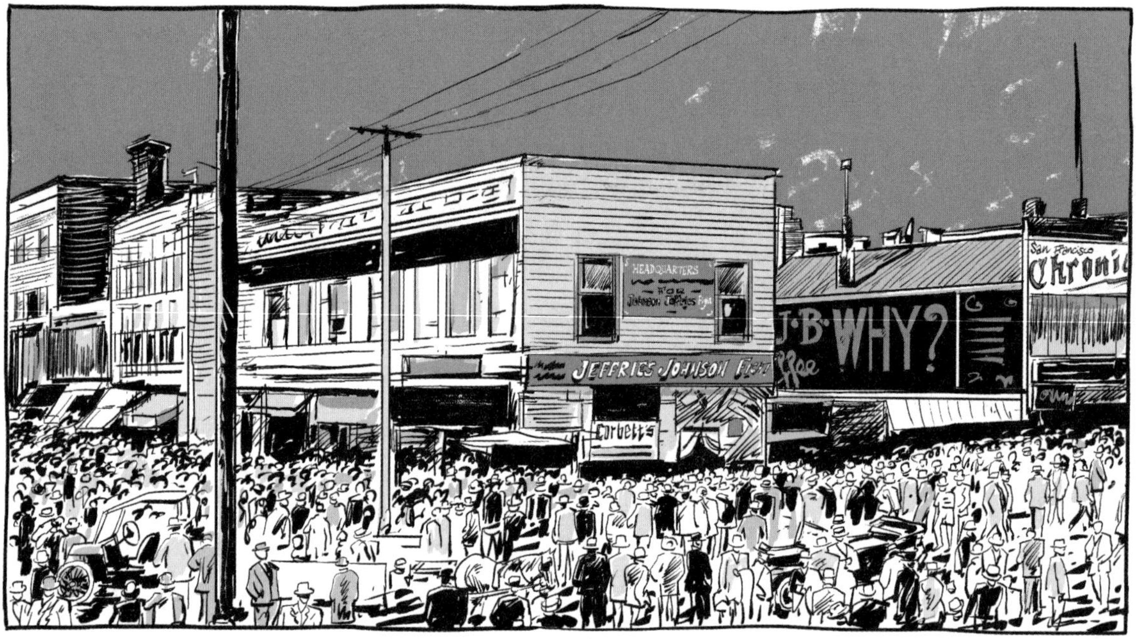
HEADQUARTERS FOR Johnson Jeffries Fight
JEFFRIES JOHNSON FIGHT
Corbett's
J·B· WHY?
San Francisco Chronic

Almost all the bets were on Jeffries.

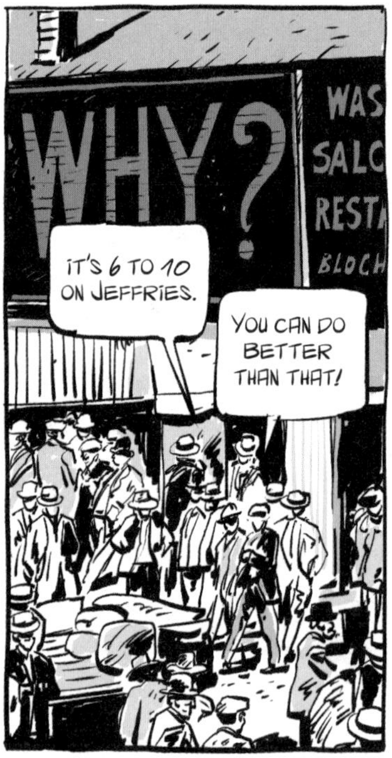
WHY?
IT'S 6 TO 10 ON JEFFRIES.
YOU CAN DO BETTER THAN THAT!

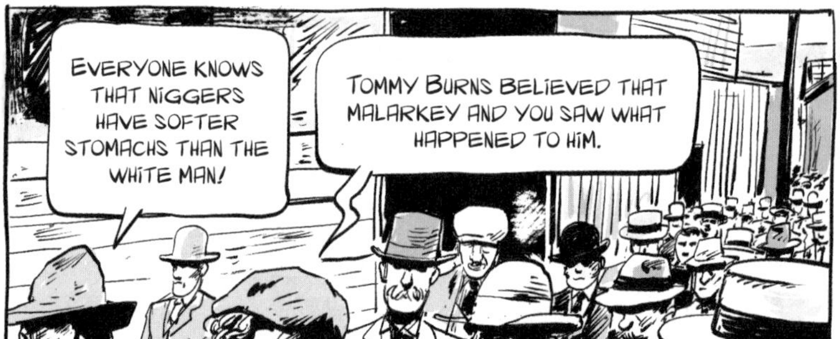
EVERYONE KNOWS THAT NIGGERS HAVE SOFTER STOMACHS THAN THE WHITE MAN!
TOMMY BURNS BELIEVED THAT MALARKEY AND YOU SAW WHAT HAPPENED TO HIM.

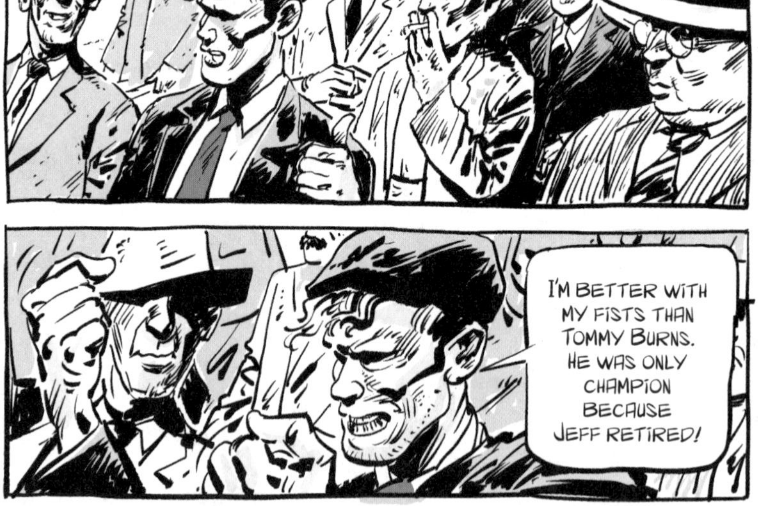
I'M BETTER WITH MY FISTS THAN TOMMY BURNS. HE WAS ONLY CHAMPION BECAUSE JEFF RETIRED!

The pickpockets & petty thieves were open for business.

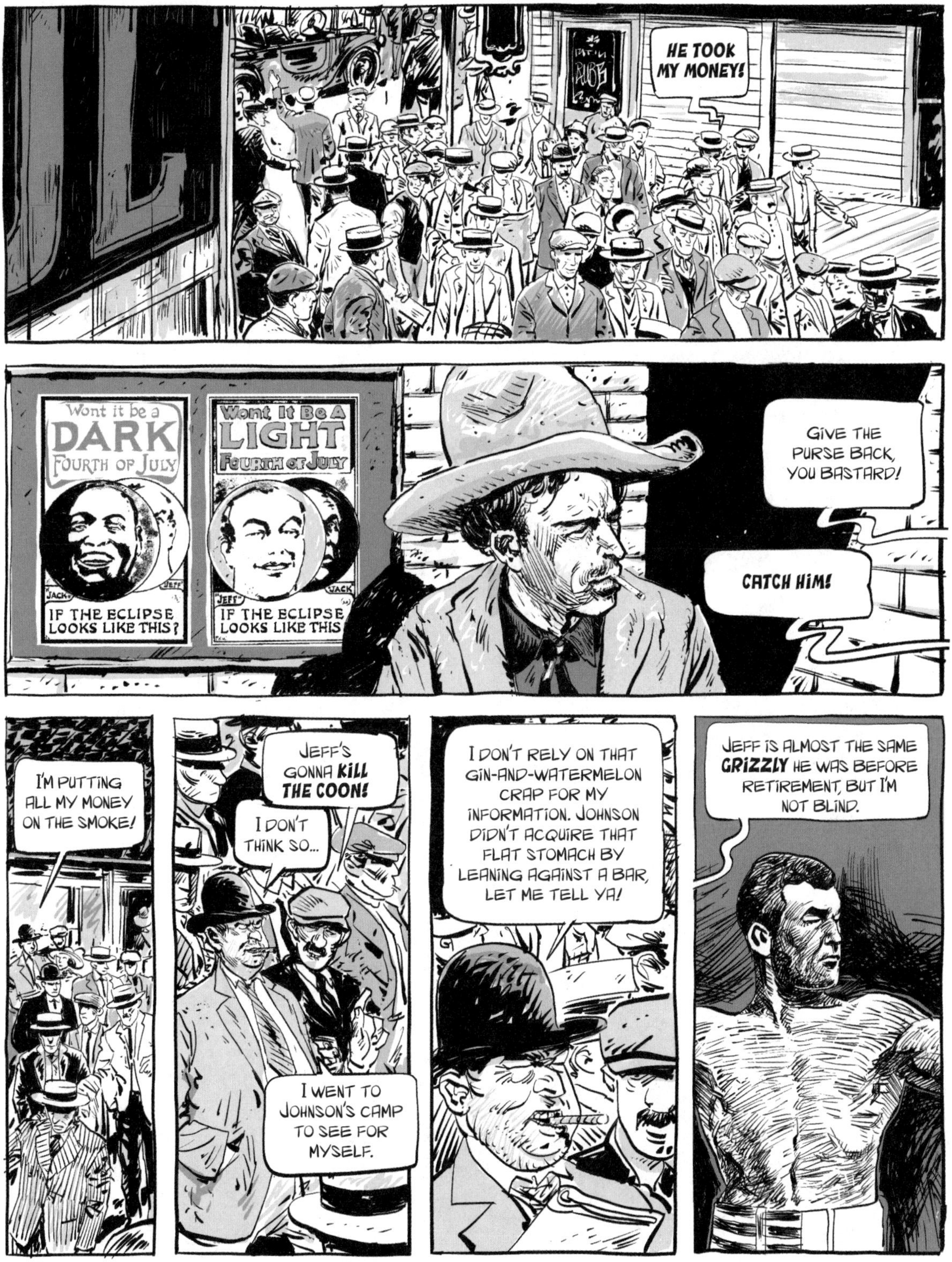
HE TOOK MY MONEY!
Wont it be a DARK FOURTH OF JULY
JACK
JEFF
IF THE ECLIPSE LOOKS LIKE THIS?
Wont It Be A LIGHT Fourth of July
"JEFF"
JACK
IF THE ECLIPSE LOOKS LIKE THIS
GIVE THE PURSE BACK, YOU BASTARD!
CATCH HIM!
I'M PUTTING ALL MY MONEY ON THE SMOKE!
JEFF'S GONNA KILL THE COON!
I DON'T THINK SO...
I WENT TO JOHNSON'S CAMP TO SEE FOR MYSELF.
I DON'T RELY ON THAT GIN-AND-WATERMELON CRAP FOR MY INFORMATION. JOHNSON DIDN'T ACQUIRE THAT FLAT STOMACH BY LEANING AGAINST A BAR, LET ME TELL YA!
JEFF IS ALMOST THE SAME GRIZZLY HE WAS BEFORE RETIREMENT, BUT I'M NOT BLIND.

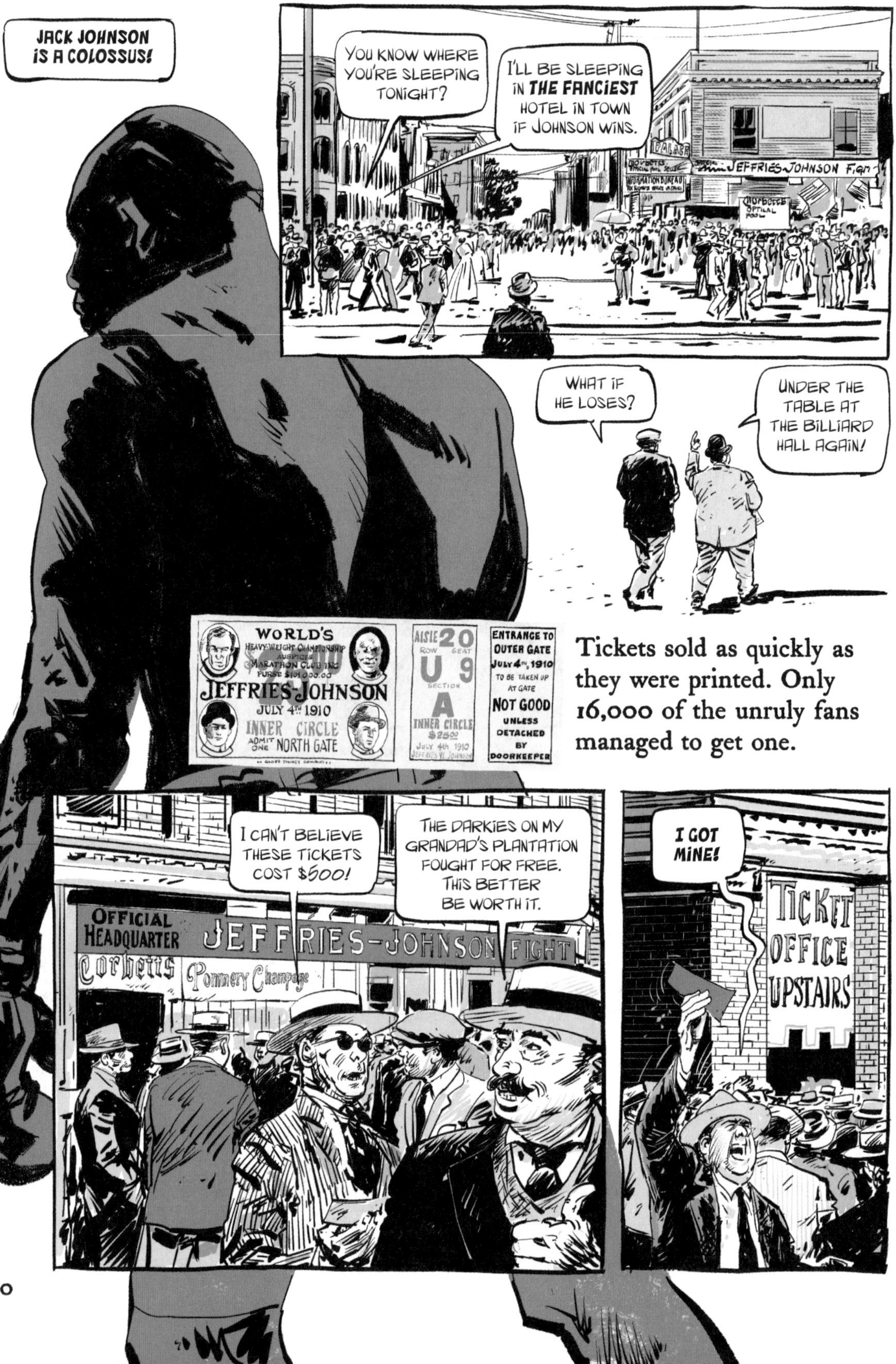
JACK JOHNSON IS A COLOSSUS!
YOU KNOW WHERE YOU'RE SLEEPING TONIGHT?
I'LL BE SLEEPING IN **THE FANCIEST** HOTEL IN TOWN IF JOHNSON WINS.
PALACE
JEFFRIES-JOHNSON FIGHT
WHAT IF HE LOSES?
UNDER THE TABLE AT THE BILLIARD HALL AGAIN!
WORLD'S HEAVY-WEIGHT CHAMPIONSHIP
JEFFRIES-JOHNSON
JULY 4TH 1910
INNER CIRCLE
ADMIT ONE NORTH GATE
AISLE 20 ROW U SEAT 9 SECTION A
INNER CIRCLE $25.00
JULY 4th 1910
ENTRANCE TO OUTER GATE
JULY 4TH, 1910
TO BE TAKEN UP AT GATE
NOT GOOD UNLESS DETACHED BY DOORKEEPER
Tickets sold as quickly as they were printed. Only 16,000 of the unruly fans managed to get one.
I CAN'T BELIEVE THESE TICKETS COST $500!
THE DARKIES ON MY GRANDAD'S PLANTATION FOUGHT FOR FREE. THIS BETTER BE WORTH IT.
OFFICIAL HEADQUARTER
JEFFRIES-JOHNSON FIGHT
Corbetts
Pommery Champagne
I GOT MINE!
TICKET OFFICE UPSTAIRS

All of these saps betting against me.
What's that saying about a fool & his money?

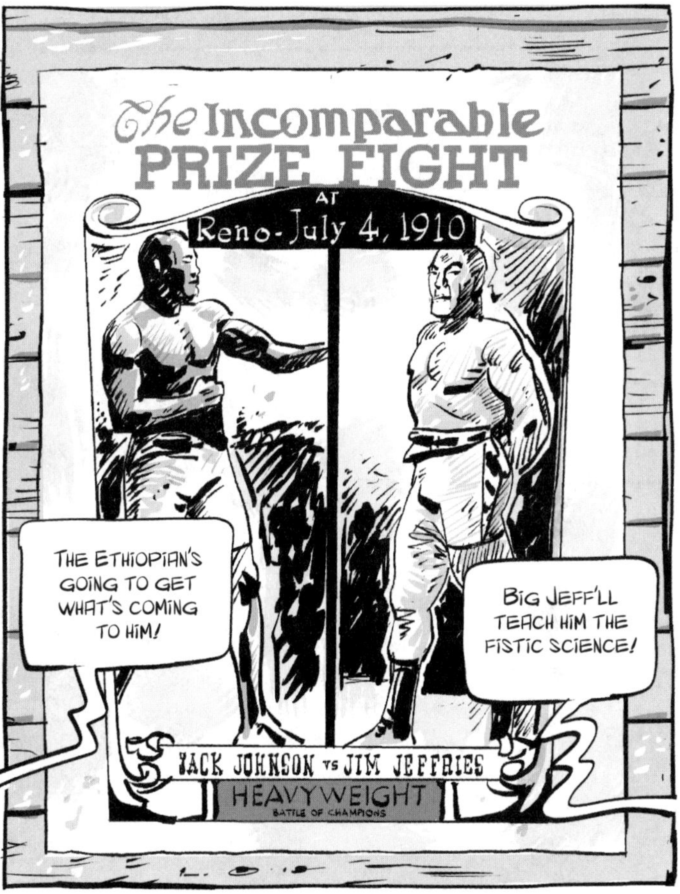
The Incomparable
PRIZE FIGHT
AT
Reno - July 4, 1910
THE ETHIOPIAN'S GOING TO GET WHAT'S COMING TO HIM!
BIG JEFF'LL TEACH HIM THE FISTIC SCIENCE!
JACK JOHNSON vs JIM JEFFRIES
HEAVYWEIGHT
BATTLE OF CHAMPIONS

The day got hotter every minute as the sun crested the bright desert, but the sports showed up in their gambling suits anyway.

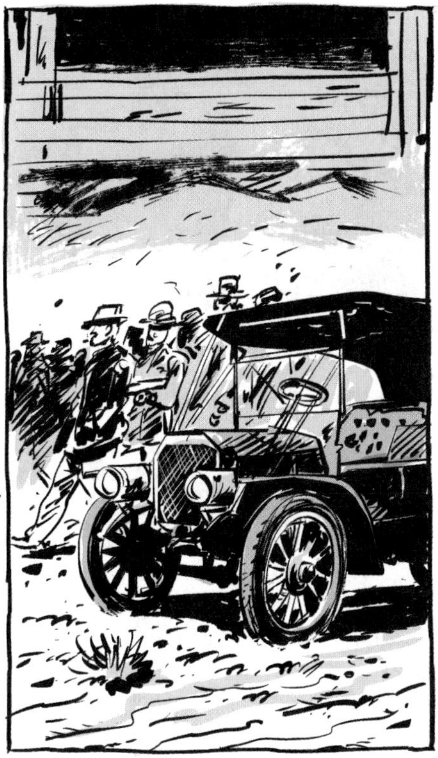

The sawmills & carpenters worked though the heat in the day & by torchlight at night to build the stadium in less than 3 weeks.

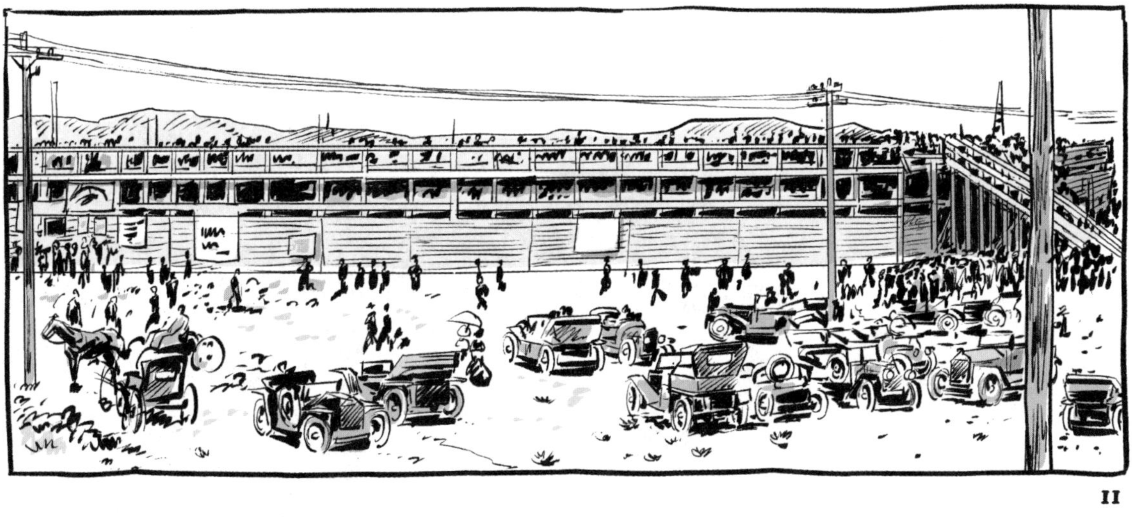

The whole place smelled like dust, sweat & the new pine used to make the bleachers. You could hear the hammers & saws still working as the spectators lined up.

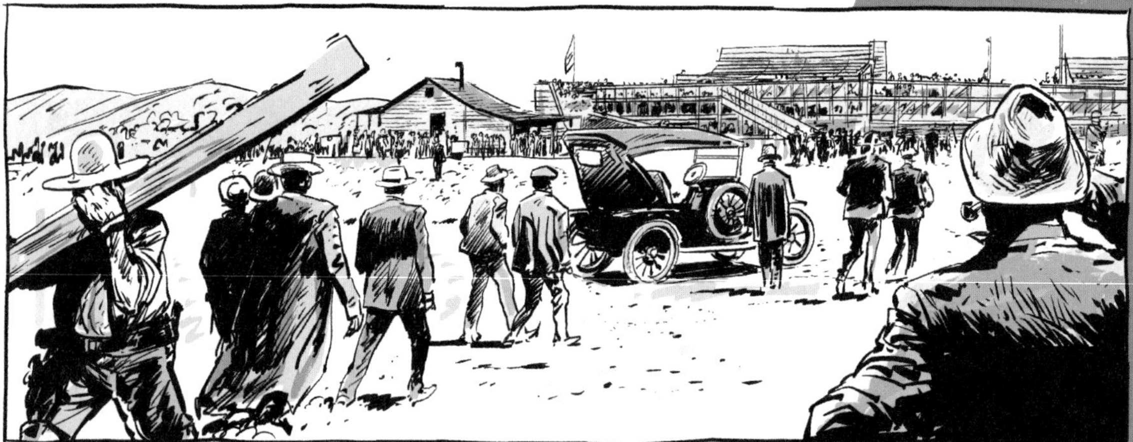

But they got it ready.

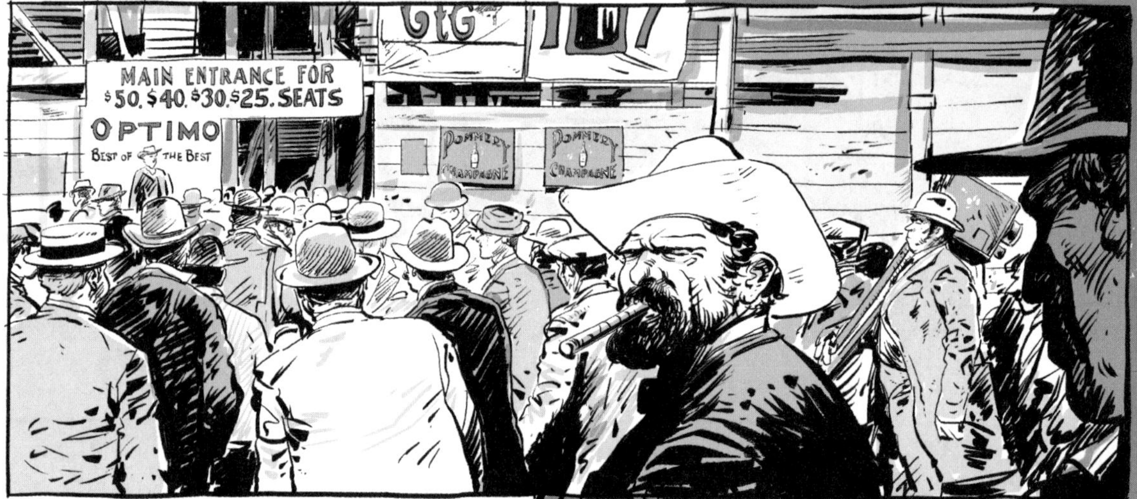
MAIN ENTRANCE FOR
$50. $40. $30. $25. SEATS
OPTIMO
BEST OF THE BEST
POMMERY CHAMPAGNE
POMMERY CHAMPAGNE

I am ready.

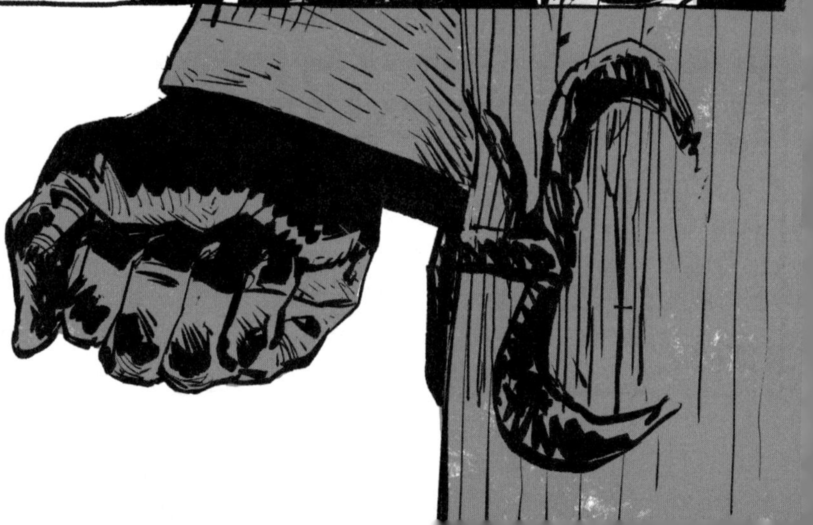

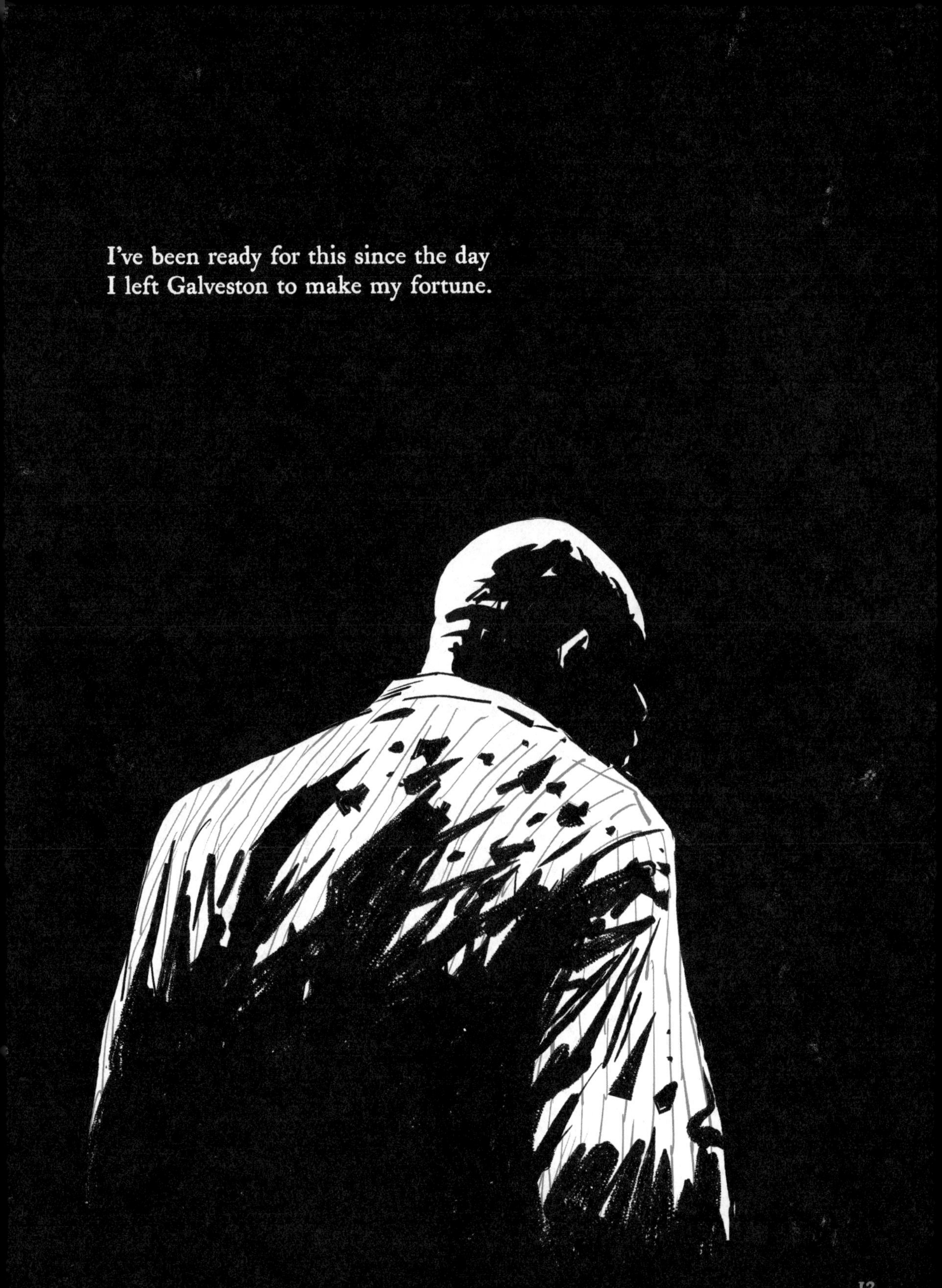
I've been ready for this since the day
I left Galveston to make my fortune.

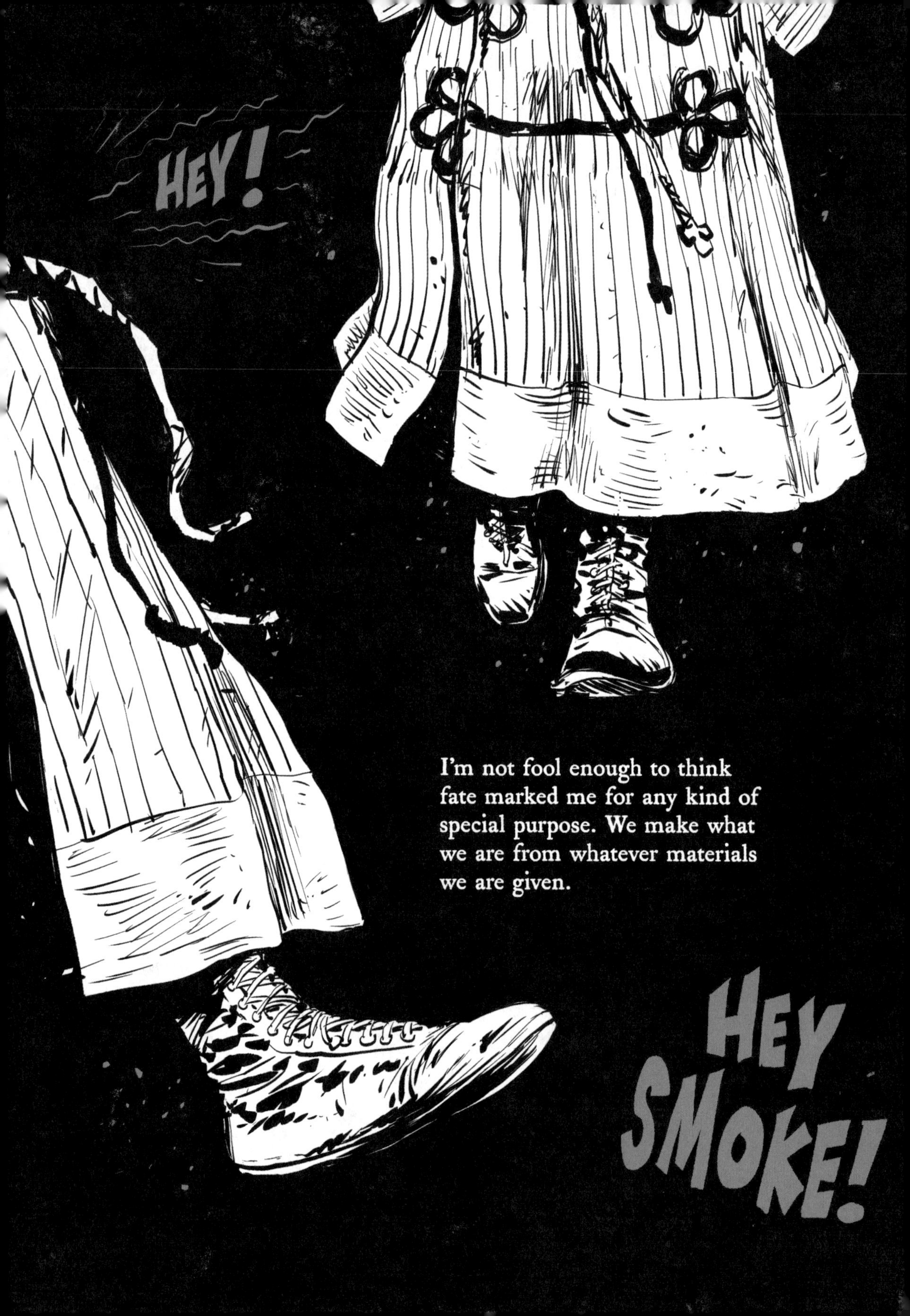
HEY!
I'm not fool enough to think fate marked me for any kind of special purpose. We make what we are from whatever materials we are given.
HEY SMOKE!

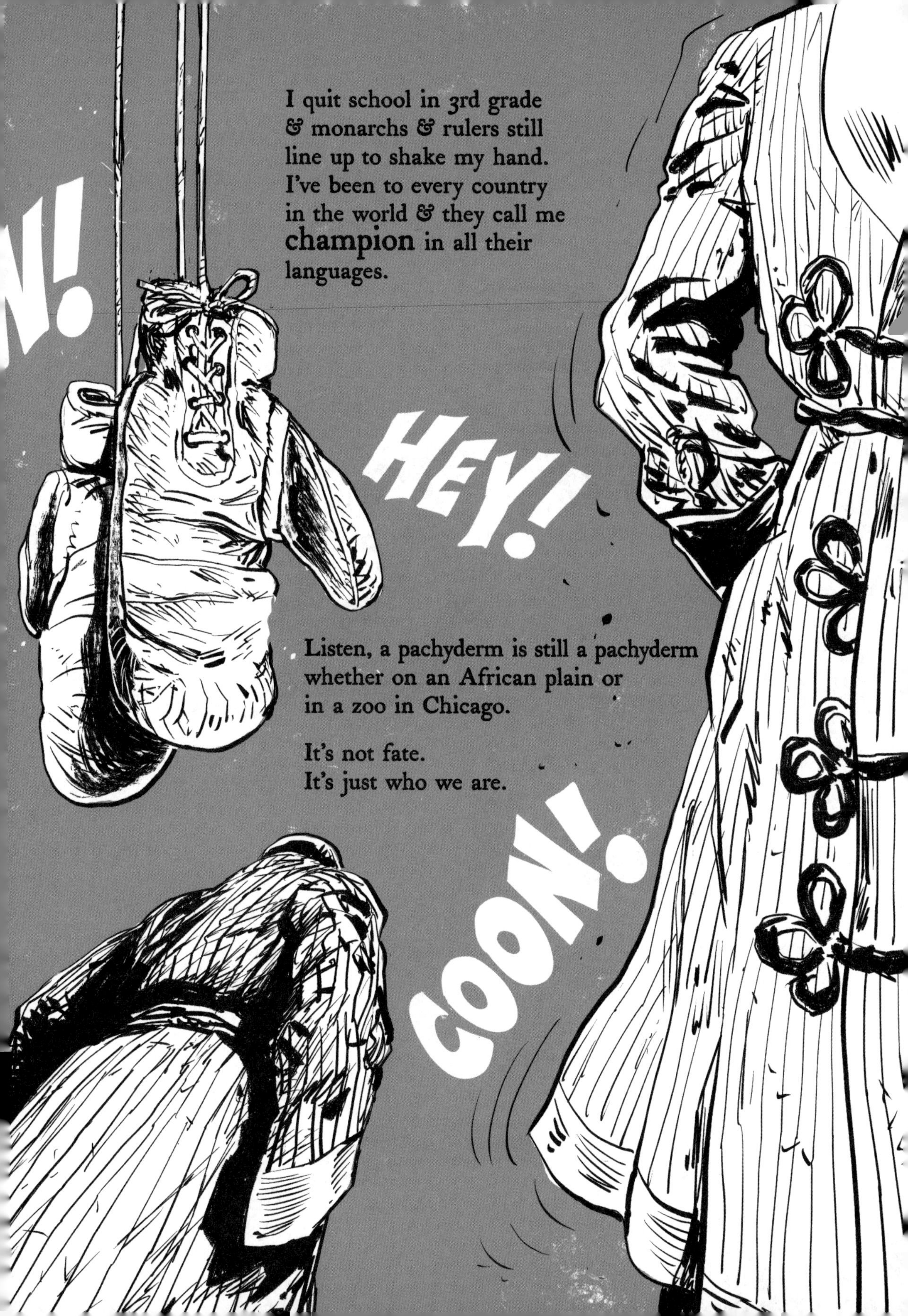
I quit school in 3rd grade & monarchs & rulers still line up to shake my hand. I've been to every country in the world & they call me **champion** in all their languages.
HEY!
Listen, a pachyderm is still a pachyderm whether on an African plain or in a zoo in Chicago.
It's not fate.
It's just who we are.
COON!

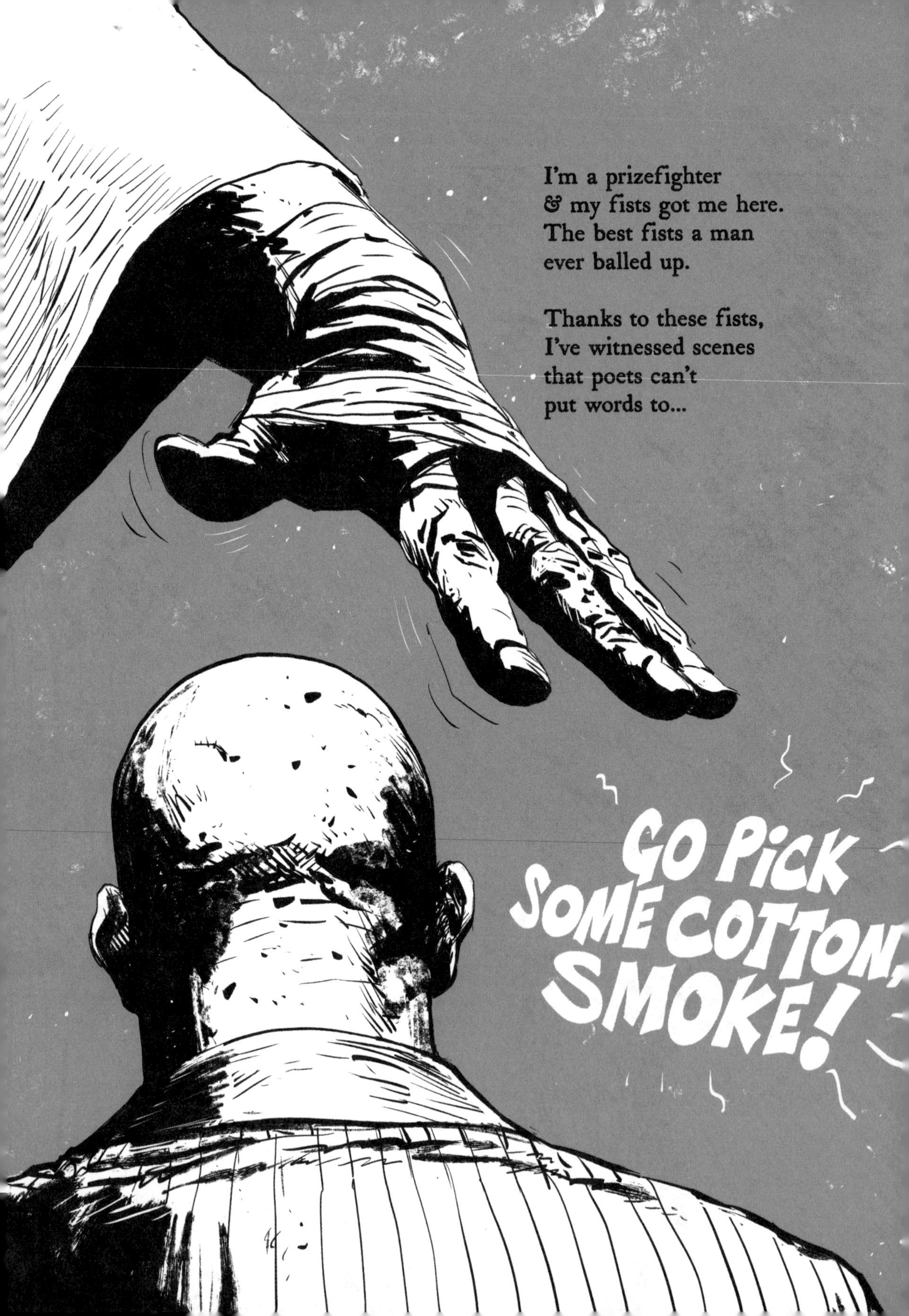
I'm a prizefighter
& my fists got me here.
The best fists a man
ever balled up.
Thanks to these fists,
I've witnessed scenes
that poets can't
put words to...
GO PICK SOME COTTON, SMOKE!

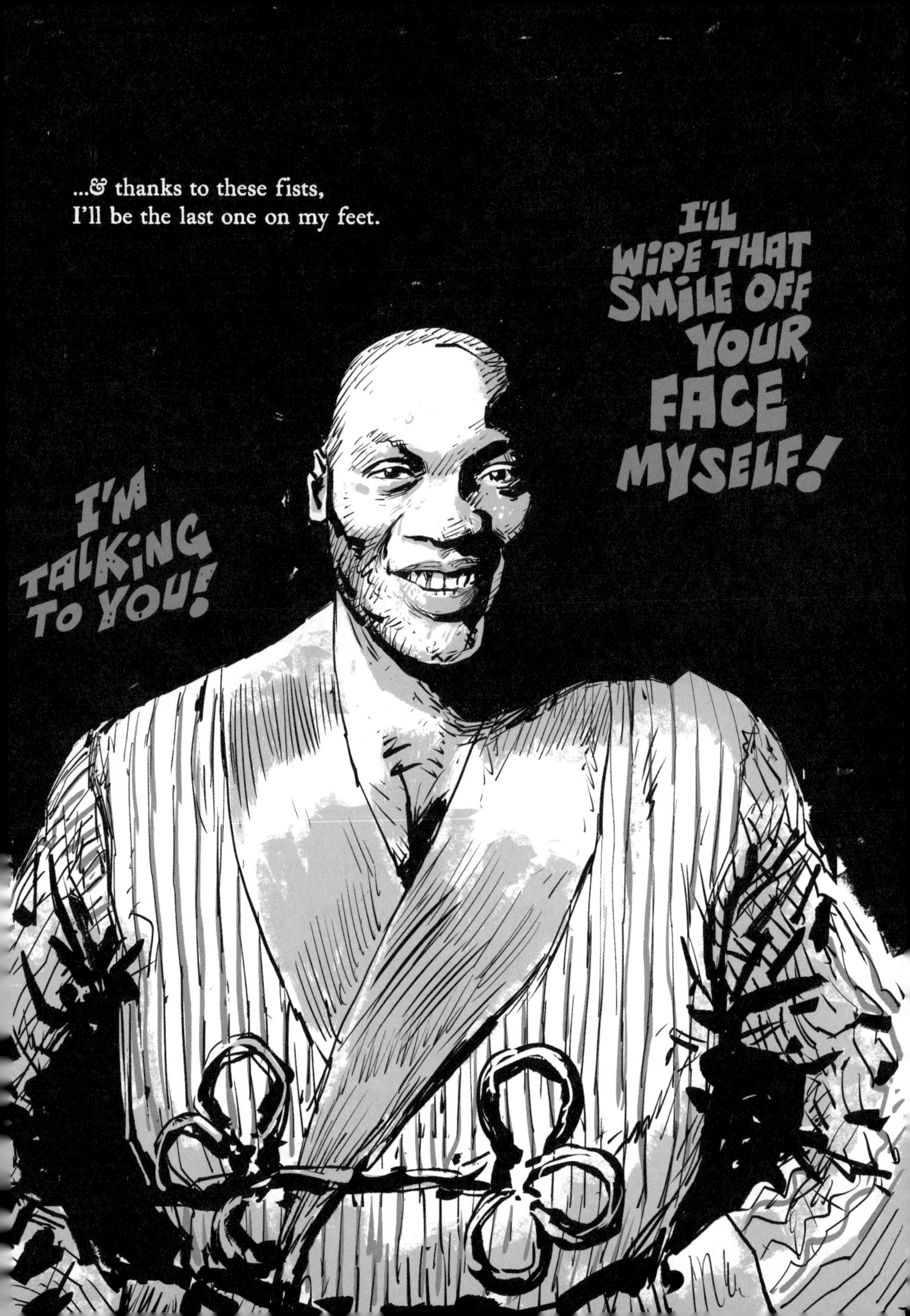
...& thanks to these fists,
I'll be the last one on my feet.
I'LL WIPE THAT SMILE OFF YOUR FACE MYSELF!
I'M TALKING TO YOU!

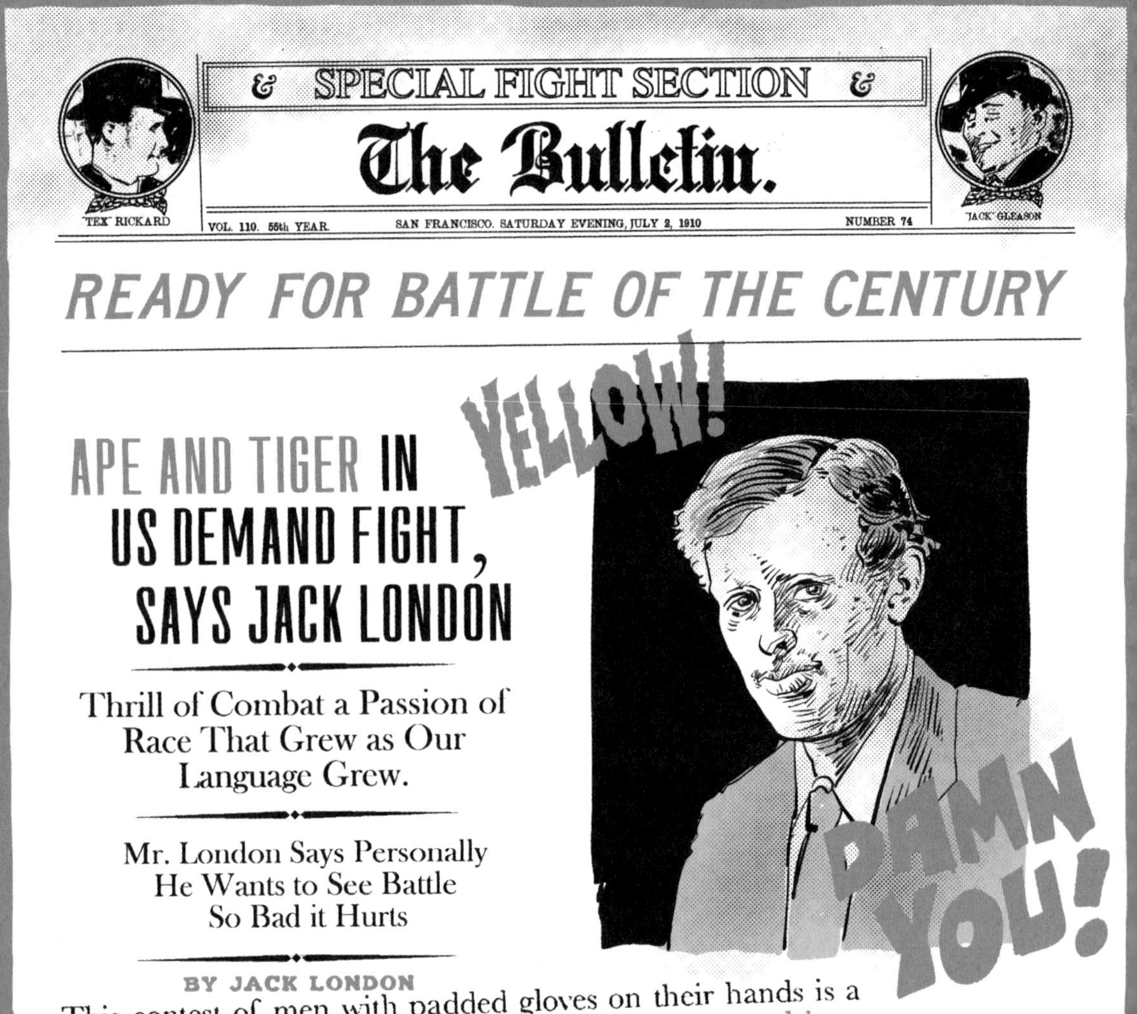
& SPECIAL FIGHT SECTION &
The Bulletin.
"TEX" RICKARD
"JACK" GLEASON
VOL. 110. 55th YEAR.
SAN FRANCISCO. SATURDAY EVENING, JULY 2, 1910
NUMBER 74
READY FOR BATTLE OF THE CENTURY
YELLOW!
APE AND TIGER IN US DEMAND FIGHT, SAYS JACK LONDON
Thrill of Combat a Passion of Race That Grew as Our Language Grew.
Mr. London Says Personally He Wants to See Battle So Bad it Hurts
DAMN YOU!
BY JACK LONDON
This contest of men with padded gloves on their hands is a sport that belongs unequivocally to the English-speaking race, and that has taken centuries for the race to develop. It is no
And why do they want to do this?
For honor and fame
and prize for $100,000
This is the ape and tiger in us.
This is the call of the wild.

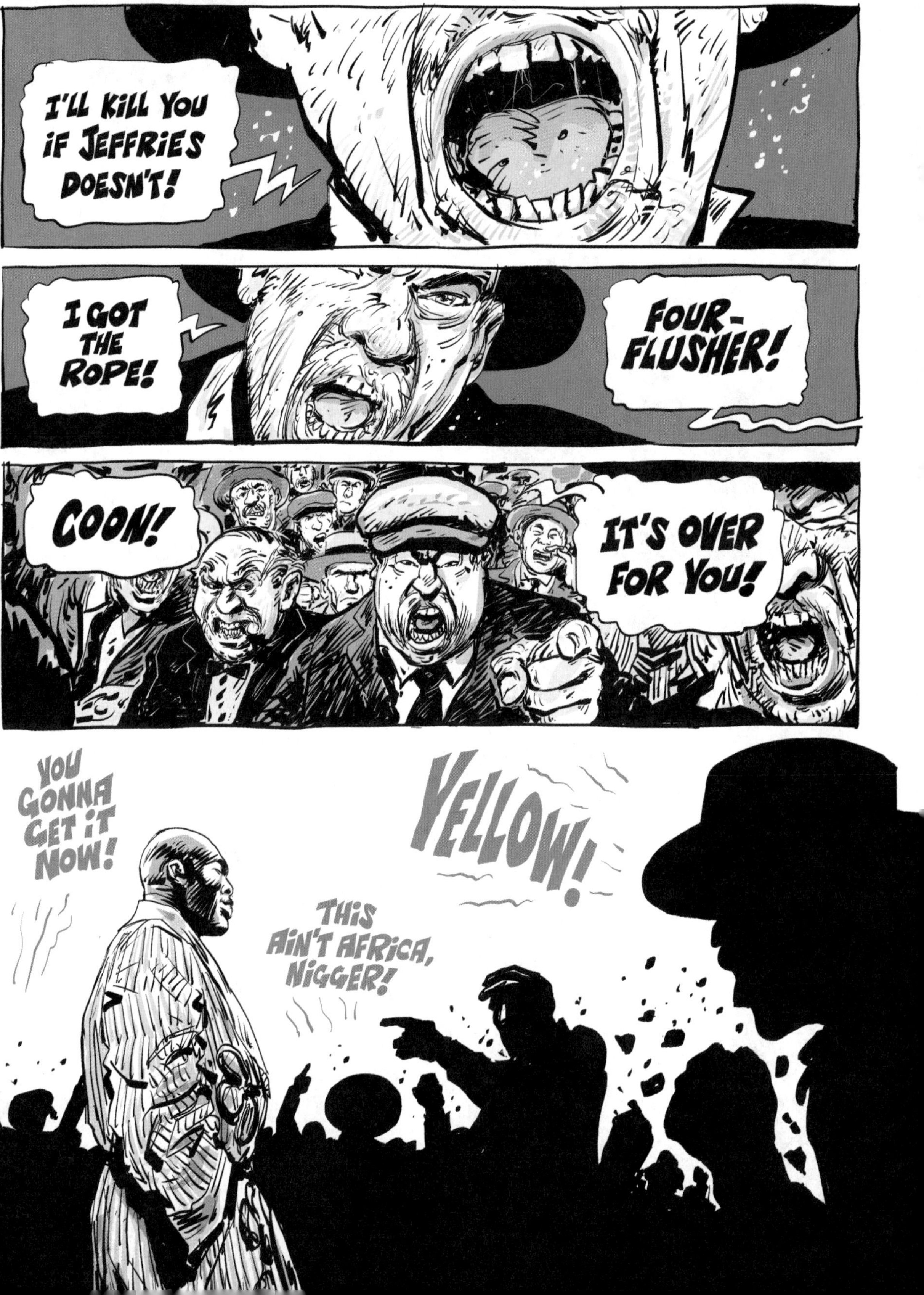
I'LL KILL YOU IF JEFFRIES DOESN'T!
I GOT THE ROPE!
FOUR-FLUSHER!
COON!
IT'S OVER FOR YOU!
YOU GONNA GET IT NOW!
YELLOW!
THIS AIN'T AFRICA, NIGGER!

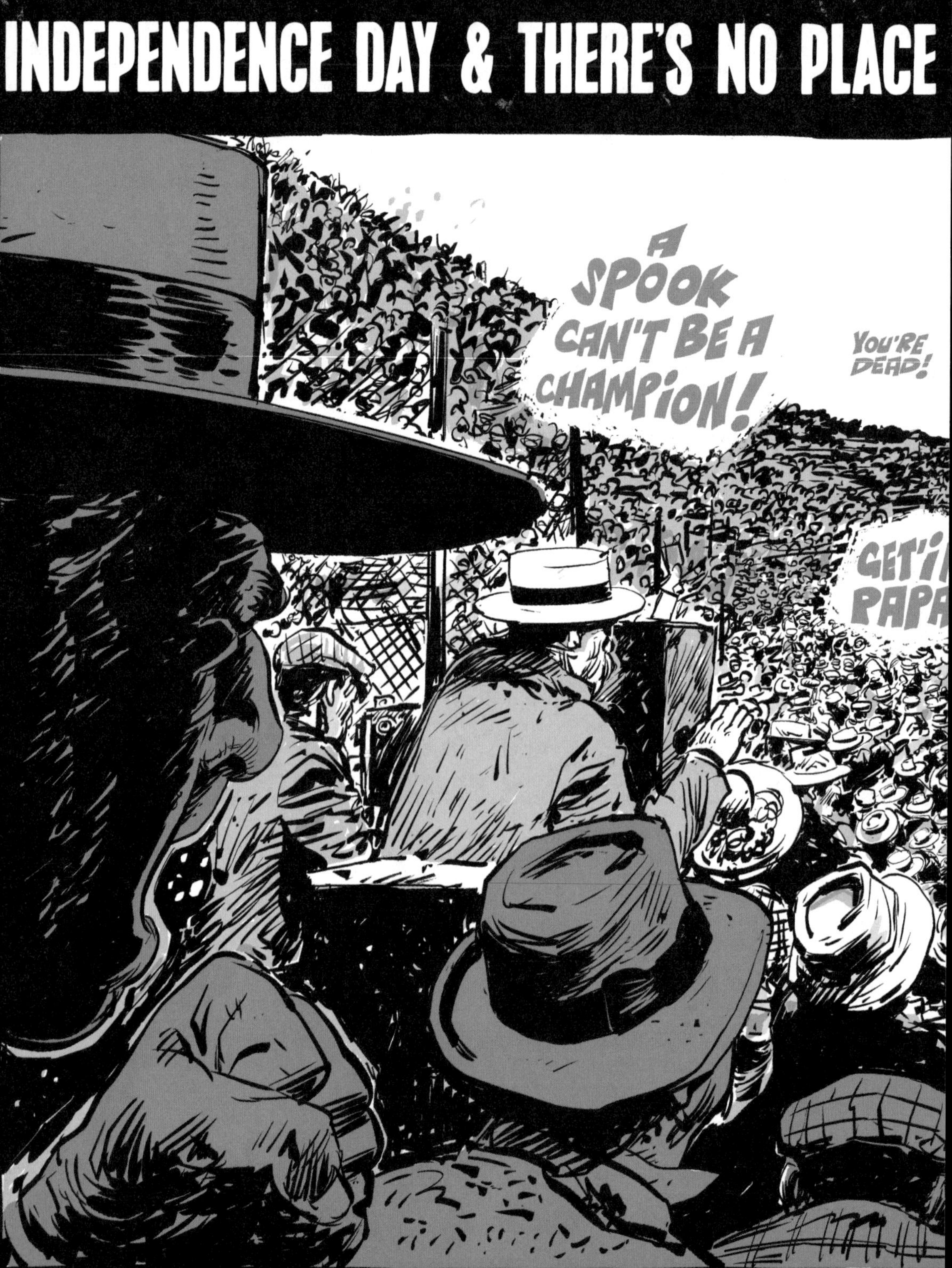
INDEPENDENCE DAY & THERE'S NO PLACE
A SPOOK CAN'T BE A CHAMPION!
YOU'RE DEAD!

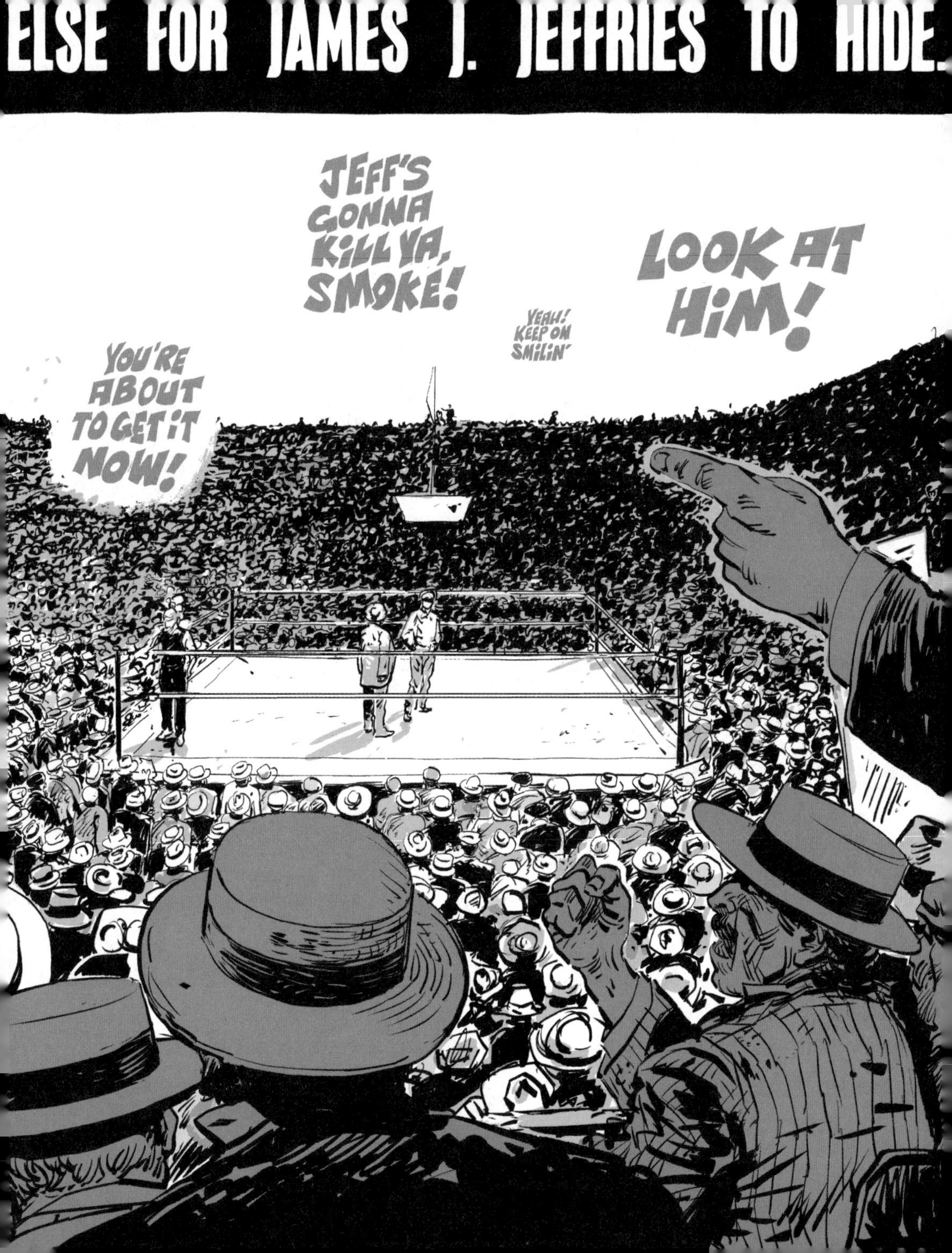
ELSE FOR JAMES J. JEFFRIES TO HIDE.
JEFF'S GONNA KILL YA, SMOKE!
YOU'RE ABOUT TO GET IT NOW!
YEAH! KEEP ON SMILIN'
LOOK AT HIM!

Jack London & the rest of white America had been waiting for this since I became champion.

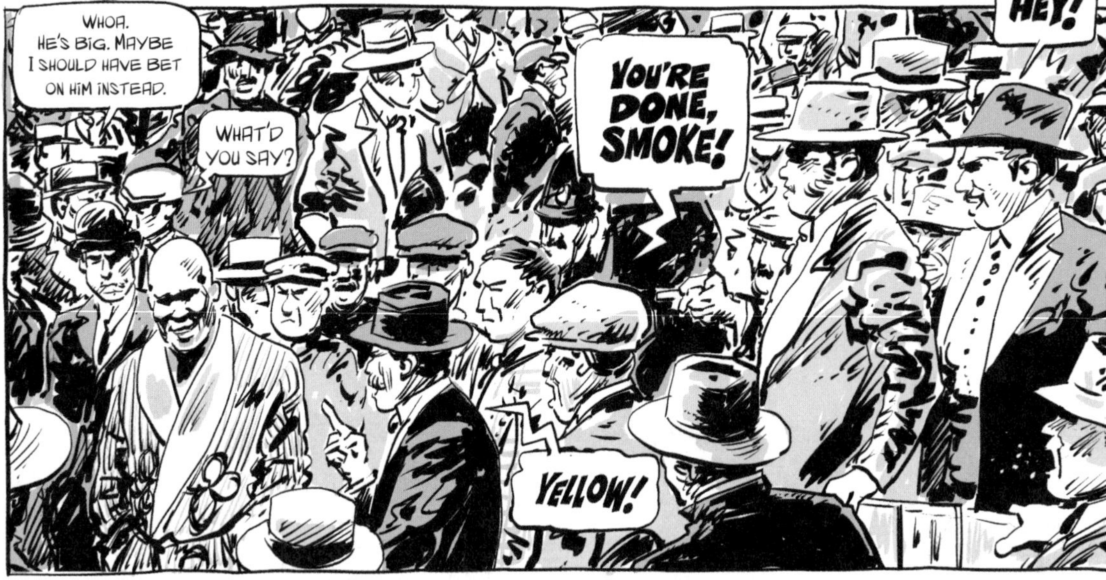
WHOA. HE'S BIG. MAYBE I SHOULD HAVE BET ON HIM INSTEAD.
WHAT'D YOU SAY?
YOU'RE DONE, SMOKE!
HEY!
YELLOW!

White people were in rows as far up as I could see, so many they looked like bales of cotton stacked on top of each other.

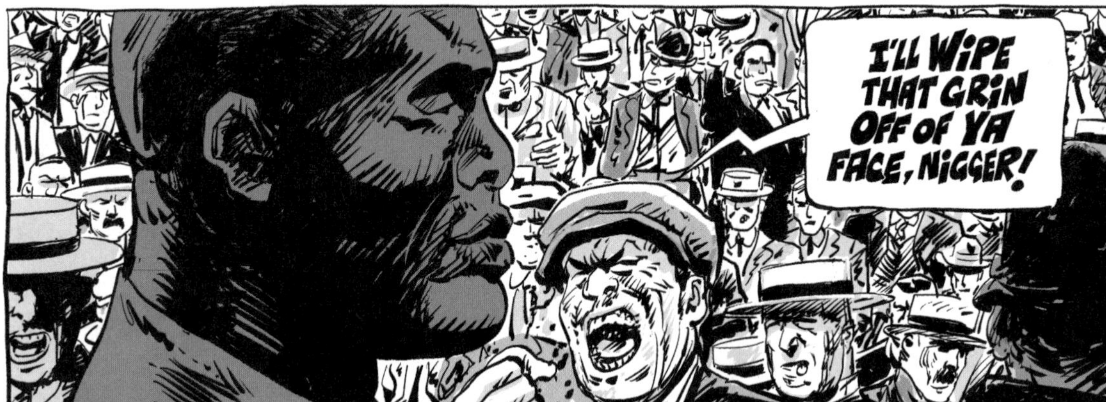
I'LL WIPE THAT GRIN OFF OF YA FACE, NIGGER!

Every one of them as afraid of my left hooks as they were of my gold smile. Every one of them waiting for me to be put down.

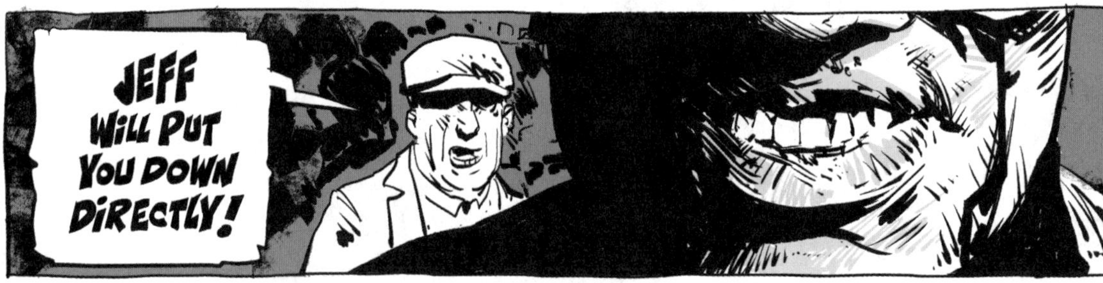
JEFF WILL PUT YOU DOWN DIRECTLY!

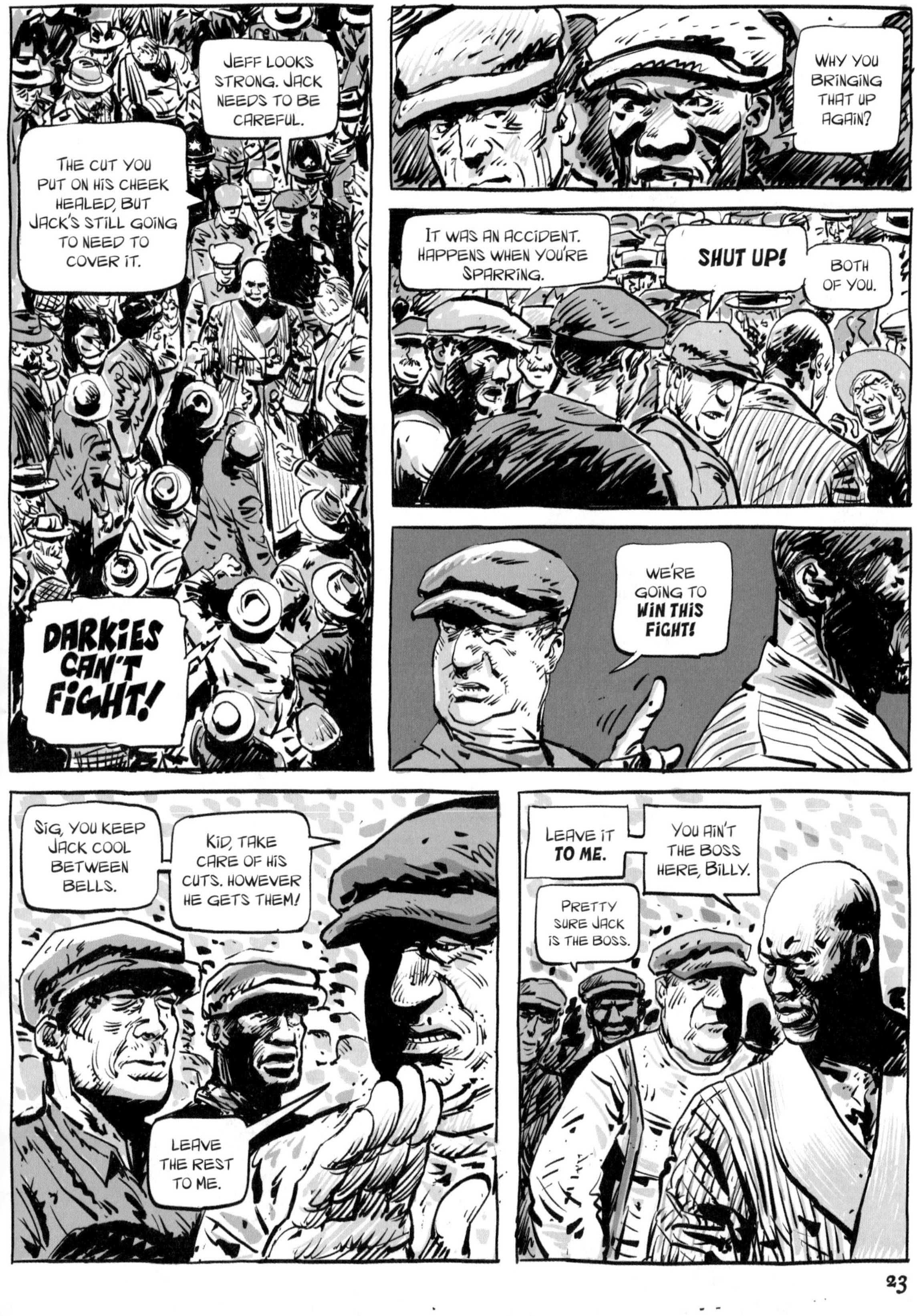
JEFF LOOKS STRONG. JACK NEEDS TO BE CAREFUL.
THE CUT YOU PUT ON HIS CHEEK HEALED, BUT JACK'S STILL GOING TO NEED TO COVER IT.
DARKIES CAN'T FIGHT!
WHY YOU BRINGING THAT UP AGAIN?
IT WAS AN ACCIDENT. HAPPENS WHEN YOU'RE SPARRING.
SHUT UP!
BOTH OF YOU.
WE'RE GOING TO WIN THIS FIGHT!
SIG, YOU KEEP JACK COOL BETWEEN BELLS.
KID, TAKE CARE OF HIS CUTS. HOWEVER HE GETS THEM!
LEAVE THE REST TO ME.
LEAVE IT TO ME.
YOU AIN'T THE BOSS HERE, BILLY.
PRETTY SURE JACK IS THE BOSS.

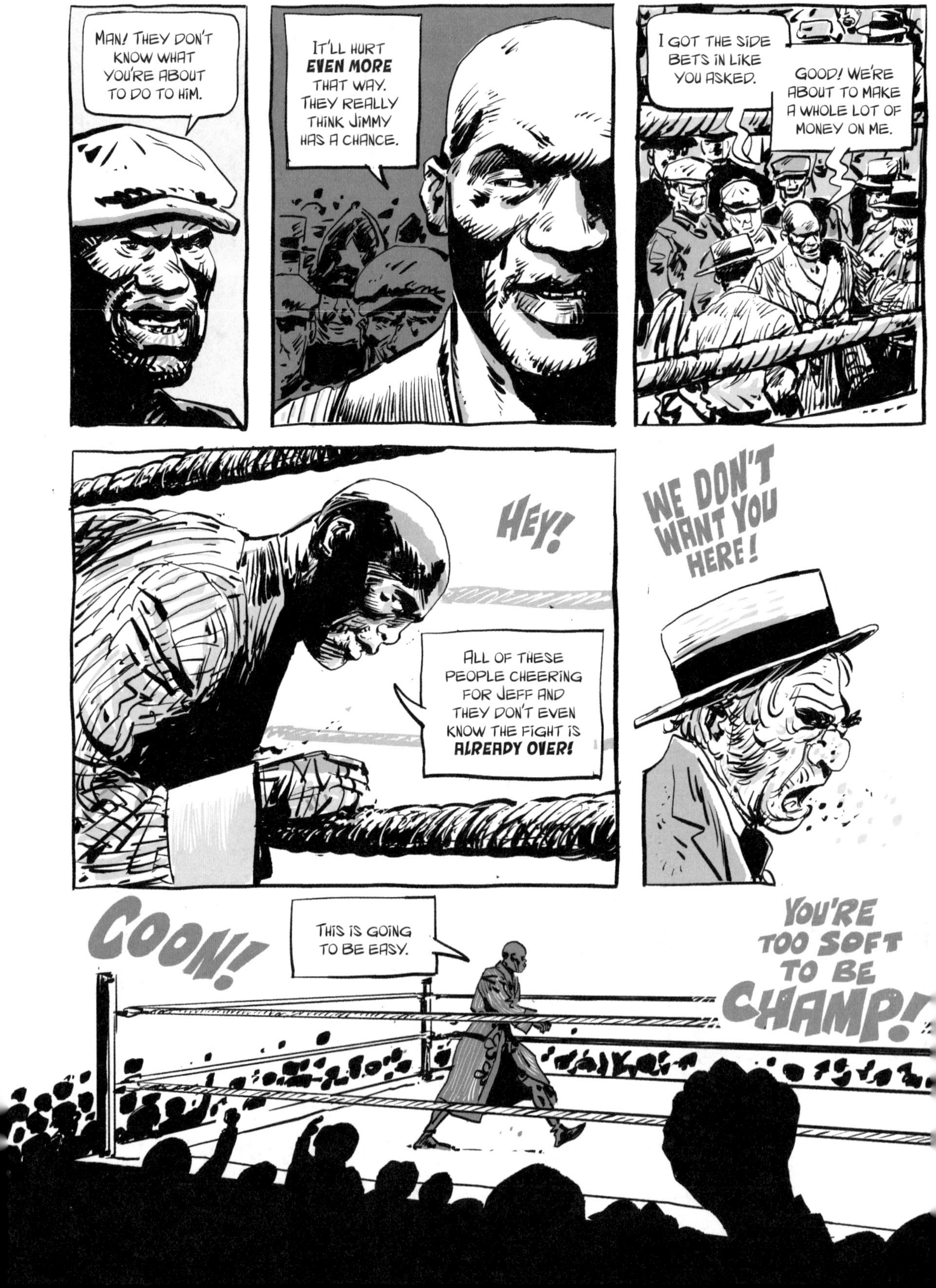
MAN! THEY DON'T KNOW WHAT YOU'RE ABOUT TO DO TO HIM.
IT'LL HURT **EVEN MORE** THAT WAY. THEY REALLY THINK JIMMY HAS A CHANCE.
I GOT THE SIDE BETS IN LIKE YOU ASKED.
GOOD! WE'RE ABOUT TO MAKE A WHOLE LOT OF MONEY ON ME.
HEY!
ALL OF THESE PEOPLE CHEERING FOR JEFF AND THEY DON'T EVEN KNOW THE FIGHT IS **ALREADY OVER!**
WE DON'T WANT YOU HERE!
COON!
THIS IS GOING TO BE EASY.
YOU'RE TOO SOFT TO BE CHAMP!

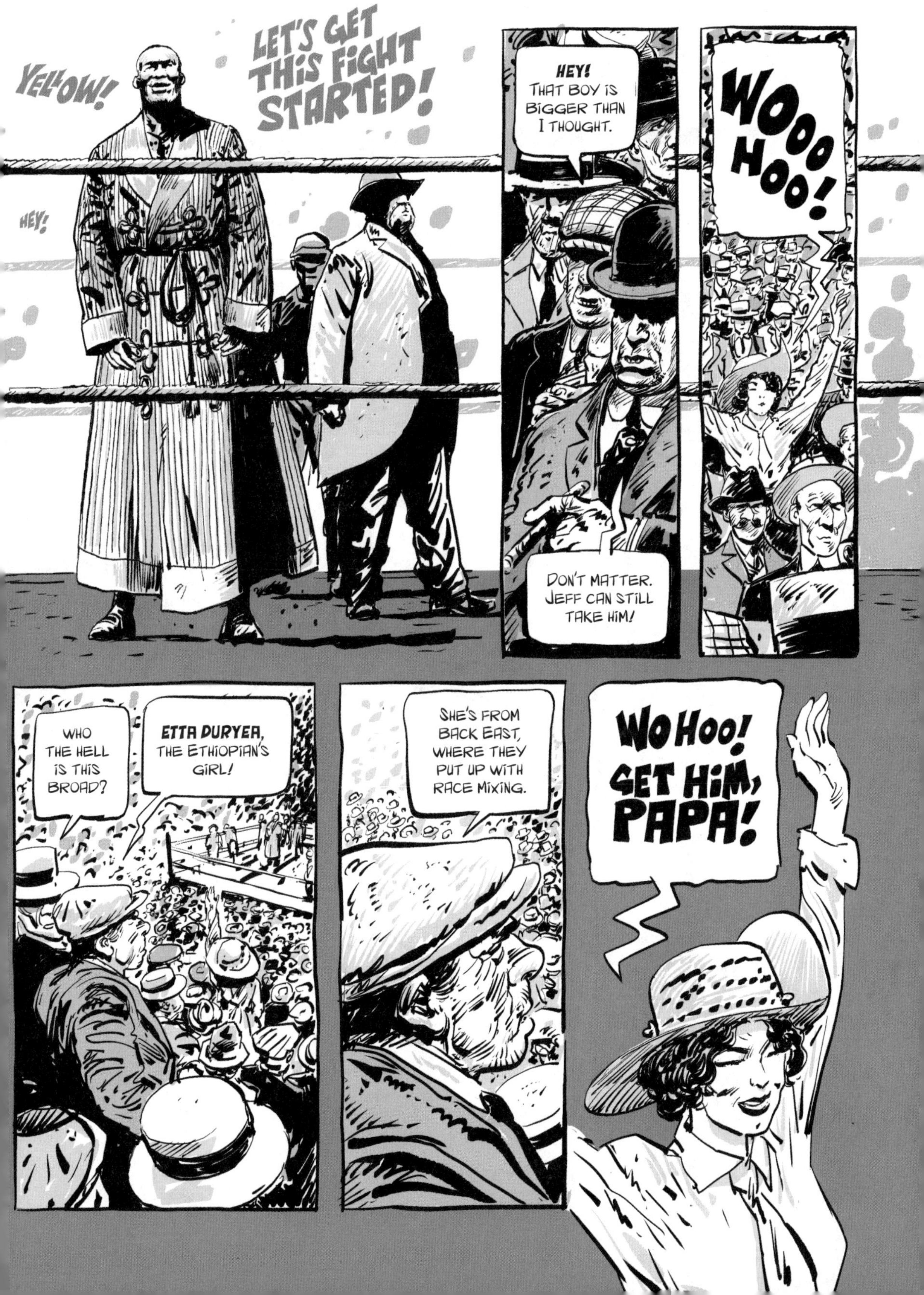
YELL-OW!
LET'S GET THIS FIGHT STARTED!
HEY!
HEY! THAT BOY IS BIGGER THAN I THOUGHT.
DON'T MATTER. JEFF CAN STILL TAKE HIM!
WOOO HOO!
WHO THE HELL IS THIS BROAD?
ETTA DURYEA, THE ETHIOPIAN'S GIRL!
SHE'S FROM BACK EAST, WHERE THEY PUT UP WITH RACE MIXING.
WO HOO! GET HIM, PAPA!

JACK'S COMPOUND, THE NIGHT BEFORE

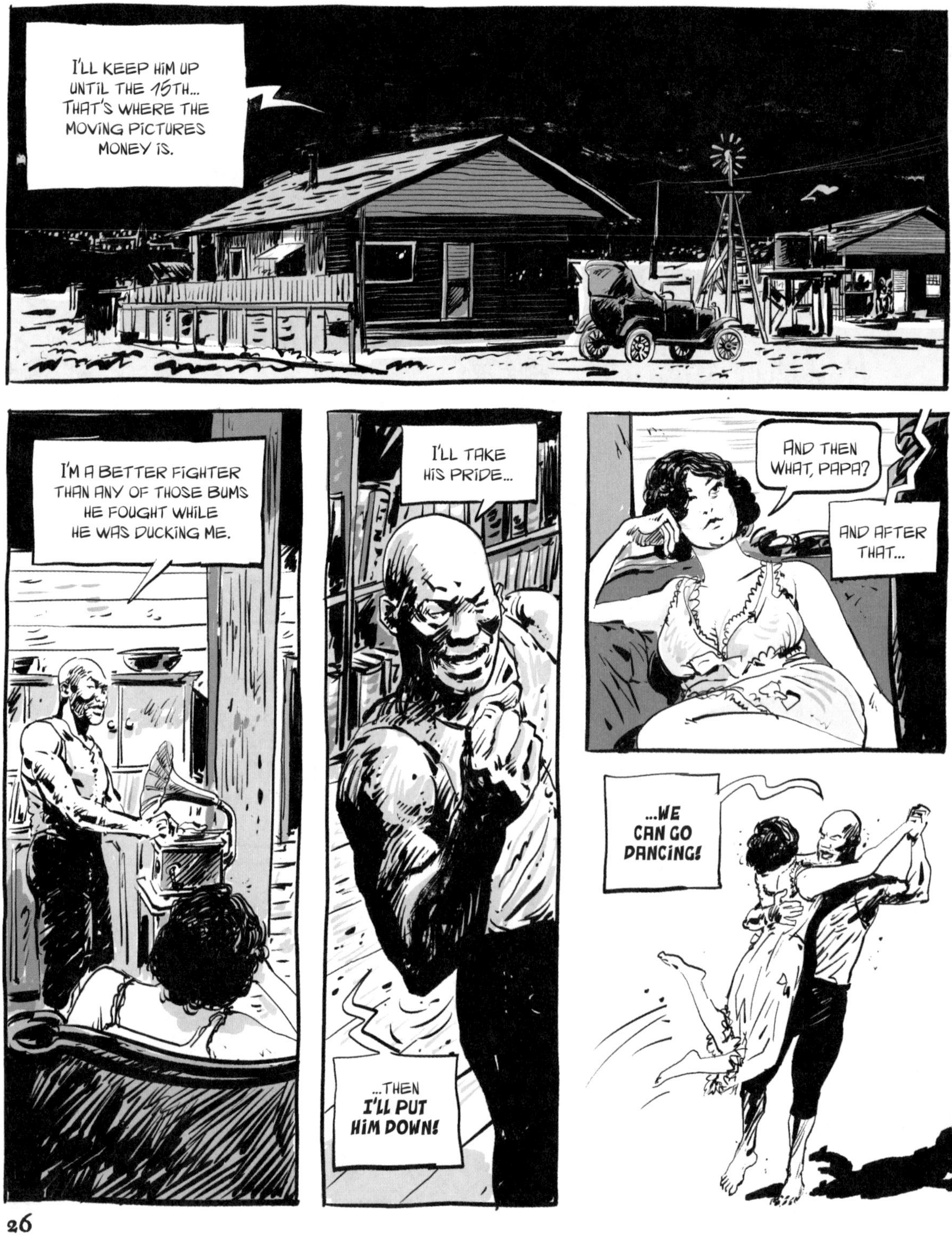
I'LL KEEP HIM UP UNTIL THE 15TH... THAT'S WHERE THE MOVING PICTURES MONEY IS.
I'M A BETTER FIGHTER THAN ANY OF THOSE BUMS HE FOUGHT WHILE HE WAS DUCKING ME.
I'LL TAKE HIS PRIDE...
...THEN I'LL PUT HIM DOWN!
AND THEN WHAT, PAPA?
AND AFTER THAT...
...WE CAN GO DANCING!

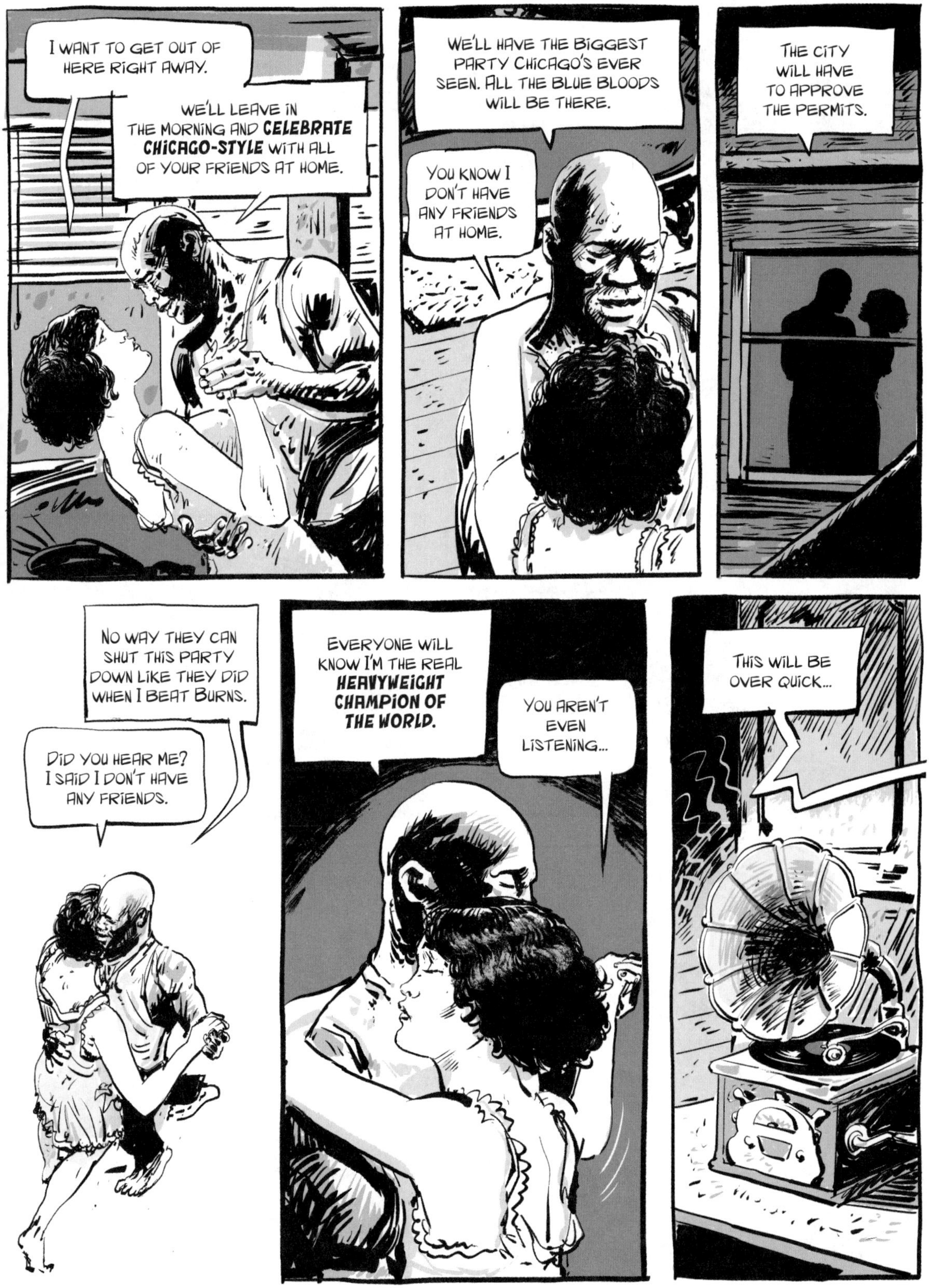
I WANT TO GET OUT OF HERE RIGHT AWAY.
WE'LL LEAVE IN THE MORNING AND **CELEBRATE CHICAGO-STYLE** WITH ALL OF YOUR FRIENDS AT HOME.
WE'LL HAVE THE BIGGEST PARTY CHICAGO'S EVER SEEN. ALL THE BLUE BLOODS WILL BE THERE.
YOU KNOW I DON'T HAVE ANY FRIENDS AT HOME.
THE CITY WILL HAVE TO APPROVE THE PERMITS.
NO WAY THEY CAN SHUT THIS PARTY DOWN LIKE THEY DID WHEN I BEAT BURNS.
DID YOU HEAR ME? I SAID I DON'T HAVE ANY FRIENDS.
EVERYONE WILL KNOW I'M THE REAL **HEAVYWEIGHT CHAMPION OF THE WORLD.**
YOU AREN'T EVEN LISTENING...
THIS WILL BE OVER QUICK...

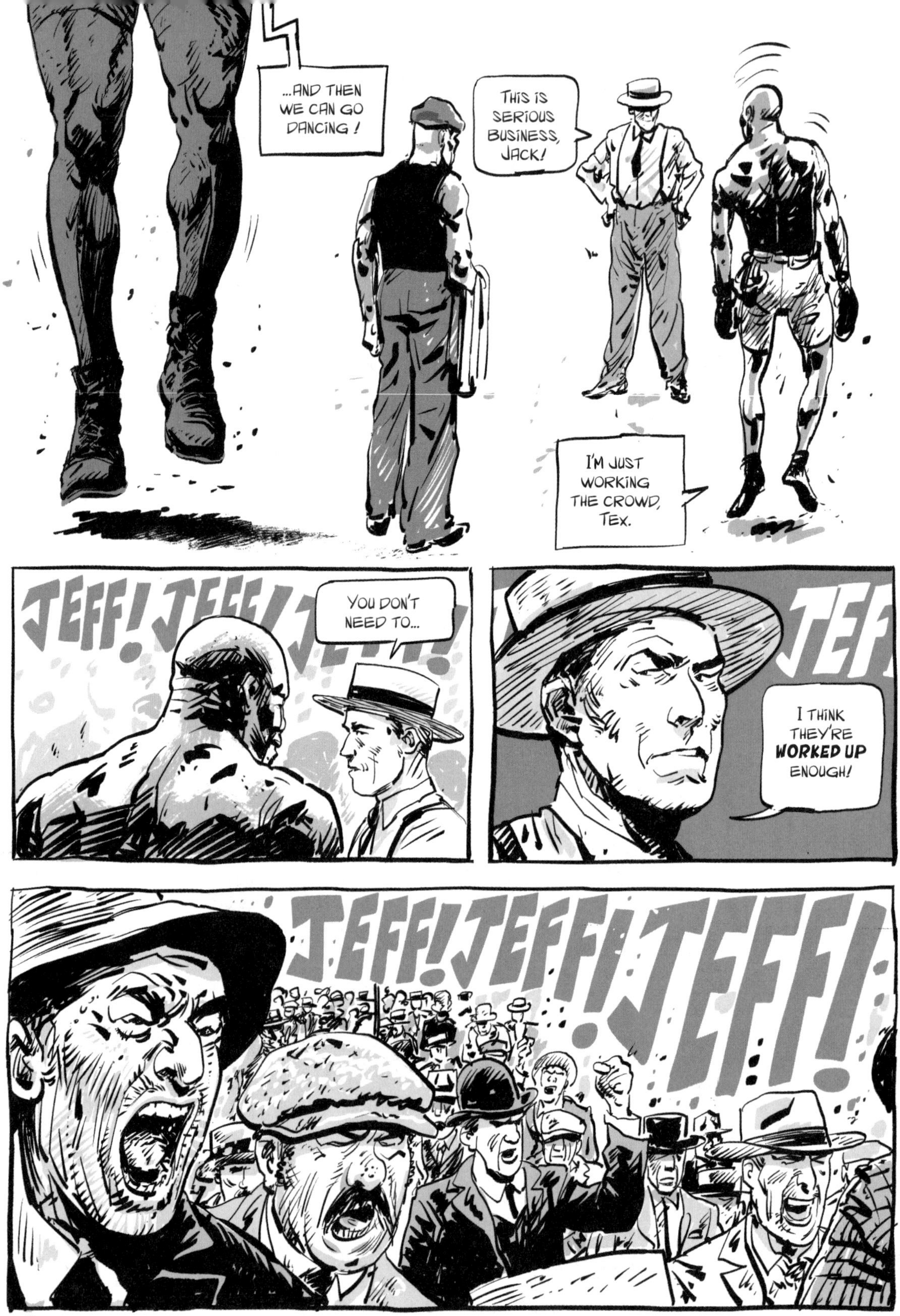
...AND THEN WE CAN GO DANCING!
THIS IS SERIOUS BUSINESS, JACK!
I'M JUST WORKING THE CROWD, TEX.
JEFF! JEFF!
YOU DON'T NEED TO...
I THINK THEY'RE **WORKED UP** ENOUGH!
JEFF! JEFF! JEFF!

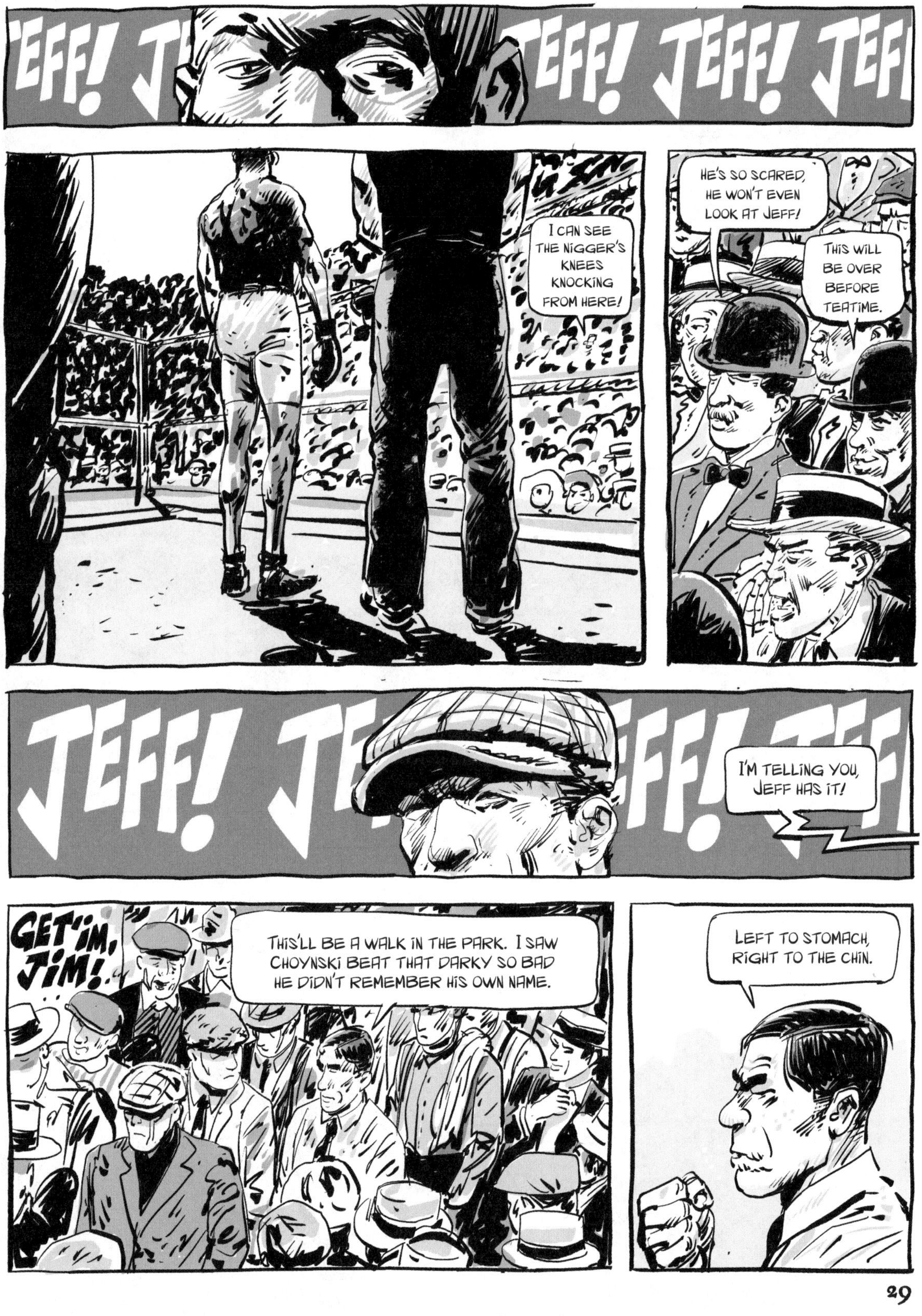
JEFF! JEFF!
I CAN SEE THE NIGGER'S KNEES KNOCKING FROM HERE!
HE'S SO SCARED, HE WON'T EVEN LOOK AT JEFF!
THIS WILL BE OVER BEFORE TEATIME.
JEFF!
I'M TELLING YOU, JEFF HAS IT!
GET 'IM, JIM!
THIS'LL BE A WALK IN THE PARK. I SAW CHOYNSKI BEAT THAT DARKY SO BAD HE DIDN'T REMEMBER HIS OWN NAME.
LEFT TO STOMACH, RIGHT TO THE CHIN.

THAT WAS 10 YEARS AGO. THE MAN'S A REAL PRIZEFIGHTER NOW.

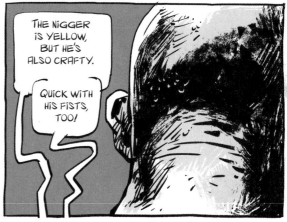

THE NIGGER IS YELLOW, BUT HE'S ALSO CRAFTY.

QUICK WITH HIS FISTS, TOO!

LIL ARTHUR'LL BE ON THE CANVAS BEFORE JEFF BREAKS A SWEAT! HE JUST HAS TO GET THE COON TO STAND UP LIKE A MAN.

EASIER SAID THAN DONE!

BET YOUR LAST COPPER. THE VAUDEVILLE SHOW IS OVER TODAY.

I WOULD CONSIDER ANY MOVE TO INTIMIDATE JOHNSON AS COWARDLY AND A DISGRACE TO THE AMERICAN SPIRIT OF FAIR PLAY.

I HEARD SOME FOUR-FLUSHERS IN THE STANDS TALKING ABOUT ATTACKING JACK JOHNSON AFTER THE FIGHT.

I EXPECT TO WHIP HIM AND THEN SHAKE HIS HAND.

IF JOHNSON SHOULD BY ANY CHANCE WIN, THOUGH, **HE MUST NOT BE HARMED.**

I DEMAND THIS.

GET'IM, JIM!

GET'IM, JIM

GET'IM, JIM!

GET'IM, JIM!

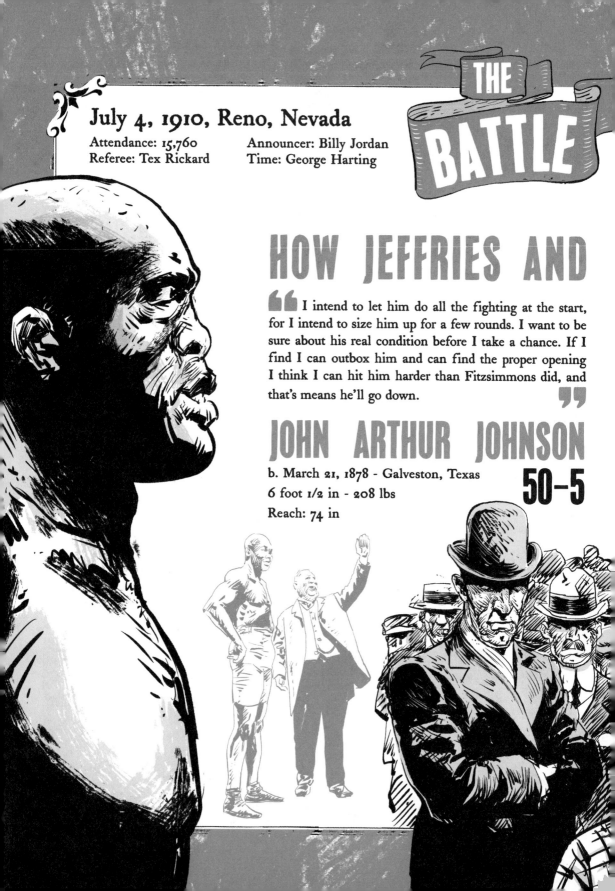

July 4, 1910, Reno, Nevada

Attendance: 15,760
Referee: Tex Rickard
Announcer: Billy Jordan
Time: George Harting

THE BATTLE

HOW JEFFRIES AND

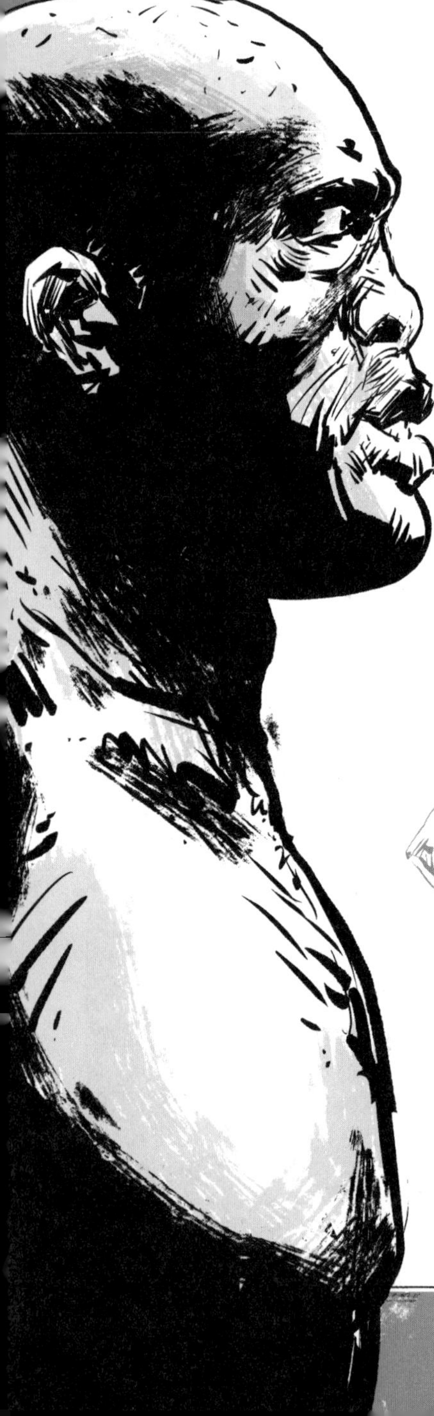

"I intend to let him do all the fighting at the start, for I intend to size him up for a few rounds. I want to be sure about his real condition before I take a chance. If I find I can outbox him and can find the proper opening I think I can hit him harder than Fitzsimmons did, and that's means he'll go down."

JOHN ARTHUR JOHNSON

b. March 21, 1878 - Galveston, Texas
6 foot 1/2 in - 208 lbs
Reach: 74 in

50–5

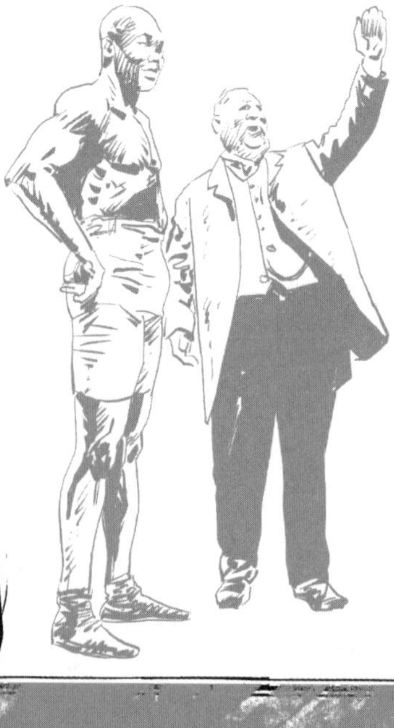

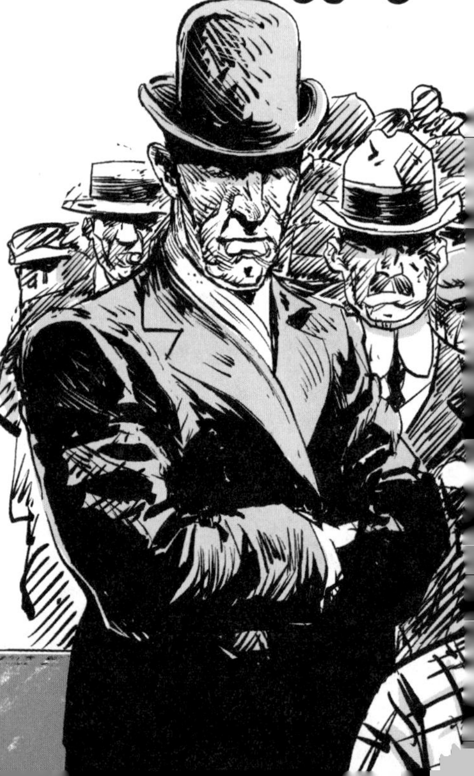

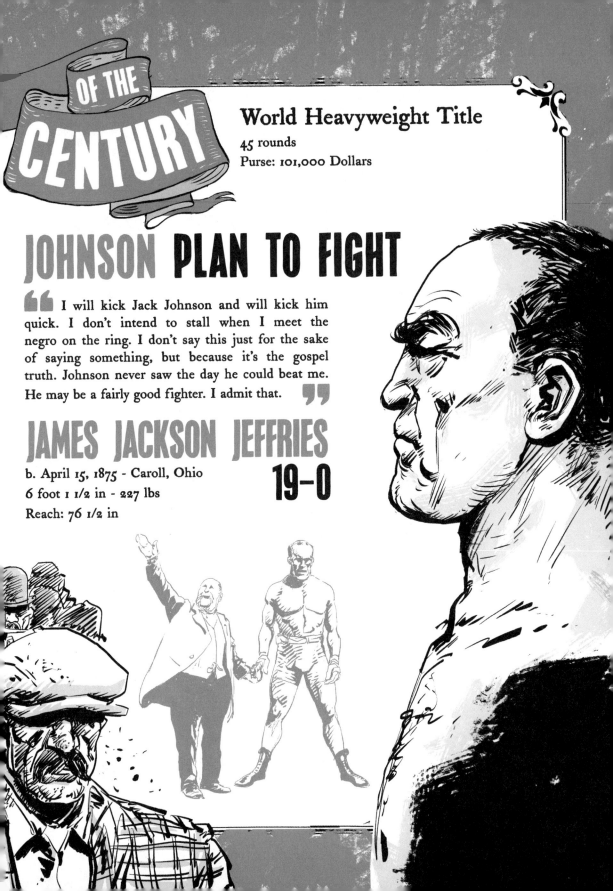

OF THE CENTURY

World Heavyweight Title
45 rounds
Purse: 101,000 Dollars

JOHNSON PLAN TO FIGHT

"I will kick Jack Johnson and will kick him quick. I don't intend to stall when I meet the negro on the ring. I don't say this just for the sake of saying something, but because it's the gospel truth. Johnson never saw the day he could beat me. He may be a fairly good fighter. I admit that."

JAMES JACKSON JEFFRIES

19-0

b. April 15, 1875 - Caroll, Ohio
6 foot 1 1/2 in - 227 lbs
Reach: 76 1/2 in

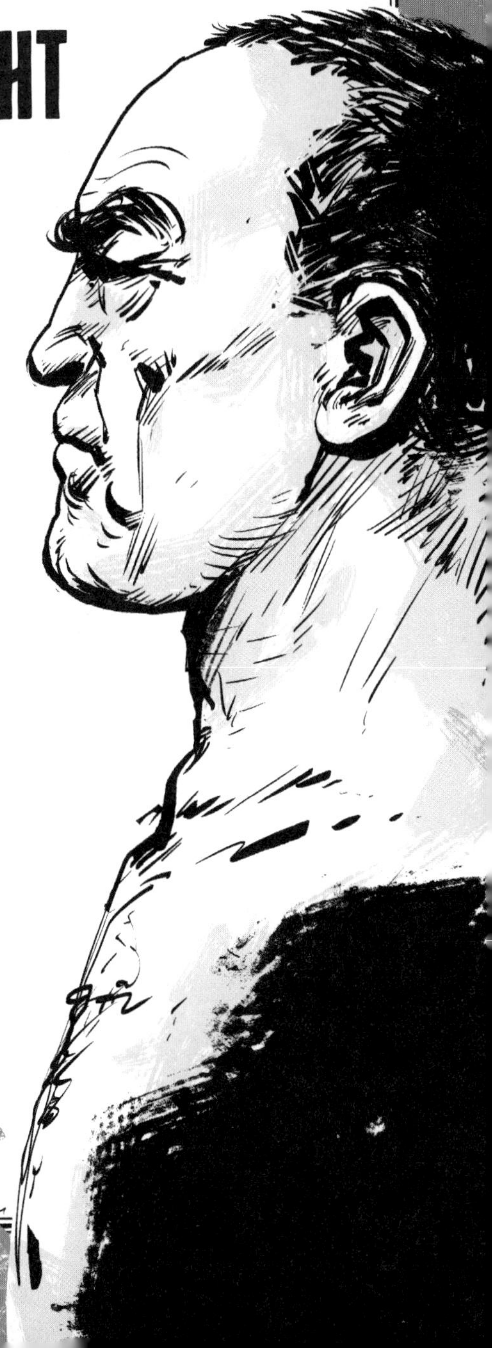

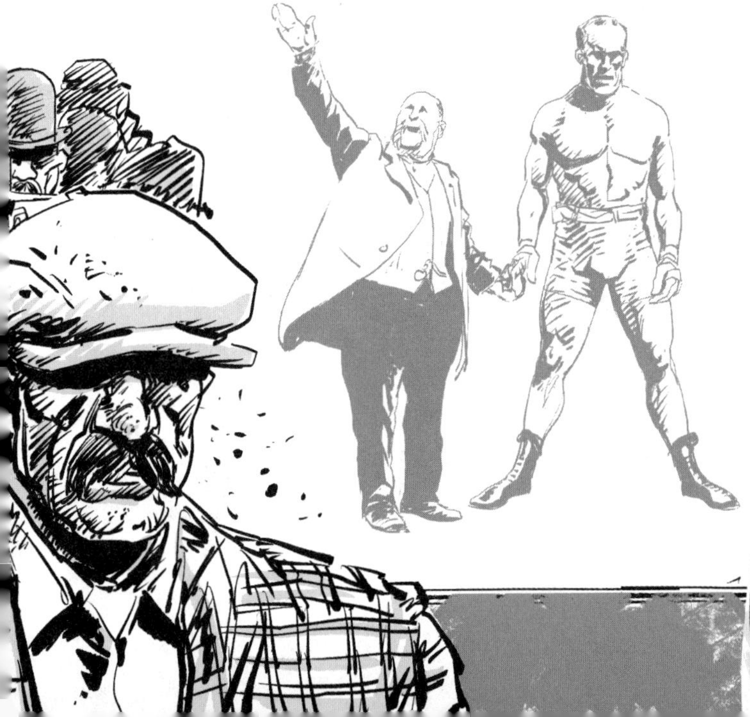

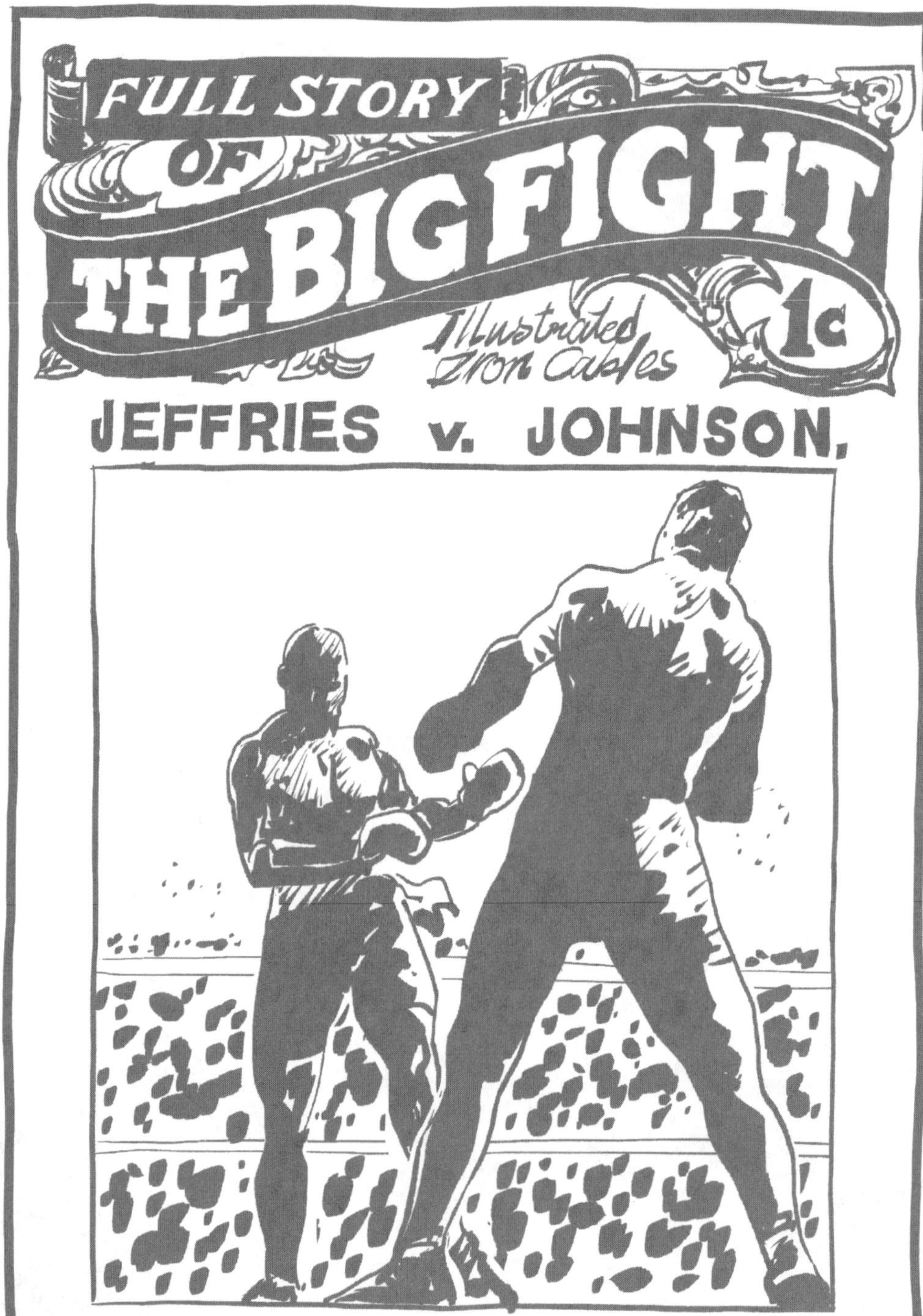
FULL STORY
OF
THE BIG FIGHT
1c
Illustrated
Iron Cables
JEFFRIES v. JOHNSON.

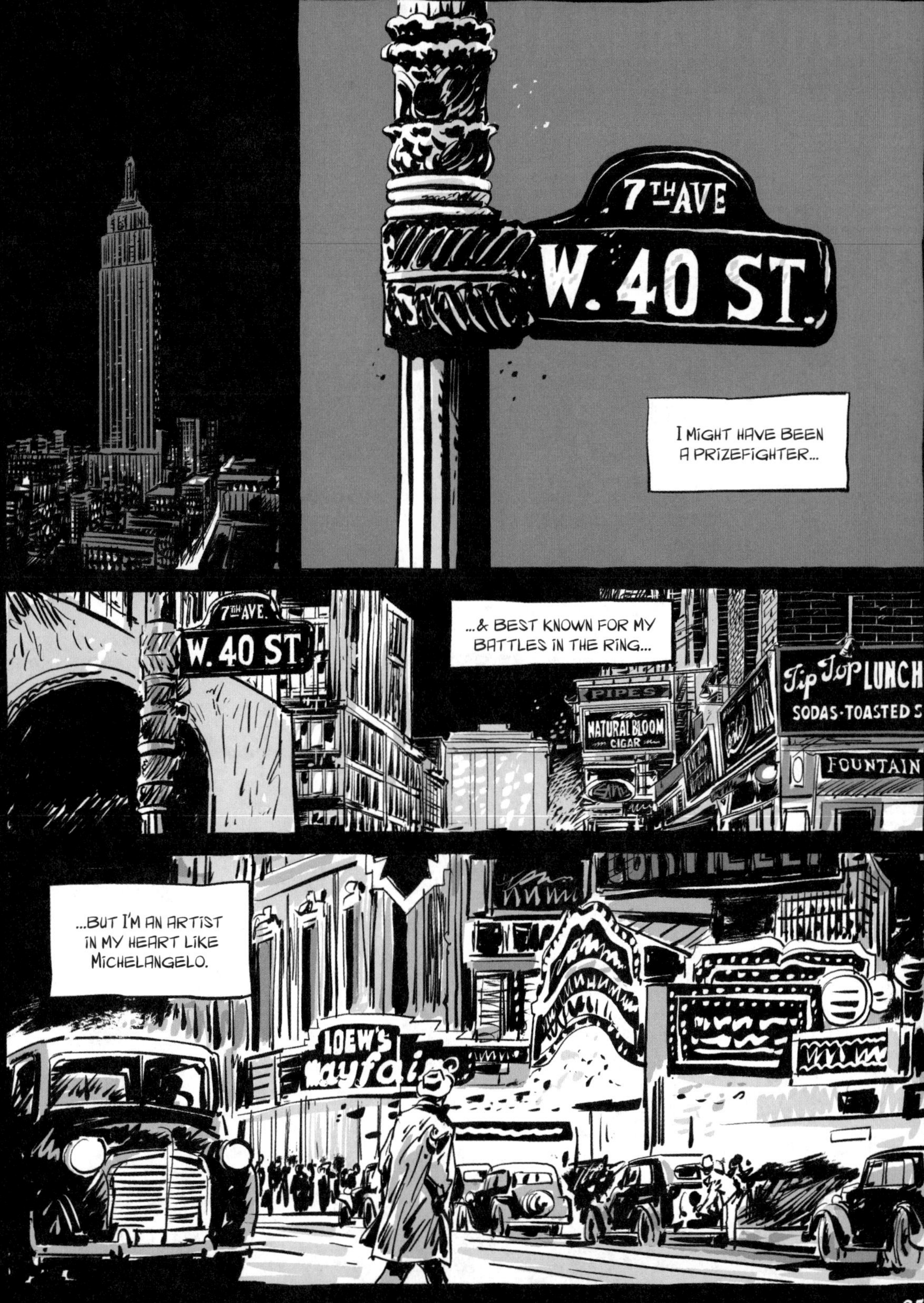
7TH AVE
W. 40 ST.
I MIGHT HAVE BEEN A PRIZEFIGHTER...
7TH AVE.
W. 40 ST
...& BEST KNOWN FOR MY BATTLES IN THE RING...
PIPES
NATURAL BLOOM CIGAR
Tip Top LUNCH
SODAS·TOASTED S
FOUNTAIN
...BUT I'M AN ARTIST IN MY HEART LIKE MICHELANGELO.
LOEW'S
Mayfai

HUBERT'S MUSEUM, A HOUSE OF ODDITIES, NY 1938

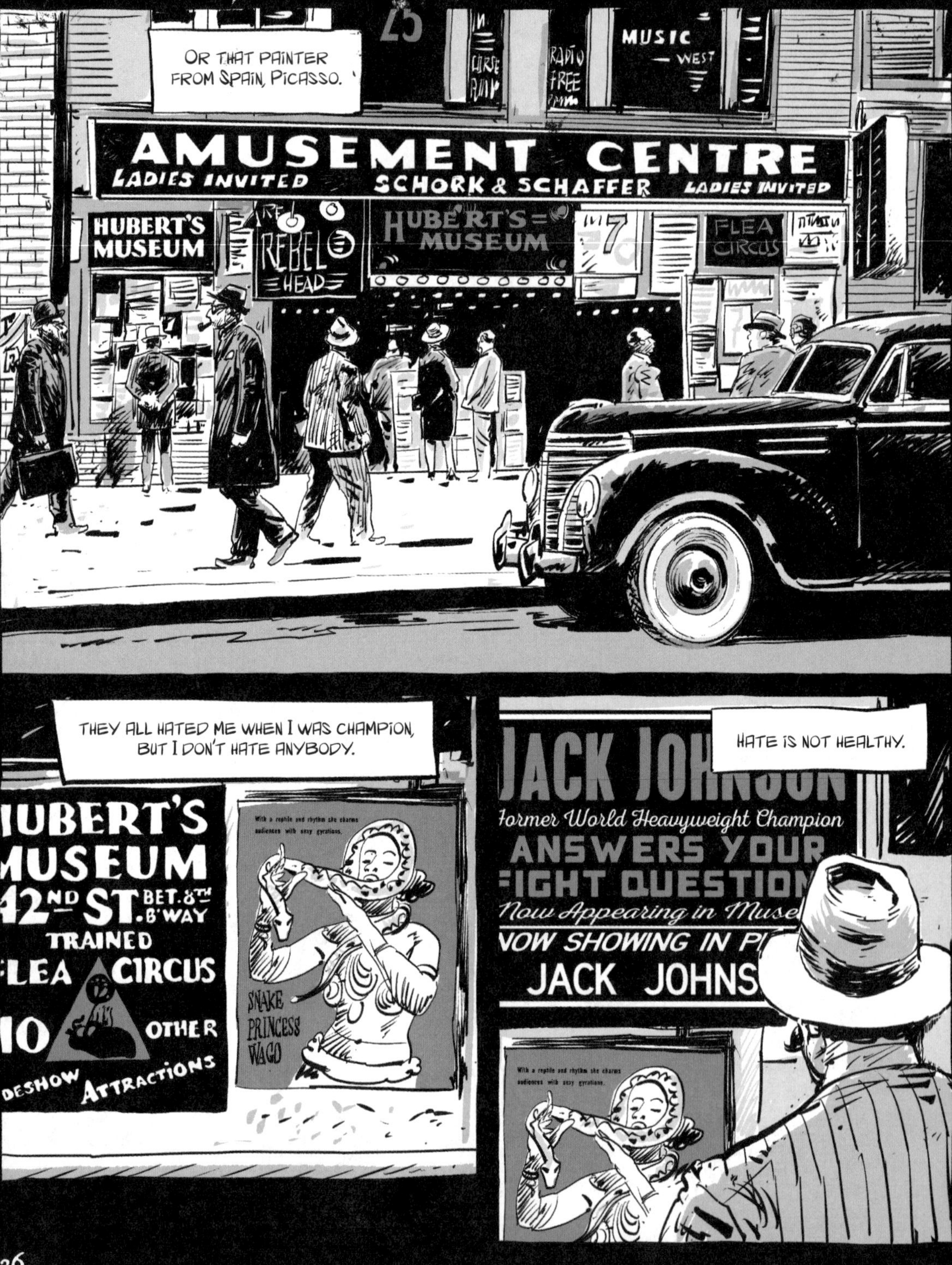

OR THAT PAINTER FROM SPAIN, PICASSO.
MUSIC WEST
RADIO FREE
AMUSEMENT CENTRE
LADIES INVITED
SCHORK & SCHAFFER
LADIES INVITED
HUBERT'S MUSEUM
REBEL HEAD
HUBERT'S MUSEUM
FLEA CIRCUS
THEY ALL HATED ME WHEN I WAS CHAMPION, BUT I DON'T HATE ANYBODY.
IUBERT'S
MUSEUM
42ND ST. BET. 8TH B'WAY
TRAINED
FLEA CIRCUS
OTHER
DESHOW ATTRACTIONS
With a reptile and rhythm she charms audiences with sexy gyrations.
SNAKE PRINCESS WAGO
HATE IS NOT HEALTHY.
JACK JOH
Former World Heavyweight Champion
ANSWERS YOUR
FIGHT QUESTIO
Now Appearing in Muse
NOW SHOWING IN P
JACK JOHNS
With a reptile and rhythm she charms audiences with sexy gyrations.

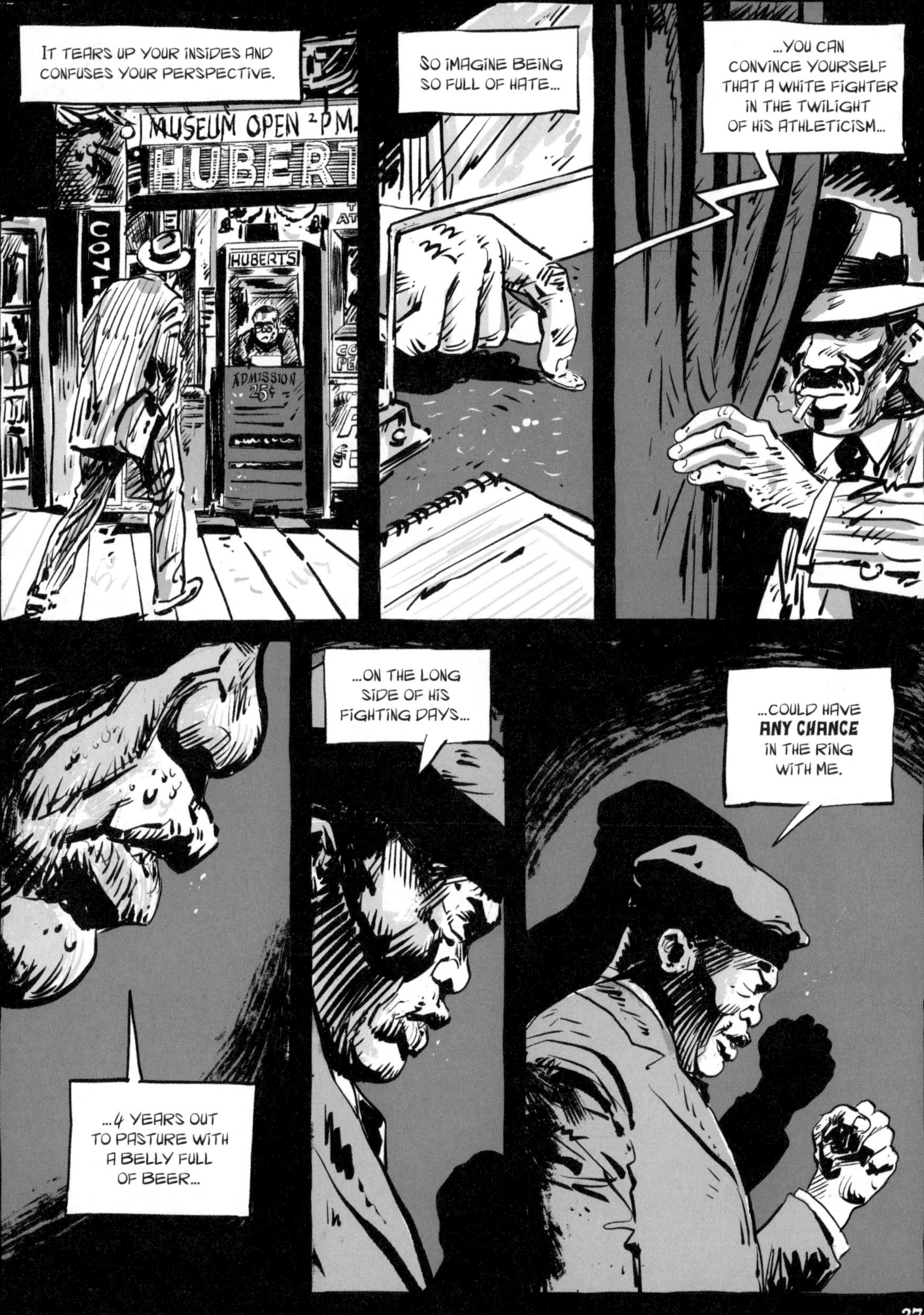

It tears up your insides and confuses your perspective.
MUSEUM OPEN 2 PM.
HUBERT'S
HUBERT'S
ADMISSION 25¢
So imagine being so full of hate...
...you can convince yourself that a white fighter in the twilight of his athleticism...
...4 years out to pasture with a belly full of beer...
...on the long side of his fighting days...
...could have **any chance** in the ring with me.

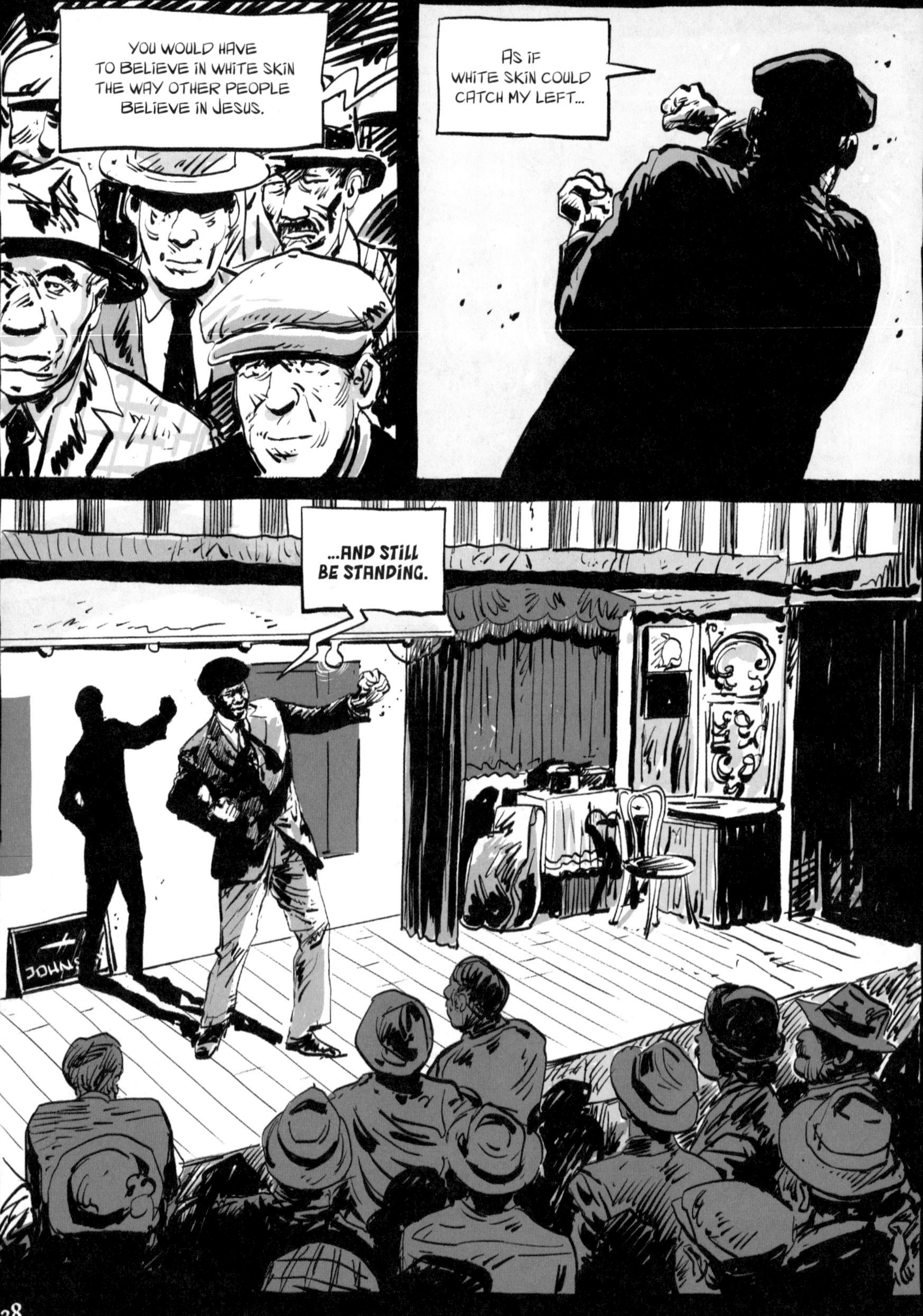
YOU WOULD HAVE TO BELIEVE IN WHITE SKIN THE WAY OTHER PEOPLE BELIEVE IN JESUS.
AS IF WHITE SKIN COULD CATCH MY LEFT...
...AND STILL BE STANDING.

As if white skin does the fighting
and not the bruising.

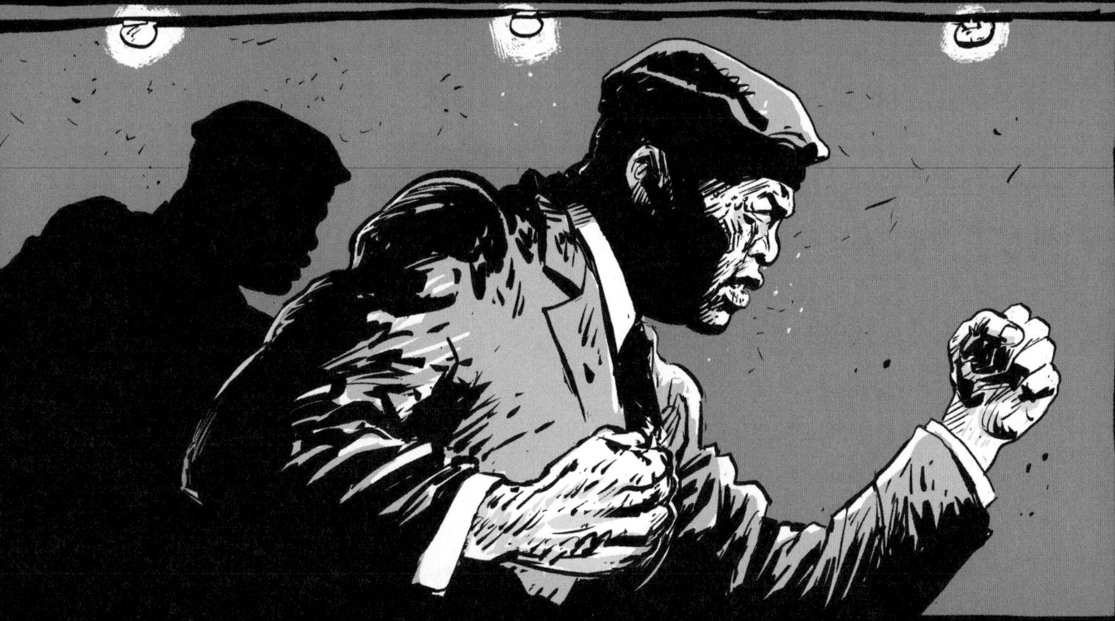

White isn't a color.

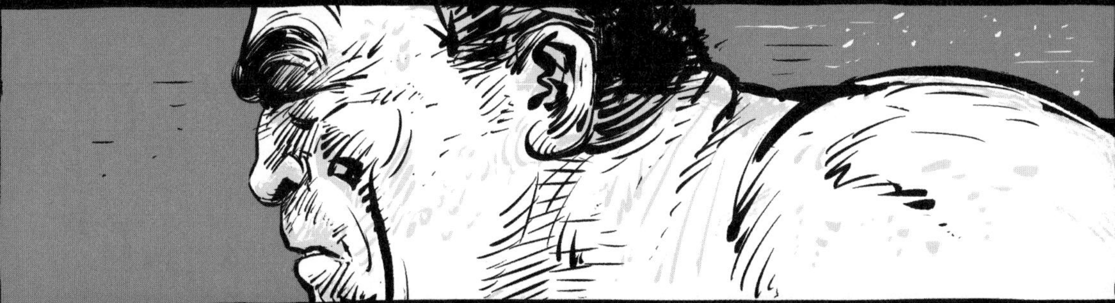

It's the absence of color.

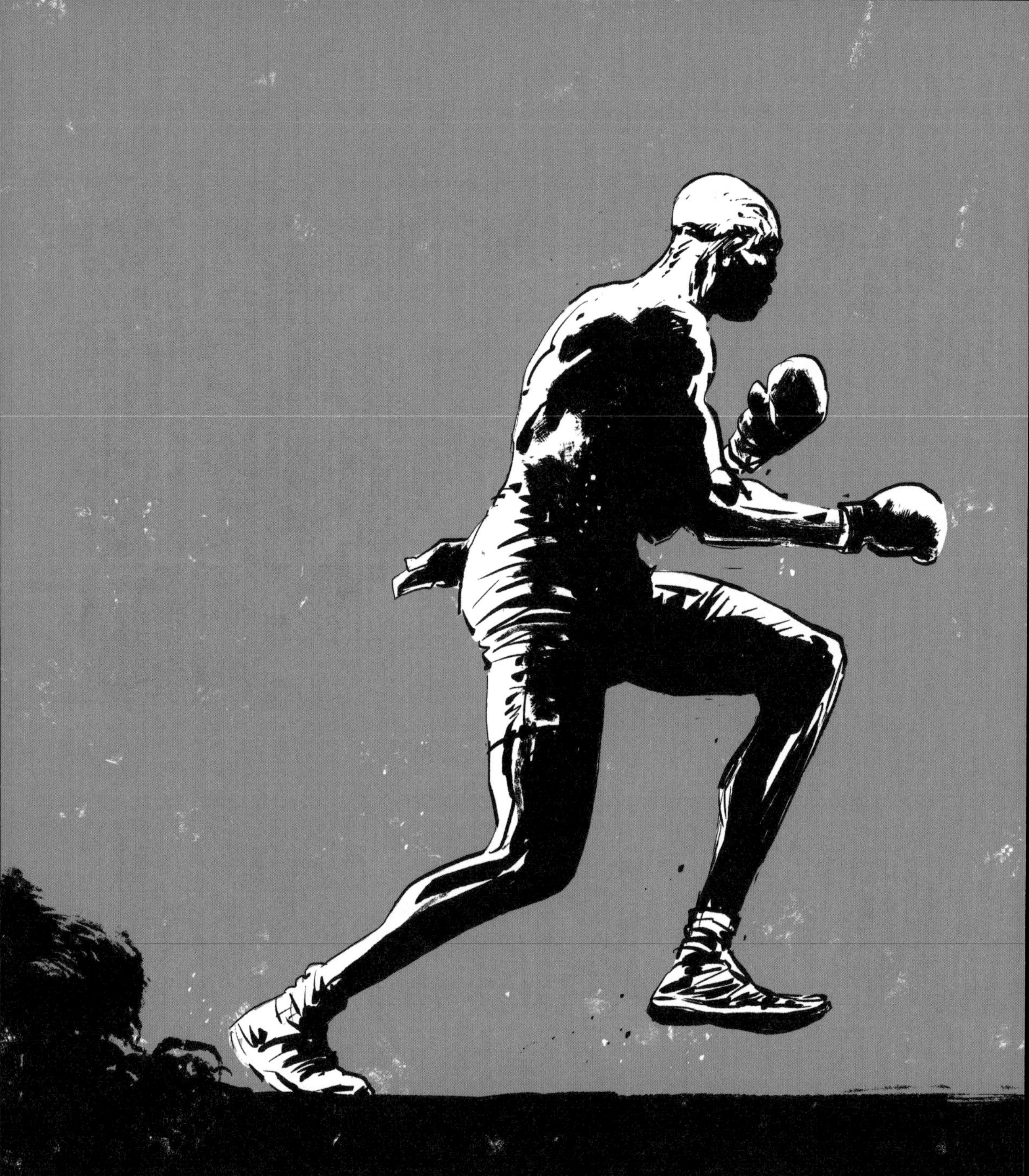

I'M READY, JEFF

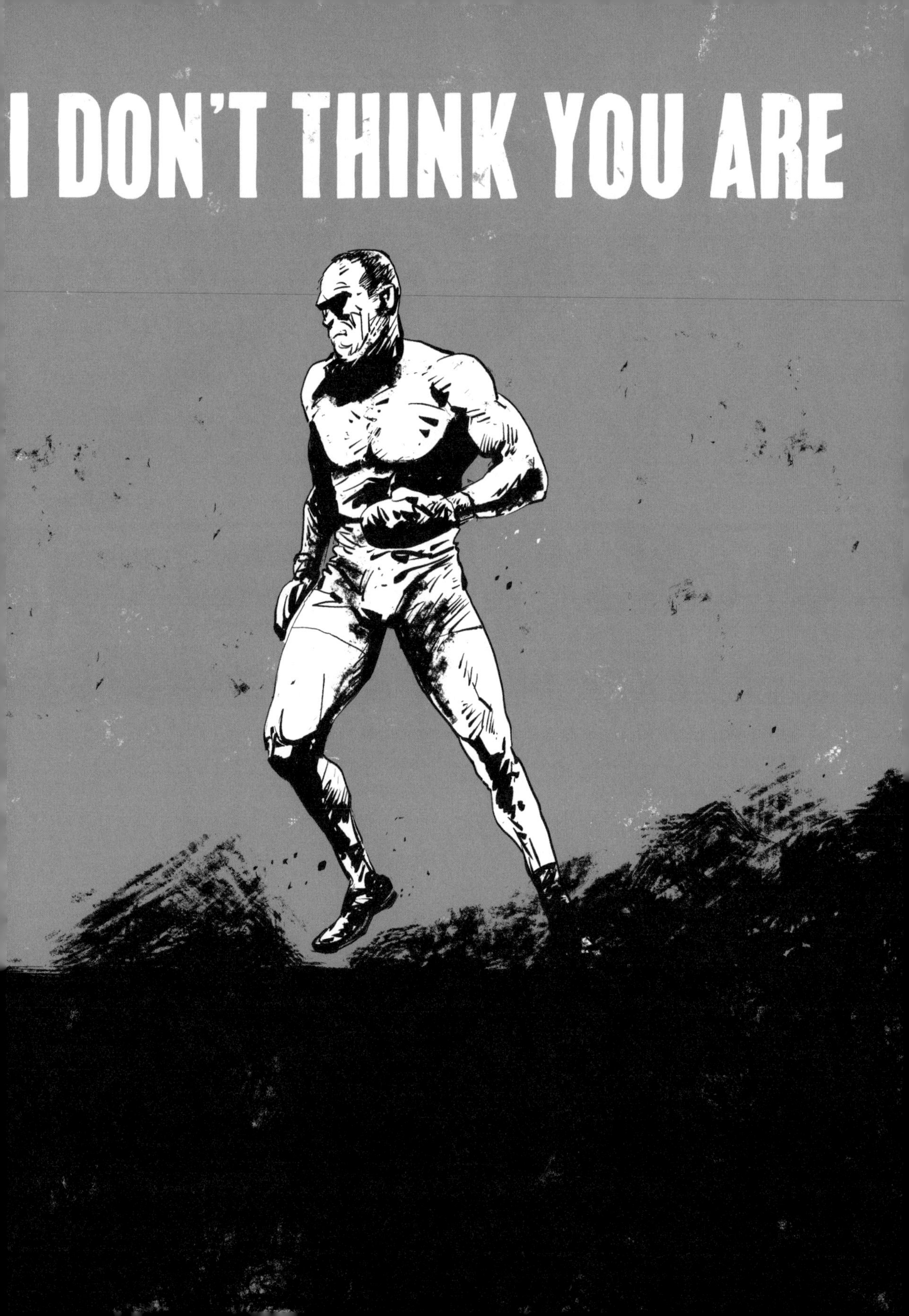
I DON'T THINK YOU ARE

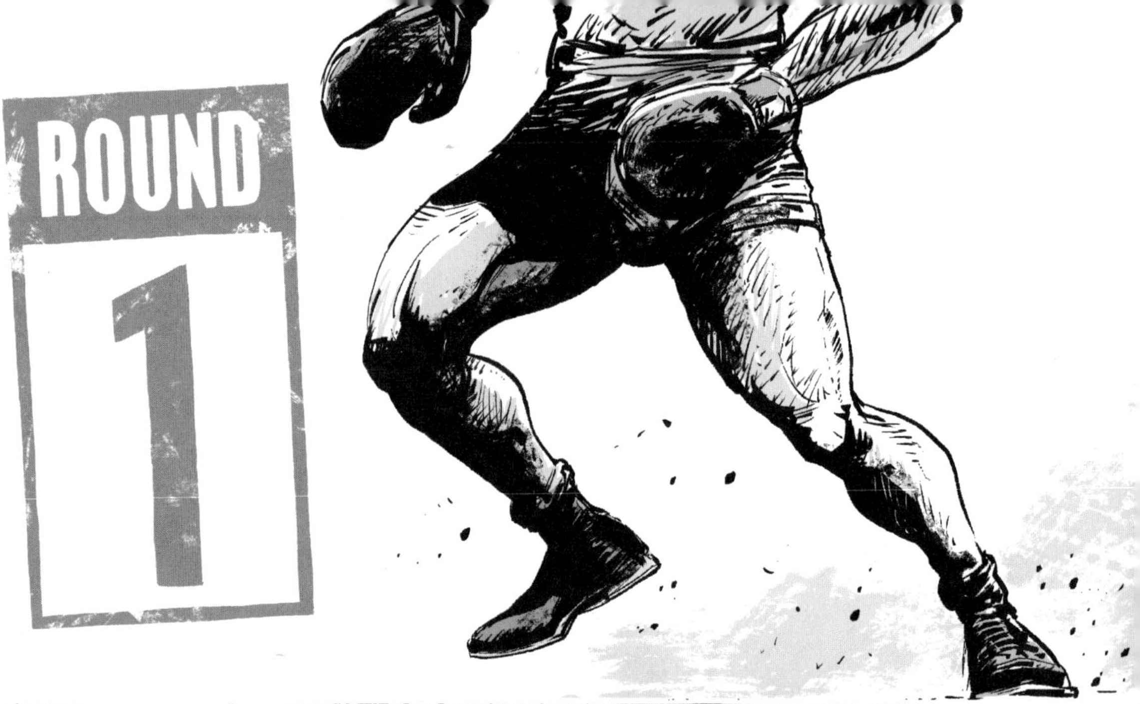
ROUND
1

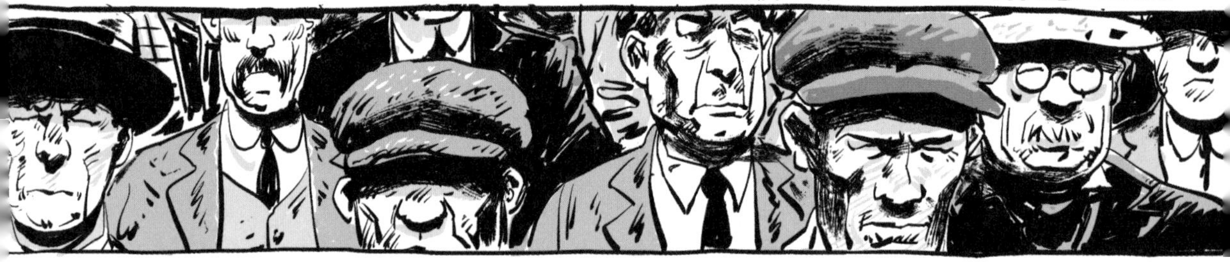

Some whites still believe they can have whatever they want from Blacks. Like it's the slave days & we're still property.

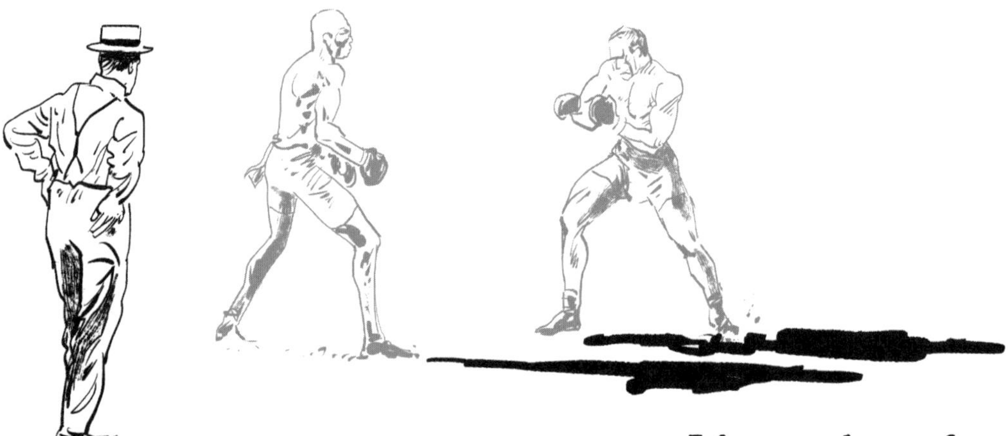

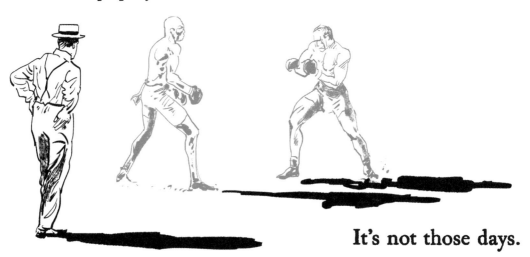

It's not those days.

I'm my own man
whether they like it or not.

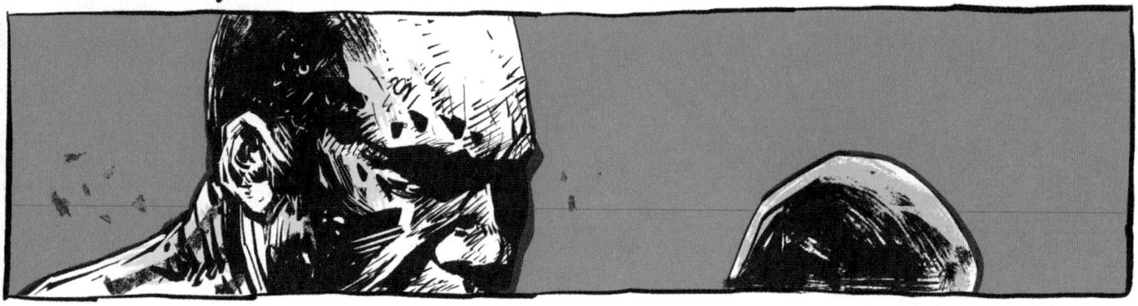

Same for Jeffries. He was
a game champion in his day.

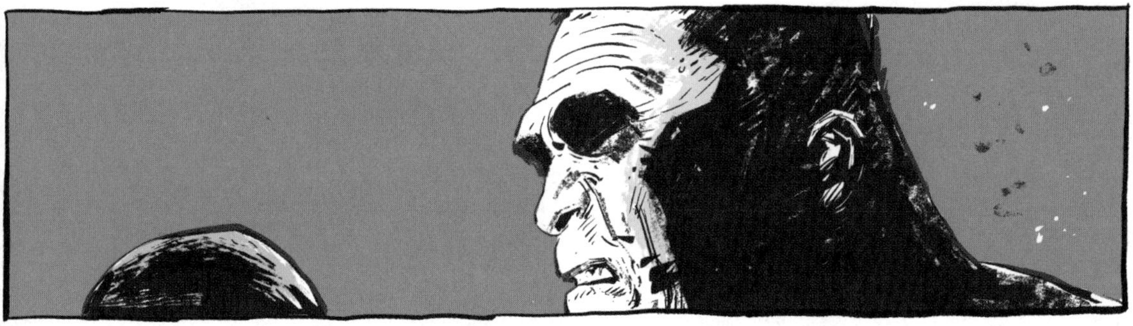

But today
isn't his day.

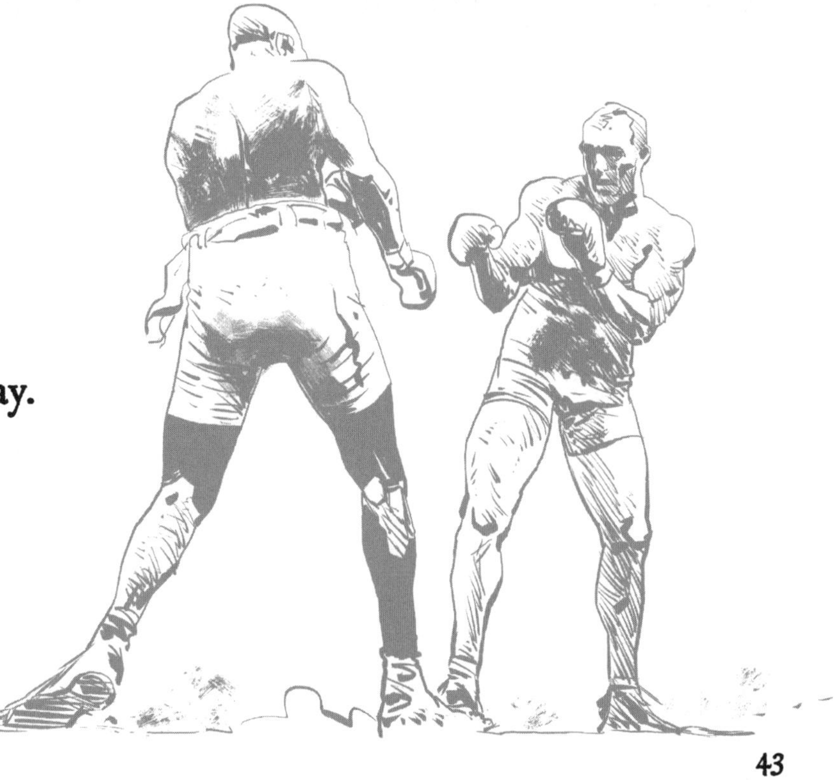

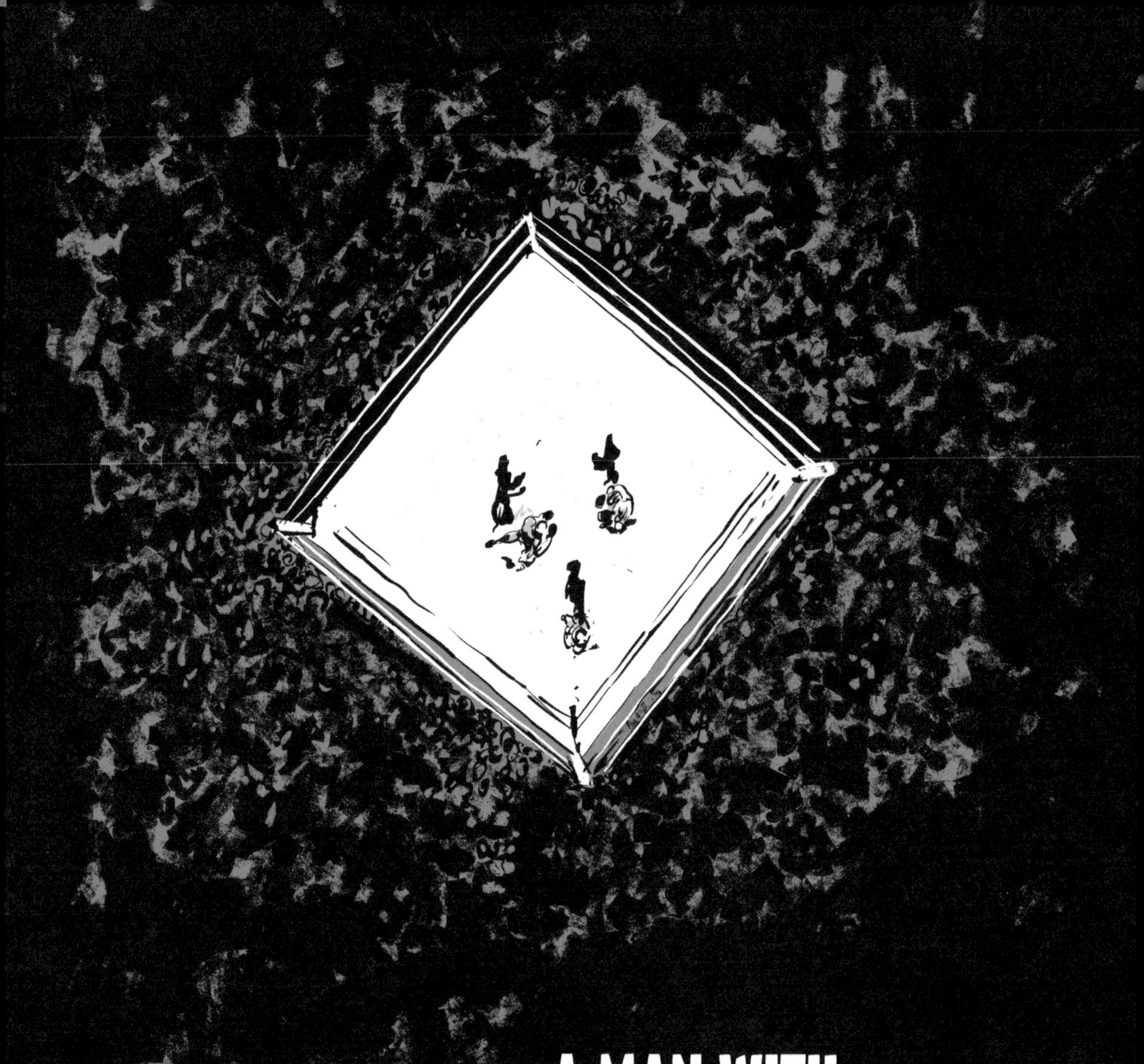

A MAN WITH PROSPECTS

As soon as I was grown enough, I hopped a boxcar in the middle of the night & headed to Chicago. I knew I had prospects past Galveston, past shoveling manure & straw out of smelly horse stalls.

I knew I was made for something
more majestic than rotting fish,
sea salt & all that stevedore sweat.

I told the boys unloading that steamer cargo, "Tossing cotton might be easy, but it don't pay enough for a shoe shine." & I knew my shoes were going to shine like shaving mirrors.

GET OFF!

GO!

HIT 'IM!

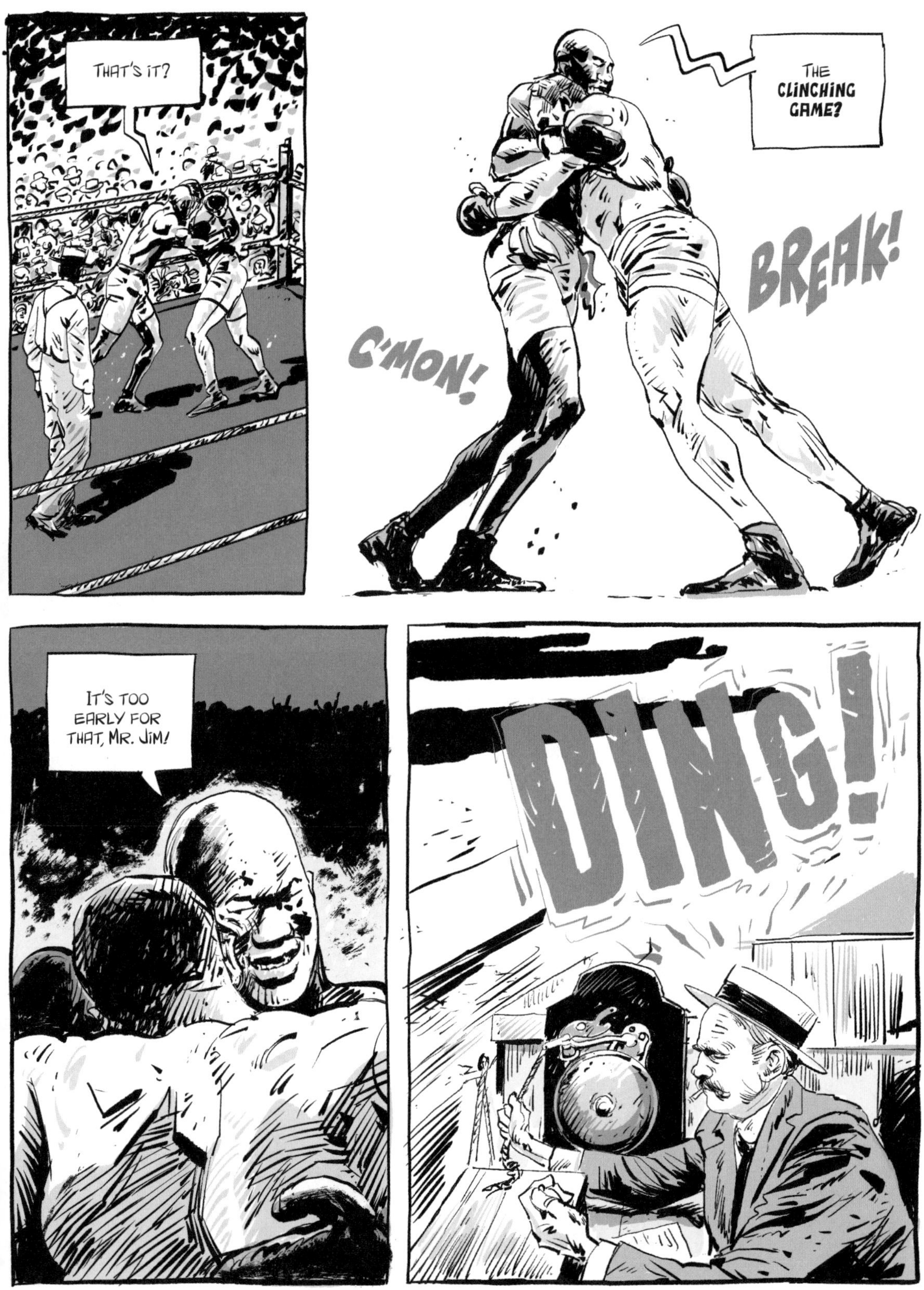
THAT'S IT?
THE CLINCHING GAME?
BREAK!
C'MON!
IT'S TOO EARLY FOR THAT, MR. JIM!
DING!

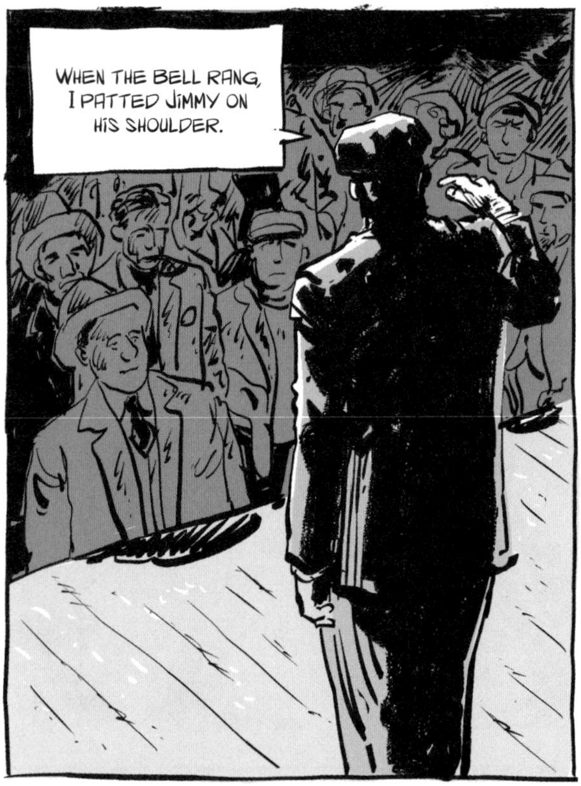
WHEN THE BELL RANG, I PATTED JIMMY ON HIS SHOULDER.

It was my last gentlemanly gesture...

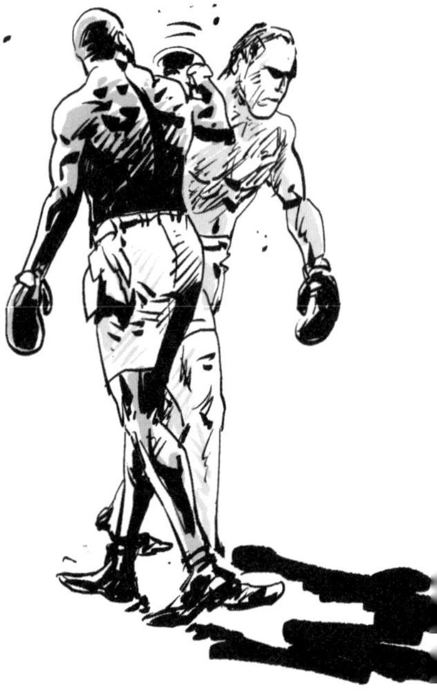

...before the hurt.

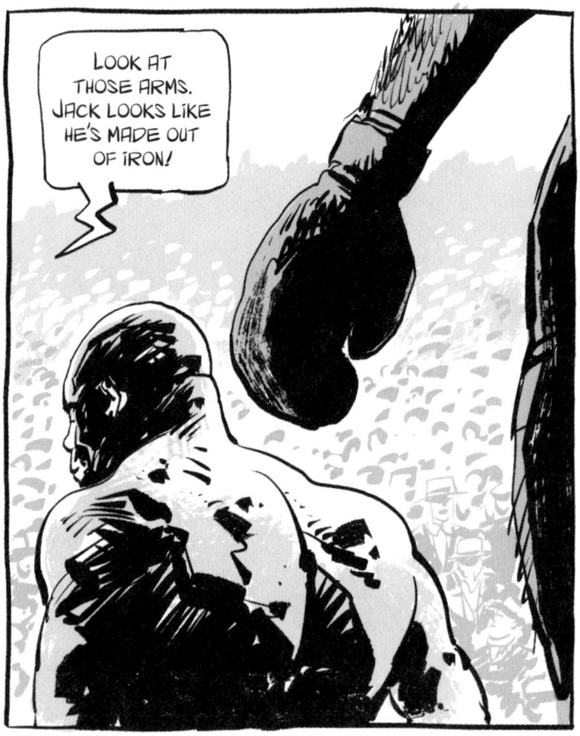
LOOK AT THOSE ARMS. JACK LOOKS LIKE HE'S MADE OUT OF IRON!

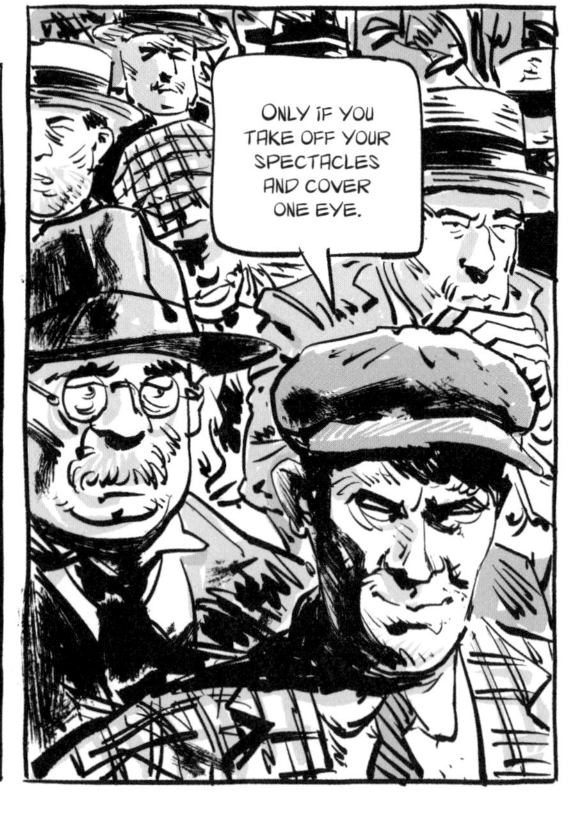
ONLY IF YOU TAKE OFF YOUR SPECTACLES AND COVER ONE EYE.

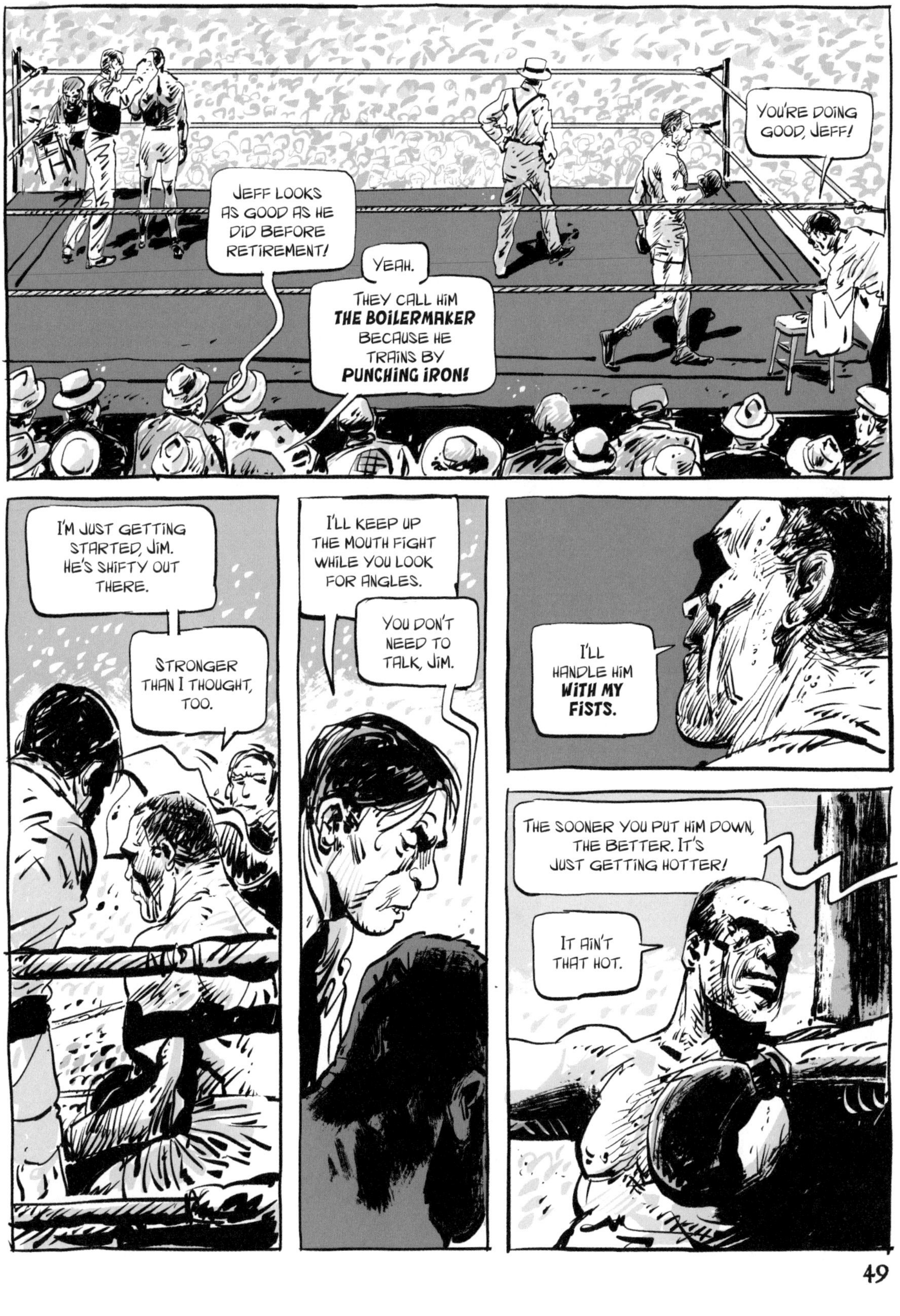
YOU'RE DOING GOOD, JEFF!
JEFF LOOKS AS GOOD AS HE DID BEFORE RETIREMENT!
YEAH.
THEY CALL HIM **THE BOILERMAKER** BECAUSE HE TRAINS BY **PUNCHING IRON!**
I'M JUST GETTING STARTED, JIM. HE'S SHIFTY OUT THERE.
STRONGER THAN I THOUGHT, TOO.
I'LL KEEP UP THE MOUTH FIGHT WHILE YOU LOOK FOR ANGLES.
YOU DON'T NEED TO TALK, JIM.
I'LL HANDLE HIM **WITH MY FISTS.**
THE SOONER YOU PUT HIM DOWN, THE BETTER. IT'S JUST GETTING HOTTER!
IT AIN'T THAT HOT.

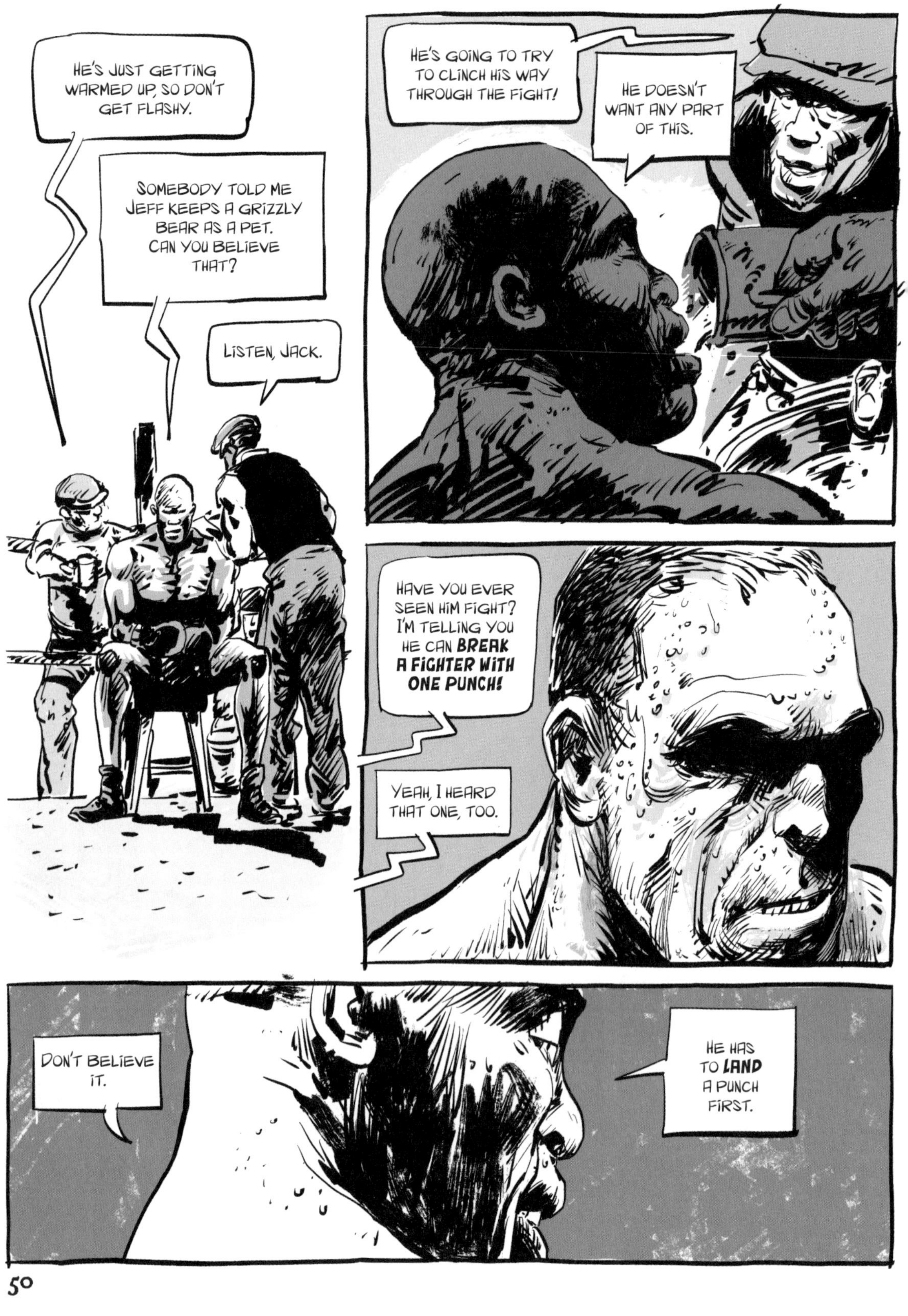
HE'S JUST GETTING WARMED UP, SO DON'T GET FLASHY.
SOMEBODY TOLD ME JEFF KEEPS A GRIZZLY BEAR AS A PET. CAN YOU BELIEVE THAT?
LISTEN, JACK.
HE'S GOING TO TRY TO CLINCH HIS WAY THROUGH THE FIGHT!
HE DOESN'T WANT ANY PART OF THIS.
HAVE YOU EVER SEEN HIM FIGHT? I'M TELLING YOU HE CAN **BREAK A FIGHTER WITH ONE PUNCH!**
YEAH, I HEARD THAT ONE, TOO.
DON'T BELIEVE IT.
HE HAS TO **LAND** A PUNCH FIRST.

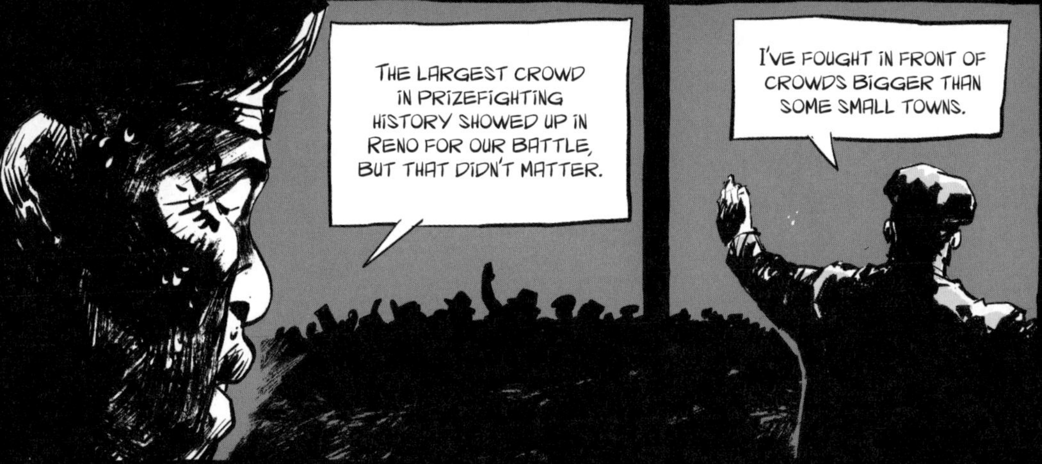
THE LARGEST CROWD IN PRIZEFIGHTING HISTORY SHOWED UP IN RENO FOR OUR BATTLE, BUT THAT DIDN'T MATTER.
I'VE FOUGHT IN FRONT OF CROWDS BIGGER THAN SOME SMALL TOWNS.

I've fought every way & everywhere:
in overalls on empty streets
& in sandlots. I fought in a three-
piece suit on a boxcar & with
one hand tied behind my back
in a cellar. Any place somebody
put up their dukes. I even fought
in a battle royal blindfolded.

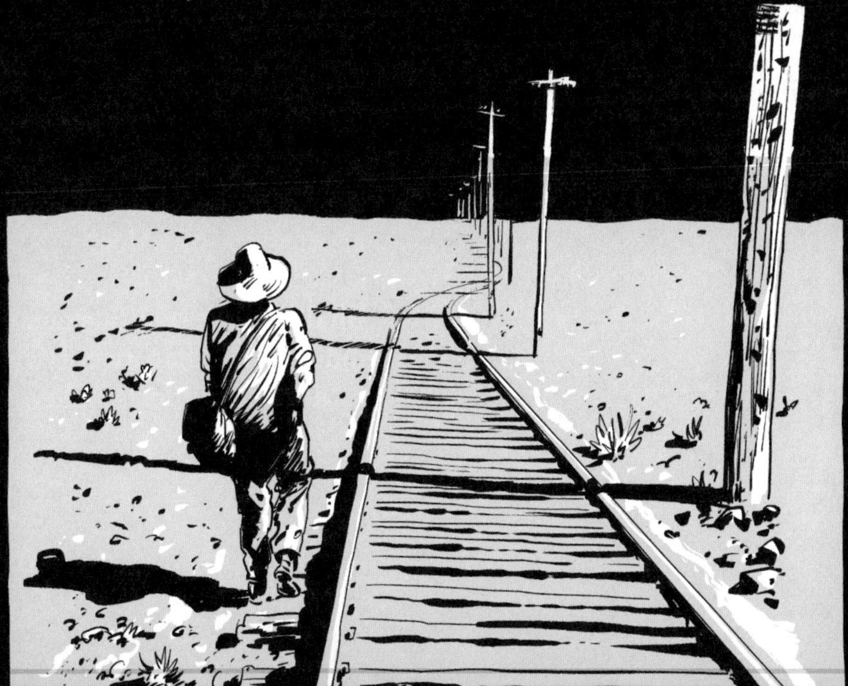

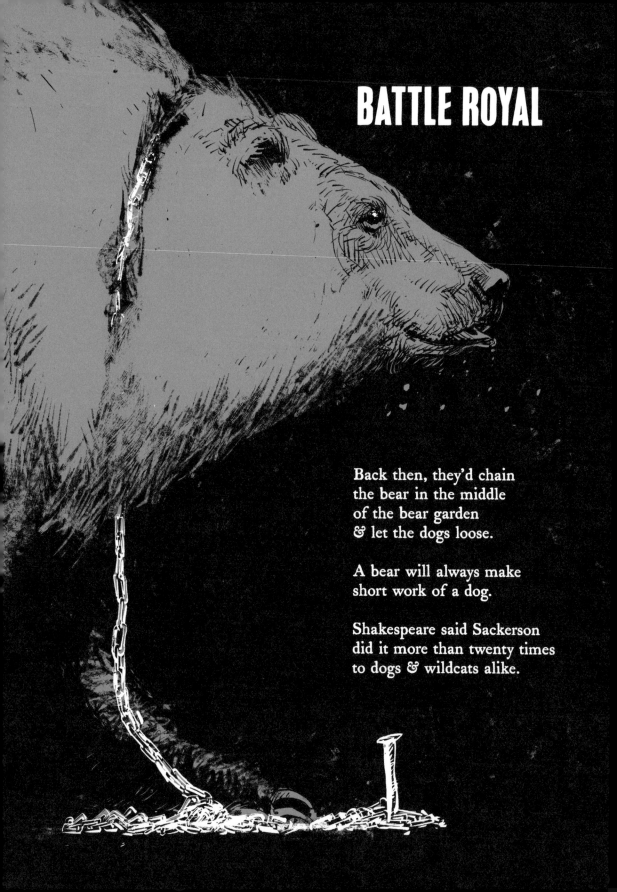

BATTLE ROYAL

Back then, they'd chain
the bear in the middle
of the bear garden
& let the dogs loose.

A bear will always make
short work of a dog.

Shakespeare said Sackerson
did it more than twenty times
to dogs & wildcats alike.

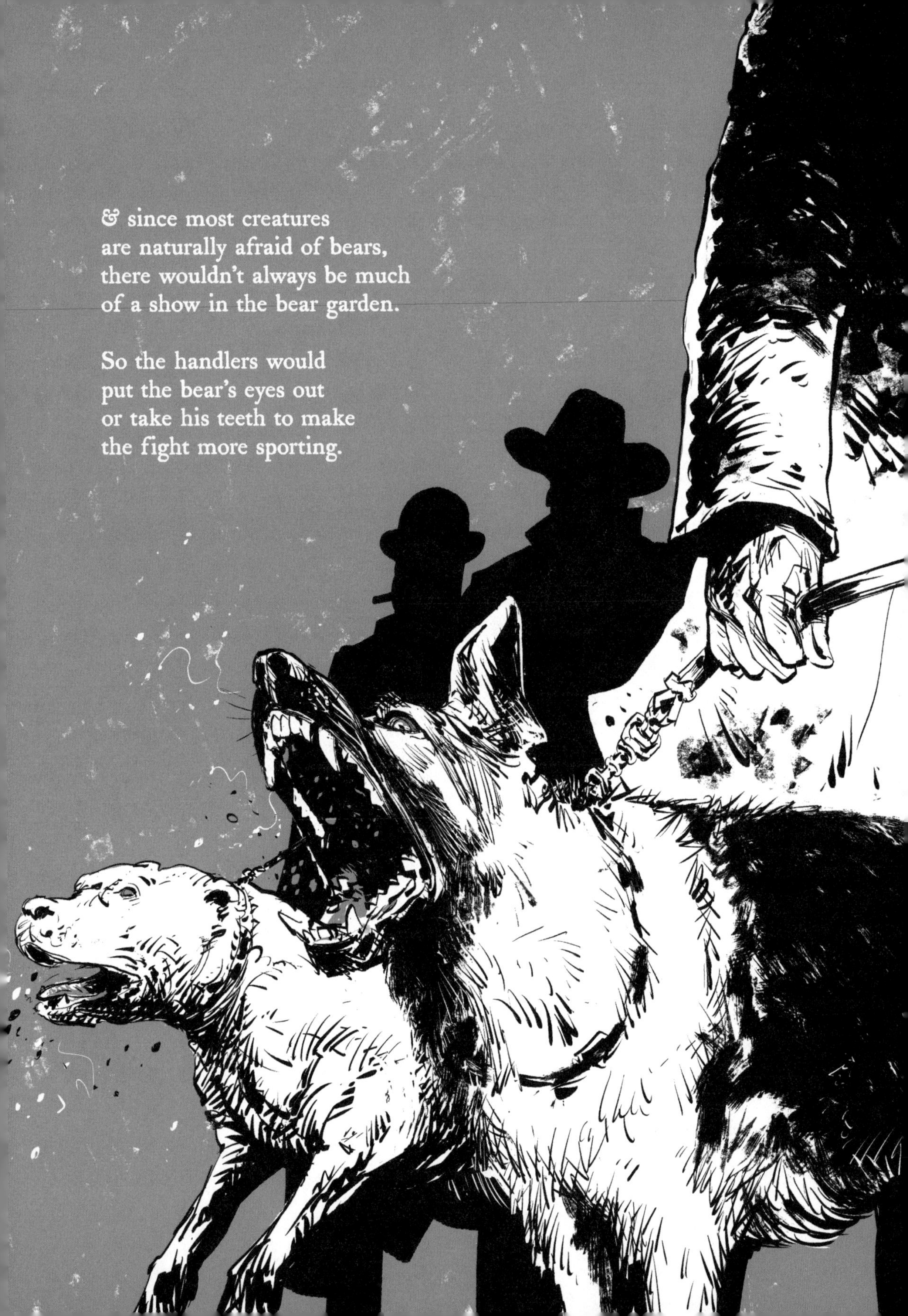
& since most creatures
are naturally afraid of bears,
there wouldn't always be much
of a show in the bear garden.
So the handlers would
put the bear's eyes out
or take his teeth to make
the fight more sporting.

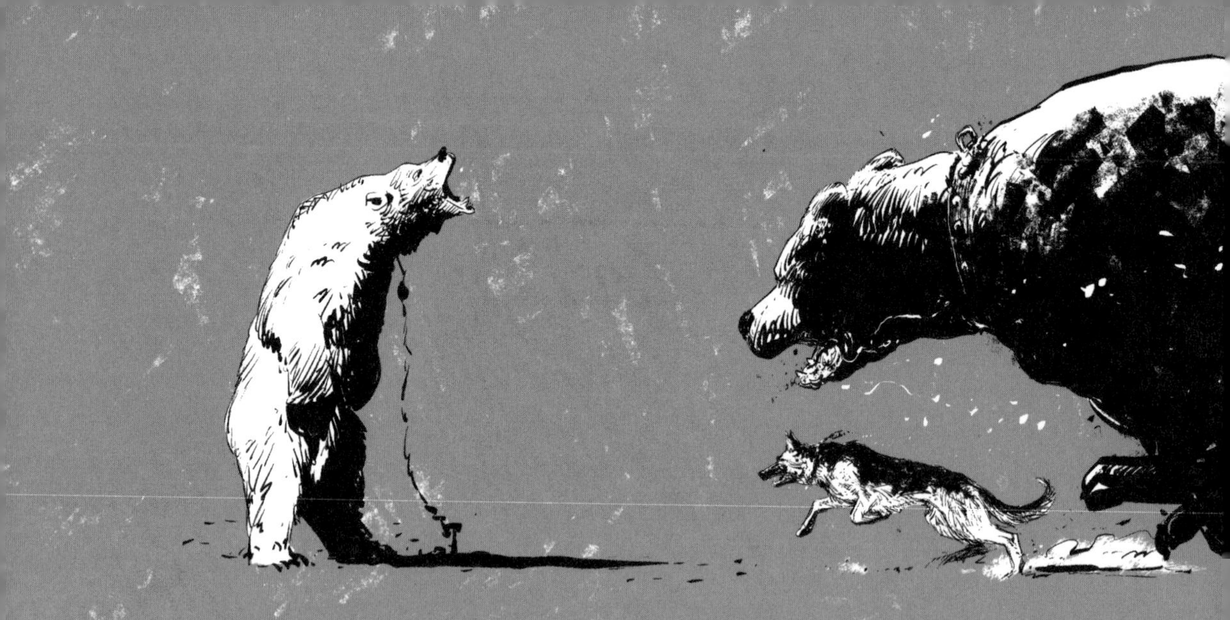

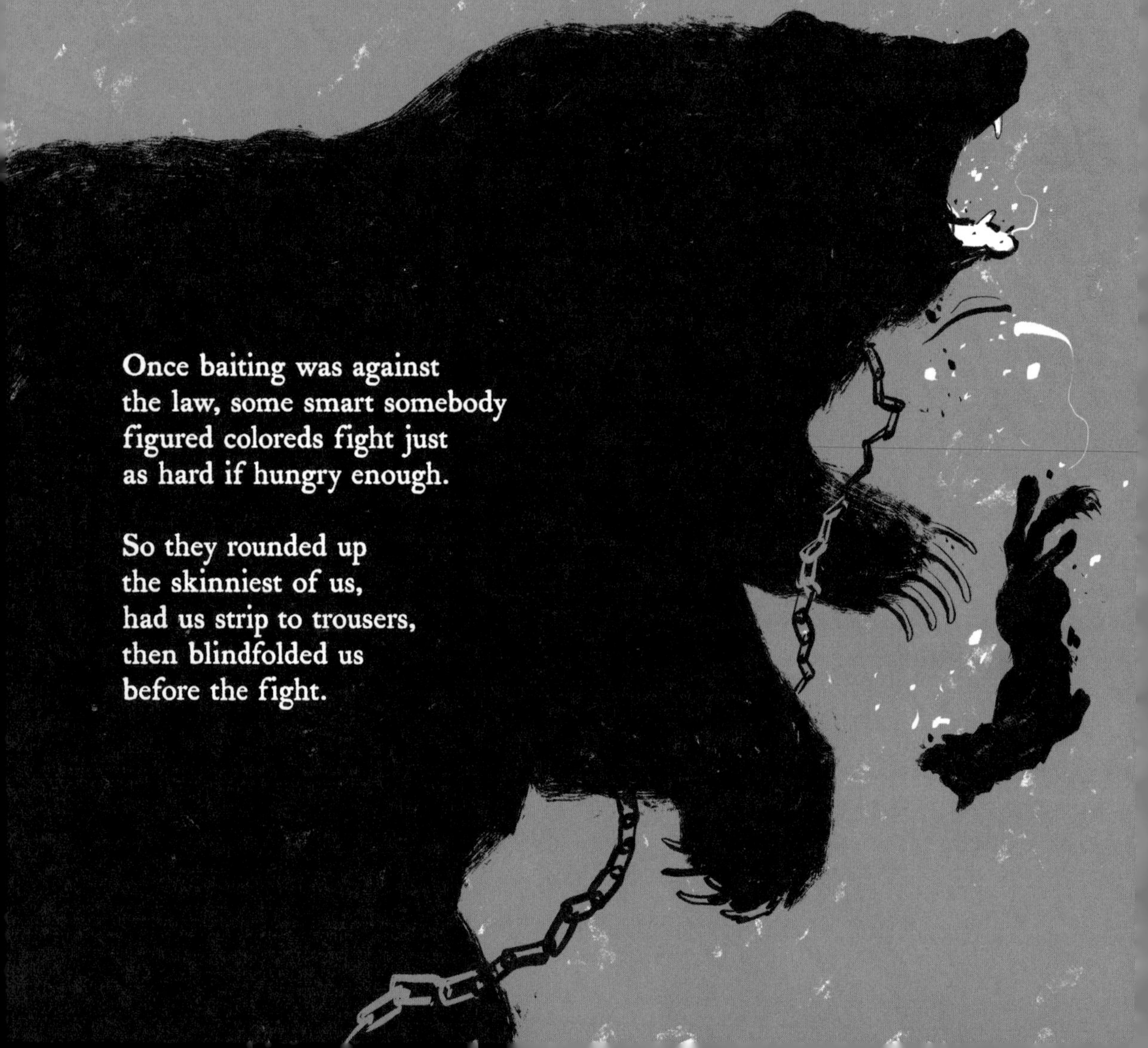

Once baiting was against
the law, some smart somebody
figured coloreds fight just
as hard if hungry enough.

So they rounded up
the skinniest of us,
had us strip to trousers,
then blindfolded us
before the fight.

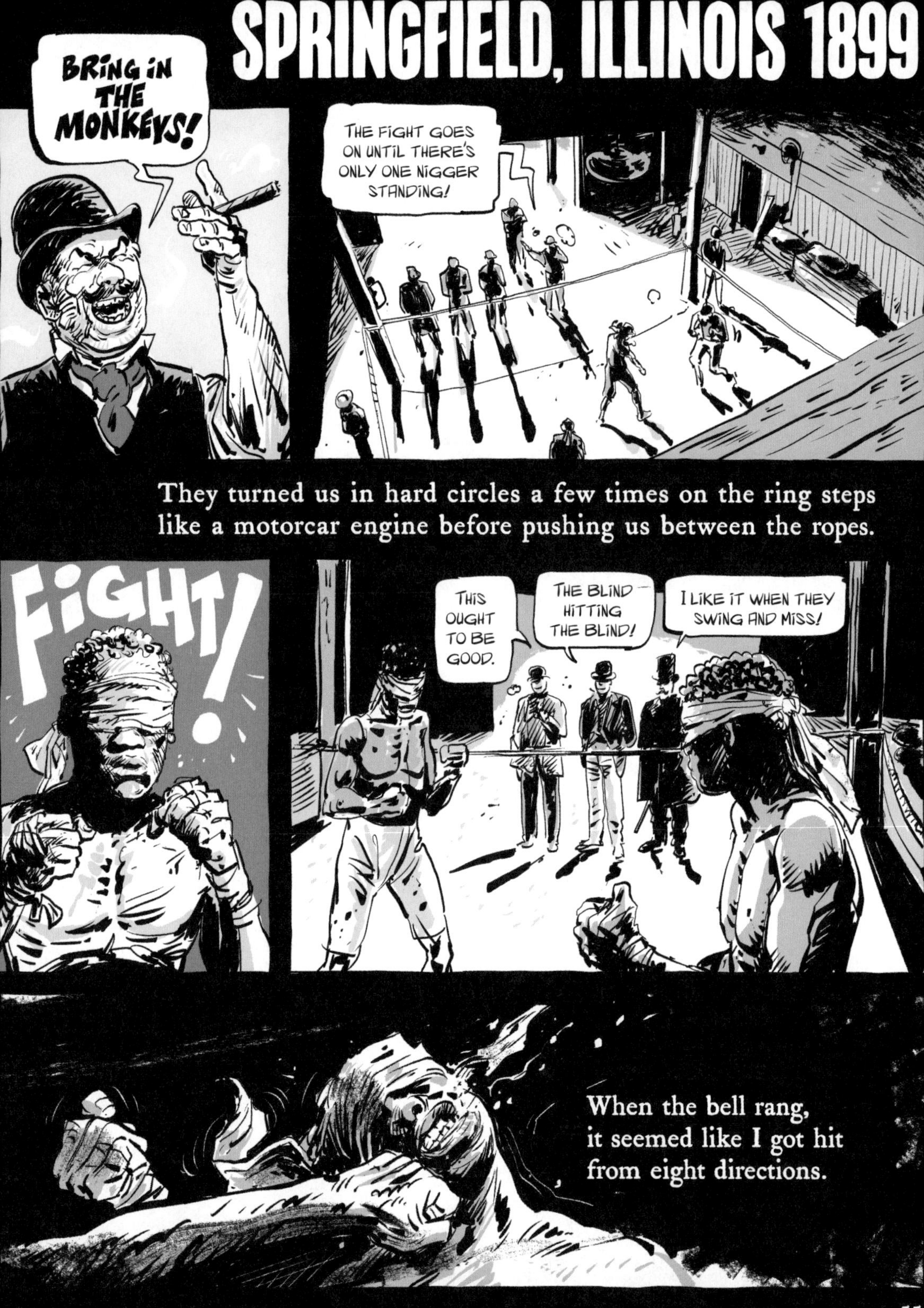
SPRINGFIELD, ILLINOIS 1899
BRING IN THE MONKEYS!
THE FIGHT GOES ON UNTIL THERE'S ONLY ONE NIGGER STANDING!
They turned us in hard circles a few times on the ring steps like a motorcar engine before pushing us between the ropes.
FIGHT!
THIS OUGHT TO BE GOOD.
THE BLIND HITTING THE BLIND!
I LIKE IT WHEN THEY SWING AND MISS!
When the bell rang, it seemed like I got hit from eight directions.

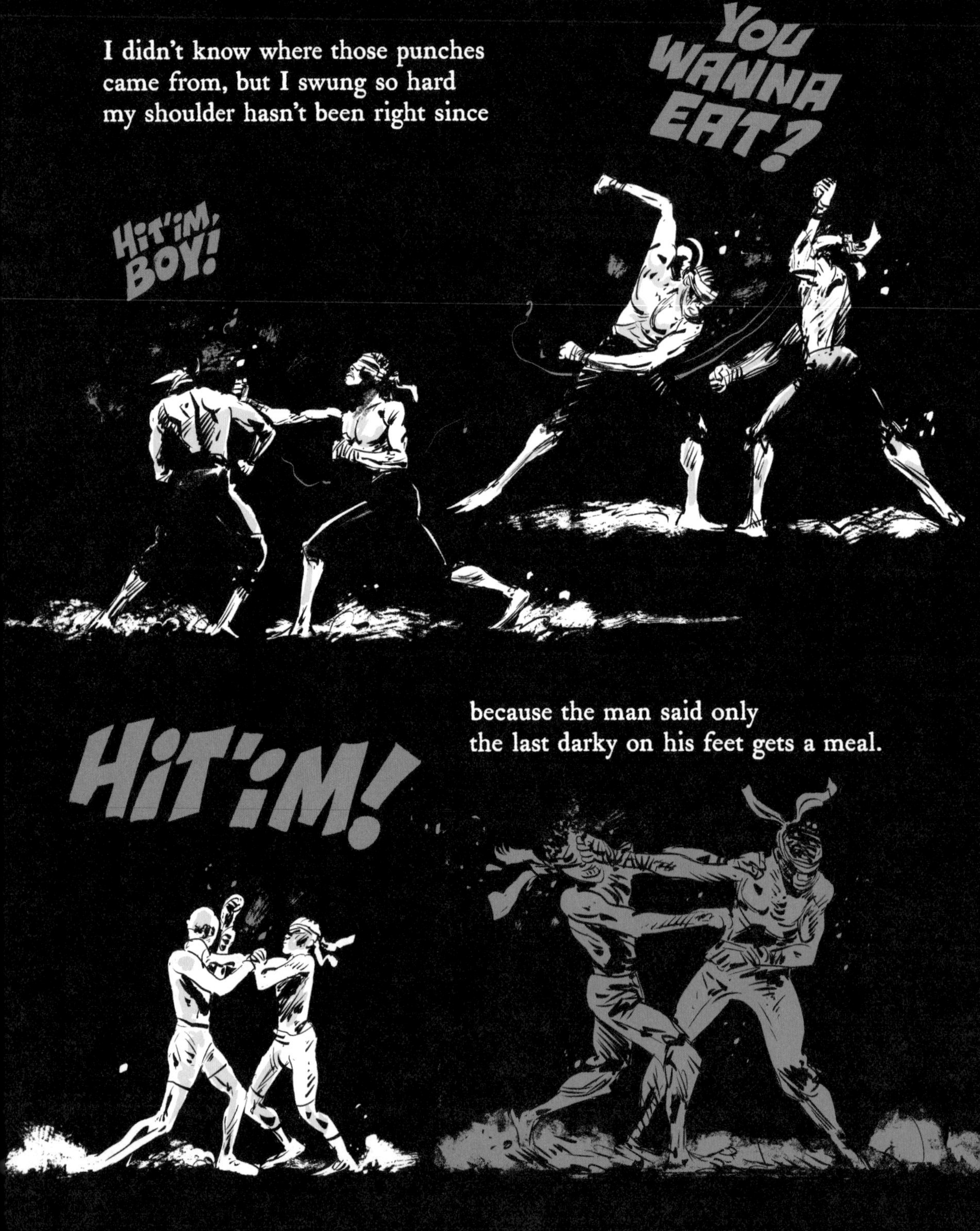
I didn't know where those punches
came from, but I swung so hard
my shoulder hasn't been right since
YOU WANNA EAT?
HIT'IM, BOY!
HIT'IM!
because the man said only
the last darky on his feet gets a meal.

Somebody was eating
that day & I already
had my fork & spoon ready.

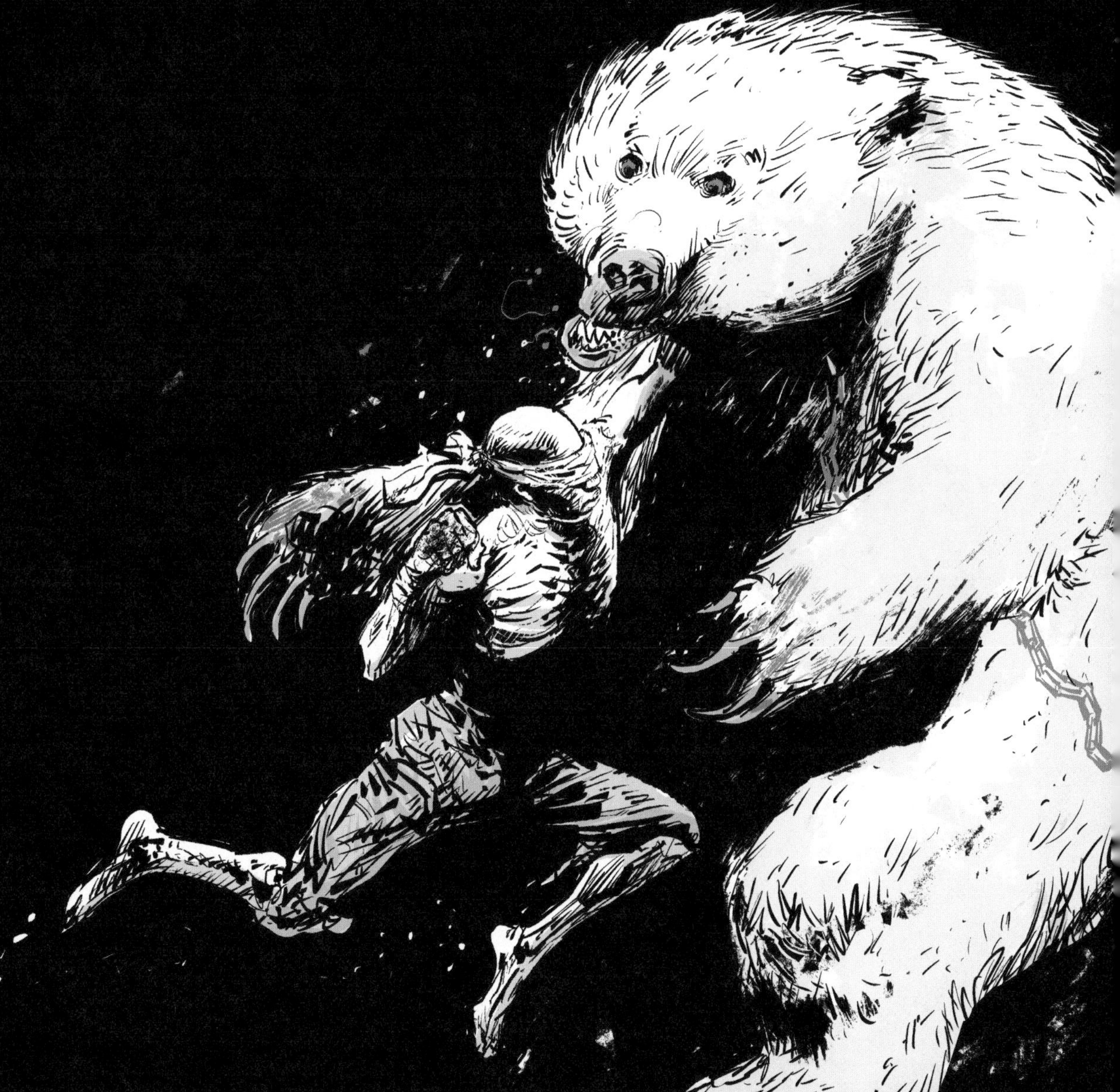

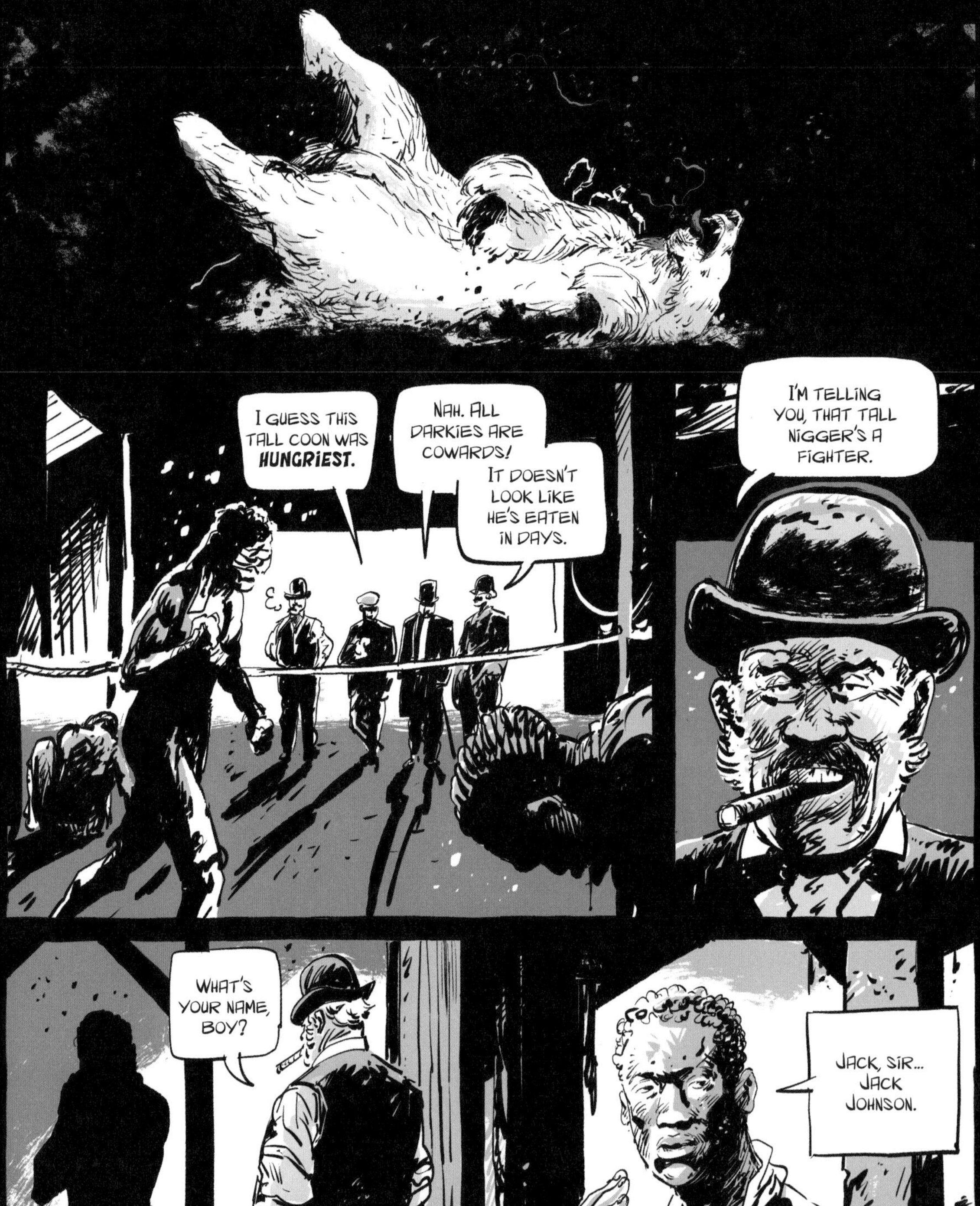
I GUESS THIS TALL COON WAS **HUNGRIEST.**
NAH. ALL DARKIES ARE COWARDS!
IT DOESN'T LOOK LIKE HE'S EATEN IN DAYS.
I'M TELLING YOU, THAT TALL NIGGER'S A FIGHTER.
WHAT'S YOUR NAME, BOY?
JACK, SIR... JACK JOHNSON.

A PIECE OF ADVICE FROM JACK JOHNSON

Understand Shakespeare. Man's behavior
is in the great poet's words. See,

politicians are as crooked as a bag of fishhooks:
give them enough money & whatever

ugly you might have done isn't so ugly
anymore. No colored in this world's got

enough money to change black to white,
so if you are going to make it

in these United States of America, you best
figure out how the bear Sackerson was still

able to beat back those hungry dogs
after the handlers pulled out all his teeth.

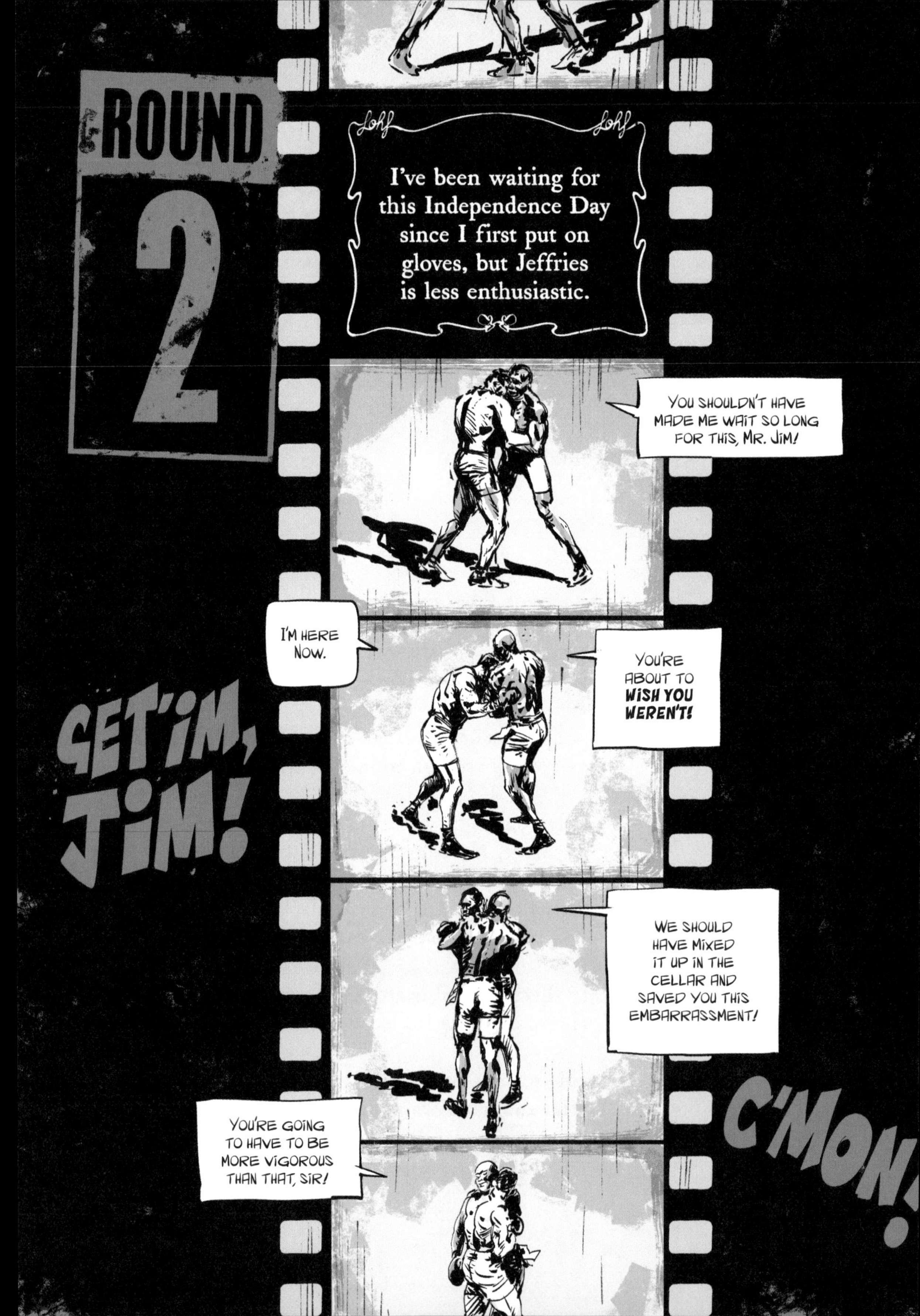
ROUND 2
I've been waiting for this Independence Day since I first put on gloves, but Jeffries is less enthusiastic.
YOU SHOULDN'T HAVE MADE ME WAIT SO LONG FOR THIS, MR. JIM!
I'M HERE NOW.
YOU'RE ABOUT TO **WISH YOU WEREN'T!**
GET 'IM, JIM!
WE SHOULD HAVE MIXED IT UP IN THE CELLAR AND SAVED YOU THIS EMBARRASSMENT!
YOU'RE GOING TO HAVE TO BE MORE VIGOROUS THAN THAT, SIR!
C'MON!

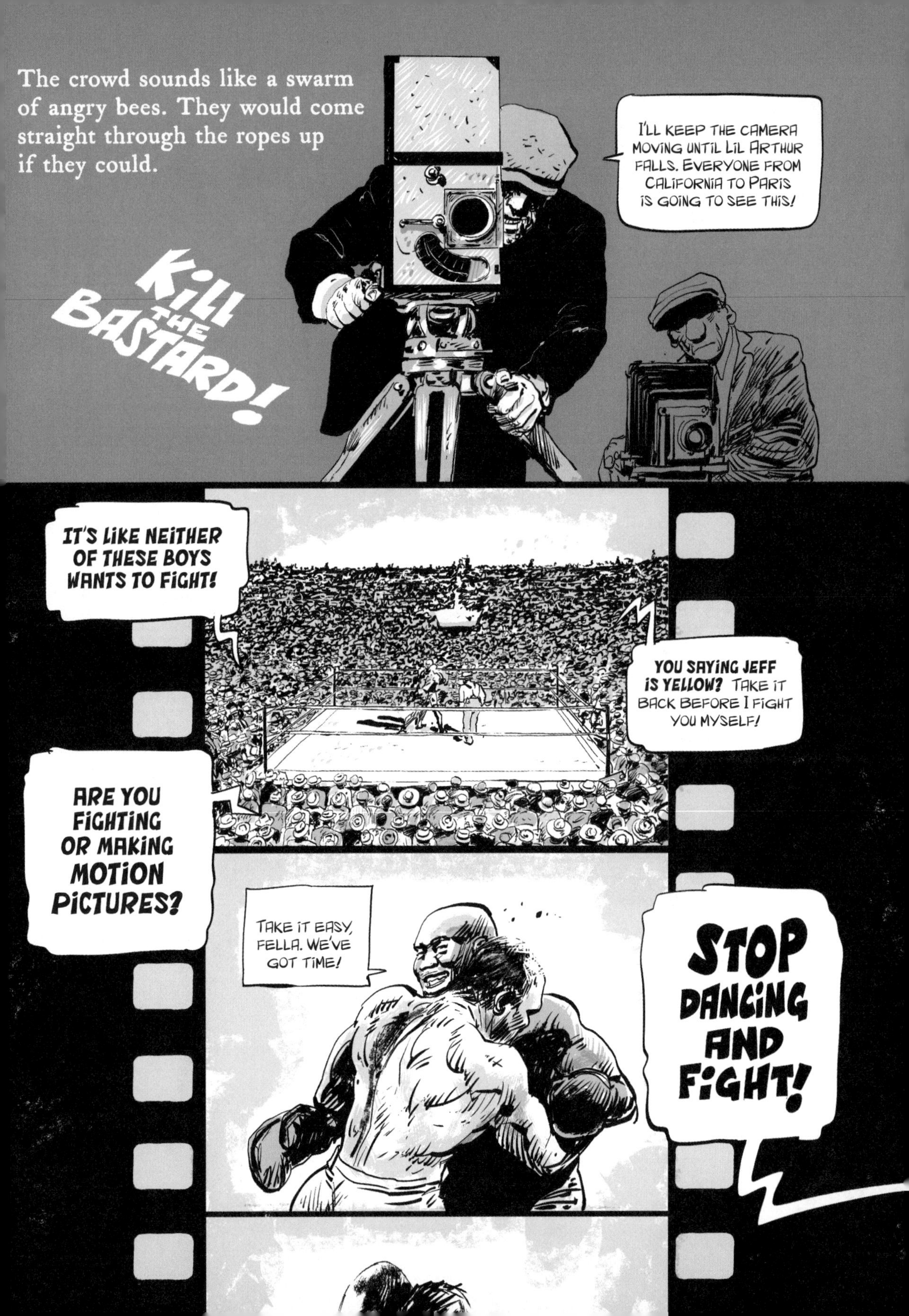

The crowd sounds like a swarm of angry bees. They would come straight through the ropes up if they could.
I'LL KEEP THE CAMERA MOVING UNTIL LIL ARTHUR FALLS. EVERYONE FROM CALIFORNIA TO PARIS IS GOING TO SEE THIS!
KILL THE BASTARD!
IT'S LIKE NEITHER OF THESE BOYS WANTS TO FIGHT!
YOU SAYING JEFF IS YELLOW? TAKE IT BACK BEFORE I FIGHT YOU MYSELF!
ARE YOU FIGHTING OR MAKING MOTION PICTURES?
TAKE IT EASY, FELLA. WE'VE GOT TIME!
STOP DANCING AND FIGHT!

What some people in the crowd don't know is the motion picture money is bigger than the prize money.

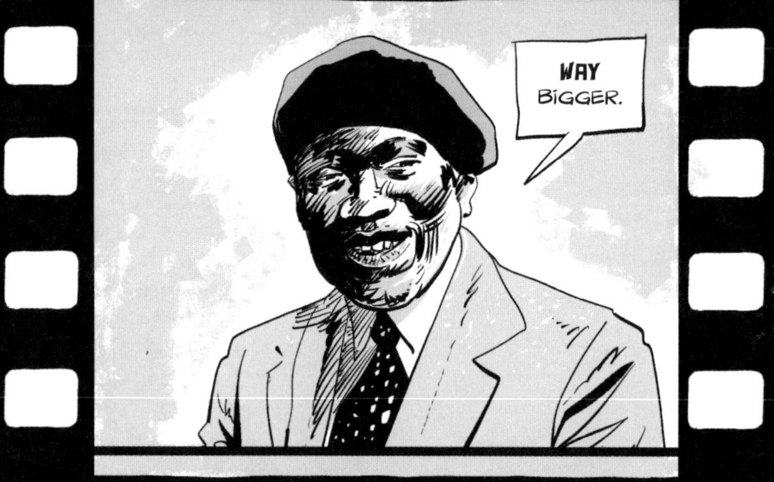
WAY BIGGER.

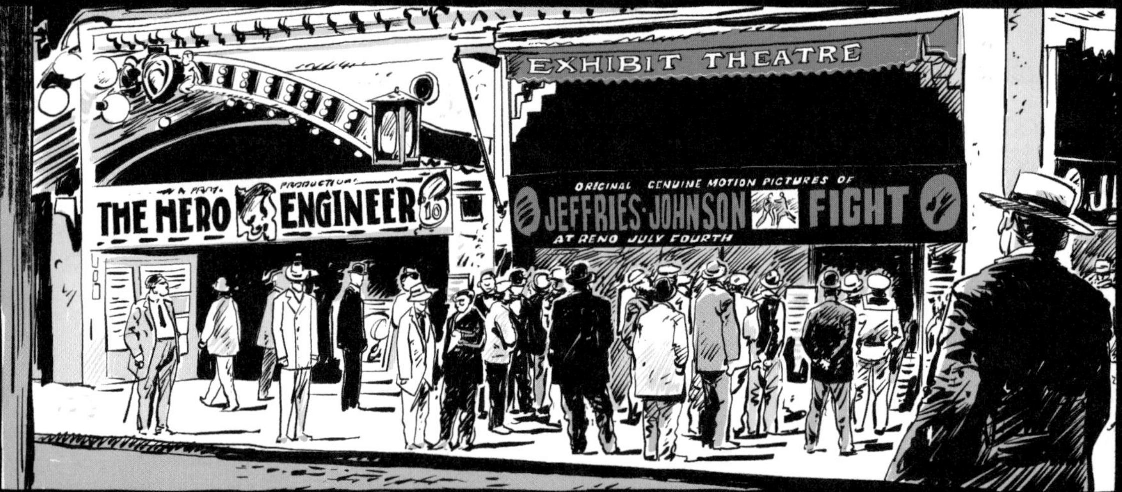
EXHIBIT THEATRE
THE HERO ENGINEER
10
ORIGINAL GENUINE MOTION PICTURES OF
JEFFRIES-JOHNSON FIGHT
AT RENO JULY FOURTH

Motion pictures started out as what they called **camera obscura**.

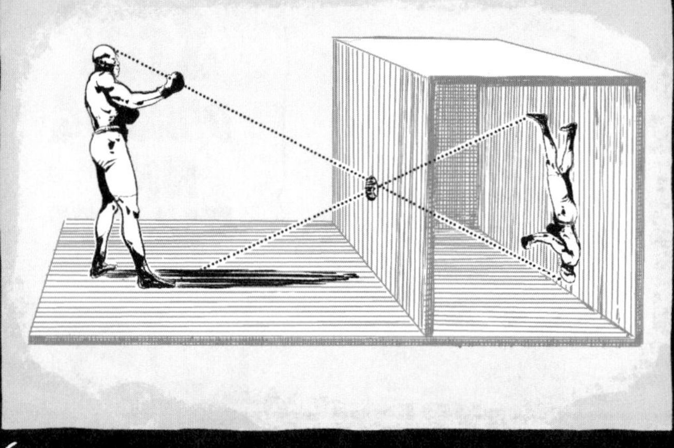

You'd look into the pinhole and see all kinds of illusions dancing inside.

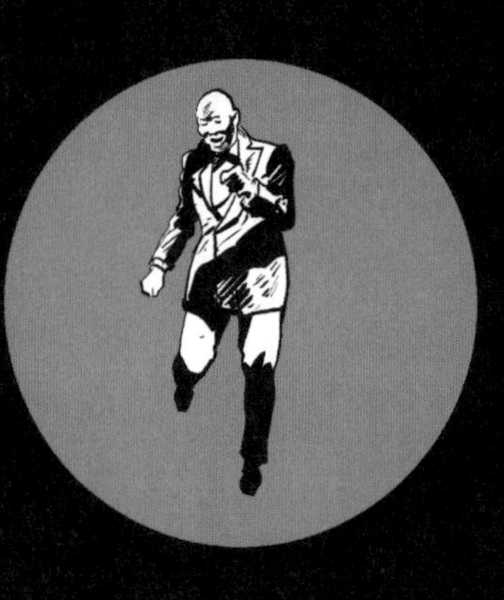

Sometimes it looked like magic pulled from a hat, other times it looked like the flashes inside the eyes right after a punch connects.

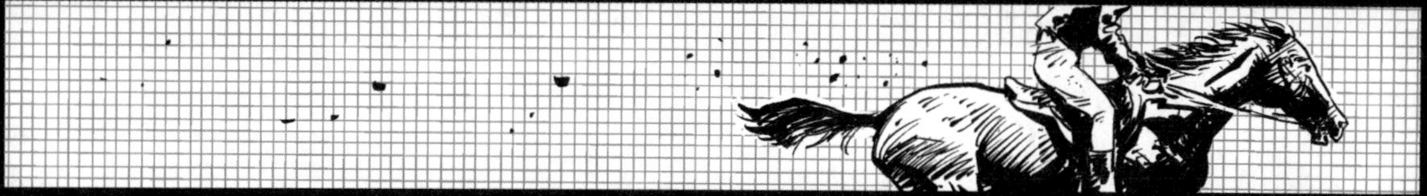

Things really got cooking when Muybridge took photographs of that Black jockey riding Sallie Gardner & made them go. Twelve pictures per second.

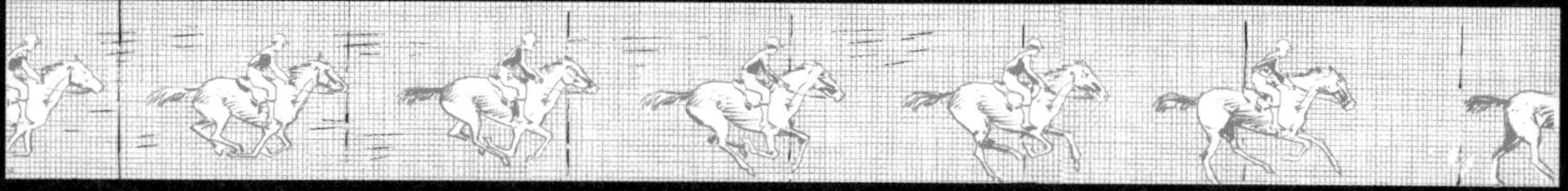

Later Edison & his Kinetographs of waterfalls & locomotive collisions. Lumière & his Cinématographe–everyone wanted pictures that move with their own locomotion.

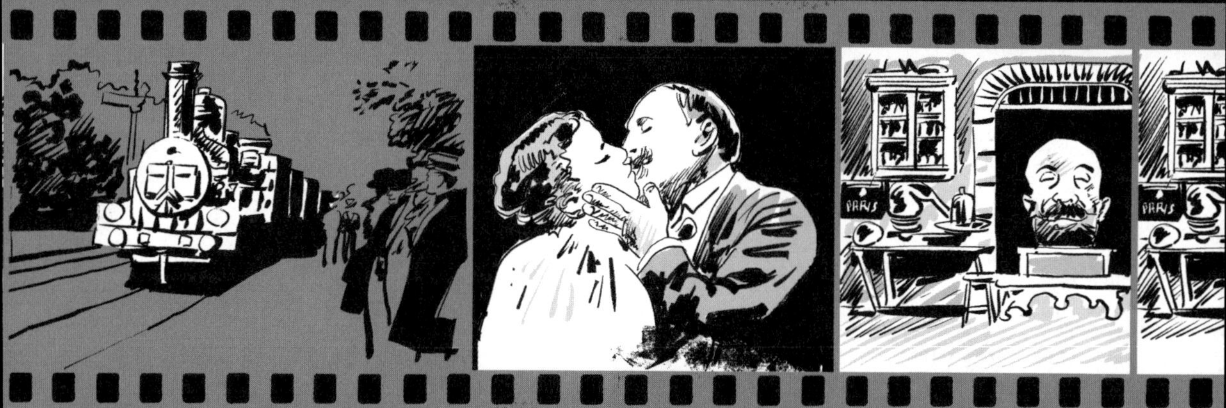
PARIS
PARIS

Their movies allowed us to see things we have never experienced in our real lives. The wonders of the world

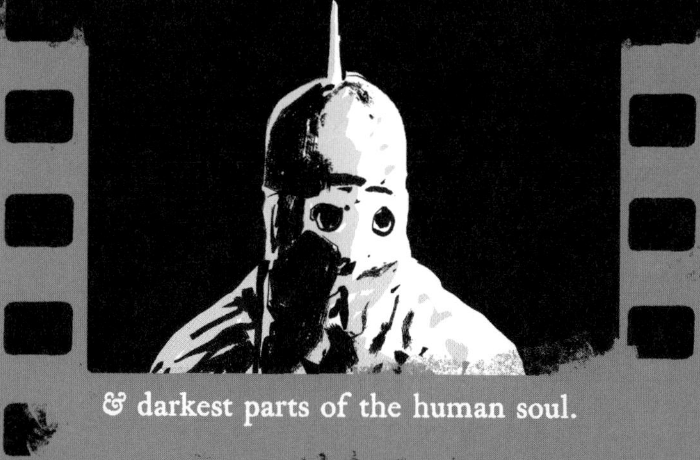

& darkest parts of the human soul.

Adapted from Thomas Dixon's novel

"The Clansman"

COPYRIGHT 1915
DAVID W. GRIFFITH
CORPORATION

COPYRIGHT 1915
EPOCH PRODUCING
CORPORATION AND
THOMAS DIXON

Griffith   *Griffith*

D. W. GRIFFITH

presents

The Birth of a Nation

Adapted from Thomas Dixon's novel

"The Clansman"

COPYRIGHT 1915
DAVID W. GRIFFITH
CORPORATION

COPYRIGHT 1915
EPOCH PRODUCING
CORPORATION AND
THOMAS DIXON

FORTY ACRES
AND A MULE
FOR EVERY COLORED CITIZEN

EQUALITY
EQUAL RIGHTS
EQUAL POLITICS
EQUAL MARRIAGE.

D. W. Griffith & his blackface
marauding. D. W. Griffith
& his grand wish for
a Confederate America.

Did you know his picture
was the first shown
in the White House?
The Confederacy lost
& they're still making
monuments to it.

I never met Griffith, but
his work lacked honesty.
President Wilson said
Griffith wrote history
with lightning...

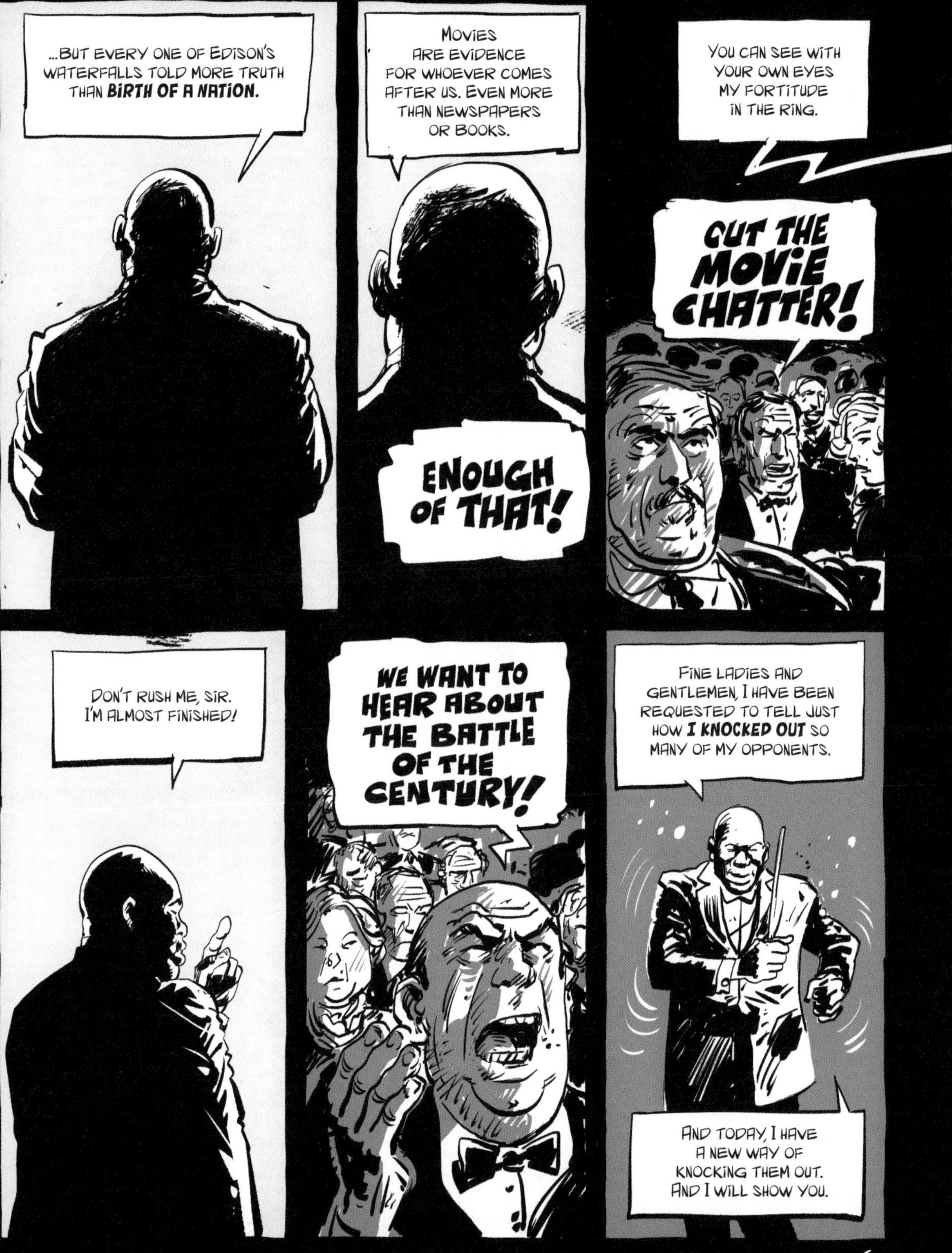
...BUT EVERY ONE OF EDISON'S WATERFALLS TOLD MORE TRUTH THAN BIRTH OF A NATION.
MOVIES ARE EVIDENCE FOR WHOEVER COMES AFTER US. EVEN MORE THAN NEWSPAPERS OR BOOKS.
ENOUGH OF THAT!
YOU CAN SEE WITH YOUR OWN EYES MY FORTITUDE IN THE RING.
CUT THE MOVIE CHATTER!
DON'T RUSH ME, SIR. I'M ALMOST FINISHED!
WE WANT TO HEAR ABOUT THE BATTLE OF THE CENTURY!
FINE LADIES AND GENTLEMEN, I HAVE BEEN REQUESTED TO TELL JUST HOW I KNOCKED OUT SO MANY OF MY OPPONENTS.
AND TODAY, I HAVE A NEW WAY OF KNOCKING THEM OUT. AND I WILL SHOW YOU.

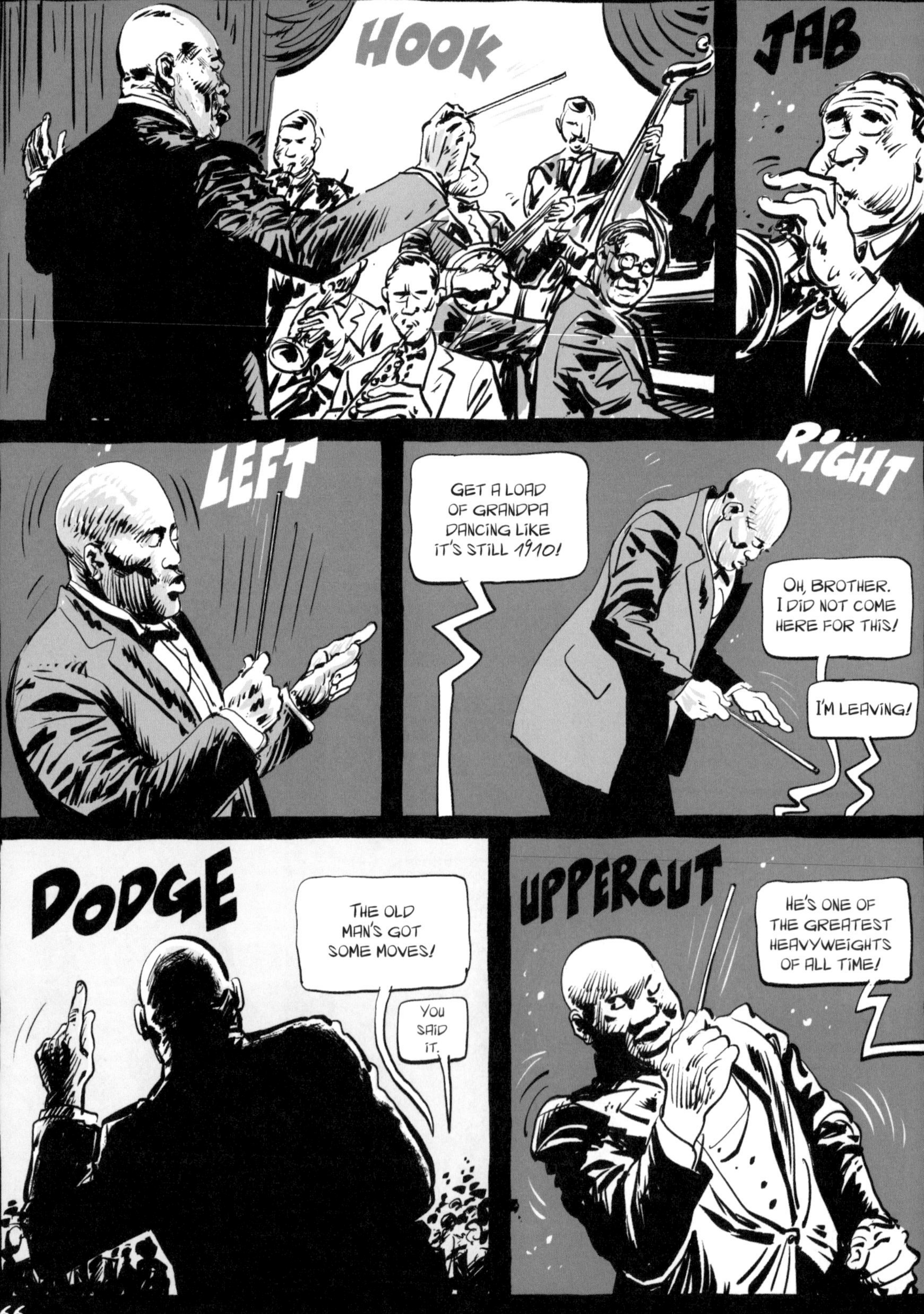
HOOK
JAB
LEFT
RIGHT
GET A LOAD OF GRANDPA DANCING LIKE IT'S STILL 1910!
OH, BROTHER. I DID NOT COME HERE FOR THIS!
I'M LEAVING!
DODGE
THE OLD MAN'S GOT SOME MOVES!
YOU SAID IT.
UPPERCUT
HE'S ONE OF THE GREATEST HEAVYWEIGHTS OF ALL TIME!

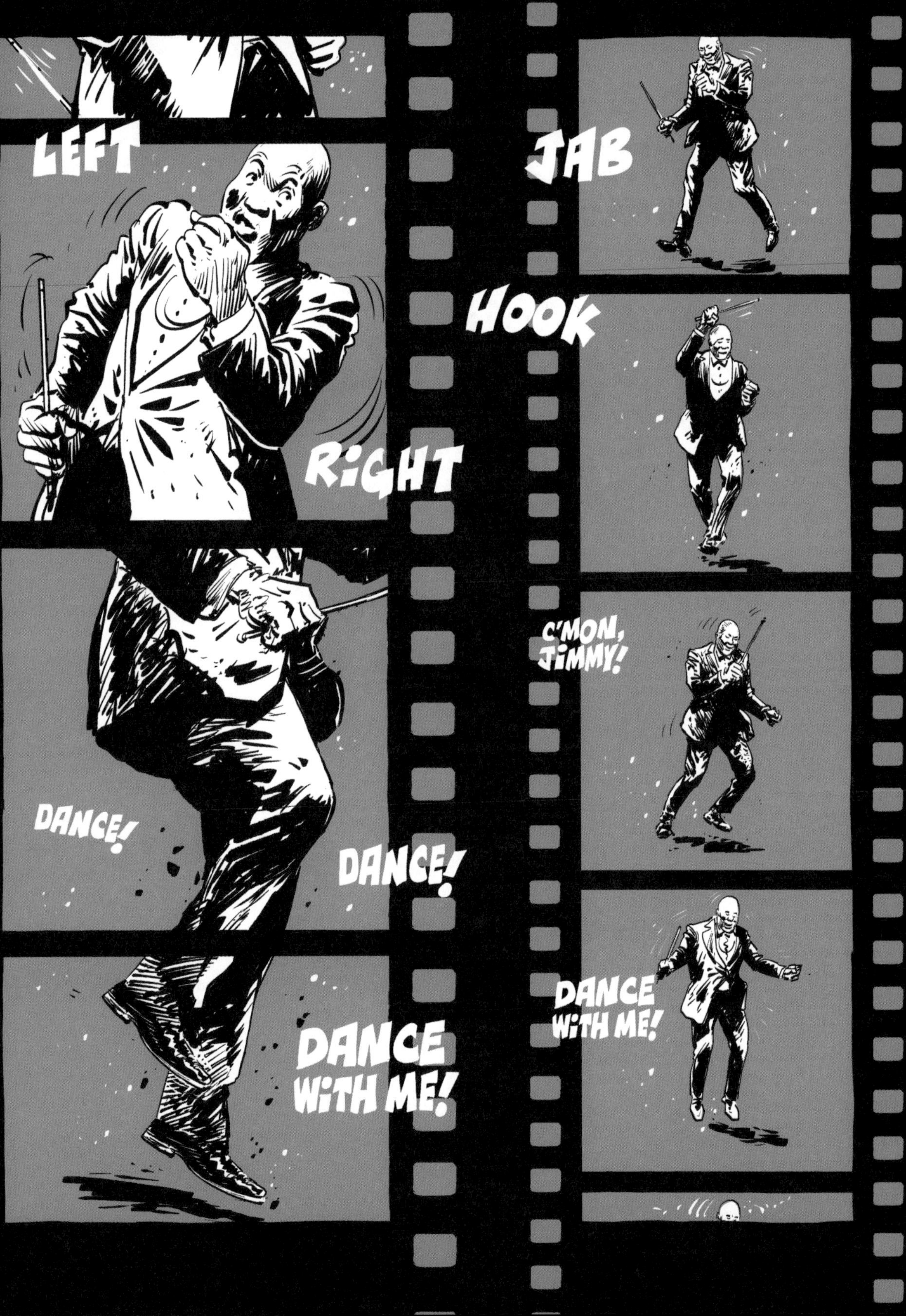
LEFT
RIGHT
DANCE!
DANCE!
DANCE WITH ME!
JAB
HOOK
C'MON, JIMMY!
DANCE WITH ME!

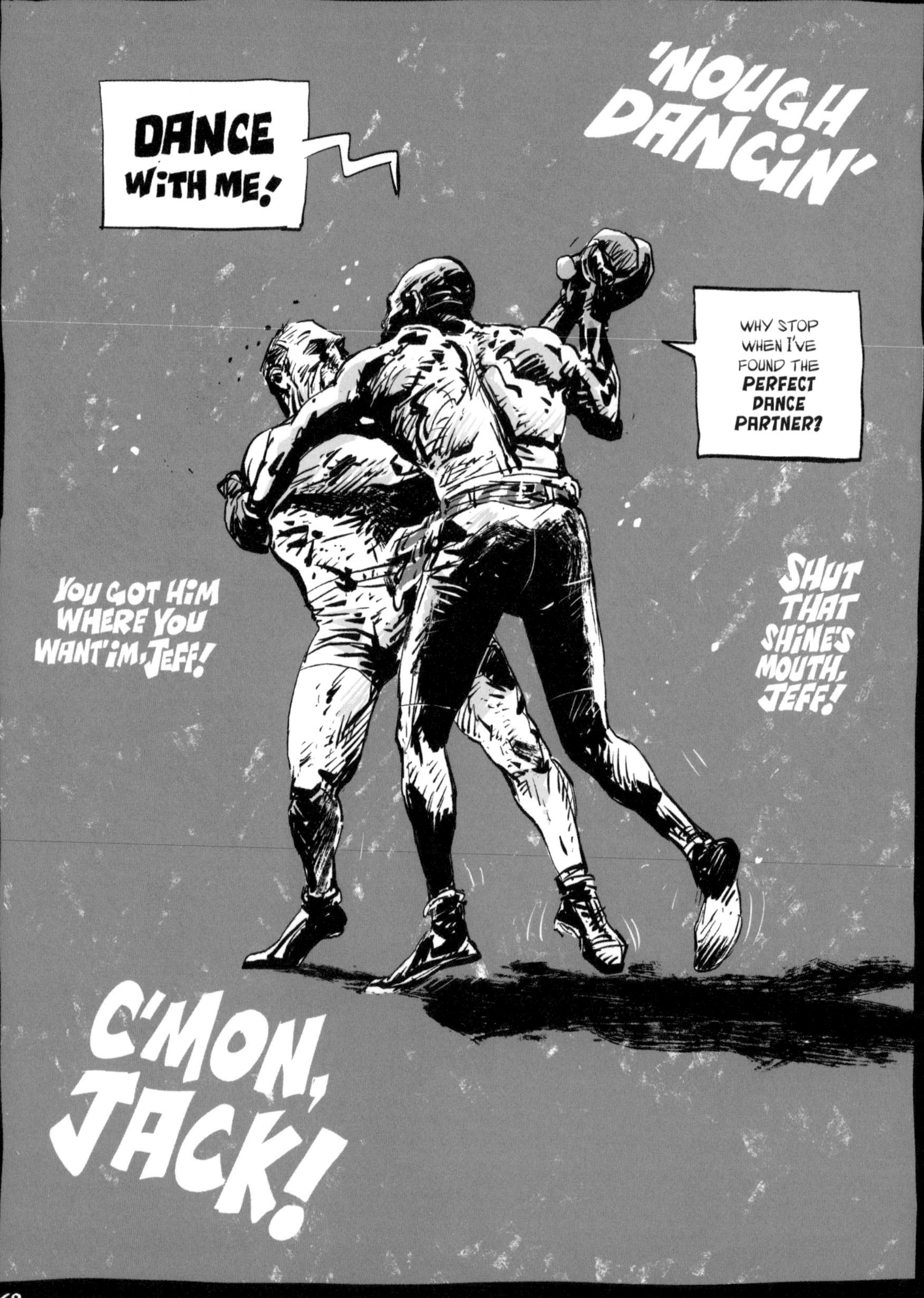
DANCE WITH ME!
'NOUGH DANCIN'
WHY STOP WHEN I'VE FOUND THE PERFECT DANCE PARTNER?
YOU GOT HIM WHERE YOU WANT'IM, JEFF!
SHUT THAT SHINE'S MOUTH, JEFF!
C'MON, JACK!

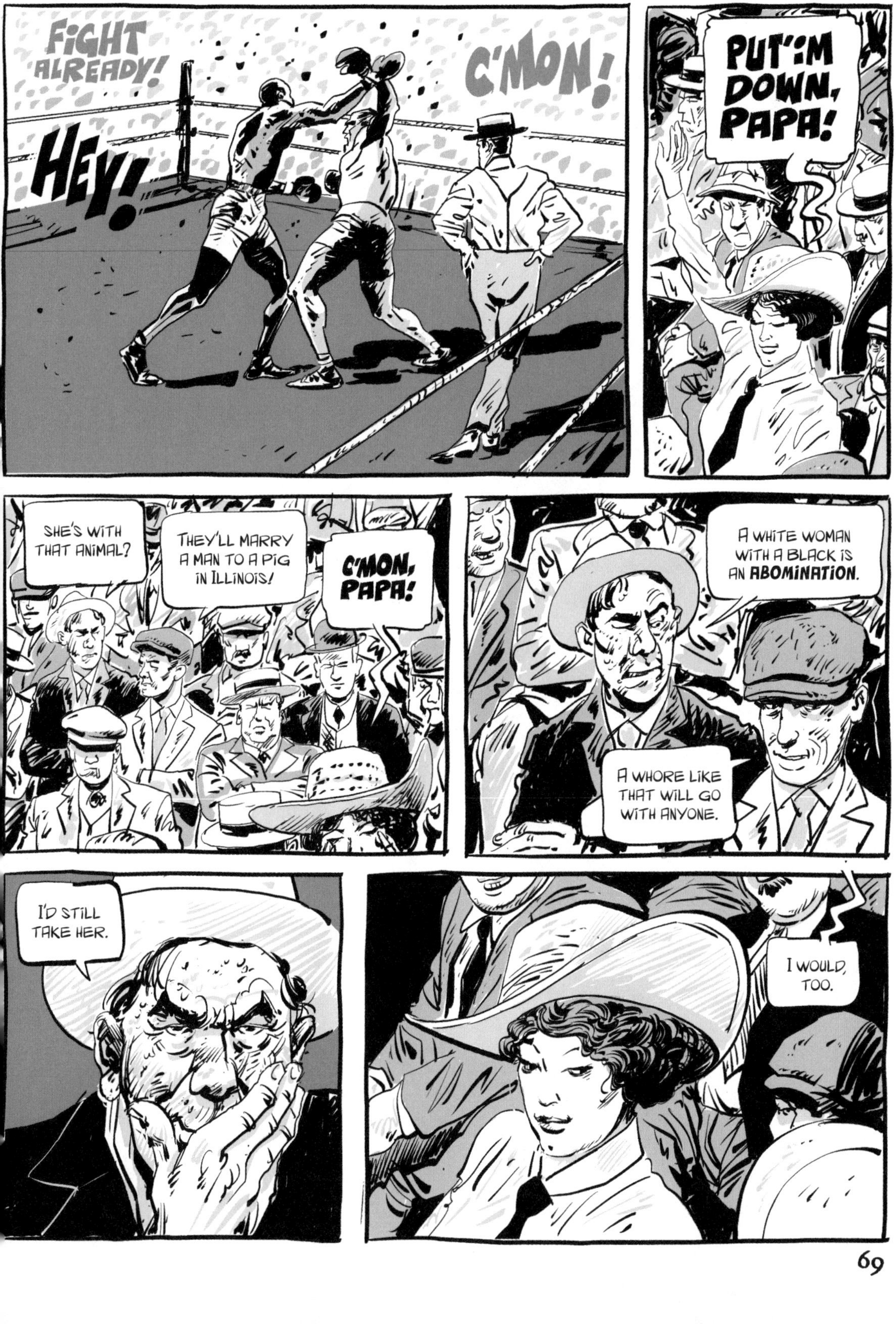
FIGHT ALREADY!
HEY!
C'MON!
PUT'IM DOWN, PAPA!
SHE'S WITH THAT ANIMAL?
THEY'LL MARRY A MAN TO A PIG IN ILLINOIS!
C'MON, PAPA!
A WHITE WOMAN WITH A BLACK IS AN **ABOMINATION**.
A WHORE LIKE THAT WILL GO WITH ANYONE.
I'D STILL TAKE HER.
I WOULD, TOO.

ROMANCE
IS EXTRA

LONG ISLAND MOTOR PARKWAY, NEW YORK 1908

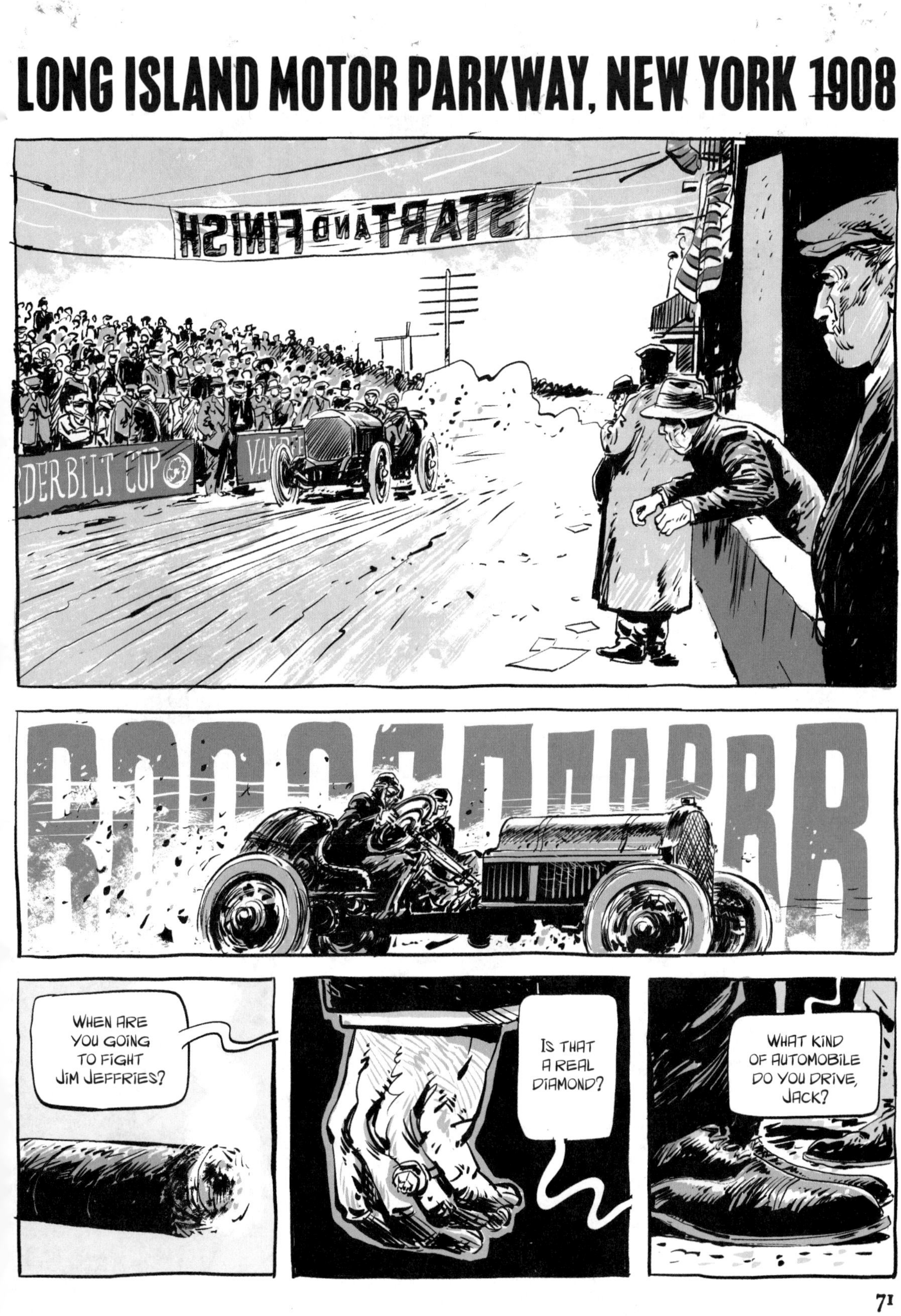
WHEN ARE YOU GOING TO FIGHT JIM JEFFRIES?
IS THAT A REAL DIAMOND?
WHAT KIND OF AUTOMOBILE DO YOU DRIVE, JACK?

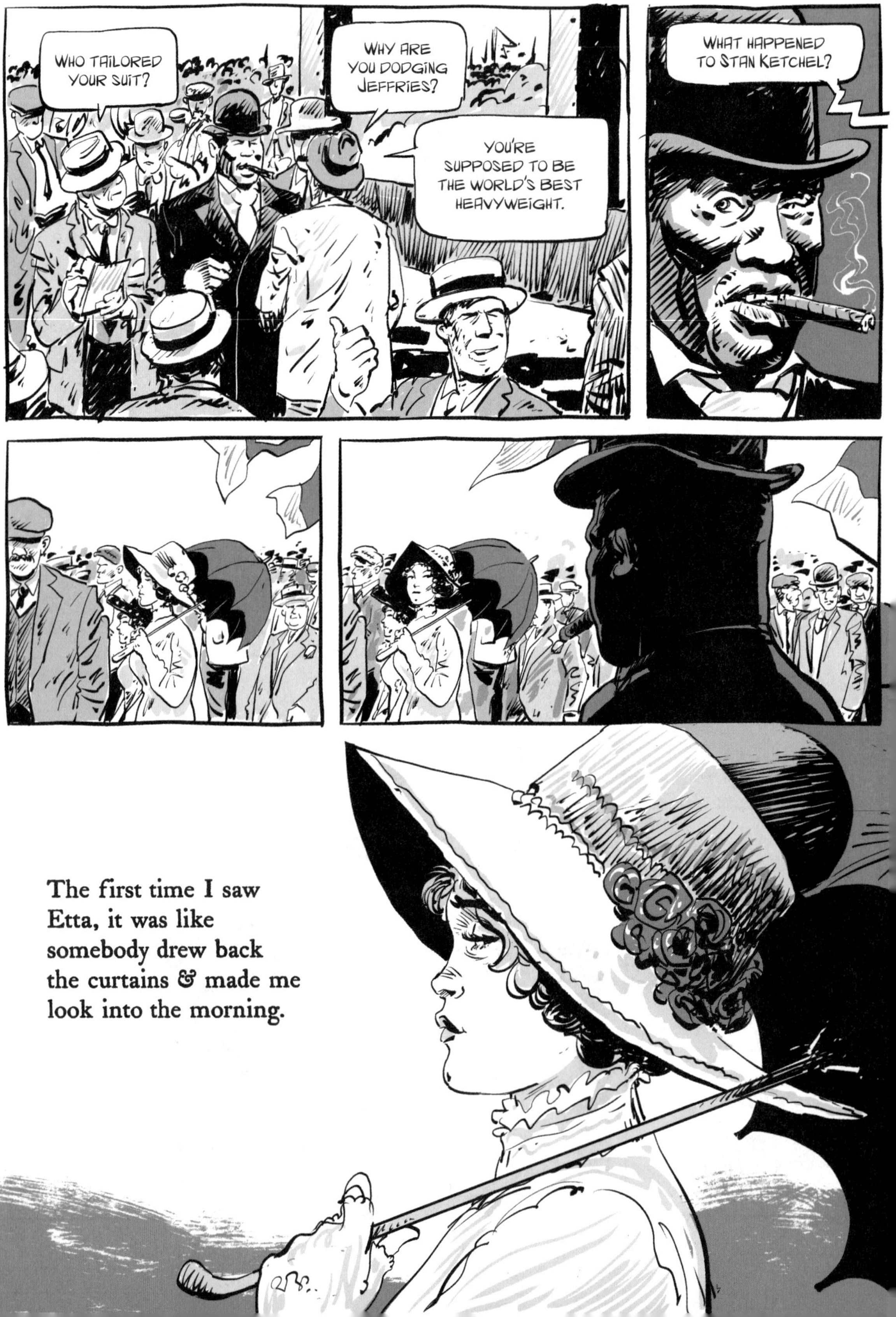
WHO TAILORED YOUR SUIT?
WHY ARE YOU DODGING JEFFRIES?
YOU'RE SUPPOSED TO BE THE WORLD'S BEST HEAVYWEIGHT.
WHAT HAPPENED TO STAN KETCHEL?
The first time I saw Etta, it was like somebody drew back the curtains & made me look into the morning.

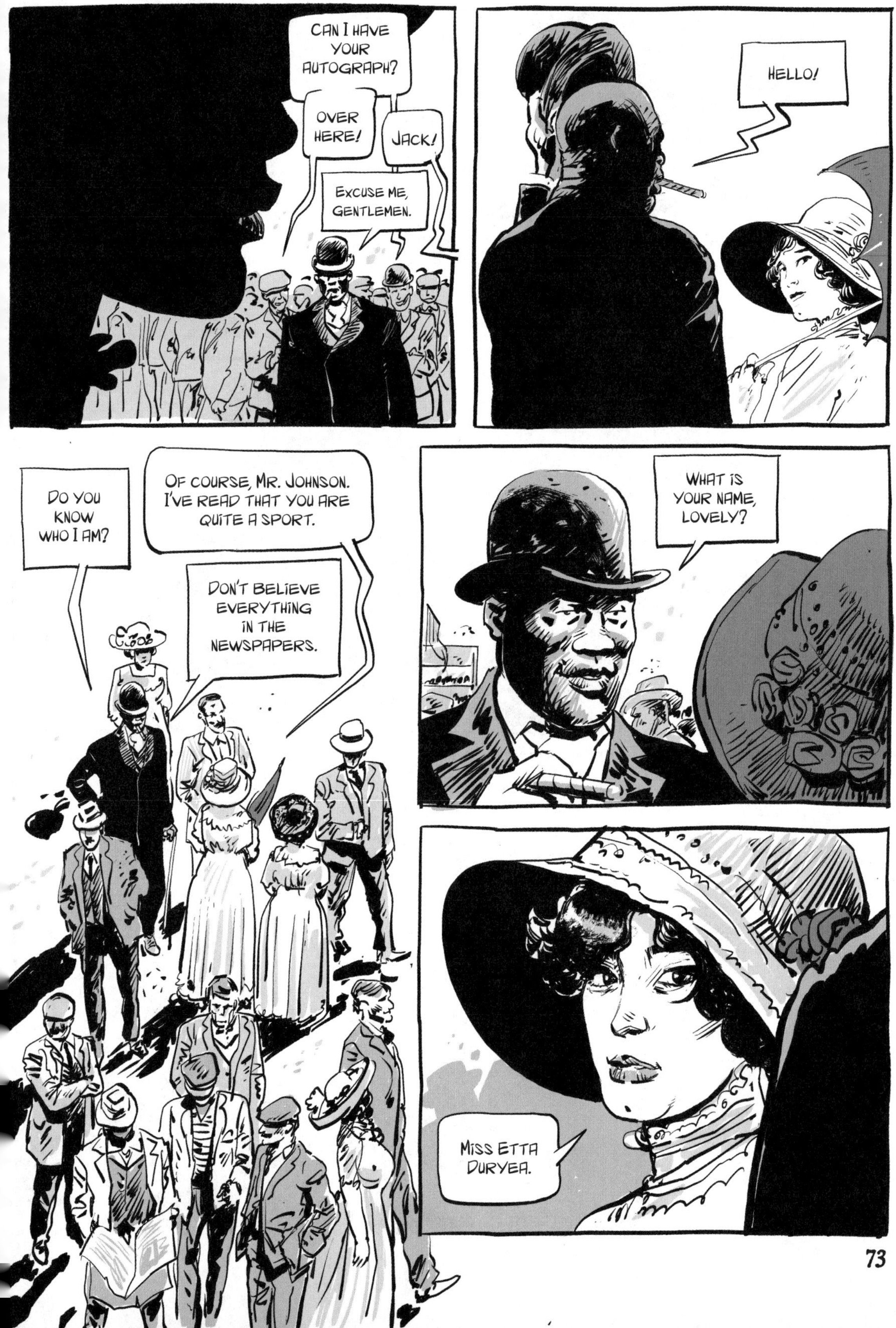
CAN I HAVE YOUR AUTOGRAPH?
OVER HERE!
JACK!
EXCUSE ME, GENTLEMEN.
HELLO!
DO YOU KNOW WHO I AM?
OF COURSE, MR. JOHNSON. I'VE READ THAT YOU ARE QUITE A SPORT.
DON'T BELIEVE EVERYTHING IN THE NEWSPAPERS.
WHAT IS YOUR NAME, LOVELY?
MISS ETTA DURYEA.

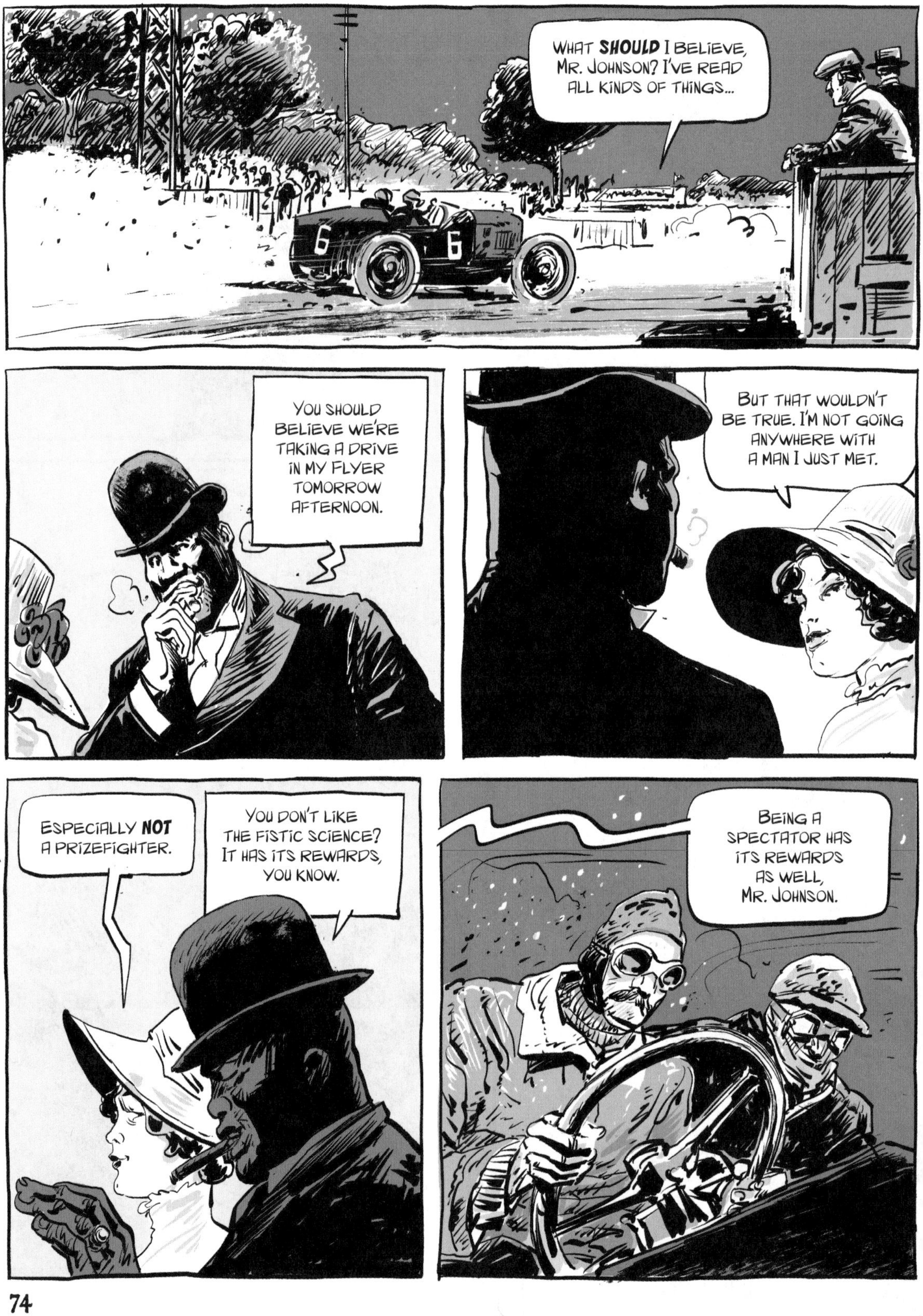
WHAT **SHOULD** I BELIEVE, MR. JOHNSON? I'VE READ ALL KINDS OF THINGS...
YOU SHOULD BELIEVE WE'RE TAKING A DRIVE IN MY FLYER TOMORROW AFTERNOON.
BUT THAT WOULDN'T BE TRUE. I'M NOT GOING ANYWHERE WITH A MAN I JUST MET.
ESPECIALLY **NOT** A PRIZEFIGHTER.
YOU DON'T LIKE THE FISTIC SCIENCE? IT HAS ITS REWARDS, YOU KNOW.
BEING A SPECTATOR HAS ITS REWARDS AS WELL, MR. JOHNSON.

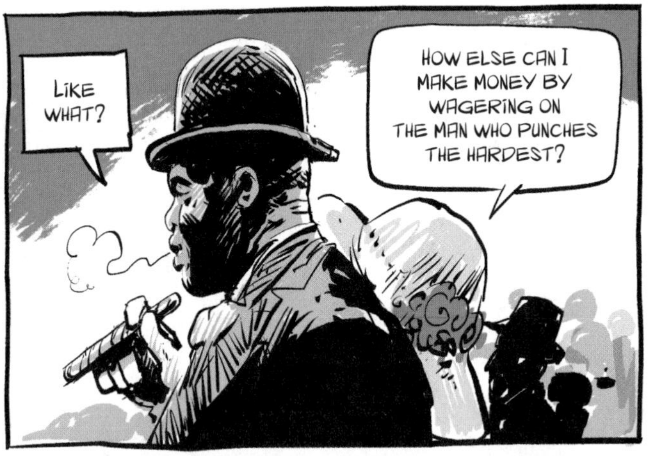
LIKE WHAT?
HOW ELSE CAN I MAKE MONEY BY WAGERING ON THE MAN WHO PUNCHES THE HARDEST?

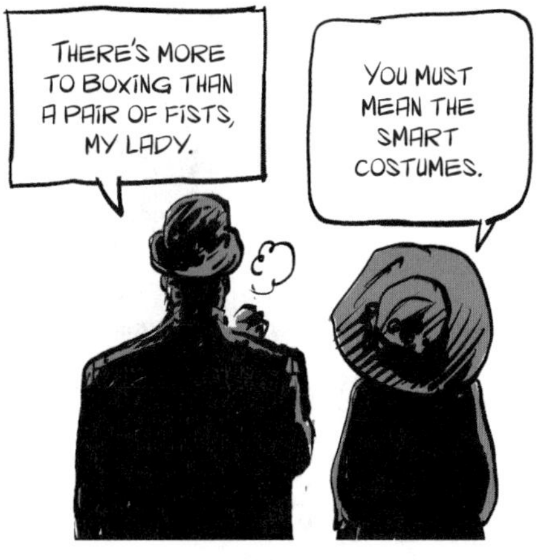
THERE'S MORE TO BOXING THAN A PAIR OF FISTS, MY LADY.
YOU MUST MEAN THE SMART COSTUMES.

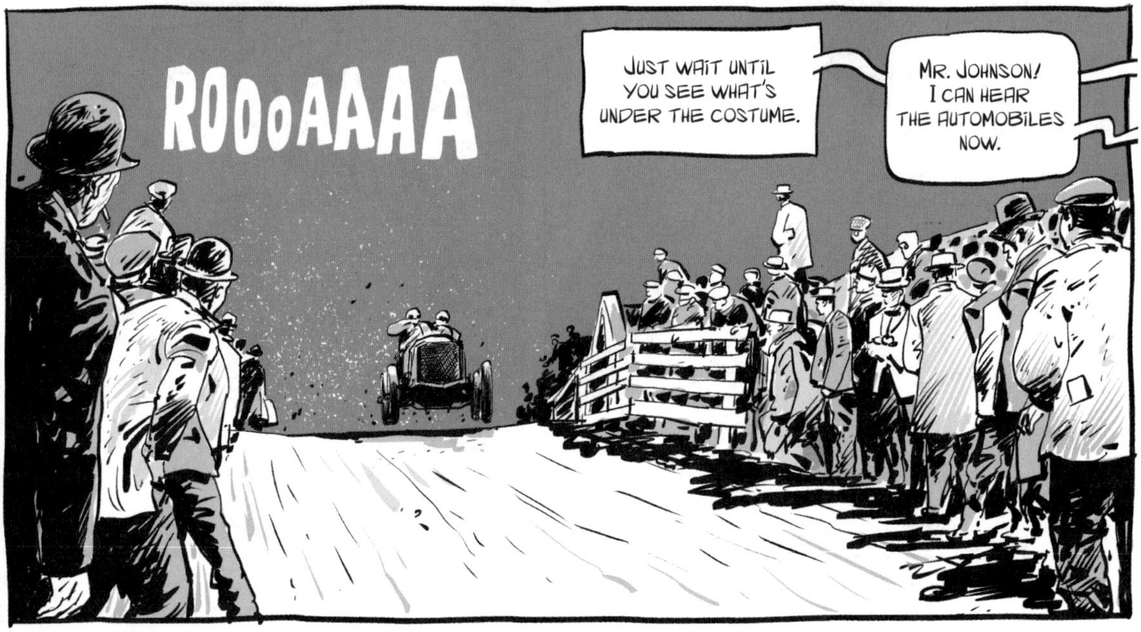
ROOoAAAA
JUST WAIT UNTIL YOU SEE WHAT'S UNDER THE COSTUME.
MR. JOHNSON! I CAN HEAR THE AUTOMOBILES NOW.

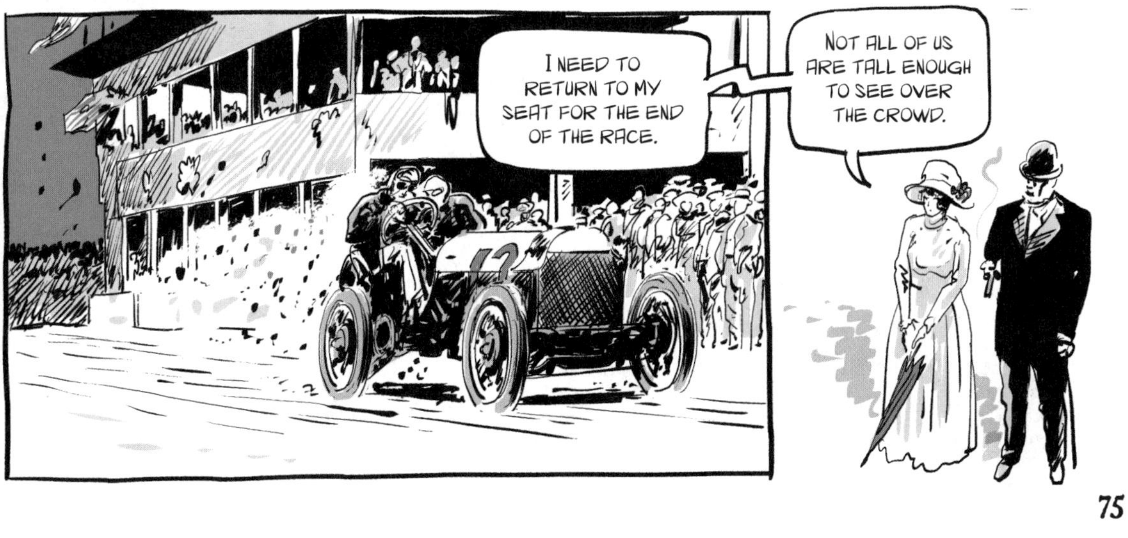
I NEED TO RETURN TO MY SEAT FOR THE END OF THE RACE.
NOT ALL OF US ARE TALL ENOUGH TO SEE OVER THE CROWD.

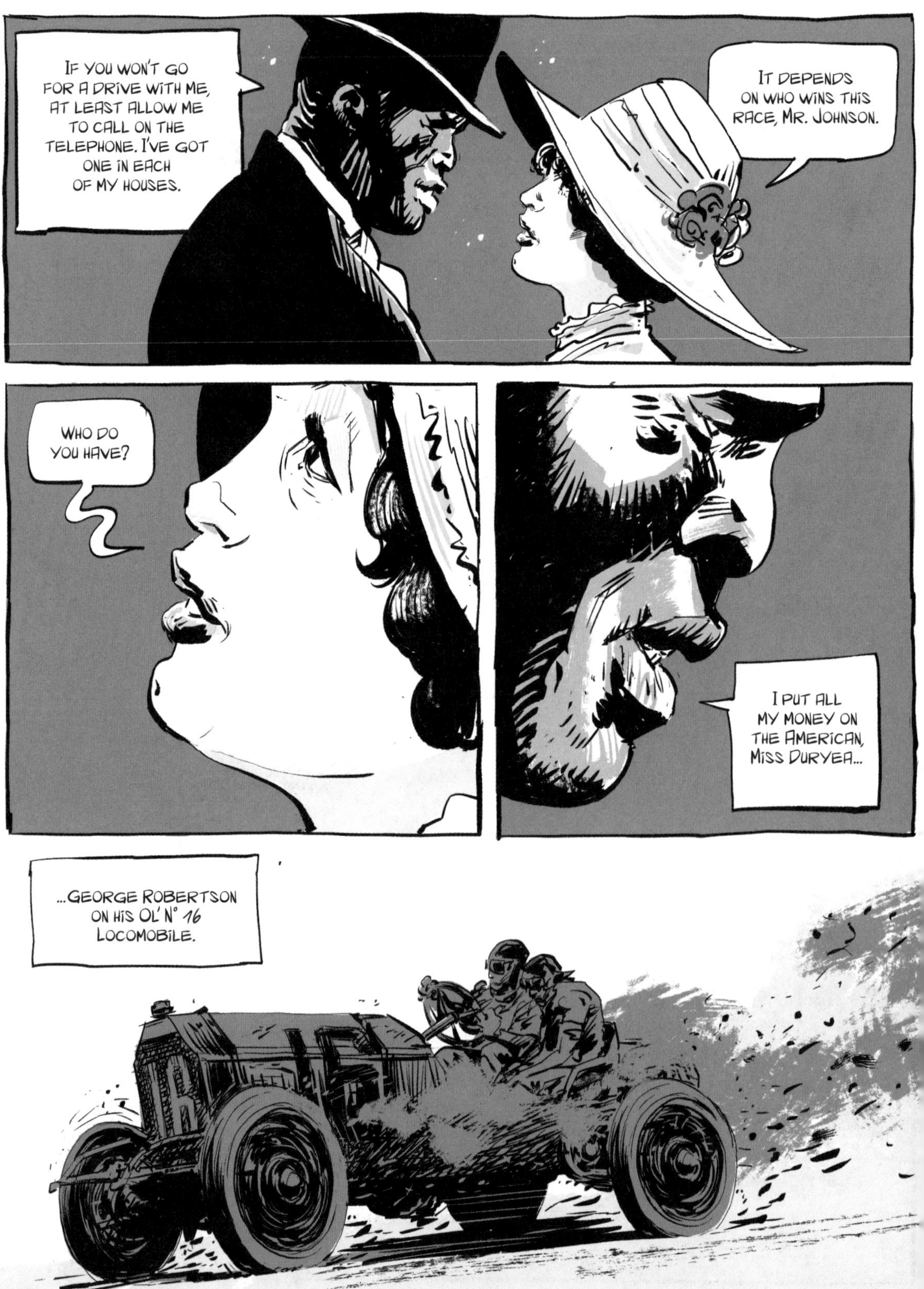
If you won't go for a drive with me, at least allow me to call on the telephone. I've got one in each of my houses.
It depends on who wins this race, Mr. Johnson.
Who do you have?
I put all my money on the American, Miss Duryea...
...George Robertson on his ol' n° 16 Locomobile.

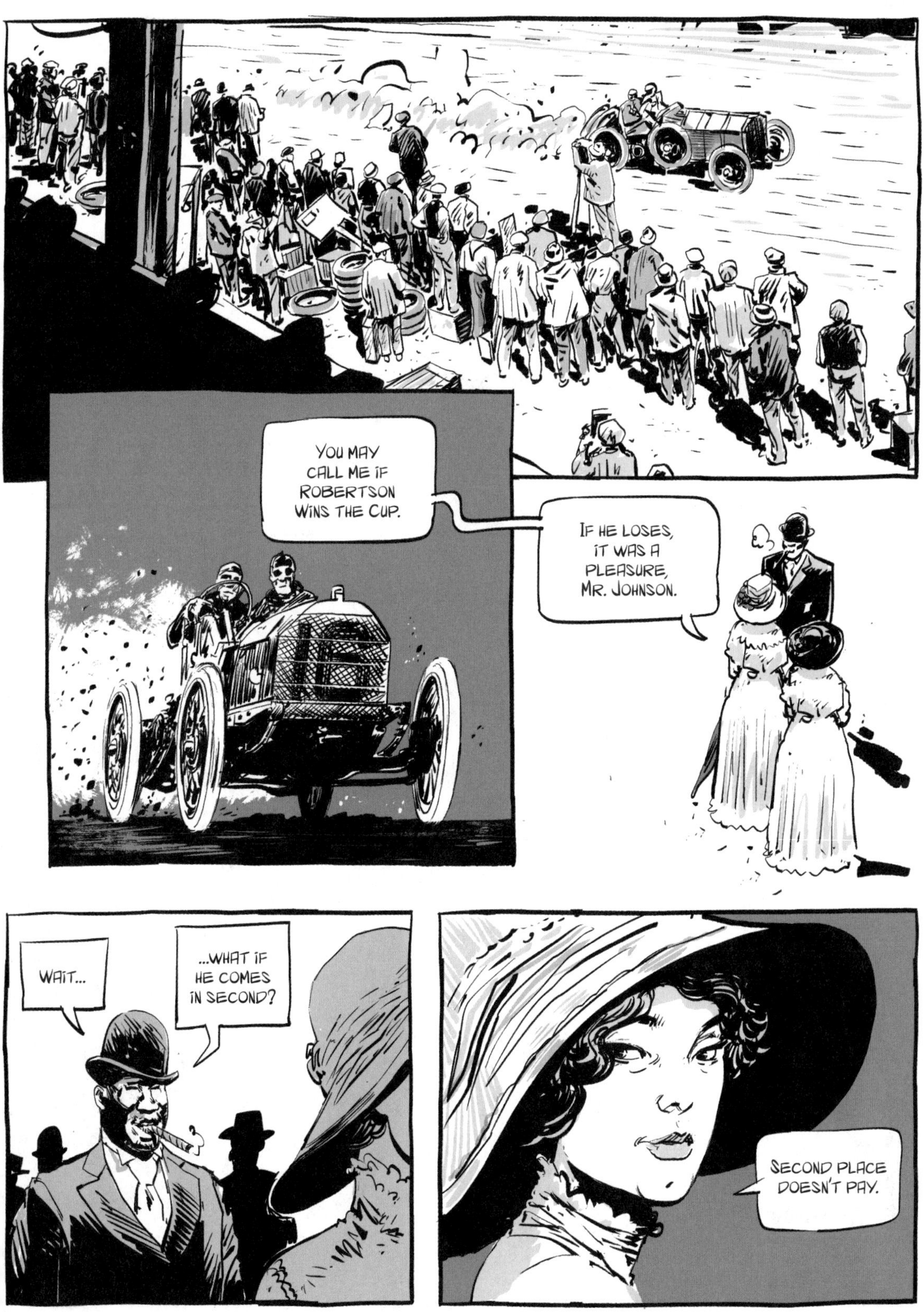
YOU MAY CALL ME IF ROBERTSON WINS THE CUP.
IF HE LOSES, IT WAS A PLEASURE, MR. JOHNSON.
WAIT...
...WHAT IF HE COMES IN SECOND?
SECOND PLACE DOESN'T PAY.

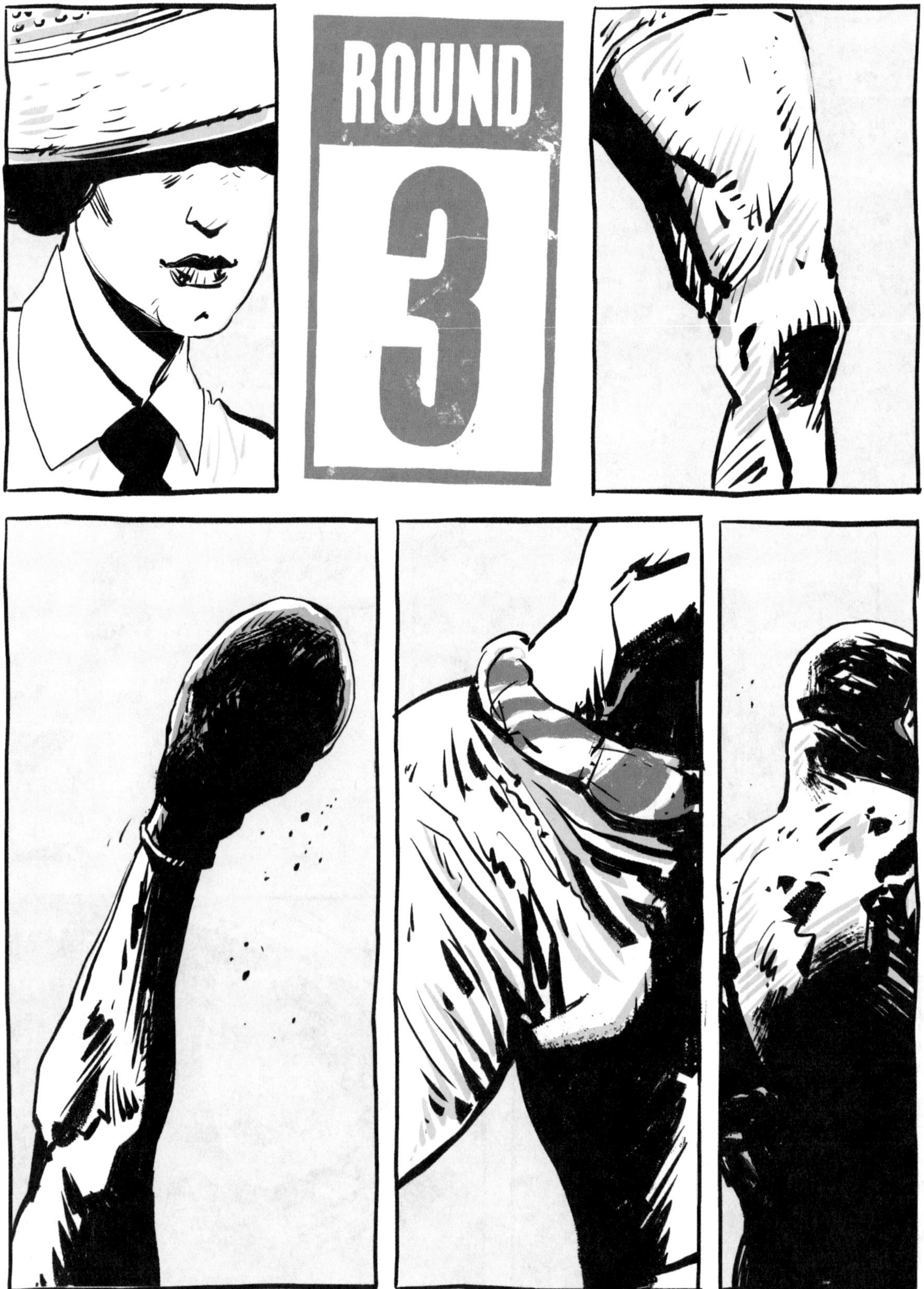
ROUND
3

Watching Papa fight is like watching something that's meant to be.

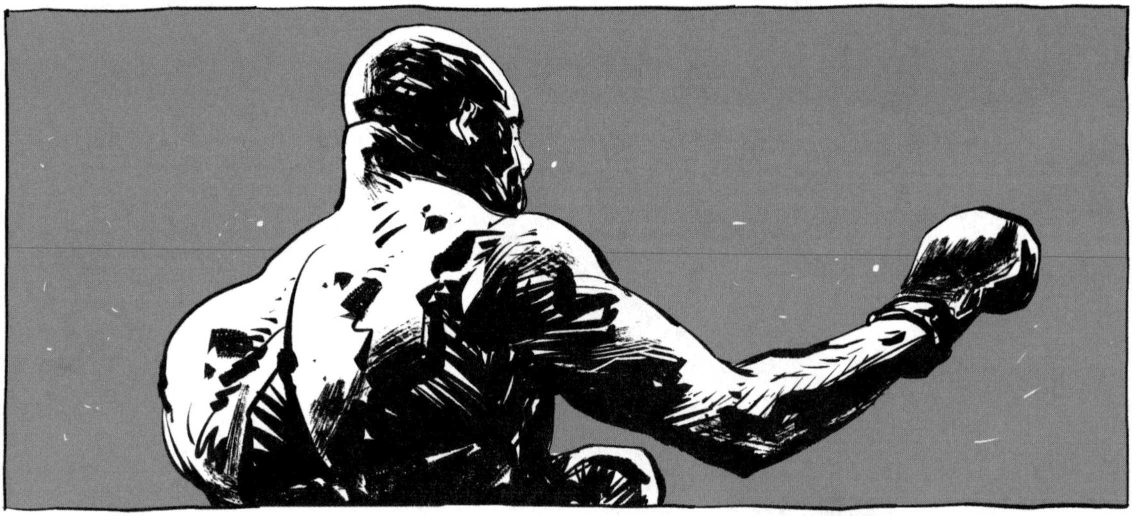

He moves in the ring like water moves toward the shore

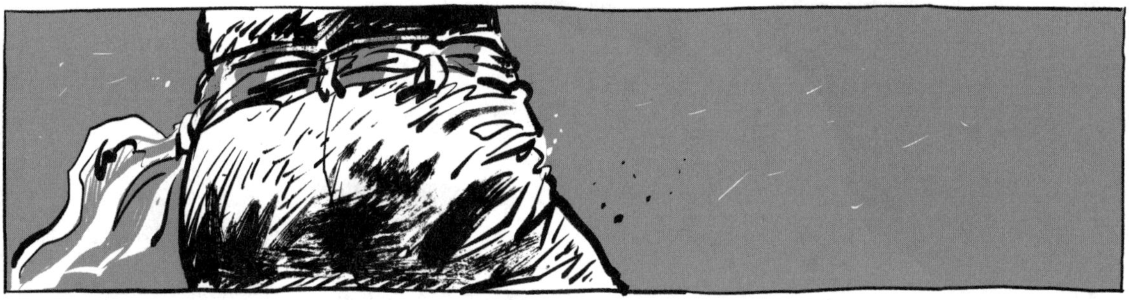

or the way the moon rises at the appointed time.

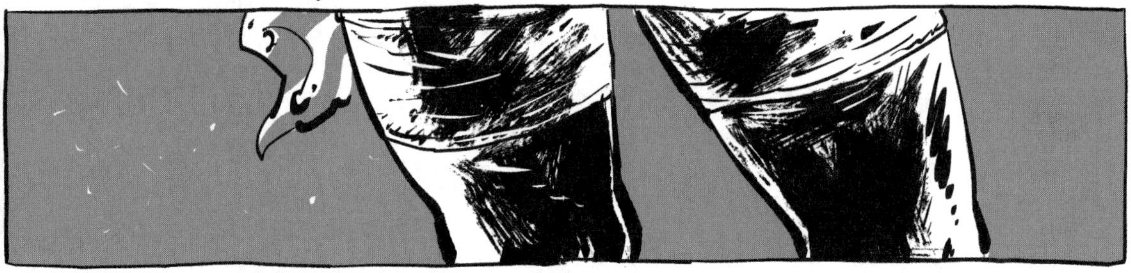

He's inevitable in the ring and out.

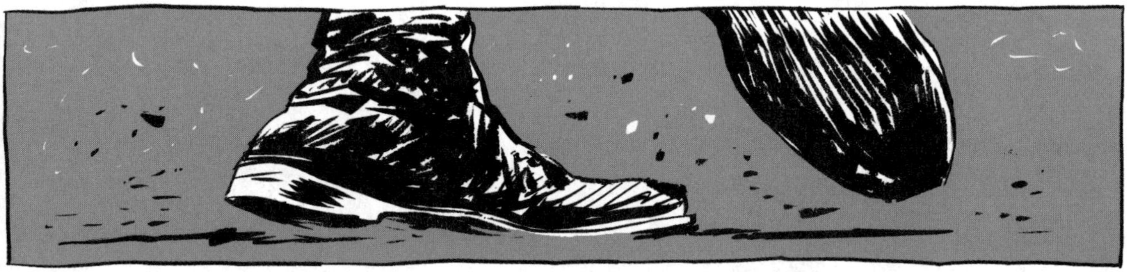

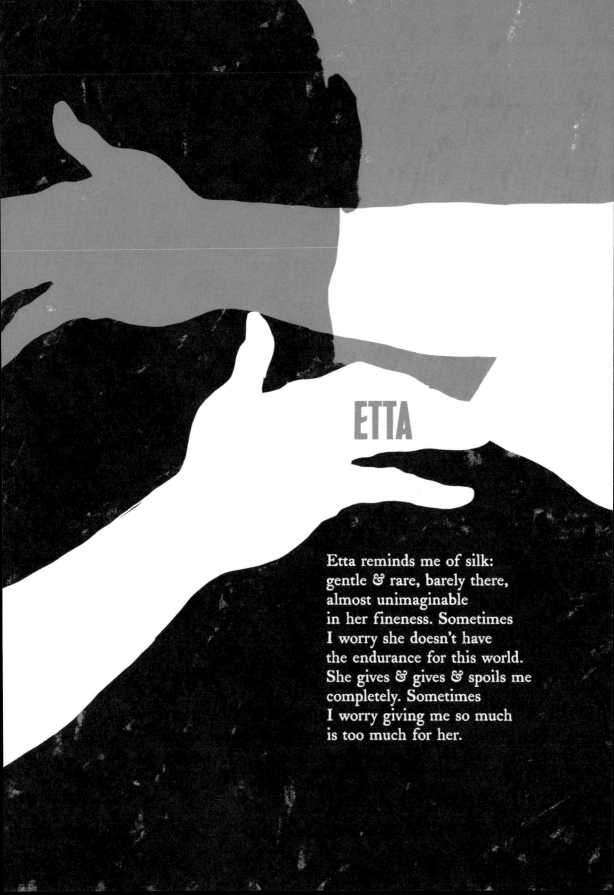

ETTA

Etta reminds me of silk:
gentle & rare, barely there,
almost unimaginable
in her fineness. Sometimes
I worry she doesn't have
the endurance for this world.
She gives & gives & spoils me
completely. Sometimes
I worry giving me so much
is too much for her.

Etta understands my pride.
She makes me feel like
the heavyweight champion
just by looking at me.
I never have to put my hands
on her. She knows
how to pamper & build me up
without any of that.

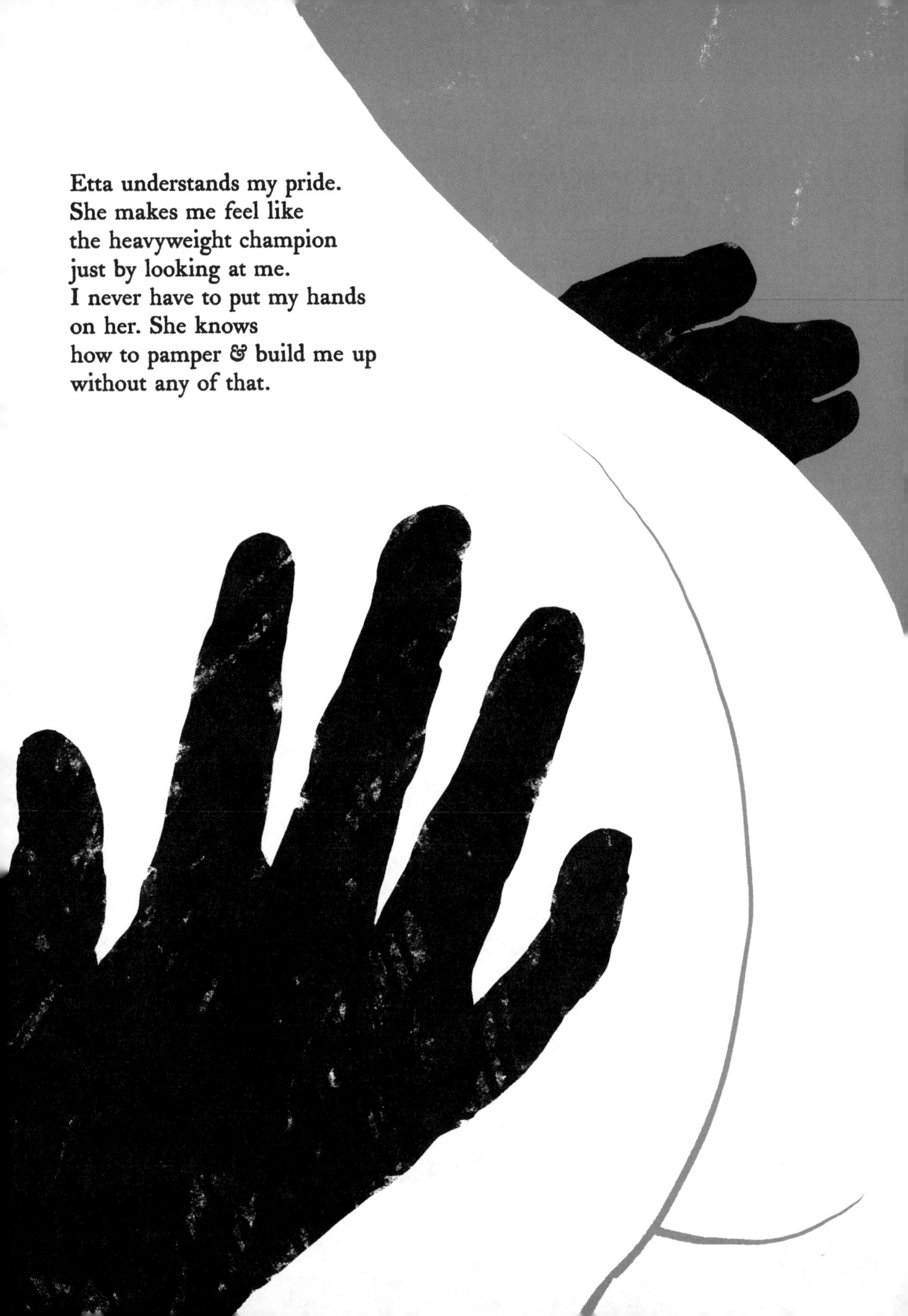

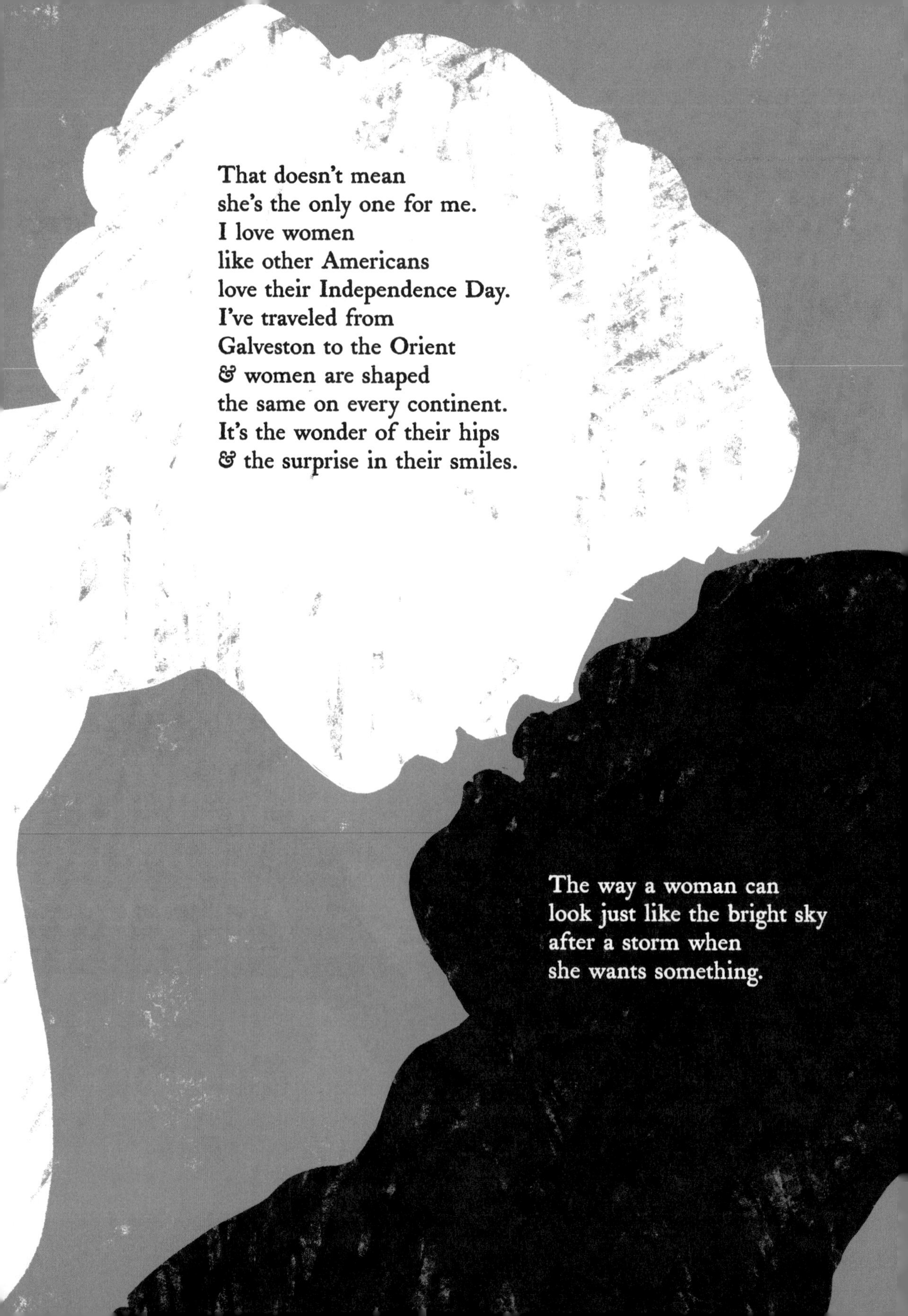

That doesn't mean
she's the only one for me.
I love women
like other Americans
love their Independence Day.
I've traveled from
Galveston to the Orient
& women are shaped
the same on every continent.
It's the wonder of their hips
& the surprise in their smiles.

The way a woman can
look just like the bright sky
after a storm when
she wants something.

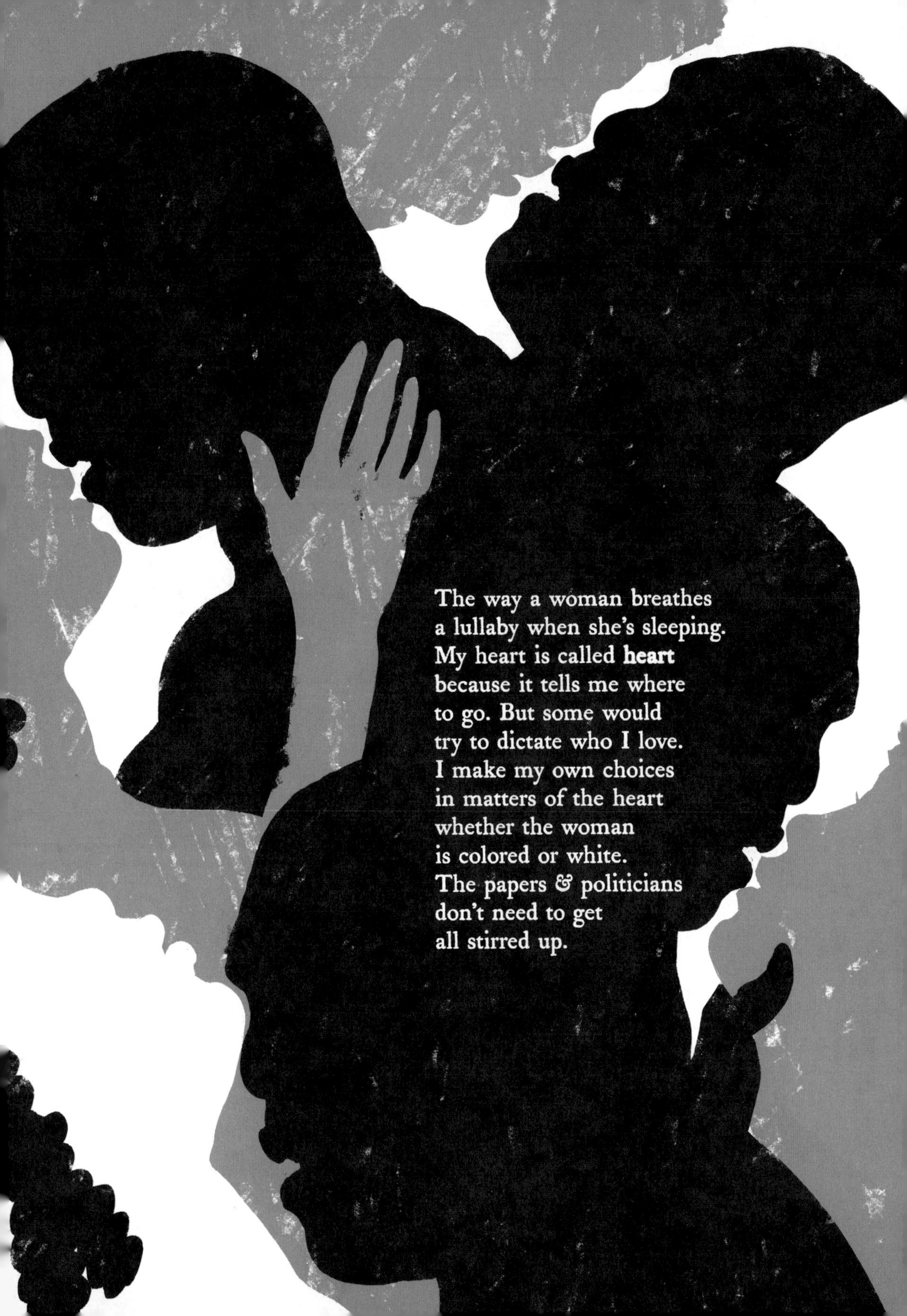

The way a woman breathes
a lullaby when she's sleeping.
My heart is called **heart**
because it tells me where
to go. But some would
try to dictate who I love.
I make my own choices
in matters of the heart
whether the woman
is colored or white.
The papers & politicians
don't need to get
all stirred up.

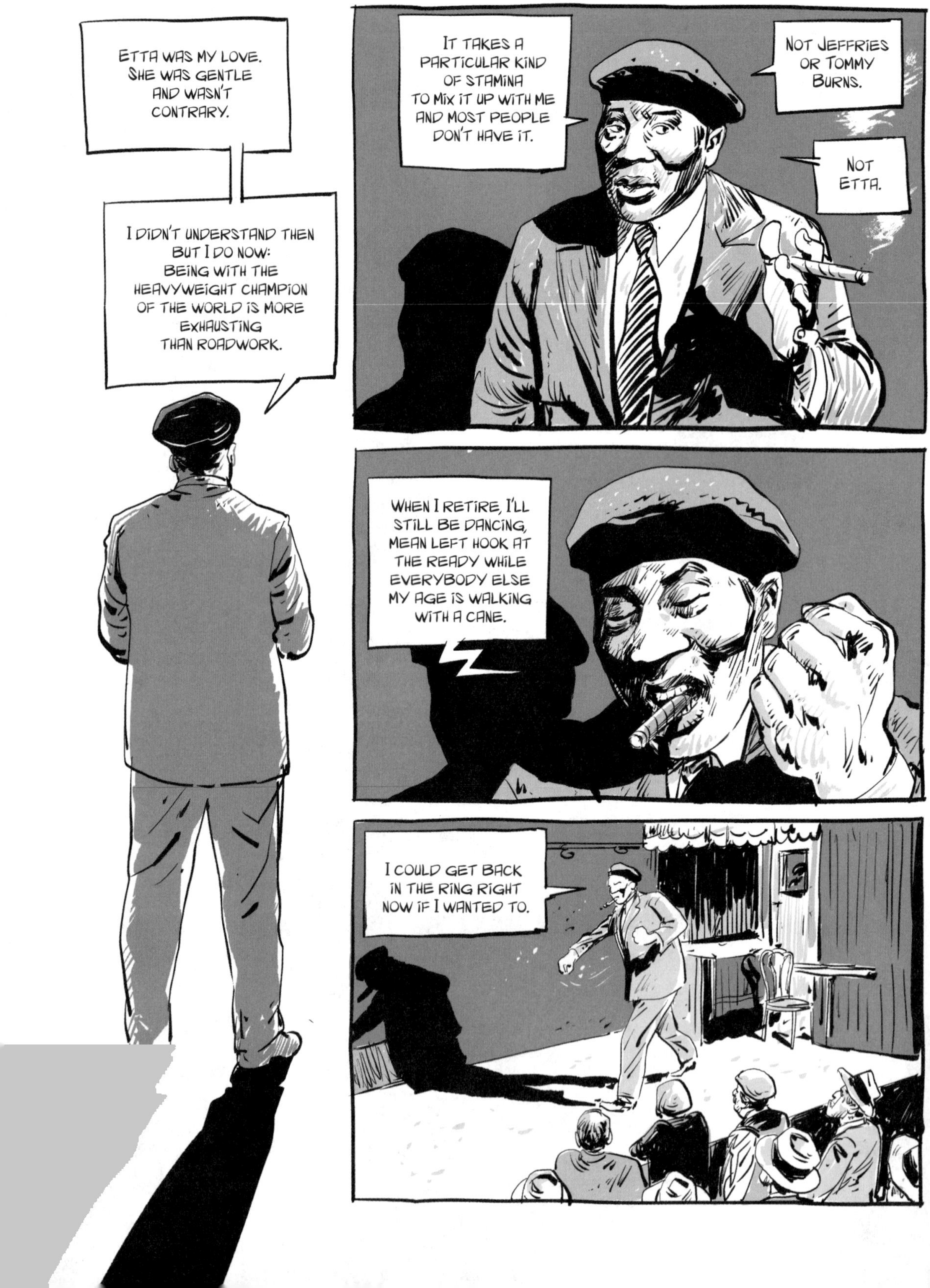
ETTA WAS MY LOVE. SHE WAS GENTLE AND WASN'T CONTRARY.
I DIDN'T UNDERSTAND THEN BUT I DO NOW: BEING WITH THE HEAVYWEIGHT CHAMPION OF THE WORLD IS MORE EXHAUSTING THAN ROADWORK.
IT TAKES A PARTICULAR KIND OF STAMINA TO MIX IT UP WITH ME AND MOST PEOPLE DON'T HAVE IT.
NOT JEFFRIES OR TOMMY BURNS.
NOT ETTA.
WHEN I RETIRE, I'LL STILL BE DANCING, MEAN LEFT HOOK AT THE READY WHILE EVERYBODY ELSE MY AGE IS WALKING WITH A CANE.
I COULD GET BACK IN THE RING RIGHT NOW IF I WANTED TO.

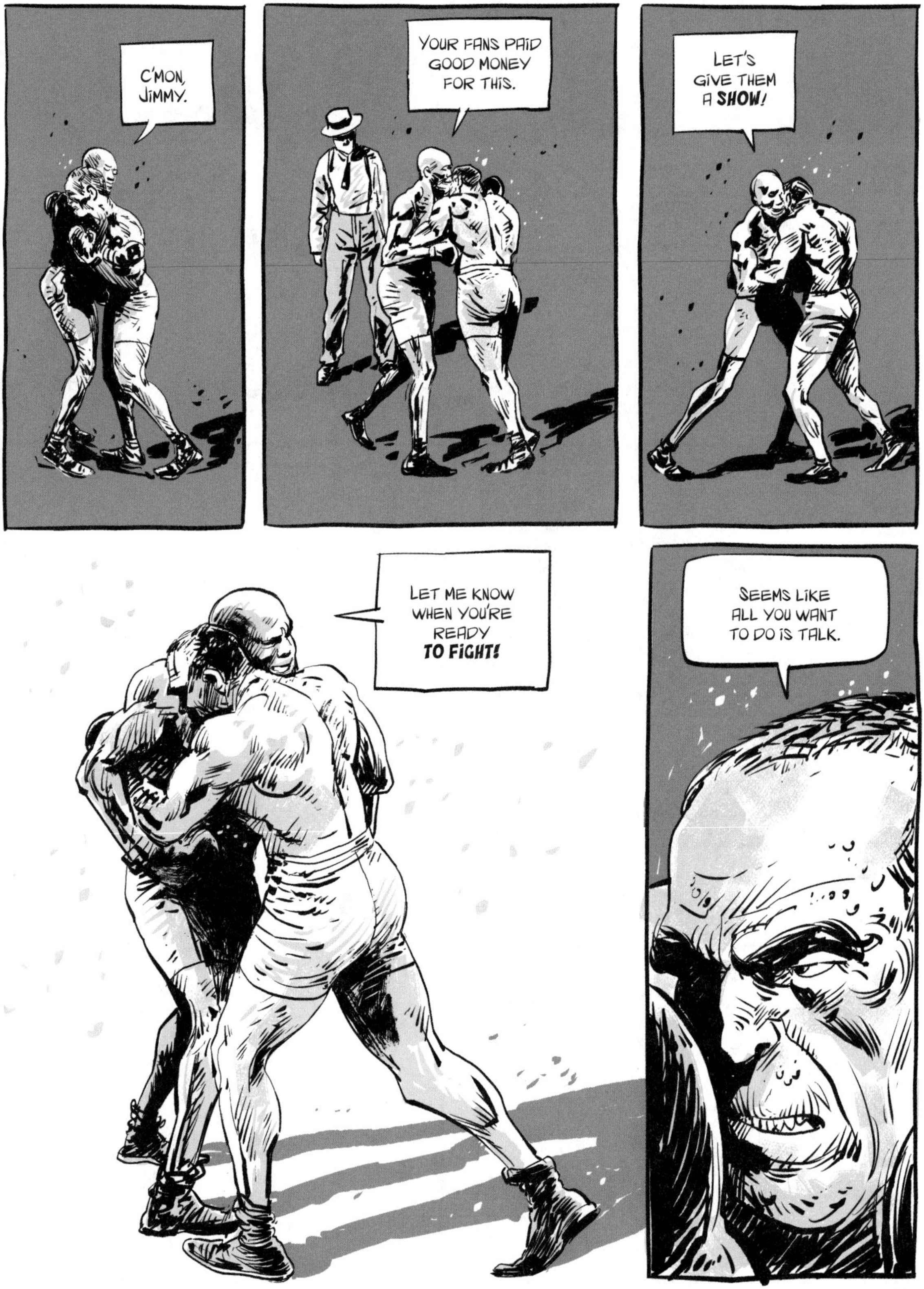
C'MON, JIMMY.
YOUR FANS PAID GOOD MONEY FOR THIS.
LET'S GIVE THEM A SHOW!
LET ME KNOW WHEN YOU'RE READY TO FIGHT!
SEEMS LIKE ALL YOU WANT TO DO IS TALK.

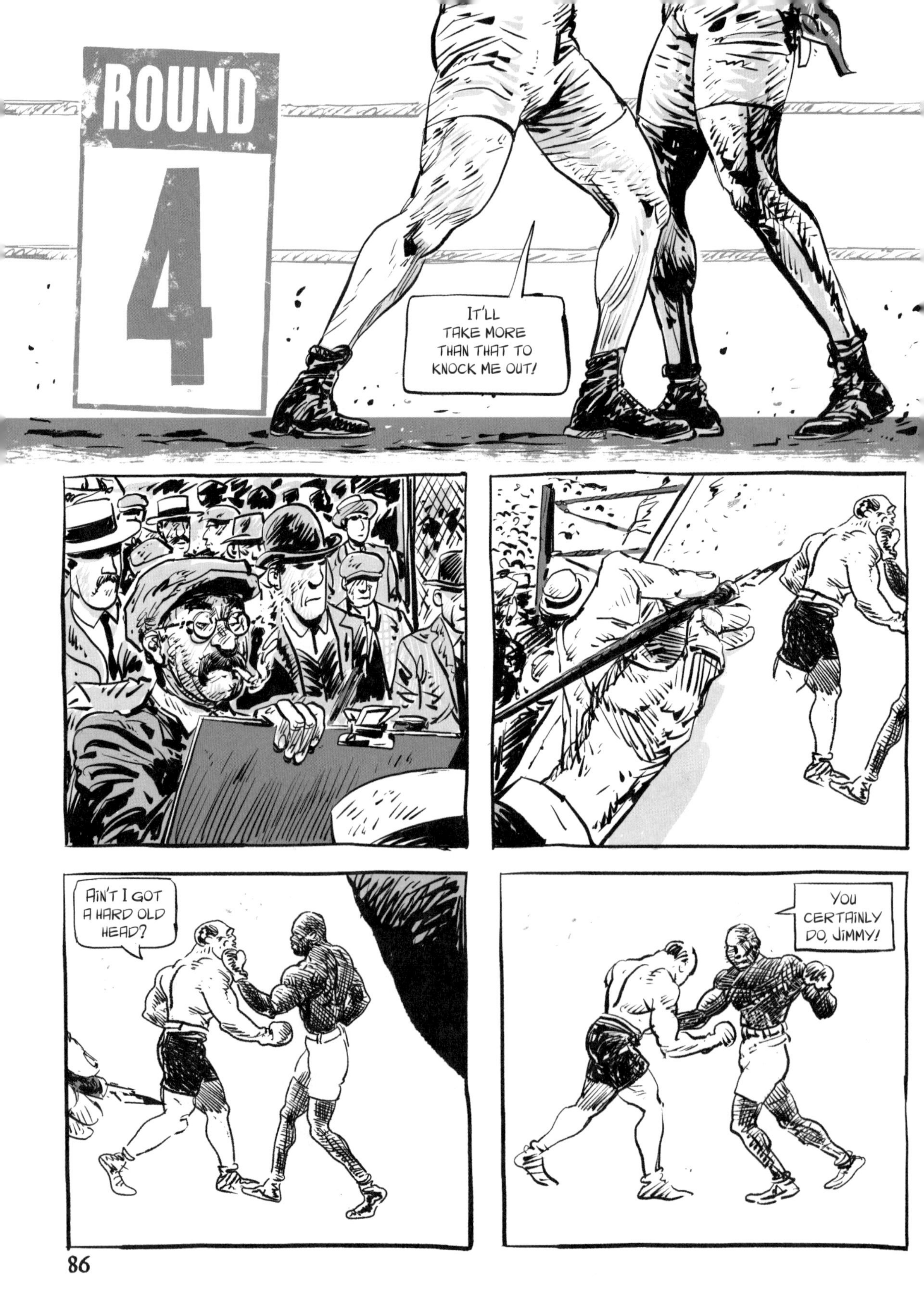

ROUND
4
IT'LL TAKE MORE THAN THAT TO KNOCK ME OUT!
AIN'T I GOT A HARD OLD HEAD?
YOU CERTAINLY DO, JIMMY!

It might seem unsportsmanlike, talking to Mr. Jim while I'm beating him so thoroughly...

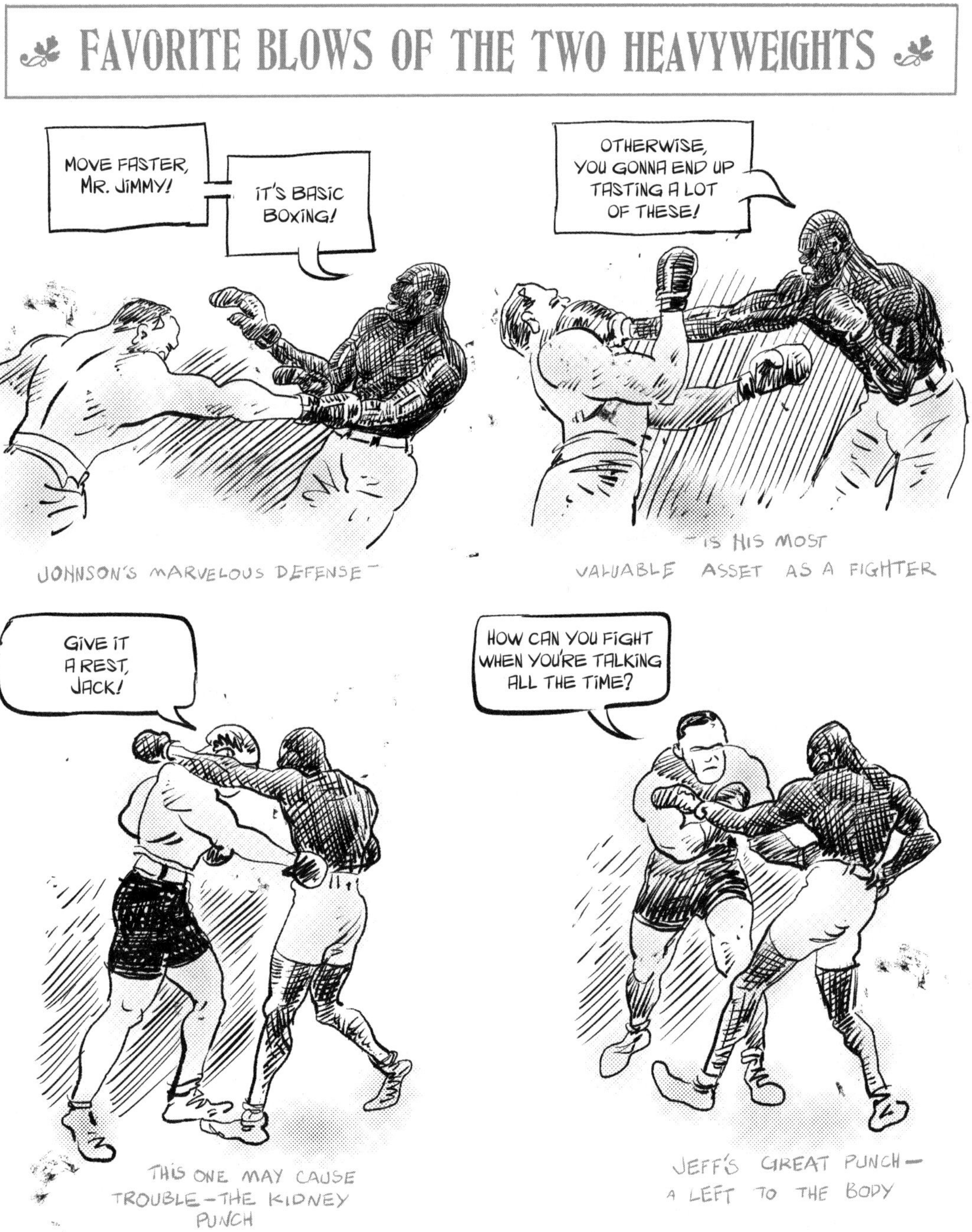
FAVORITE BLOWS OF THE TWO HEAVYWEIGHTS
MOVE FASTER, MR. JIMMY!
IT'S BASIC BOXING!
OTHERWISE, YOU GONNA END UP TASTING A LOT OF THESE!
JOHNSON'S MARVELOUS DEFENSE—
—IS HIS MOST VALUABLE ASSET AS A FIGHTER
GIVE IT A REST, JACK!
HOW CAN YOU FIGHT WHEN YOU'RE TALKING ALL THE TIME?
THIS ONE MAY CAUSE TROUBLE—THE KIDNEY PUNCH
JEFF'S GREAT PUNCH— A LEFT TO THE BODY

...but mouth fighting has always been part of the show.

The right kind of talk can make
a weak fighter wild. It's even better
when the cornermen get involved.

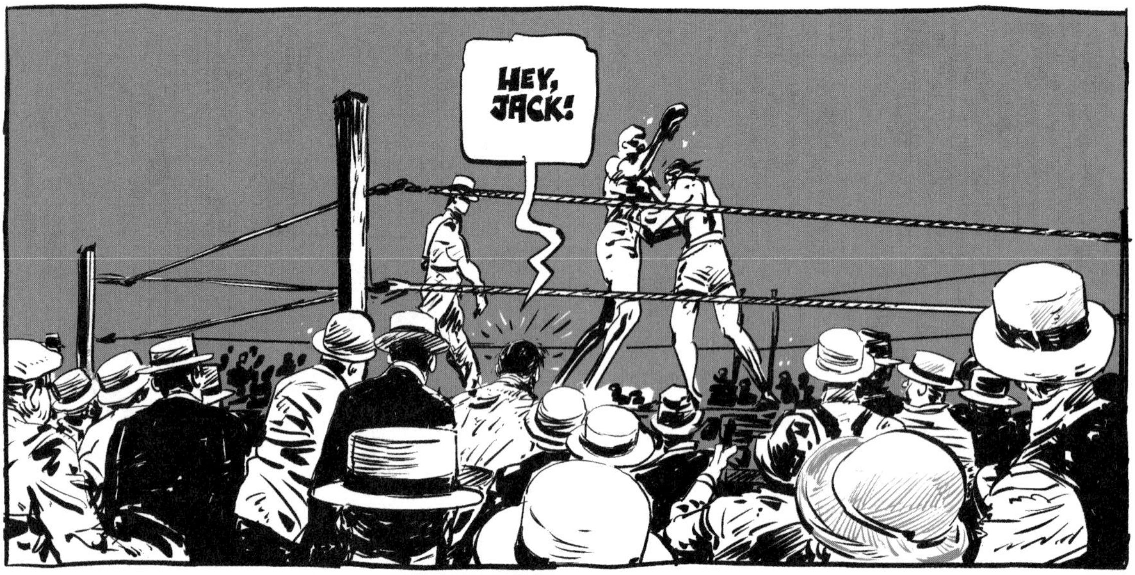
HEY, JACK!

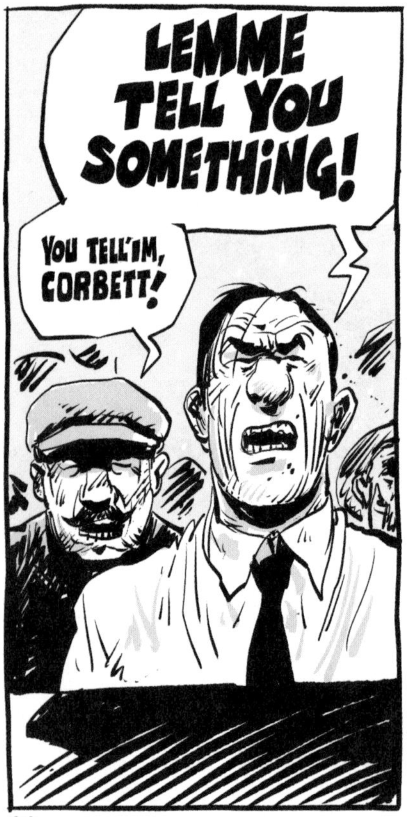
LEMME TELL YOU SOMETHING!
YOU TELL'IM, CORBETT!

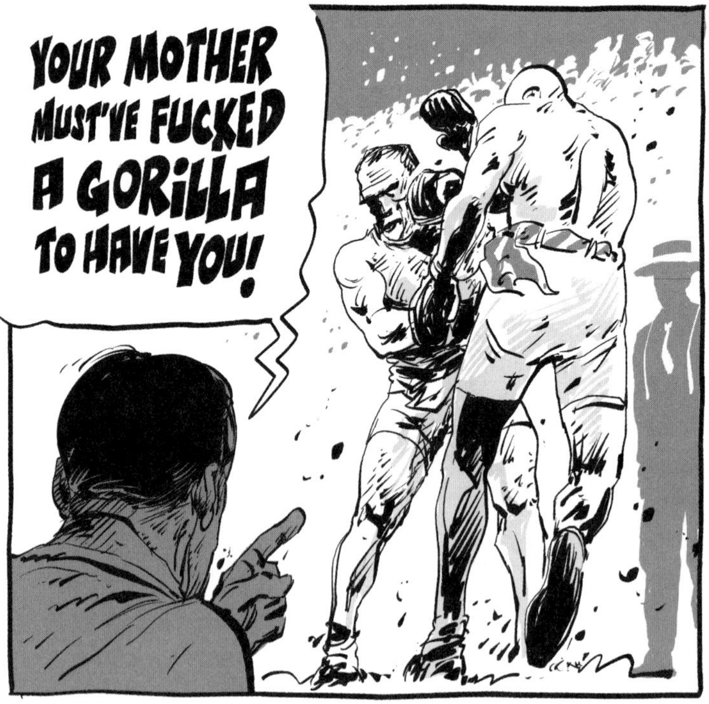
YOUR MOTHER MUST'VE FUCKED A GORILLA TO HAVE YOU!

Corbett's out there, saying unrepeatable
things about my dear mother.

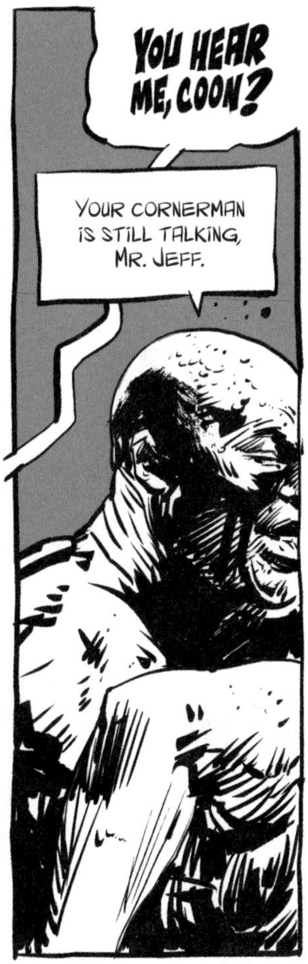
YOU HEAR ME, COON?
YOUR CORNERMAN IS STILL TALKING, MR. JEFF.

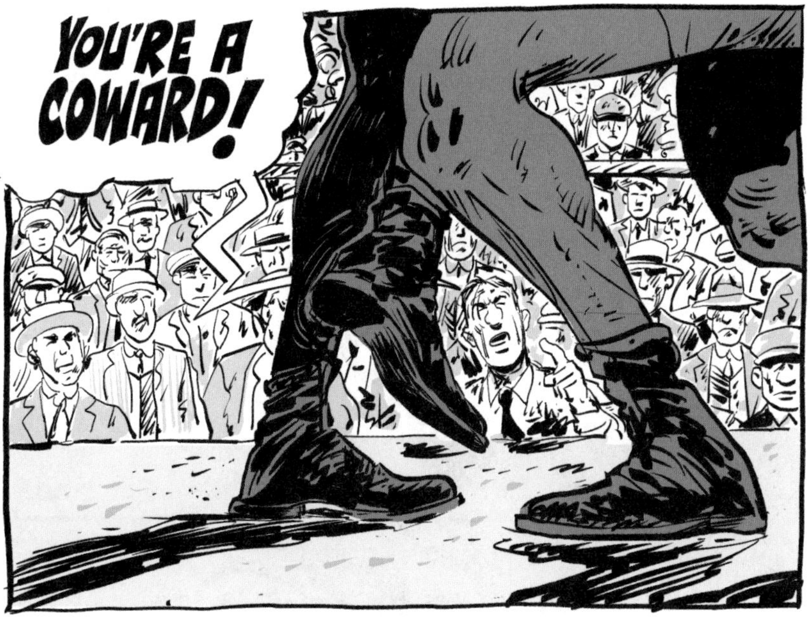
YOU'RE A COWARD!

He paced outside the ring just like a circus tiger before the man with the whip shows up.

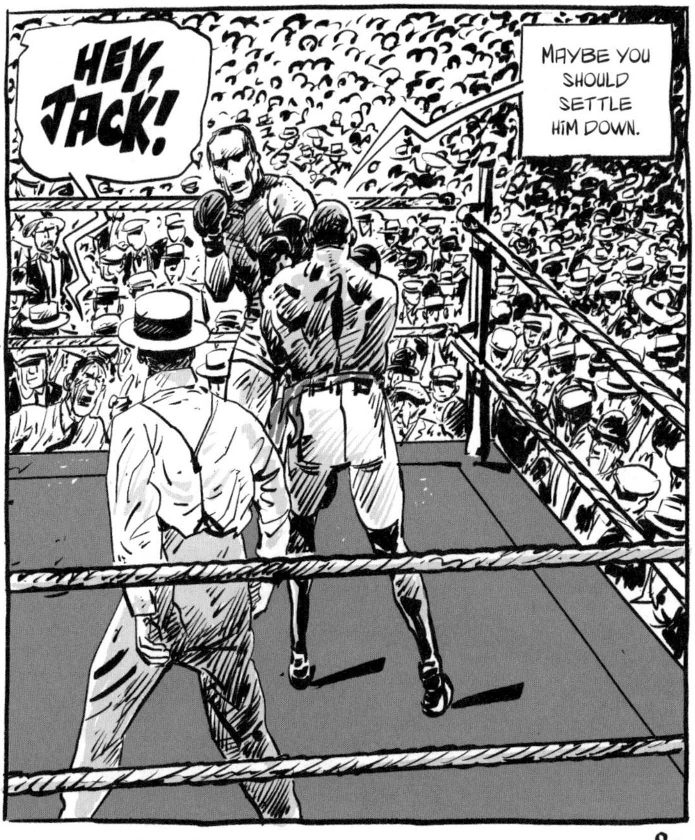
HEY, JACK!
MAYBE YOU SHOULD SETTLE HIM DOWN.

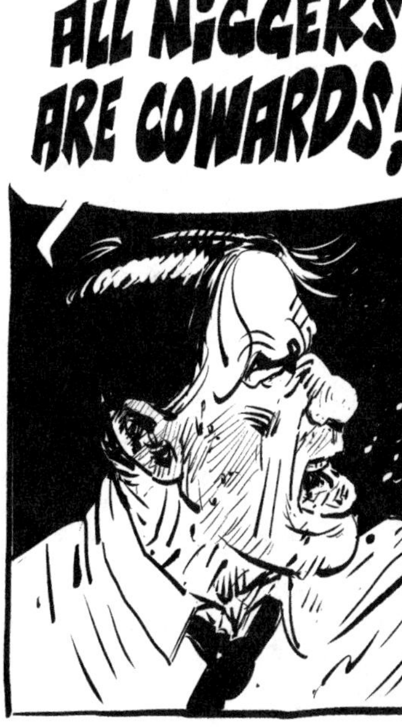
ALL NIGGERS ARE COWARDS!

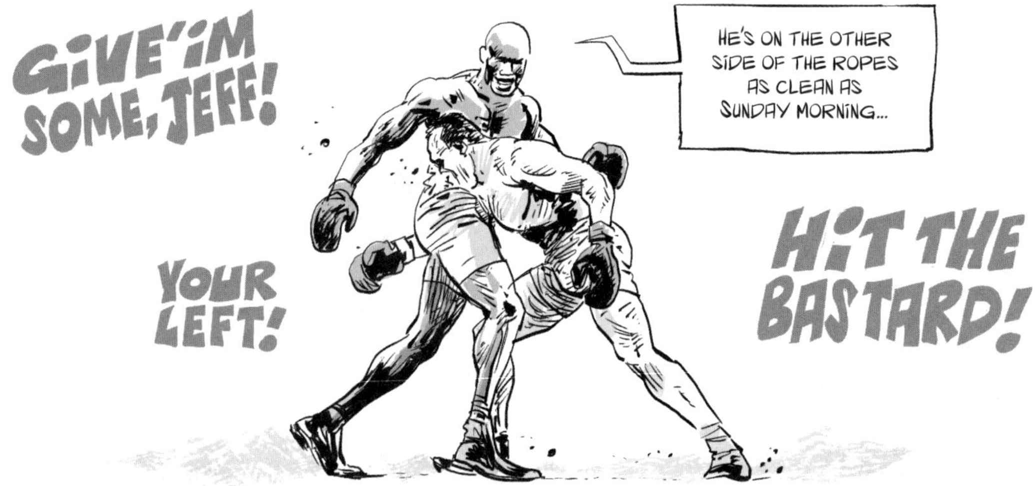
GIVE 'IM SOME, JEFF!
HE'S ON THE OTHER SIDE OF THE ROPES AS CLEAN AS SUNDAY MORNING...
YOUR LEFT!
HIT THE BASTARD!

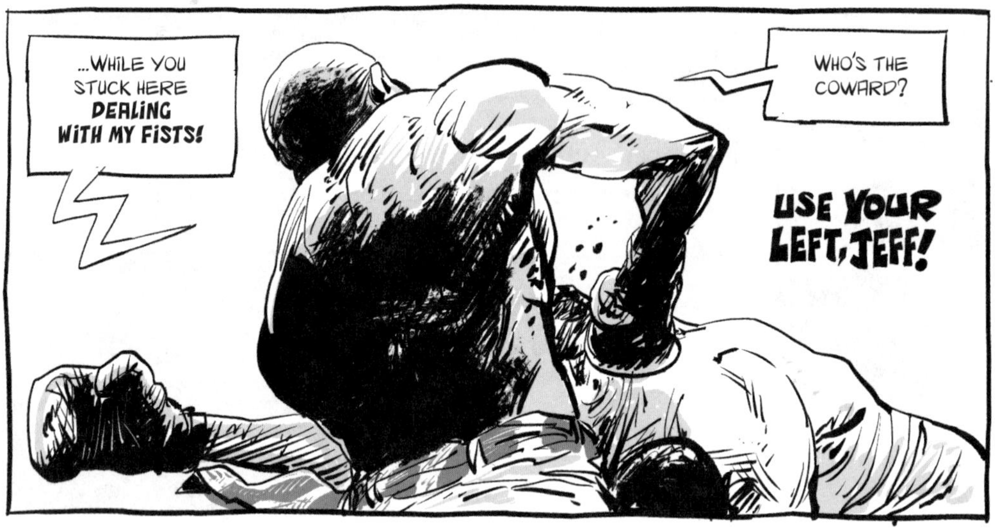
...WHILE YOU STUCK HERE **DEALING WITH MY FISTS!**
WHO'S THE COWARD?
USE YOUR LEFT, JEFF!

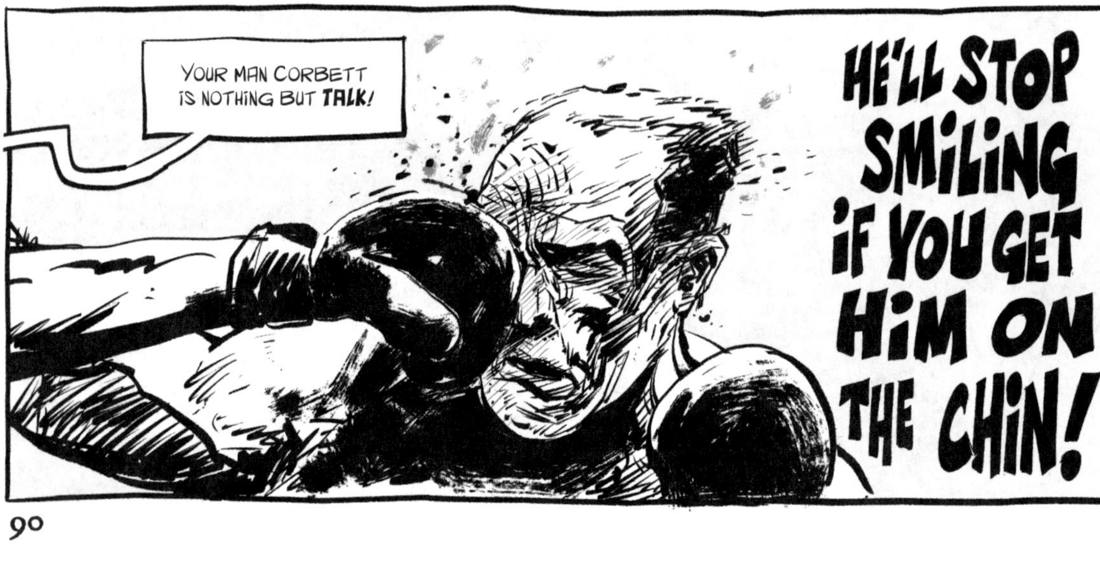
YOUR MAN CORBETT IS NOTHING BUT **TALK!**
HE'LL STOP SMILING IF YOU GET HIM ON THE CHIN!

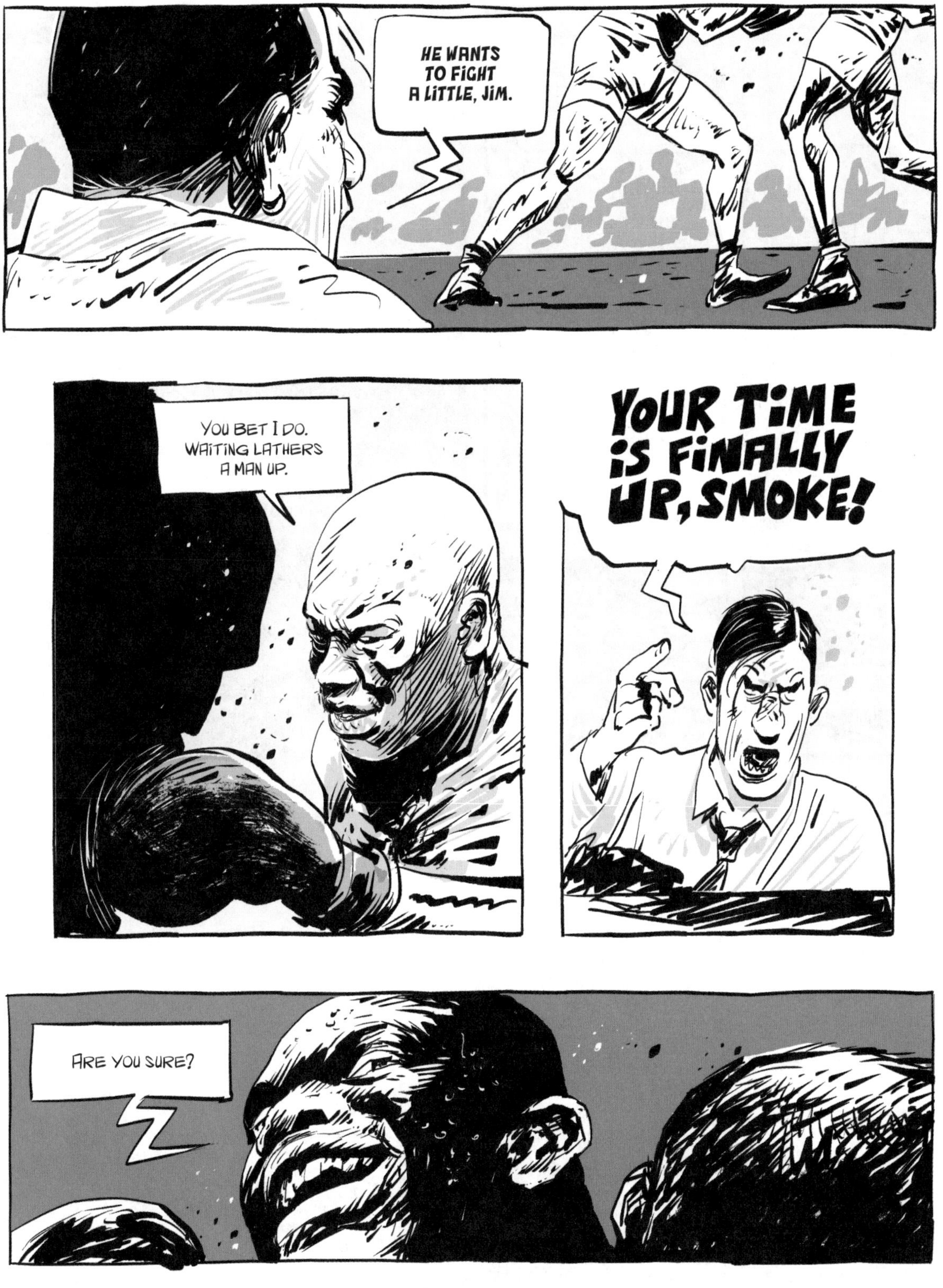
HE WANTS TO FIGHT A LITTLE, JIM.
YOU BET I DO. WAITING LATHERS A MAN UP.
YOUR TIME IS FINALLY UP, SMOKE!
ARE YOU SURE?

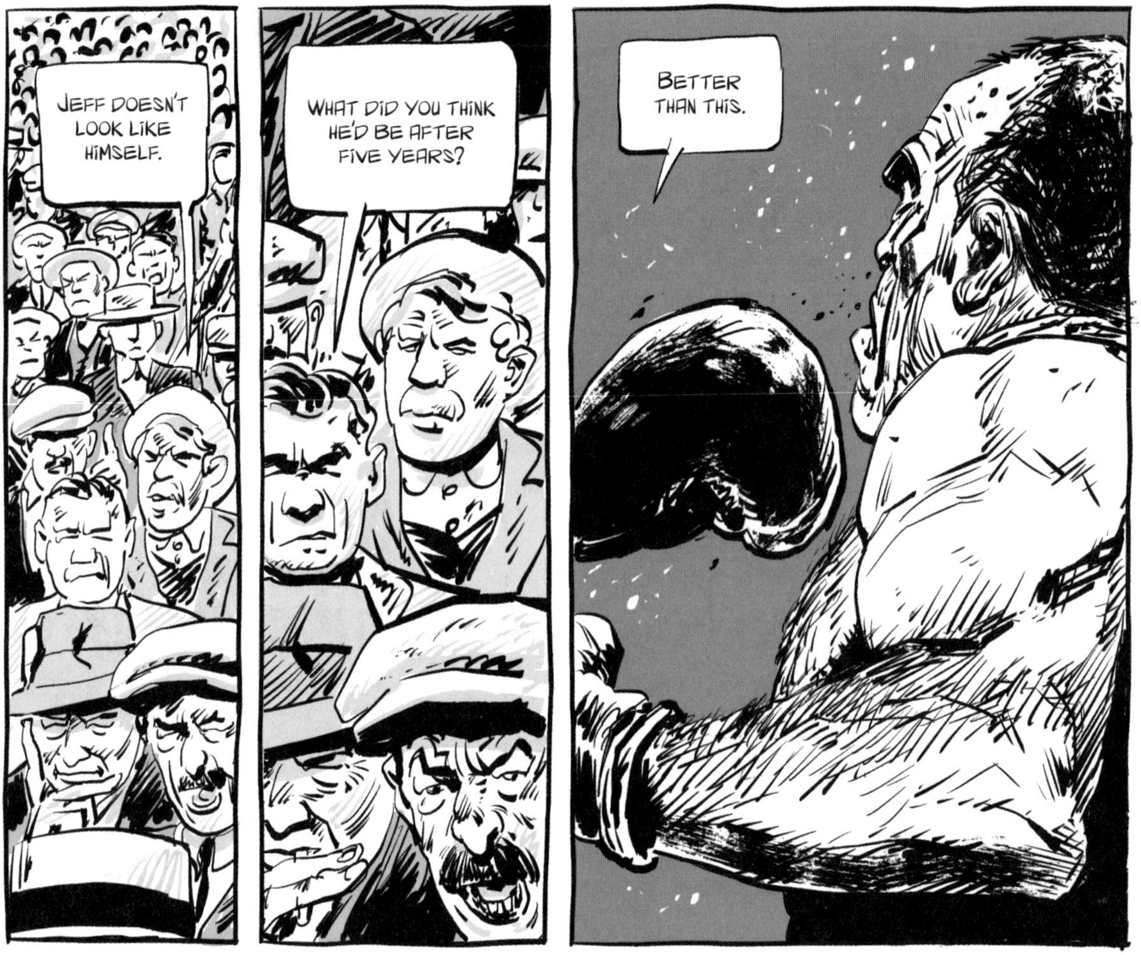
JEFF DOESN'T LOOK LIKE HIMSELF.
WHAT DID YOU THINK HE'D BE AFTER FIVE YEARS?
BETTER THAN THIS.

Corbett's mouth fighting had no sophistication, but the crowd loved to hear him say what they were thinking.

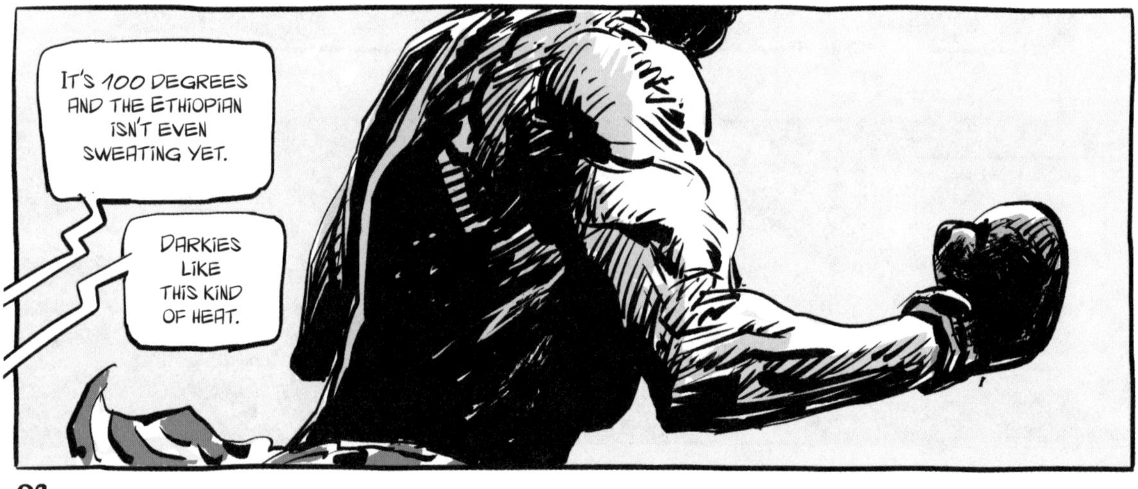
IT'S *100* DEGREES AND THE ETHIOPIAN ISN'T EVEN SWEATING YET.
DARKIES LIKE THIS KIND OF HEAT.

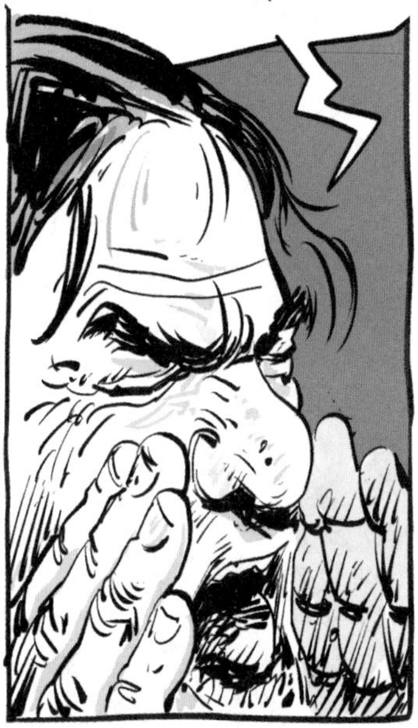
YOUR MOTHER'S A MONKEY!

The mouth fight is as important as fists or footwork. An angry fighter is a sloppy fighter.

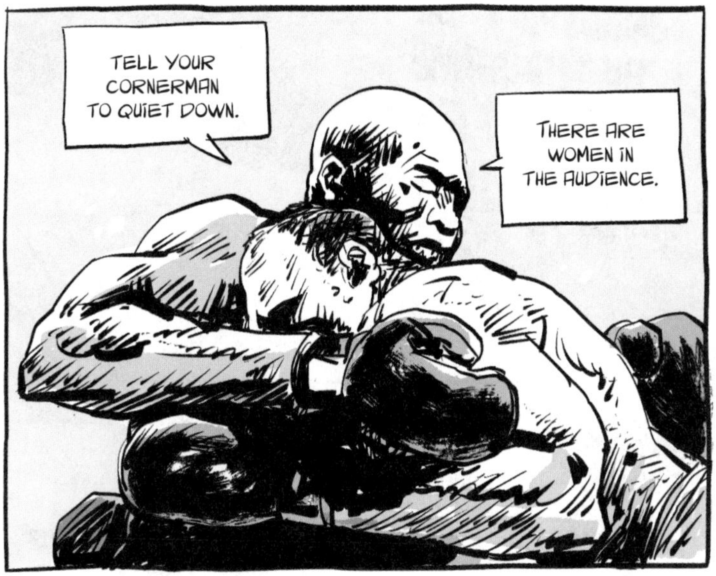
TELL YOUR CORNERMAN TO QUIET DOWN.
THERE ARE WOMEN IN THE AUDIENCE.

How are they supposed to solve my defense...

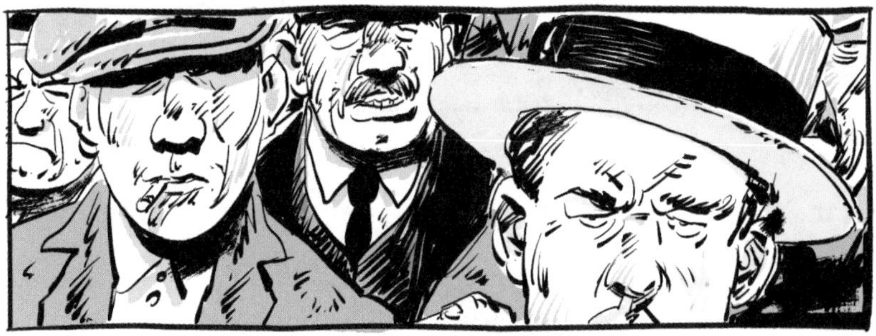

...when they're like a bull seeing a muleta?

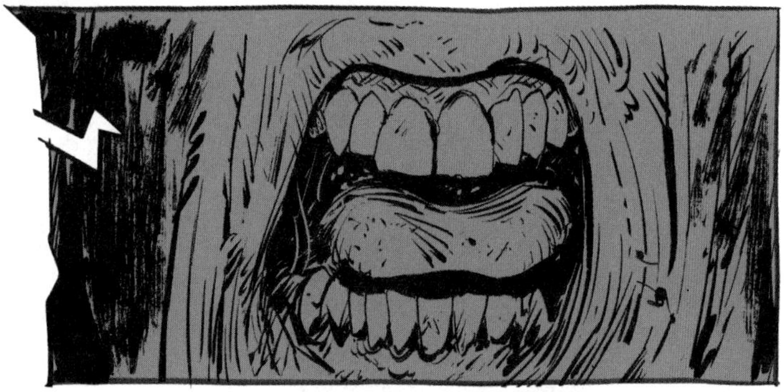
YOU'RE A MONKEY!

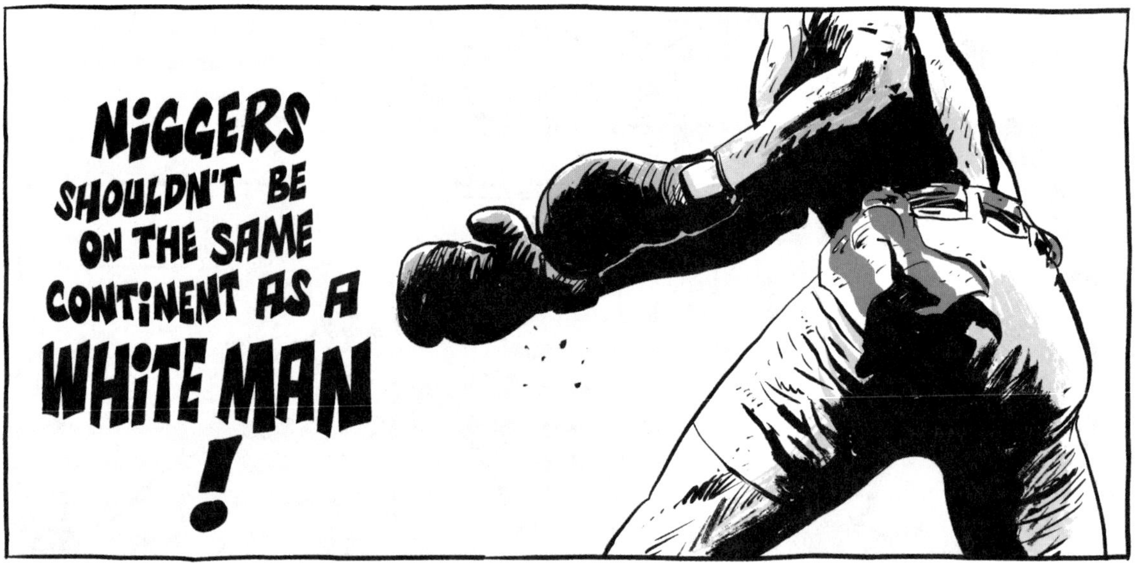
NiGGERS SHOULDN'T BE ON THE SAME CONTiNENT AS A WHiTE MAN !

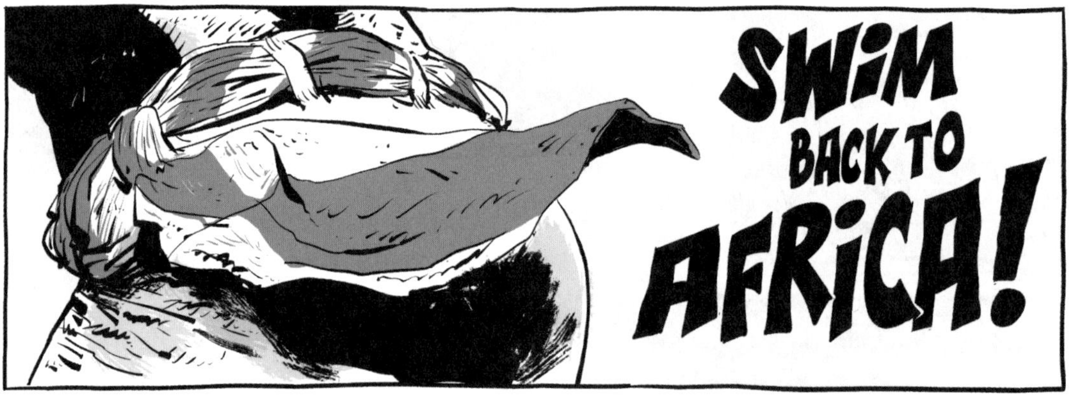
SWiM BACK TO AFRiCA!

Corbett still doesn't get
I'm a modern Black man.

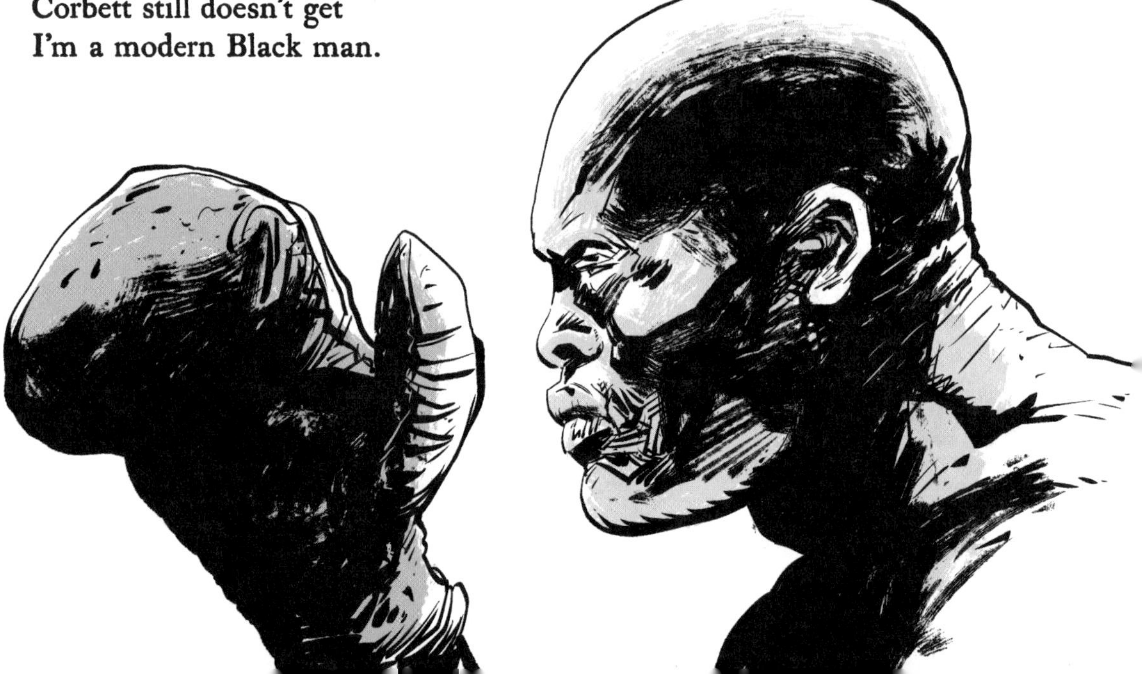

I'm the newest fashion.

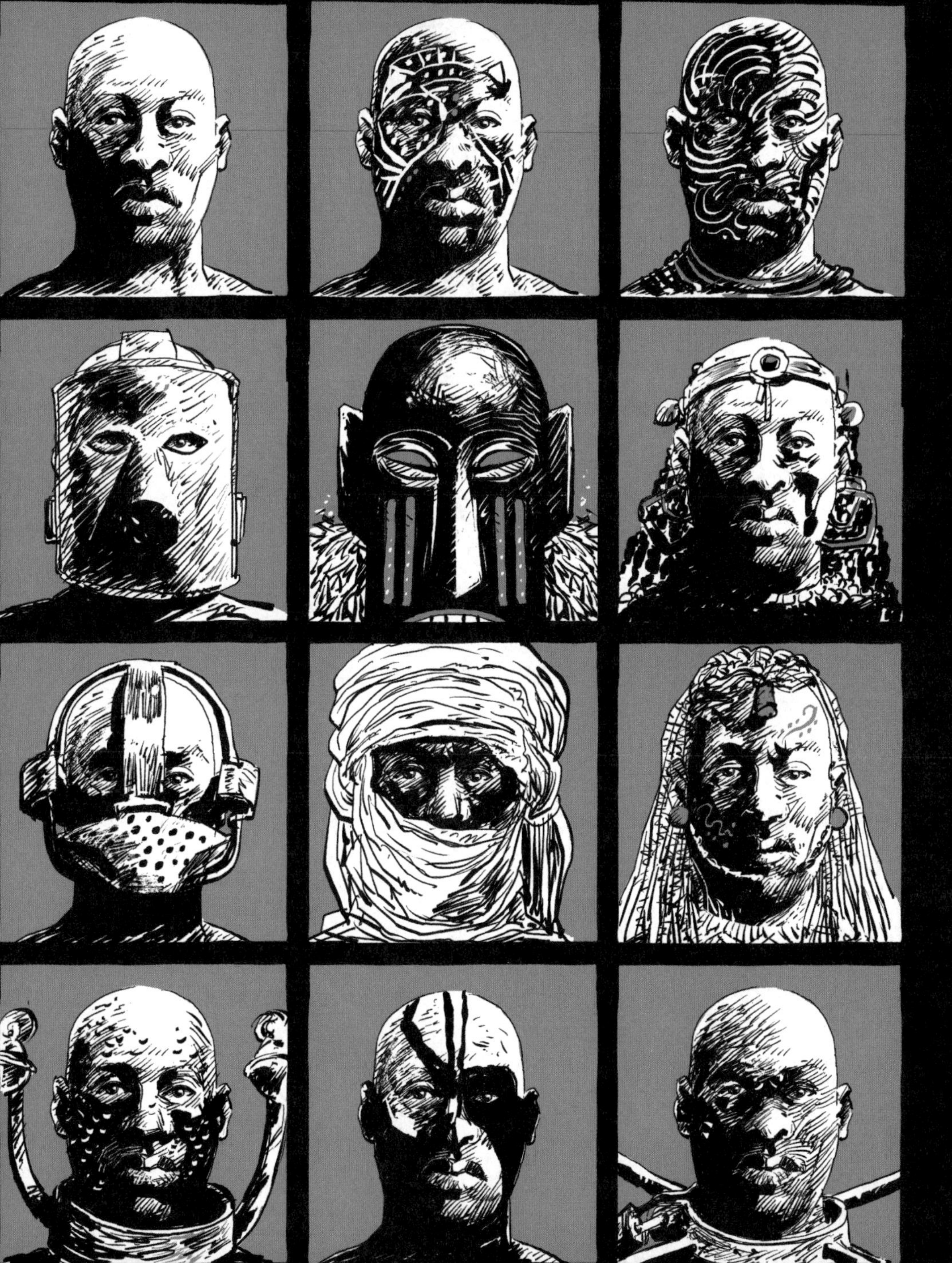

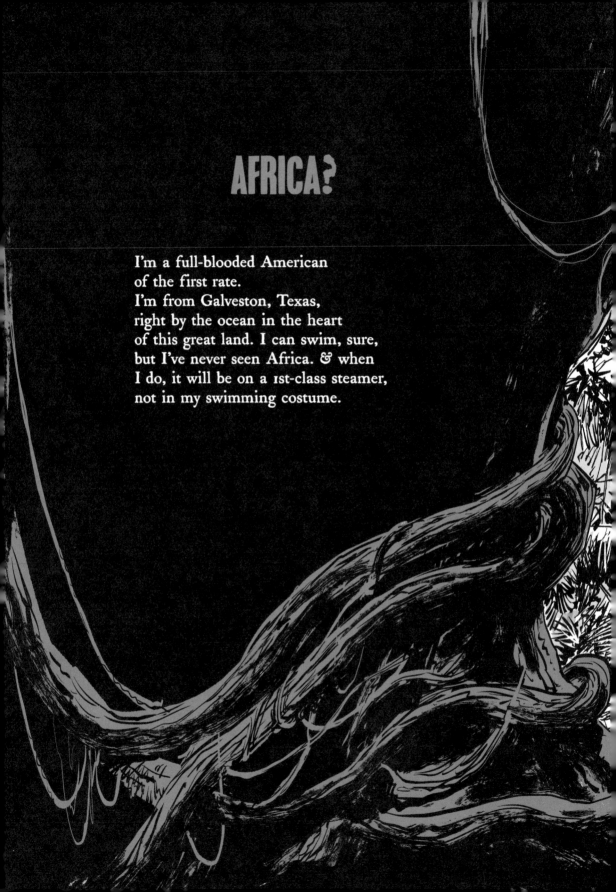

AFRICA?

I'm a full-blooded American
of the first rate.
I'm from Galveston, Texas,
right by the ocean in the heart
of this great land. I can swim, sure,
but I've never seen Africa. & when
I do, it will be on a 1st-class steamer,
not in my swimming costume.

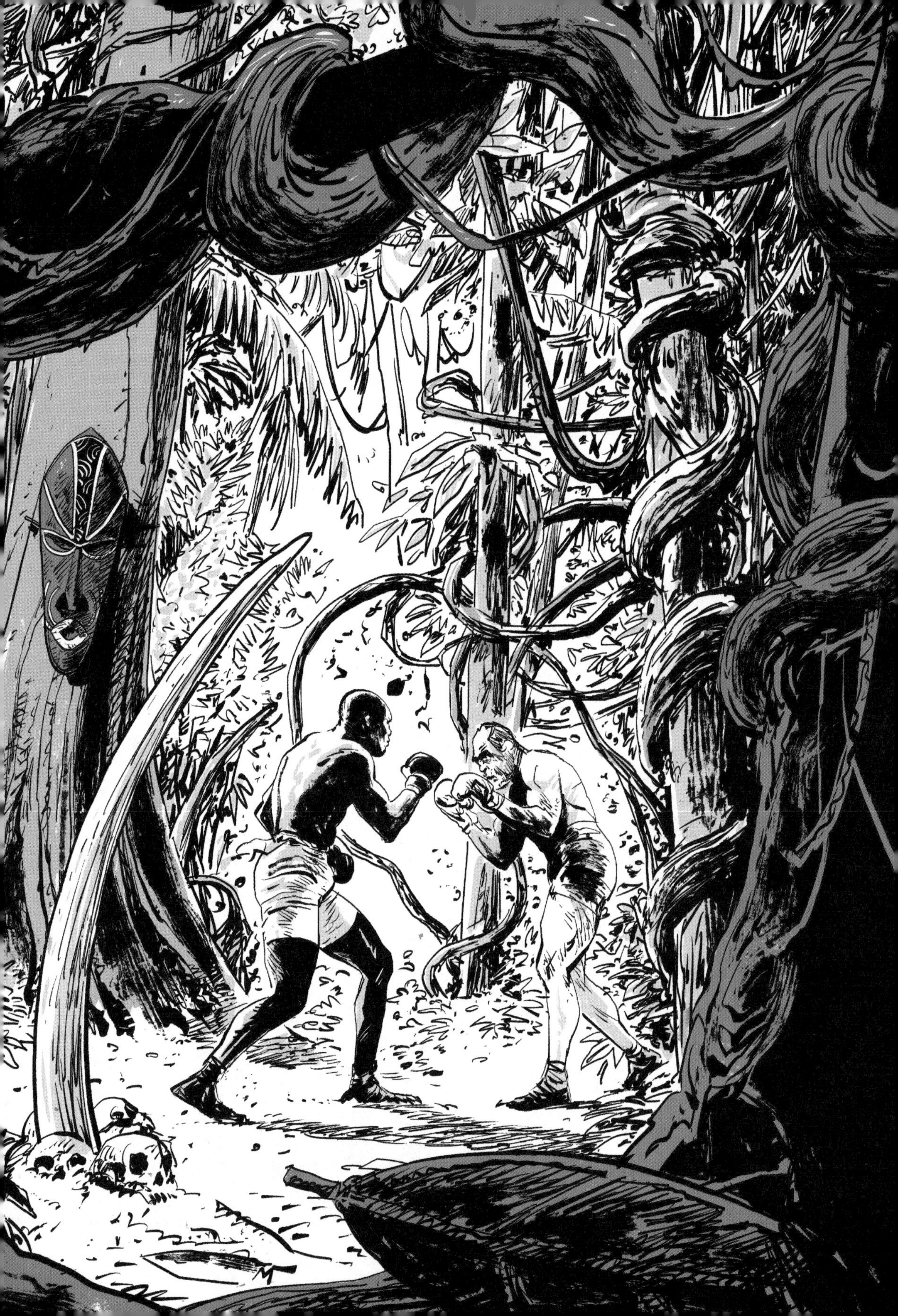

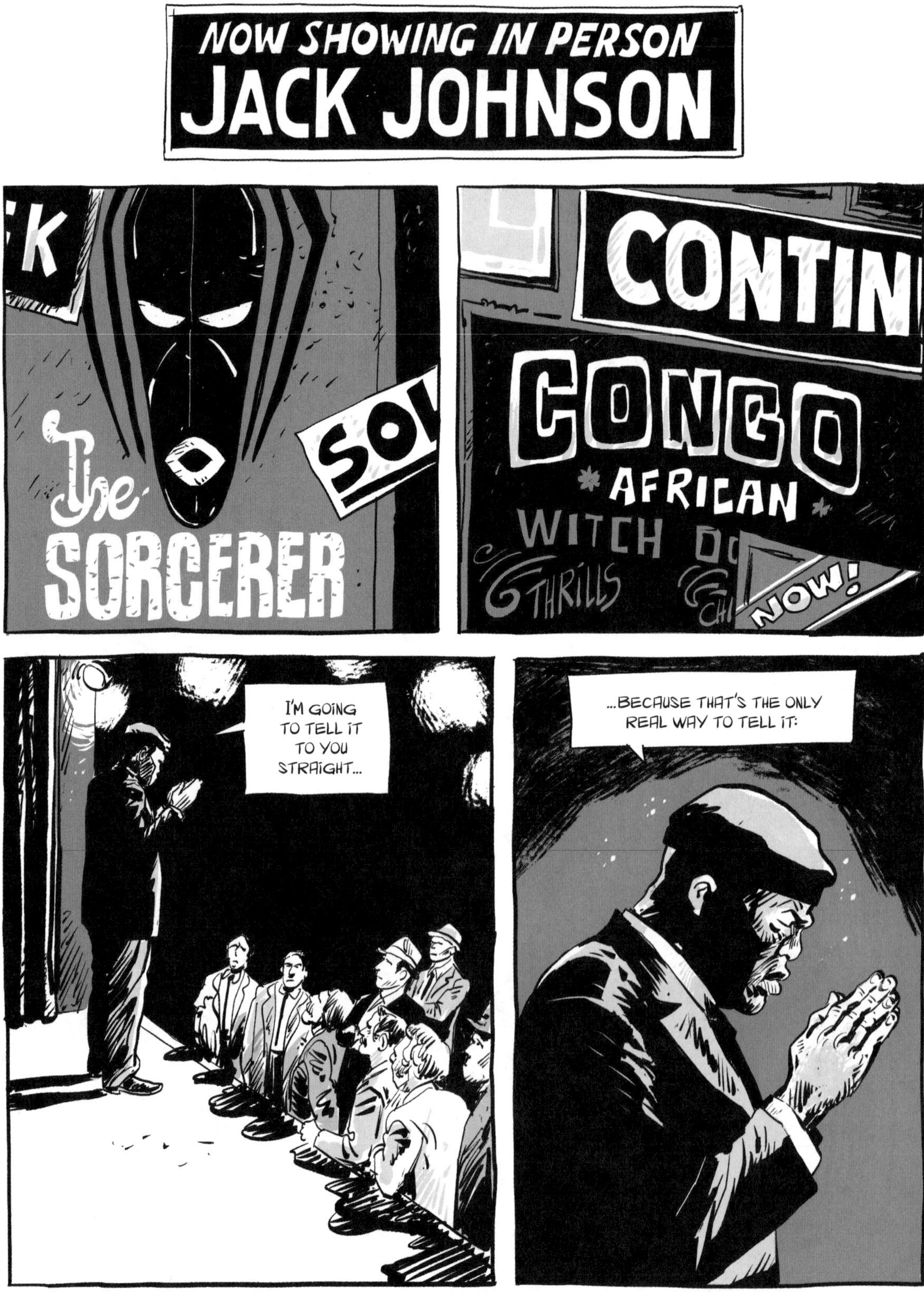
NOW SHOWING IN PERSON
JACK JOHNSON
K
The SORCERER
SO
CONTIN
CONGO
AFRICAN
WITCH D
THRILLS
NOW!
I'M GOING TO TELL IT TO YOU STRAIGHT...
...BECAUSE THAT'S THE ONLY REAL WAY TO TELL IT:

THE SAN FRANCISCO CALL. THURSDAY, JUNE 9, 1910

Call's Page of Sports

BEING AN ORIGINAL IS LONELY BUSINESS.

It might have seemed like
I was having a good time,
but I've been angry most
of my life. You would be,
too, if people questioned
your heart, your smarts
& your manhood everyday.
I got tired of the jokes.
I got tired of all the insinuations
about my skin. So I started
writing a book of advice
for the next Jack Johnson.
I don't want him to go through
the things I've gone through.

Chicago Examiner

TWENTIETH CENTURY NEWSPAPER

My whole life whites have antagonized
me & insulted me. They refuse to see
that I'm a man no matter how quickly
I put their great hopes to sleep.

THE NEW SENSATION
ALL COONS LOOK ALIKE TO ME.
A DARKEY MISUNDERSTANDING
WRITTEN & COMPOSED BY
ERNEST HOGAN.

"ABYSMAL BRUTE"
$

Y

NEW YORK EVENING JOURNAL, JUN

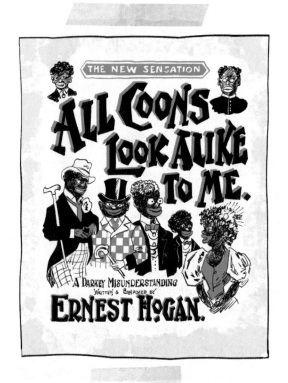

EVENING JOURN

JOHNSON WAS BOXING WI

HE WAS JUST READY GETTING READY TO SEE THE FIGHT WHEN THE

Los Angeles Examiner
Racing Sporting & Section An other

JOHNSON PAINTS HIS CHRISTMAS PRESENT BLACK

WORLD'S HEAVYWEIGHT CHAMPIONSHIP
AH'M A REGULAR CHAWLES DANA GIBJOHNSON
AH'SE LOOKIN FO A CROWN TO DISCOLOR MAN SELF
JOHNSON.
LANGFORD.
LILY WHITE
TAR
TAR
COLOR LINE
ROYAL BLACK
GEO HERRIMAN

CHICKENS VS. THE CHAMPIONSHIP

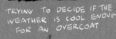

IF AHM ASLEEP — FO' LOR' SAKE DON'T WAKE ME! — SLING ANOTHER SQUAWKER
WHY! YOU HAVE EATEN TEN ALREADY!
ITS "ONLY "NATCHEL" THAT JACK HAS A LIKING FOR POULTRY —— SINCE, HE IS A DESCENDANT OF HAM AND THE CHICKENS COME FROM EGGS —— — AND YOU KNOW THAT HAM AND EGGS ALWAYS DID GO WELL TOGETHER —— (CURTAIN)

I WONDAH IF DIS HERE CHICKEN DIET EFFECTS YO' HEART?

DO YOU GET JACK IN HIS LATEST RING COSTUME

EXCLUSIVE STUDIES OF JACK JOHNSON'S FIGHTING FACE —By GOLDBERG

ARTISTIC STUDY OF JACK JOHNSON'S HEAD.

COMPARING THE RELATIVE MERITS OF ANNA HELD AND DOCTEUR COOK

TRYING TO DECIDE IF THE WEATHER IS COOL ENOUGH FOR AN OVERCOAT

DRINKING A PINT OF STEWED RHUBARB

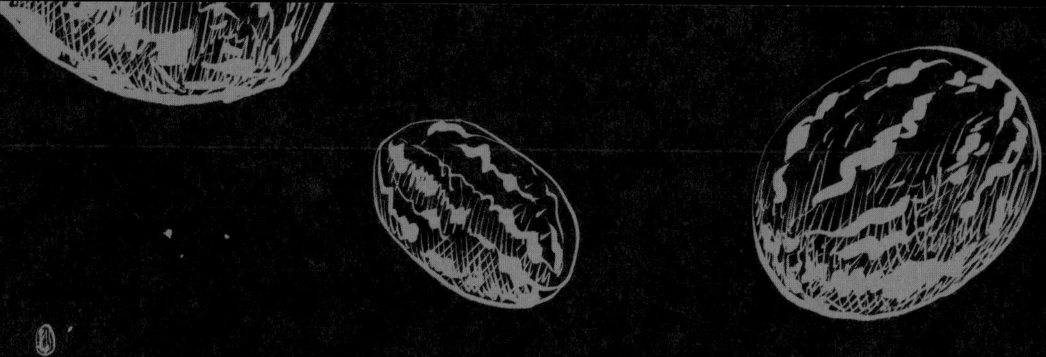

It's as if they have never seen a Black man up close.
Who can eat with lips bigger than their whole face?
Who can smile with a watermelon instead of a mouth?
Who can smell with a bone through the middle of his nose?

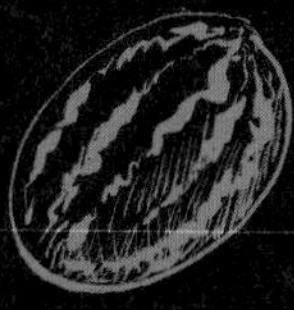

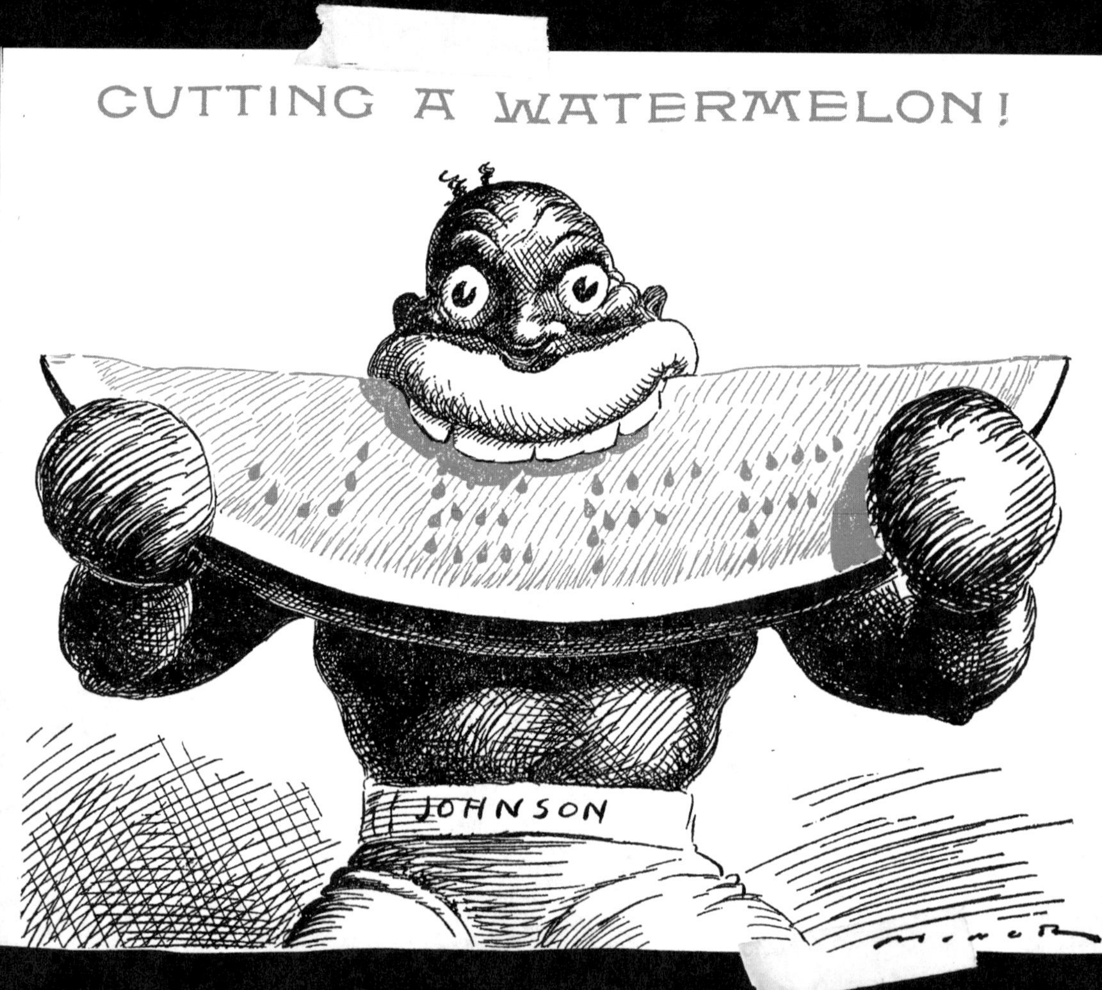
CUTTING A WATERMELON!
JOHNSON

After I beat this white hope, I hope
they remember all their illustrations
of me—licking cartoon lips & chewing
watermelons, dressed up as an ape
lounging in some unknown part of Africa.

I hope they remember the indignities
because I remember every one
of them & you best believe I'm thinking
about those drawings every time
I catch their man with an uppercut.

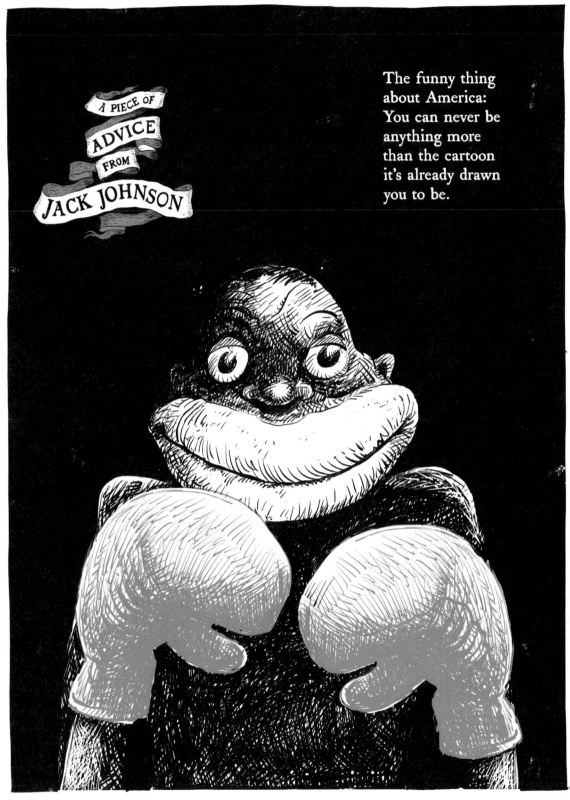

A PIECE OF **ADVICE** FROM **JACK JOHNSON**

The funny thing about America: You can never be anything more than the cartoon it's already drawn you to be.

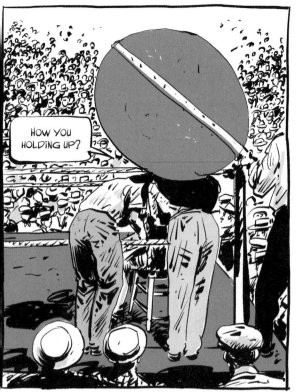

HOW YOU HOLDING UP?

HE'S CLEVER. I JUST WISH HE DIDN'T TALK SO MUCH. YOU INSULTING HIS MOTHER DON'T HELP.

HE'S A CLOWN WITH GOLD TEETH.

HE CAN FIGHT A LITTLE, BUT HE CAN'T HANDLE YOUR FISTS *IF YOU ATTACK!*

I'M LOOKING FOR THE RIGHT ANGLES.

ALL RIGHT...

NOW, STOP HUNTING ANGLES AND *START SWINGING!*

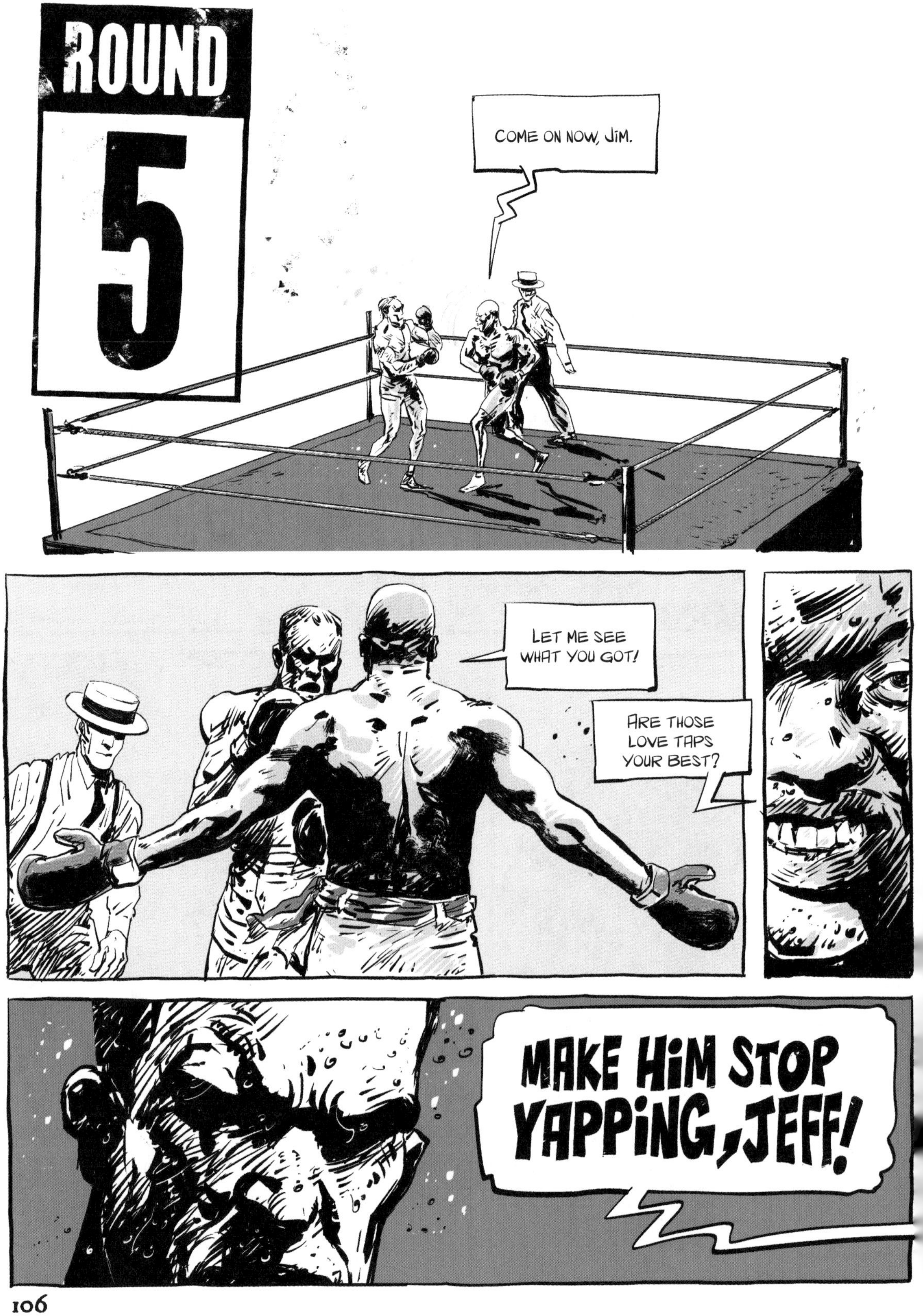
ROUND
5
COME ON NOW, JIM.
LET ME SEE WHAT YOU GOT!
ARE THOSE LOVE TAPS YOUR BEST?
MAKE HIM STOP YAPPING, JEFF!

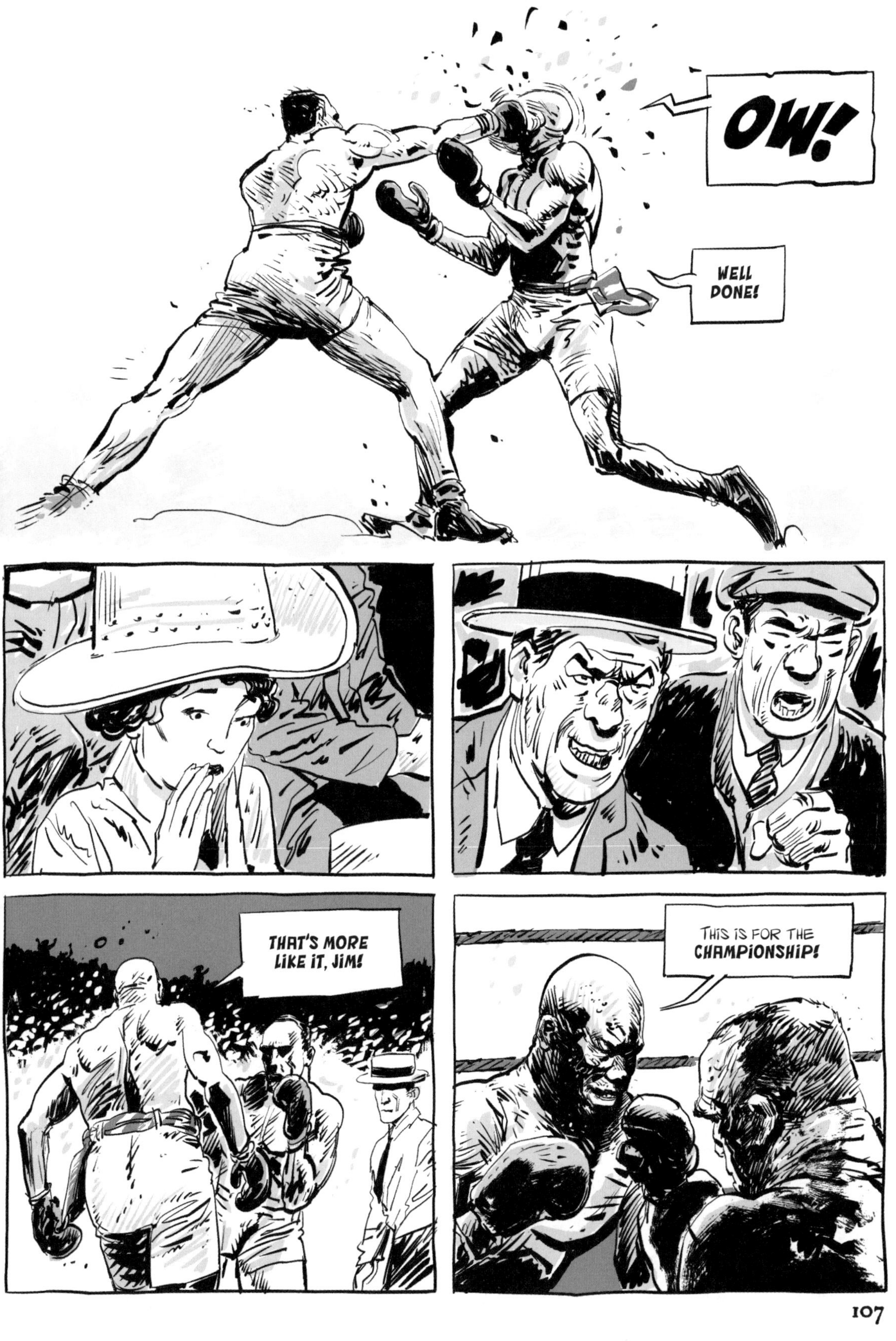
OW!
WELL DONE!
THAT'S MORE LIKE IT, JIM!
THIS IS FOR THE CHAMPIONSHIP!

PRIZEFIGHTING IS THE MOST FISTIC OF ALL SCIENCES

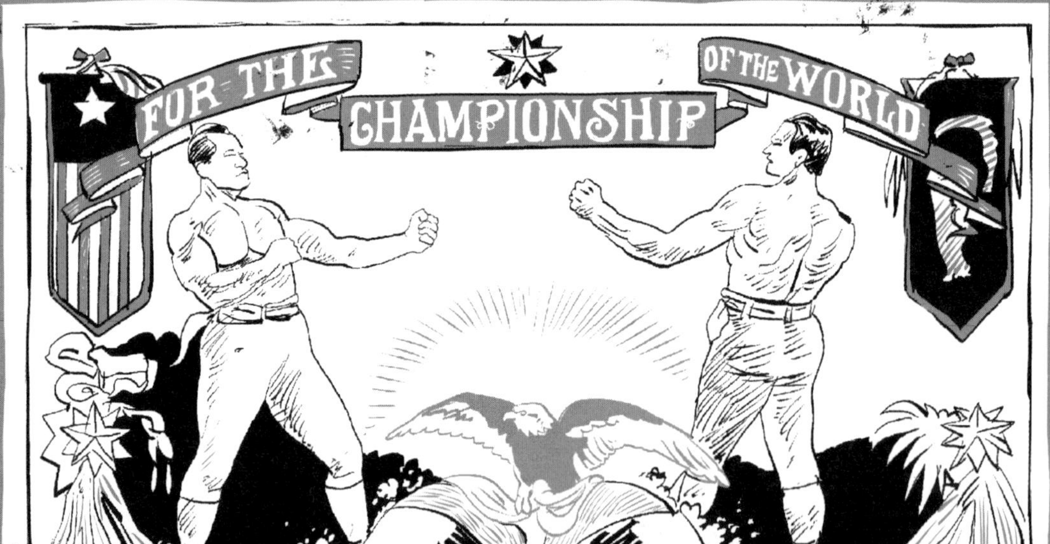
FOR THE
CHAMPIONSHIP
OF THE WORLD
J.L. SULLIVAN
JAKE KILRAIN

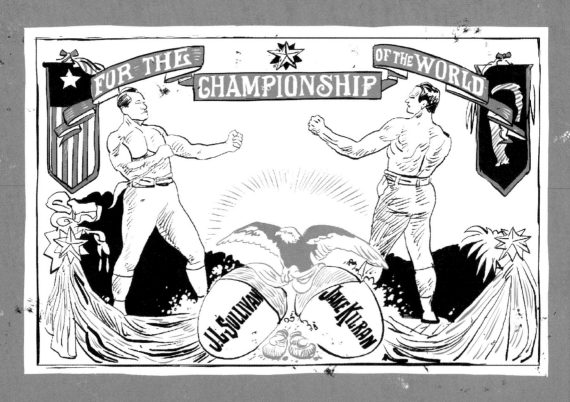

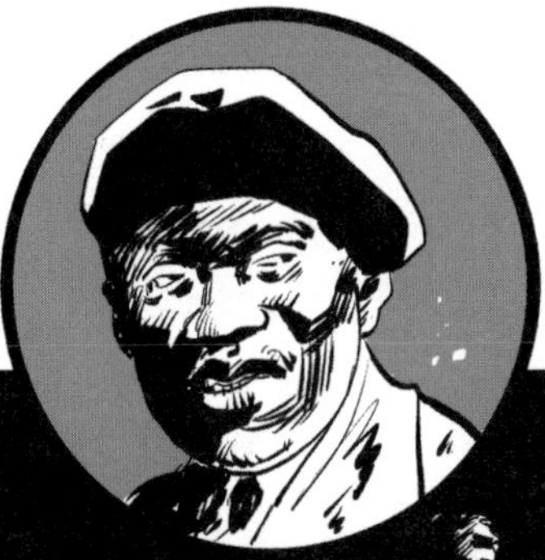

Jim Jeffries was a game champion in his day, but prizefighting started with John L. Sullivan.

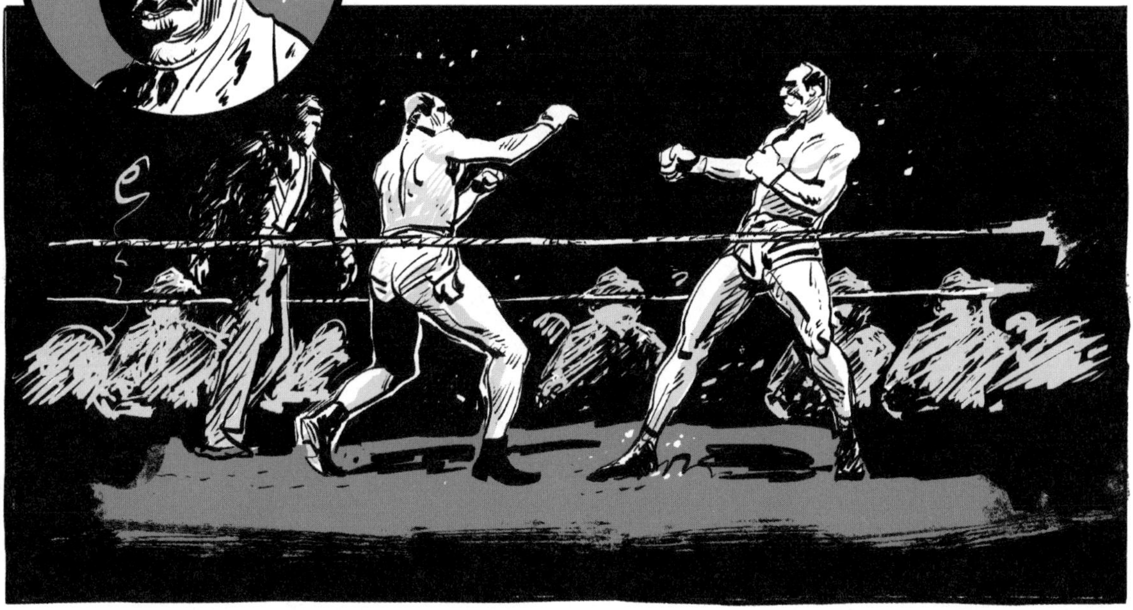

They called him the Boston Strongboy.

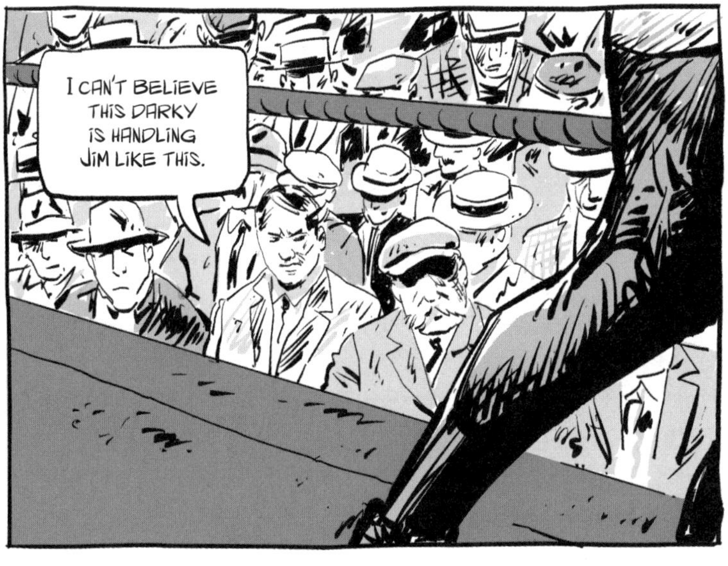
I CAN'T BELIEVE THIS DARKY IS HANDLING JIM LIKE THIS.

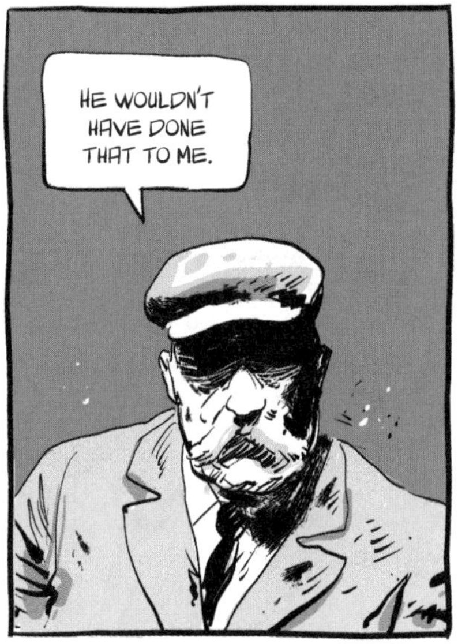
HE WOULDN'T HAVE DONE THAT TO ME.

No man could match his ferocity or tenacity.

He could drink with the best of them & his mustache was always curled to perfection. He was the first to draw the color line.

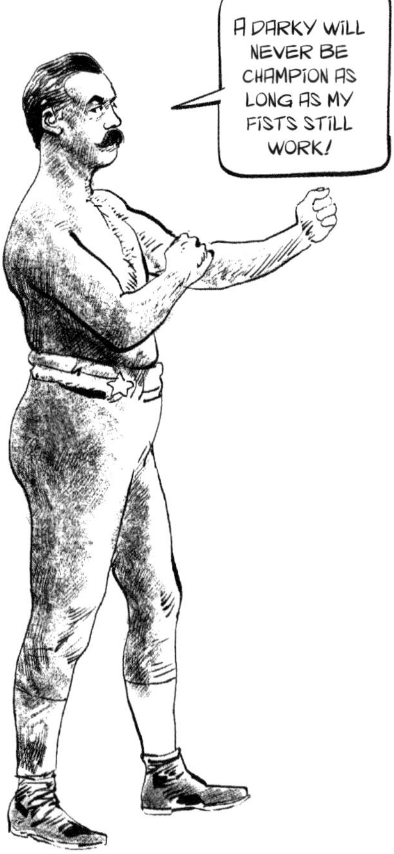
A DARKY WILL NEVER BE CHAMPION AS LONG AS MY FISTS STILL WORK!

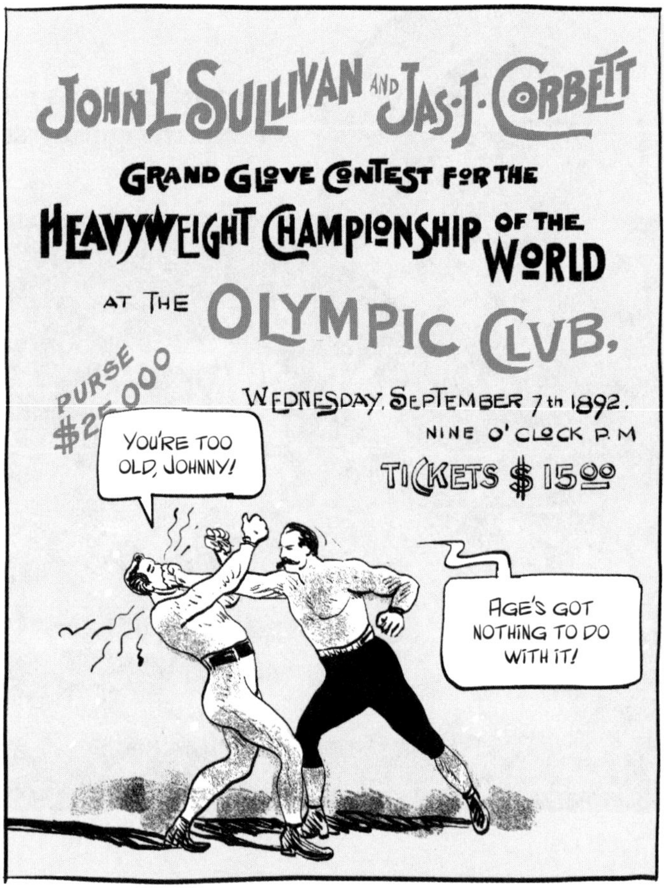
JOHN L. SULLIVAN AND JAS. J. CORBETT
GRAND GLOVE CONTEST FOR THE
HEAVYWEIGHT CHAMPIONSHIP OF THE WORLD
AT THE OLYMPIC CLUB,
PURSE
WEDNESDAY, SEPTEMBER 7th 1892.
NINE O' CLOCK P.M
TICKETS $ 15.00
YOU'RE TOO OLD, JOHNNY!
AGE'S GOT NOTHING TO DO WITH IT!

No man could match knuckles with him until James J. Corbett. Corbett had a new kind of panache. Something between brawling & dancing, & it confused the old pugilists.

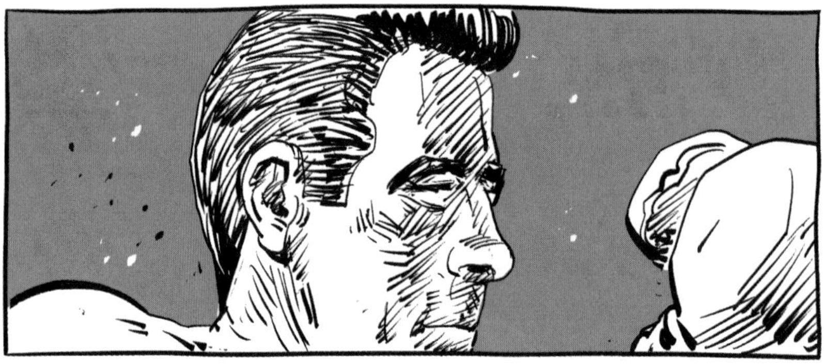

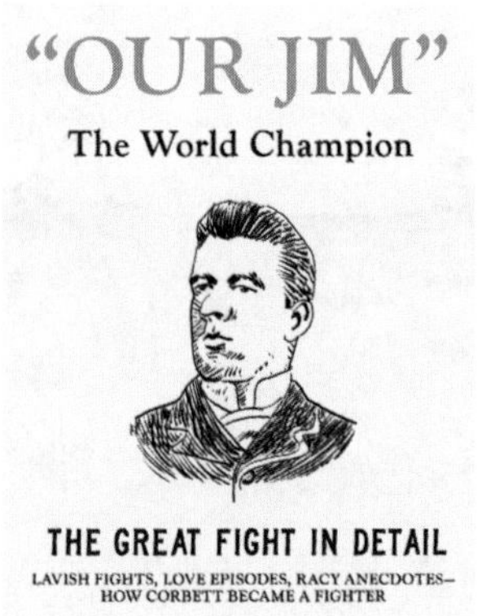
"OUR JIM"
The World Champion
THE GREAT FIGHT IN DETAIL
LAVISH FIGHTS, LOVE EPISODES, RACY ANECDOTES—HOW CORBETT BECAME A FIGHTER

"Gentleman" James J. Corbett
World Heavyweight Champion
1892-1897

Corbett was too clever for them & he hated Black people almost as much as he hated losing. I can't even repeat the things he said during my battle with Jeffries.

Like most white prizefighters, Corbett was more worried about the color of the man than his skills in the ring.

Corbett was just about to retire when I first started boxing.

He wouldn't have lasted more than 3 rounds in the ring with me.

White fighters acted like the color line was a law, but it was just cowardice.

From 1903 to 1909, I demolished every fighter who challenged me. Even the fiercest colored pugilists.

Sam McVey,
Frank Childs,
Sandy Ferguson,
Marvin Hart,
Joe Jeanette...

I was the best & every one of them knew it.

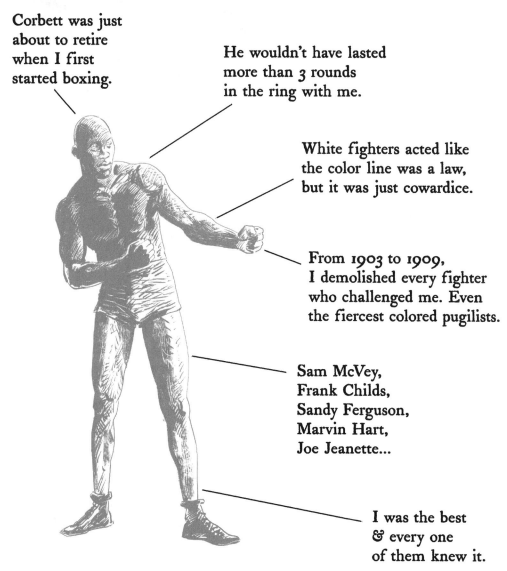

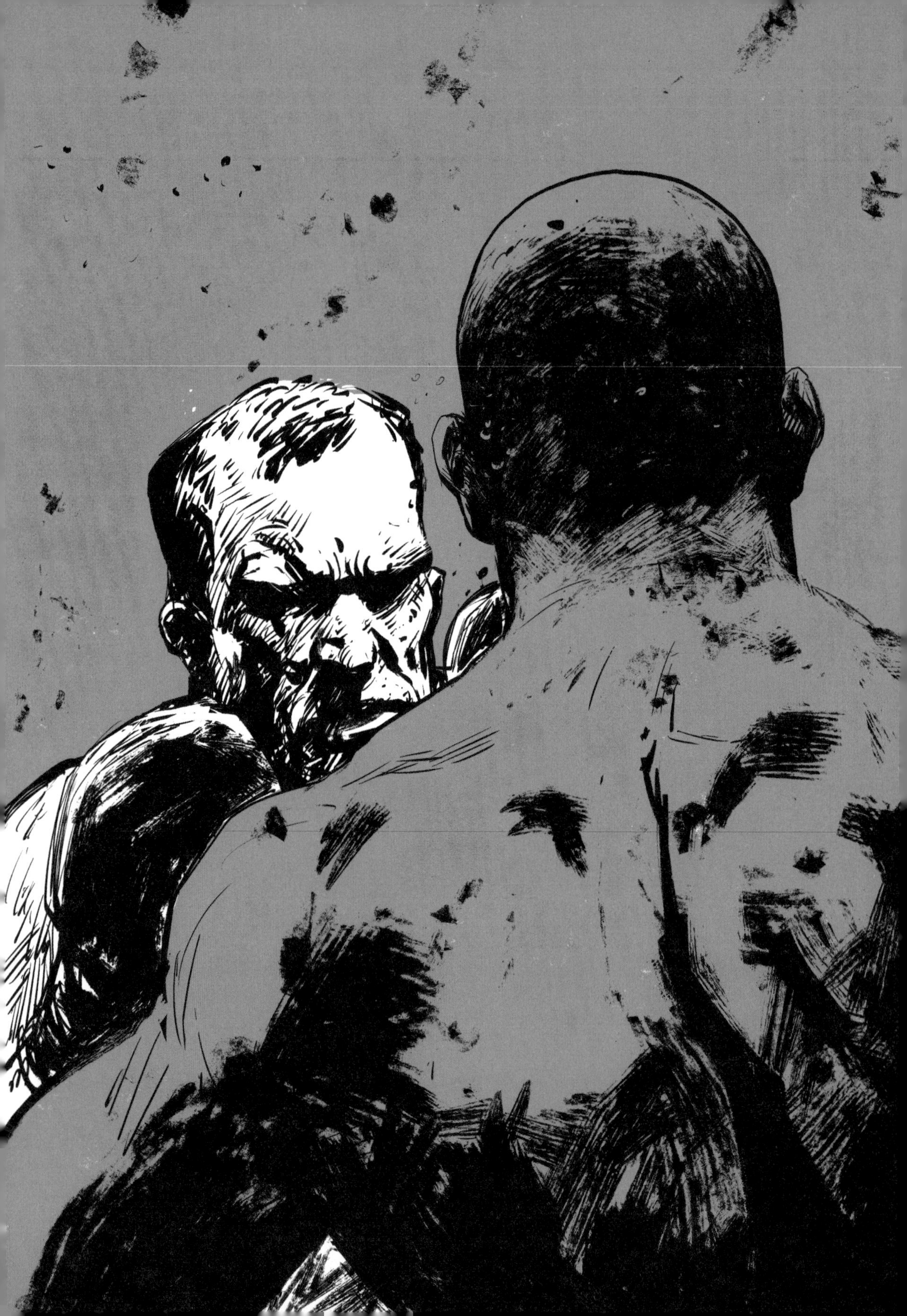

THE COLOR LINE

Imagine being the best at what you do
& the folks in your profession won't
allow you to ply your trade. You might
be the best carpenter in New York State
& nobody will hire you to pick up a hammer.
You might be the finest surgeon
in the entire United States, but nobody
will let you operate. That's what it was
like for me. I was the best to ever put
on gloves & none of the white prizefighters
would give me a shot at the prize.

WEATHER FORECAST.
CHICAGO AND VICINITY—Generally fair and not so warm Tuesday; Wednesday probably fair; fresh to brisk westerly winds Tuesday, becoming northwesterly Wednesday in the morning.

Chicago Examiner

THE TWENTIETH CENTURY NEWSPAPER

If Dissatisfied
With your present room, make a change to a better one. Look at the large list published in the Examiner "Rooms to Rent" columns and you will surely find a desirable place.

VOL. VI, NO. [illegible], A. M. ★★ FRIDAY, FEBRUARY 7, 1908, 12 PAGES. PRICE ONE CENT Delivered by Carrier, 20 Cents per Month.

WEATHER FORECAST —— **BASEBALL AND OTHER SPORTS** —— FRIDAY, FEBRUARY 7, 1908.

JOHNSON CHASES BURNS ACROSS THE GLOBE BUT THE CHAMP SAYS NO TO THE CHALLENGER

CUBS READY FOR SPRING TRAINING

Team Heads to Vicksburg to prepare for season

It's tough to win a World Series like the Chicago Cubs did last year. It might be even tougher to win a second one. Lucky for the Cubs and their fans, starting pitchers Orval Overall and Three Finger Brown return along with the double playmaking in field of Frank Chance, Johnny Evers, and Joe Tinker. All of their defensive dexterity is matched by their offense. All of the starters batted above .200 with Frank Chance batting an impressive .293. If the bats are swinging with the same accuracy in 1908, opposing teams better watch out. Also of note...

WORLD CHAMPIONSHIP
BURNS
GLOVES
PUGILANIA

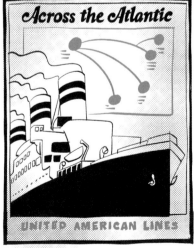

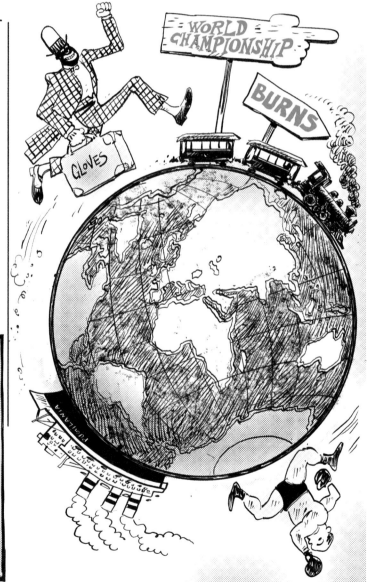

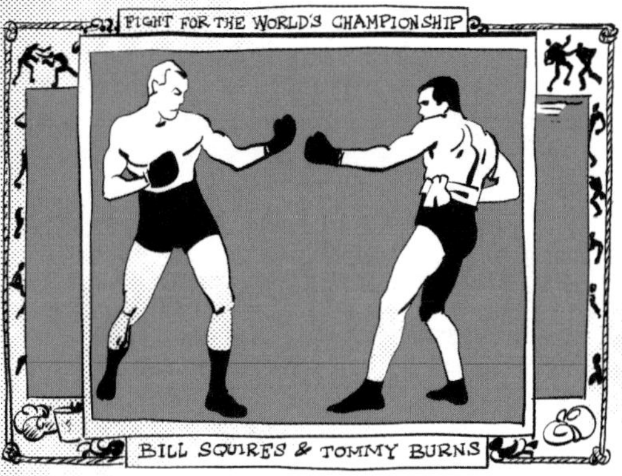
FIGHT FOR THE WORLD'S CHAMPIONSHIP
BILL SQUIRES & TOMMY BURNS

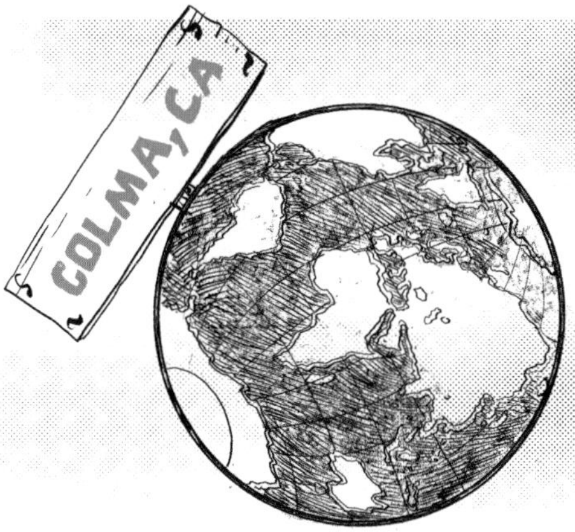
COLMA, CA

IS TOMMY BURNS A PRIZEFIGHTER OR A TRACK ATHLETE?

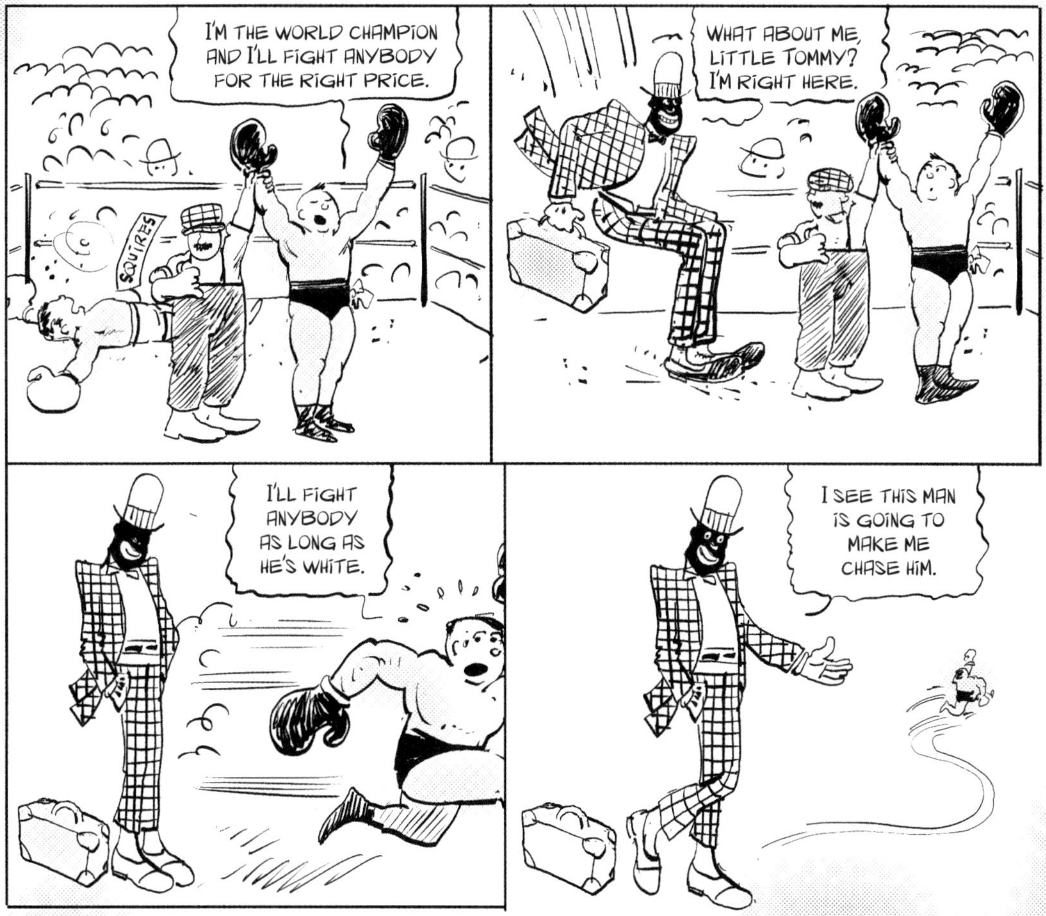
I'M THE WORLD CHAMPION AND I'LL FIGHT ANYBODY FOR THE RIGHT PRICE.
SQUIRES
WHAT ABOUT ME, LITTLE TOMMY? I'M RIGHT HERE.
I'LL FIGHT ANYBODY AS LONG AS HE'S WHITE.
I SEE THIS MAN IS GOING TO MAKE ME CHASE HIM.

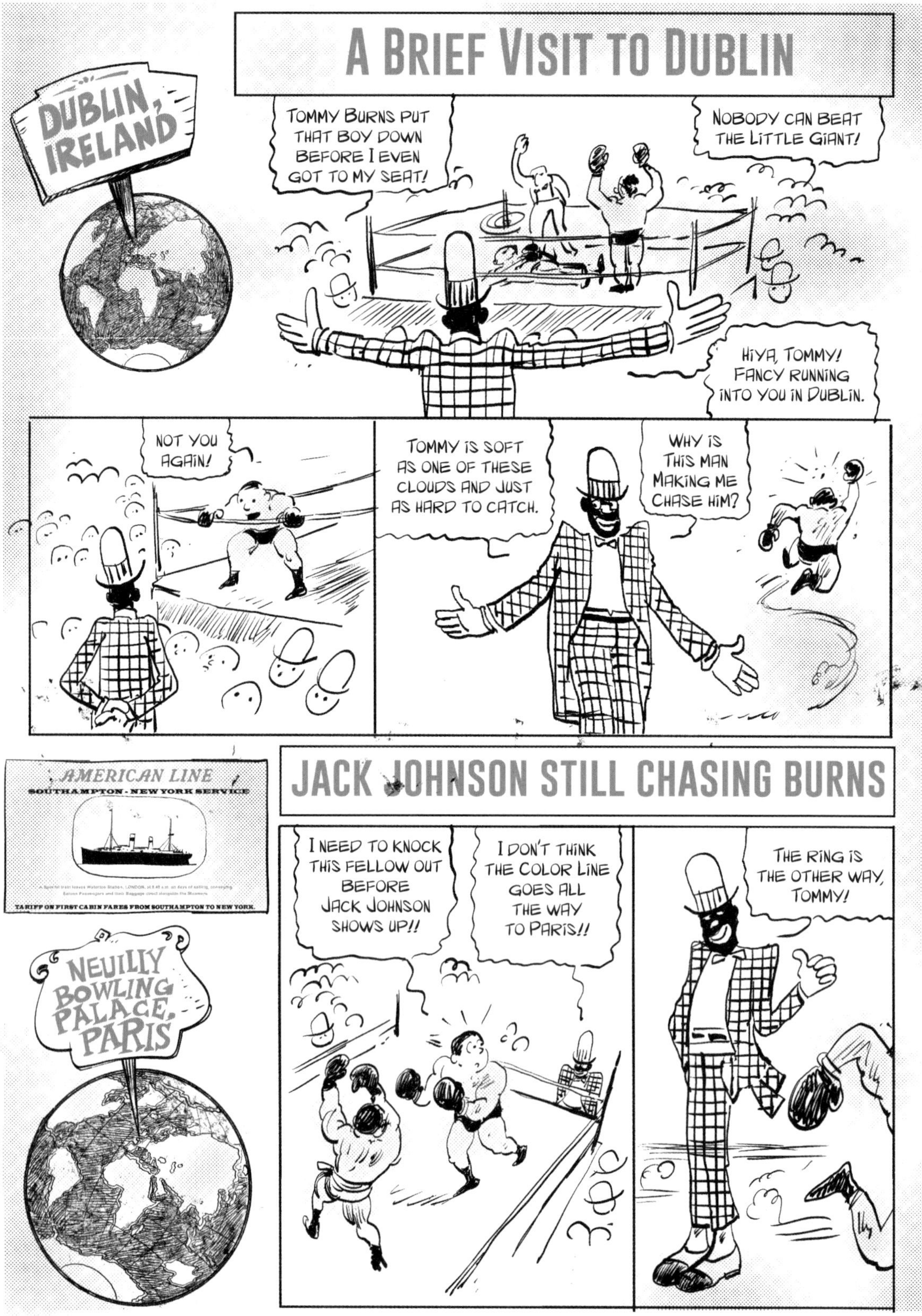
A BRIEF VISIT TO DUBLIN
DUBLIN, IRELAND
TOMMY BURNS PUT THAT BOY DOWN BEFORE I EVEN GOT TO MY SEAT!
NOBODY CAN BEAT THE LITTLE GIANT!
HIYA, TOMMY! FANCY RUNNING INTO YOU IN DUBLIN.
NOT YOU AGAIN!
TOMMY IS SOFT AS ONE OF THESE CLOUDS AND JUST AS HARD TO CATCH.
WHY IS THIS MAN MAKING ME CHASE HIM?
AMERICAN LINE
SOUTHAMPTON - NEW YORK SERVICE
TARIFF ON FIRST CABIN FARES FROM SOUTHAMPTON TO NEW YORK.
JACK JOHNSON STILL CHASING BURNS
NEUILLY BOWLING PALACE, PARIS
I NEED TO KNOCK THIS FELLOW OUT BEFORE JACK JOHNSON SHOWS UP!!
I DON'T THINK THE COLOR LINE GOES ALL THE WAY TO PARIS!!
THE RING IS THE OTHER WAY, TOMMY!

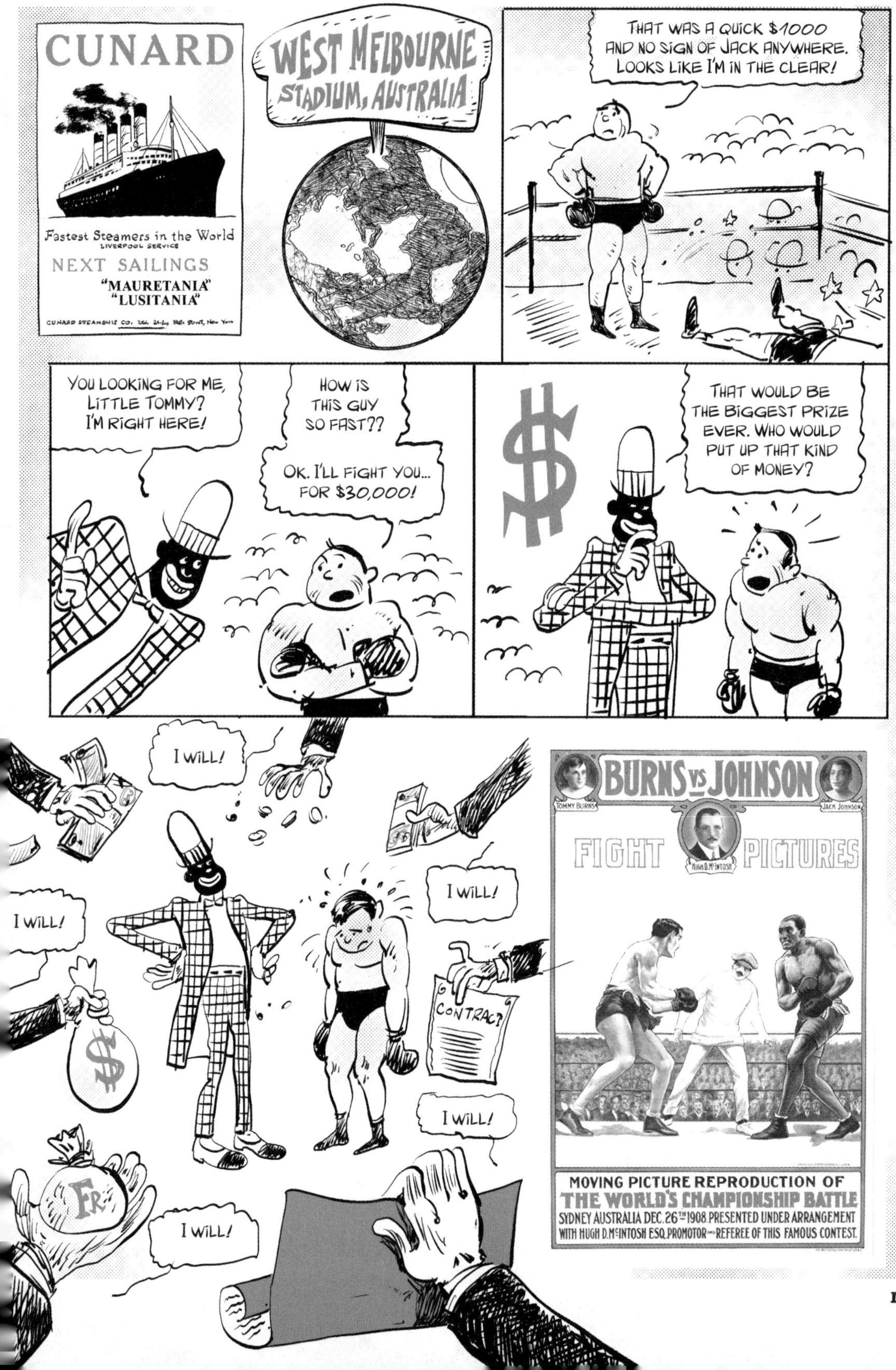
CUNARD
Fastest Steamers in the World
LIVERPOOL SERVICE
NEXT SAILINGS
"MAURETANIA"
"LUSITANIA"
WEST MELBOURNE STADIUM, AUSTRALIA
THAT WAS A QUICK $1000 AND NO SIGN OF JACK ANYWHERE. LOOKS LIKE I'M IN THE CLEAR!
YOU LOOKING FOR ME, LITTLE TOMMY? I'M RIGHT HERE!
HOW IS THIS GUY SO FAST??
OK. I'LL FIGHT YOU... FOR $30,000!
$
THAT WOULD BE THE BIGGEST PRIZE EVER. WHO WOULD PUT UP THAT KIND OF MONEY?
I WILL!
I WILL!
I WILL!
I WILL!
I WILL!
$
CONTRACT
FR
BURNS VS JOHNSON
TOMMY BURNS
JACK JOHNSON
FIGHT PICTURES
HUGH D. MCINTOSH
MOVING PICTURE REPRODUCTION OF
THE WORLD'S CHAMPIONSHIP BATTLE
SYDNEY AUSTRALIA DEC. 26TH 1908. PRESENTED UNDER ARRANGEMENT WITH HUGH D. MCINTOSH ESQ. PROMOTOR AND REFEREE OF THIS FAMOUS CONTEST.

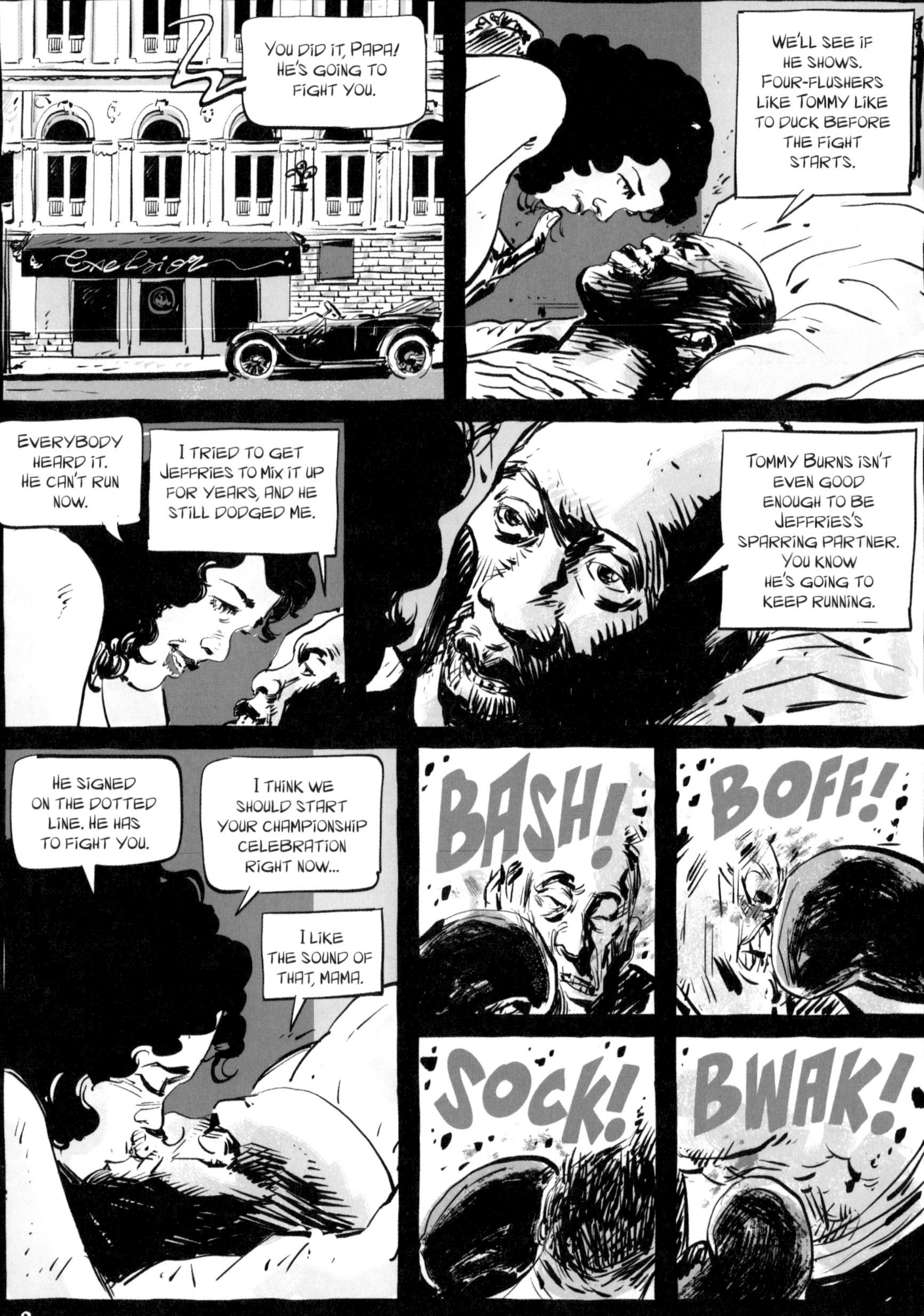

YOU DID IT, PAPA! HE'S GOING TO FIGHT YOU.
WE'LL SEE IF HE SHOWS. FOUR-FLUSHERS LIKE TOMMY LIKE TO DUCK BEFORE THE FIGHT STARTS.
EVERYBODY HEARD IT. HE CAN'T RUN NOW.
I TRIED TO GET JEFFRIES TO MIX IT UP FOR YEARS, AND HE STILL DODGED ME.
TOMMY BURNS ISN'T EVEN GOOD ENOUGH TO BE JEFFRIES'S SPARRING PARTNER. YOU KNOW HE'S GOING TO KEEP RUNNING.
HE SIGNED ON THE DOTTED LINE. HE HAS TO FIGHT YOU.
I THINK WE SHOULD START YOUR CHAMPIONSHIP CELEBRATION RIGHT NOW...
I LIKE THE SOUND OF THAT, MAMA.
BASH!
BOFF!
SOCK!
BWAK!

SYDNEY, AUSTRALIA DECEMBER 26, 1908

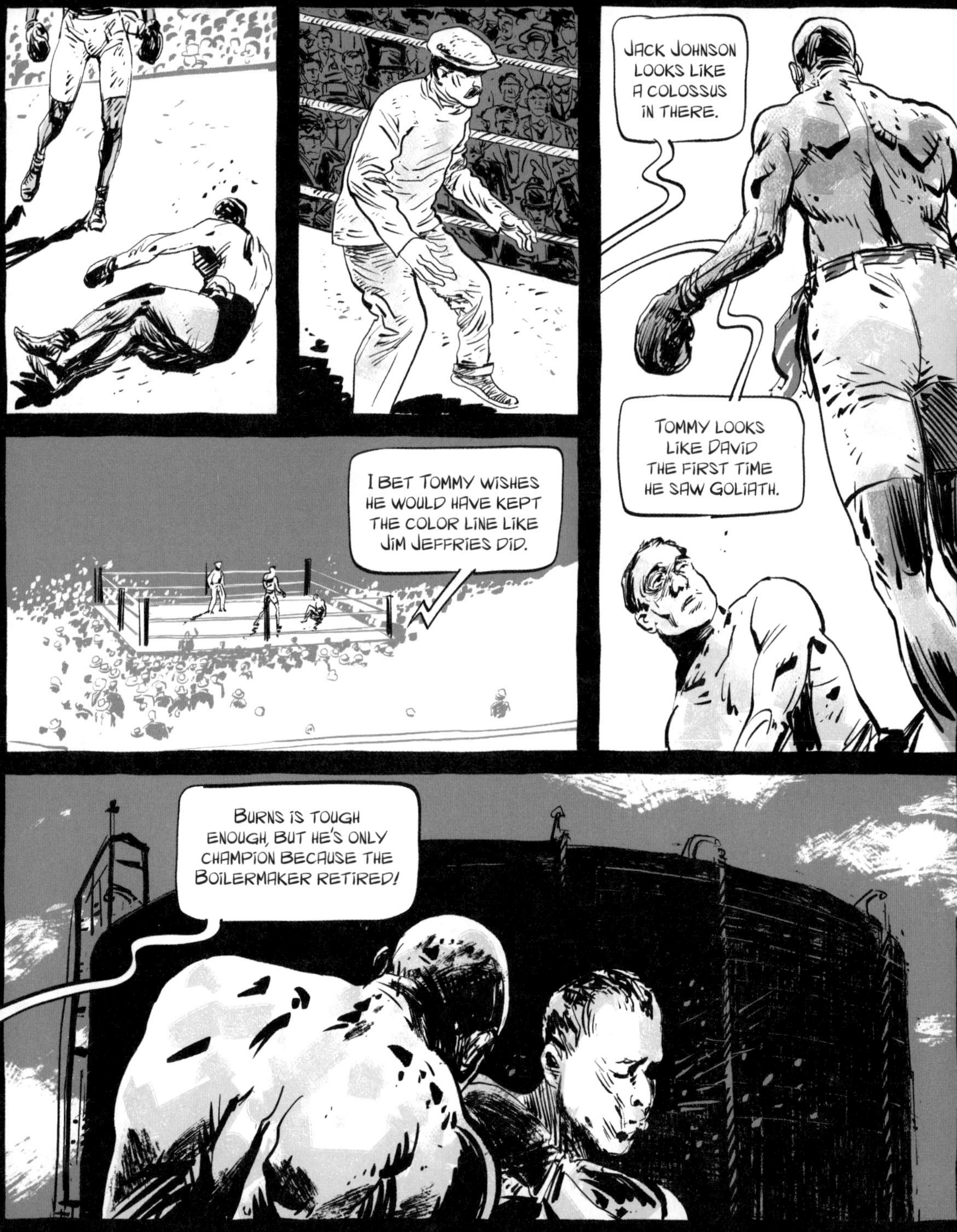

JACK JOHNSON LOOKS LIKE A COLOSSUS IN THERE.
TOMMY LOOKS LIKE DAVID THE FIRST TIME HE SAW GOLIATH.
I BET TOMMY WISHES HE WOULD HAVE KEPT THE COLOR LINE LIKE JIM JEFFRIES DID.
BURNS IS TOUGH ENOUGH, BUT HE'S ONLY CHAMPION BECAUSE THE BOILERMAKER RETIRED!

ALWAYS ON THE DODGE

Tommy Burns was a pretend champion from the start & like all paper champions he didn't have the stomach for a fight.

He beat Marvin Hart for the title—a man who knew about as much about the fistic science as a horse knows about driving a Thomas Flyer.

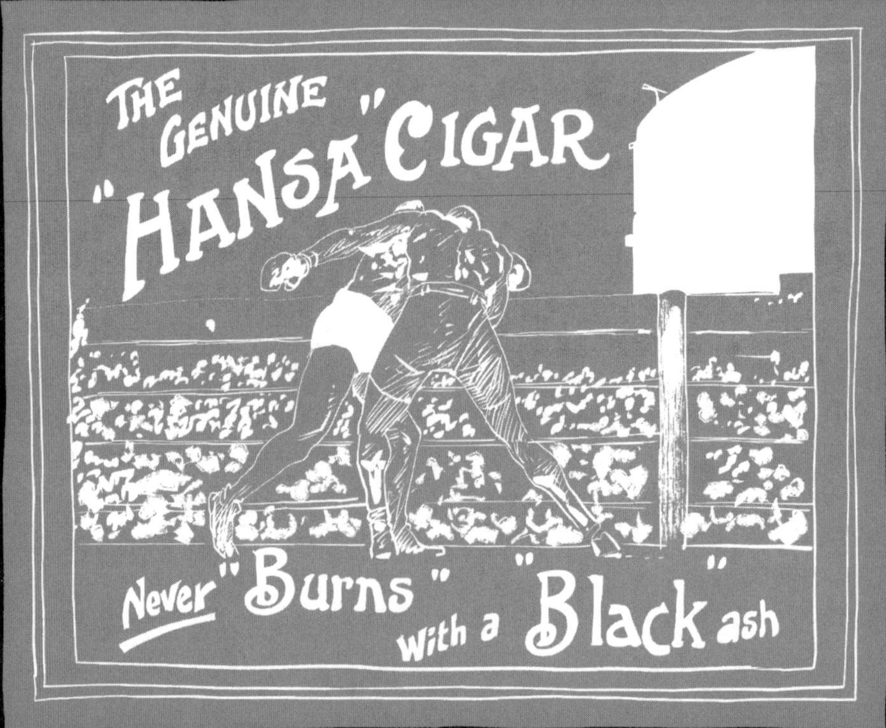
THE GENUINE "HANSA" CIGAR
Never "Burns" with a "Black" ash

One time, Burns told an Australian
reporter that I was the one dodging
him. Like I hadn't spent my last
copper on steamer ships following

him to England & France.
When we finally fought, they fixed it
to give me a lemon. I didn't fall
for the game. The promoters couldn't

handle me any better than their boy
Burns. He was a four-flusher all the way
up to the moment I knocked him out
& the cameraman stopped filming.

The police stepped in when he
was on his way down. Otherwise
Ol' Tommy's bad day would
have gotten even worse.

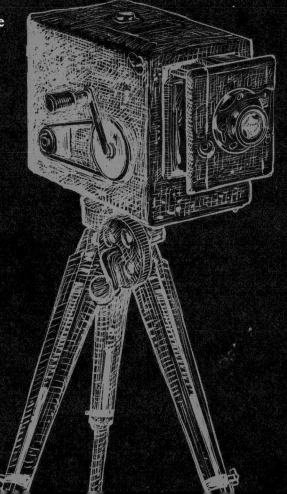

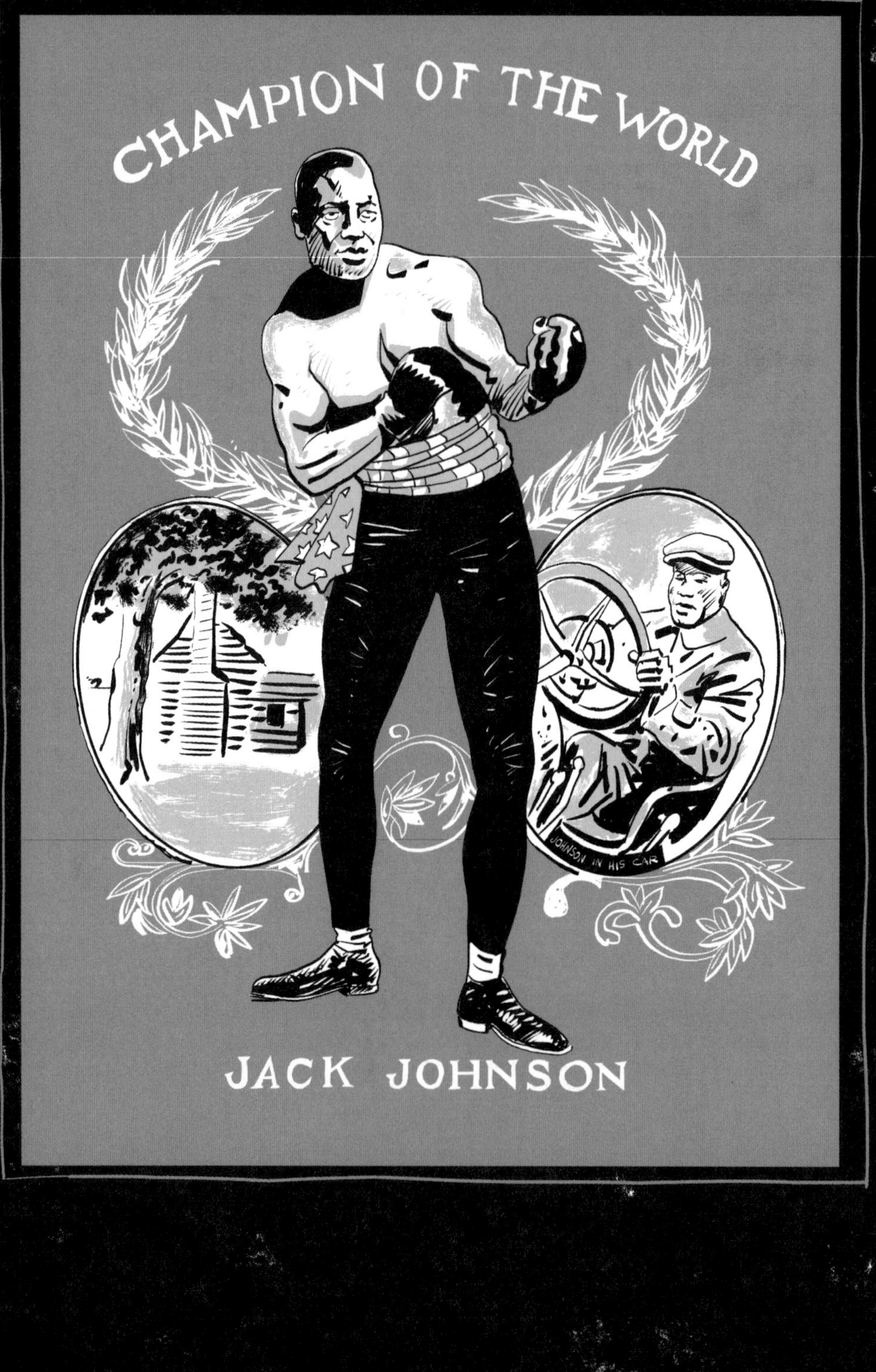
CHAMPION OF THE WORLD
JOHNSON IN HIS CAR
JACK JOHNSON

THE EVENING WORLD, TUESDAY, JANUARY 9, 1912.

BEST SPORTING PAGE IN NEW YORK

T'WAS A DARK DAY IN AUSTRALIA

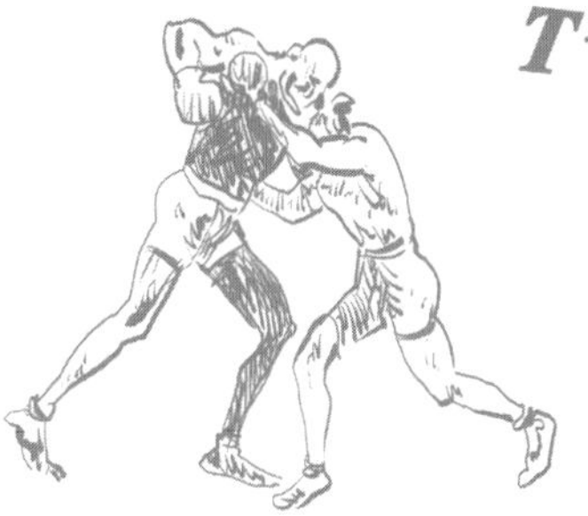

The first Black to hold the heavyweight title.
The greatest colored man who ever lived.
If they would have kept the camera turning,
you would have seen the crowd leaving so quietly
it could have been the middle of the night.
I raised my own arms in victory behind
a line of officers & nobody cheered but me.
If they would have kept the camera going,
everybody would have seen Tommy, his face
puffed up & bleeding, telling the referee
that he could still fight: "The darky's getting
tired," he mumbled with a busted jaw.
I took the title from him, but Tommy
was never the real champion.
A champion is the best of his generation,
ready to fight anybody anywhere.
Somebody with fortitude & cleverness
to match their courage in the ring.
Tommy Burns was no champion.
He was just white & in the right place.
Jim Jeffries was the real champion
& to be the best I had to beat the best.

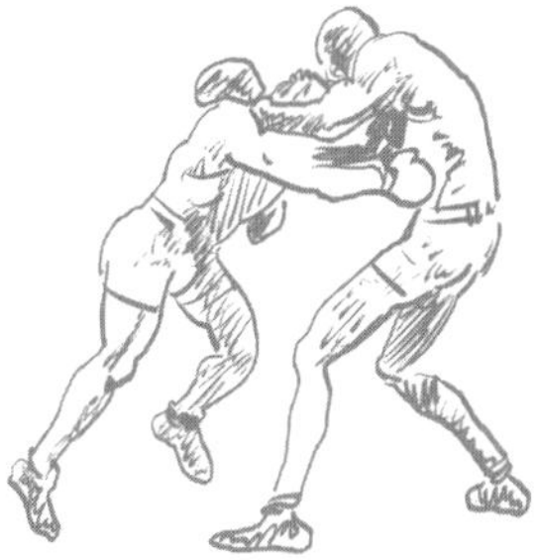

CORBETT'S POOL ROOM, SAN FRANCISCO, CALIFORNIA 1909

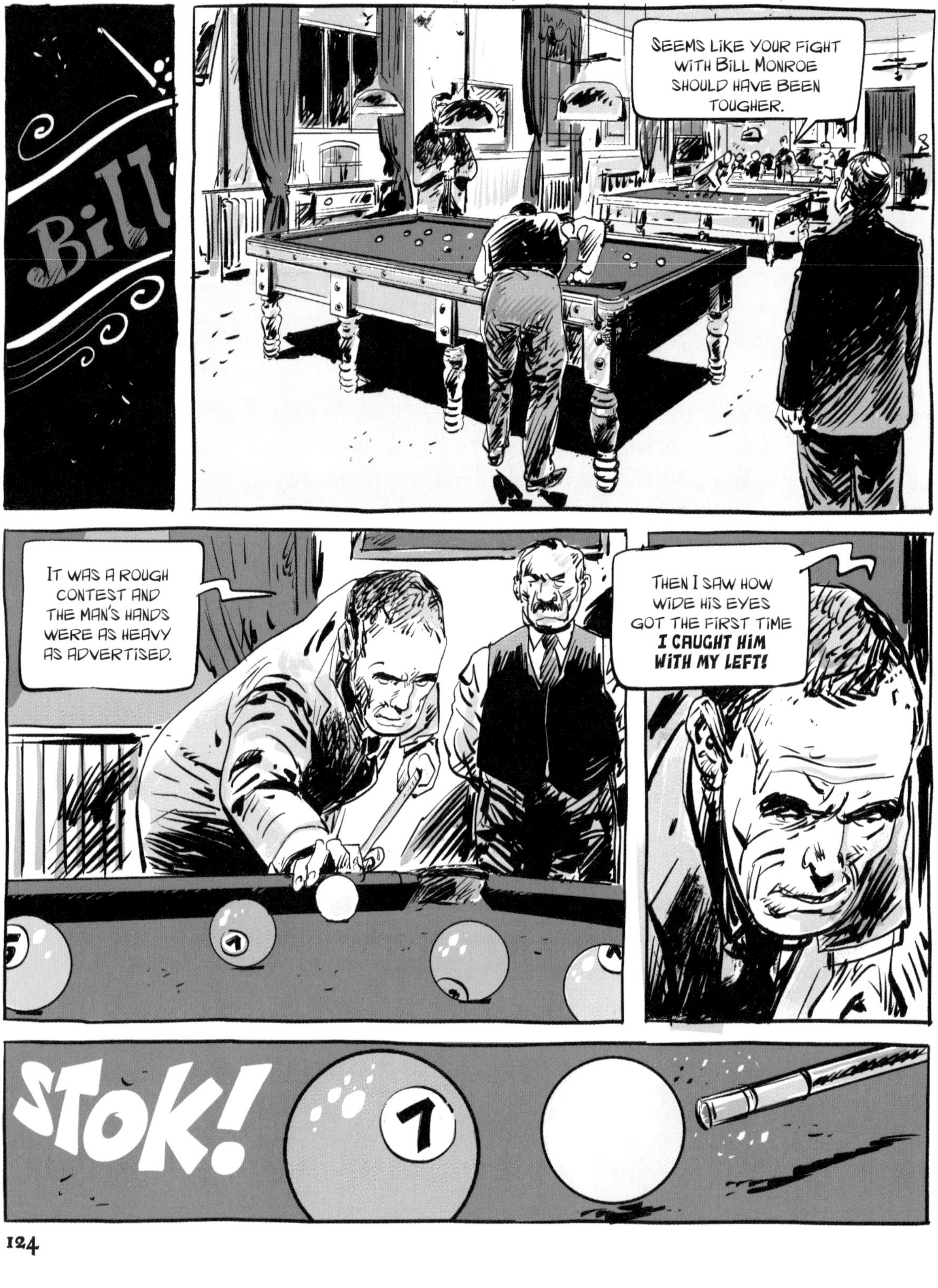
Bill
SEEMS LIKE YOUR FIGHT WITH BILL MONROE SHOULD HAVE BEEN TOUGHER.
IT WAS A ROUGH CONTEST AND THE MAN'S HANDS WERE AS HEAVY AS ADVERTISED.
THEN I SAW HOW WIDE HIS EYES GOT THE FIRST TIME **I CAUGHT HIM WITH MY LEFT!**
STOK!
7

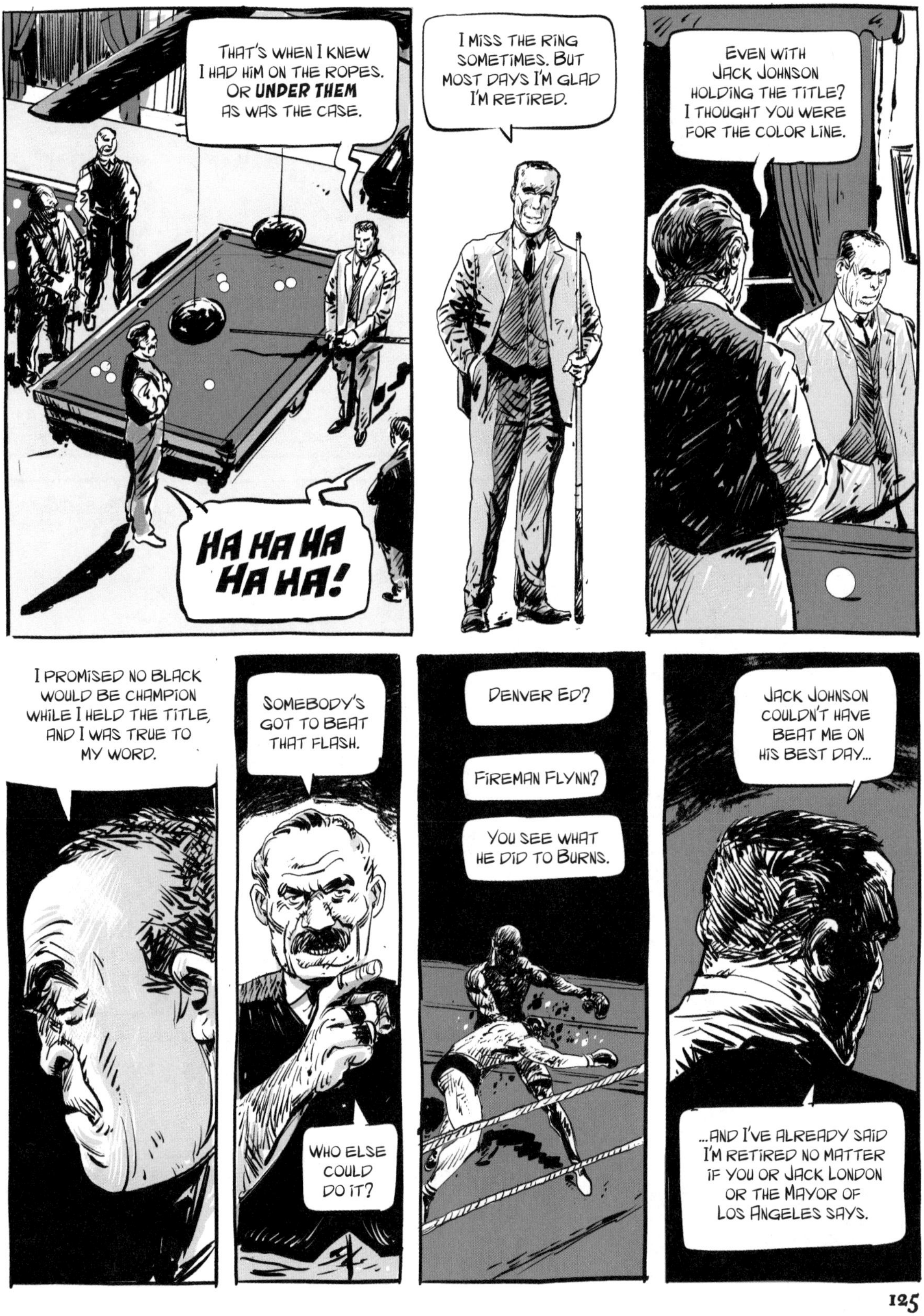
THAT'S WHEN I KNEW I HAD HIM ON THE ROPES. OR **UNDER THEM** AS WAS THE CASE.
HA HA HA HA HA!
I MISS THE RING SOMETIMES. BUT MOST DAYS I'M GLAD I'M RETIRED.
EVEN WITH JACK JOHNSON HOLDING THE TITLE? I THOUGHT YOU WERE FOR THE COLOR LINE.
I PROMISED NO BLACK WOULD BE CHAMPION WHILE I HELD THE TITLE, AND I WAS TRUE TO MY WORD.
SOMEBODY'S GOT TO BEAT THAT FLASH.
WHO ELSE COULD DO IT?
DENVER ED?
FIREMAN FLYNN?
YOU SEE WHAT HE DID TO BURNS.
JACK JOHNSON COULDN'T HAVE BEAT ME ON HIS BEST DAY...
...AND I'VE ALREADY SAID I'M RETIRED NO MATTER IF YOU OR JACK LONDON OR THE MAYOR OF LOS ANGELES SAYS.

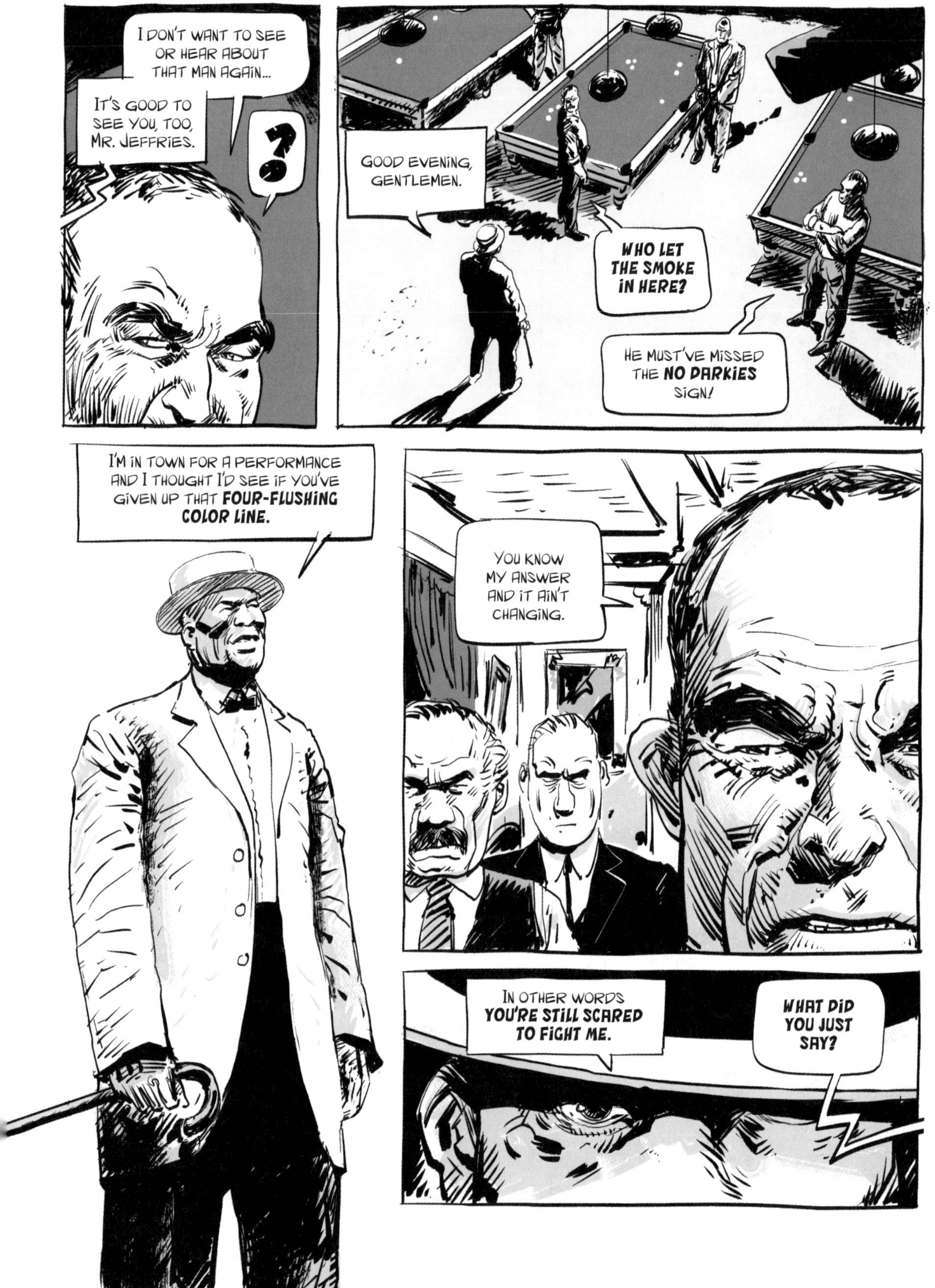
I DON'T WANT TO SEE OR HEAR ABOUT THAT MAN AGAIN...
IT'S GOOD TO SEE YOU, TOO, MR. JEFFRIES.
?
GOOD EVENING, GENTLEMEN.
WHO LET THE SMOKE IN HERE?
HE MUST'VE MISSED THE NO DARKIES SIGN!
I'M IN TOWN FOR A PERFORMANCE AND I THOUGHT I'D SEE IF YOU'VE GIVEN UP THAT FOUR-FLUSHING COLOR LINE.
YOU KNOW MY ANSWER AND IT AIN'T CHANGING.
IN OTHER WORDS YOU'RE STILL SCARED TO FIGHT ME.
WHAT DID YOU JUST SAY?

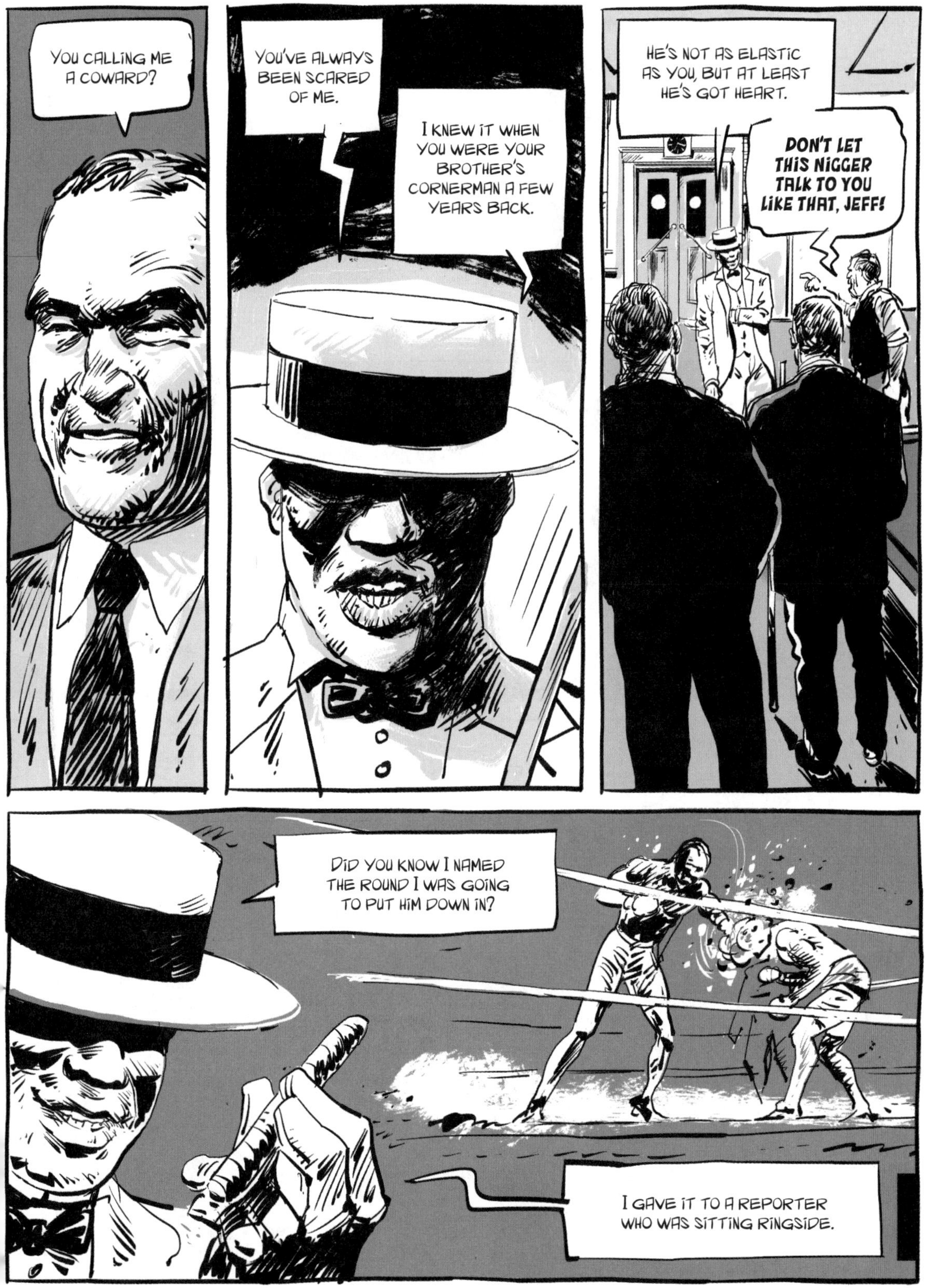
YOU CALLING ME A COWARD?
YOU'VE ALWAYS BEEN SCARED OF ME.
I KNEW IT WHEN YOU WERE YOUR BROTHER'S CORNERMAN A FEW YEARS BACK.
HE'S NOT AS ELASTIC AS YOU, BUT AT LEAST HE'S GOT HEART.
DON'T LET THIS NIGGER TALK TO YOU LIKE THAT, JEFF!
DID YOU KNOW I NAMED THE ROUND I WAS GOING TO PUT HIM DOWN IN?
I GAVE IT TO A REPORTER WHO WAS SITTING RINGSIDE.

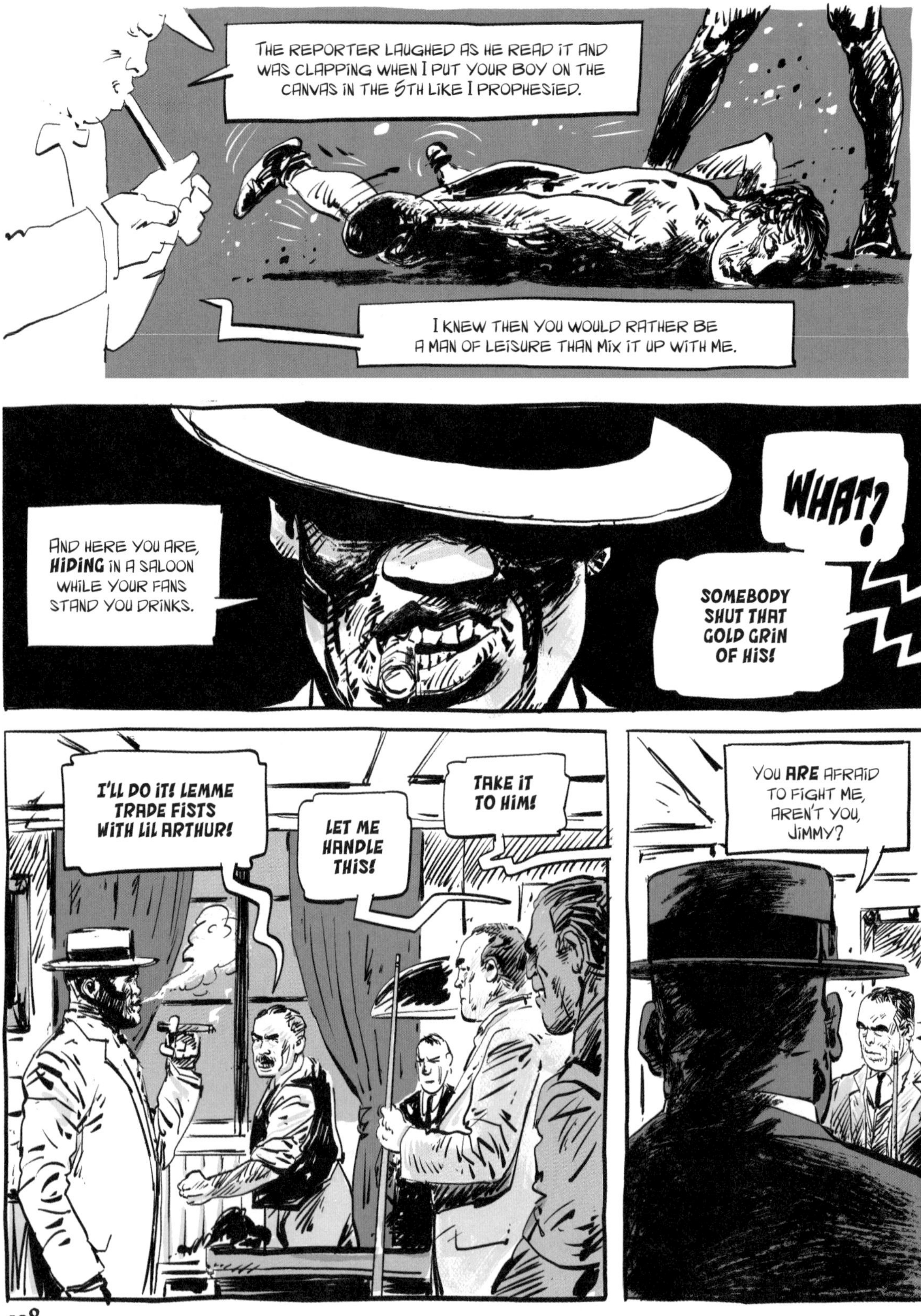
THE REPORTER LAUGHED AS HE READ IT AND WAS CLAPPING WHEN I PUT YOUR BOY ON THE CANVAS IN THE 5TH LIKE I PROPHESIED.
I KNEW THEN YOU WOULD RATHER BE A MAN OF LEISURE THAN MIX IT UP WITH ME.
AND HERE YOU ARE, HIDING IN A SALOON WHILE YOUR FANS STAND YOU DRINKS.
WHAT?
SOMEBODY SHUT THAT GOLD GRIN OF HIS!
I'LL DO IT! LEMME TRADE FISTS WITH LIL ARTHUR!
LET ME HANDLE THIS!
TAKE IT TO HIM!
YOU ARE AFRAID TO FIGHT ME, AREN'T YOU, JIMMY?

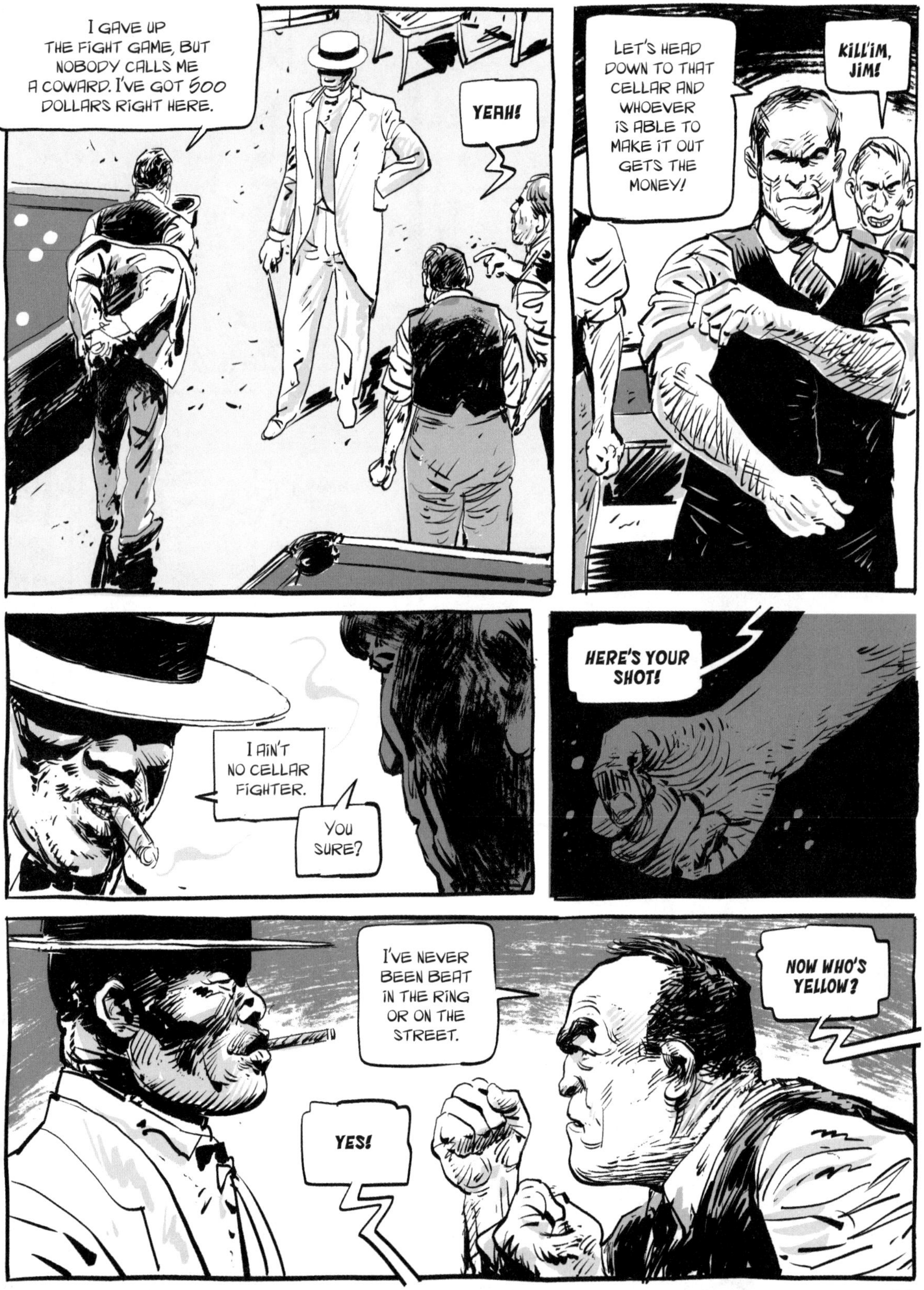
I GAVE UP THE FIGHT GAME, BUT NOBODY CALLS ME A COWARD. I'VE GOT 500 DOLLARS RIGHT HERE.
YEAH!
LET'S HEAD DOWN TO THAT CELLAR AND WHOEVER IS ABLE TO MAKE IT OUT GETS THE MONEY!
KILL'IM, JIM!
I AIN'T NO CELLAR FIGHTER.
YOU SURE?
HERE'S YOUR SHOT!
I'VE NEVER BEEN BEAT IN THE RING OR ON THE STREET.
NOW WHO'S YELLOW?
YES!

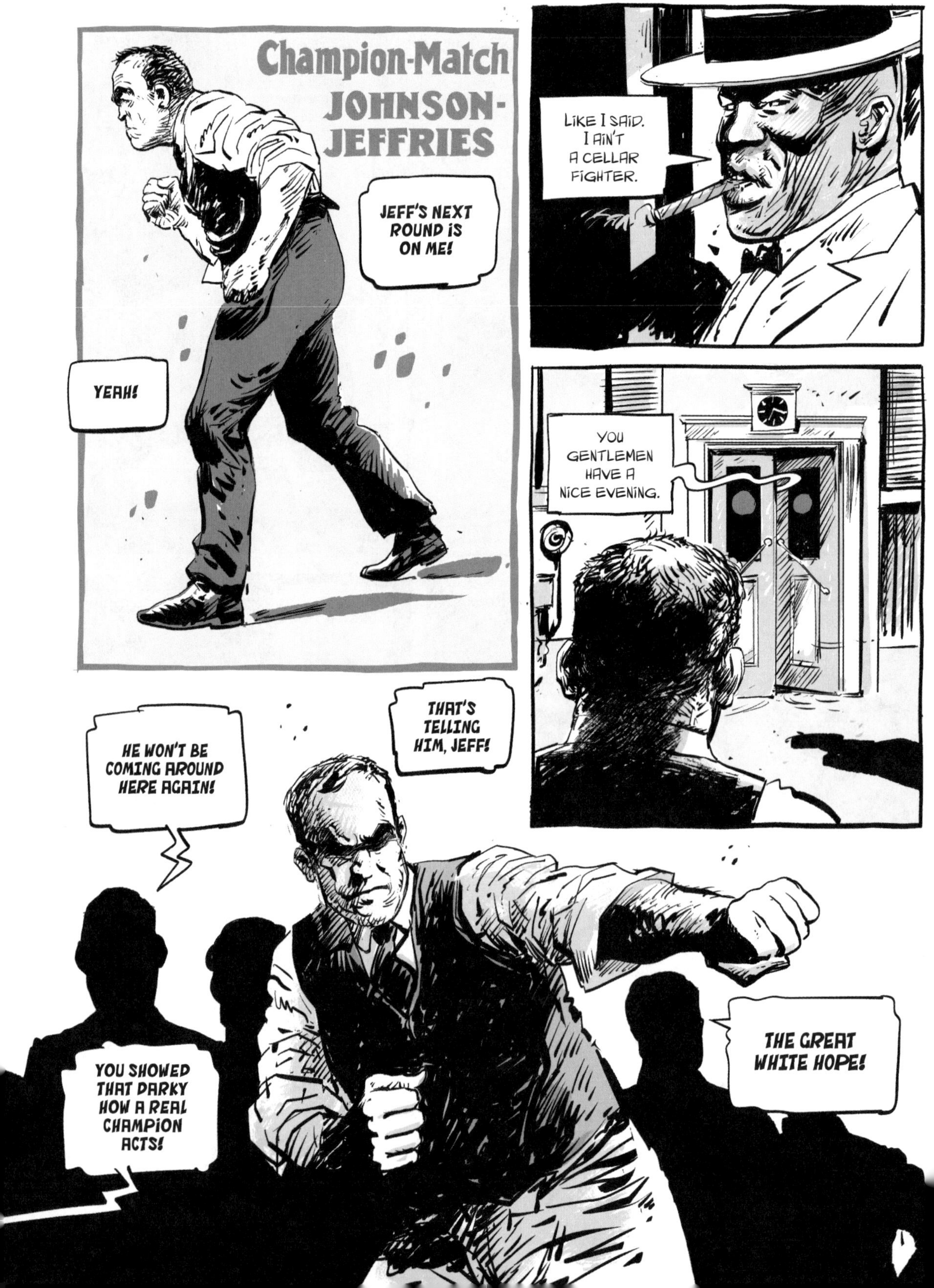
Champion-Match
JOHNSON-JEFFRIES
JEFF'S NEXT ROUND IS ON ME!
YEAH!
LIKE I SAID. I AIN'T A CELLAR FIGHTER.
YOU GENTLEMEN HAVE A NICE EVENING.
THAT'S TELLING HIM, JEFF!
HE WON'T BE COMING AROUND HERE AGAIN!
YOU SHOWED THAT DARKY HOW A REAL CHAMPION ACTS!
THE GREAT WHITE HOPE!

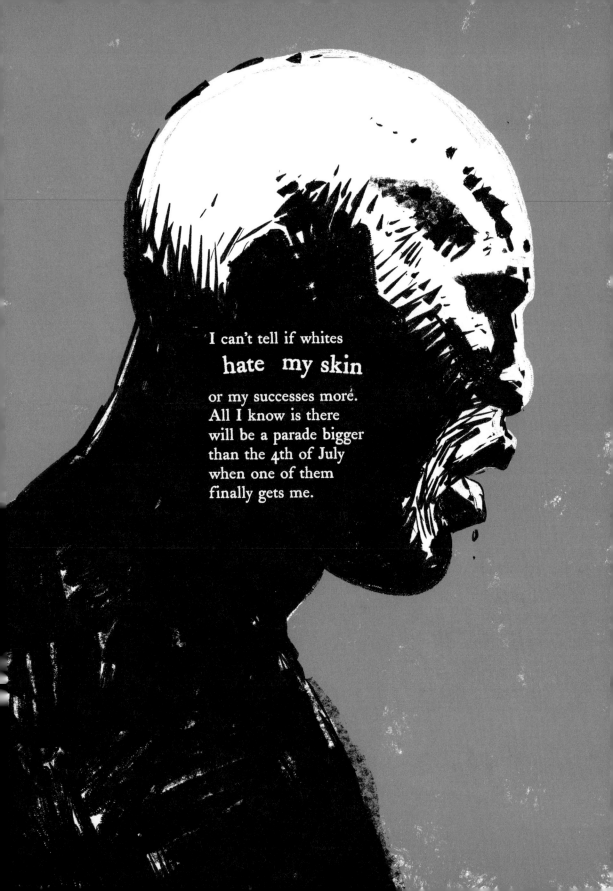

I can't tell if whites
hate my skin

or my successes more.
All I know is there
will be a parade bigger
than the 4th of July
when one of them
finally gets me.

ROUND 6

I took the heavyweight championship from
Tommy Burns & nobody was taking it from me.

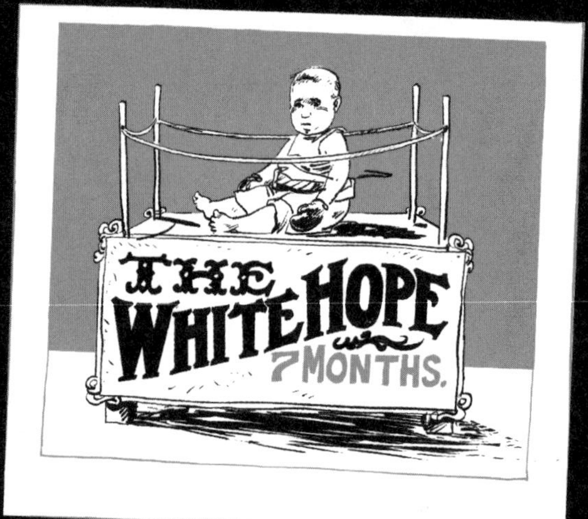
THE
WHITE HOPE
7 MONTHS.

Not President Roosevelt or Tex Rickard,
or the Great White Hopes.
There were so many of them.
George Rodel's chin was so weak
they called him the Diving Venus.

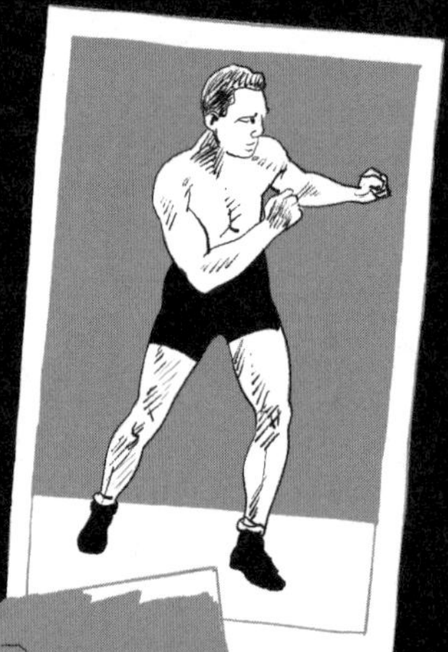

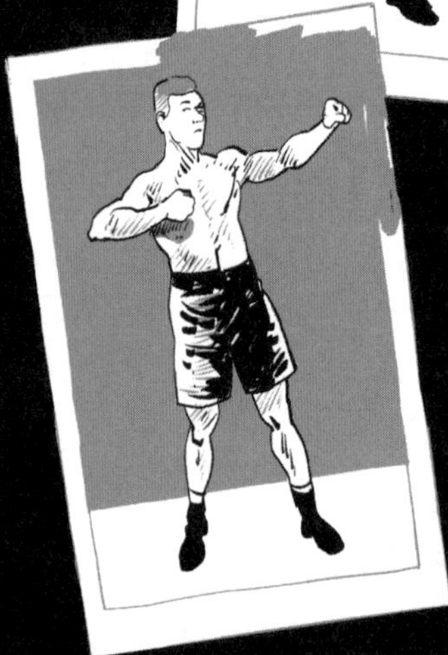

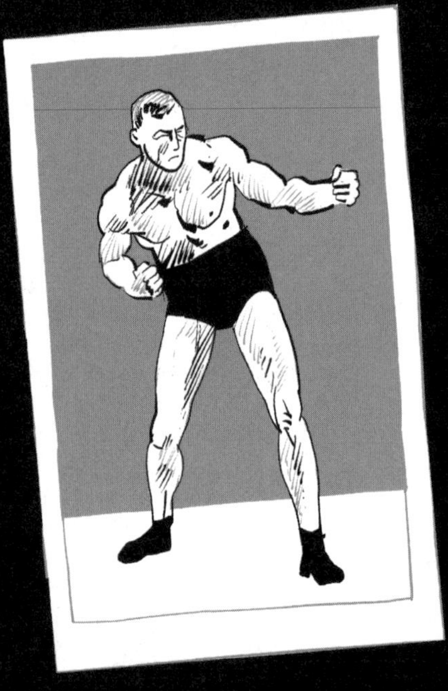

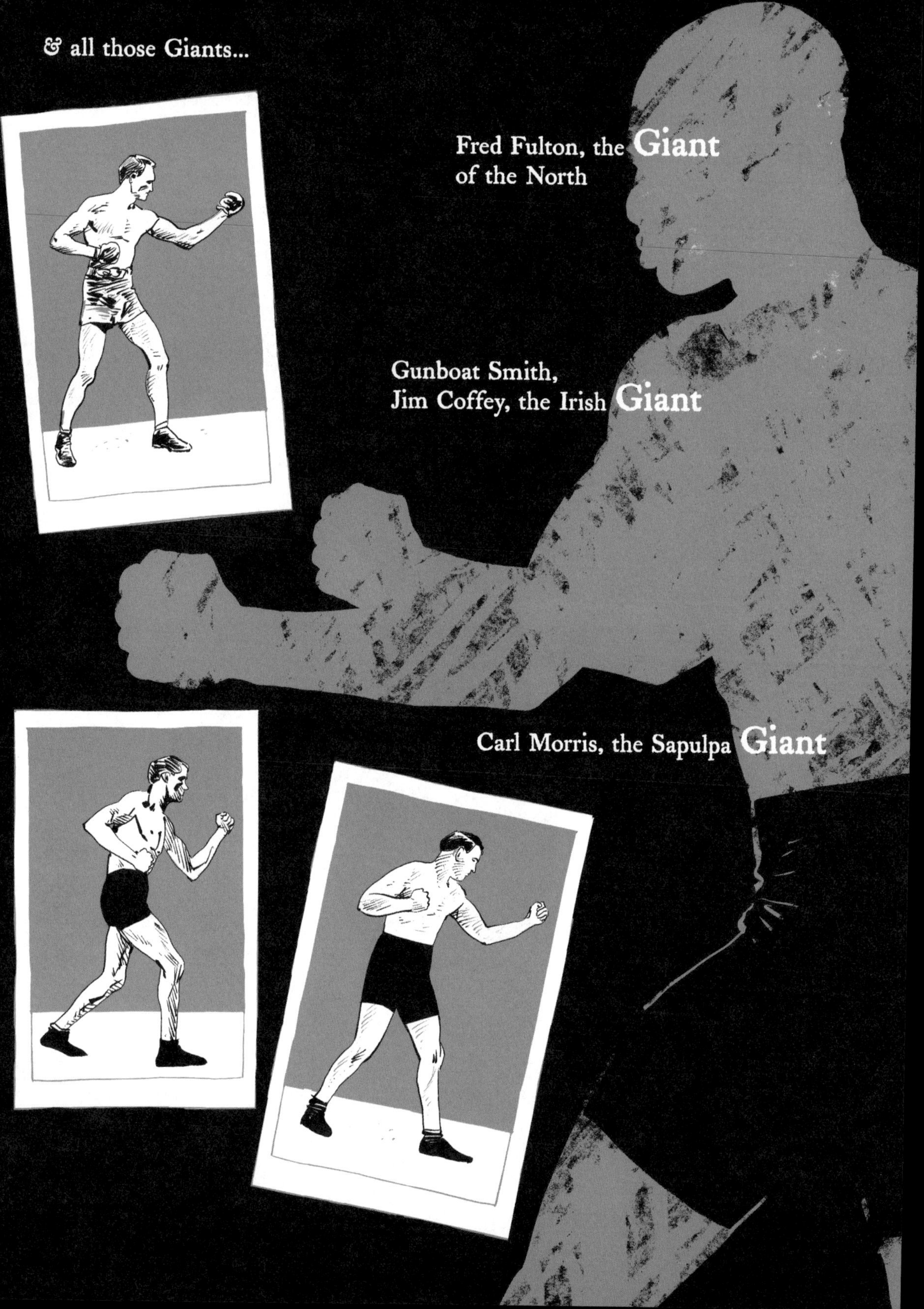
& all those Giants...
Fred Fulton, the Giant of the North
Gunboat Smith,
Jim Coffey, the Irish Giant
Carl Morris, the Sapulpa Giant

They tried & they all got dropped
just like cherries from a tree.
Jim Jeffries couldn't have stayed
in the ring with me before retirement.

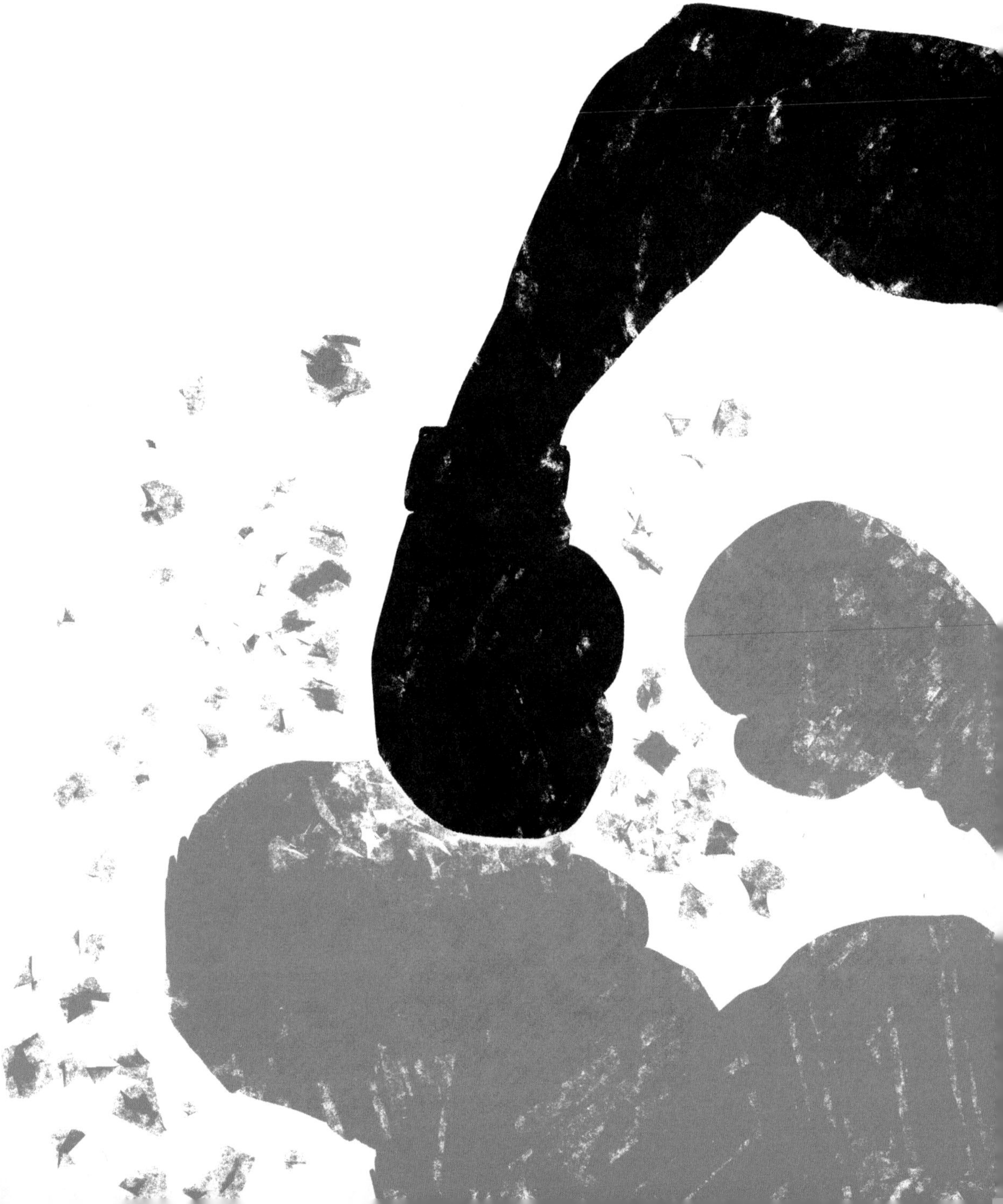

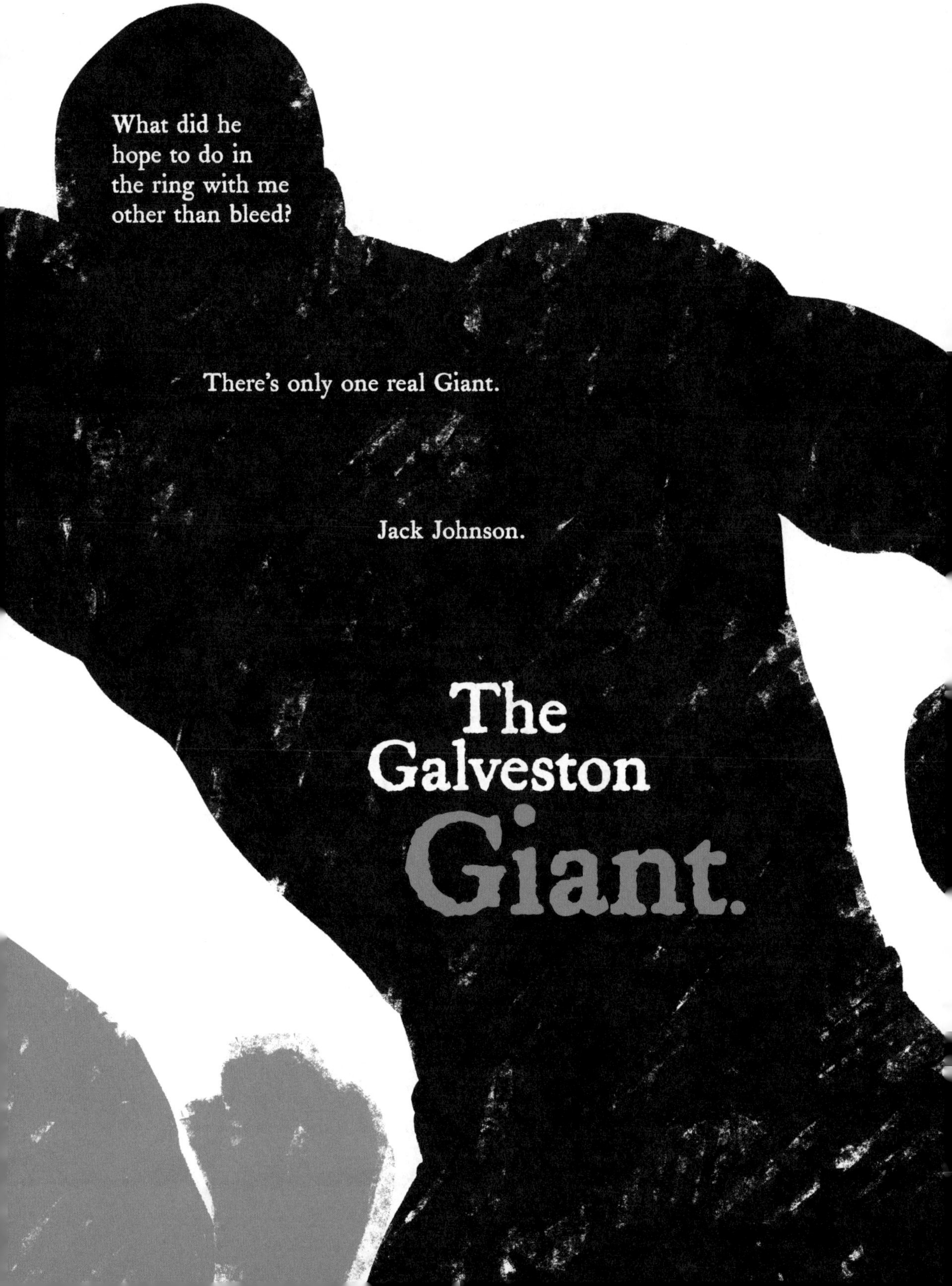
What did he hope to do in the ring with me other than bleed?
There's only one real Giant.
Jack Johnson.
The Galveston Giant.

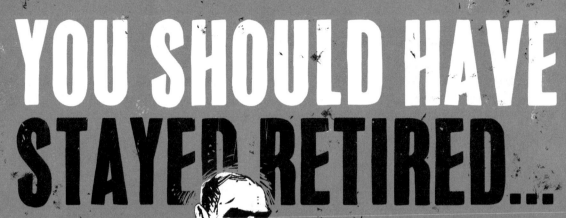
YOU SHOULD HAVE STAYED RETIRED...

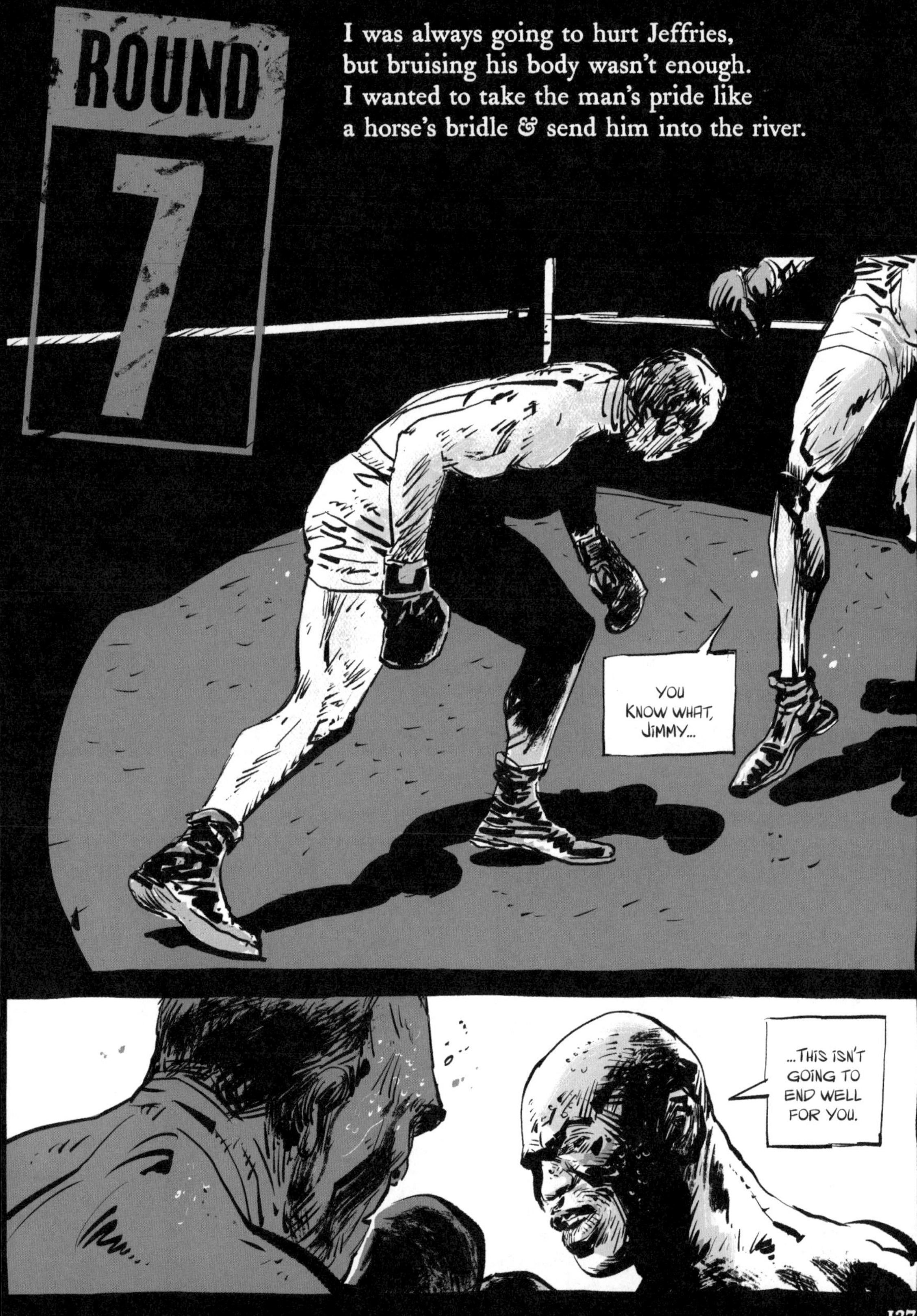
ROUND 7
I was always going to hurt Jeffries, but bruising his body wasn't enough. I wanted to take the man's pride like a horse's bridle & send him into the river.
YOU KNOW WHAT, JIMMY...
...THIS ISN'T GOING TO END WELL FOR YOU.

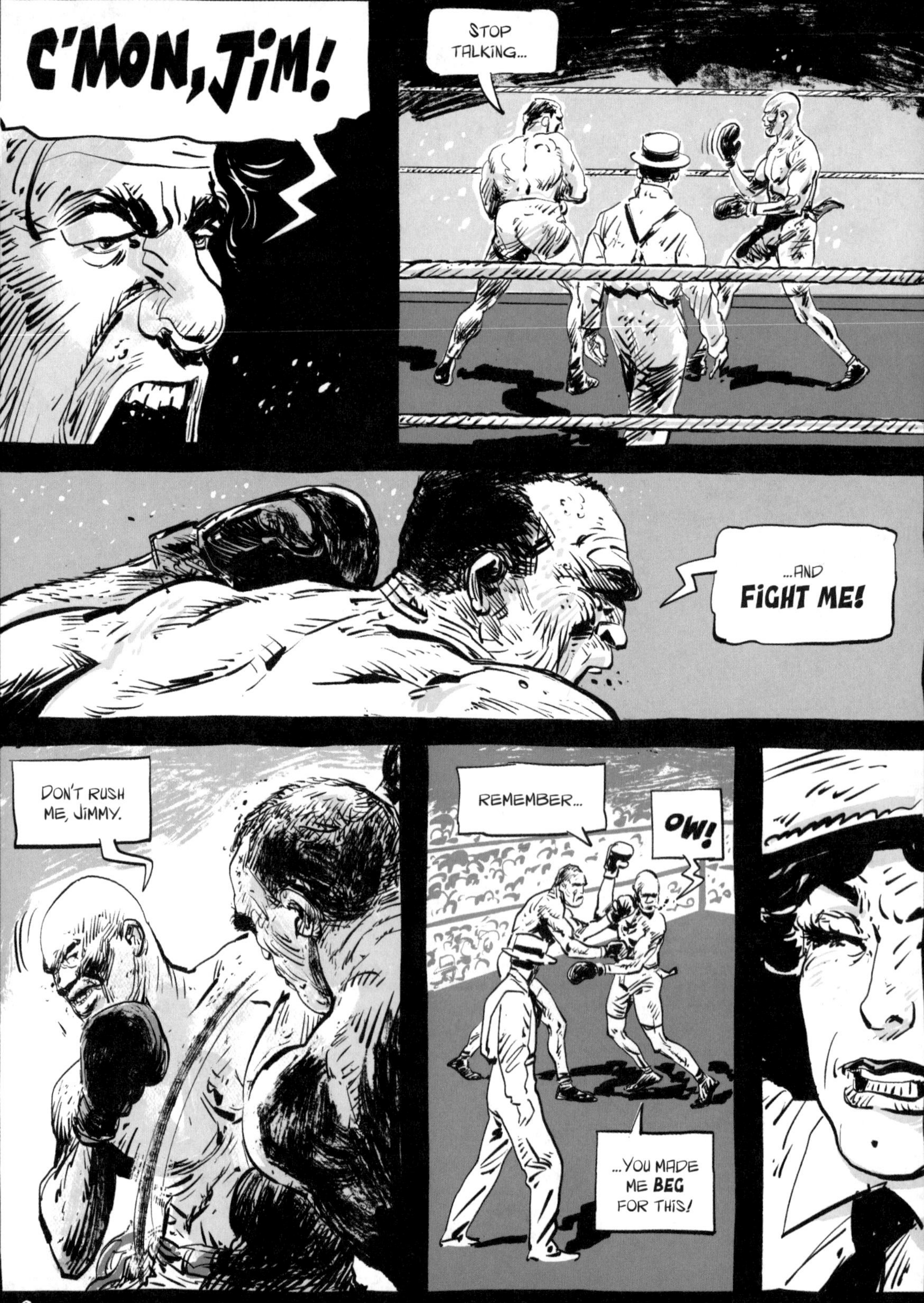

C'MON, JIM!
STOP TALKING...
...AND FIGHT ME!
DON'T RUSH ME, JIMMY.
REMEMBER...
OW!
...YOU MADE ME BEG FOR THIS!

I could tell I was winning the mouth fight, because Jeffries was starting to fight wild.

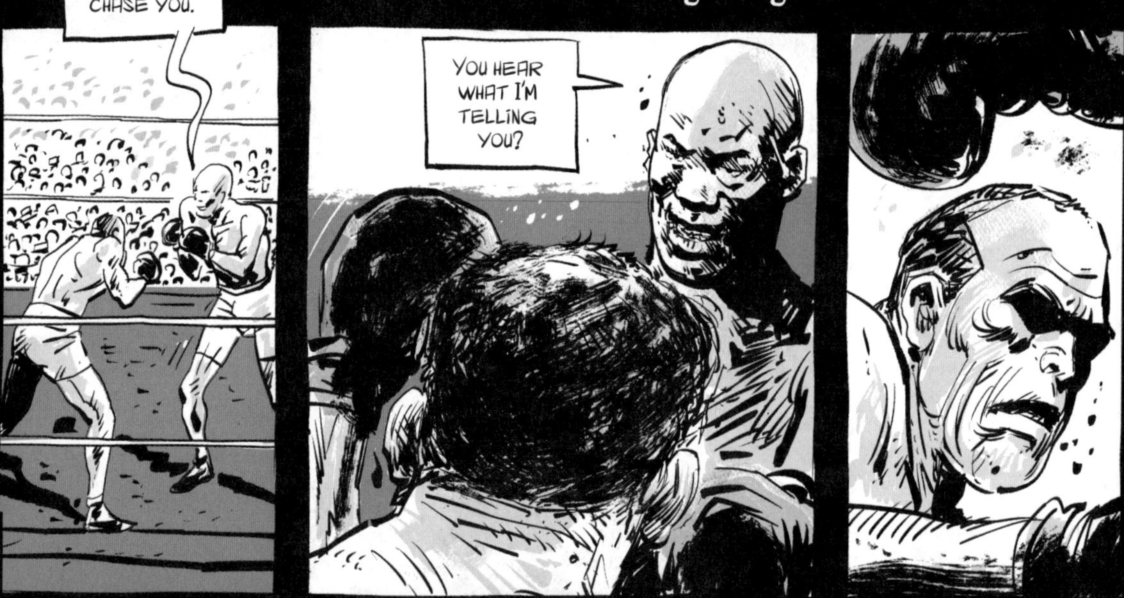
I HAD TO CHASE YOU.
YOU HEAR WHAT I'M TELLING YOU?

Then he hit me with a left-handed lead to the stomach that sounded like an automobile crash.

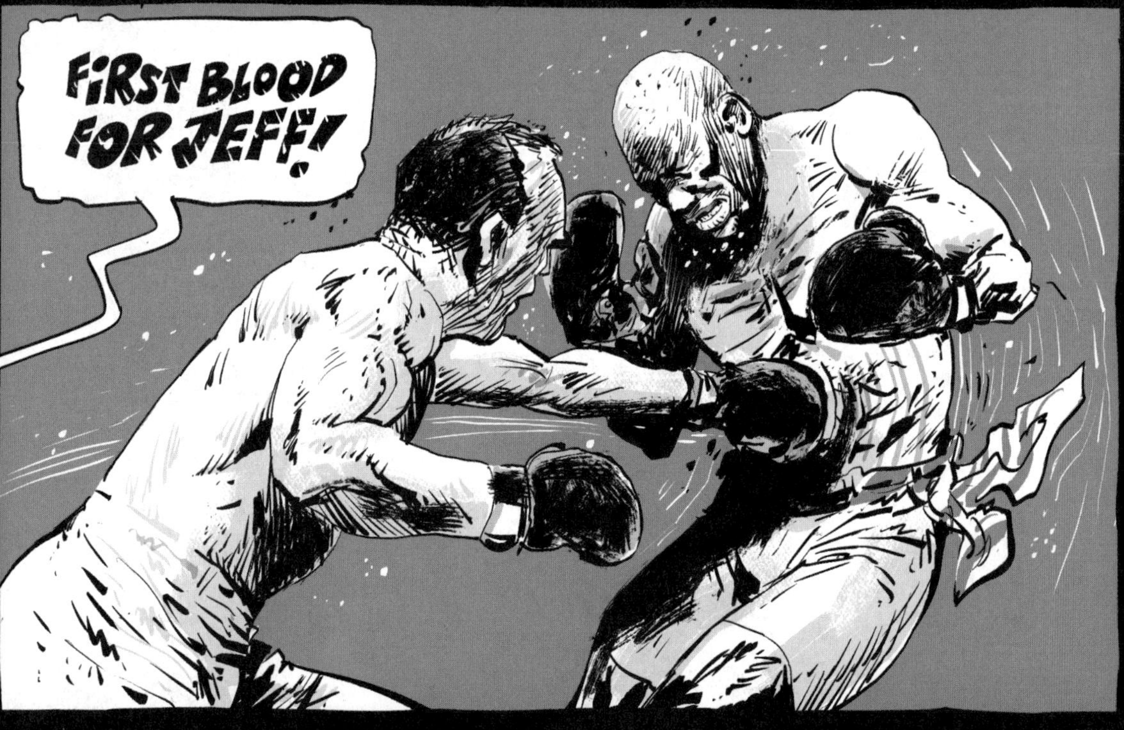
FIRST BLOOD FOR JEFF!

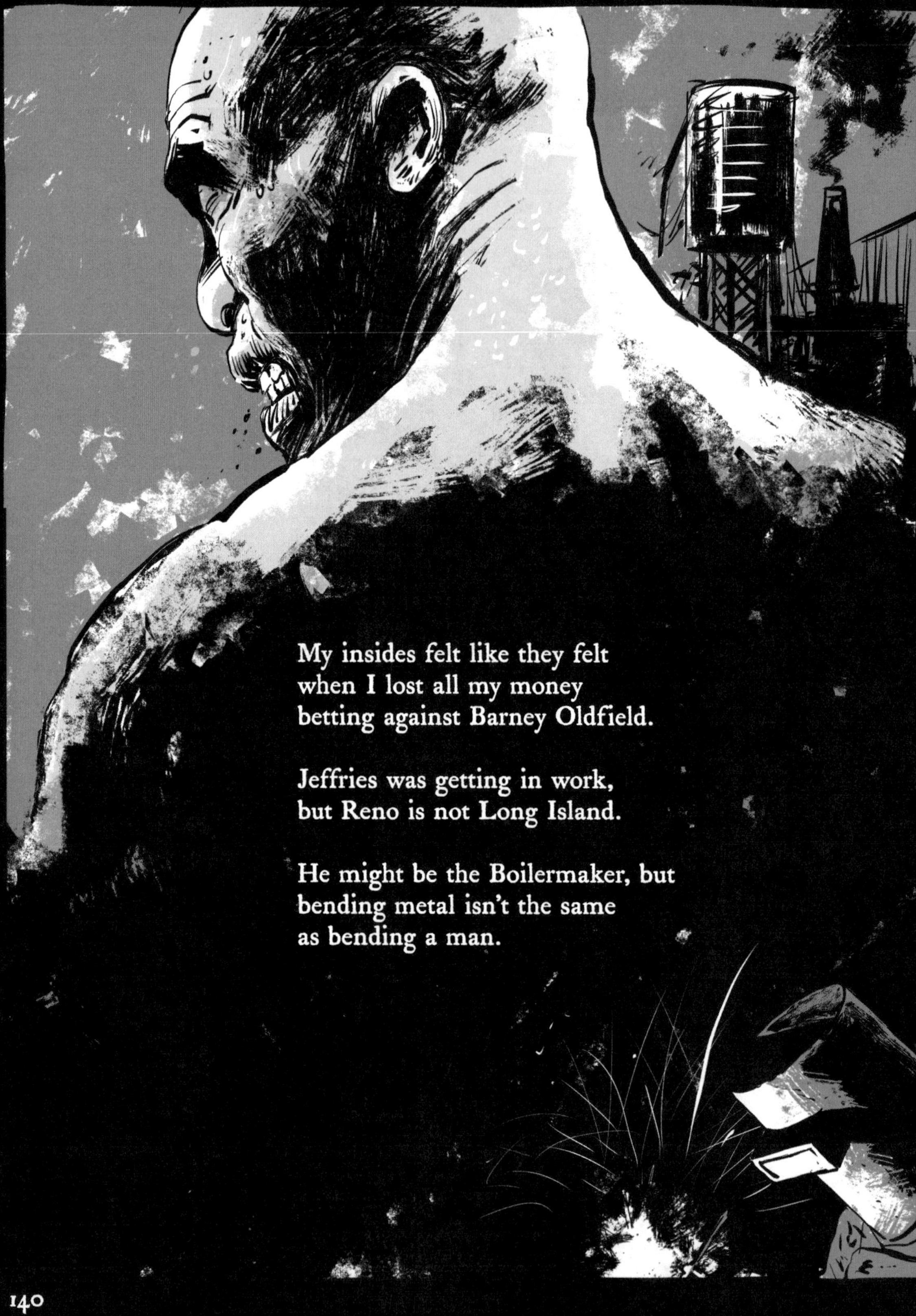
My insides felt like they felt
when I lost all my money
betting against Barney Oldfield.

Jeffries was getting in work,
but Reno is not Long Island.

He might be the Boilermaker, but
bending metal isn't the same
as bending a man.

MULHOLLAND STEEL, LOS ANGELES, CALIFORNIA 1891

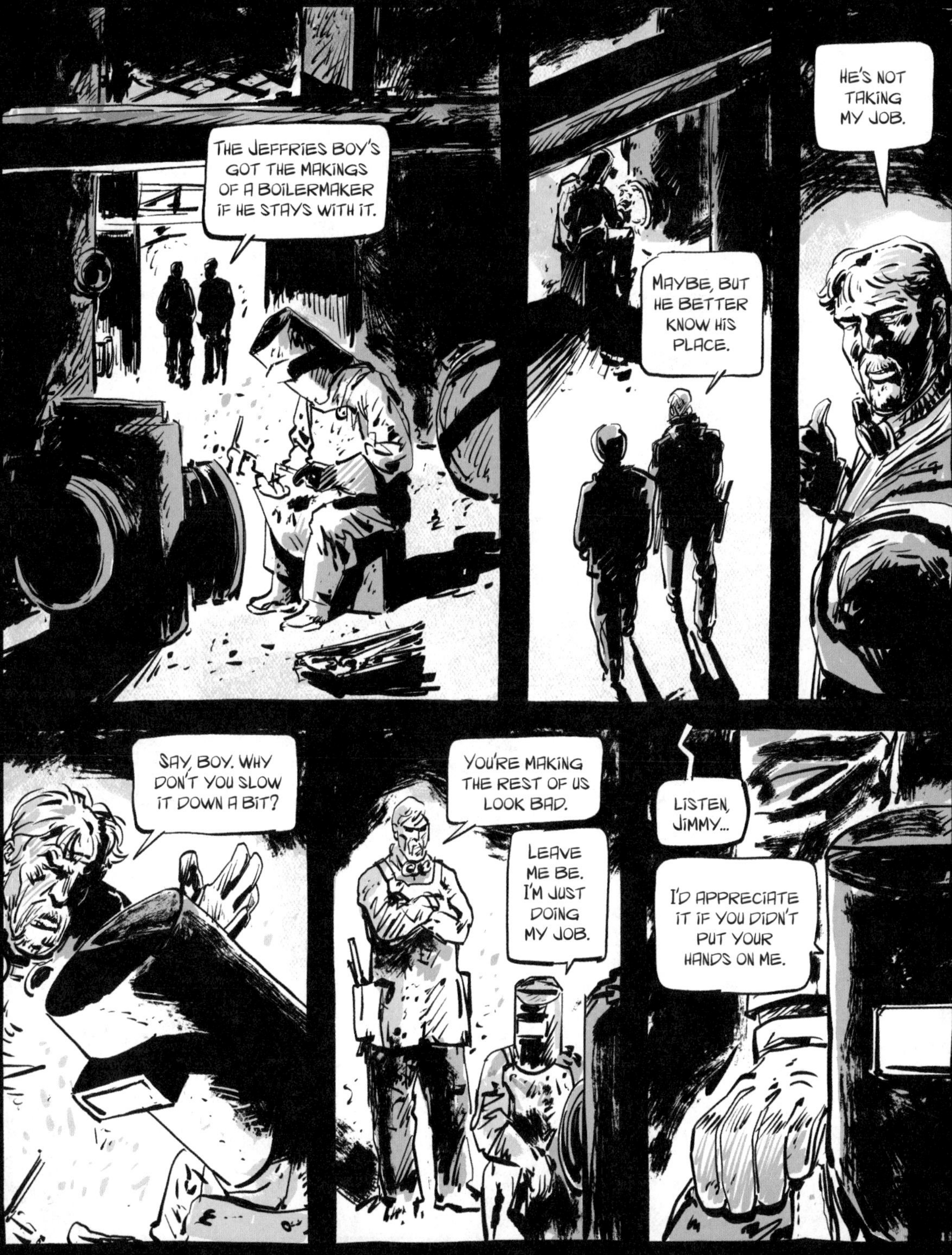

THE JEFFRIES BOY'S GOT THE MAKINGS OF A BOILERMAKER IF HE STAYS WITH IT.
MAYBE, BUT HE BETTER KNOW HIS PLACE.
HE'S NOT TAKING MY JOB.
SAY, BOY. WHY DON'T YOU SLOW IT DOWN A BIT?
YOU'RE MAKING THE REST OF US LOOK BAD.
LEAVE ME BE. I'M JUST DOING MY JOB.
LISTEN, JIMMY...
I'D APPRECIATE IT IF YOU DIDN'T PUT YOUR HANDS ON ME.

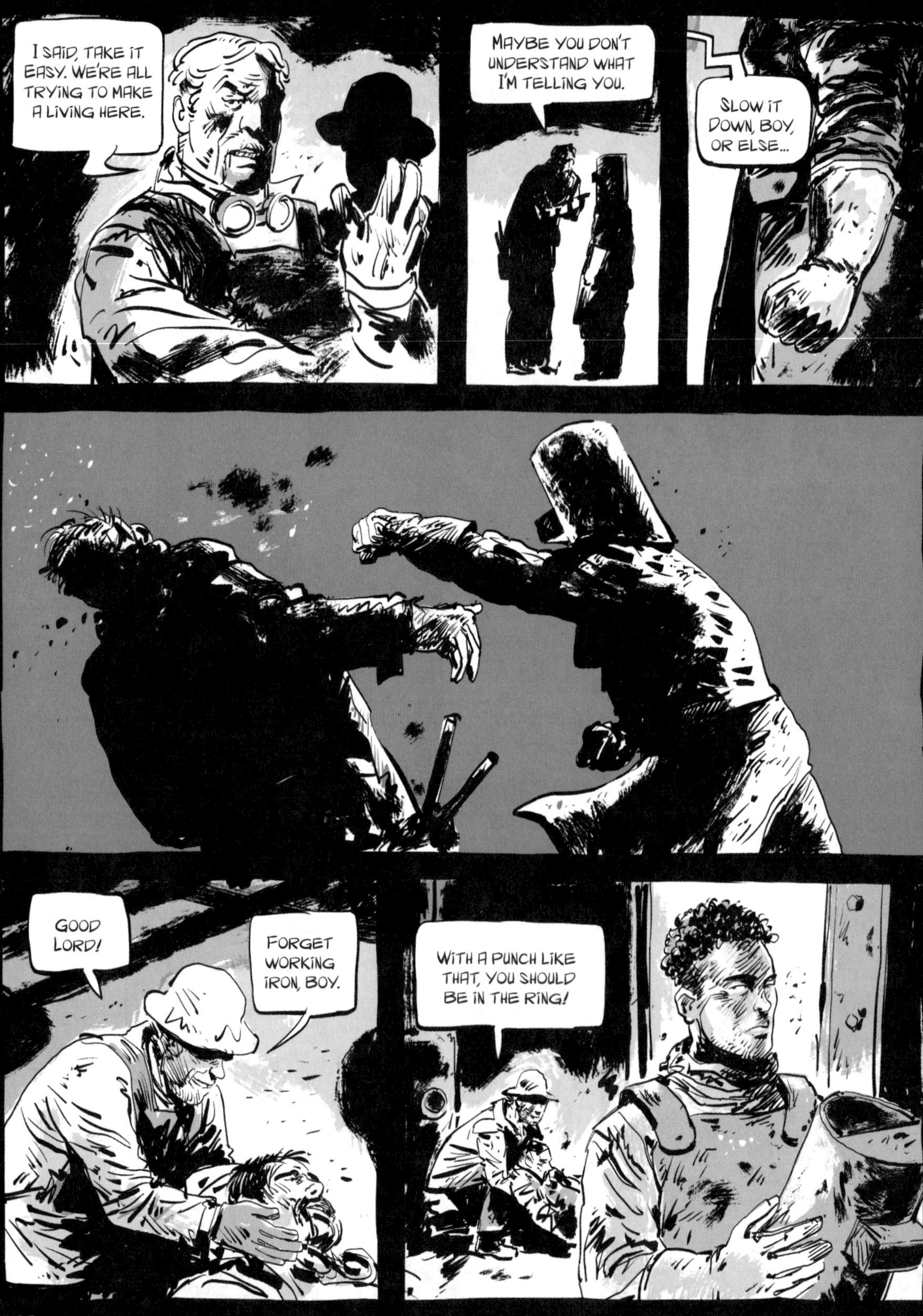
I SAID, TAKE IT EASY. WE'RE ALL TRYING TO MAKE A LIVING HERE.
MAYBE YOU DON'T UNDERSTAND WHAT I'M TELLING YOU.
SLOW IT DOWN, BOY, OR ELSE...
GOOD LORD!
FORGET WORKING IRON, BOY.
WITH A PUNCH LIKE THAT, YOU SHOULD BE IN THE RING!

Excuse after excuse to avoid me, even when that writer Jack London begged him to take the championship back for the white race.

ROUND 8

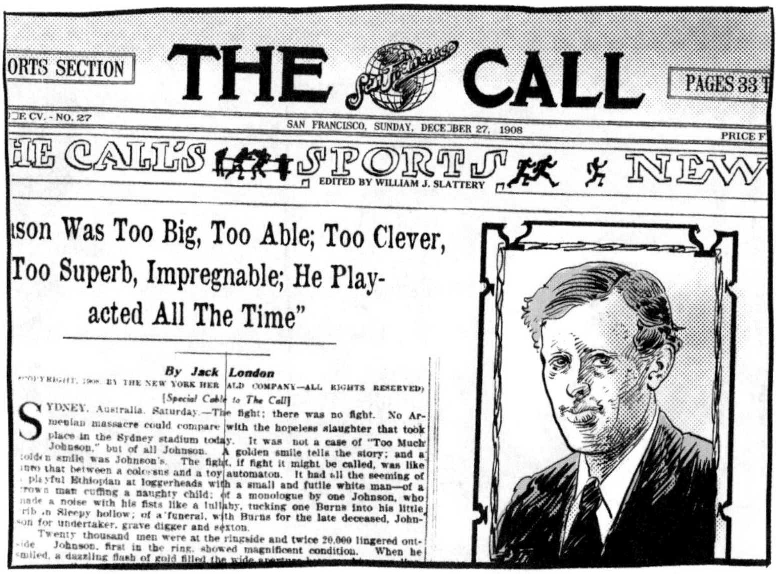
ORTS SECTION THE CALL PAGES 33 T

E CV. - NO. 27 SAN FRANCISCO, SUNDAY, DECEMBER 27, 1908 PRICE F

HE CALL'S SPORTS NEW

EDITED BY WILLIAM J. SLATTERY

ison Was Too Big, Too Able; Too Clever, Too Superb, Impregnable; He Play-acted All The Time"

By Jack London

COPYRIGHT, 1908, BY THE NEW YORK HERALD COMPANY—ALL RIGHTS RESERVED)

[Special Cable to The Call]

SYDNEY, Australia, Saturday.—The fight; there was no fight. No Armenian massacre could compare with the hopeless slaughter that took place in the Sydney stadium today. It was not a case of "Too Much Johnson," but of all Johnson. A golden smile tells the story; and a golden smile was Johnson's. The fight, if fight it might be called, was like unto that between a colossus and a toy automaton. It had all the seeming of a playful Ethiopian at loggerheads with a small and futile white man—of a grown man cuffing a naughty child; of a monologue by one Johnson, who made a noise with his fists like a lullaby, tucking one Burns into his little crib in Sleepy hollow; of a funeral, with Burns for the late deceased, Johnson for undertaker, grave digger and sexton.

Twenty thousand men were at the ringside and twice 20,000 lingered outside. Johnson, first in the ring, showed magnificent condition. When he smiled, a dazzling flash of gold filled the wide

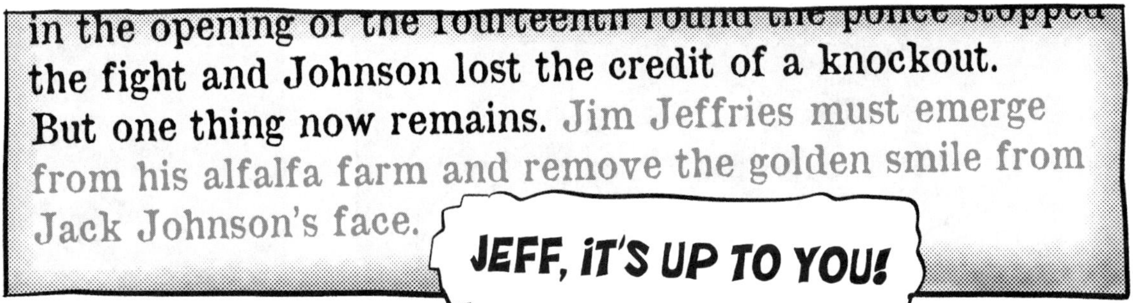

in the opening of the fourteenth round the police stopped the fight and Johnson lost the credit of a knockout. But one thing now remains. Jim Jeffries must emerge from his alfalfa farm and remove the golden smile from Jack Johnson's face.
JEFF, IT'S UP TO YOU!

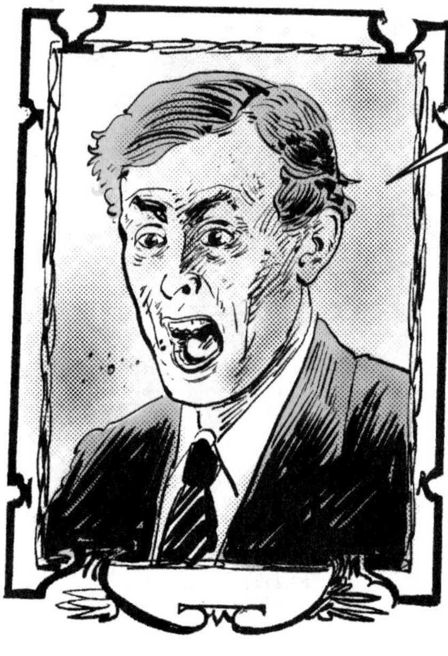

I never liked the man's wilderness tales anyway. His language was primitive on its best day.

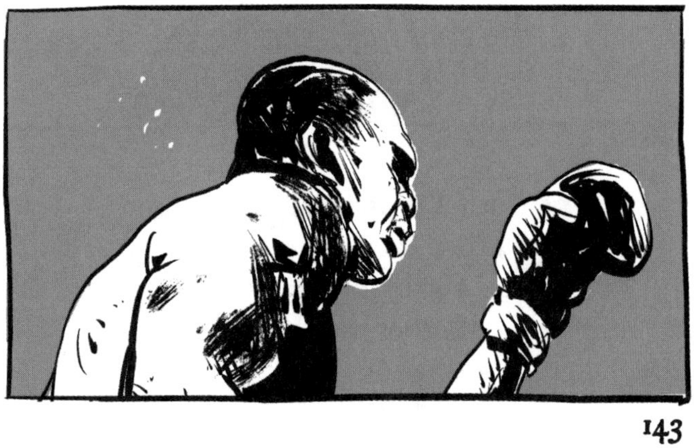

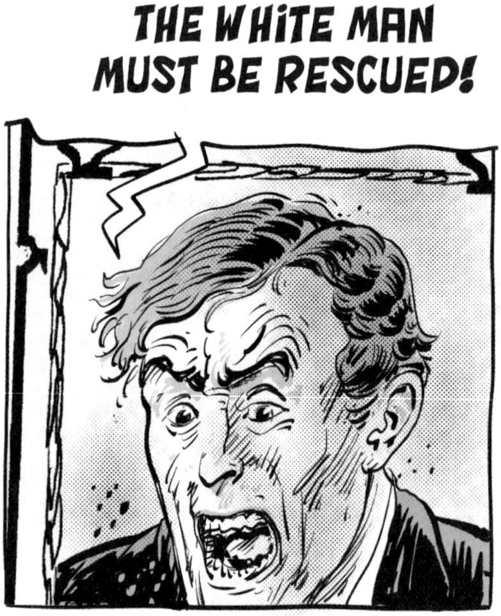
THE WHITE MAN
MUST BE RESCUED!

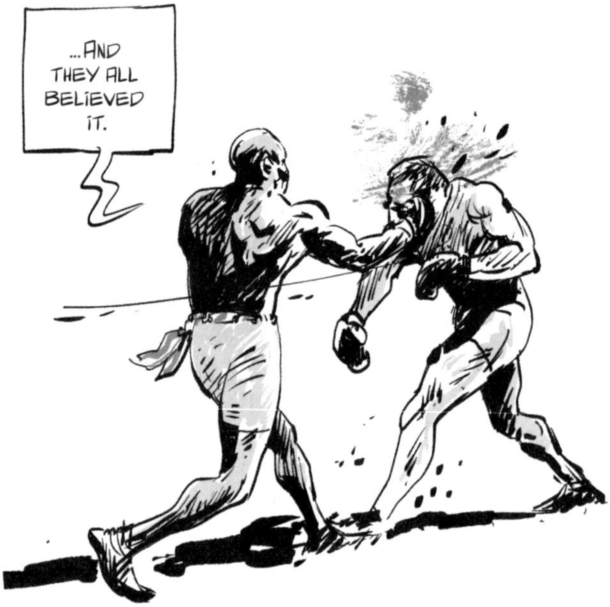
...AND THEY ALL BELIEVED IT.

The way Jeff told it, he retired undefeated because he'd beaten everybody there was to beat.

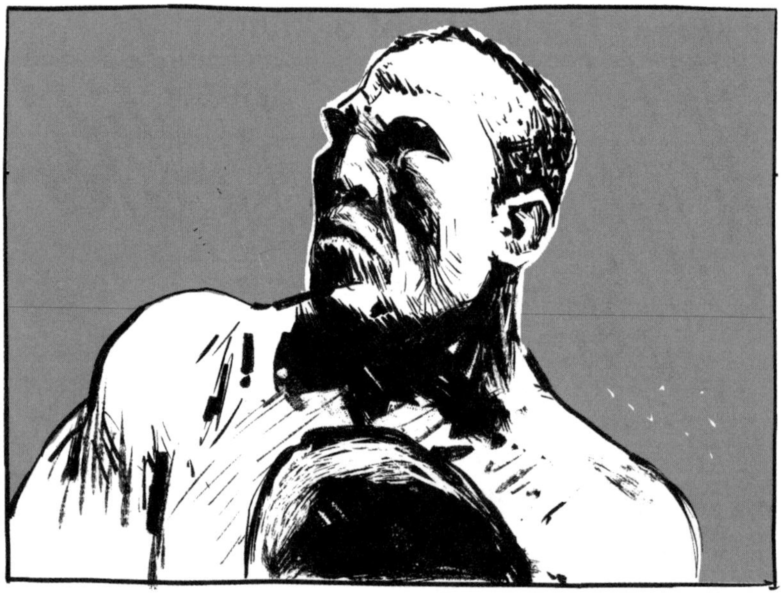

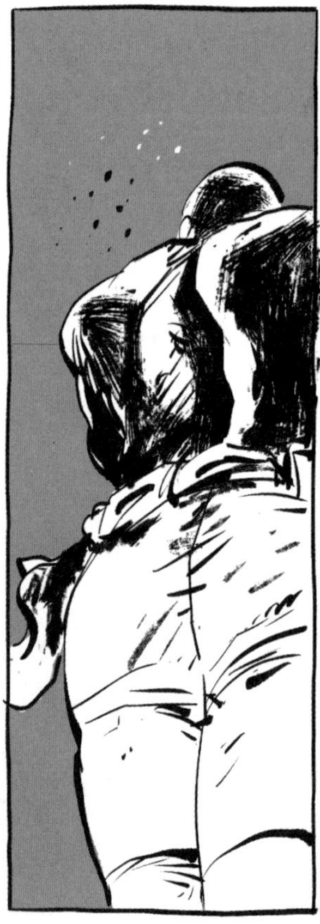

But in truth **I'm** the reason he quit & bought that farm. **I'm** the reason he became a saloon keeper, telling stories to whoever would listen.

CARNAHAN BAR, VERNON, CALIFORNIA 1909

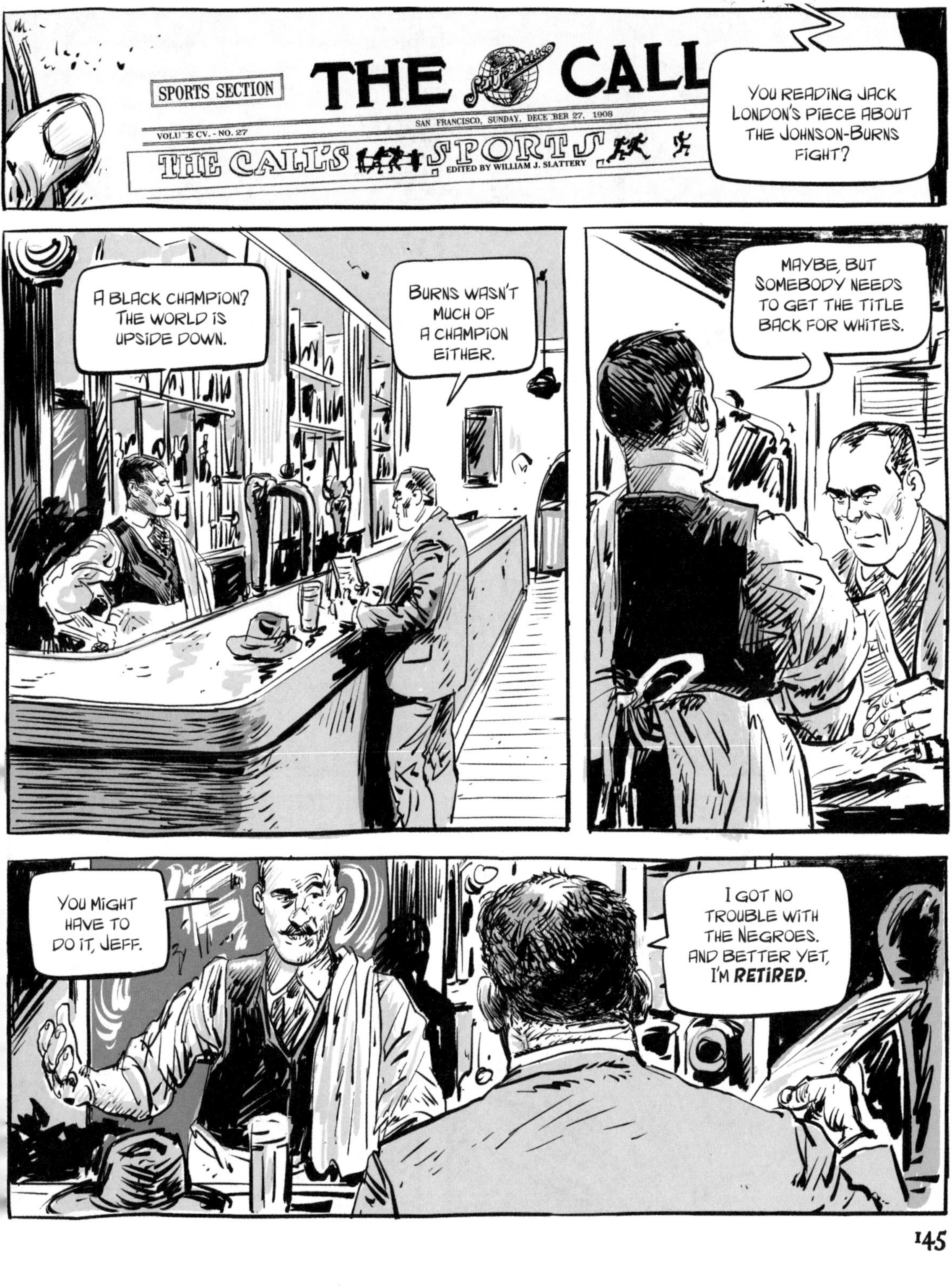
SPORTS SECTION
THE CALL
SAN FRANCISCO, SUNDAY, DECE BER 27, 1908
VOLU E CV. - NO. 27
THE CALL'S SPORTS
EDITED BY WILLIAM J. SLATTERY
YOU READING JACK LONDON'S PIECE ABOUT THE JOHNSON-BURNS FIGHT?
A BLACK CHAMPION? THE WORLD IS UPSIDE DOWN.
BURNS WASN'T MUCH OF A CHAMPION EITHER.
MAYBE, BUT SOMEBODY NEEDS TO GET THE TITLE BACK FOR WHITES.
YOU MIGHT HAVE TO DO IT, JEFF.
I GOT NO TROUBLE WITH THE NEGROES. AND BETTER YET, I'M ***RETIRED***.

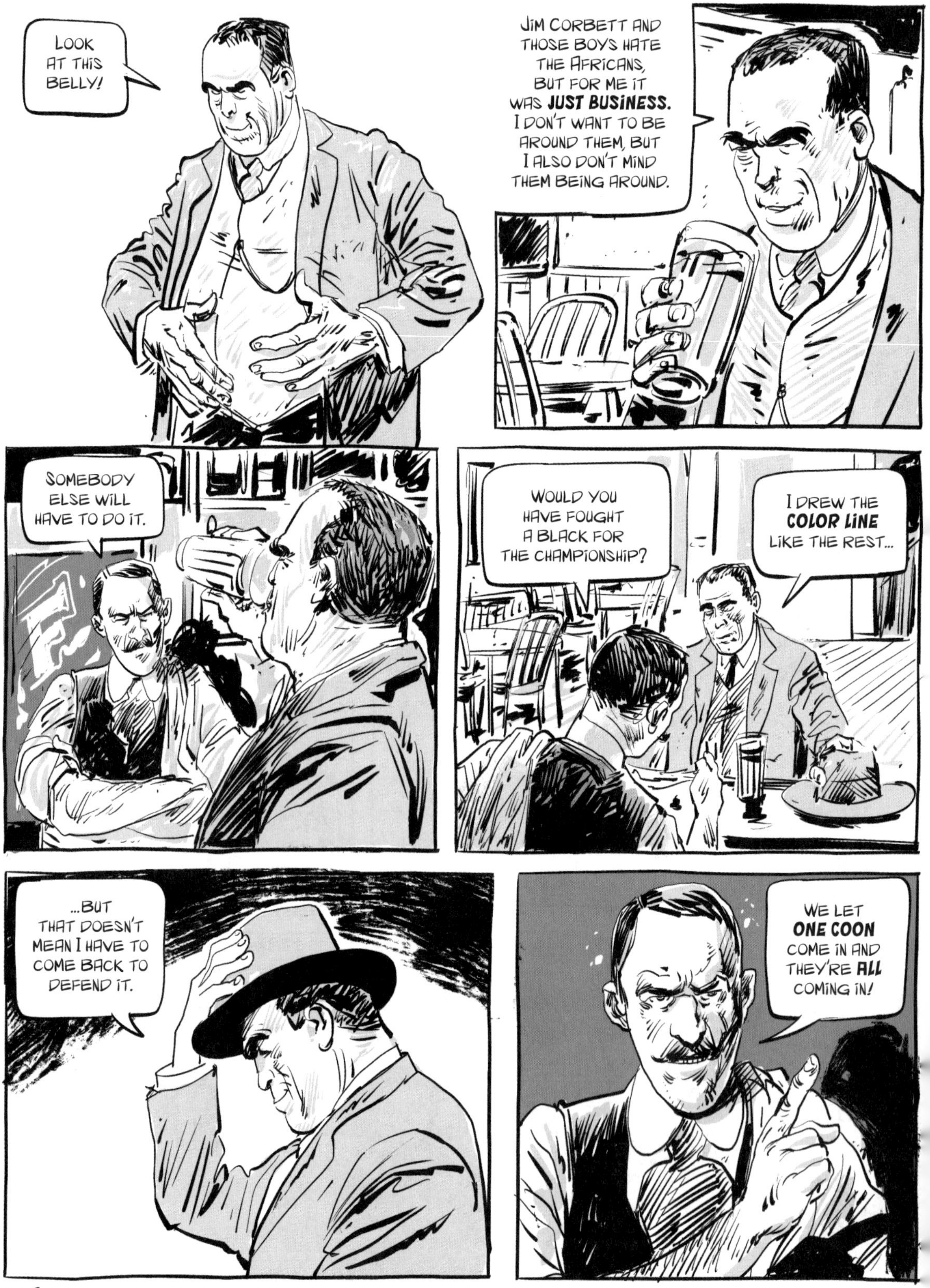
LOOK AT THIS BELLY!
JIM CORBETT AND THOSE BOYS HATE THE AFRICANS, BUT FOR ME IT WAS **JUST BUSINESS.** I DON'T WANT TO BE AROUND THEM, BUT I ALSO DON'T MIND THEM BEING AROUND.
SOMEBODY ELSE WILL HAVE TO DO IT.
WOULD YOU HAVE FOUGHT A BLACK FOR THE CHAMPIONSHIP?
I DREW THE **COLOR LINE** LIKE THE REST...
...BUT THAT DOESN'T MEAN I HAVE TO COME BACK TO DEFEND IT.
WE LET **ONE COON** COME IN AND THEY'RE **ALL** COMING IN!

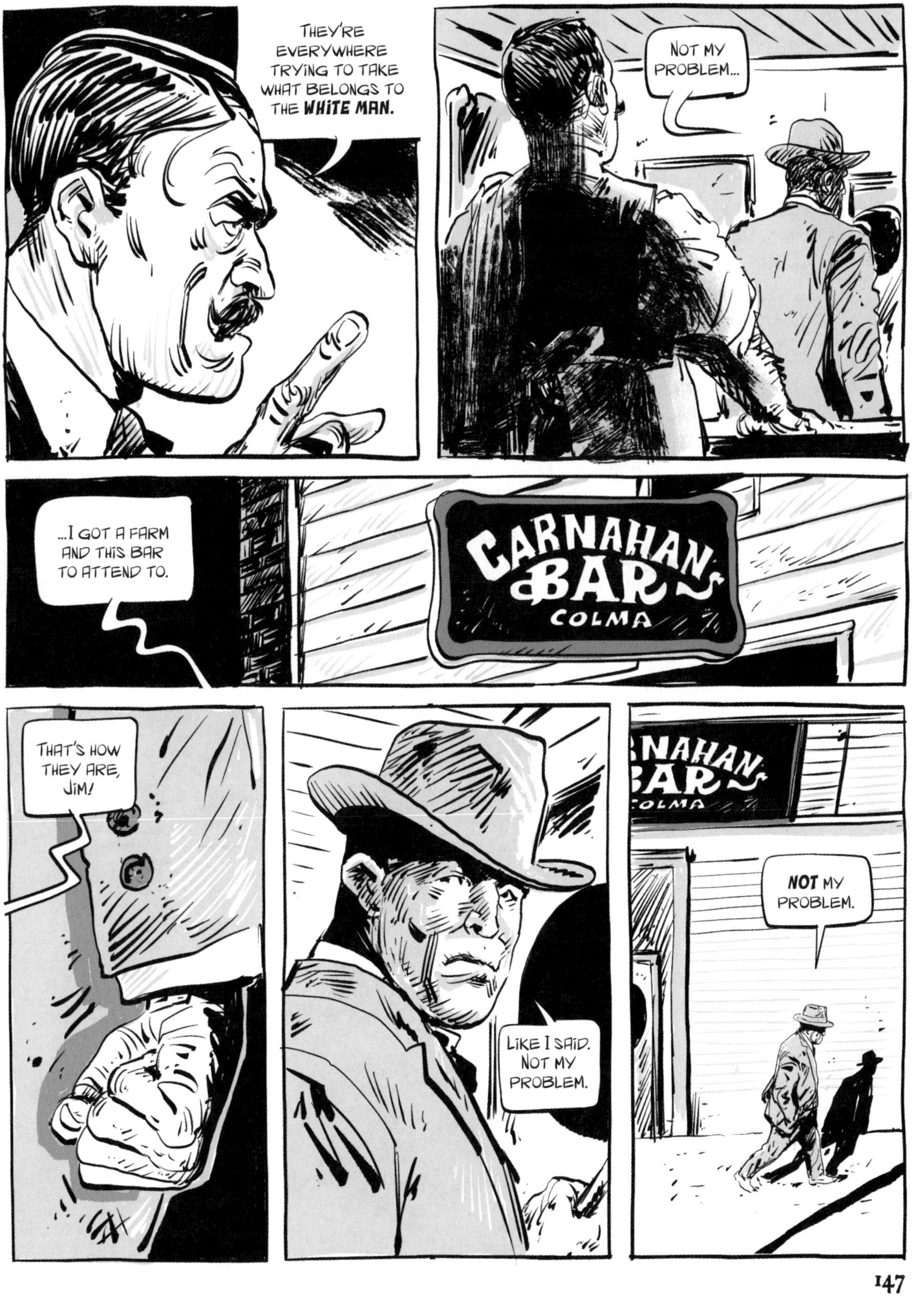
THEY'RE EVERYWHERE TRYING TO TAKE WHAT BELONGS TO THE **WHITE MAN.**
NOT MY PROBLEM...
...I GOT A FARM AND THIS BAR TO ATTEND TO.
CARNAHAN BAR COLMA
THAT'S HOW THEY ARE, JIM!
LIKE I SAID. NOT MY PROBLEM.
NOT MY PROBLEM.

ROOOO

JEFFRIES'S ALFALFA FARM, VERNON, CA 1908

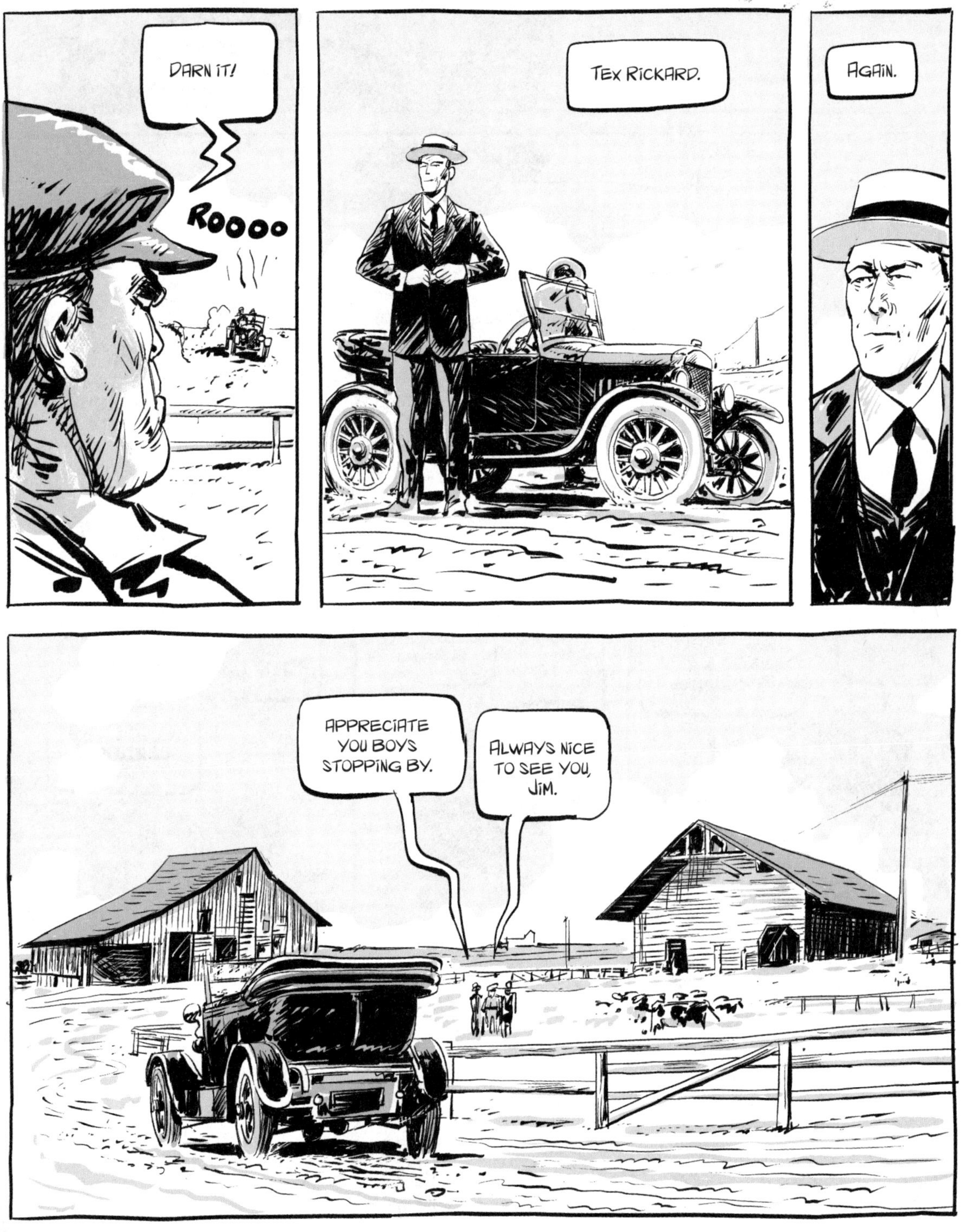
DARN IT!
ROOOO
TEX RICKARD.
AGAIN.
APPRECIATE YOU BOYS STOPPING BY.
ALWAYS NICE TO SEE YOU, JIM.

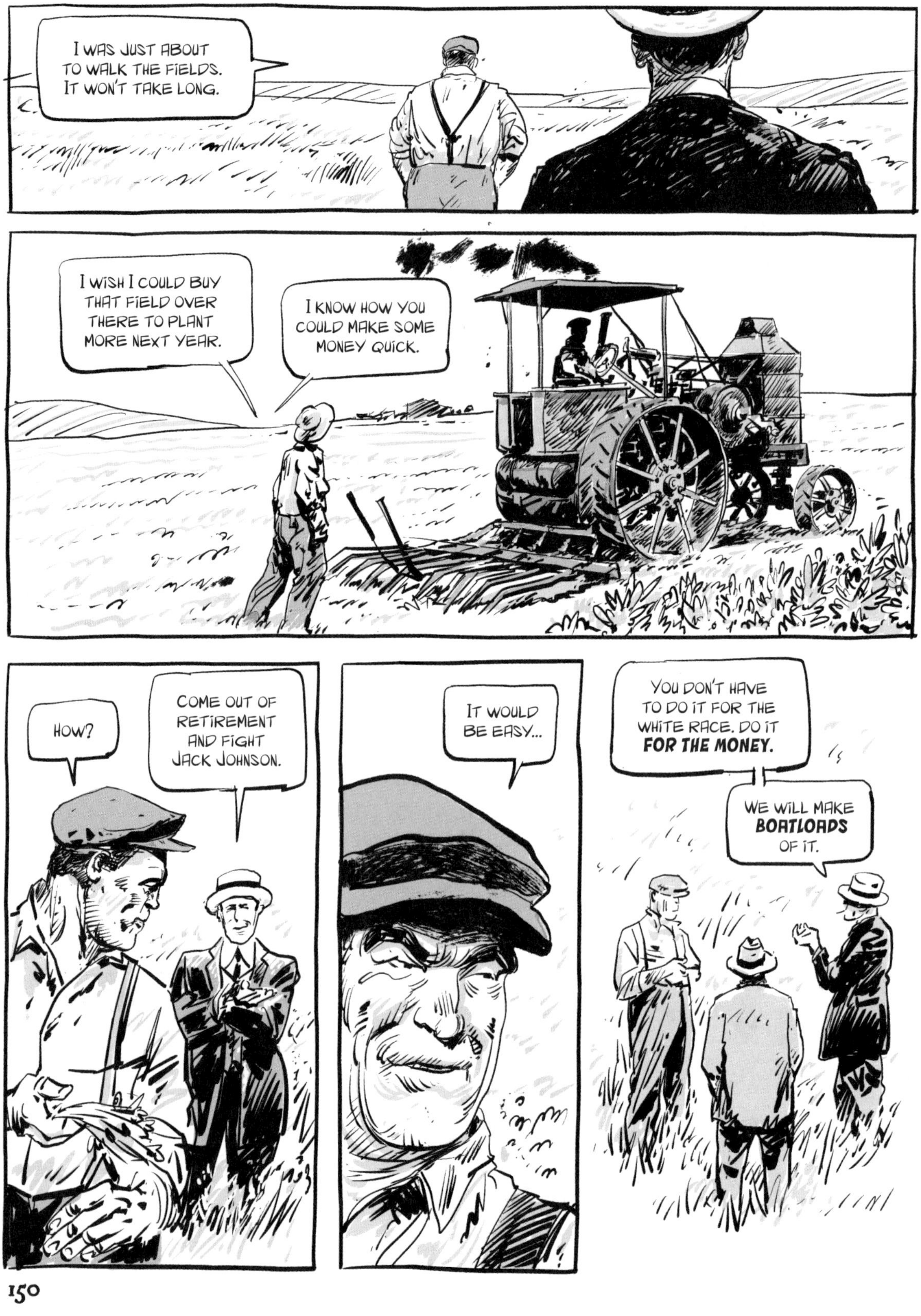
I WAS JUST ABOUT TO WALK THE FIELDS. IT WON'T TAKE LONG.
I WISH I COULD BUY THAT FIELD OVER THERE TO PLANT MORE NEXT YEAR.
I KNOW HOW YOU COULD MAKE SOME MONEY QUICK.
HOW?
COME OUT OF RETIREMENT AND FIGHT JACK JOHNSON.
IT WOULD BE EASY...
YOU DON'T HAVE TO DO IT FOR THE WHITE RACE. DO IT **FOR THE MONEY.**
WE WILL MAKE **BOATLOADS** OF IT.

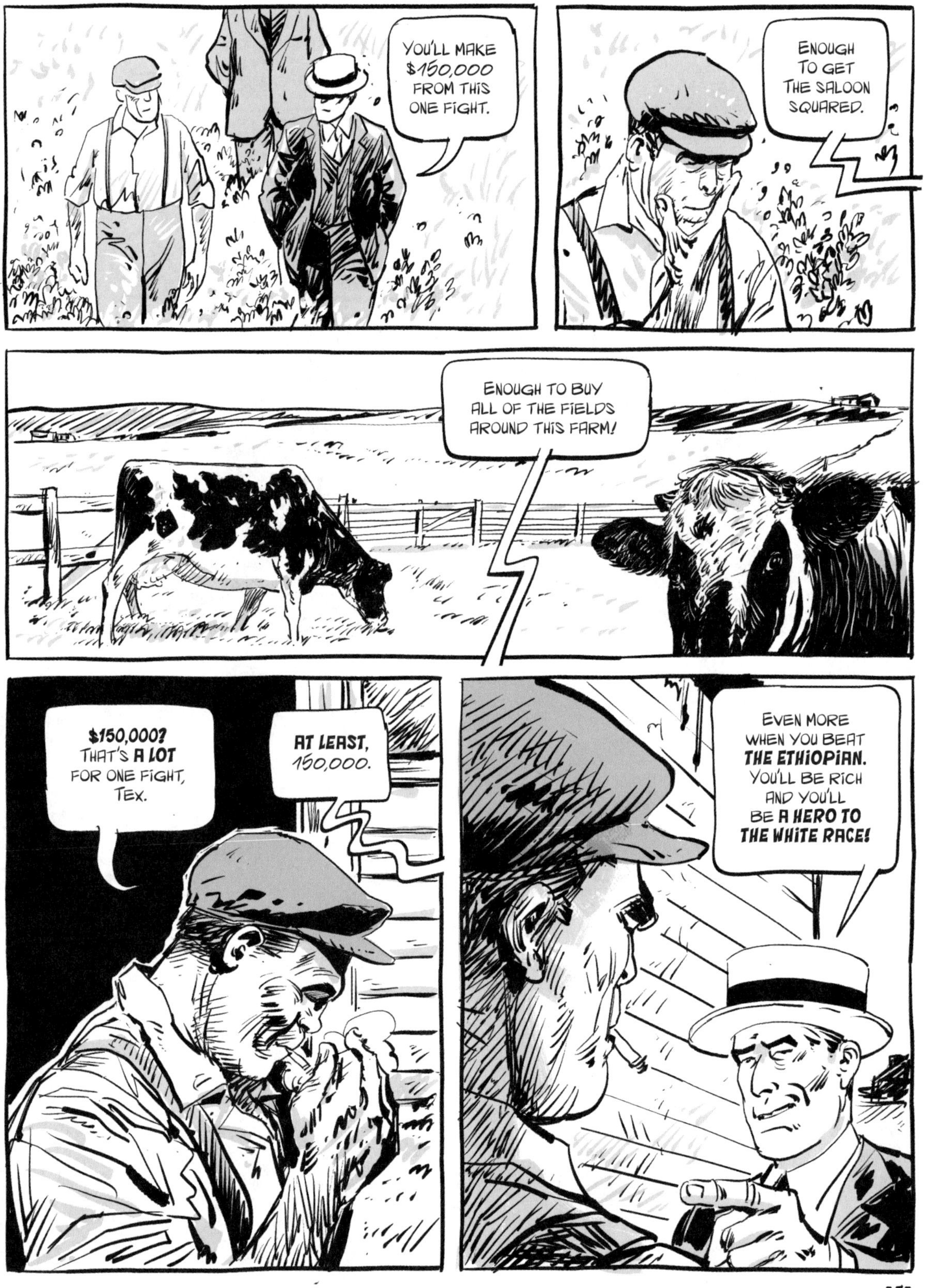
YOU'LL MAKE $150,000 FROM THIS ONE FIGHT.
ENOUGH TO GET THE SALOON SQUARED.
ENOUGH TO BUY ALL OF THE FIELDS AROUND THIS FARM!
$150,000? THAT'S A LOT FOR ONE FIGHT, TEX.
AT LEAST, 150,000.
EVEN MORE WHEN YOU BEAT THE ETHIOPIAN. YOU'LL BE RICH AND YOU'LL BE A HERO TO THE WHITE RACE!

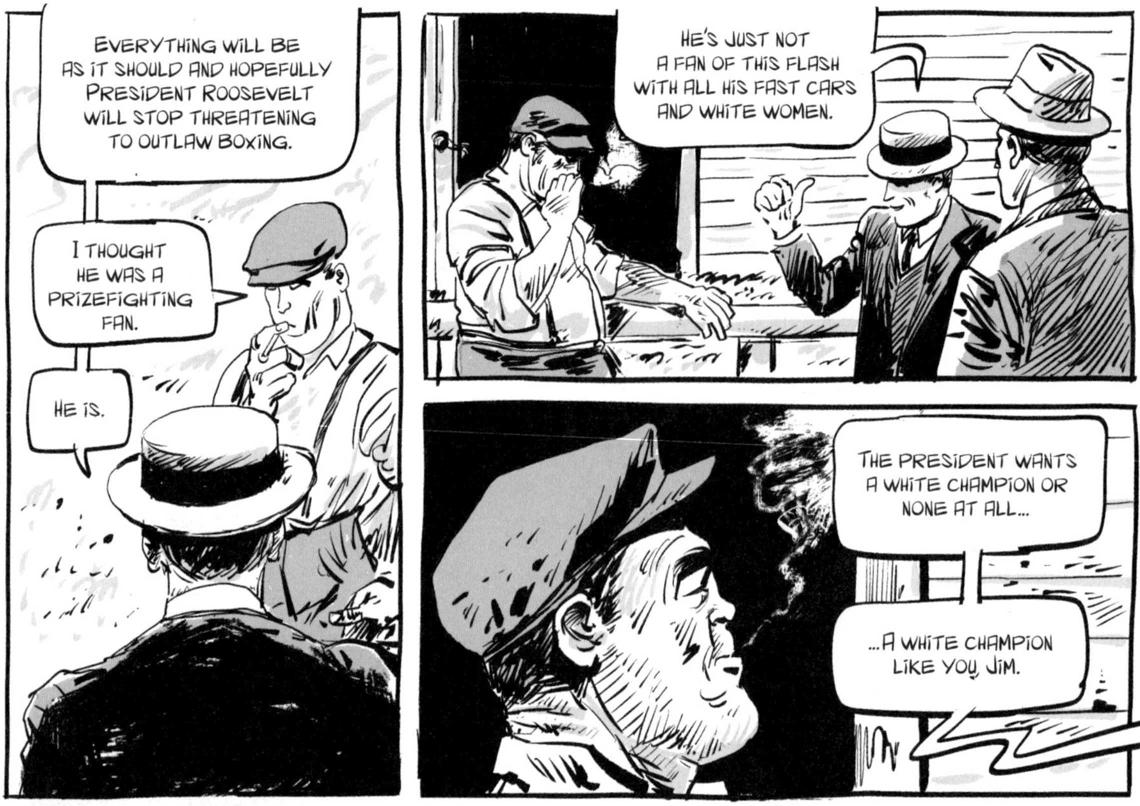
EVERYTHING WILL BE AS IT SHOULD AND HOPEFULLY PRESIDENT ROOSEVELT WILL STOP THREATENING TO OUTLAW BOXING.
I THOUGHT HE WAS A PRIZEFIGHTING FAN.
HE IS.
HE'S JUST NOT A FAN OF THIS FLASH WITH ALL HIS FAST CARS AND WHITE WOMEN.
THE PRESIDENT WANTS A WHITE CHAMPION OR NONE AT ALL...
...A WHITE CHAMPION LIKE YOU, JIM.

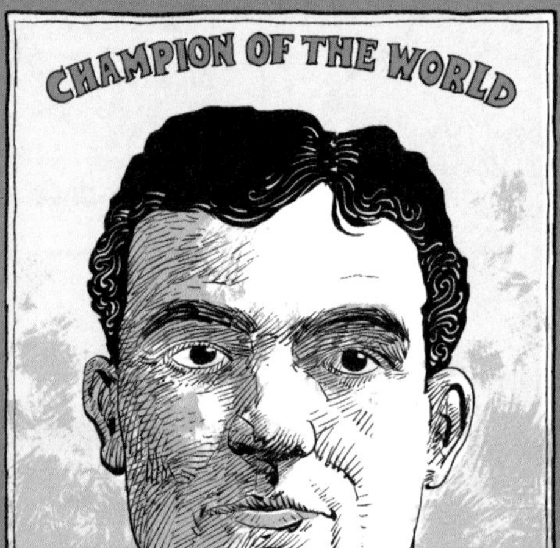
CHAMPION OF THE WORLD
JAMES J. JEFFRIES
THE ONLY UNDEFEATED HEAVYWEIGHT LIVING

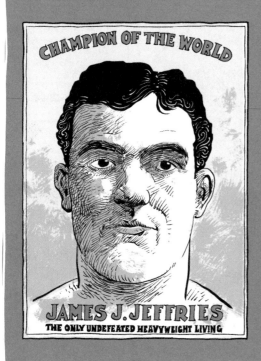

James J. Jeffries is the ideal American: White, powerful, true to his family and friends. He's what all other champions aspire to. Forget all of the other great hopes who have battled Jack Johnson and lost. None of them had the stature, stamina, or integrity of the Boilermaker, James J. Jeffries. If this paper wasn't such a fan of our beloved President Roosevelt, we'd nominate Mr. Jeffries for executive office!

—*Dallas Morning Star*, March 7, 1910

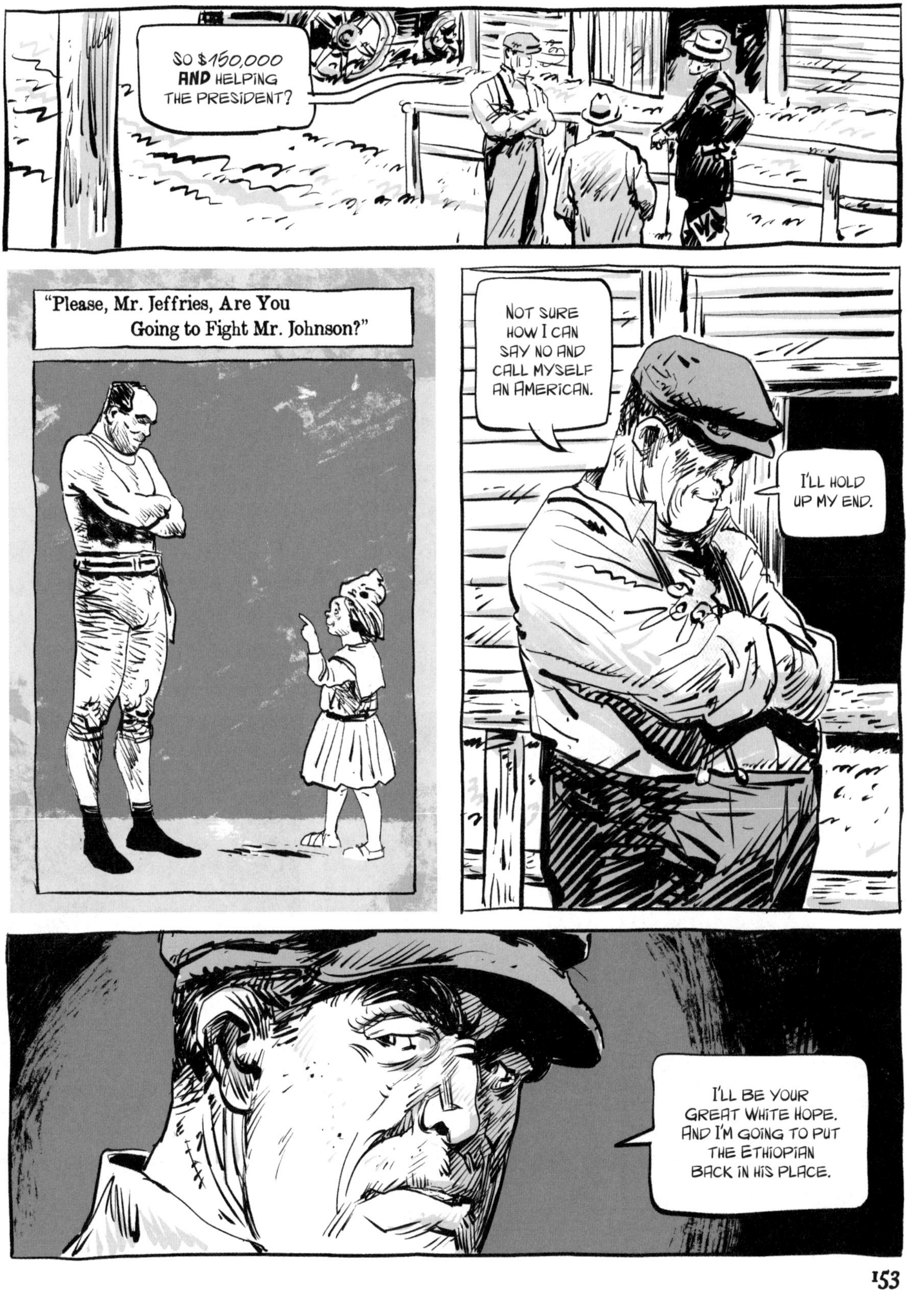

SO $150,000 AND HELPING THE PRESIDENT?
"Please, Mr. Jeffries, Are You Going to Fight Mr. Johnson?"
NOT SURE HOW I CAN SAY NO AND CALL MYSELF AN AMERICAN.
I'LL HOLD UP MY END.
I'LL BE YOUR GREAT WHITE HOPE. AND I'M GOING TO PUT THE ETHIOPIAN BACK IN HIS PLACE.

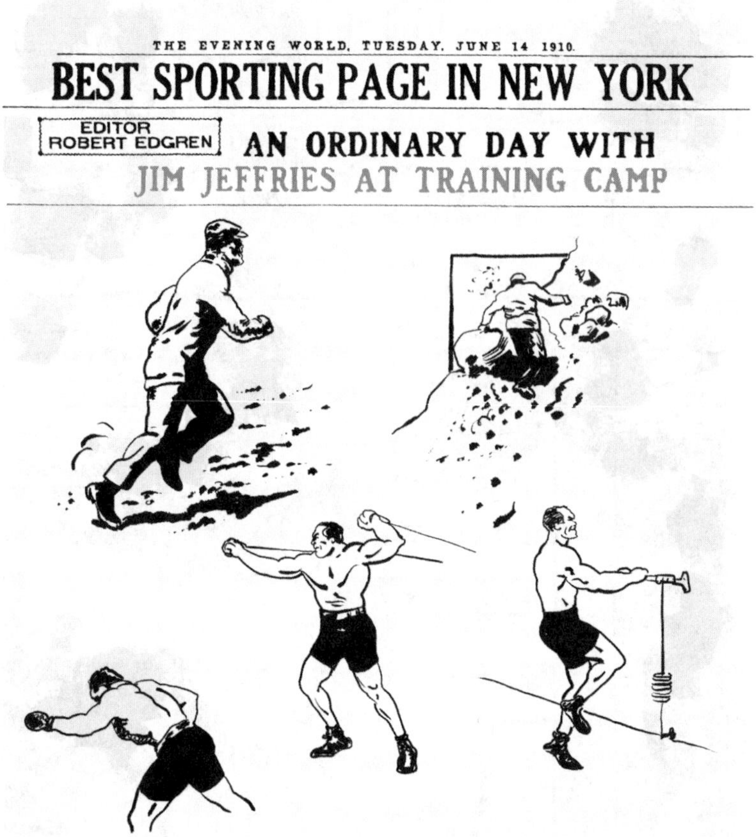
THE EVENING WORLD, TUESDAY, JUNE 14 1910.
BEST SPORTING PAGE IN NEW YORK
EDITOR ROBERT EDGREN
AN ORDINARY DAY WITH
JIM JEFFRIES AT TRAINING CAMP

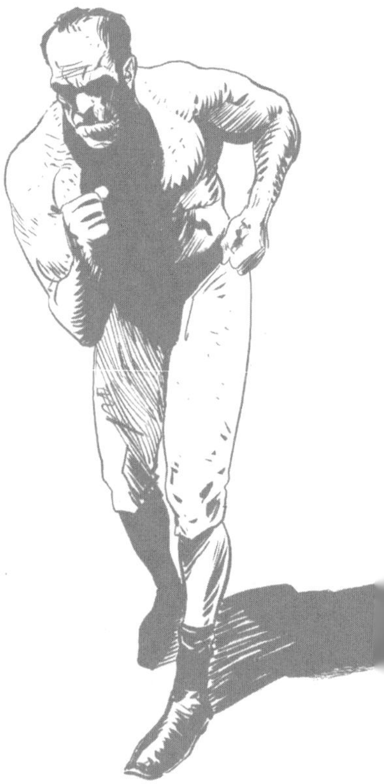

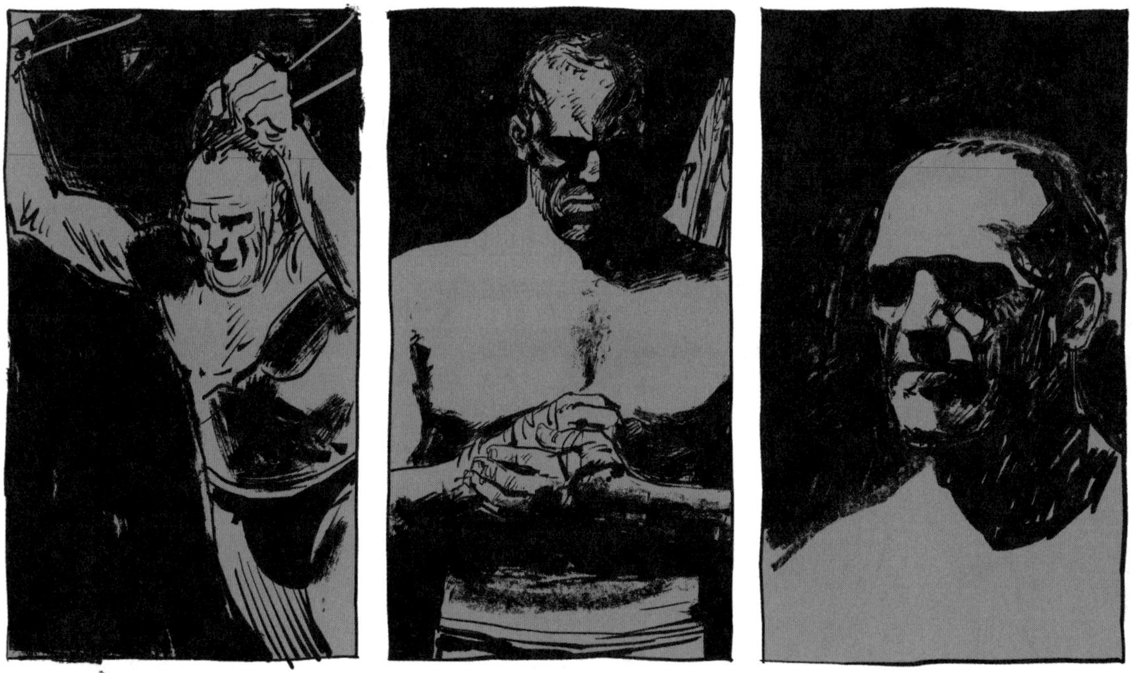

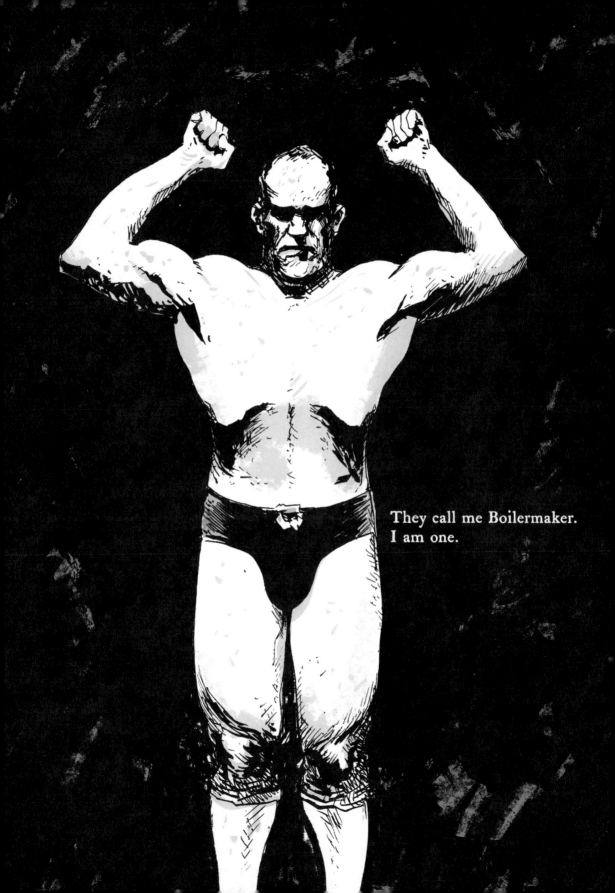

They call me Boilermaker.
I am one.

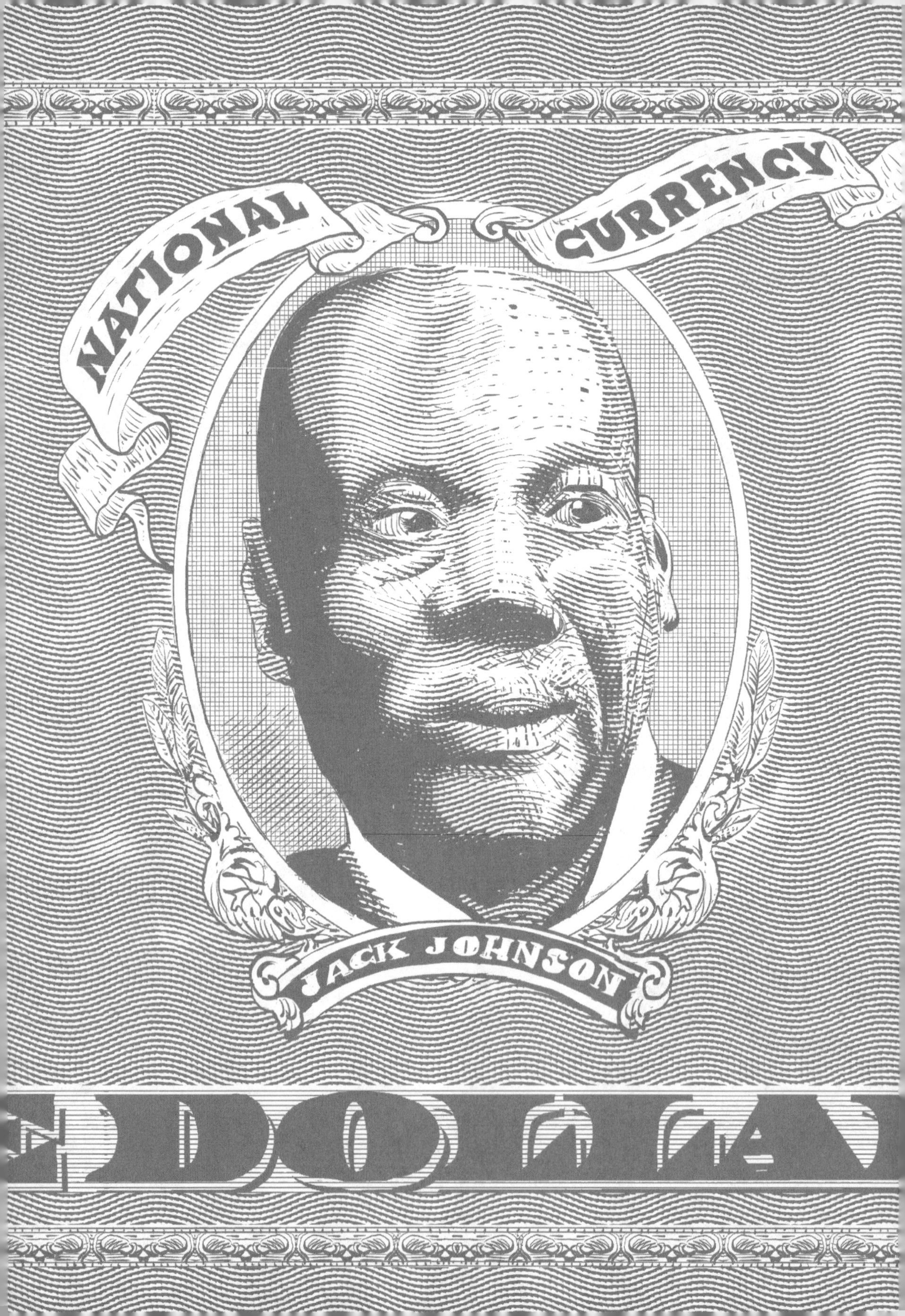
NATIONAL CURRENCY
JACK JOHNSON

IT'S ALWAYS THE MONEY

Some people want
to be mayor or president.
Some people want to be doctors
to fix bones or hearts.
Or opera singers with the kind
of vibrato in their throats
can change weather & reshape
clouds. I would have loved
to be a doctor or a singer.
I didn't want to be heavyweight
champion until I finally
understood my science is fistic.
Now I'm a doctor with an uppercut.
I'm an aria with a fist.

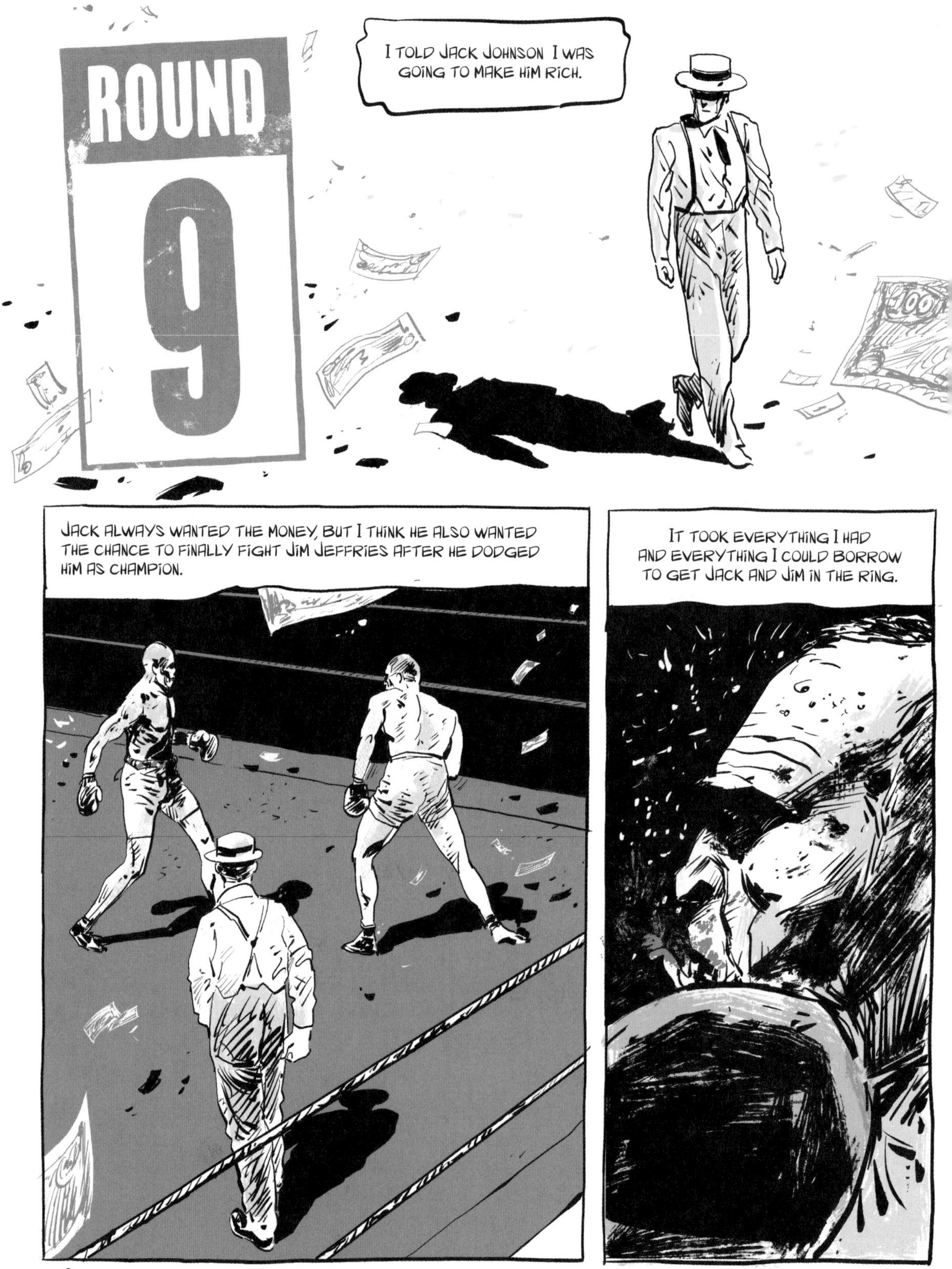
ROUND
9
I TOLD JACK JOHNSON I WAS GOING TO MAKE HIM RICH.
JACK ALWAYS WANTED THE MONEY, BUT I THINK HE ALSO WANTED THE CHANCE TO FINALLY FIGHT JIM JEFFRIES AFTER HE DODGED HIM AS CHAMPION.
IT TOOK EVERYTHING I HAD AND EVERYTHING I COULD BORROW TO GET JACK AND JIM IN THE RING.

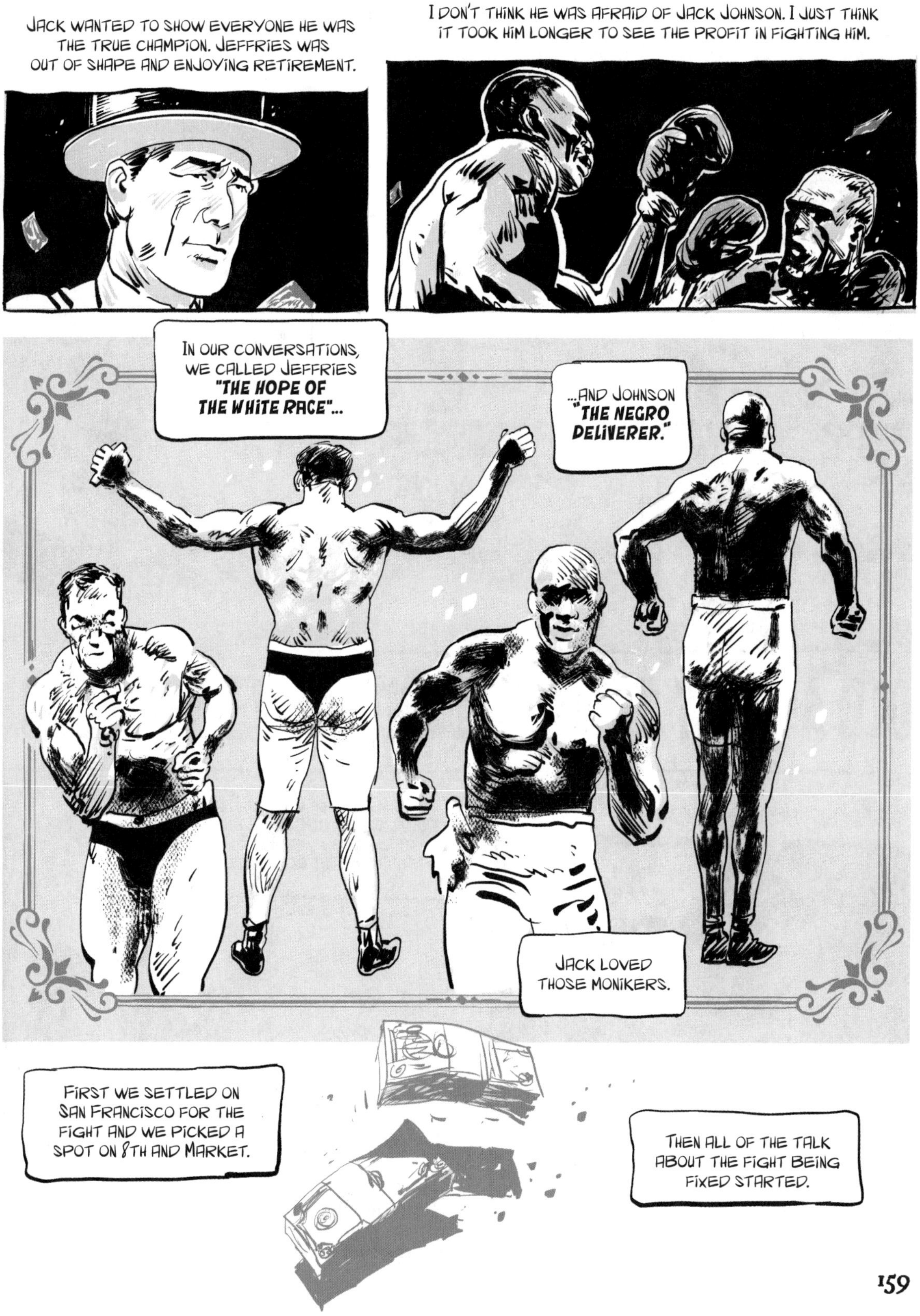
JACK WANTED TO SHOW EVERYONE HE WAS THE TRUE CHAMPION. JEFFRIES WAS OUT OF SHAPE AND ENJOYING RETIREMENT.
I DON'T THINK HE WAS AFRAID OF JACK JOHNSON. I JUST THINK IT TOOK HIM LONGER TO SEE THE PROFIT IN FIGHTING HIM.
IN OUR CONVERSATIONS, WE CALLED JEFFRIES "THE HOPE OF THE WHITE RACE"...
...AND JOHNSON "THE NEGRO DELIVERER."
JACK LOVED THOSE MONIKERS.
FIRST WE SETTLED ON SAN FRANCISCO FOR THE FIGHT AND WE PICKED A SPOT ON 8TH AND MARKET.
THEN ALL OF THE TALK ABOUT THE FIGHT BEING FIXED STARTED.

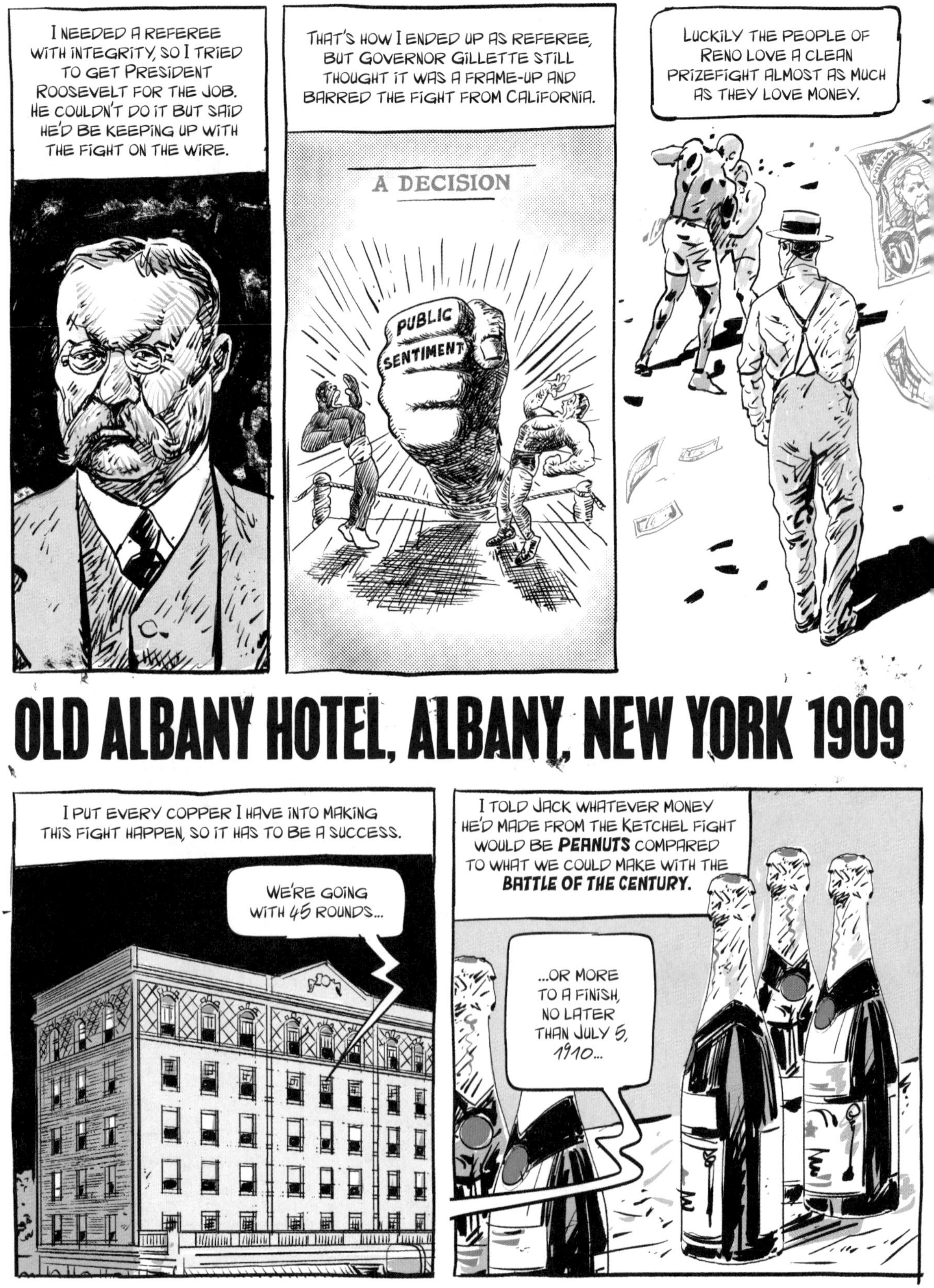
I NEEDED A REFEREE WITH INTEGRITY, SO I TRIED TO GET PRESIDENT ROOSEVELT FOR THE JOB. HE COULDN'T DO IT BUT SAID HE'D BE KEEPING UP WITH THE FIGHT ON THE WIRE.
THAT'S HOW I ENDED UP AS REFEREE, BUT GOVERNOR GILLETTE STILL THOUGHT IT WAS A FRAME-UP AND BARRED THE FIGHT FROM CALIFORNIA.
A DECISION
PUBLIC SENTIMENT
LUCKILY THE PEOPLE OF RENO LOVE A CLEAN PRIZEFIGHT ALMOST AS MUCH AS THEY LOVE MONEY.
OLD ALBANY HOTEL, ALBANY, NEW YORK 1909
I PUT EVERY COPPER I HAVE INTO MAKING THIS FIGHT HAPPEN, SO IT HAS TO BE A SUCCESS.
WE'RE GOING WITH 45 ROUNDS...
I TOLD JACK WHATEVER MONEY HE'D MADE FROM THE KETCHEL FIGHT WOULD BE **PEANUTS** COMPARED TO WHAT WE COULD MAKE WITH THE **BATTLE OF THE CENTURY.**
...OR MORE TO A FINISH, NO LATER THAN JULY 5, 1910...

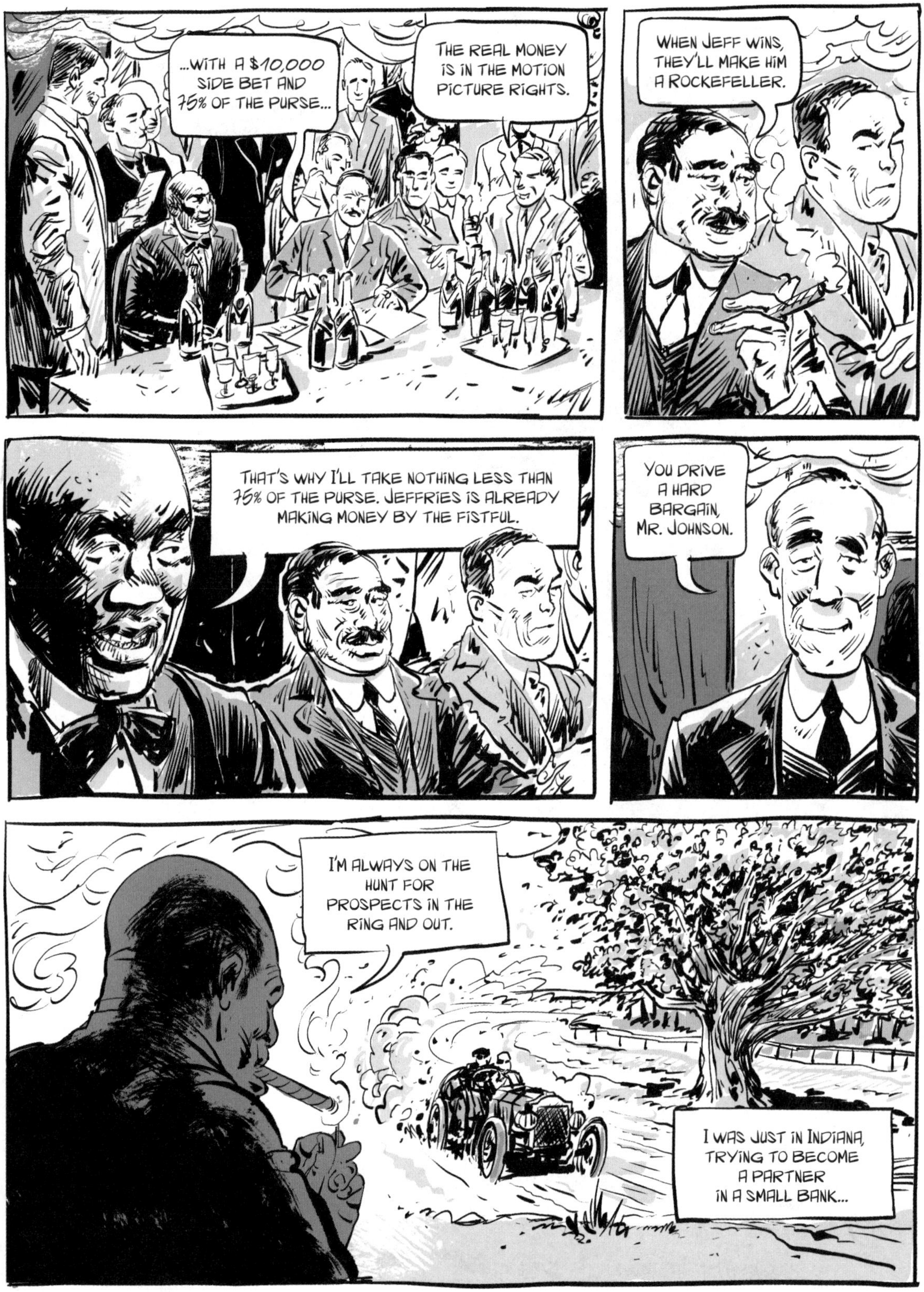
...WITH A $10,000 SIDE BET AND 75% OF THE PURSE...
THE REAL MONEY IS IN THE MOTION PICTURE RIGHTS.
WHEN JEFF WINS, THEY'LL MAKE HIM A ROCKEFELLER.
THAT'S WHY I'LL TAKE NOTHING LESS THAN 75% OF THE PURSE. JEFFRIES IS ALREADY MAKING MONEY BY THE FISTFUL.
YOU DRIVE A HARD BARGAIN, MR. JOHNSON.
I'M ALWAYS ON THE HUNT FOR PROSPECTS IN THE RING AND OUT.
I WAS JUST IN INDIANA, TRYING TO BECOME A PARTNER IN A SMALL BANK...

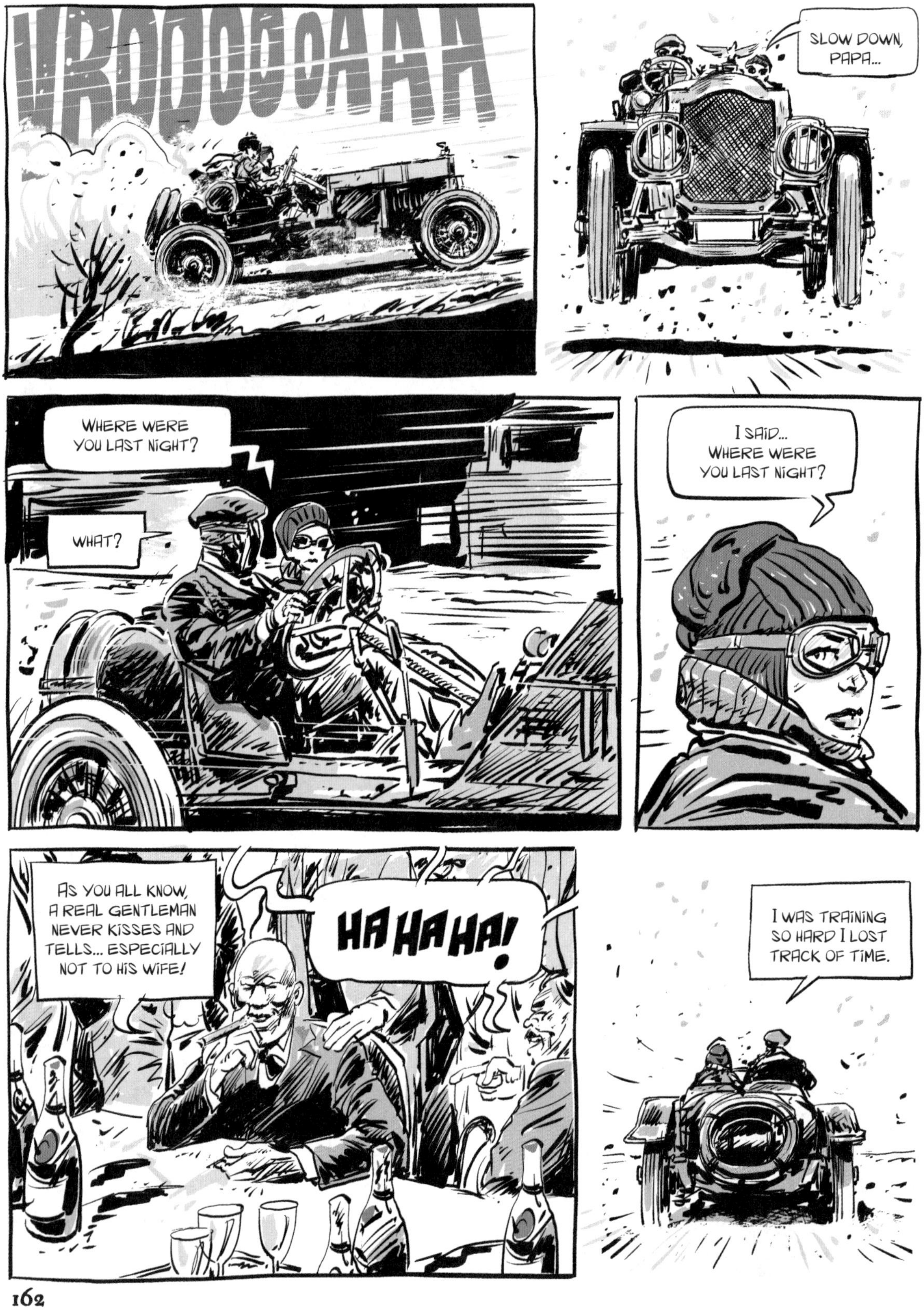
VROOOOOAAA
SLOW DOWN, PAPA...
WHERE WERE YOU LAST NIGHT?
WHAT?
I SAID... WHERE WERE YOU LAST NIGHT?
AS YOU ALL KNOW, A REAL GENTLEMAN NEVER KISSES AND TELLS... ESPECIALLY NOT TO HIS WIFE!
HA HA HA!
I WAS TRAINING SO HARD I LOST TRACK OF TIME.

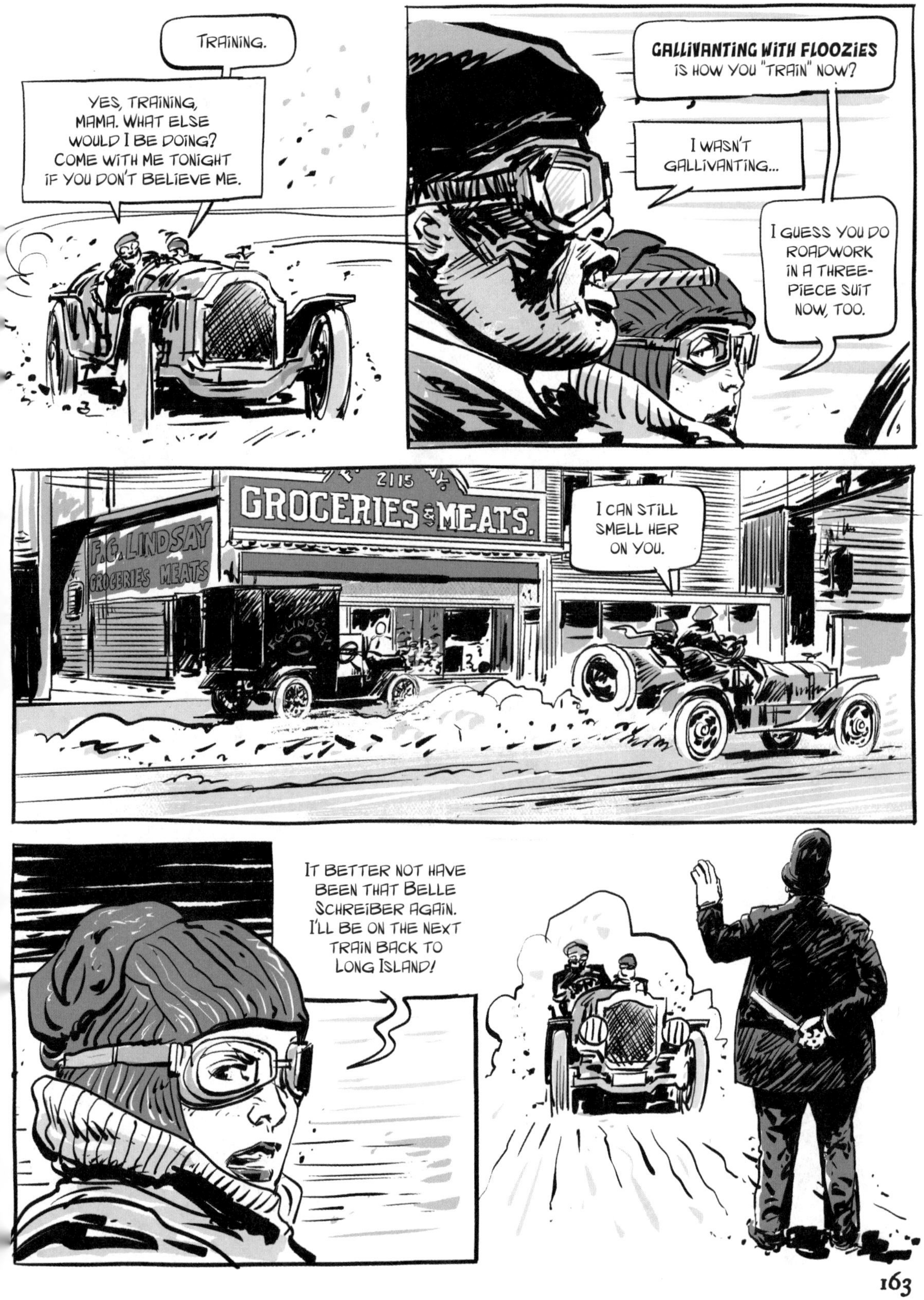
TRAINING.
YES, TRAINING, MAMA. WHAT ELSE WOULD I BE DOING? COME WITH ME TONIGHT IF YOU DON'T BELIEVE ME.
GALLIVANTING WITH FLOOZIES IS HOW YOU "TRAIN" NOW?
I WASN'T GALLIVANTING...
I GUESS YOU DO ROADWORK IN A THREE-PIECE SUIT NOW, TOO.
2115
GROCERIES & MEATS.
F.G. LINDSAY
GROCERIES MEATS
F.G. LINDSEY
I CAN STILL SMELL HER ON YOU.
IT BETTER NOT HAVE BEEN THAT BELLE SCHREIBER AGAIN. I'LL BE ON THE NEXT TRAIN BACK TO LONG ISLAND!

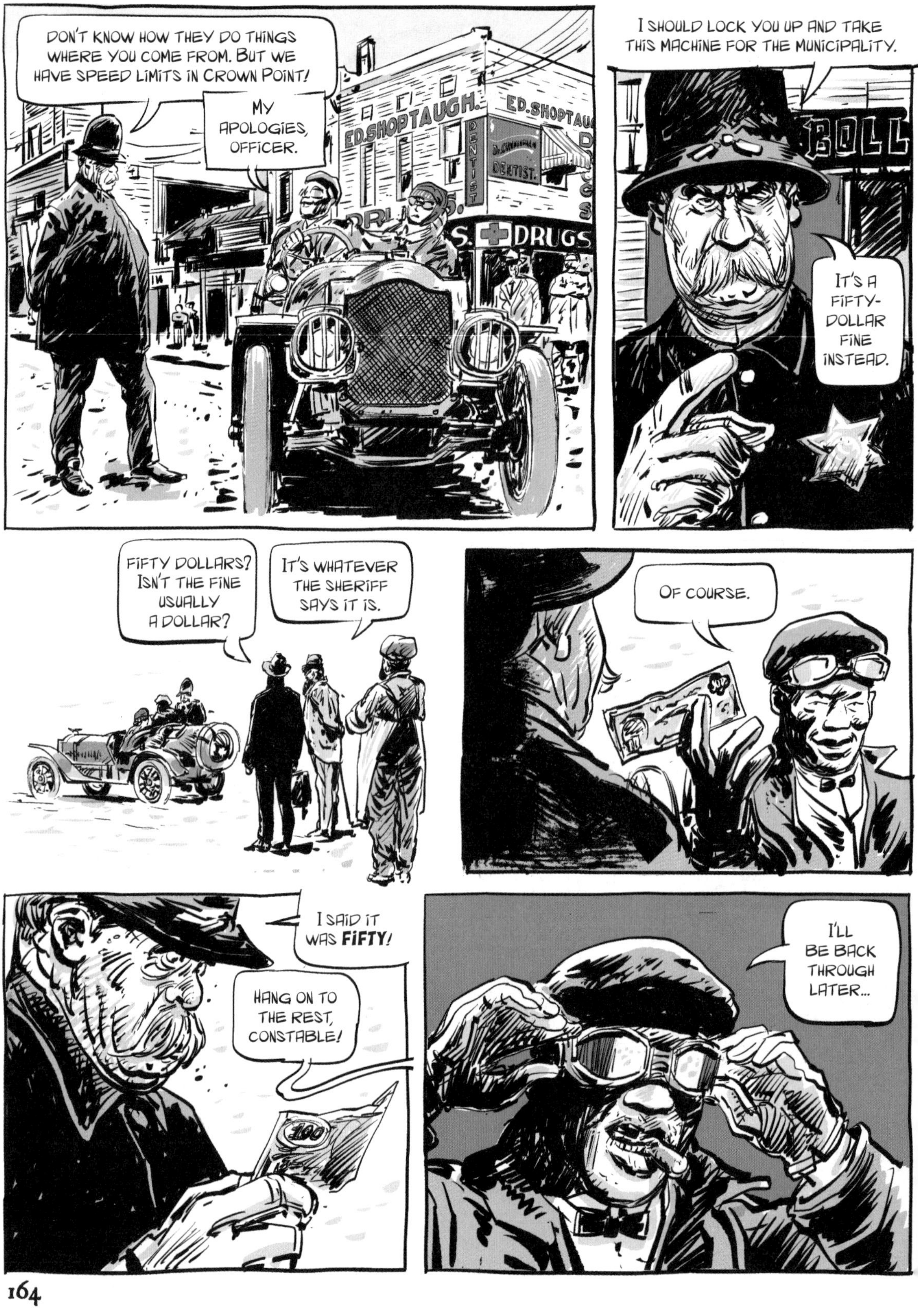

DON'T KNOW HOW THEY DO THINGS WHERE YOU COME FROM. BUT WE HAVE SPEED LIMITS IN CROWN POINT!
MY APOLOGIES, OFFICER.
ED. SHOPTAUGH.
DENTIST
DENTIST.
DRUGS
I SHOULD LOCK YOU UP AND TAKE THIS MACHINE FOR THE MUNICIPALITY.
IT'S A FIFTY-DOLLAR FINE INSTEAD.
FIFTY DOLLARS? ISN'T THE FINE USUALLY A DOLLAR?
IT'S WHATEVER THE SHERIFF SAYS IT IS.
OF COURSE.
I SAID IT WAS **FIFTY**!
HANG ON TO THE REST, CONSTABLE!
100
I'LL BE BACK THROUGH LATER...

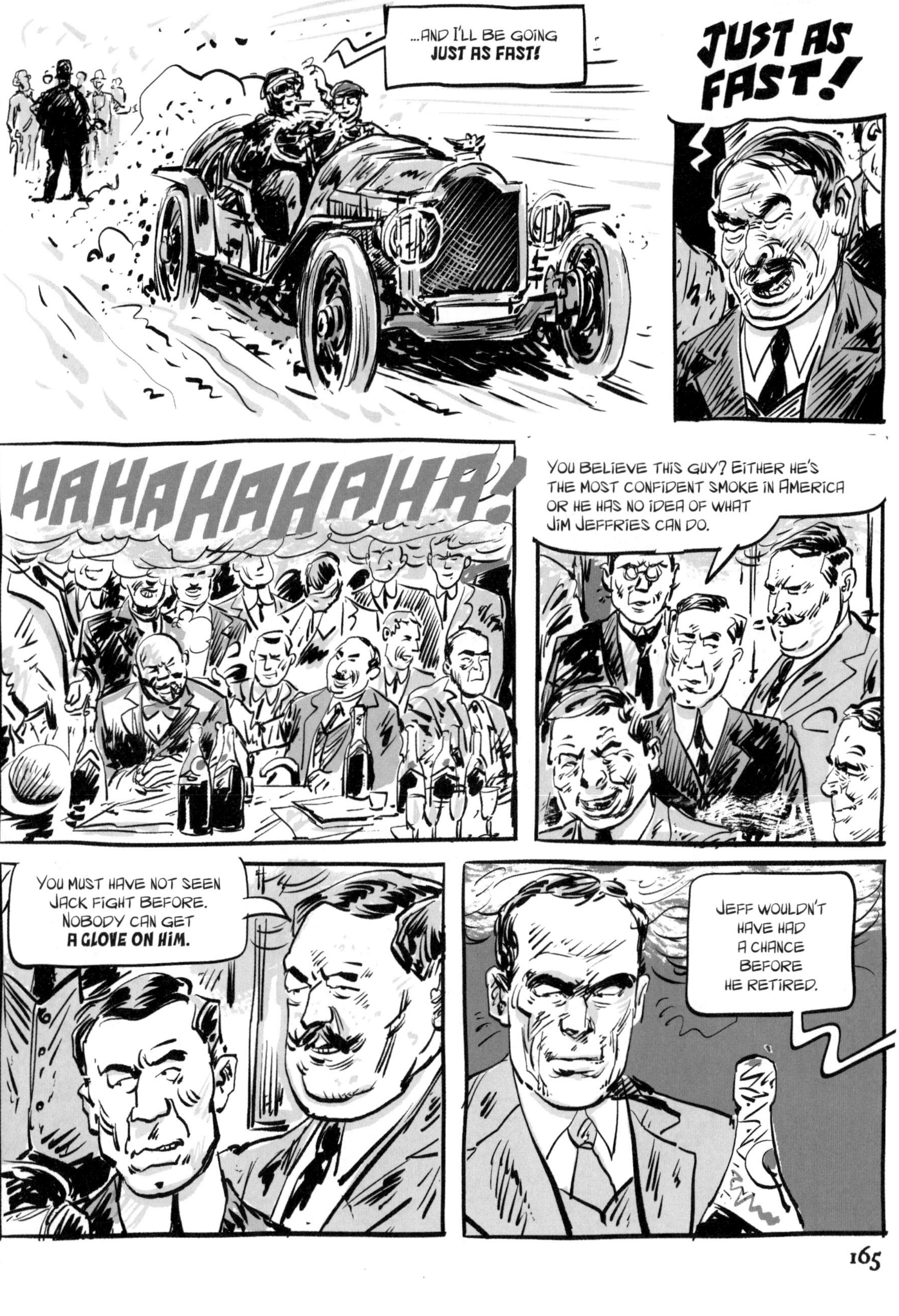
...AND I'LL BE GOING JUST AS FAST!
JUST AS FAST!
HAHAHAHAHAHA!
YOU BELIEVE THIS GUY? EITHER HE'S THE MOST CONFIDENT SMOKE IN AMERICA OR HE HAS NO IDEA OF WHAT JIM JEFFRIES CAN DO.
YOU MUST HAVE NOT SEEN JACK FIGHT BEFORE. NOBODY CAN GET A GLOVE ON HIM.
JEFF WOULDN'T HAVE HAD A CHANCE BEFORE HE RETIRED.

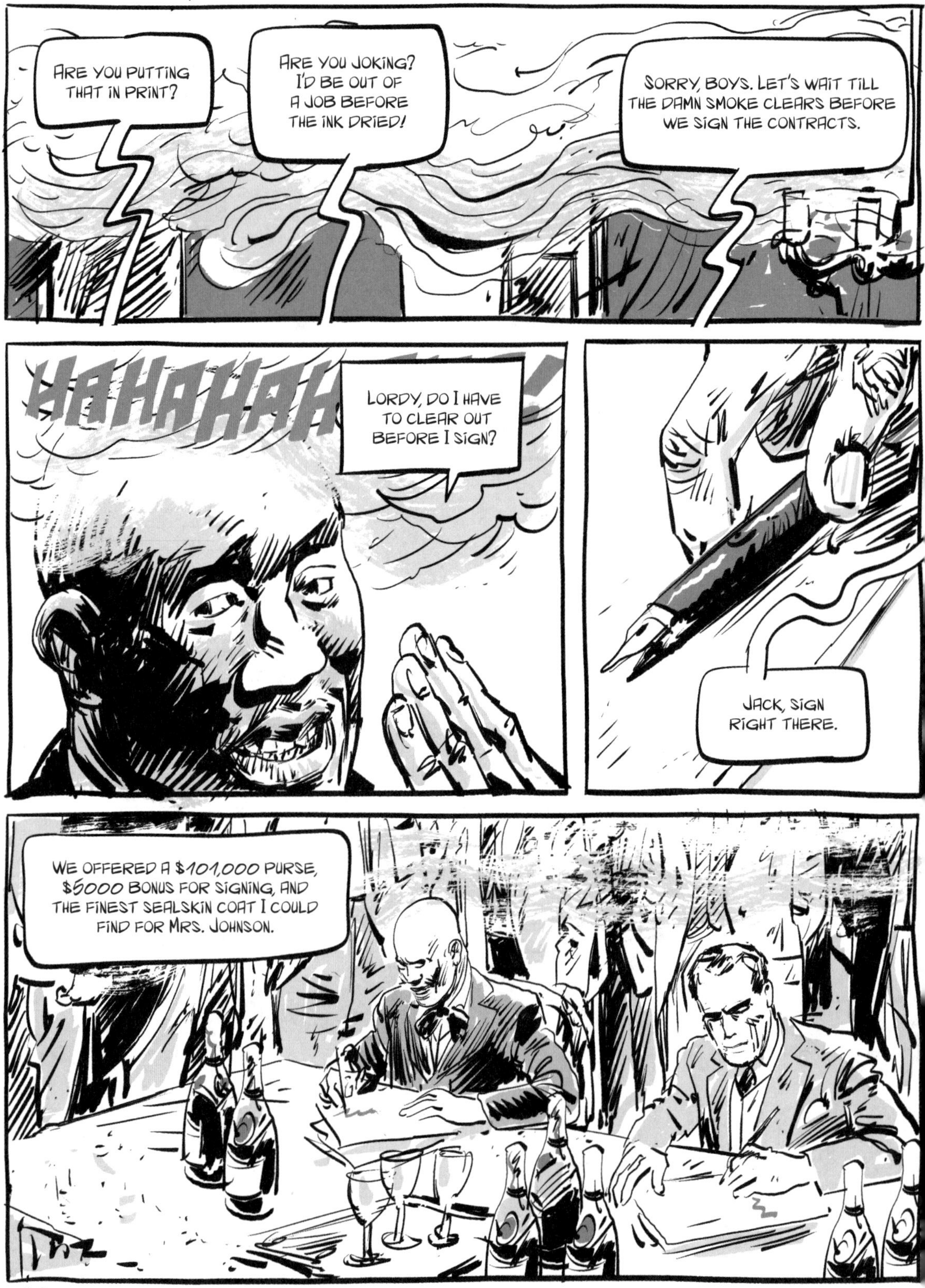
ARE YOU PUTTING THAT IN PRINT?
ARE YOU JOKING? I'D BE OUT OF A JOB BEFORE THE INK DRIED!
SORRY, BOYS. LET'S WAIT TILL THE DAMN SMOKE CLEARS BEFORE WE SIGN THE CONTRACTS.
HAHAHAH
LORDY, DO I HAVE TO CLEAR OUT BEFORE I SIGN?
JACK, SIGN RIGHT THERE.
WE OFFERED A $101,000 PURSE, $5000 BONUS FOR SIGNING, AND THE FINEST SEALSKIN COAT I COULD FIND FOR MRS. JOHNSON.

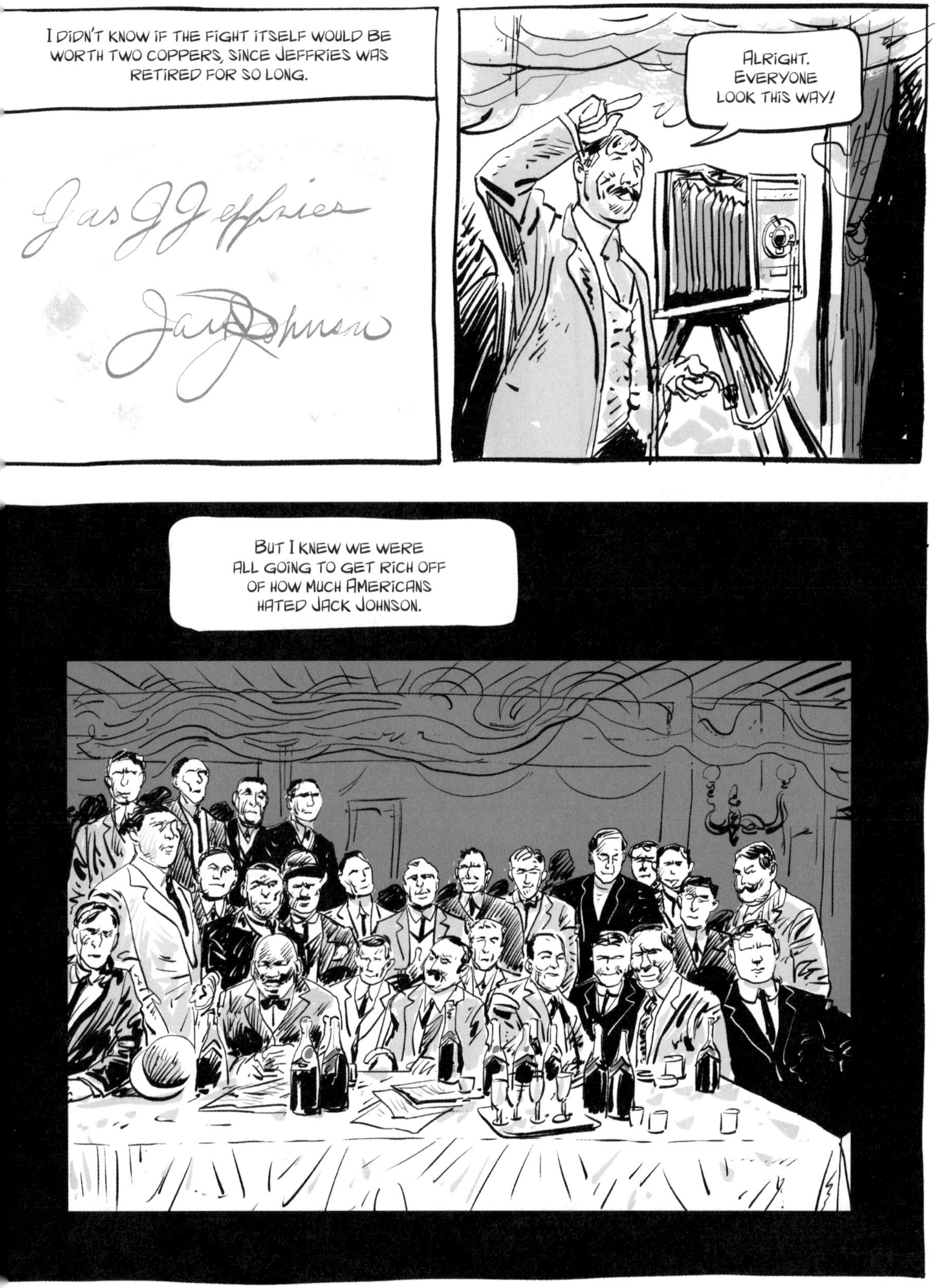
I DIDN'T KNOW IF THE FIGHT ITSELF WOULD BE WORTH TWO COPPERS, SINCE JEFFRIES WAS RETIRED FOR SO LONG.
Jas J Jeffries
Jack Johnson
ALRIGHT. EVERYONE LOOK THIS WAY!
BUT I KNEW WE WERE ALL GOING TO GET RICH OFF OF HOW MUCH AMERICANS HATED JACK JOHNSON.

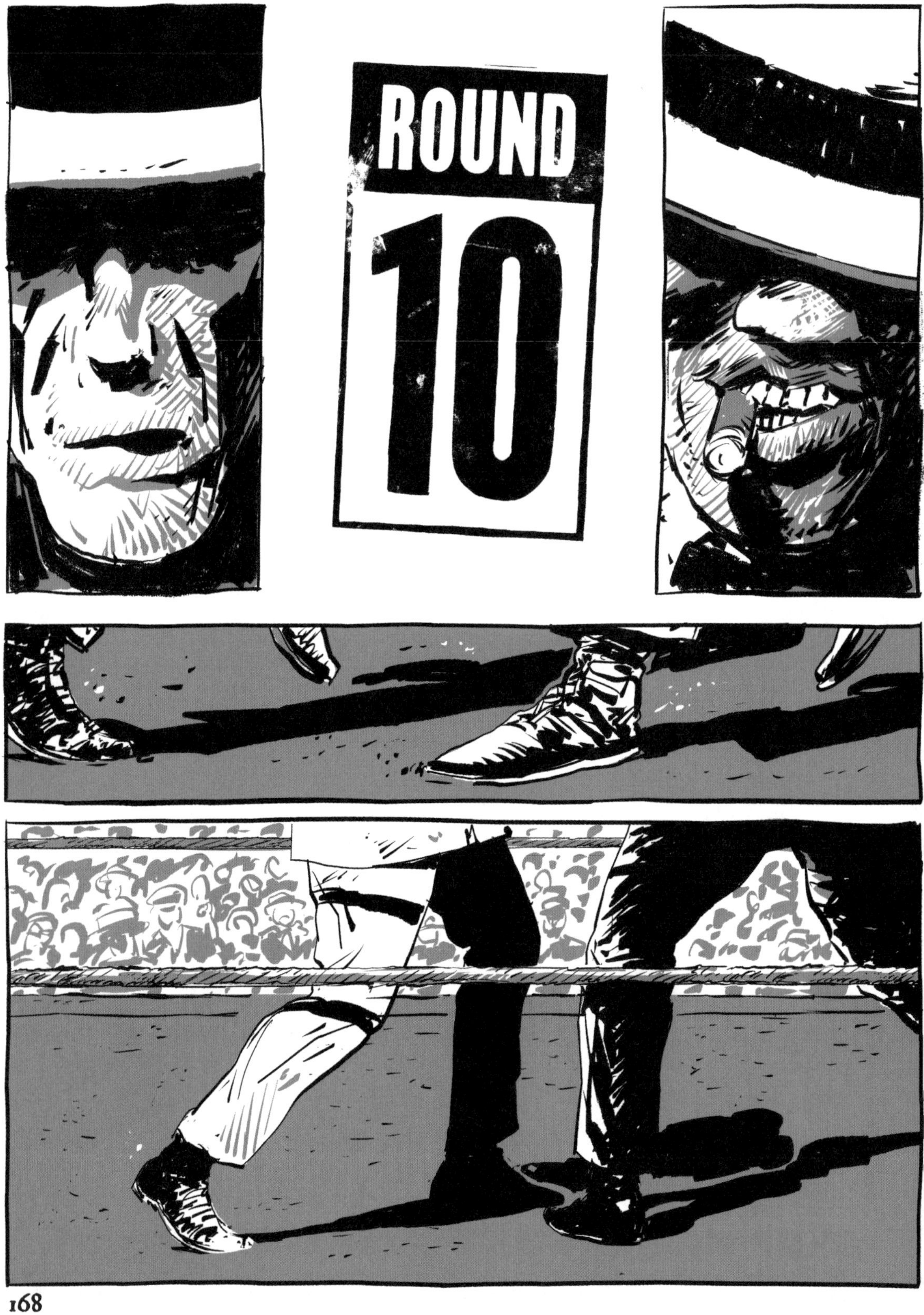
ROUND
10

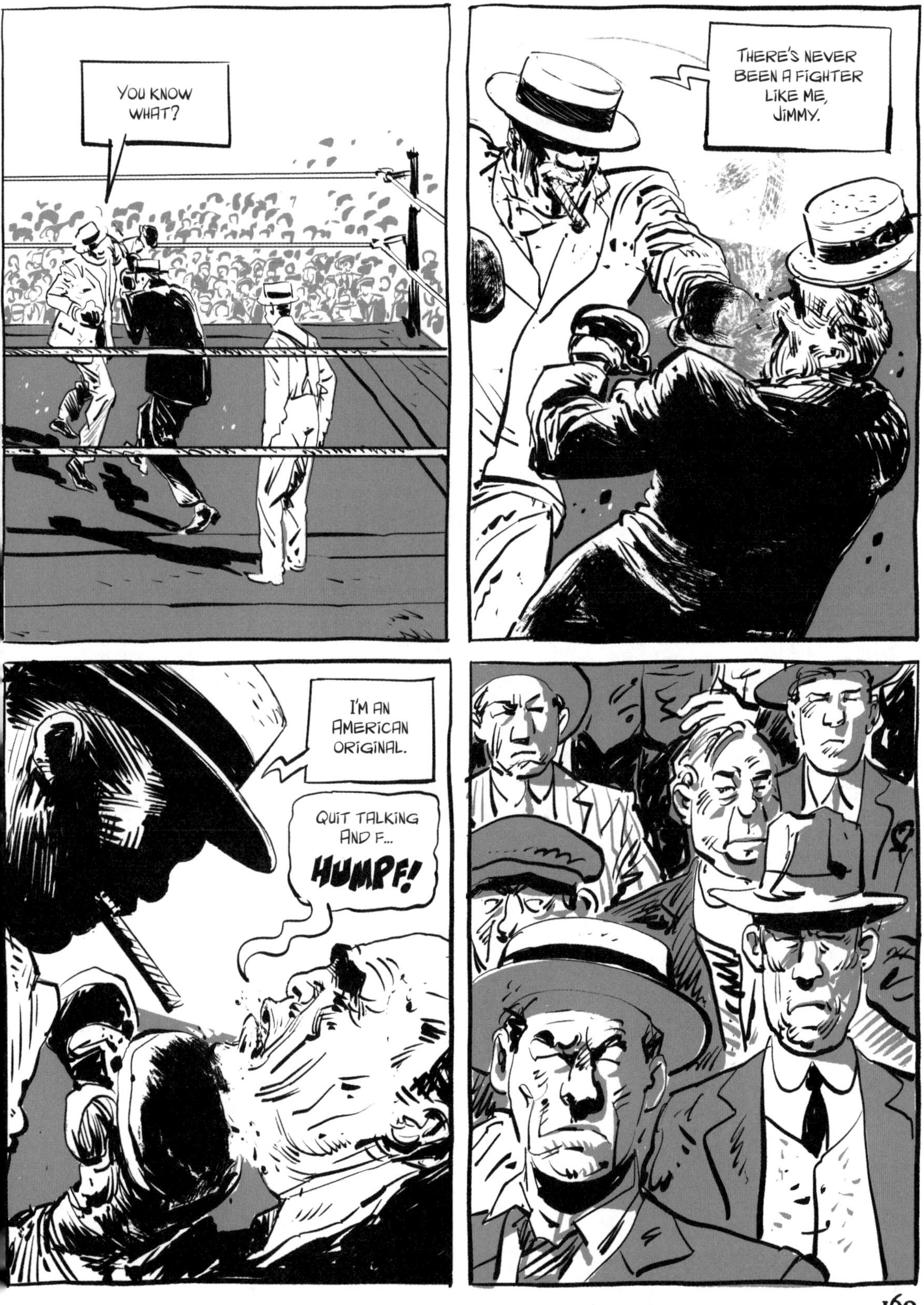
YOU KNOW WHAT?
THERE'S NEVER BEEN A FIGHTER LIKE ME, JIMMY.
I'M AN AMERICAN ORIGINAL.
QUIT TALKING AND F...
HUMPF!

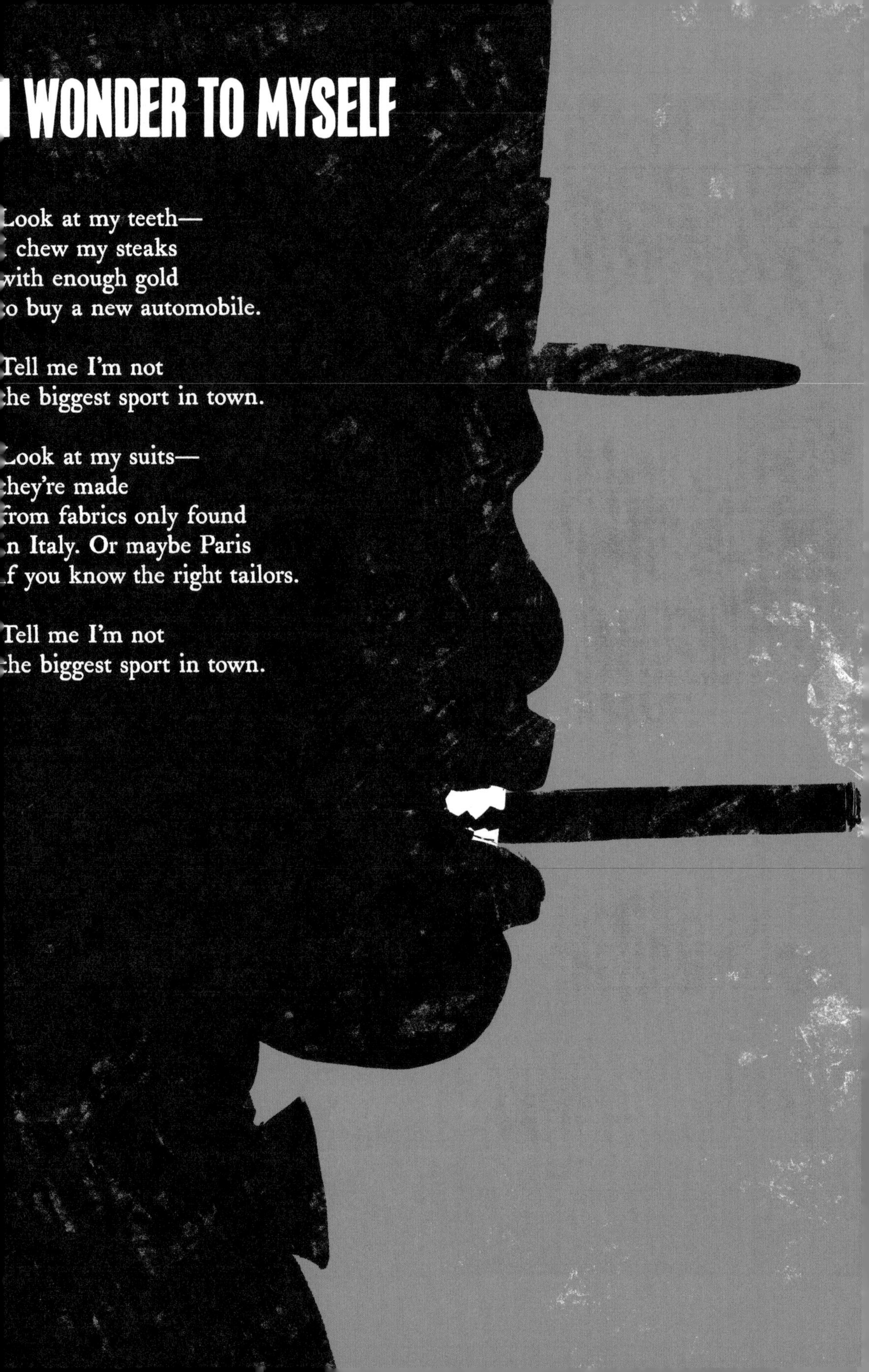

I WONDER TO MYSELF

Look at my teeth—
I chew my steaks
with enough gold
to buy a new automobile.

Tell me I'm not
the biggest sport in town.

Look at my suits—
they're made
from fabrics only found
in Italy. Or maybe Paris
if you know the right tailors.

Tell me I'm not
the biggest sport in town.

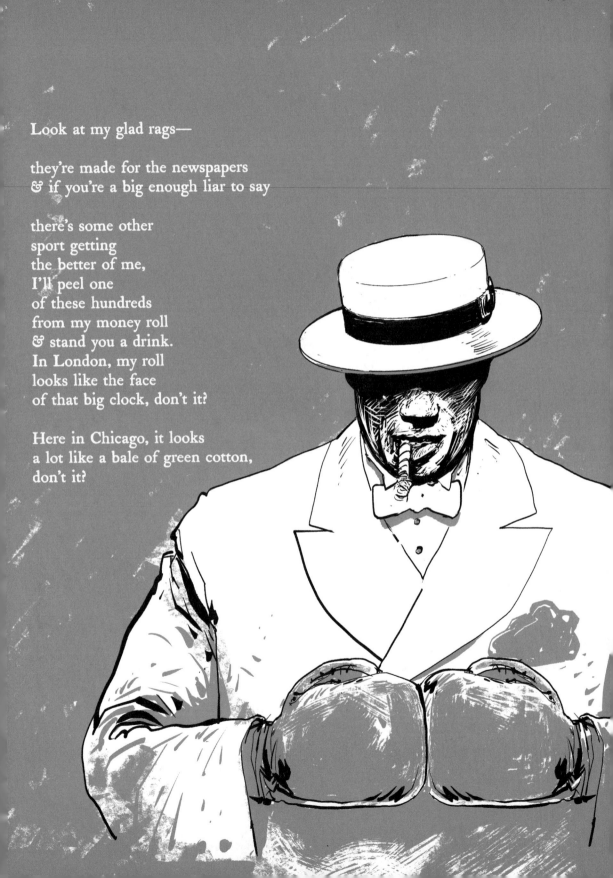

Look at my glad rags—

they're made for the newspapers
& if you're a big enough liar to say

there's some other
sport getting
the better of me,
I'll peel one
of these hundreds
from my money roll
& stand you a drink.
In London, my roll
looks like the face
of that big clock, don't it?

Here in Chicago, it looks
a lot like a bale of green cotton,
don't it?

Look at the Café de Champion—

It used to be called Turner Hall & Blacks were only allowed in if they were carrying serving trays. The minute I bought it, I changed the name so everyone would know it was my new headquarters...

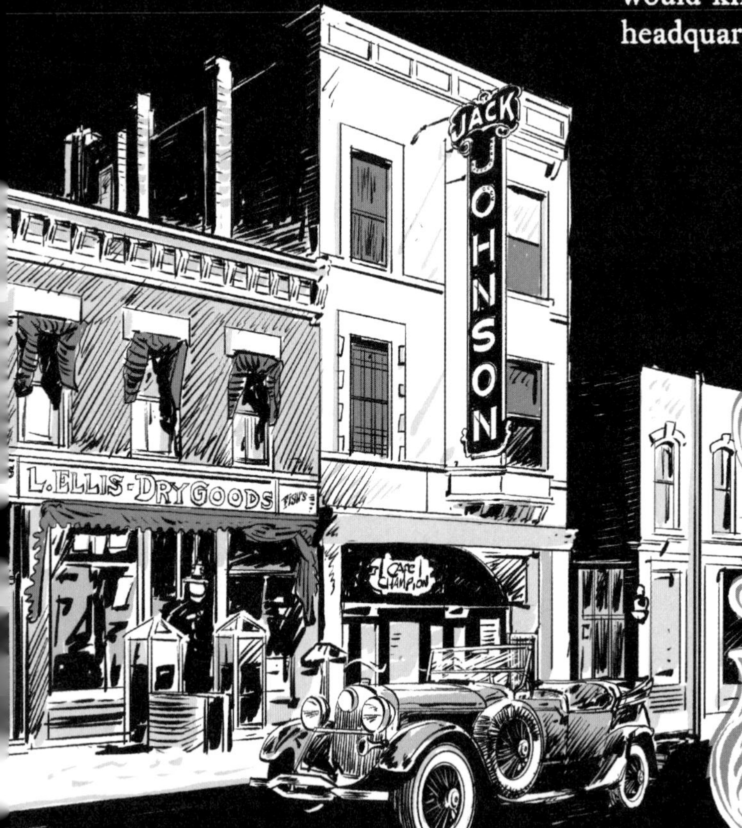
JACK
JOHNSON
L. ELLIS - DRY GOODS
CAFE CHAMPION

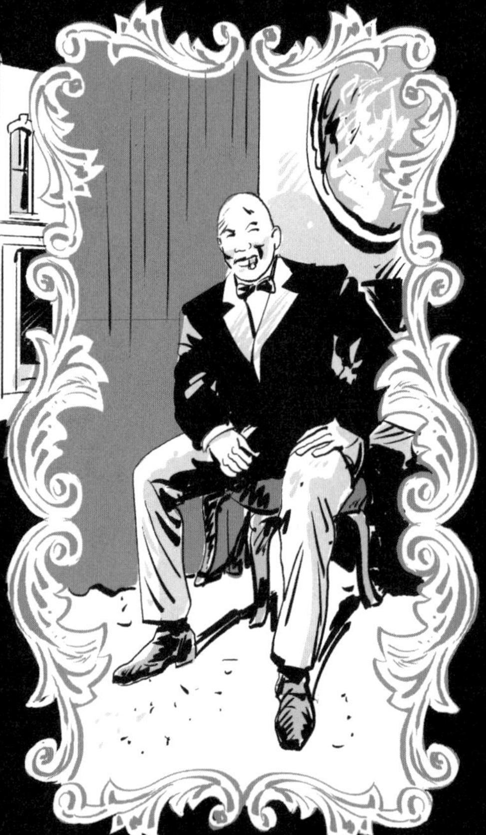

...& I renovated the joint to reflect my extravagant tastes.

I started from the front door and worked back: gold inlays everywhere, mahogany for all the wood. This is a Jack Johnson enterprise. Everything is expensive.

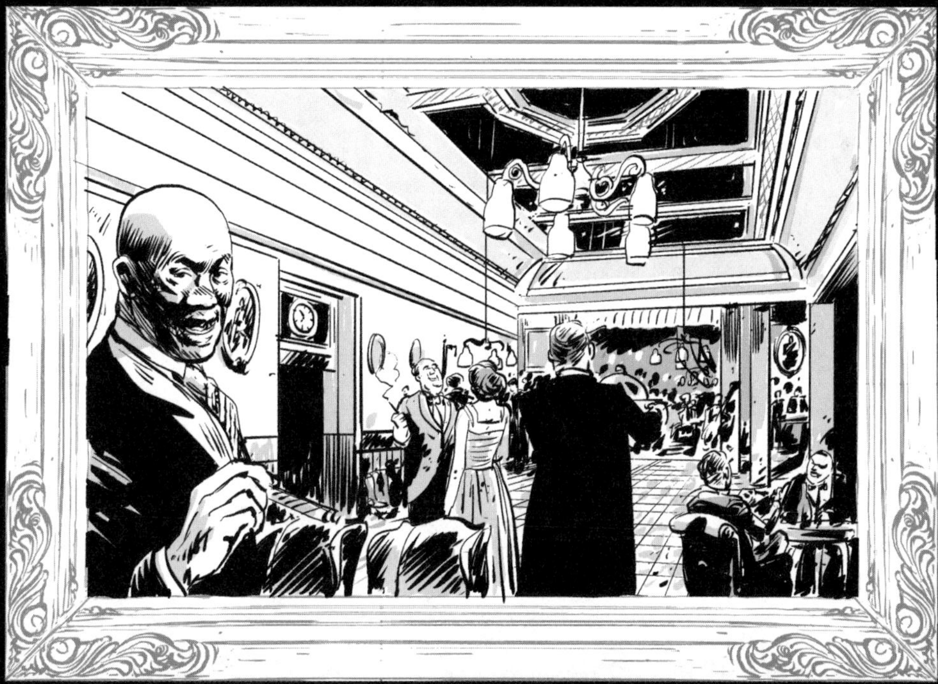

All the waiters wear tuxedoes and white gloves. All the women are beauties.

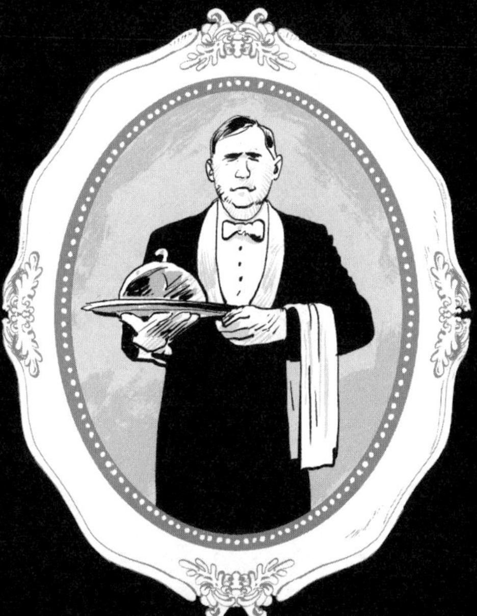

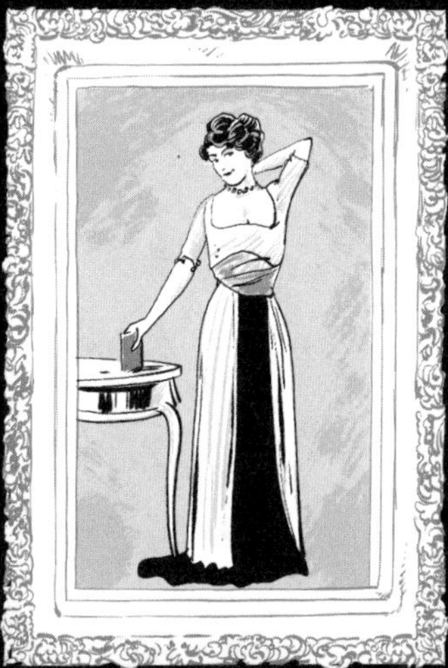

The mosaic on the floor was imported from London. The bar was hand carved in Barcelona. See those spittoons winking along the bar? Pure silver & they cost $60 each.

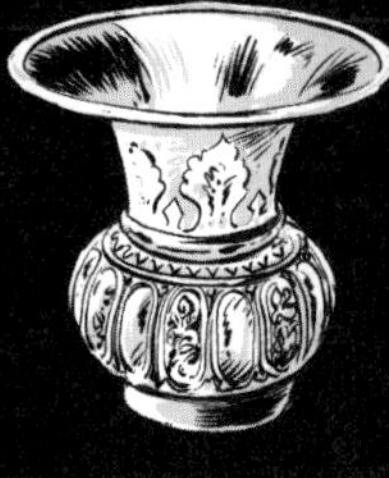

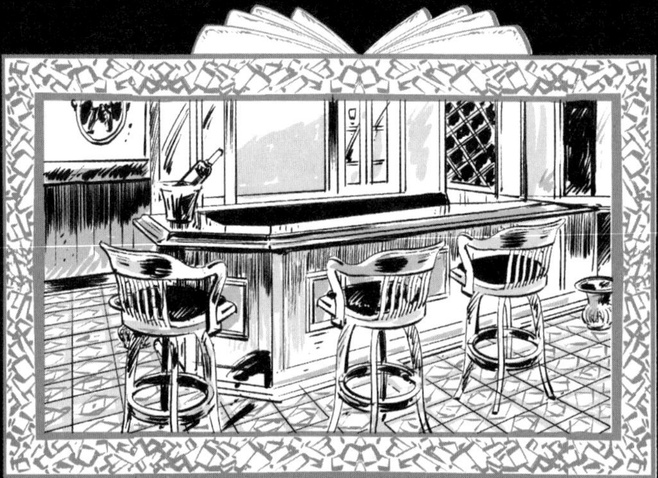

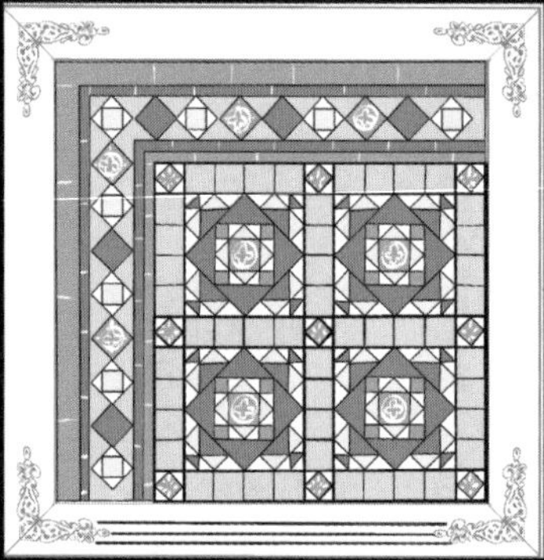

The artwork was painted by the finest artists from all over the world. My favorite is the one of Etta & me. Even a painting of her is the most beautiful thing in any room.

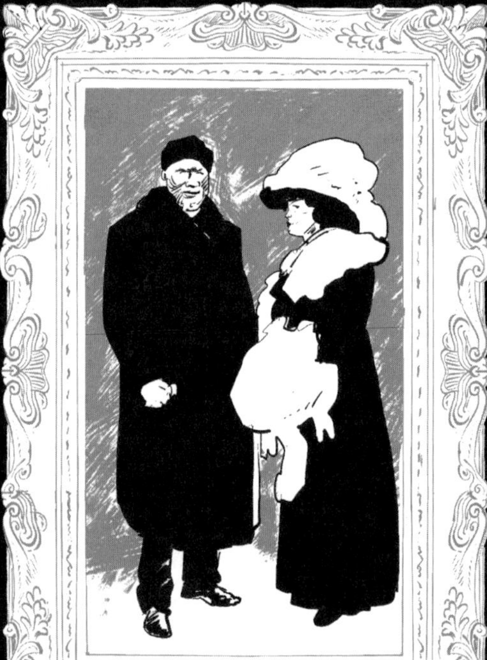

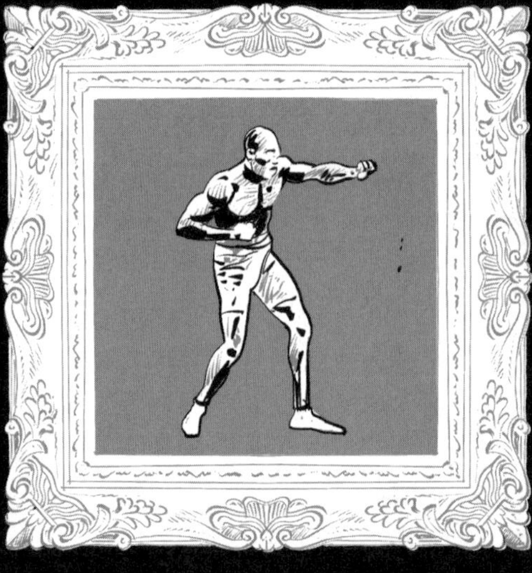

I told you this is a Jack Johnson enterprise.

Upstairs are the private dining areas where we serve Chicago's finest lobster and steak.

That door? That door leads to Etta's rooms.

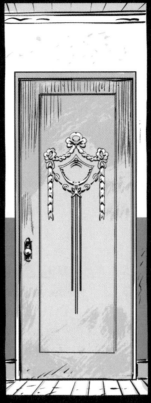

IT WOULDN'T BE PROPER FOR ME TO TAKE YOU UP THERE WHILE SHE'S RESTING.

It's easy for me to talk about
my victories & my automobiles
& my resplendent accoutrement.
You can see all of that yourselves.
What's not so easy are the nights
I slept on dirt floors or in the backs
of boxcars with my arm as a pillow
trying to get a little bit of this
American Dream. Or the days
I was so hungry I would have
cooked up the leather on my shoes
if it wasn't already worn down
to nothing. It's hard to do much
of anything when your stomach
is so empty it won't growl anymore.

What's not easy to talk about are
the times I got cheated, sometimes
by managers, other times by people
I counted as my friends. Like that
time in Paris with Frank Moran
when the organizers disappeared
with the prize money & left me
with nothing but wishes in my
wallet. Or that time in Colma with
Stanley Ketchel when he tried
to double-cross me when the fix
was already in. Sometimes
I lost even when I thought
I was winning.

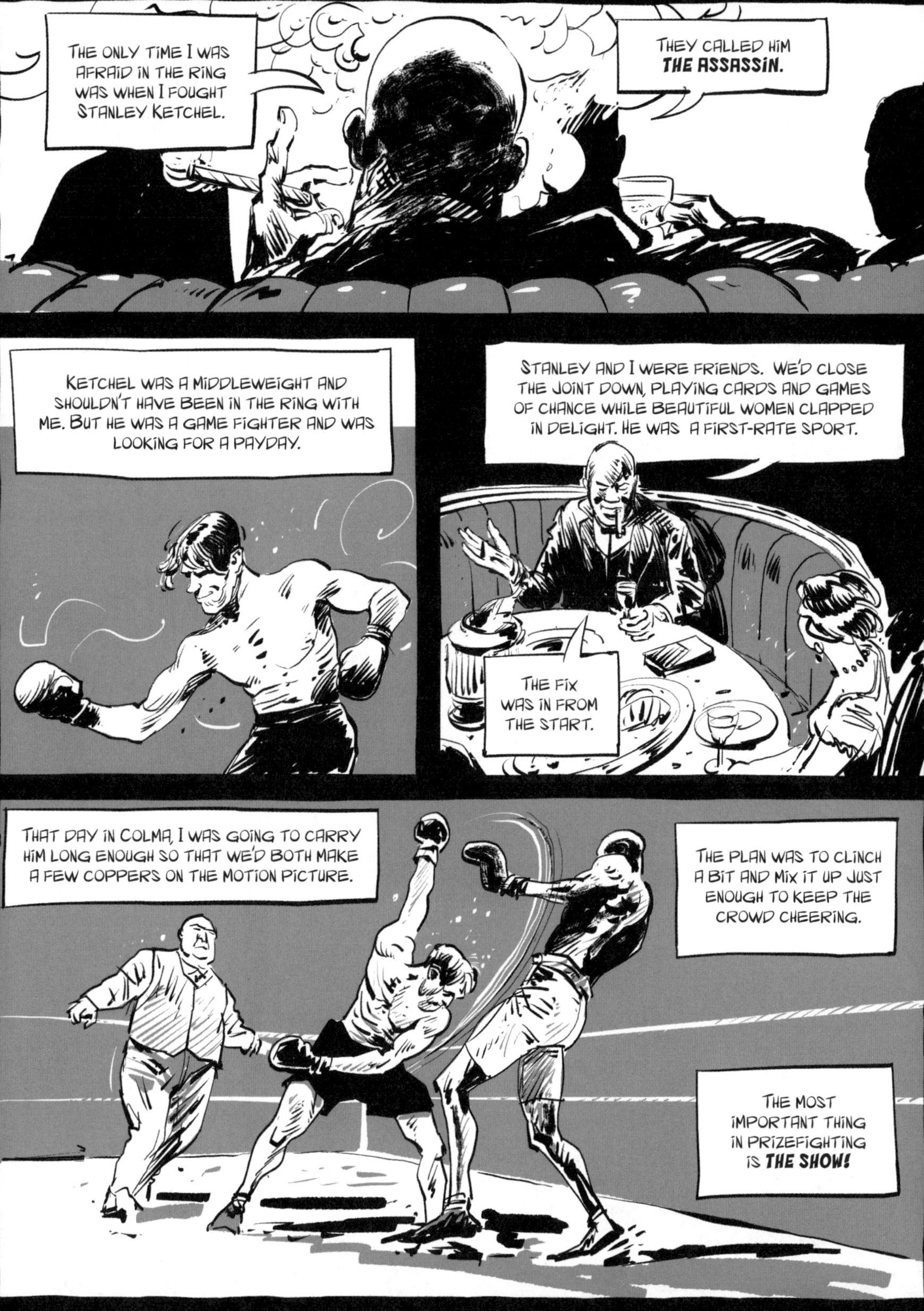
THE ONLY TIME I WAS AFRAID IN THE RING WAS WHEN I FOUGHT STANLEY KETCHEL.
THEY CALLED HIM **THE ASSASSIN.**
KETCHEL WAS A MIDDLEWEIGHT AND SHOULDN'T HAVE BEEN IN THE RING WITH ME. BUT HE WAS A GAME FIGHTER AND WAS LOOKING FOR A PAYDAY.
STANLEY AND I WERE FRIENDS. WE'D CLOSE THE JOINT DOWN, PLAYING CARDS AND GAMES OF CHANCE WHILE BEAUTIFUL WOMEN CLAPPED IN DELIGHT. HE WAS A FIRST-RATE SPORT.
THE FIX WAS IN FROM THE START.
THAT DAY IN COLMA, I WAS GOING TO CARRY HIM LONG ENOUGH SO THAT WE'D BOTH MAKE A FEW COPPERS ON THE MOTION PICTURE.
THE PLAN WAS TO CLINCH A BIT AND MIX IT UP JUST ENOUGH TO KEEP THE CROWD CHEERING.
THE MOST IMPORTANT THING IN PRIZEFIGHTING IS **THE SHOW!**

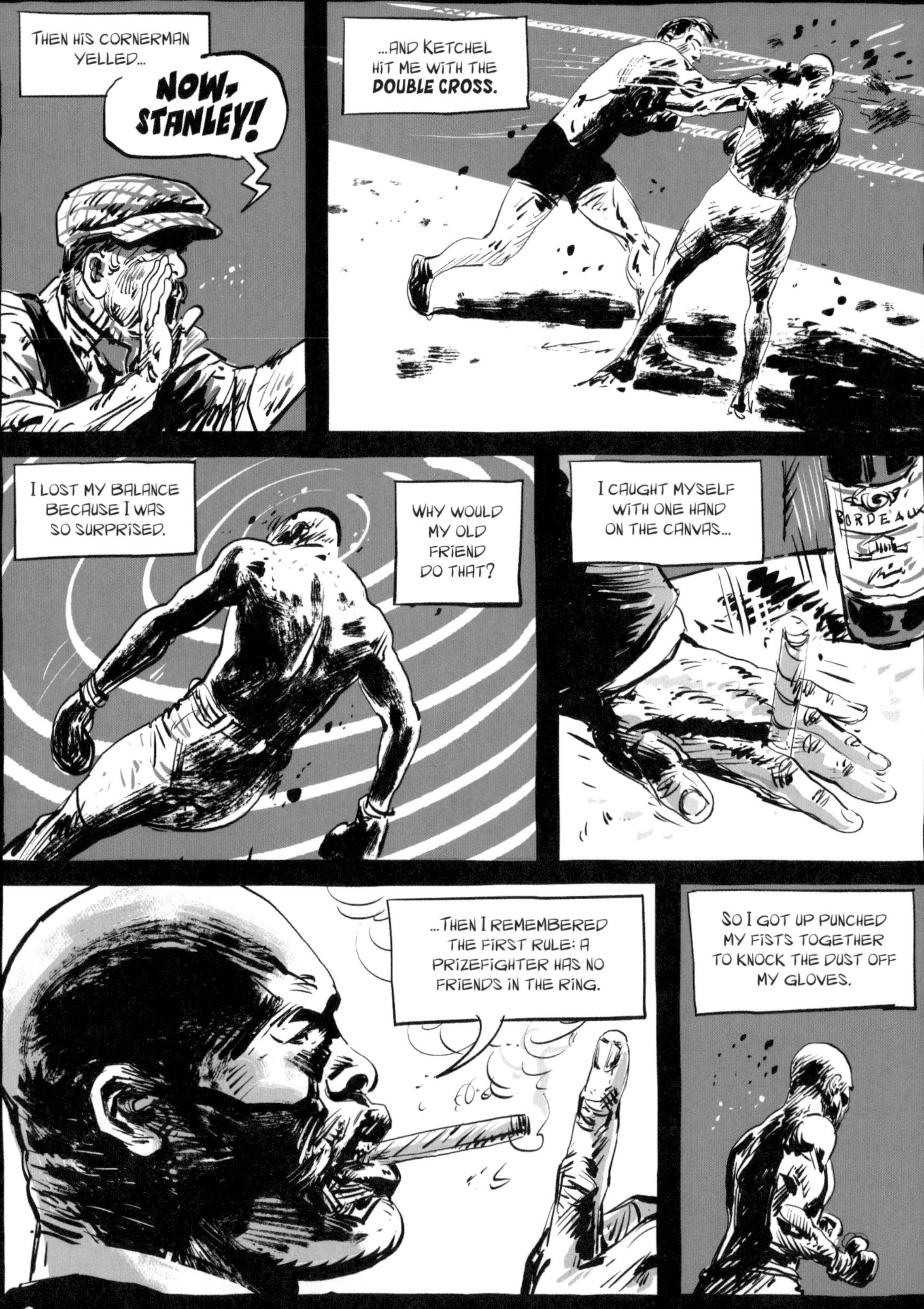
THEN HIS CORNERMAN YELLED...
NOW, STANLEY!
...AND KETCHEL HIT ME WITH THE **DOUBLE CROSS.**
I LOST MY BALANCE BECAUSE I WAS SO SURPRISED.
WHY WOULD MY OLD FRIEND DO THAT?
I CAUGHT MYSELF WITH ONE HAND ON THE CANVAS...
BORDEAUX
...THEN I REMEMBERED THE FIRST RULE: A PRIZEFIGHTER HAS NO FRIENDS IN THE RING.
SO I GOT UP PUNCHED MY FISTS TOGETHER TO KNOCK THE DUST OFF MY GLOVES.

I COULD SEE IN KETCHEL'S EYES HE KNEW HE'D MADE A MISTAKE. THAT PUNCH WAS HIS BEST AND IT DIDN'T EVEN MOVE ME.

I HIT HIM SO HARD *WE BOTH* WENT TO THE CANVAS.

I STAYED BACK, LEANING ON THE ROPES AS HE LAID THERE.

THE CROWD WAS AS QUIET AS CHURCH ON TUESDAY.

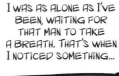

I WAS AS ALONE AS I'VE BEEN, WAITING FOR THAT MAN TO TAKE A BREATH. THAT'S WHEN I NOTICED SOMETHING...

...TWO OF HIS TEETH WERE STUCK IN MY GLOVE!

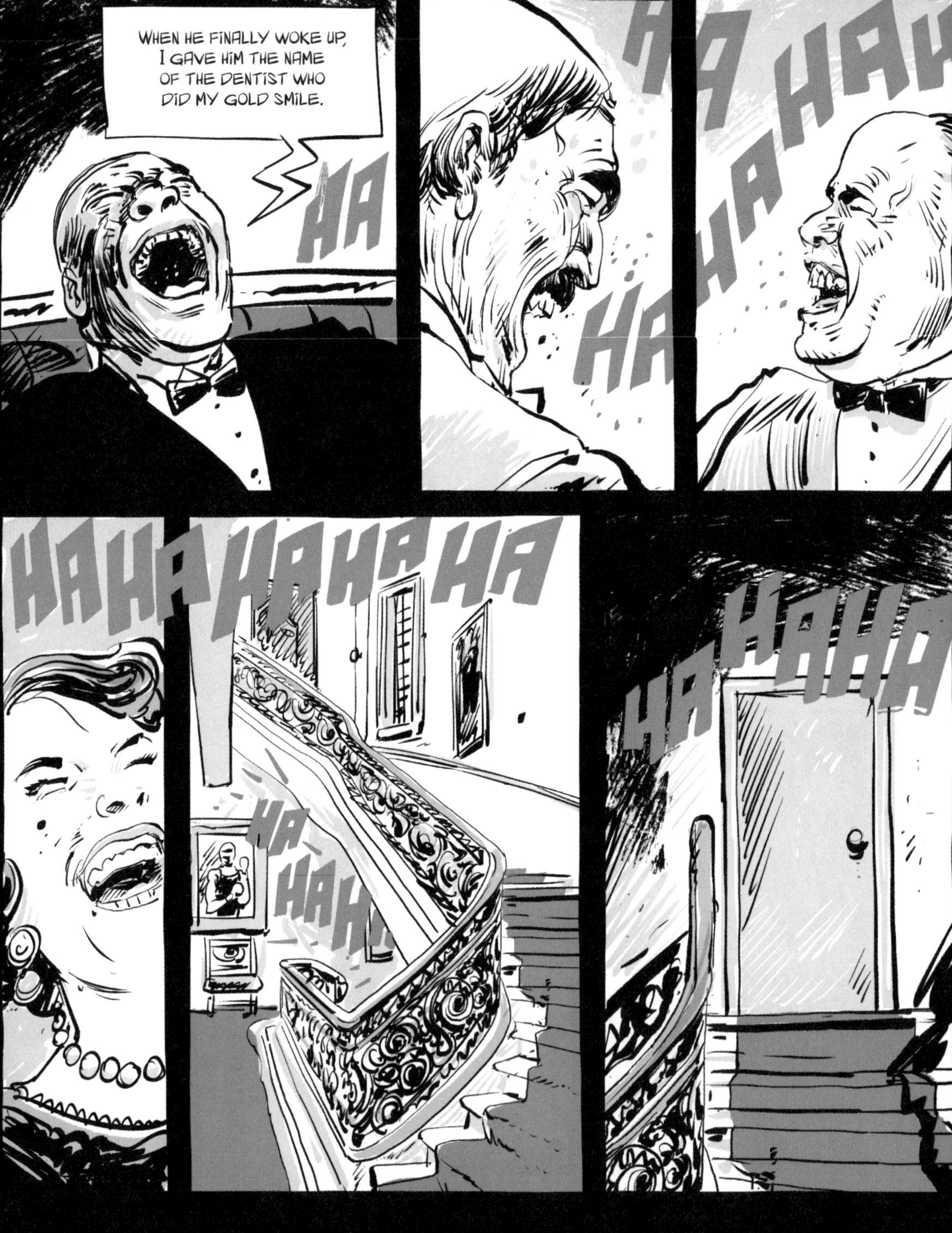
WHEN HE FINALLY WOKE UP, I GAVE HIM THE NAME OF THE DENTIST WHO DID MY GOLD SMILE.
HA
HAHAHAHA
HAHAHAHAHAHA
HA
HAHA
HAHAHAHA

People want to take on the world with their fists like he does.

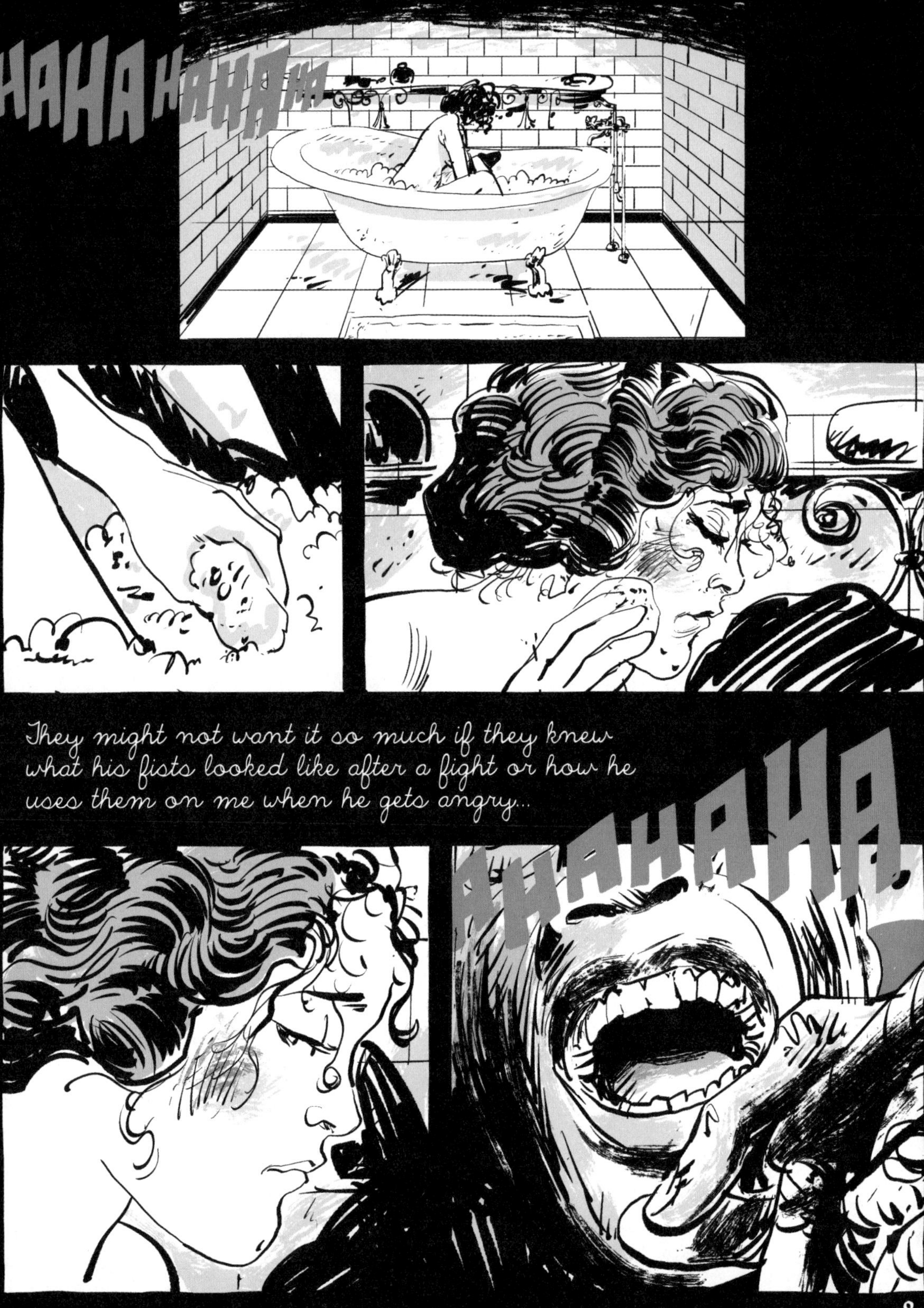
HAHAHAHAHAHA
They might not want it so much if they knew what his fists looked like after a fight or how he uses them on me when he gets angry...
AHAHAHAHA

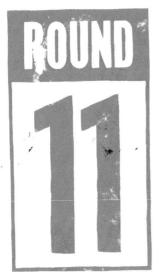

ROUND 11

Jeffries got in his shots & I gave them right back. Only he couldn't smile after & if he could, it wouldn't have been very pretty.

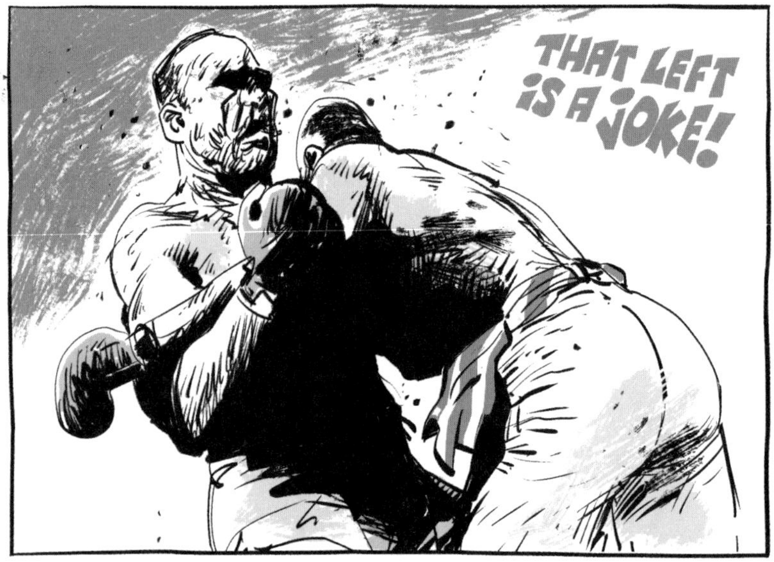
THAT LEFT IS A JOKE!

KILL THE COON!

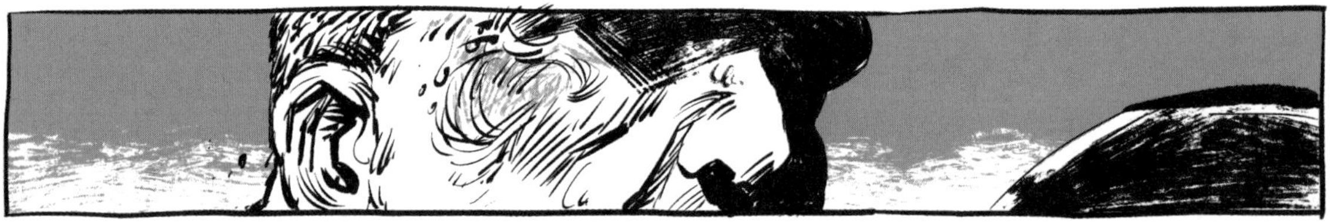

I know what that look means. The old ship is sinking.

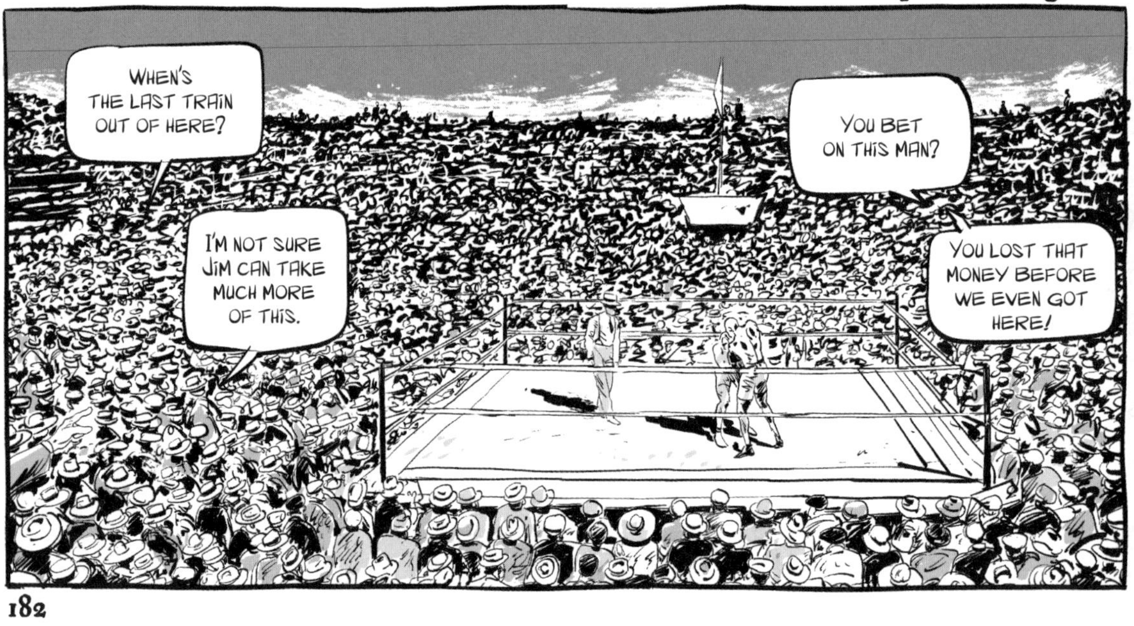
WHEN'S THE LAST TRAIN OUT OF HERE?
I'M NOT SURE JIM CAN TAKE MUCH MORE OF THIS.
YOU BET ON THIS MAN?
YOU LOST THAT MONEY BEFORE WE EVEN GOT HERE!

An angry crowd burning up in the heat.

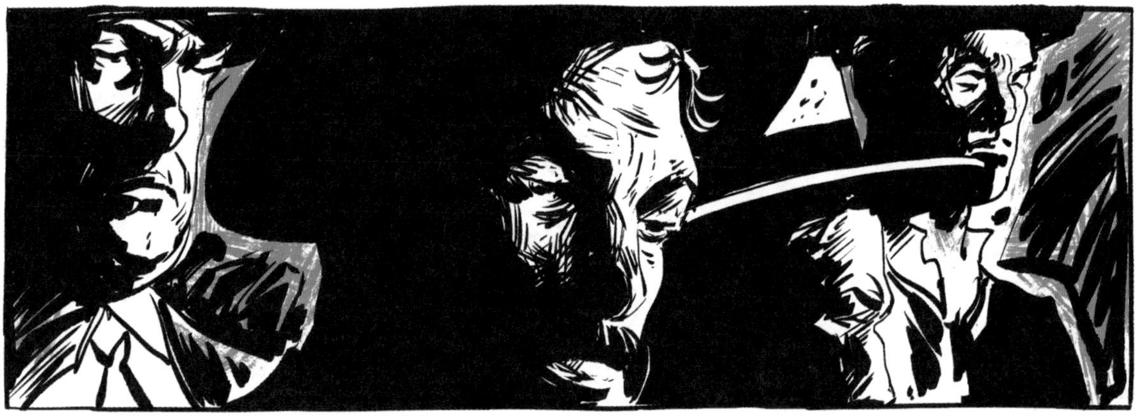

Corbett pacing outside the ring covered in sweat with nothing left to say.

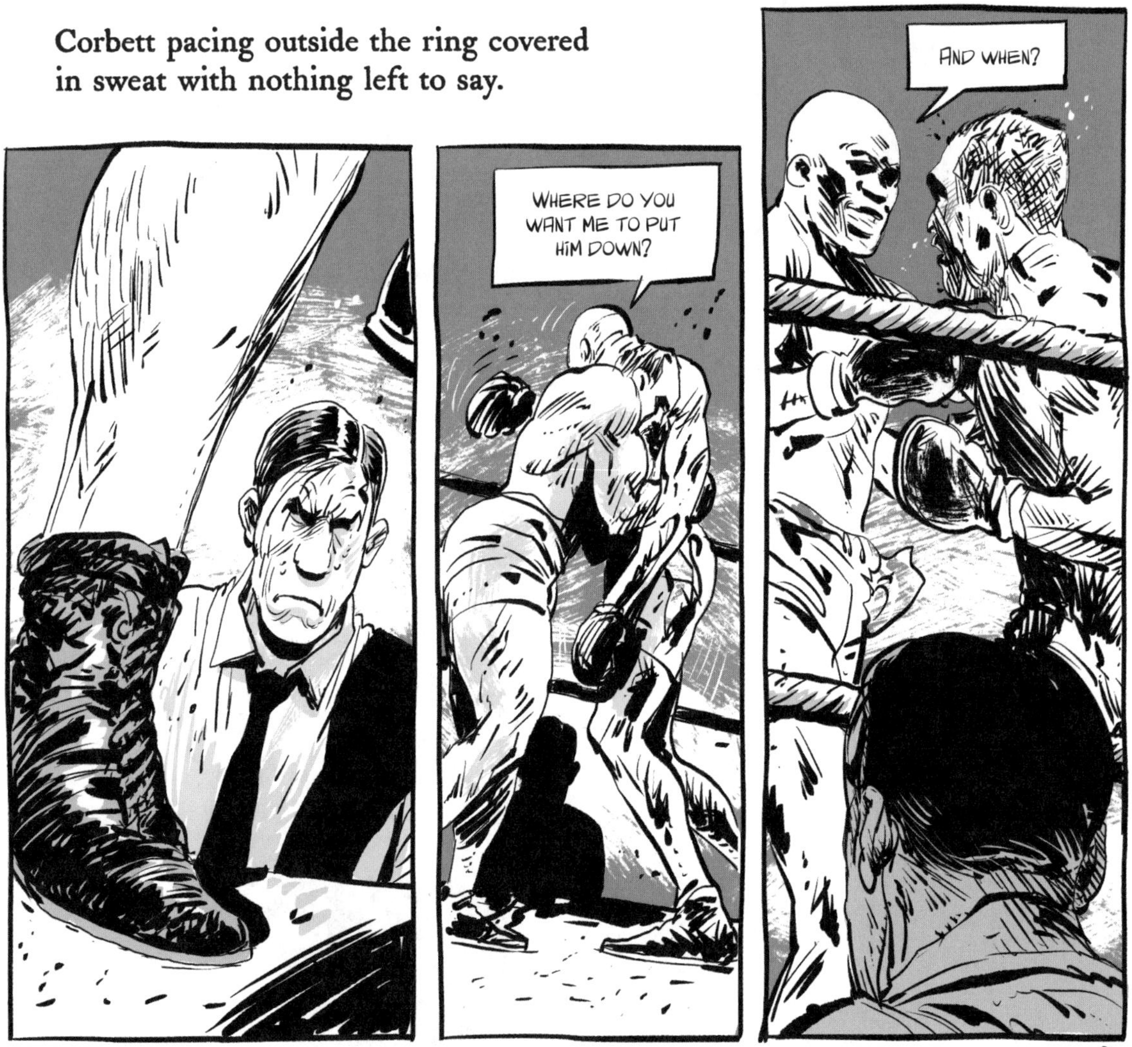
WHERE DO YOU WANT ME TO PUT HIM DOWN?
AND WHEN?

A straight right cut Jeffries's left cheek.

A straight left blocked up his right eye & Tex Rickard pulling me away from my victim.

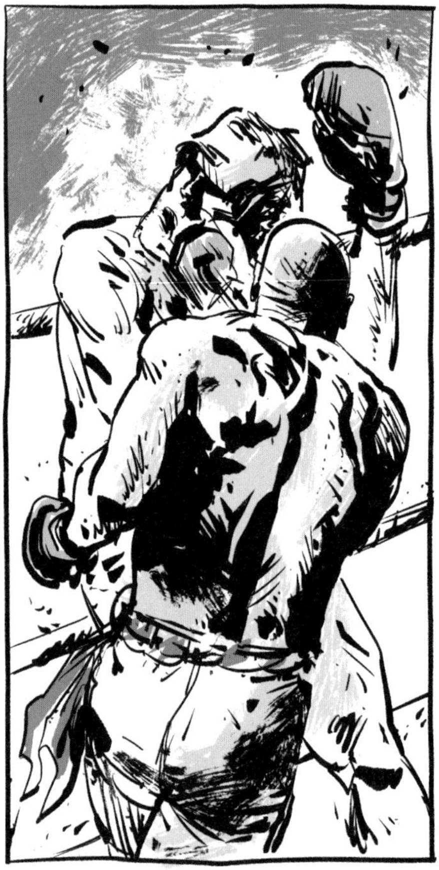

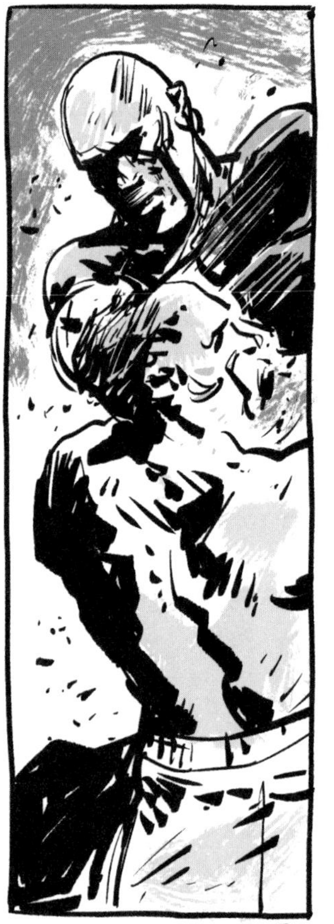

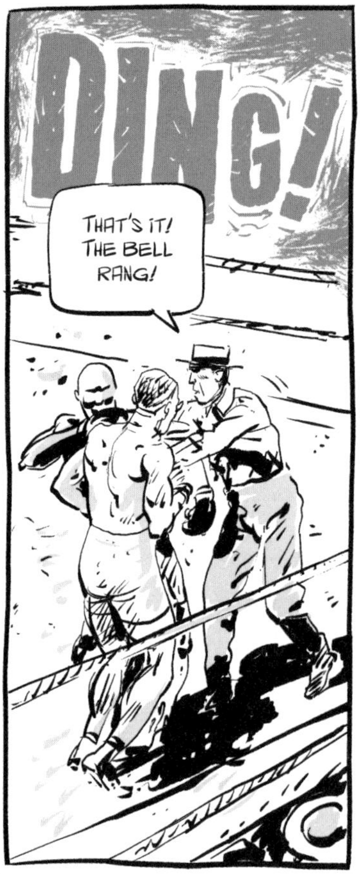
DING!
THAT'S IT! THE BELL RANG!

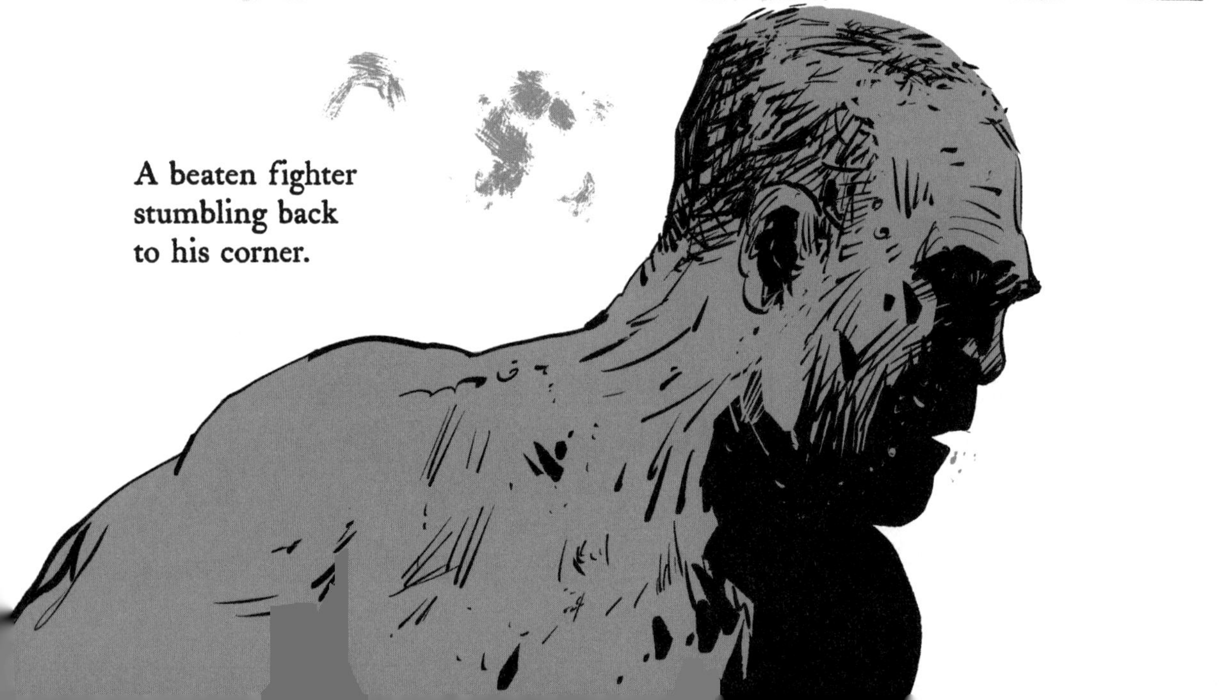
A beaten fighter stumbling back to his corner.

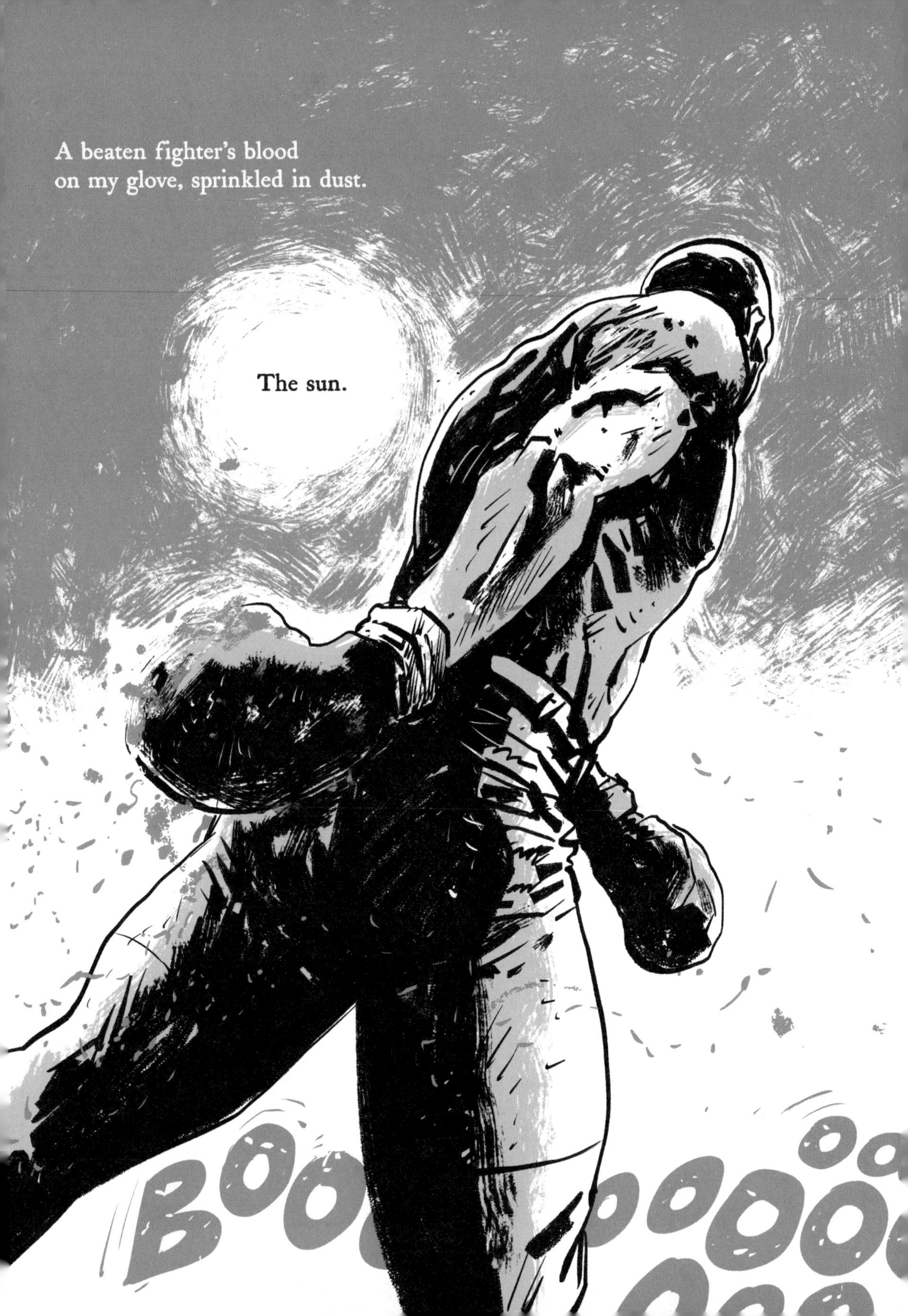
A beaten fighter's blood
on my glove, sprinkled in dust.
The sun.
BOOOOOOOOO

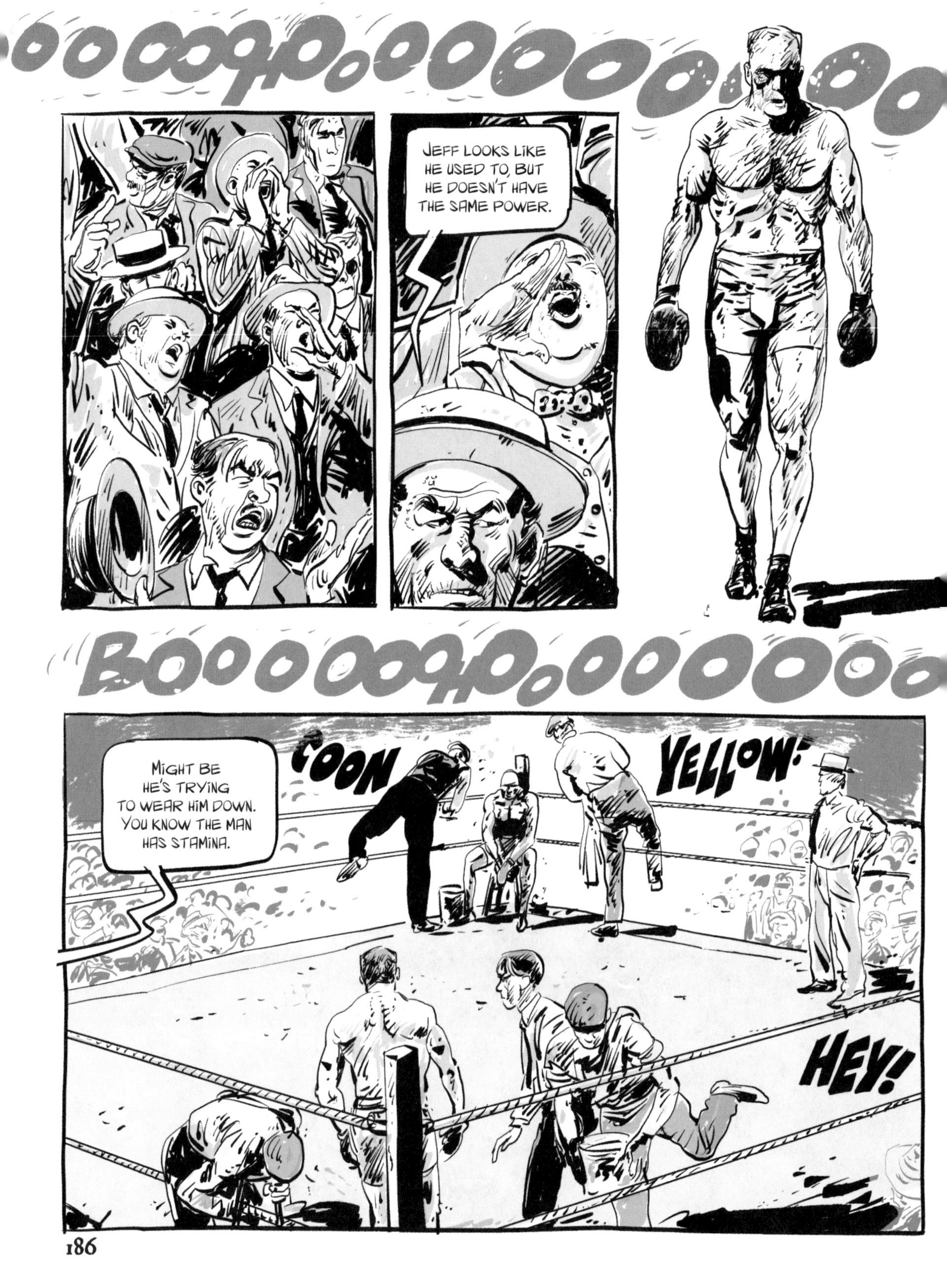

JEFF LOOKS LIKE HE USED TO, BUT HE DOESN'T HAVE THE SAME POWER.
BOOOOOOOOOOOO
MIGHT BE HE'S TRYING TO WEAR HIM DOWN. YOU KNOW THE MAN HAS STAMINA.
COON
YELLOW!
HEY!

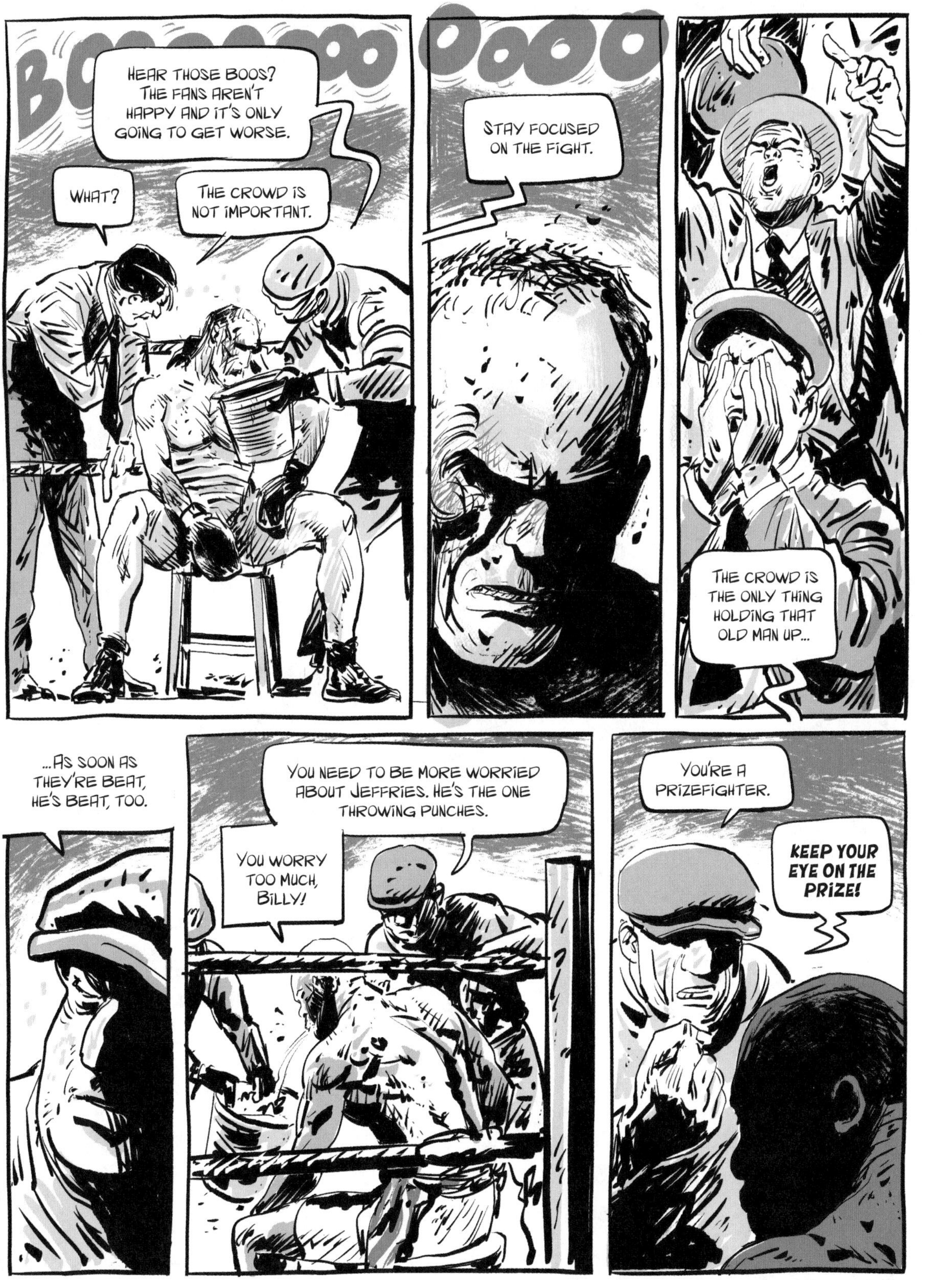
BOOOOOOOOOOOOO
HEAR THOSE BOOS? THE FANS AREN'T HAPPY AND IT'S ONLY GOING TO GET WORSE.
WHAT?
THE CROWD IS NOT IMPORTANT.
STAY FOCUSED ON THE FIGHT.
THE CROWD IS THE ONLY THING HOLDING THAT OLD MAN UP...
...AS SOON AS THEY'RE BEAT, HE'S BEAT, TOO.
YOU NEED TO BE MORE WORRIED ABOUT JEFFRIES. HE'S THE ONE THROWING PUNCHES.
YOU WORRY TOO MUCH, BILLY!
YOU'RE A PRIZEFIGHTER.
KEEP YOUR EYE ON THE PRIZE!

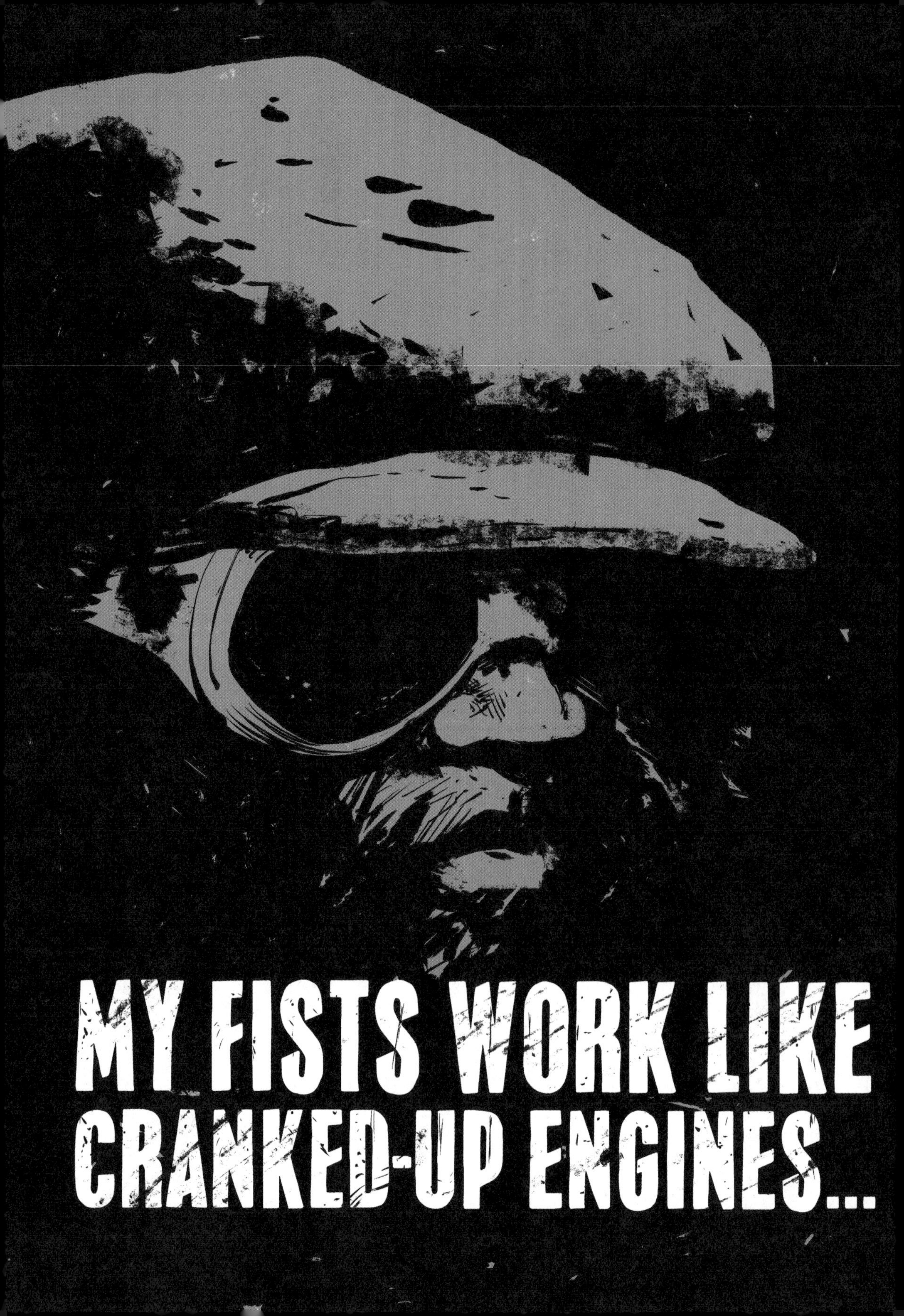
MY FISTS WORK LIKE
CRANKED-UP ENGINES...

I might make my money in the ring,
but automobiles are my **business.**

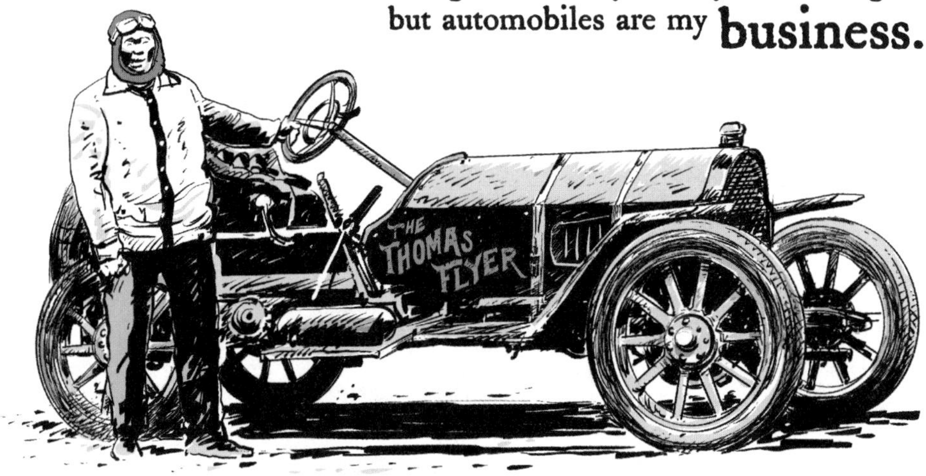
THE THOMAS FLYER

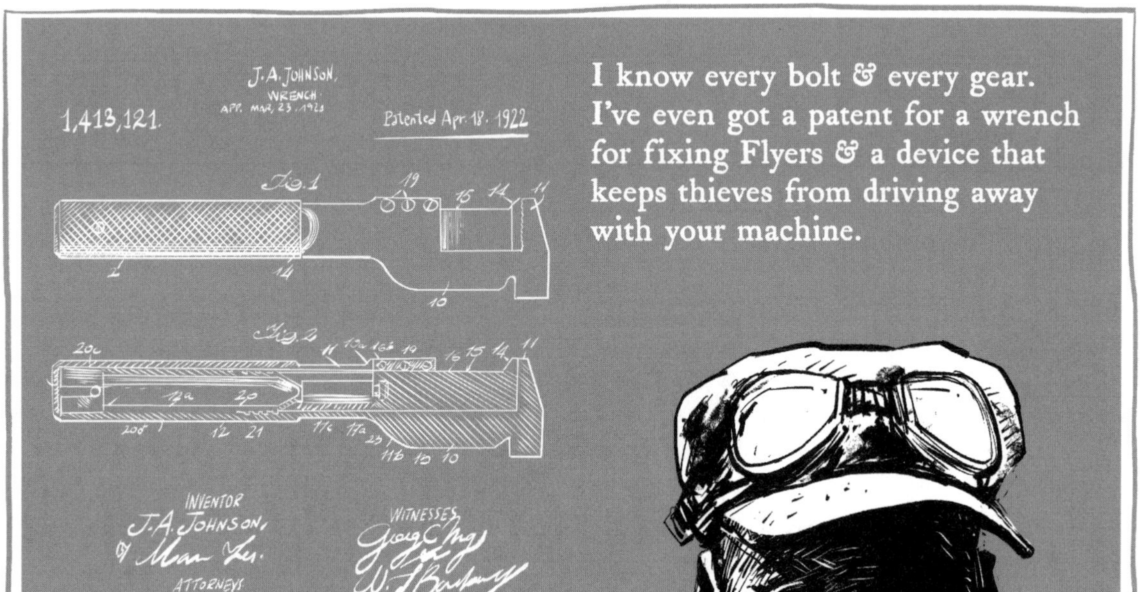
J.A. JOHNSON,
WRENCH.
APP. MAR. 23, 1921.
1,413,121.
Patented Apr. 18. 1922
INVENTOR
J.A. JOHNSON,
ATTORNEYS
WITNESSES
I know every bolt & every gear. I've even got a patent for a wrench for fixing Flyers & a device that keeps thieves from driving away with your machine.

Everybody knows you have to best
a champion to be a champion.
That's why I challenged Barney
Oldfield to a race.

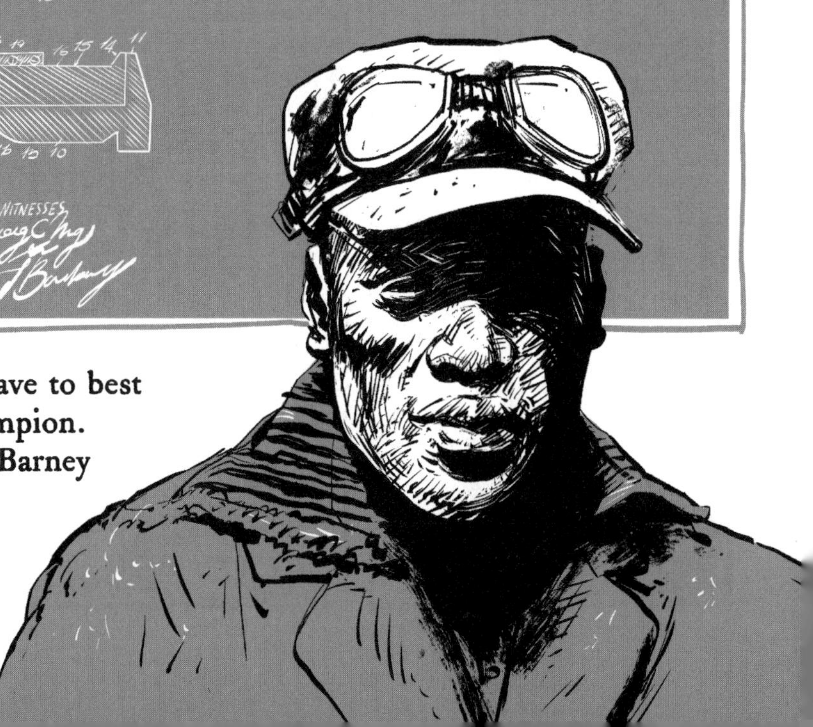

SHEEPSHEAD BAY RACE TRACK, BROOKLYN, NEW YORK 1910

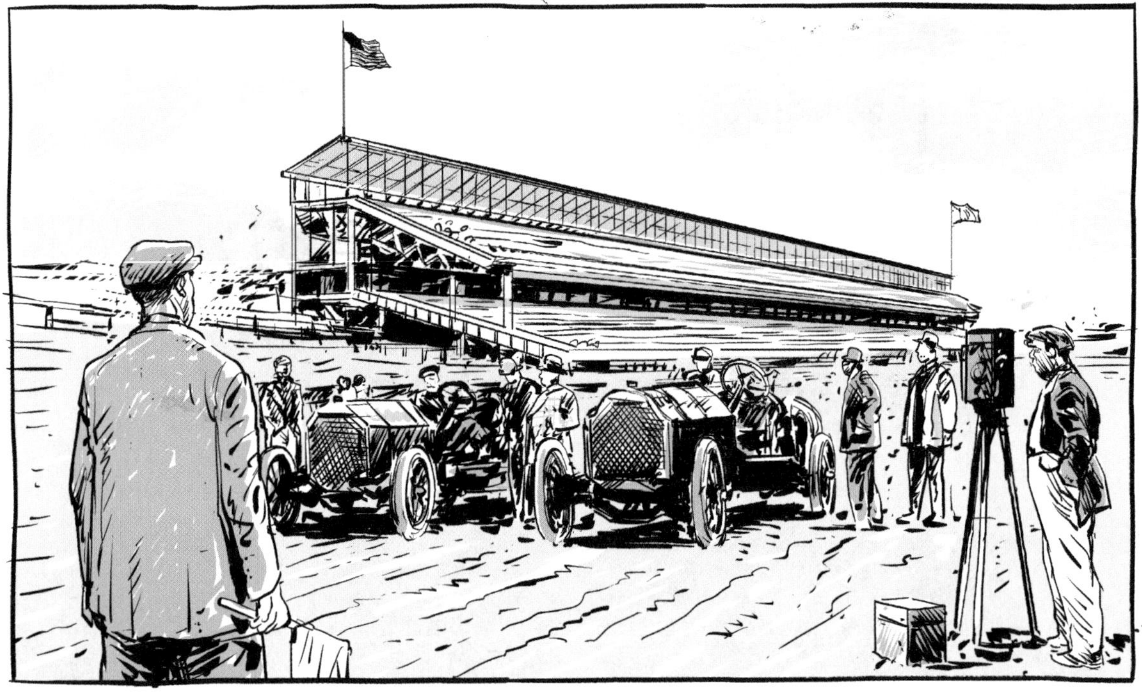

Oldfield lived for speed. Before he was a champion automobilist, he was a champion bicyclist. He agreed to race as soon as he saw the money.

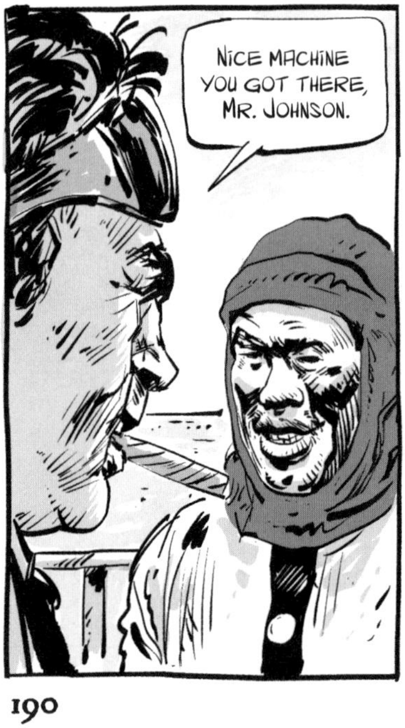
NICE MACHINE YOU GOT THERE, MR. JOHNSON.

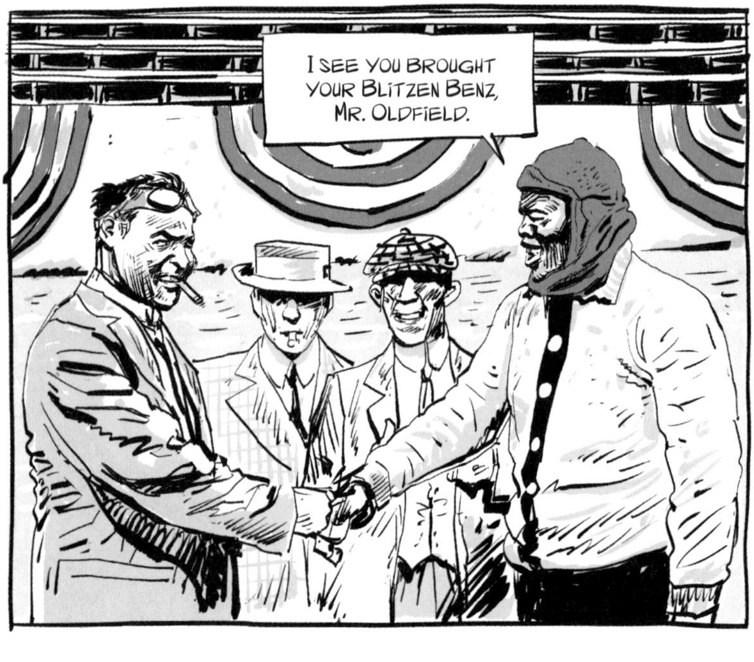
I SEE YOU BROUGHT YOUR BLITZEN BENZ, MR. OLDFIELD.

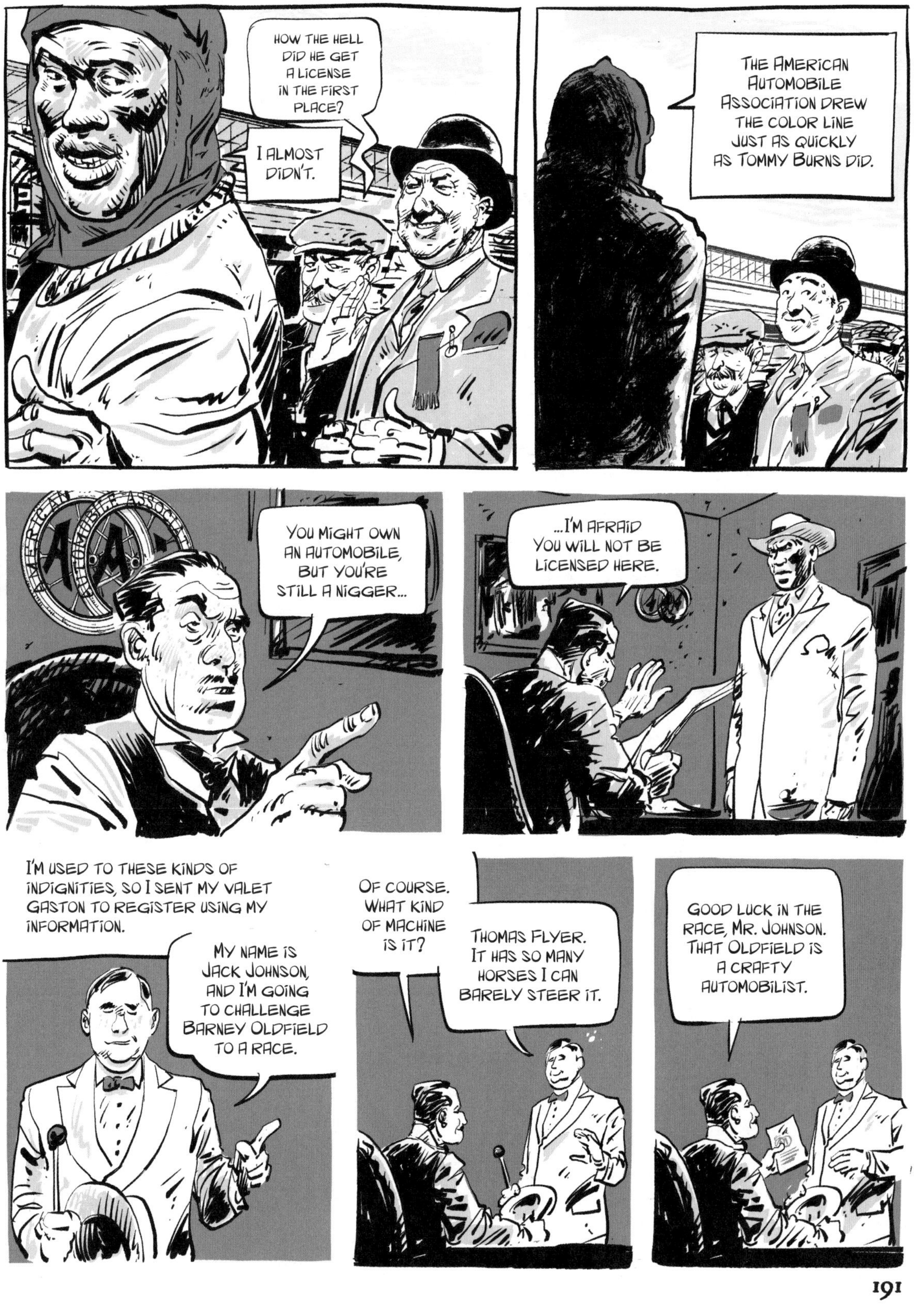
HOW THE HELL DID HE GET A LICENSE IN THE FIRST PLACE?
I ALMOST DIDN'T.
THE AMERICAN AUTOMOBILE ASSOCIATION DREW THE COLOR LINE JUST AS QUICKLY AS TOMMY BURNS DID.
YOU MIGHT OWN AN AUTOMOBILE, BUT YOU'RE STILL A NIGGER...
...I'M AFRAID YOU WILL NOT BE LICENSED HERE.
I'M USED TO THESE KINDS OF INDIGNITIES, SO I SENT MY VALET GASTON TO REGISTER USING MY INFORMATION.
MY NAME IS JACK JOHNSON, AND I'M GOING TO CHALLENGE BARNEY OLDFIELD TO A RACE.
OF COURSE. WHAT KIND OF MACHINE IS IT?
THOMAS FLYER. IT HAS SO MANY HORSES I CAN BARELY STEER IT.
GOOD LUCK IN THE RACE, MR. JOHNSON. THAT OLDFIELD IS A CRAFTY AUTOMOBILIST.

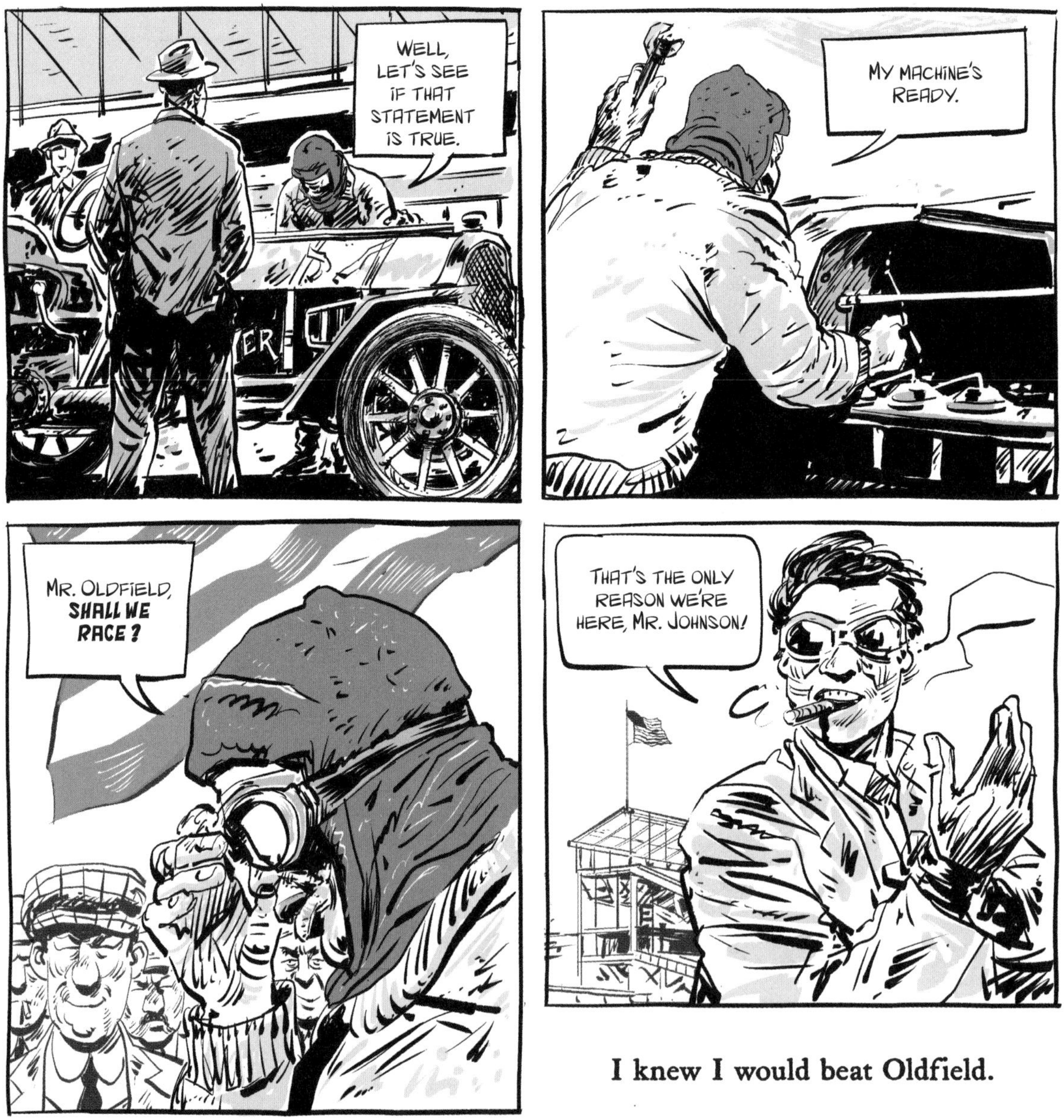
WELL, LET'S SEE IF THAT STATEMENT IS TRUE.
MY MACHINE'S READY.
MR. OLDFIELD, **SHALL WE RACE?**
THAT'S THE ONLY REASON WE'RE HERE, MR. JOHNSON!

I knew I would beat Oldfield.

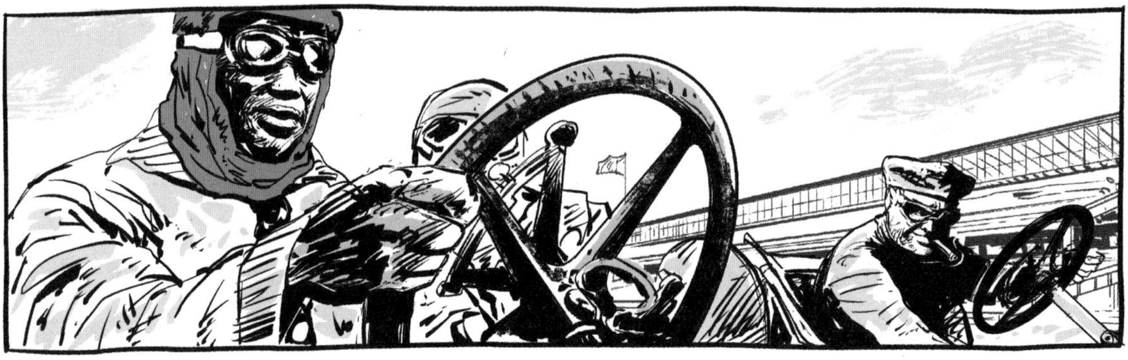

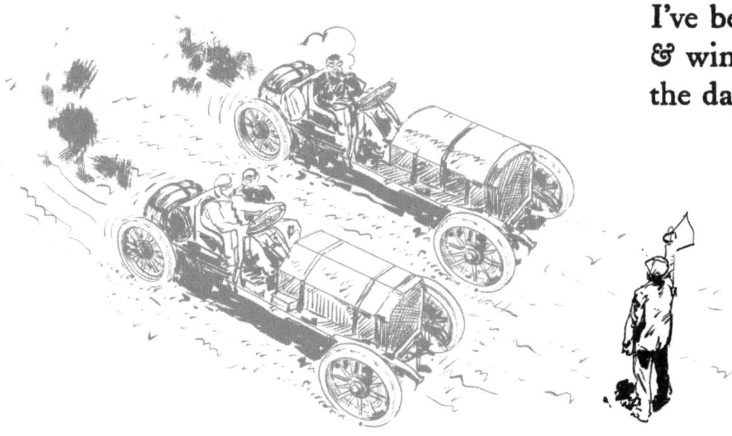

I've been competing
& winning since
the day I could walk.

Automobile racing is just another way to outrun another man. Anybody who has watched horses knows they spend the whole day trying to run faster than the next horse.

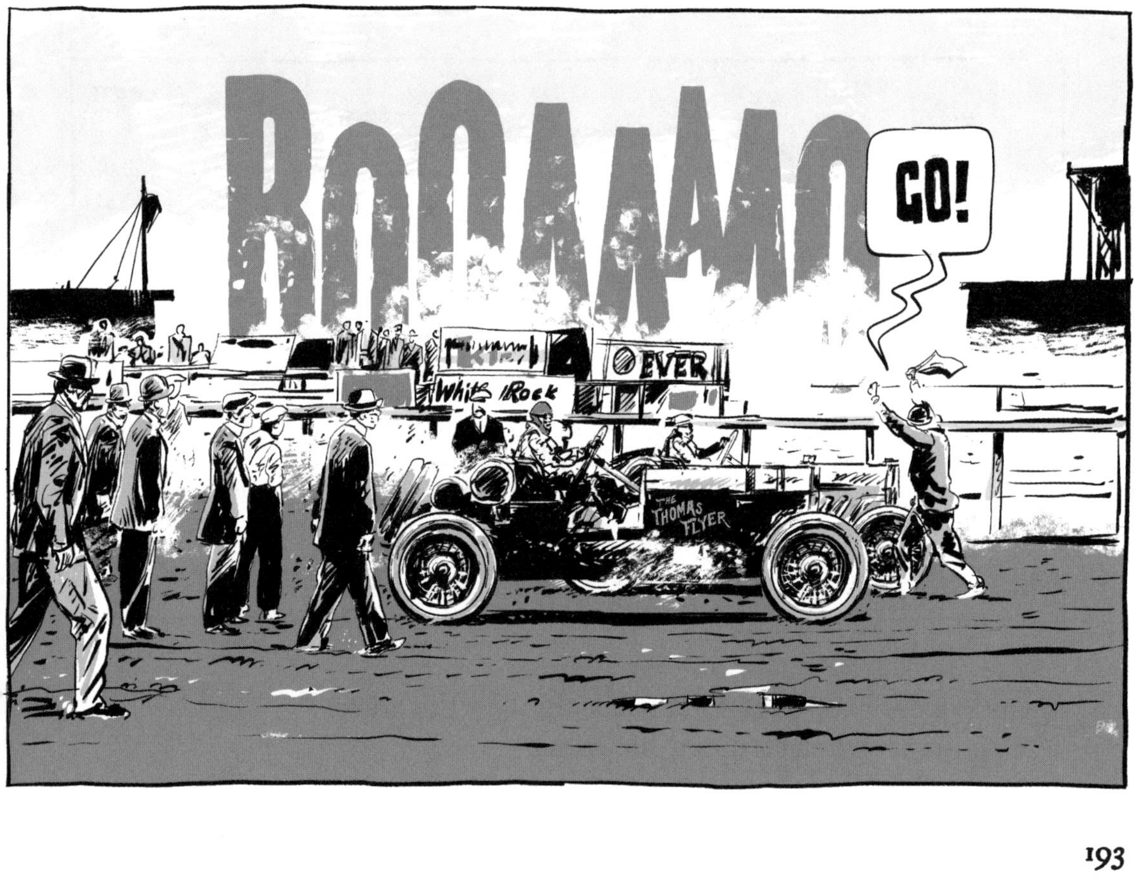
ROOAAMO
GO!
EVER
THE THOMAS FLYER

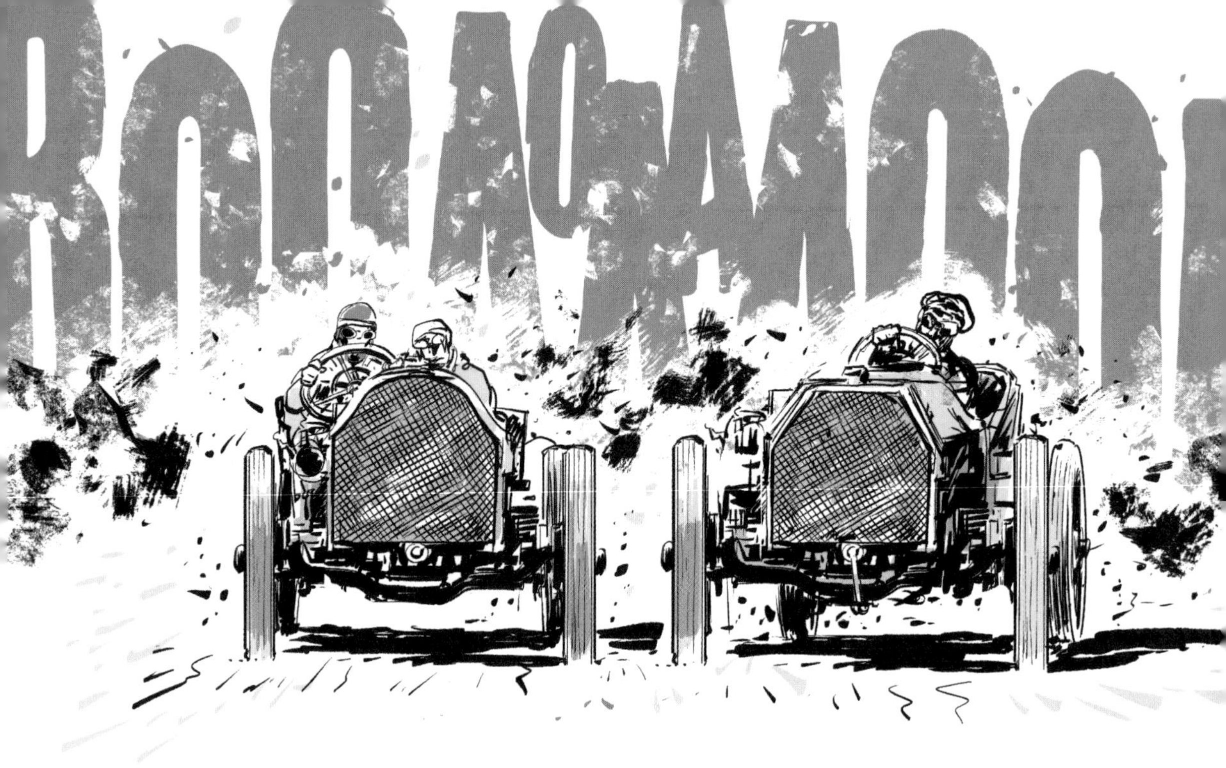

The day Jack Johnson doesn't go faster than another man is the day you best make amends because the trumpets are coming directly.

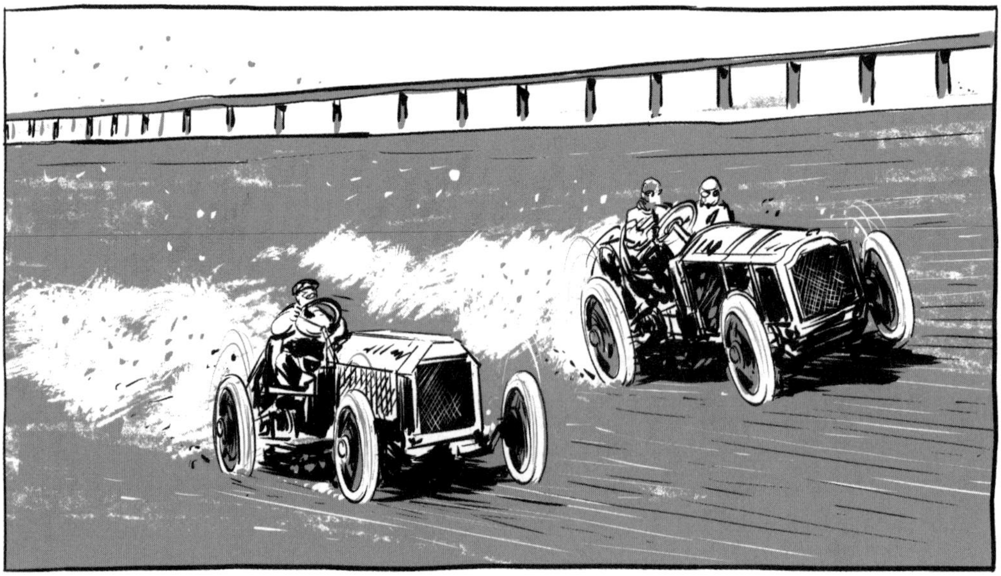

I gave Oldfield a tough time through our two heats, keeping close enough to see his car through the gravel & dust his tires kicked up on the turns.

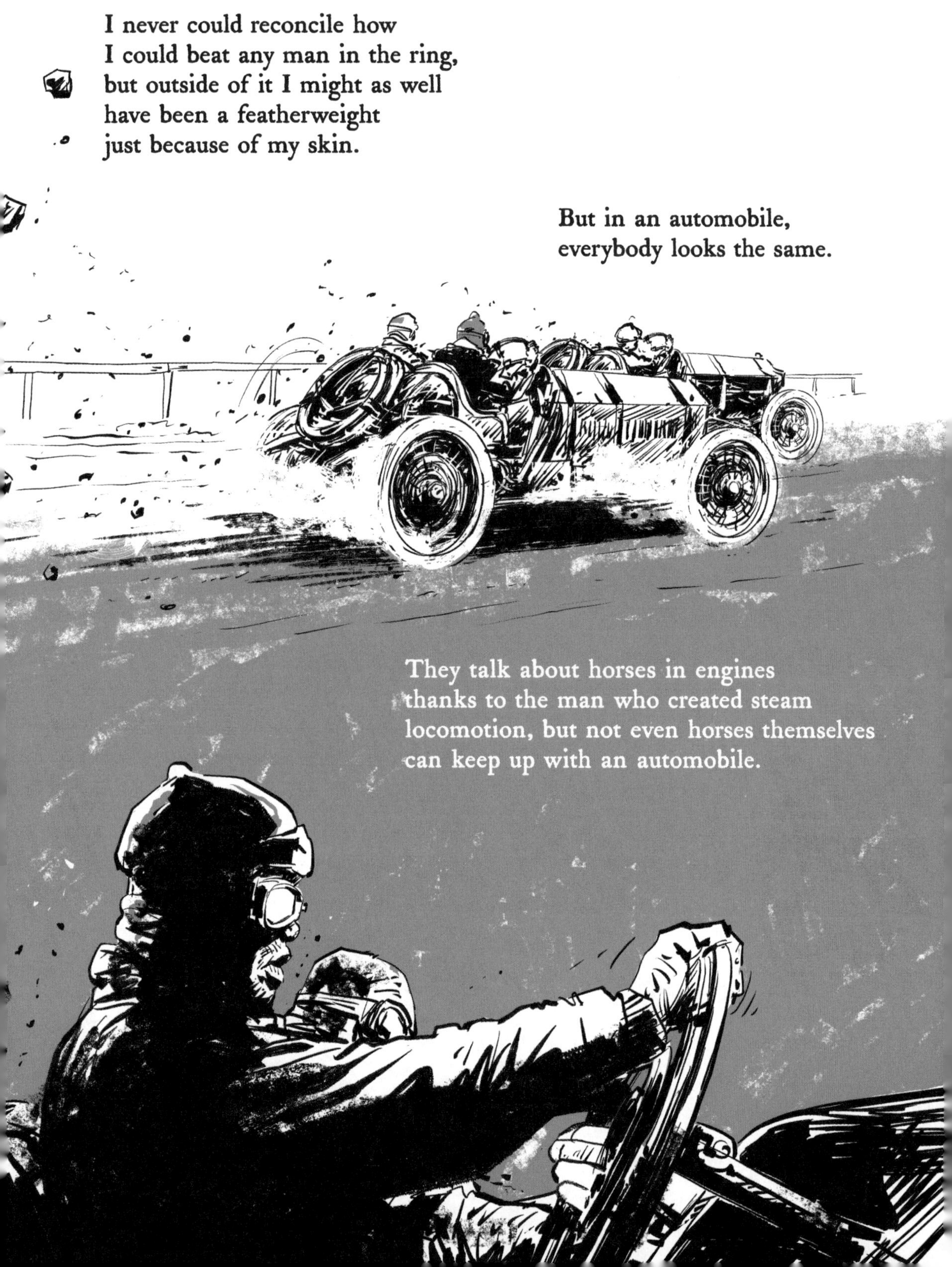
I never could reconcile how I could beat any man in the ring, but outside of it I might as well have been a featherweight just because of my skin.
But in an automobile, everybody looks the same.
They talk about horses in engines thanks to the man who created steam locomotion, but not even horses themselves can keep up with an automobile.

I am six foot, two inches tall
& I weigh two hundred & fifty pounds.

I am so strong I could plant
my feet & keep Father Time
from moving forward.

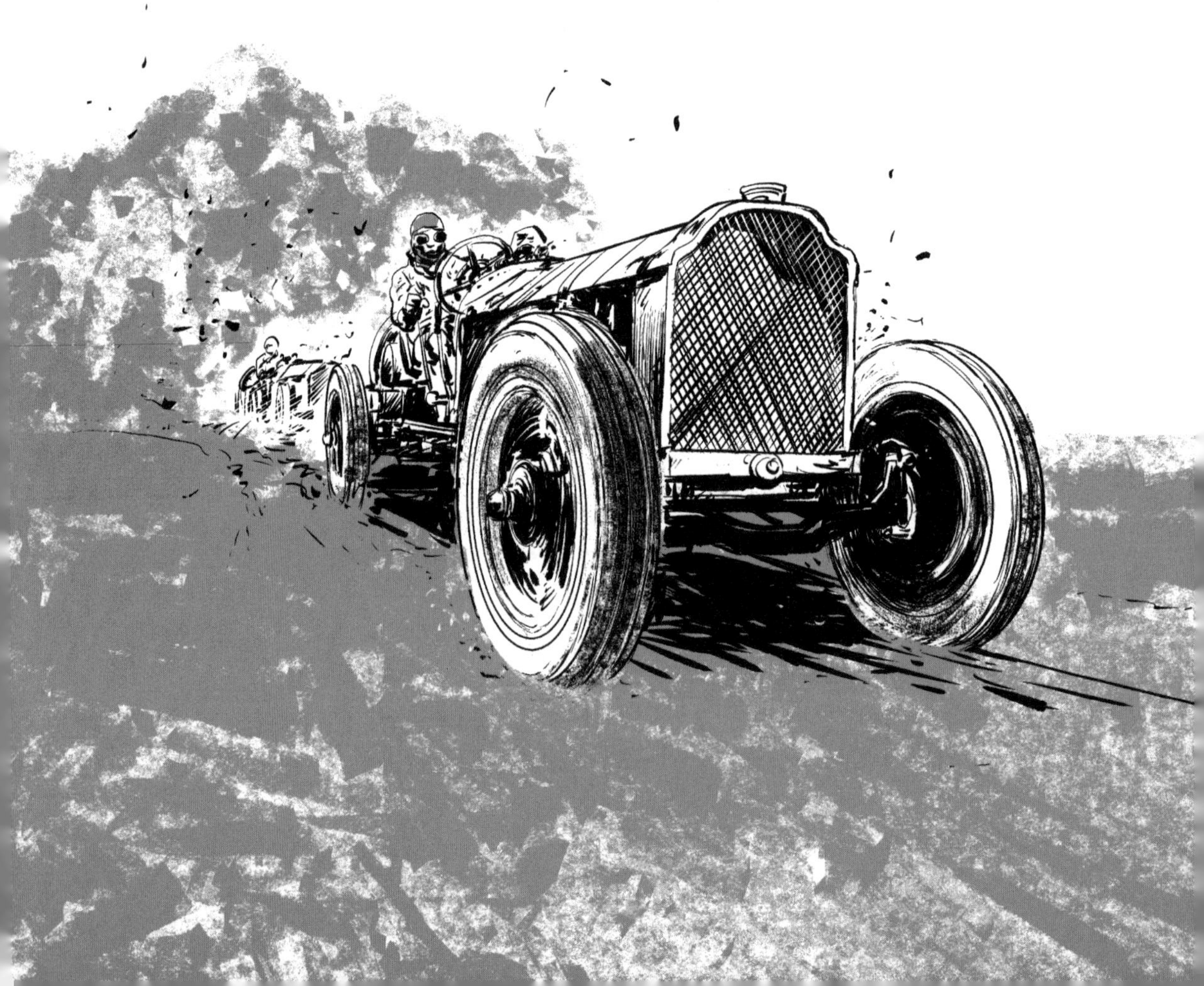

None of that—not my muscles
or my money could keep whites from
coming for me in the ring.
Or on the street. Or in court.
Or on the racetrack. Whites
have made my whole life a horse race.

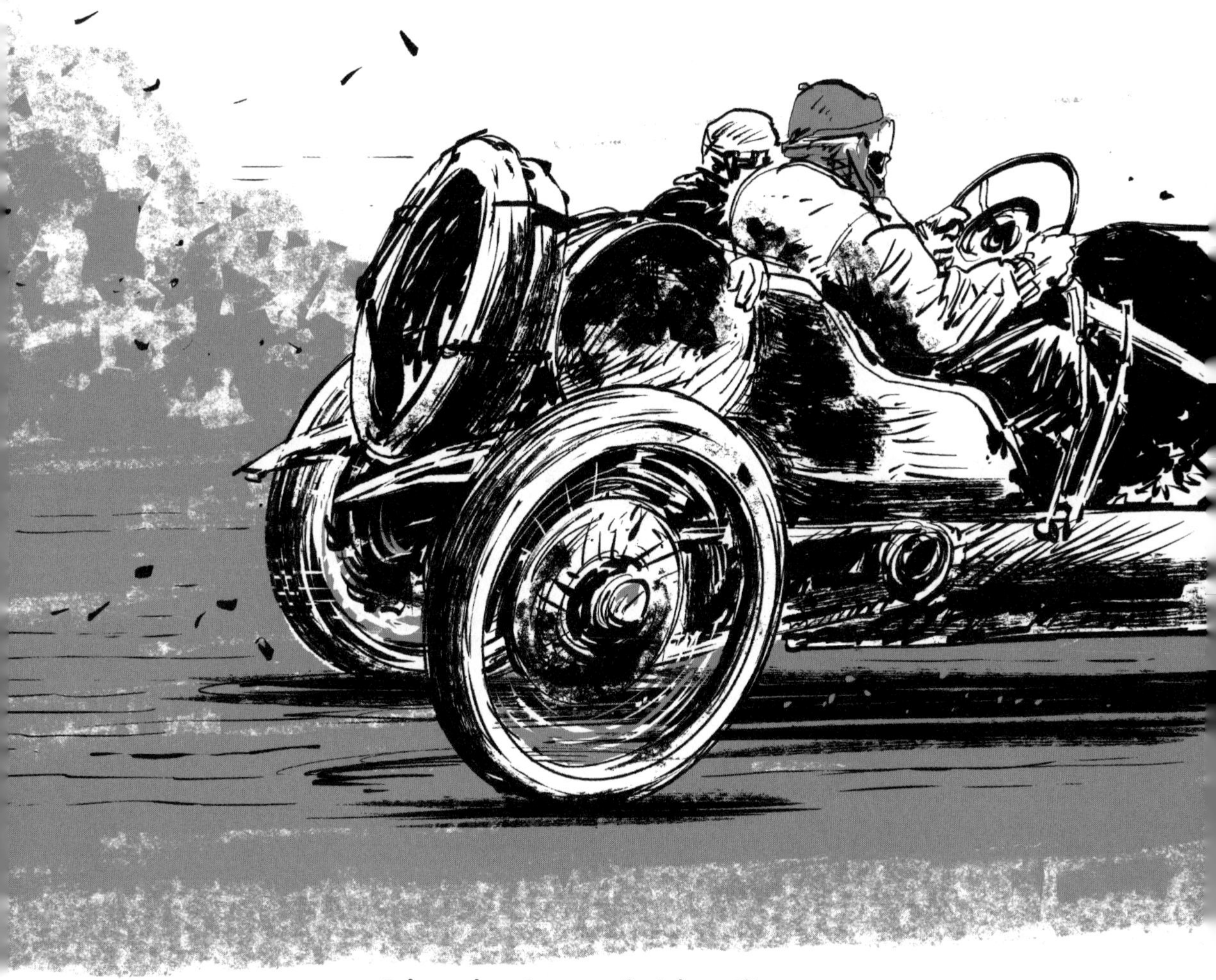

I imagine horses feel just like my opponents,
watching as the future gets further and further
ahead of them.

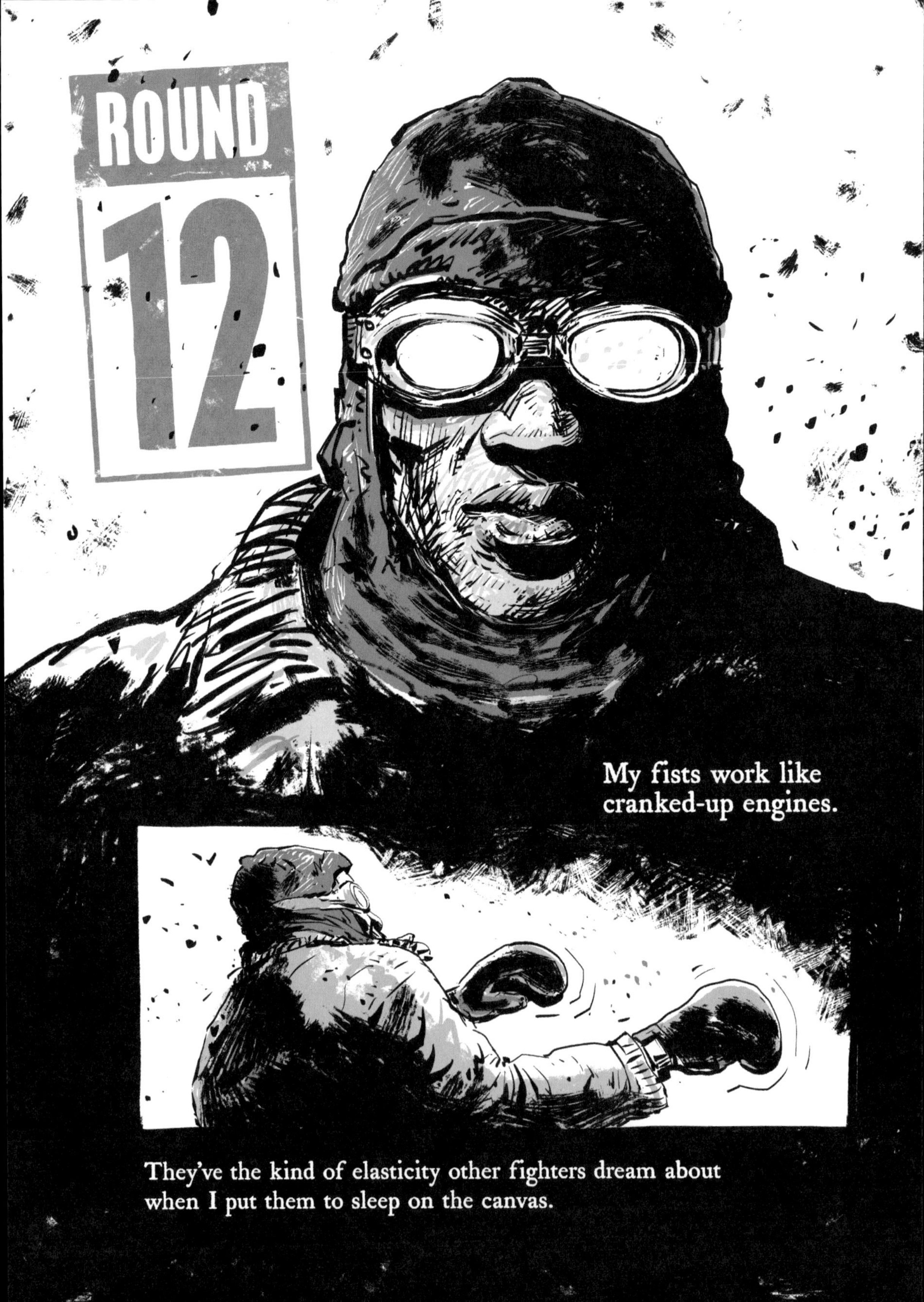
ROUND
12
My fists work like cranked-up engines.
They've the kind of elasticity other fighters dream about when I put them to sleep on the canvas.

When I hook a man,
it's like being hit
by **frustration.**

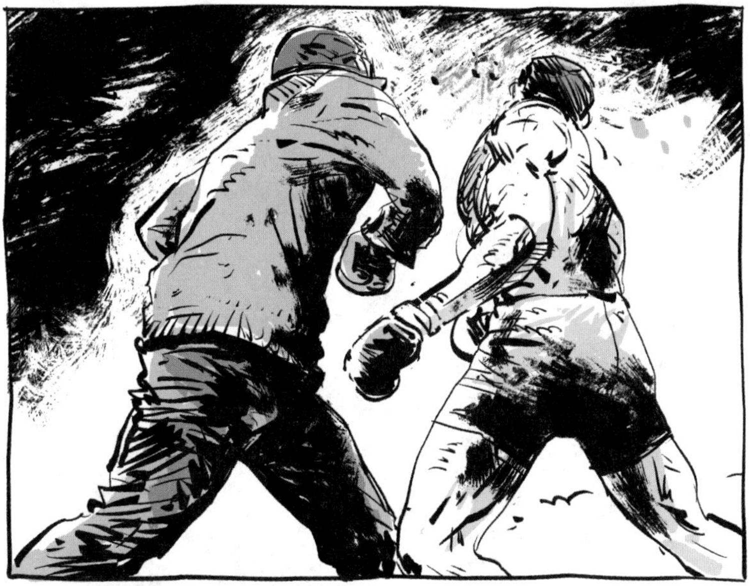

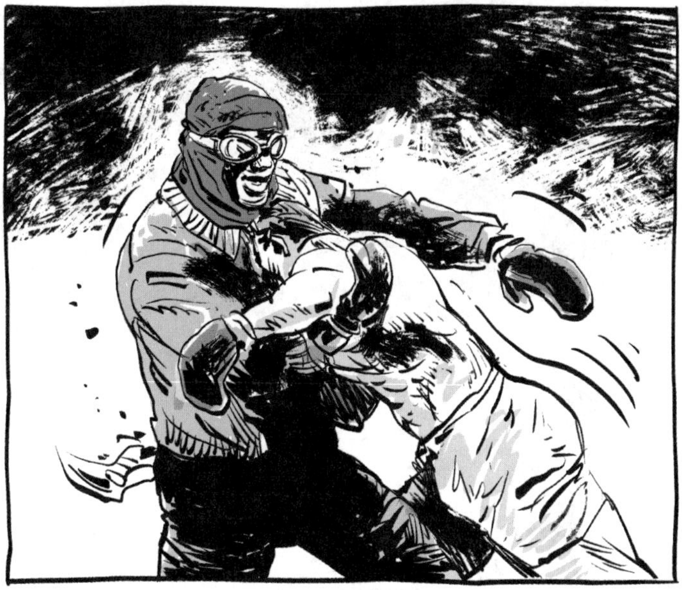

When I clinch a man,
it's like being swaddled
in **forgiveness.**

I won't forgive them for how they've treated me and my people.

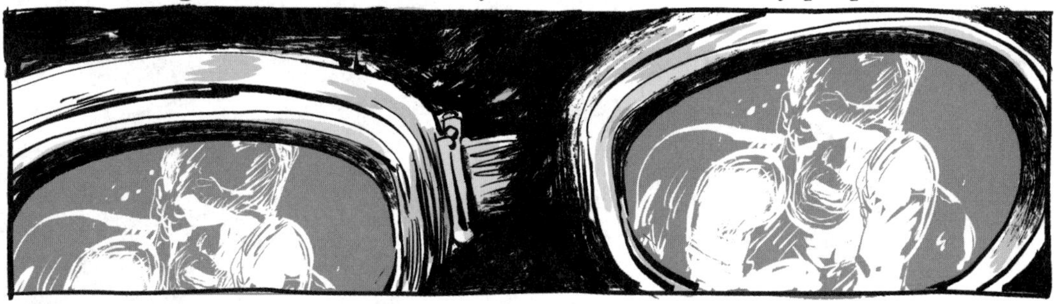

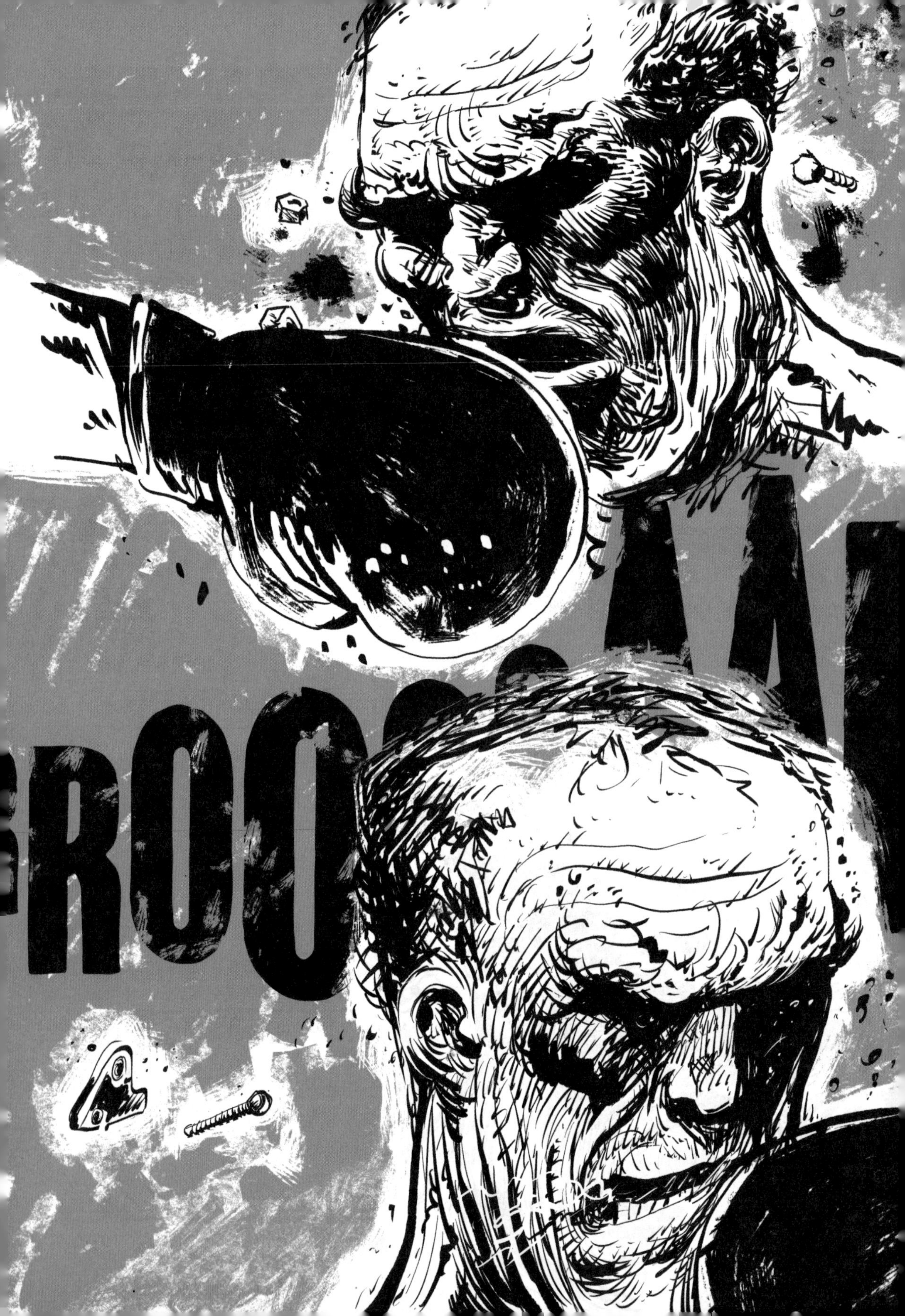

It's a fact:
The more money I make,
the more dangerous I am.
The more dangerous I am,
the blacker I become.

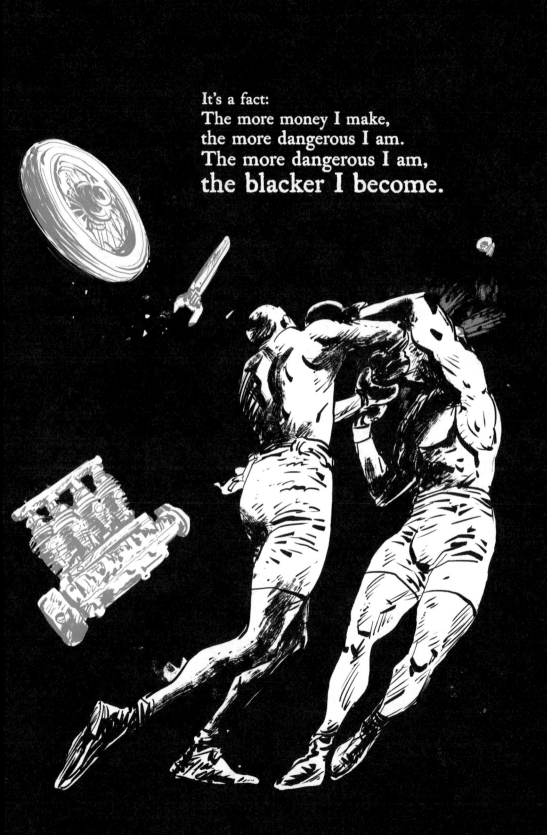

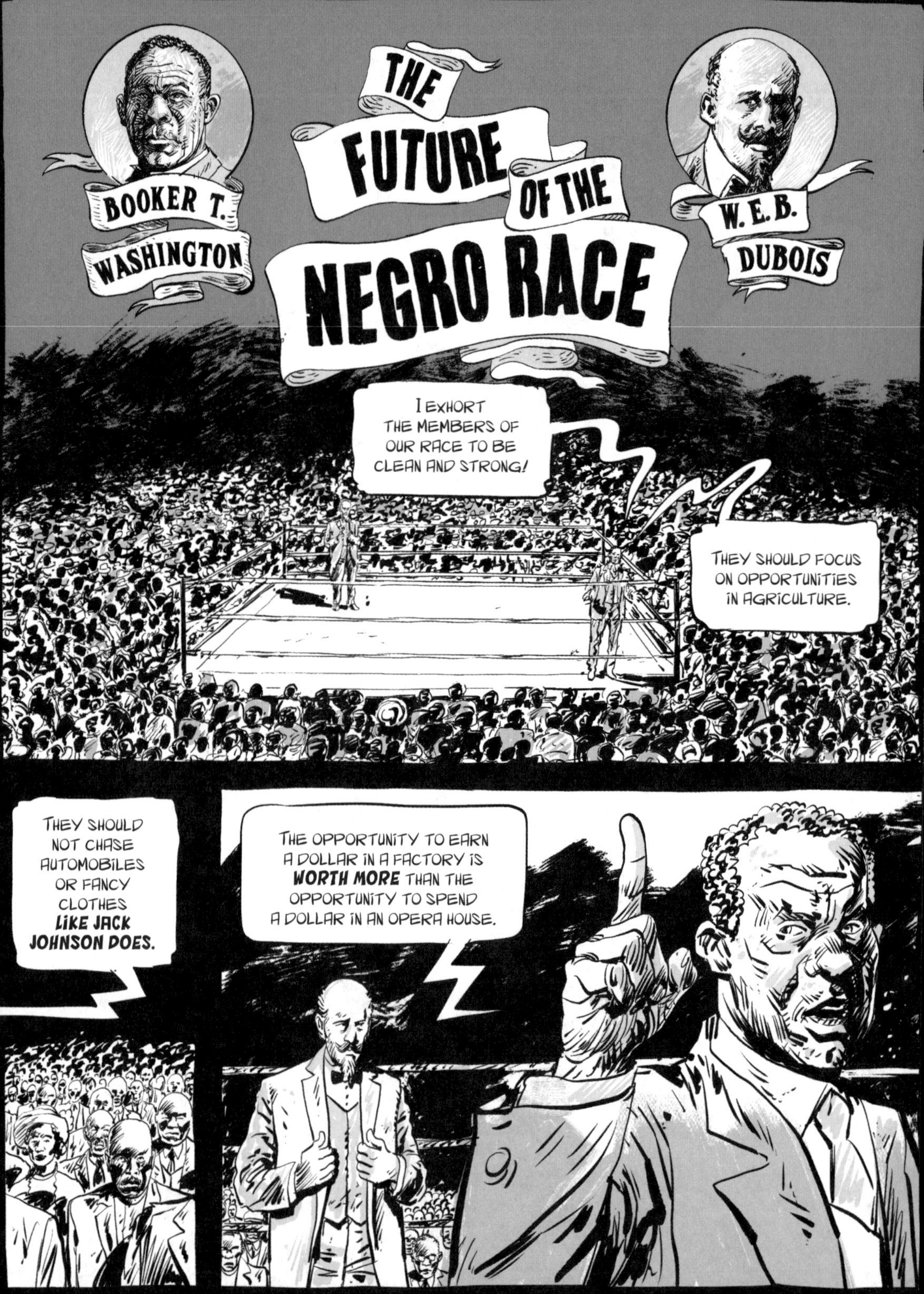
BOOKER T. WASHINGTON
THE FUTURE OF THE NEGRO RACE
W. E. B. DUBOIS
I EXHORT THE MEMBERS OF OUR RACE TO BE CLEAN AND STRONG!
THEY SHOULD FOCUS ON OPPORTUNITIES IN AGRICULTURE.
THEY SHOULD NOT CHASE AUTOMOBILES OR FANCY CLOTHES **LIKE JACK JOHNSON DOES.**
THE OPPORTUNITY TO EARN A DOLLAR IN A FACTORY IS **WORTH MORE** THAN THE OPPORTUNITY TO SPEND A DOLLAR IN AN OPERA HOUSE.

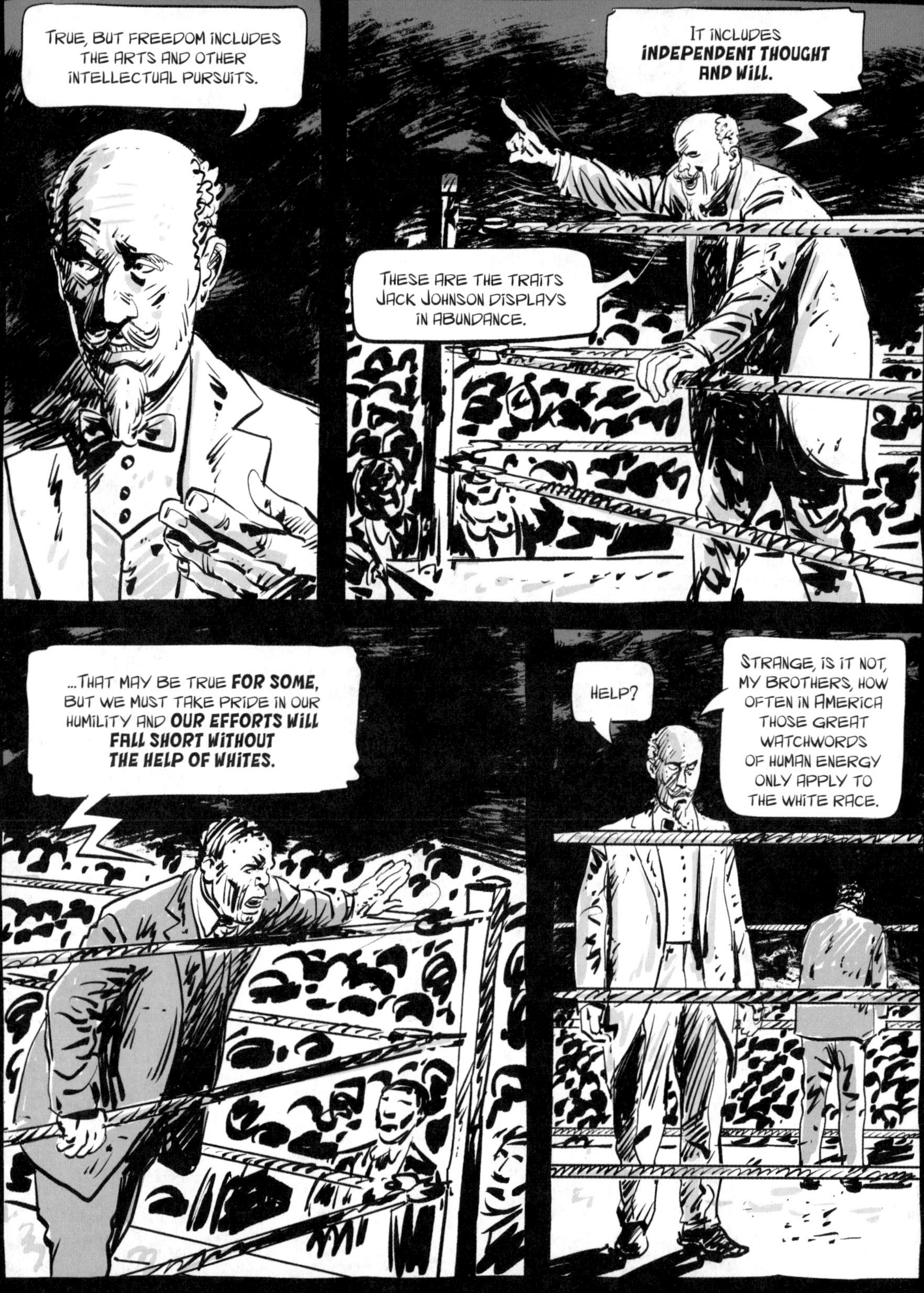
TRUE, BUT FREEDOM INCLUDES THE ARTS AND OTHER INTELLECTUAL PURSUITS.
IT INCLUDES **INDEPENDENT THOUGHT AND WILL.**
THESE ARE THE TRAITS JACK JOHNSON DISPLAYS IN ABUNDANCE.
...THAT MAY BE TRUE **FOR SOME,** BUT WE MUST TAKE PRIDE IN OUR HUMILITY AND **OUR EFFORTS WILL FALL SHORT WITHOUT THE HELP OF WHITES.**
HELP?
STRANGE, IS IT NOT, MY BROTHERS, HOW OFTEN IN AMERICA THOSE GREAT WATCHWORDS OF HUMAN ENERGY ONLY APPLY TO THE WHITE RACE.

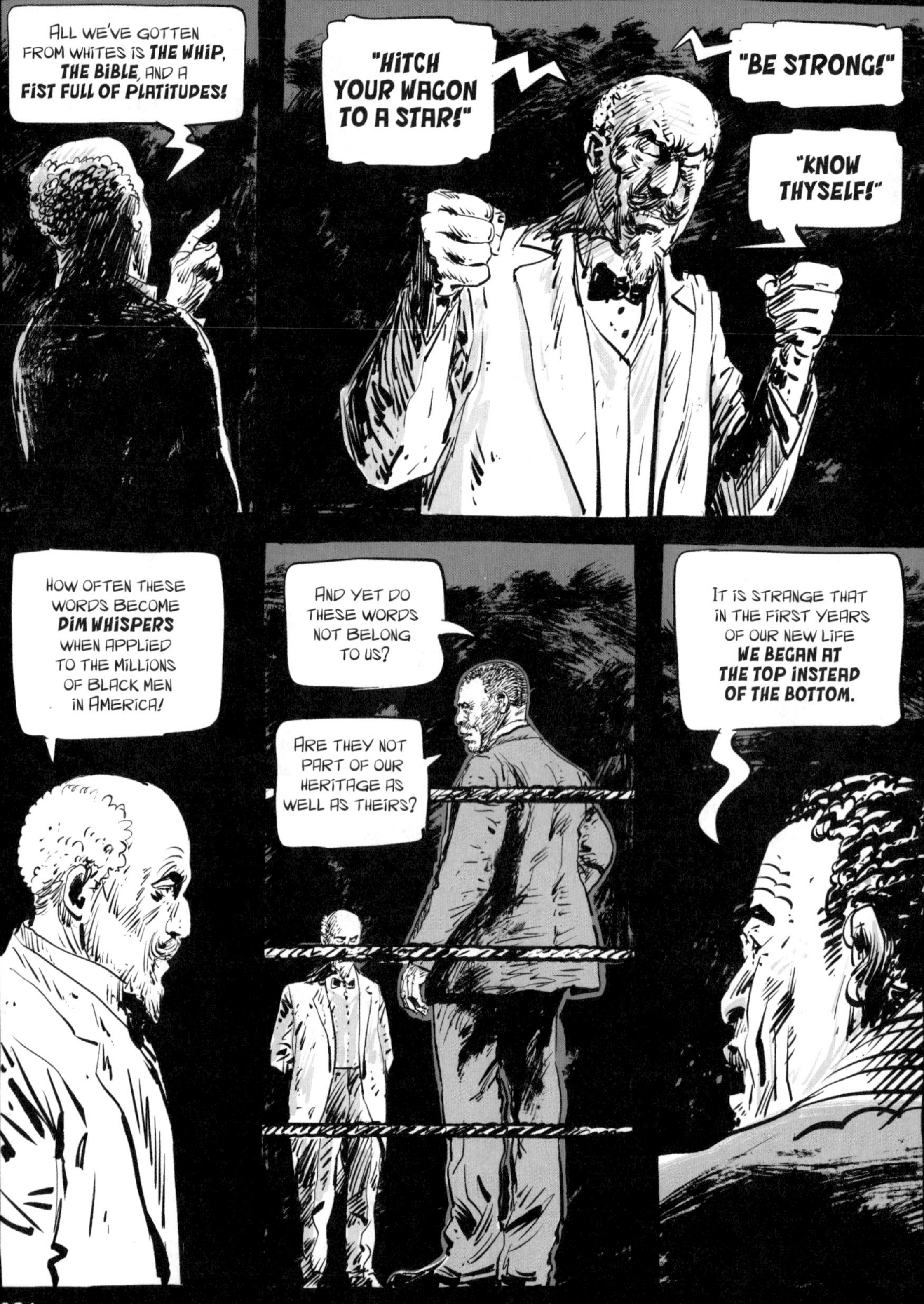
ALL WE'VE GOTTEN FROM WHITES IS THE WHIP, THE BIBLE, AND A FIST FULL OF PLATITUDES!
"HITCH YOUR WAGON TO A STAR!"
"BE STRONG!"
"KNOW THYSELF!"
HOW OFTEN THESE WORDS BECOME DIM WHISPERS WHEN APPLIED TO THE MILLIONS OF BLACK MEN IN AMERICA!
AND YET DO THESE WORDS NOT BELONG TO US?
ARE THEY NOT PART OF OUR HERITAGE AS WELL AS THEIRS?
IT IS STRANGE THAT IN THE FIRST YEARS OF OUR NEW LIFE WE BEGAN AT THE TOP INSTEAD OF THE BOTTOM.

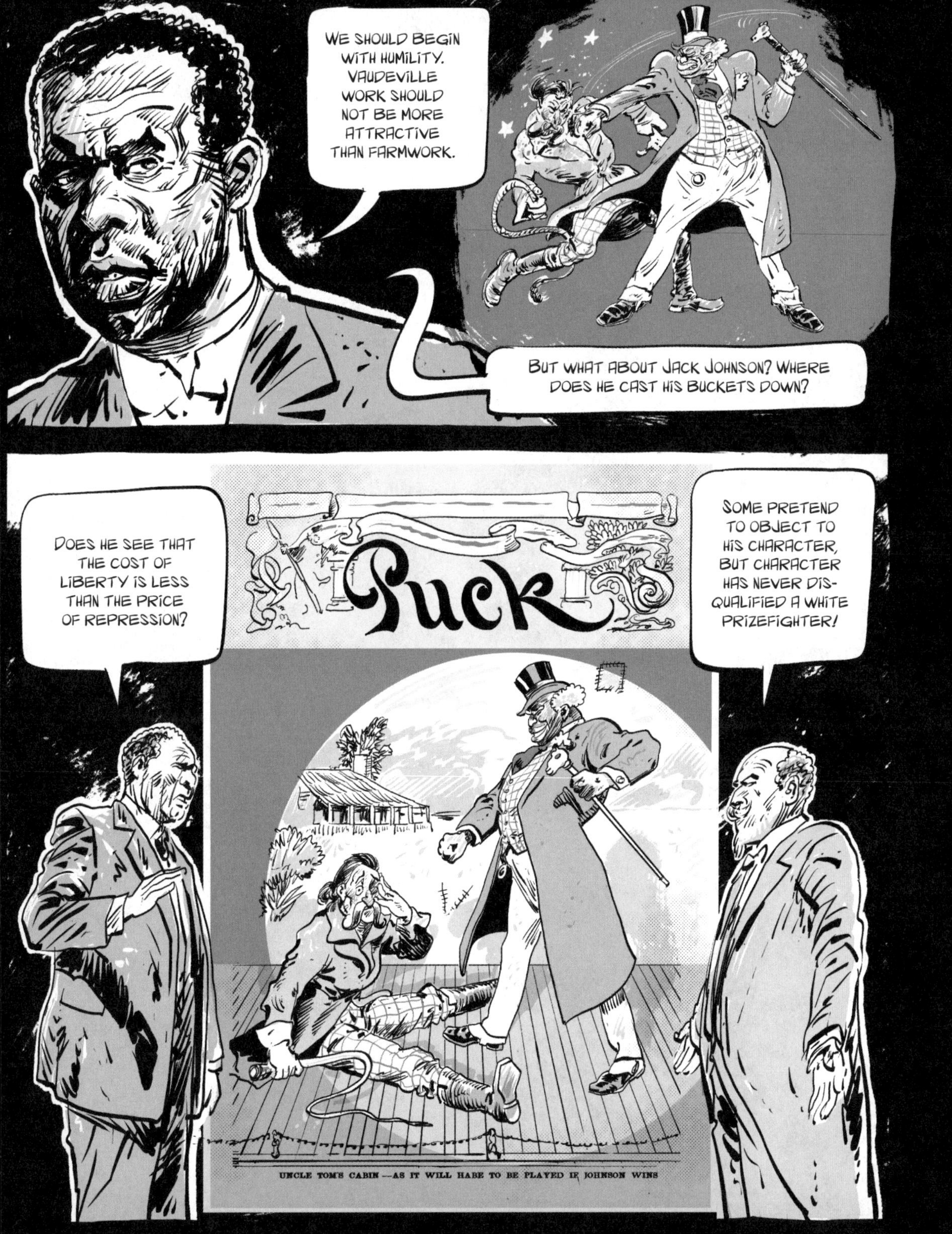
WE SHOULD BEGIN WITH HUMILITY. VAUDEVILLE WORK SHOULD NOT BE MORE ATTRACTIVE THAN FARMWORK.
BUT WHAT ABOUT JACK JOHNSON? WHERE DOES HE CAST HIS BUCKETS DOWN?
DOES HE SEE THAT THE COST OF LIBERTY IS LESS THAN THE PRICE OF REPRESSION?
Puck
SOME PRETEND TO OBJECT TO HIS CHARACTER, BUT CHARACTER HAS NEVER DIS-QUALIFIED A WHITE PRIZEFIGHTER!
UNCLE TOM'S CABIN —AS IT WILL HABE TO BE PLAYED IF JOHNSON WINS

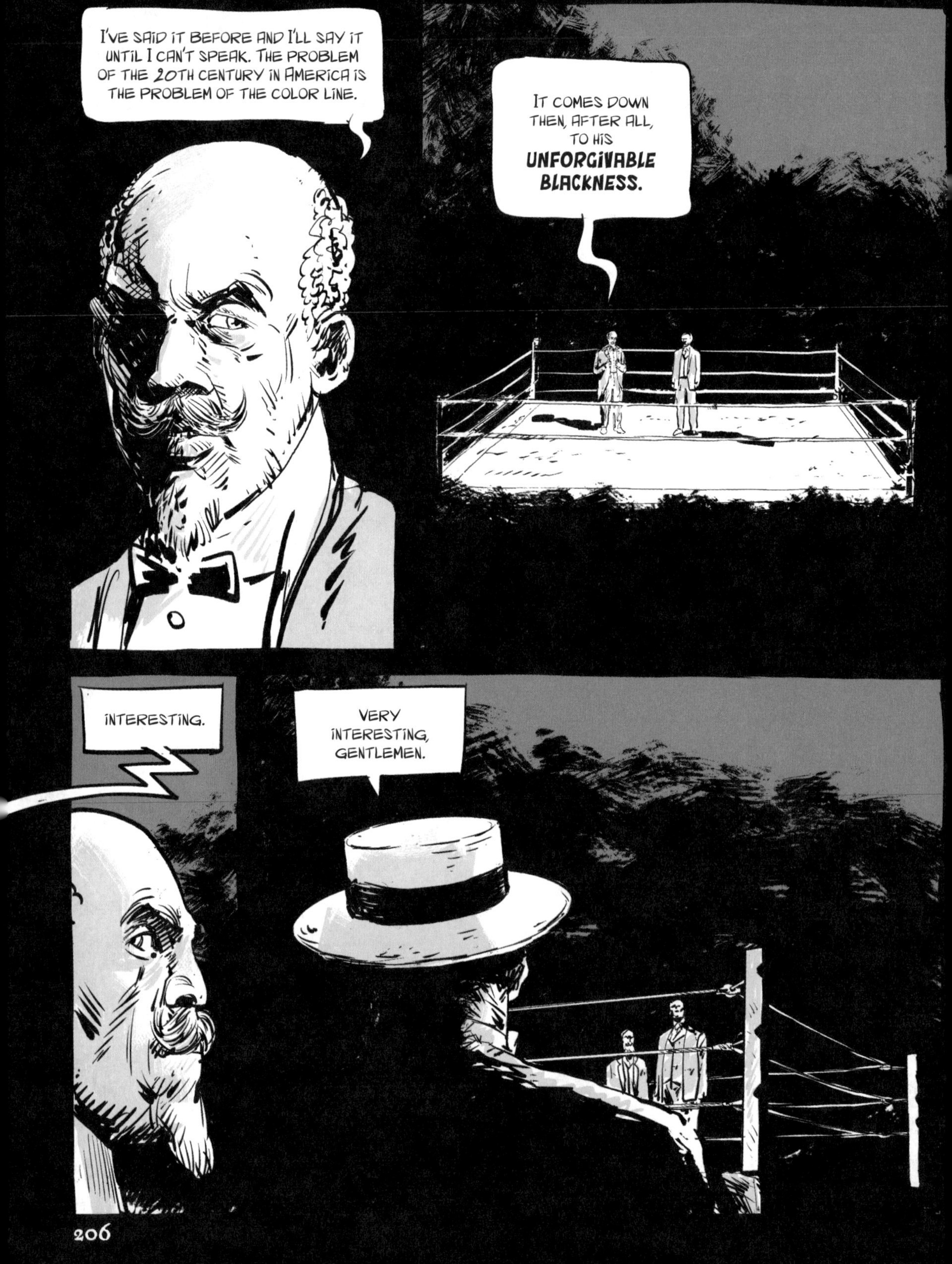
I'VE SAID IT BEFORE AND I'LL SAY IT UNTIL I CAN'T SPEAK. THE PROBLEM OF THE 20TH CENTURY IN AMERICA IS THE PROBLEM OF THE COLOR LINE.
IT COMES DOWN THEN, AFTER ALL, TO HIS **UNFORGIVABLE BLACKNESS.**
INTERESTING.
VERY INTERESTING, GENTLEMEN.

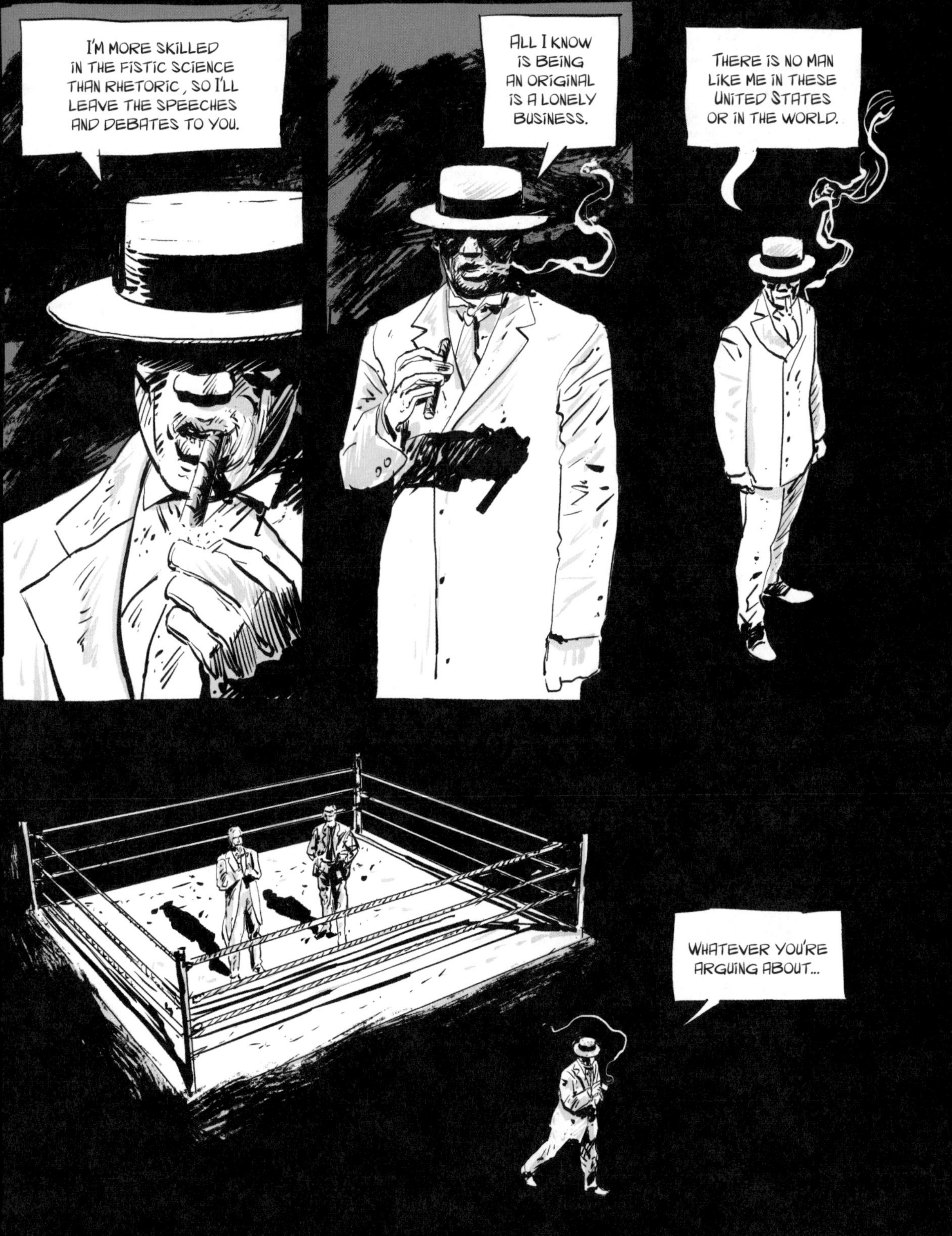
I'M MORE SKILLED IN THE FISTIC SCIENCE THAN RHETORIC, SO I'LL LEAVE THE SPEECHES AND DEBATES TO YOU.
ALL I KNOW IS BEING AN ORIGINAL IS A LONELY BUSINESS.
THERE IS NO MAN LIKE ME IN THESE UNITED STATES OR IN THE WORLD.
WHATEVER YOU'RE ARGUING ABOUT...

I'M A FREE MAN

We're supposed to be
able to be anything
we can make of ourselves.
We're supposed to be
able to pull ourselves
up & find our fortune
wherever it may be.
Funny how all the men
in the bootstrap stories
are white. Some made
it by striking oil. Others
from the railroads.
I made my fortune through
my wits & fists.

Now I've got so much
money I can wreck one
of my automobiles
& get a new one the next
day. I can change suits
five times a day & still
have suits to spare.
But since I am Black,
freedom is only an idea.
You know the French
gave us the Statue
of Liberty to honor
America's commitment
to liberty & freedom?
Seems like the French
believed in America
more than America
believes in itself.

I'm a free man. But like Shakespeare said, anybody who lives by their own measure can sit on a bench & wait for hardship to find them.

My mother & father survived what some smart somebody called the "peculiar institution." Like "peculiar" is the right word for whips & chains.

My mother hardly ever talked about what happened before freedom.

Black people didn't ask to come to America.

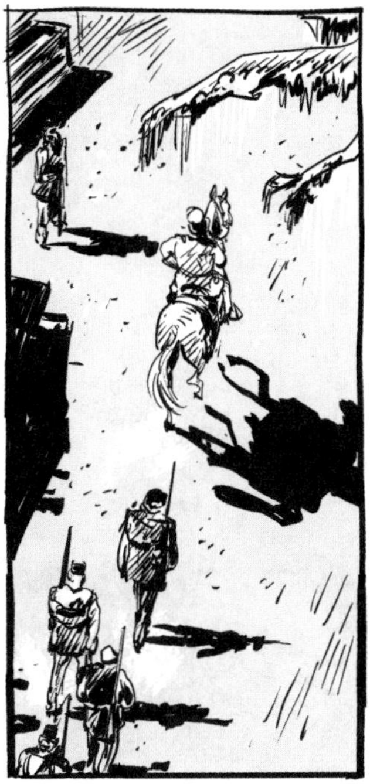

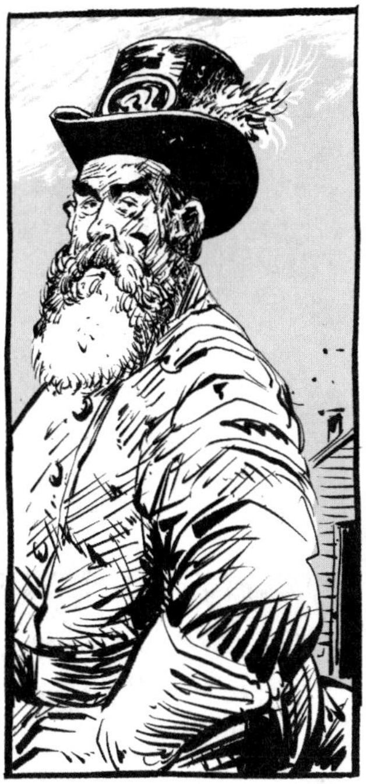

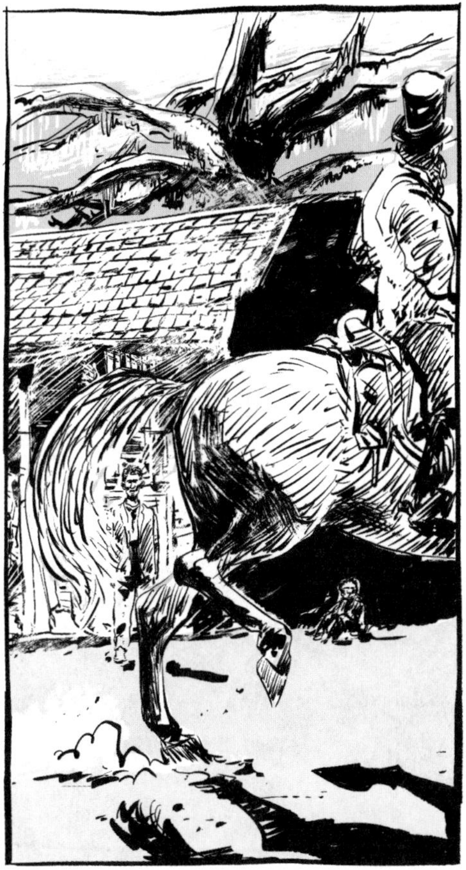

Time & time again, this country made new laws to keep us from having rights because they don't think we're human.

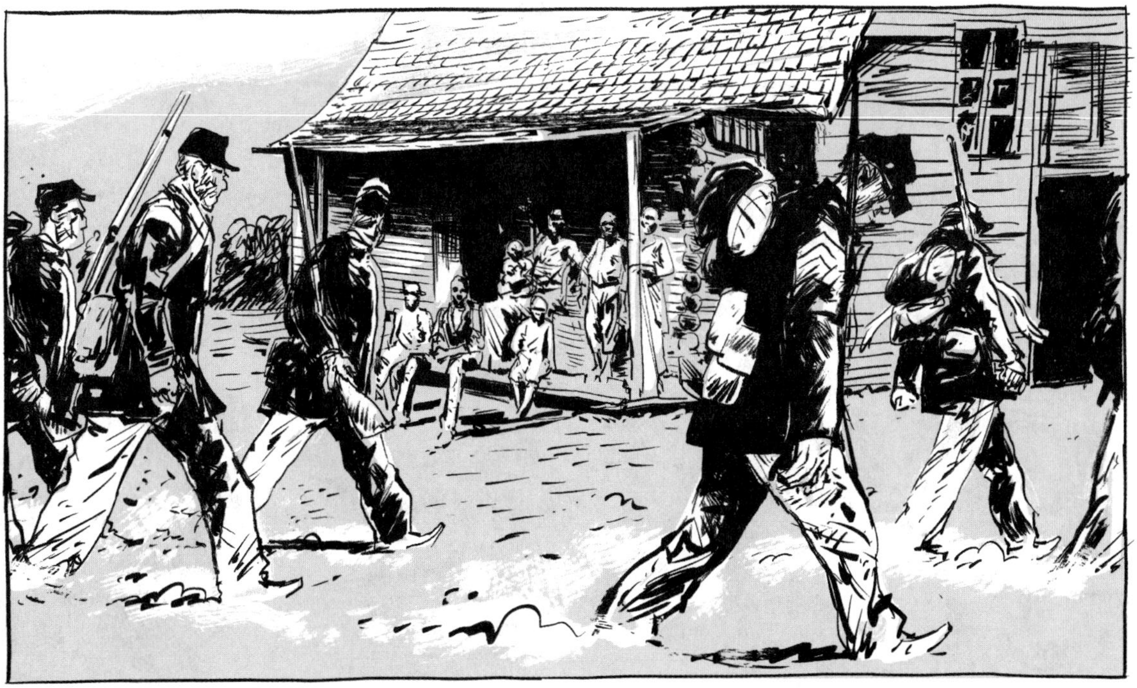

My dear mother Tiny &
my father were both born
on plantations before
the Civil War.
They saw all of it.

It wasn't even legal for us to
be free in most places.
When President Lincoln
finally freed us, they came up
with other ways to keep us down.

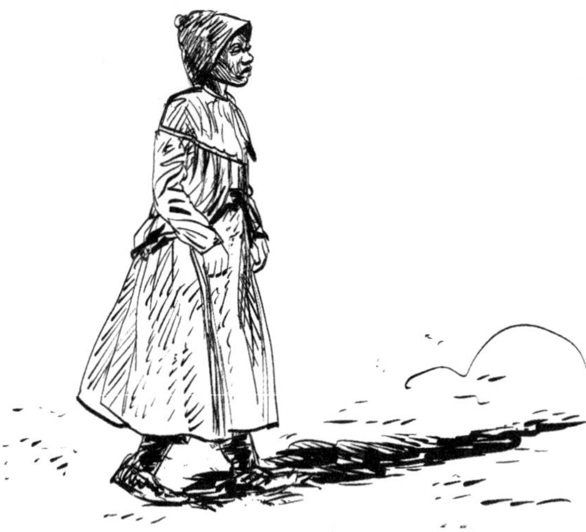

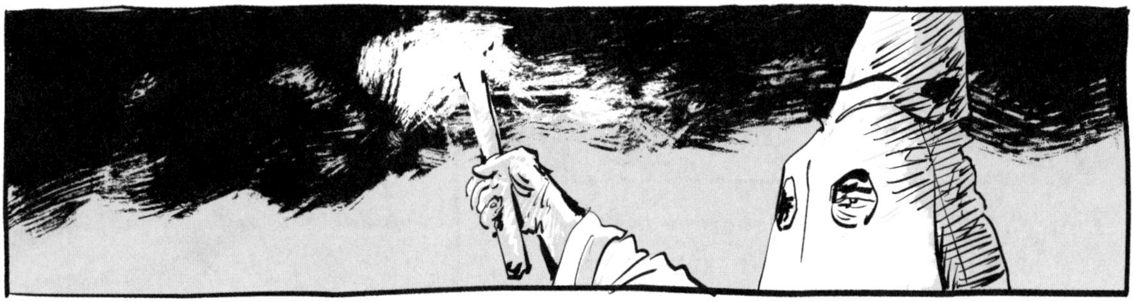

They use whips & nooses & guns. They use the Klan, the sheriffs,
& the politicians. They even use the Department of Justice.

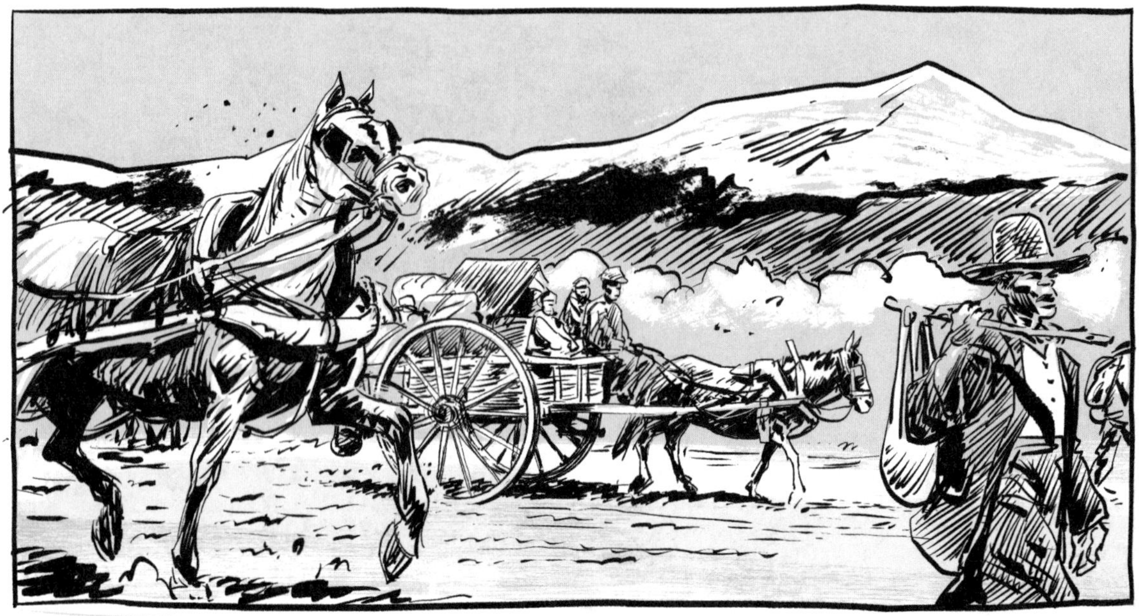

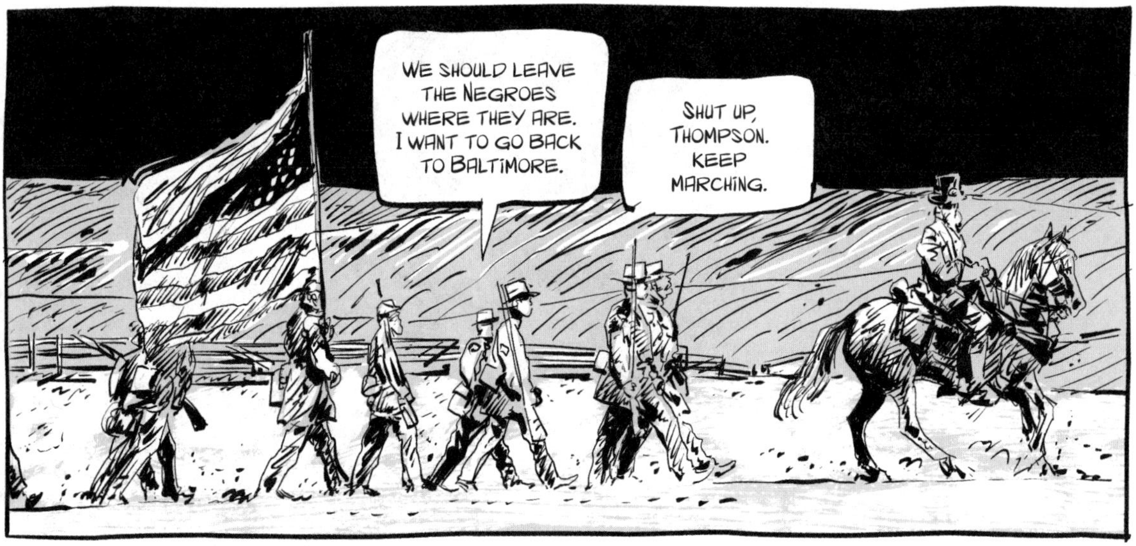
WE SHOULD LEAVE THE NEGROES WHERE THEY ARE. I WANT TO GO BACK TO BALTIMORE.
SHUT UP, THOMPSON. KEEP MARCHING.

The Mann Act is another way
they're trying to shackle me.
Just like they did my mother
& my mother's mother.

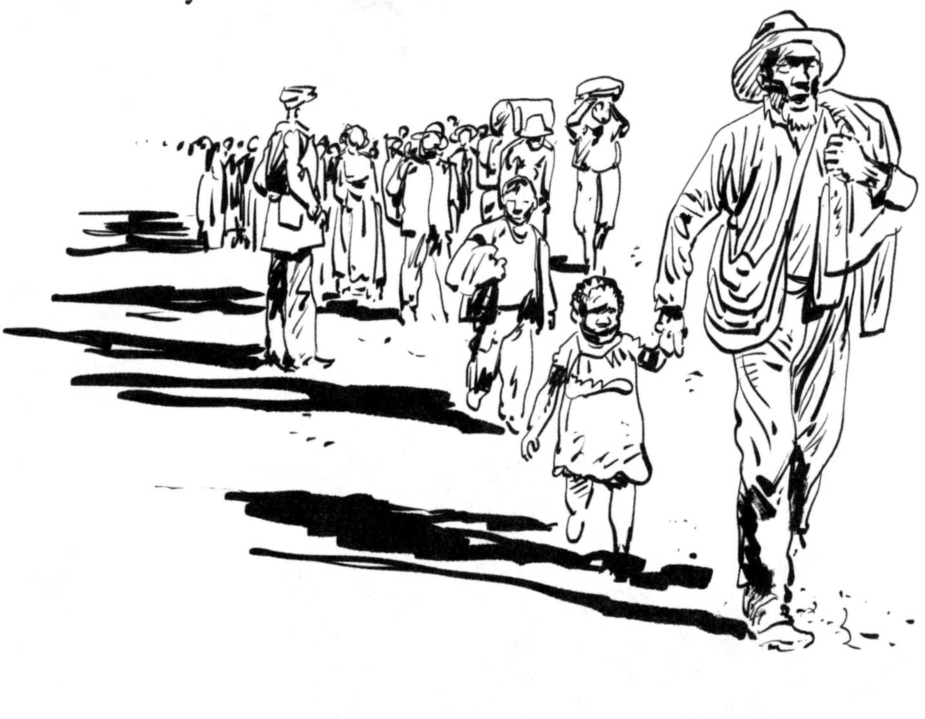

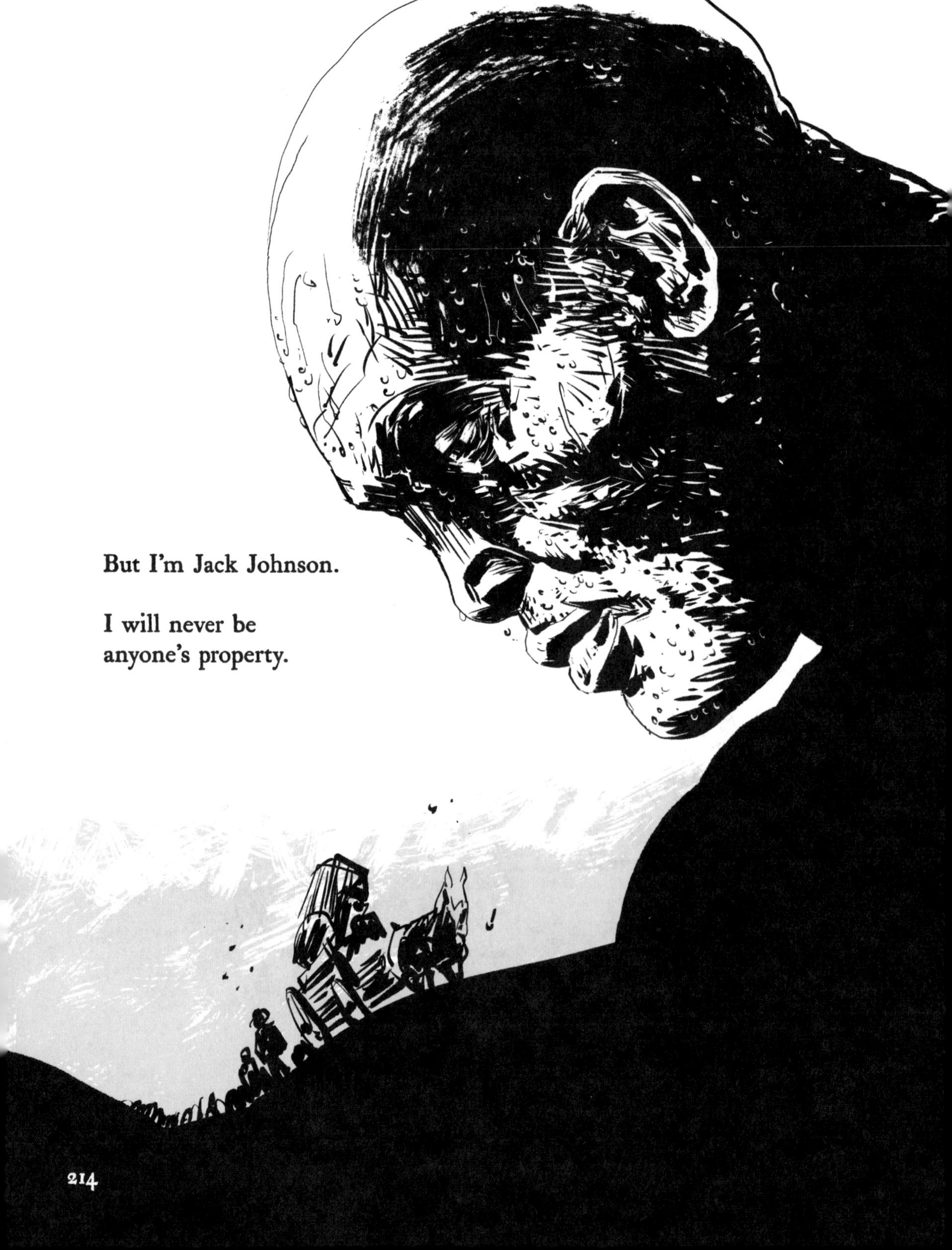
But I'm Jack Johnson.
I will never be
anyone's property.

FREEDOM IS

You want me to tell you
about the condition of being
colored in America? It's true
whites draw the color line
through everything from
apartment buildings to train cars
to championship prizefights,
but I don't pay attention
to their lines. I say again,
I am a full-blooded American
& it's my right to live as I see fit.
The day I don't live as a free man
with eyes & a heart to guide me,
it is time to lock me up
in the lunatic asylum.

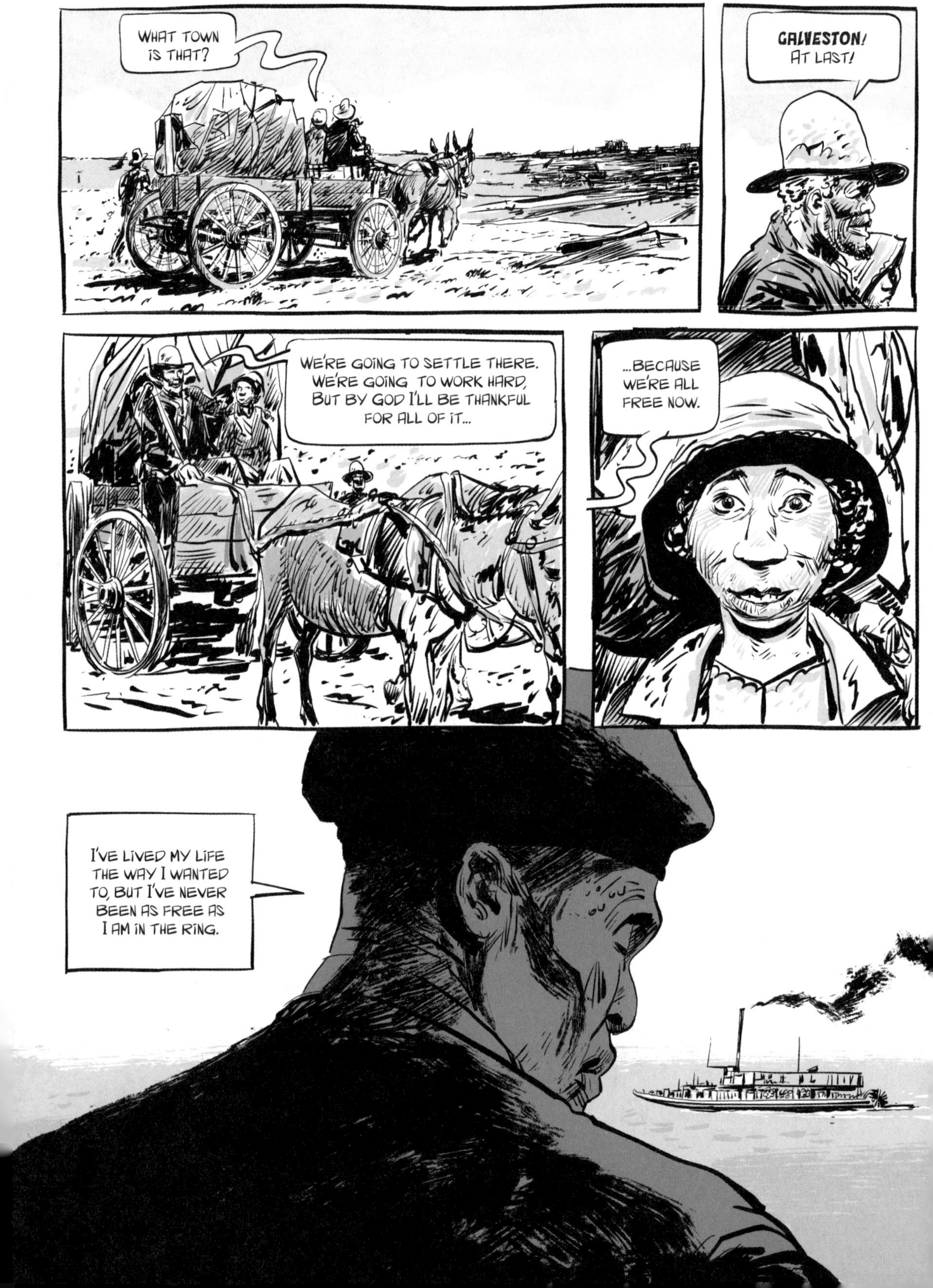
WHAT TOWN IS THAT?
GALVESTON! AT LAST!
WE'RE GOING TO SETTLE THERE. WE'RE GOING TO WORK HARD, BUT BY GOD I'LL BE THANKFUL FOR ALL OF IT...
...BECAUSE WE'RE ALL FREE NOW.
I'VE LIVED MY LIFE THE WAY I WANTED TO, BUT I'VE NEVER BEEN AS FREE AS I AM IN THE RING.

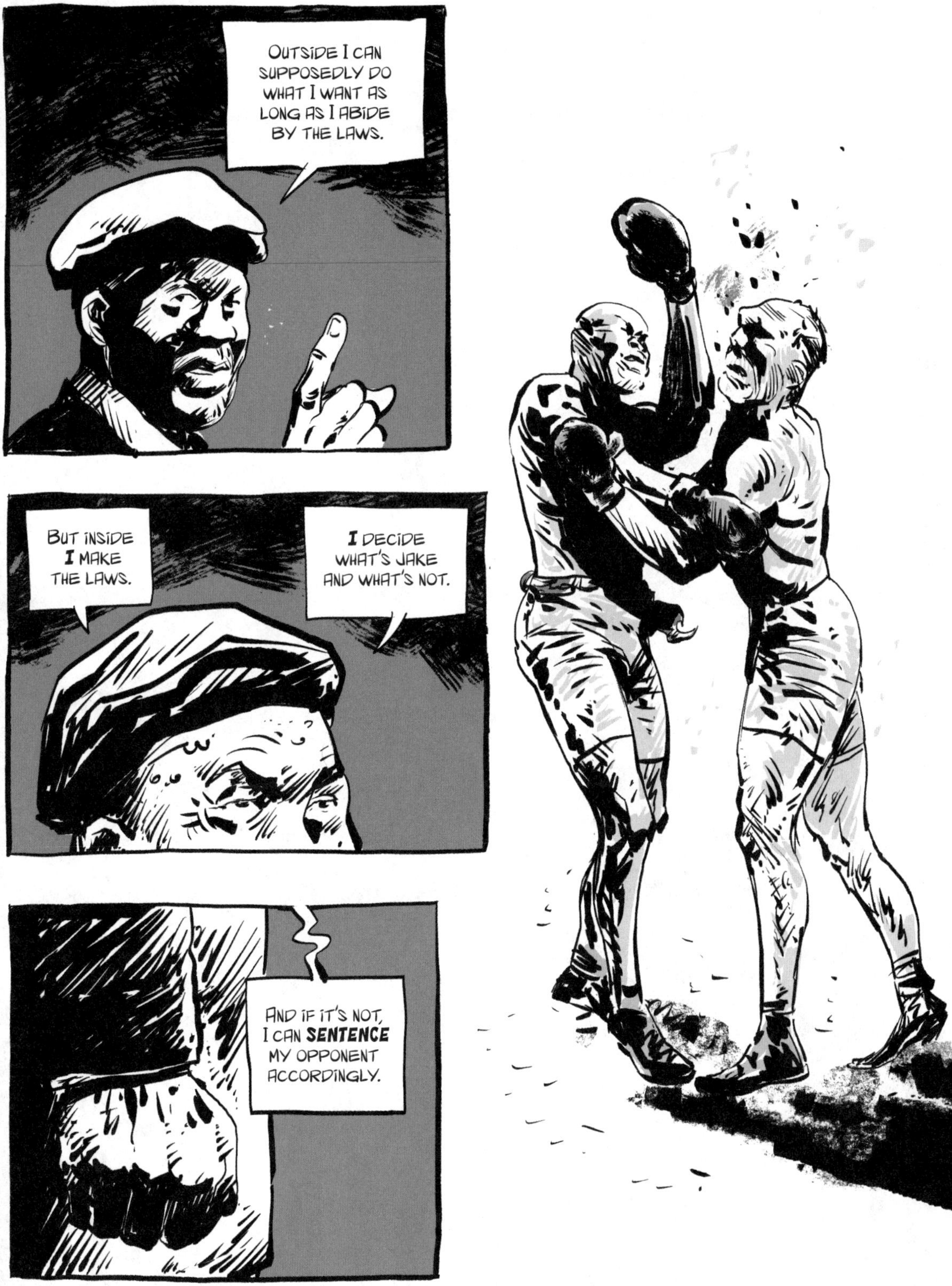
OUTSIDE I CAN SUPPOSEDLY DO WHAT I WANT AS LONG AS I ABIDE BY THE LAWS.
BUT INSIDE **I** MAKE THE LAWS.
I DECIDE WHAT'S JAKE AND WHAT'S NOT.
AND IF IT'S NOT, I CAN **SENTENCE** MY OPPONENT ACCORDINGLY.

THIS WAS JEFF'S WATERLOO

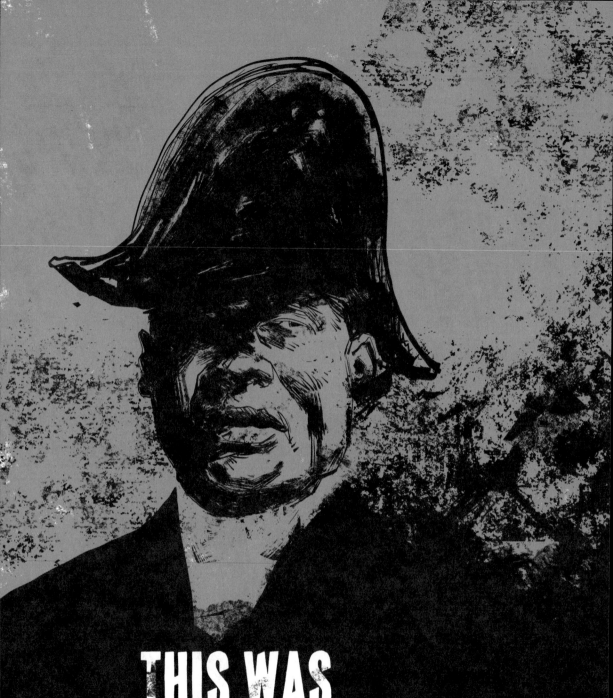

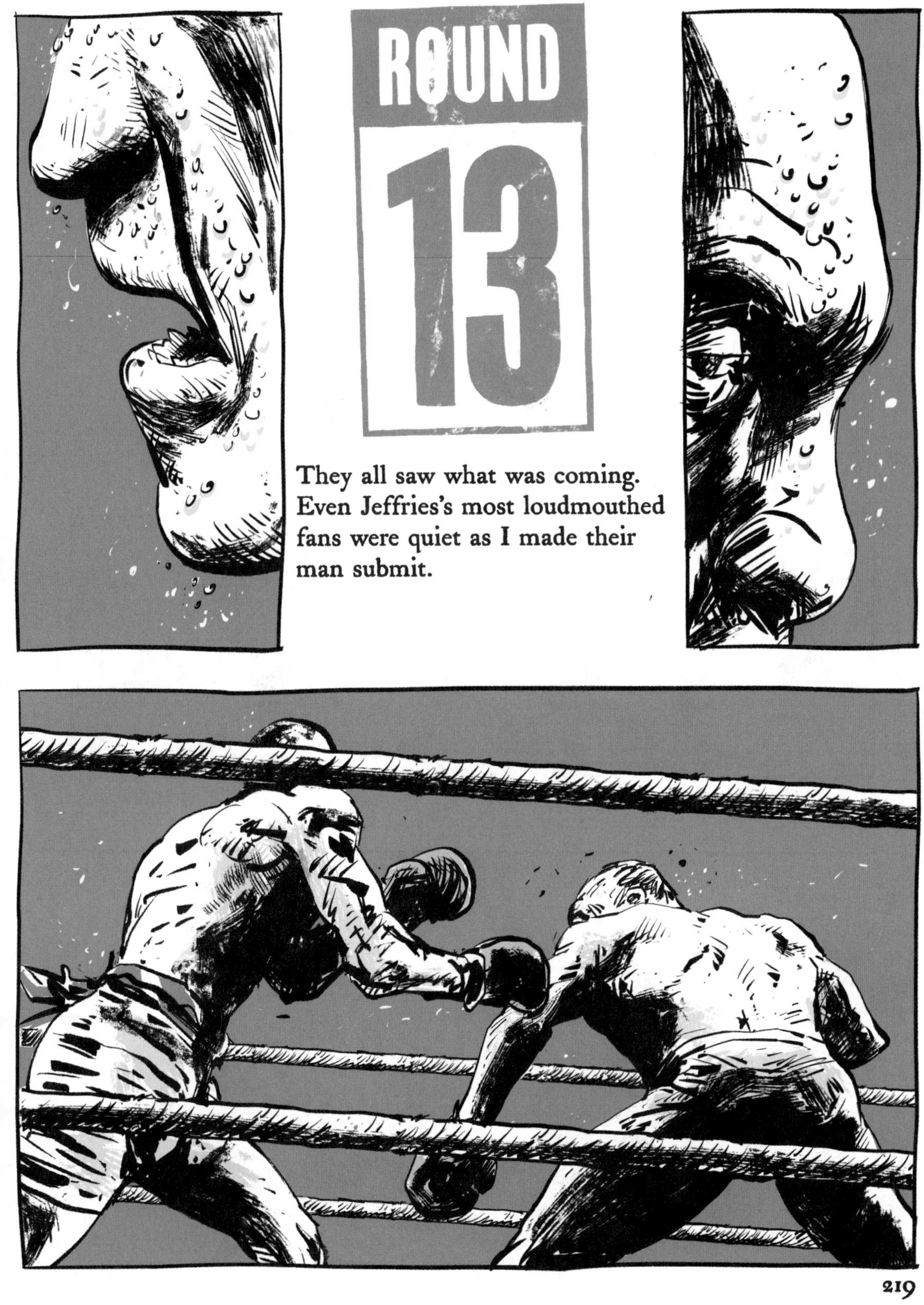
ROUND
13
They all saw what was coming. Even Jeffries's most loudmouthed fans were quiet as I made their man submit.

Questions bring as much hurt as fists do.

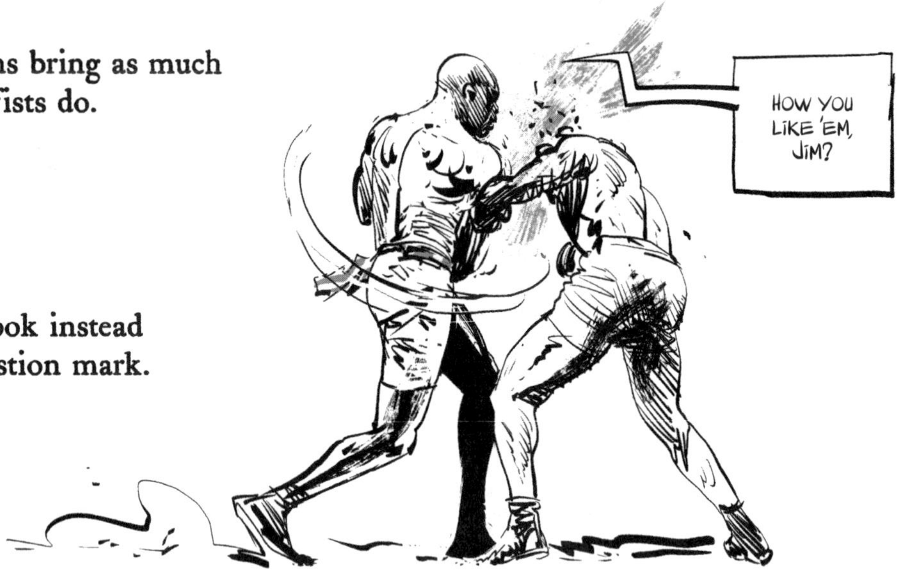
HOW YOU LIKE 'EM, JIM?

Right hook instead of a question mark.

Left then right, straight to the face like a Galveston wind.

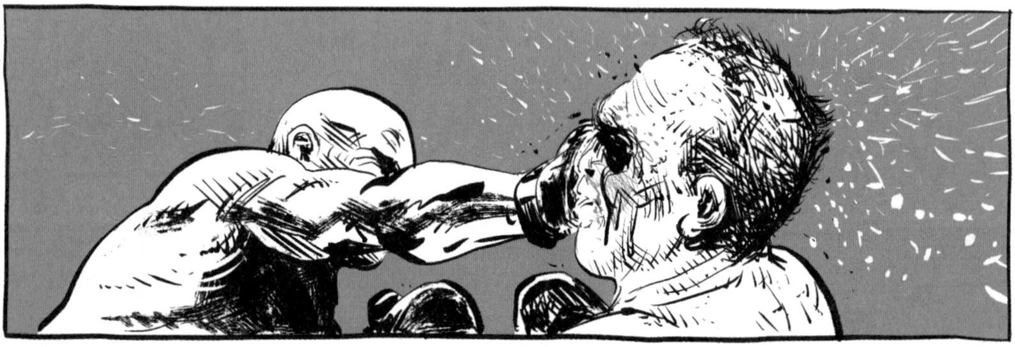

Right jab, then a crunching like eggshells.

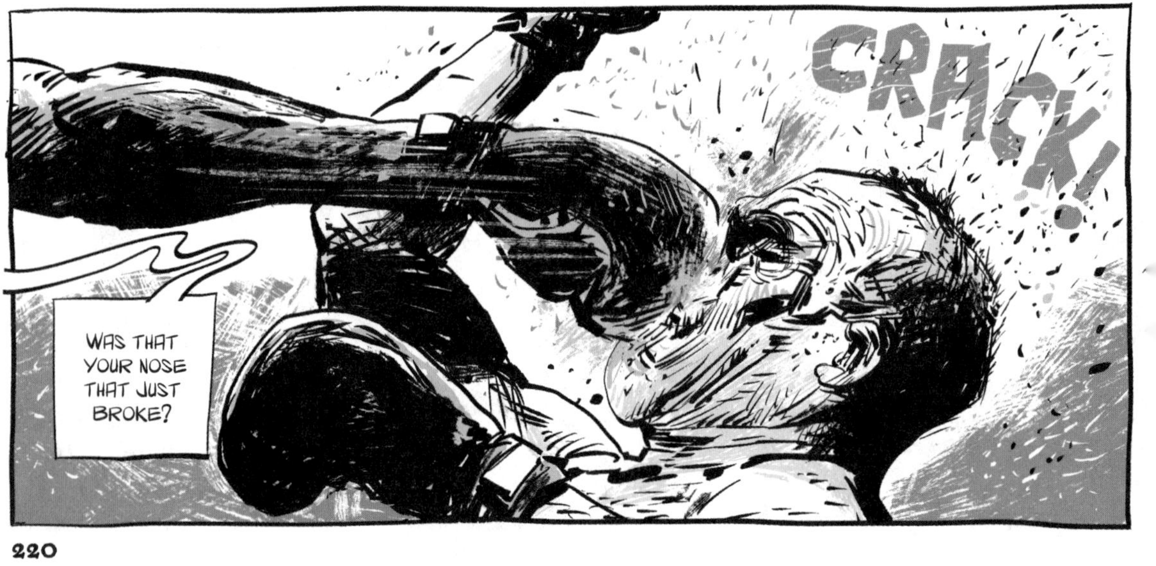
CRACK!
WAS THAT YOUR NOSE THAT JUST BROKE?

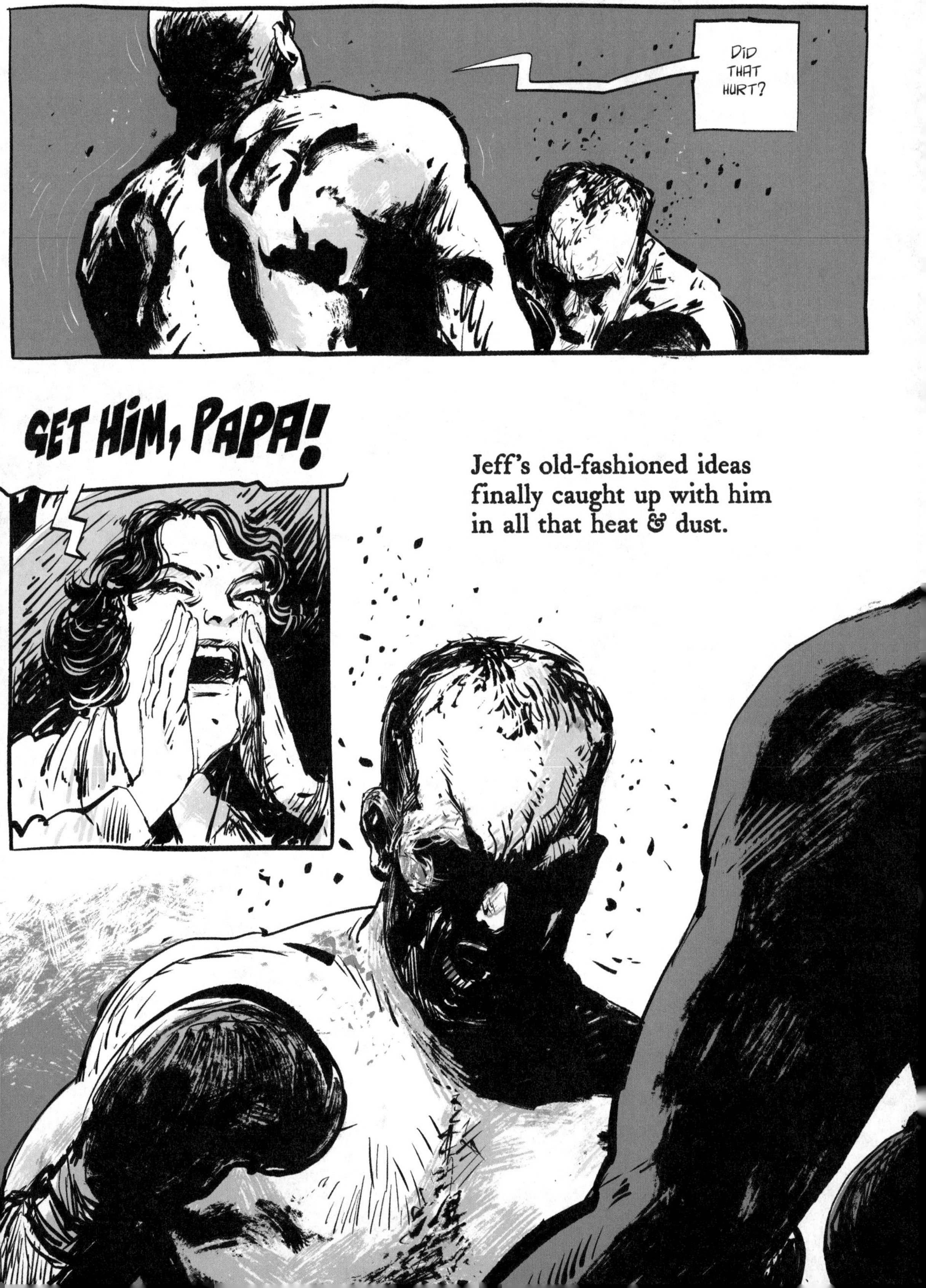
DID THAT HURT?
GET HIM, PAPA!
Jeff's old-fashioned ideas finally caught up with him in all that heat & dust.

CAFÉ DE CHAMPION, CHICAGO, IL 1912

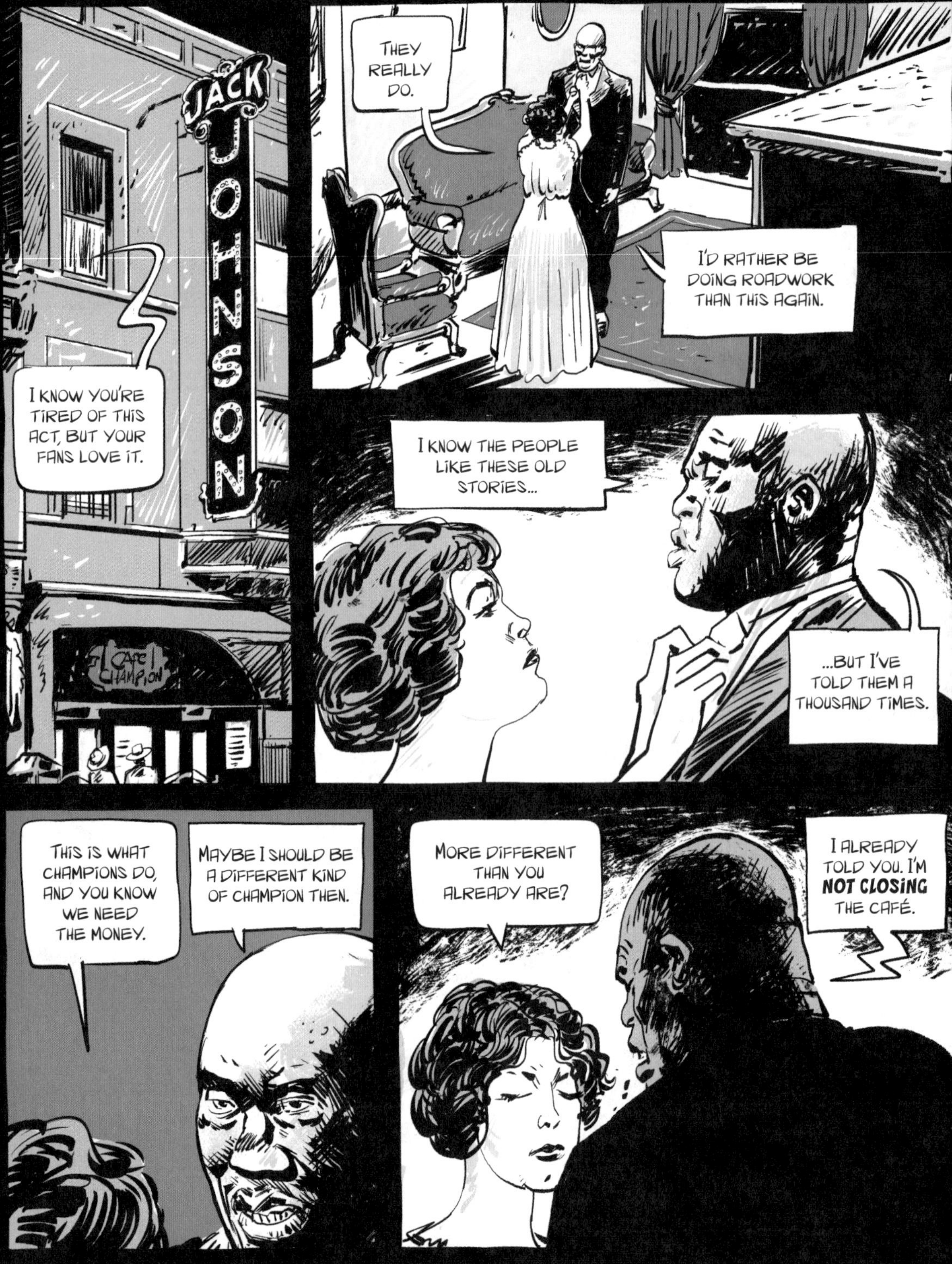
JACK
JOHNSON
CAFE CHAMPION
I KNOW YOU'RE TIRED OF THIS ACT, BUT YOUR FANS LOVE IT.
THEY REALLY DO.
I'D RATHER BE DOING ROADWORK THAN THIS AGAIN.
I KNOW THE PEOPLE LIKE THESE OLD STORIES...
...BUT I'VE TOLD THEM A THOUSAND TIMES.
THIS IS WHAT CHAMPIONS DO, AND YOU KNOW WE NEED THE MONEY.
MAYBE I SHOULD BE A DIFFERENT KIND OF CHAMPION THEN.
MORE DIFFERENT THAN YOU ALREADY ARE?
I ALREADY TOLD YOU. I'M **NOT CLOSING** THE CAFÉ.

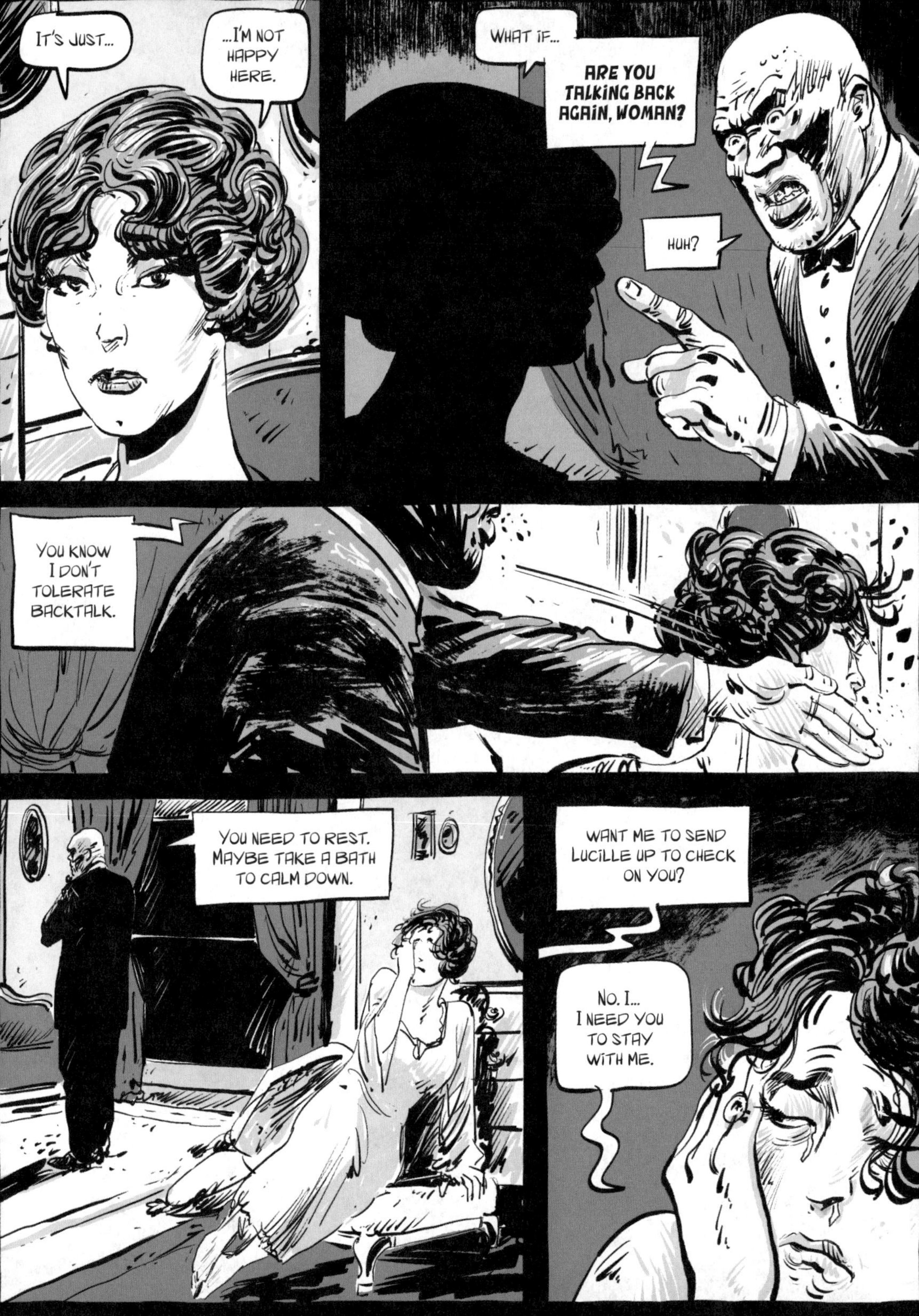
IT'S JUST...
...I'M NOT HAPPY HERE.
WHAT IF...
ARE YOU TALKING BACK AGAIN, WOMAN?
HUH?
YOU KNOW I DON'T TOLERATE BACKTALK.
YOU NEED TO REST. MAYBE TAKE A BATH TO CALM DOWN.
WANT ME TO SEND LUCILLE UP TO CHECK ON YOU?
NO. I... I NEED YOU TO STAY WITH ME.

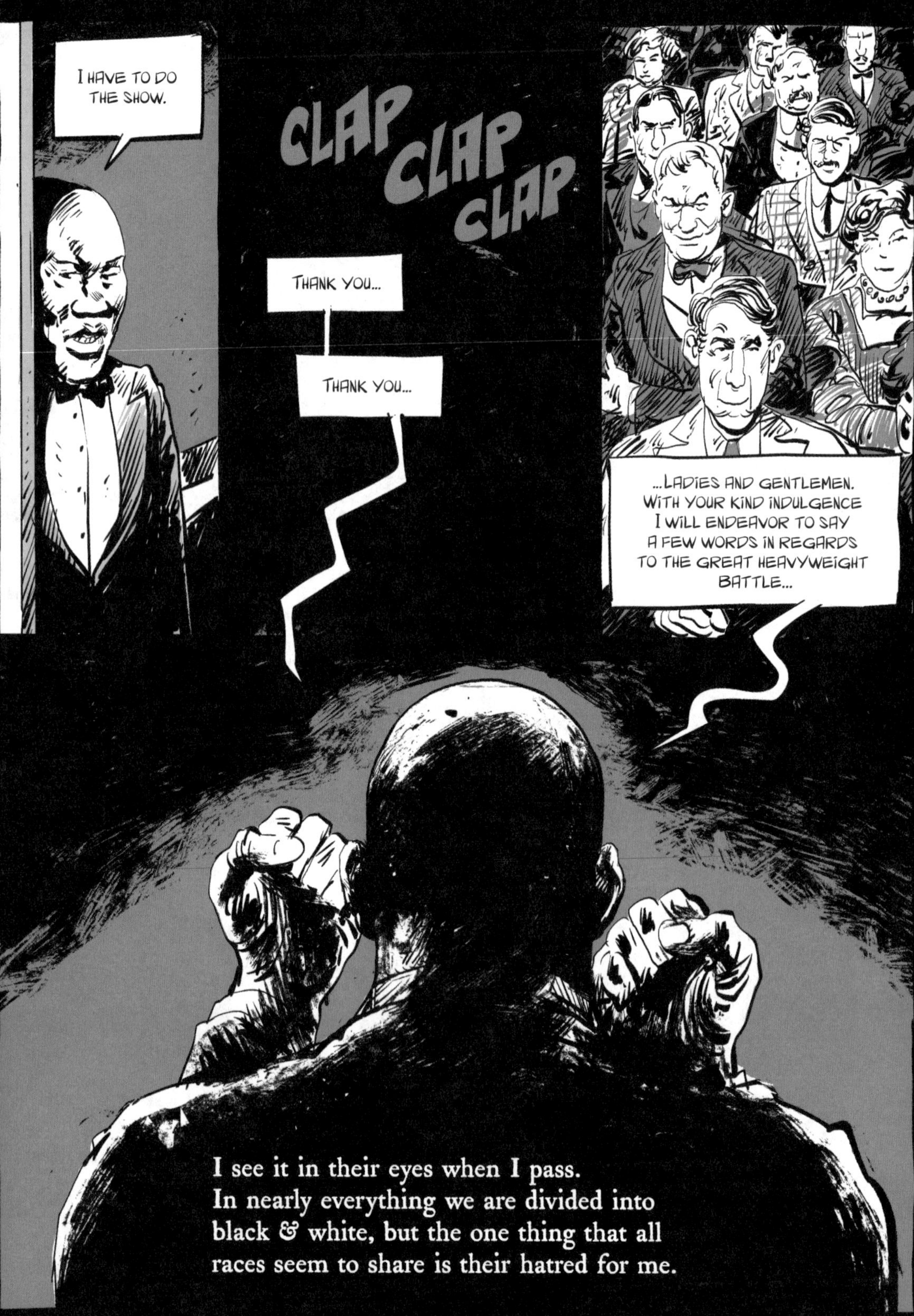
I HAVE TO DO THE SHOW.
CLAP CLAP CLAP
THANK YOU...
THANK YOU...
...LADIES AND GENTLEMEN. WITH YOUR KIND INDULGENCE I WILL ENDEAVOR TO SAY A FEW WORDS IN REGARDS TO THE GREAT HEAVYWEIGHT BATTLE...
I see it in their eyes when I pass. In nearly everything we are divided into black & white, but the one thing that all races seem to share is their hatred for me.

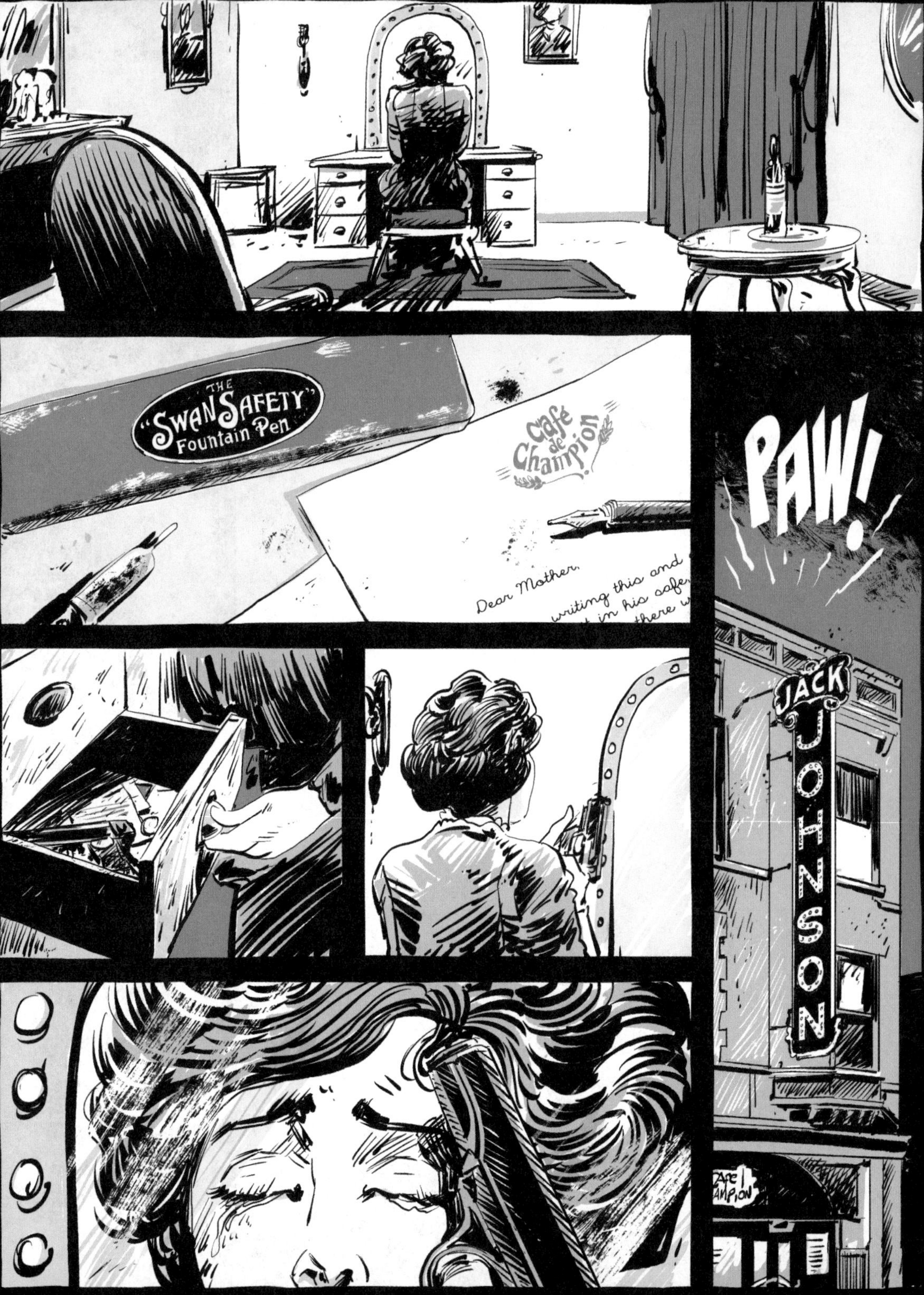
THE "SWAN SAFETY" Fountain Pen
Café de Champion
Dear Mother,
writing this and
in his safe,
there
PAW!
JACK JOHNSON

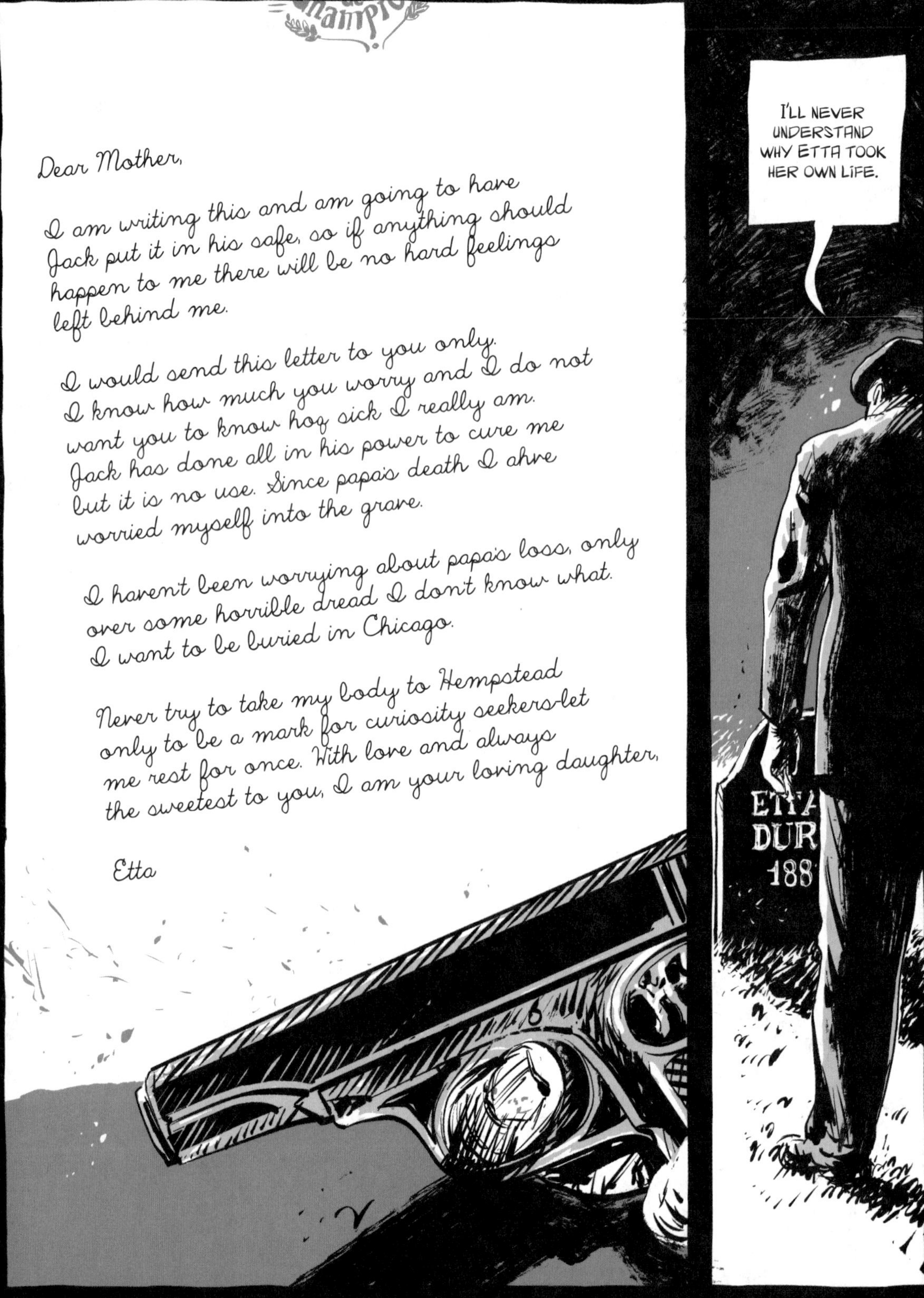
Dear Mother,
I am writing this and am going to have Jack put it in his safe, so if anything should happen to me there will be no hard feelings left behind me.
I would send this letter to you only. I know how much you worry and I do not want you to know hoq sick I really am. Jack has done all in his power to cure me but it is no use. Since papa's death I ahve worried myself into the grave.
I haven't been worrying about papa's loss, only over some horrible dread I don't know what. I want to be buried in Chicago.
Never try to take my body to Hempstead only to be a mark for curiosity seekers-let me rest for once. With love and always the sweetest to you, I am your loving daughter,
Etta
I'LL NEVER UNDERSTAND WHY ETTA TOOK HER OWN LIFE.
ETTA
DUR
188

JOHNSON'S WIFE COMMITS SUICIDE AT HER NEW HOME

Mrs. Etta Duryea Johnson Ends Life By Sending Bullet Into Her Brain.

WAS MARRIED IN THIS CITY

Chicago, Ill.—A little more than two years ago, Etta Duryea, divorced wife of Clarence Duryea, a millionaire of New York horseman, married a black man, the champion pugilist of modern times. Despite the pleading of her family and friends, she became Mrs. Jack Johnson. Today she lies dead by her own hand.

Dismissing her maids Wednesday night with the injunction that they "pray for her," Mrs. Johnson went to her rooms above her husband's cafe—the Cafe De Champ[...] 3:30 Thursday morning [...] were alarmed by [...] Rushing upsta[...] pugilist's w[...] floor, a b[...] rushed [...] out reg[...]

Ett[...] wife [...] club[...] Islan[...] got a d[...]

The firs[...] racial marria[...] friends in the e[...] her. Then cam[...] full realization o[...] her friends a[...] "conquest of [...] son built a p[...] avenue, and [...] family there. [...] son's menage[...] outcast from [...] thought she wa[...]

Mrs. Johnson [...] night for Las [...] Shortly before tim[...] eloped an attack o[...] the trip was postpo[...] After dismissing [...] Johnson went to her [...] cafe. The shoot[...] minutes later [...] Jack Jo[...] whe[...]

JACK JOHNSON'S WIFE SELF-SHOT

White Spouse of Prize Fighter Asks Her Maids' Prayers and Pulls Trigger.

ONCE A SOCIETY WOMAN.

Etta H. Duryea became the bride of John Arthur Johnson of Pittsburgh, January 18, 1911, although the fact of their being married here did not eak out until a year after that date. The ceremony was performed by Al[...] [...]man John A. Fugassi, in the par[...] [...] hotel, 518 Wy[...] [...]etor being a [...]mpion pugilist. [...] an engagement [...]inning January [...]y of Music in [...]oyed by fire [...] The marriage li[...] [...]use was taken out in the local mar[...] [...] office opposite the courthouse. [...] A. Johnson, [...]

JACK JOHNSON TORTURED WHITE WIFE.

Why Didn't Jeff Kill 'Im?

THE STORY OF A BEAST.

Jack Johnson Drove His Wife to Suicide.

Terrible Revelations by Her Mother.

"I Ask God to Send Him His Punishment."

I GUESS THE WORLD WAS TOO MUCH FOR HER.

MAYBE IF I'D STAYED WITH HER INSTEAD OF DOING THE DAMN SHOW.

MAYBE IF I'D TAKEN HER TO DINNER INSTEAD OF CAROUSING.

MAYBE IF...

227

ROUND 14

Sometimes the time
between a punch
& when it connects
feels like a year.

Time gets slow, but it's not
like you can see the future.
Not really.

I didn't see Etta in her room
with a gun in her hand.

I didn't hear the gunshot over
the dancers turkey-trotting
right below where her blood
made her a halo on the floor.

The future is full of fear.
I've never been afraid
in the ring because there's
nothing frightening about
the hurt business.

There's a simple science to it:
it's better to avoid a punch
than to clinch. It's better to whip
somebody than it is to be whipped.

There are some things you can't beat no matter how many gut hooks you throw.

The women in my life have hurt me more than any fighter ever could.

I will never understand the science of women.

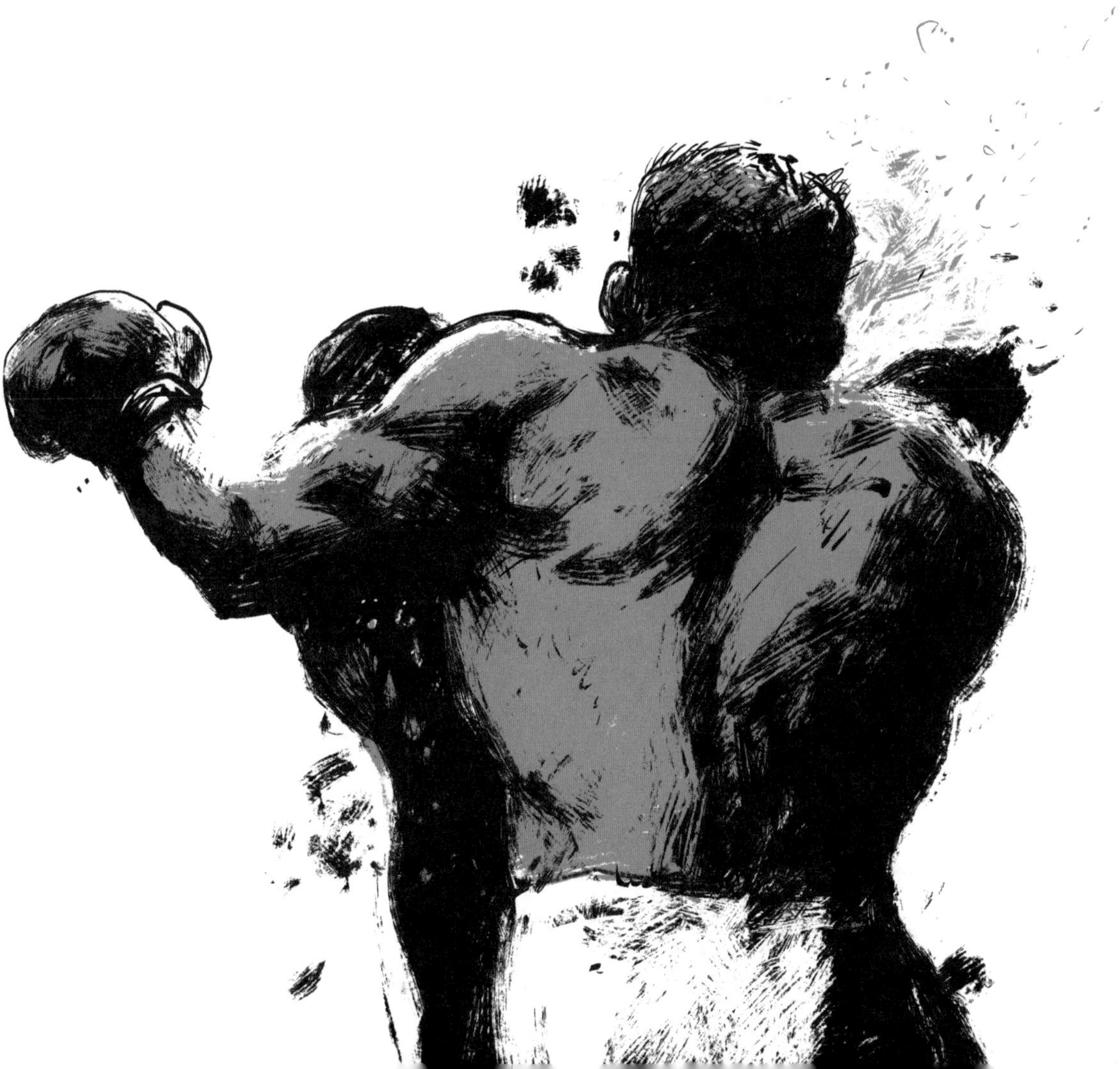

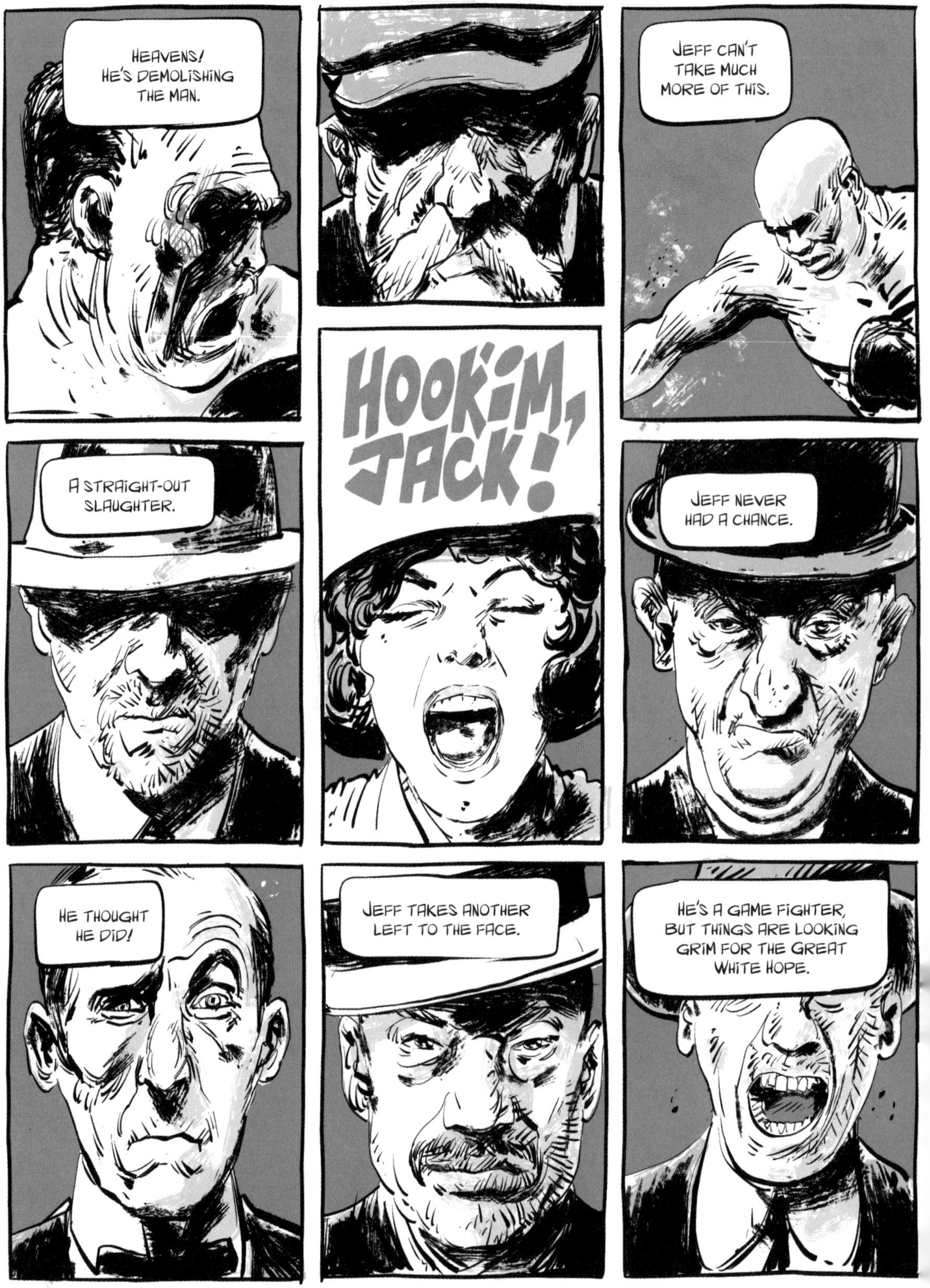
HEAVENS! HE'S DEMOLISHING THE MAN.
JEFF CAN'T TAKE MUCH MORE OF THIS.
HOOK 'IM, JACK!
A STRAIGHT-OUT SLAUGHTER.
JEFF NEVER HAD A CHANCE.
HE THOUGHT HE DID!
JEFF TAKES ANOTHER LEFT TO THE FACE.
HE'S A GAME FIGHTER, BUT THINGS ARE LOOKING GRIM FOR THE GREAT WHITE HOPE.

BRING UP YOUR LEFT!

YOUR LEFT!

I chose to keep you upright, Jeff.

HIT'IM!

I KEPT YOU UP **LONG ENOUGH,** JIMMY!

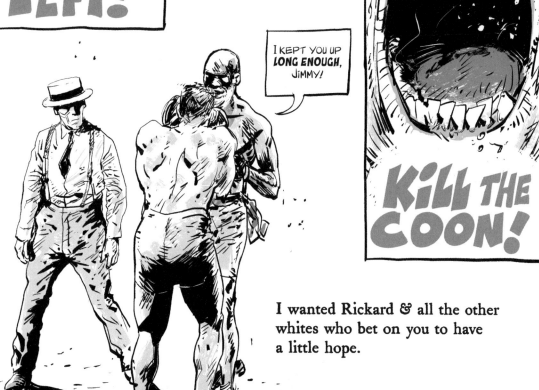

KILL THE COON!

I wanted Rickard & all the other whites who bet on you to have a little hope.

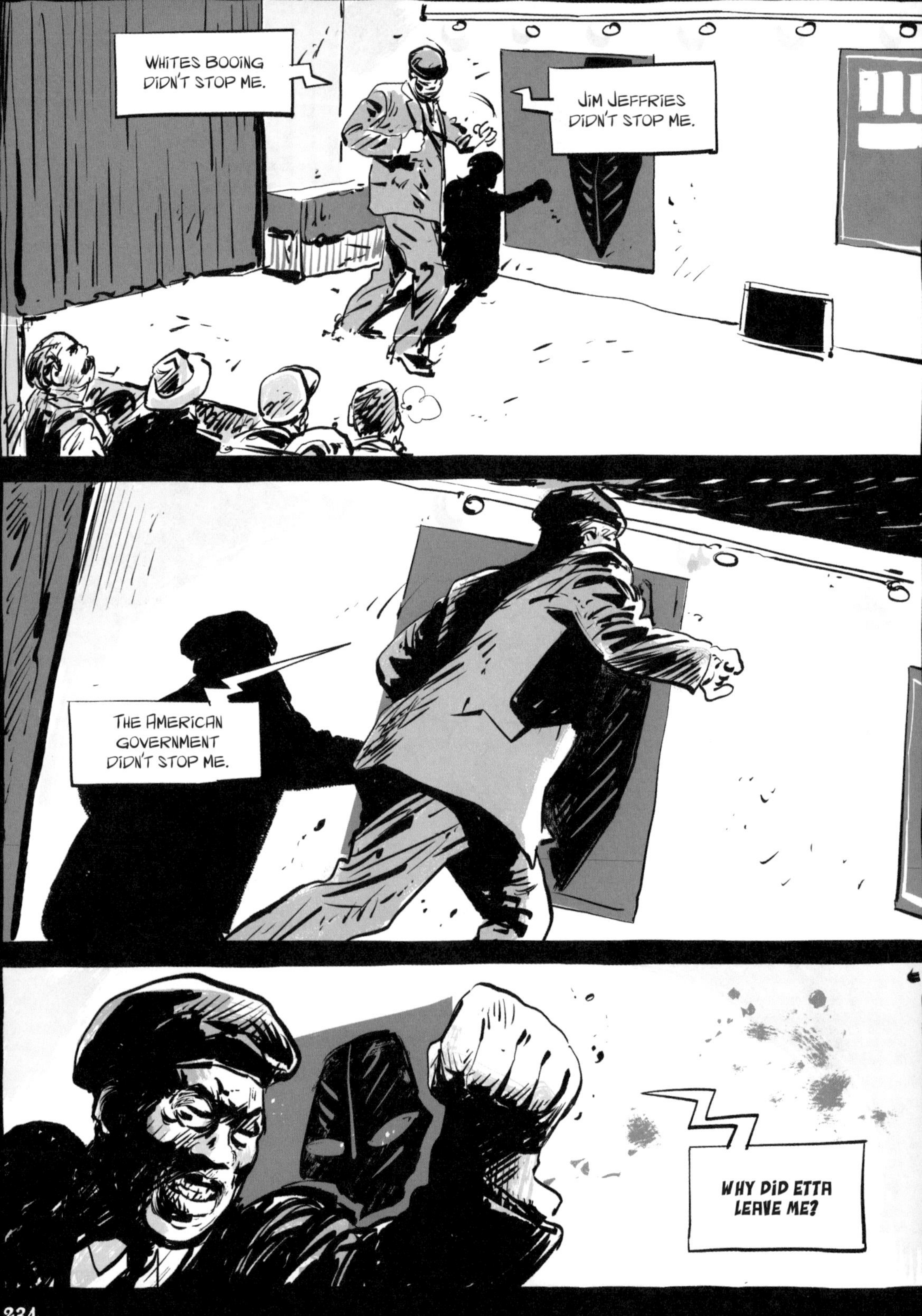
WHITES BOOING DIDN'T STOP ME.
JIM JEFFRIES DIDN'T STOP ME.
THE AMERICAN GOVERNMENT DIDN'T STOP ME.
WHY DID ETTA LEAVE ME?

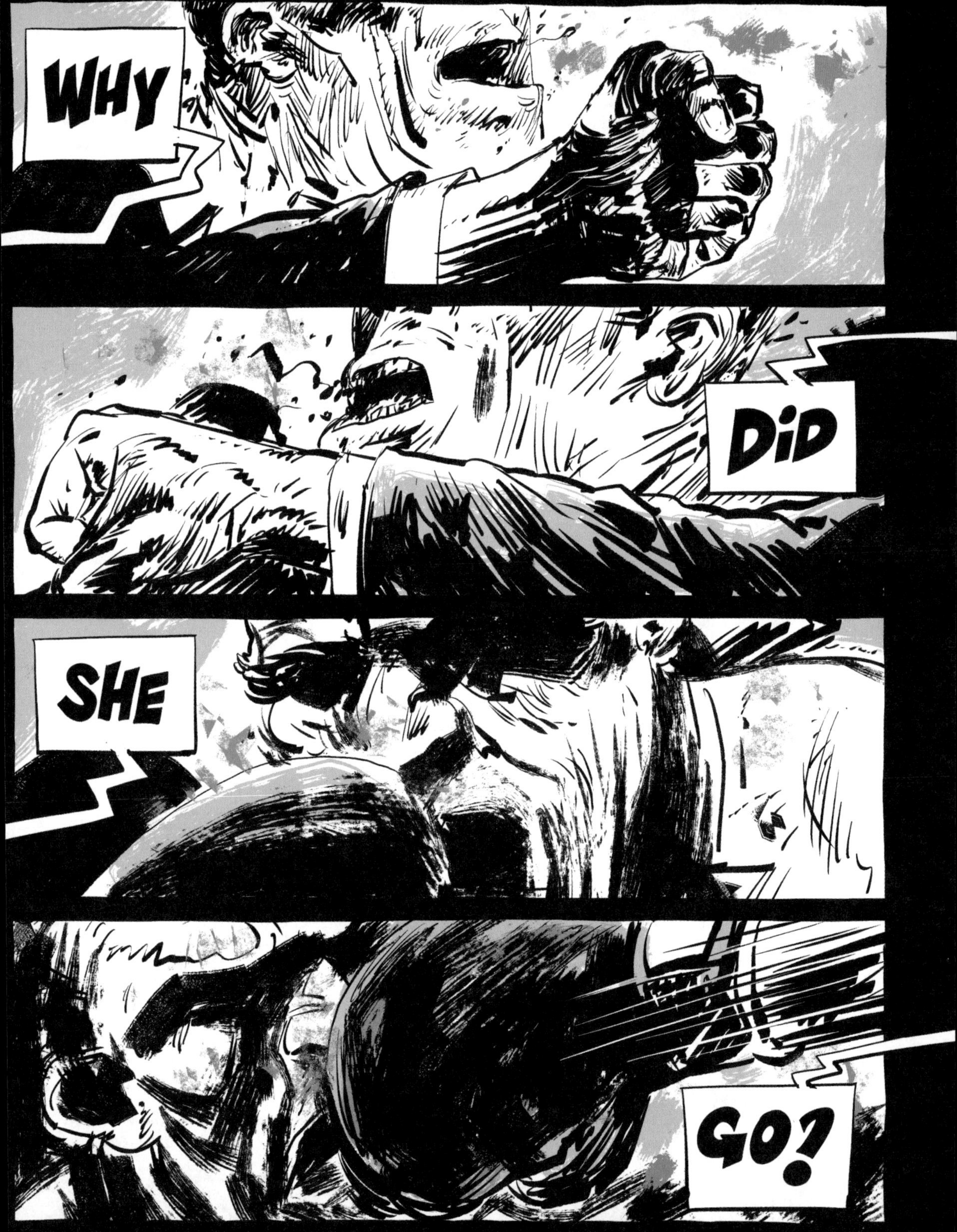
WHY
DID
SHE
GO?

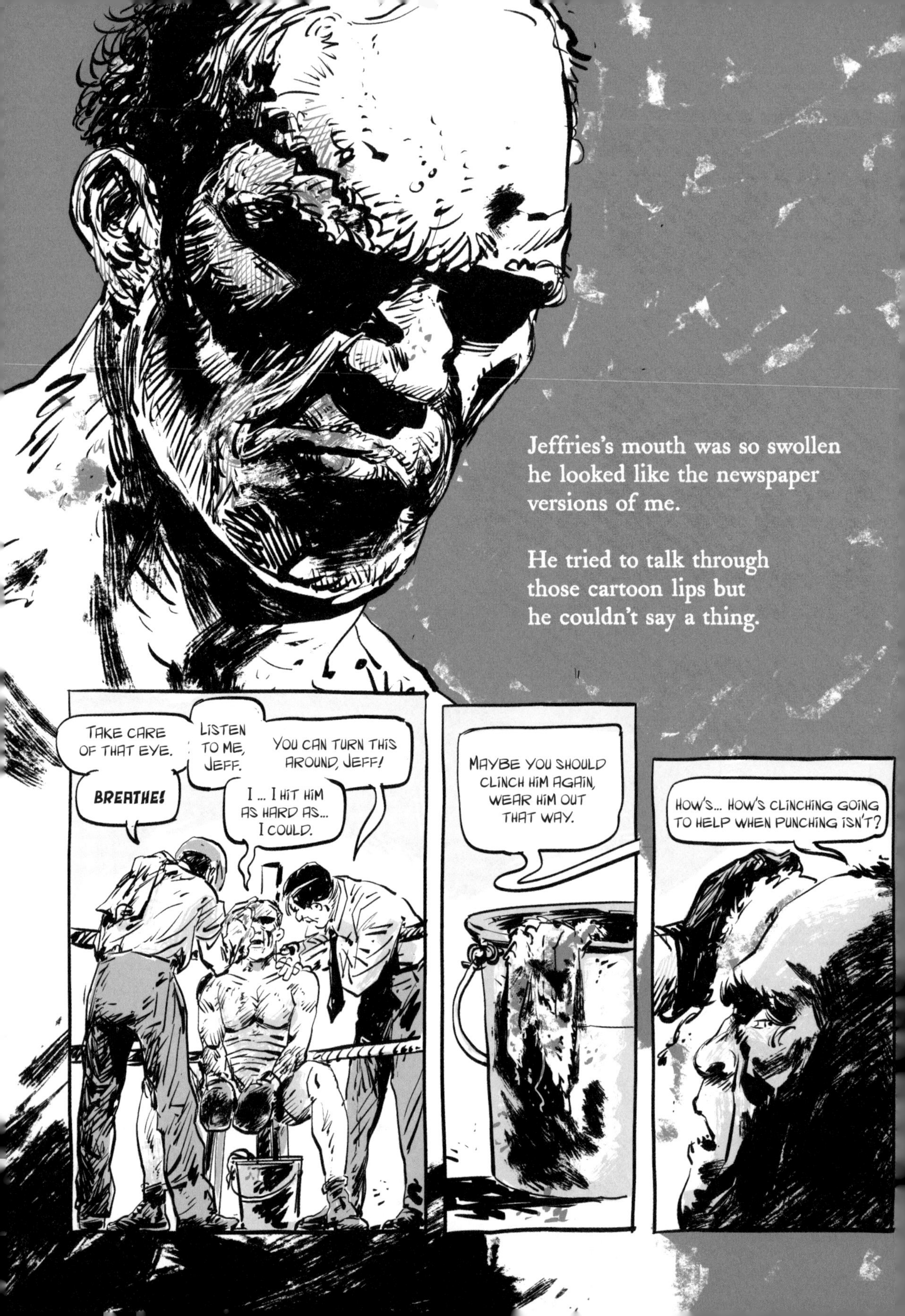

Jeffries's mouth was so swollen he looked like the newspaper versions of me.
He tried to talk through those cartoon lips but he couldn't say a thing.
TAKE CARE OF THAT EYE.
BREATHE!
LISTEN TO ME, JEFF.
YOU CAN TURN THIS AROUND, JEFF!
I ... I HIT HIM AS HARD AS... I COULD.
MAYBE YOU SHOULD CLINCH HIM AGAIN, WEAR HIM OUT THAT WAY.
HOW'S... HOW'S CLINCHING GOING TO HELP WHEN PUNCHING ISN'T?

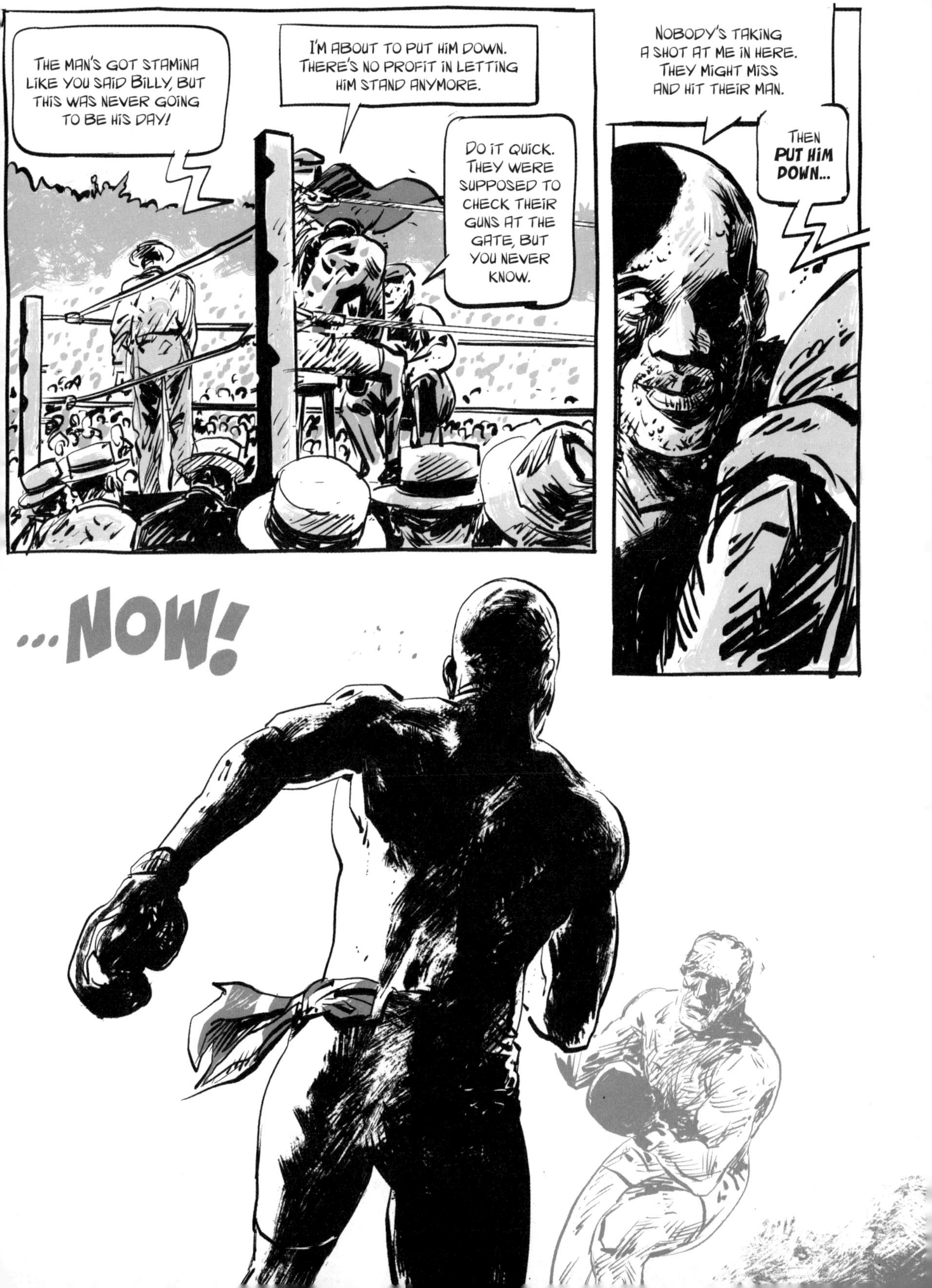
THE MAN'S GOT STAMINA LIKE YOU SAID BILLY, BUT THIS WAS NEVER GOING TO BE HIS DAY!
I'M ABOUT TO PUT HIM DOWN. THERE'S NO PROFIT IN LETTING HIM STAND ANYMORE.
DO IT QUICK. THEY WERE SUPPOSED TO CHECK THEIR GUNS AT THE GATE, BUT YOU NEVER KNOW.
NOBODY'S TAKING A SHOT AT ME IN HERE. THEY MIGHT MISS AND HIT THEIR MAN.
THEN **PUT HIM DOWN...**
...NOW!

ROUND 15

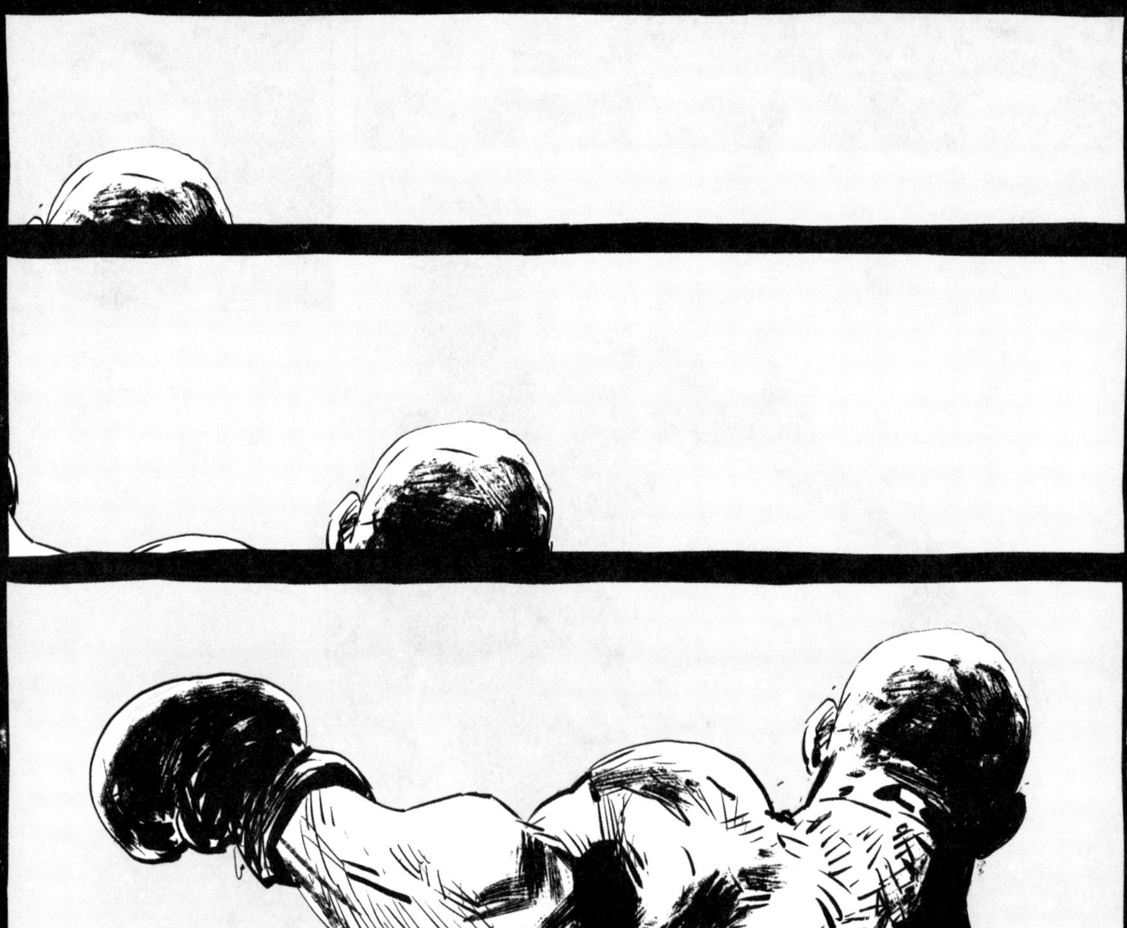

SOMETIMES THE TIME BETWEEN A THROWN JAB AND THE IMPACT FEELS LIKE A MINUTE

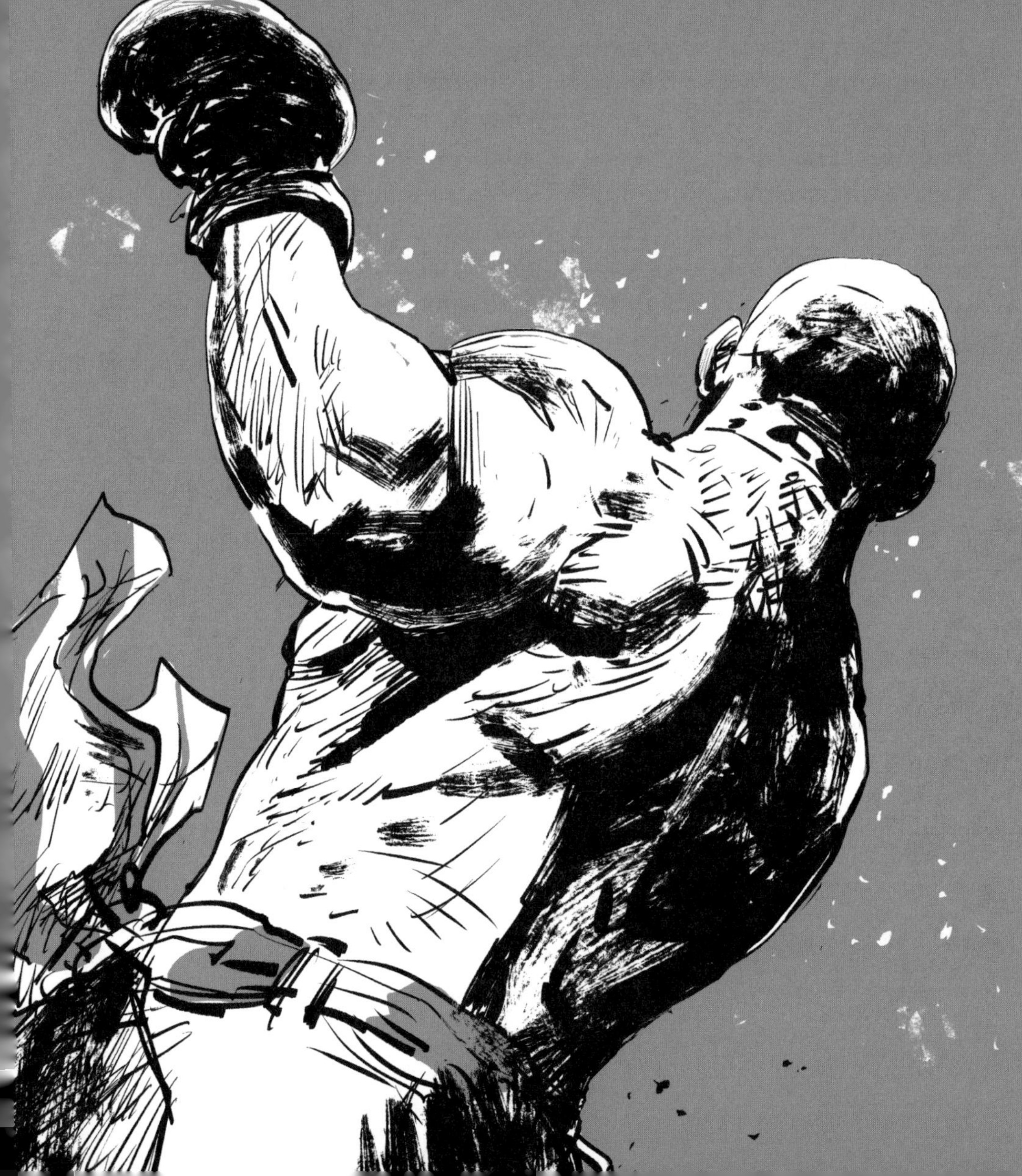

THE MANN ACT

The Mann Act was supposed to keep white women from
prostitution. But what if they were already in the trade like
Belle? I'm going to jail for her misdeeds, while she gets away
scot-free. The Mann Act was invented to keep men from
kidnapping women & forcing them to become prostitutes.
It reminds me of those villains in the silent pictures: all
in black with a hat, mustache & goatee who would tie a girl
to the train tracks. I always wondered why the bad guys did that.
Just before the locomotive runs the girl over, the hero always
rides to the rescue. I guess the marshals thought they'd be
the heroes saving helpless damsels from me. But I've never had
a mustache & Belle Schreiber was no damsel. She was a favorite
of many local politicians & law keepers when she worked
at the Everleigh Club.

I PROMISED TO TELL
YOU THE PLAIN TRUTH,
AND IT DOESN'T GET ANY
TRUER THAN THIS:

THE FIX
WAS IN
FROM THE
START.

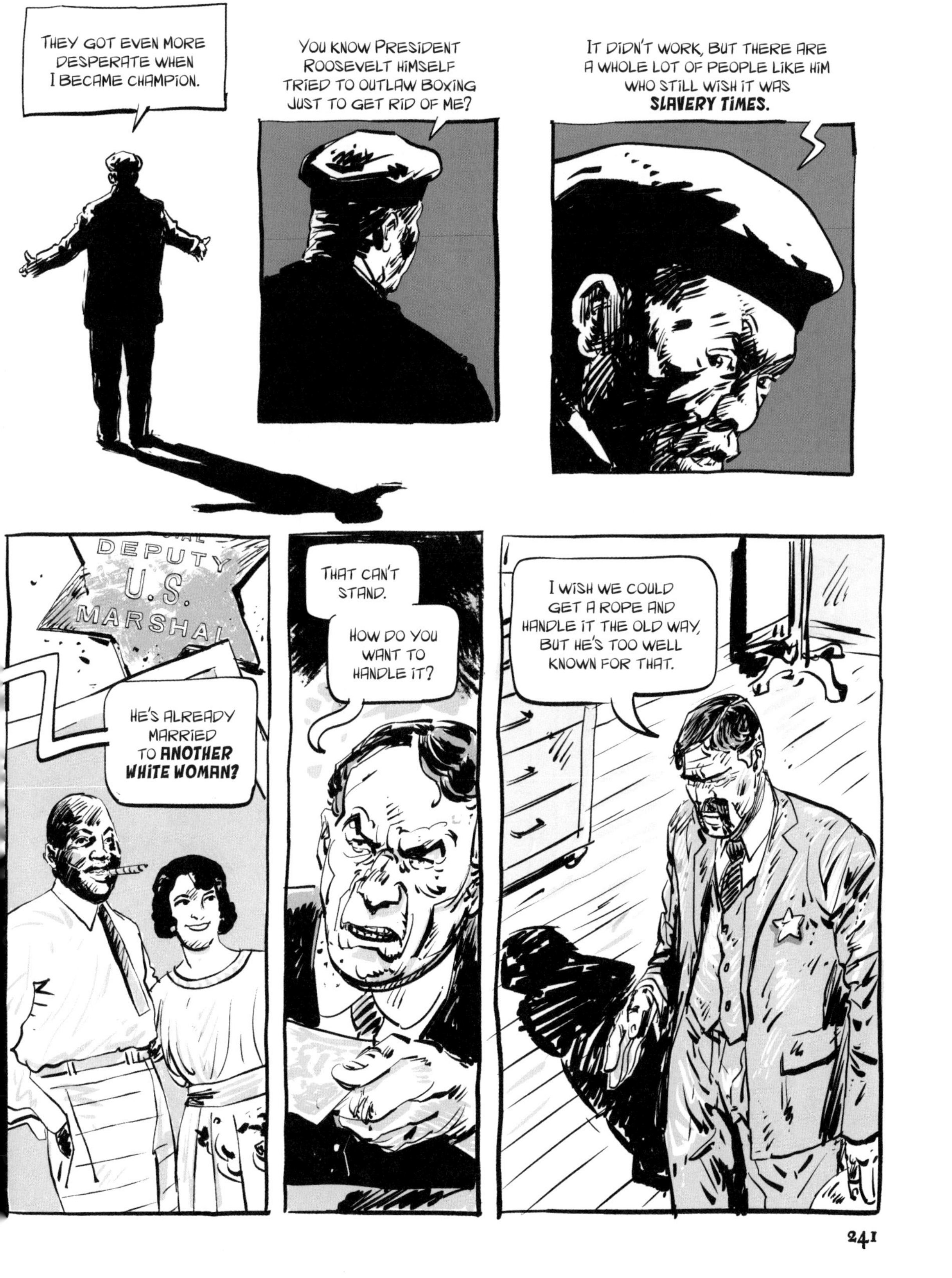
THEY GOT EVEN MORE DESPERATE WHEN I BECAME CHAMPION.
YOU KNOW PRESIDENT ROOSEVELT HIMSELF TRIED TO OUTLAW BOXING JUST TO GET RID OF ME?
IT DIDN'T WORK, BUT THERE ARE A WHOLE LOT OF PEOPLE LIKE HIM WHO STILL WISH IT WAS **SLAVERY TIMES.**
DEPUTY U.S. MARSHAL
HE'S ALREADY MARRIED TO **ANOTHER WHITE WOMAN?**
THAT CAN'T STAND.
HOW DO YOU WANT TO HANDLE IT?
I WISH WE COULD GET A ROPE AND HANDLE IT THE OLD WAY, BUT HE'S TOO WELL KNOWN FOR THAT.

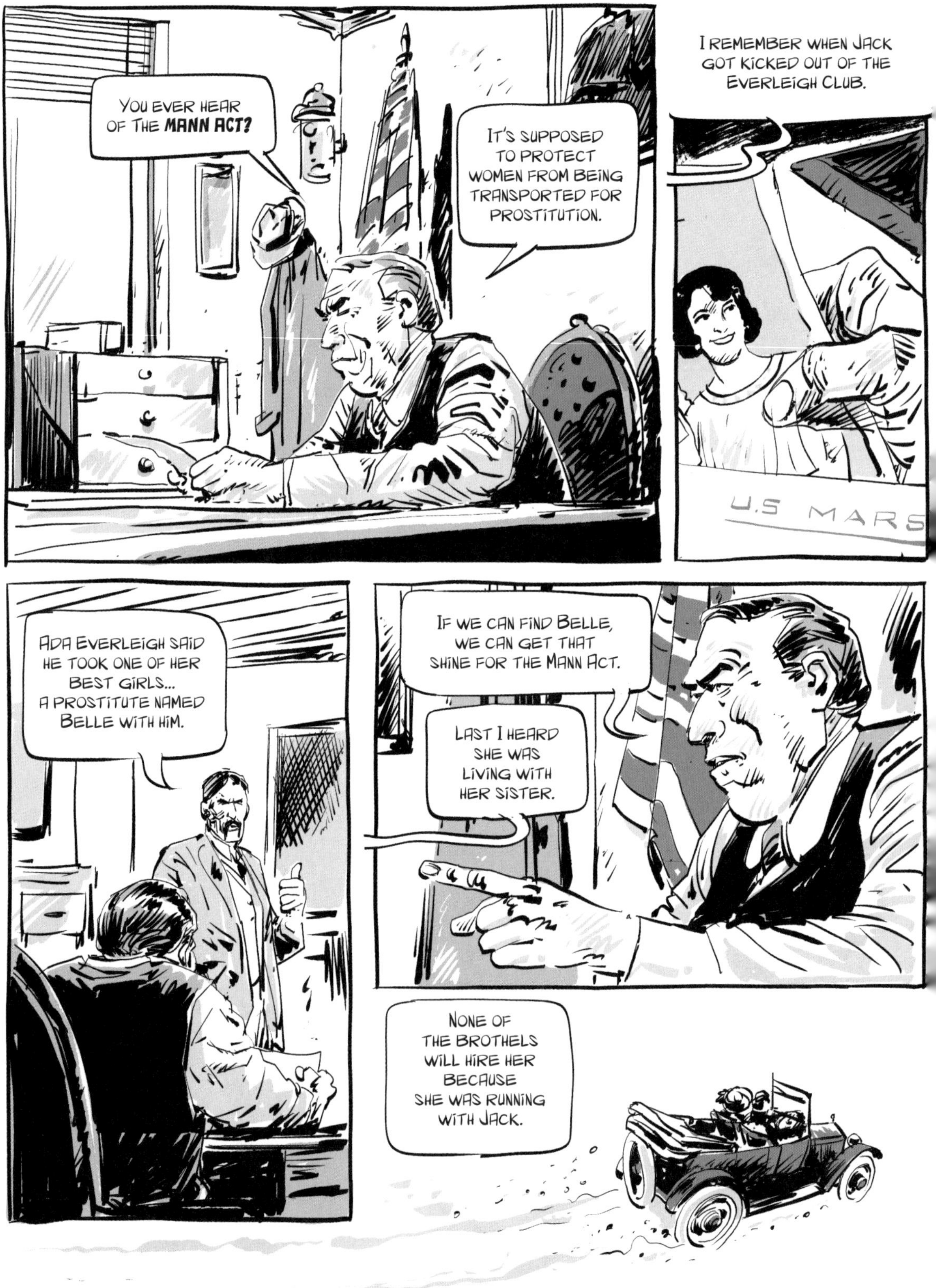
YOU EVER HEAR OF THE **MANN ACT?**
IT'S SUPPOSED TO PROTECT WOMEN FROM BEING TRANSPORTED FOR PROSTITUTION.
I REMEMBER WHEN JACK GOT KICKED OUT OF THE EVERLEIGH CLUB.
U.S MARS
ADA EVERLEIGH SAID HE TOOK ONE OF HER BEST GIRLS... A PROSTITUTE NAMED BELLE WITH HIM.
IF WE CAN FIND BELLE, WE CAN GET THAT SHINE FOR THE MANN ACT.
LAST I HEARD SHE WAS LIVING WITH HER SISTER.
NONE OF THE BROTHELS WILL HIRE HER BECAUSE SHE WAS RUNNING WITH JACK.

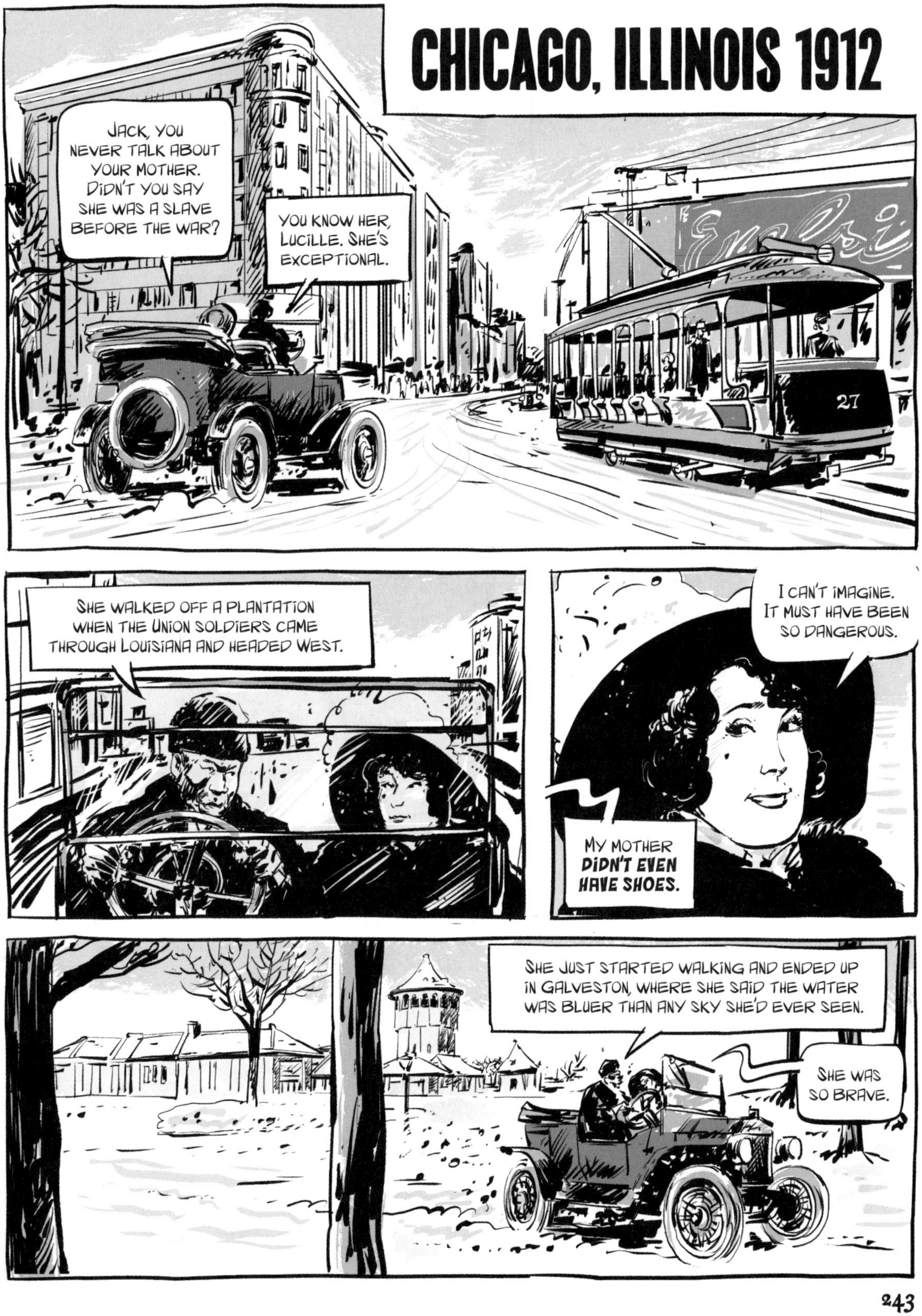
CHICAGO, ILLINOIS 1912
JACK, YOU NEVER TALK ABOUT YOUR MOTHER. DIDN'T YOU SAY SHE WAS A SLAVE BEFORE THE WAR?
YOU KNOW HER, LUCILLE. SHE'S EXCEPTIONAL.
27
SHE WALKED OFF A PLANTATION WHEN THE UNION SOLDIERS CAME THROUGH LOUISIANA AND HEADED WEST.
I CAN'T IMAGINE. IT MUST HAVE BEEN SO DANGEROUS.
MY MOTHER DIDN'T EVEN HAVE SHOES.
SHE JUST STARTED WALKING AND ENDED UP IN GALVESTON, WHERE SHE SAID THE WATER WAS BLUER THAN ANY SKY SHE'D EVER SEEN.
SHE WAS SO BRAVE.

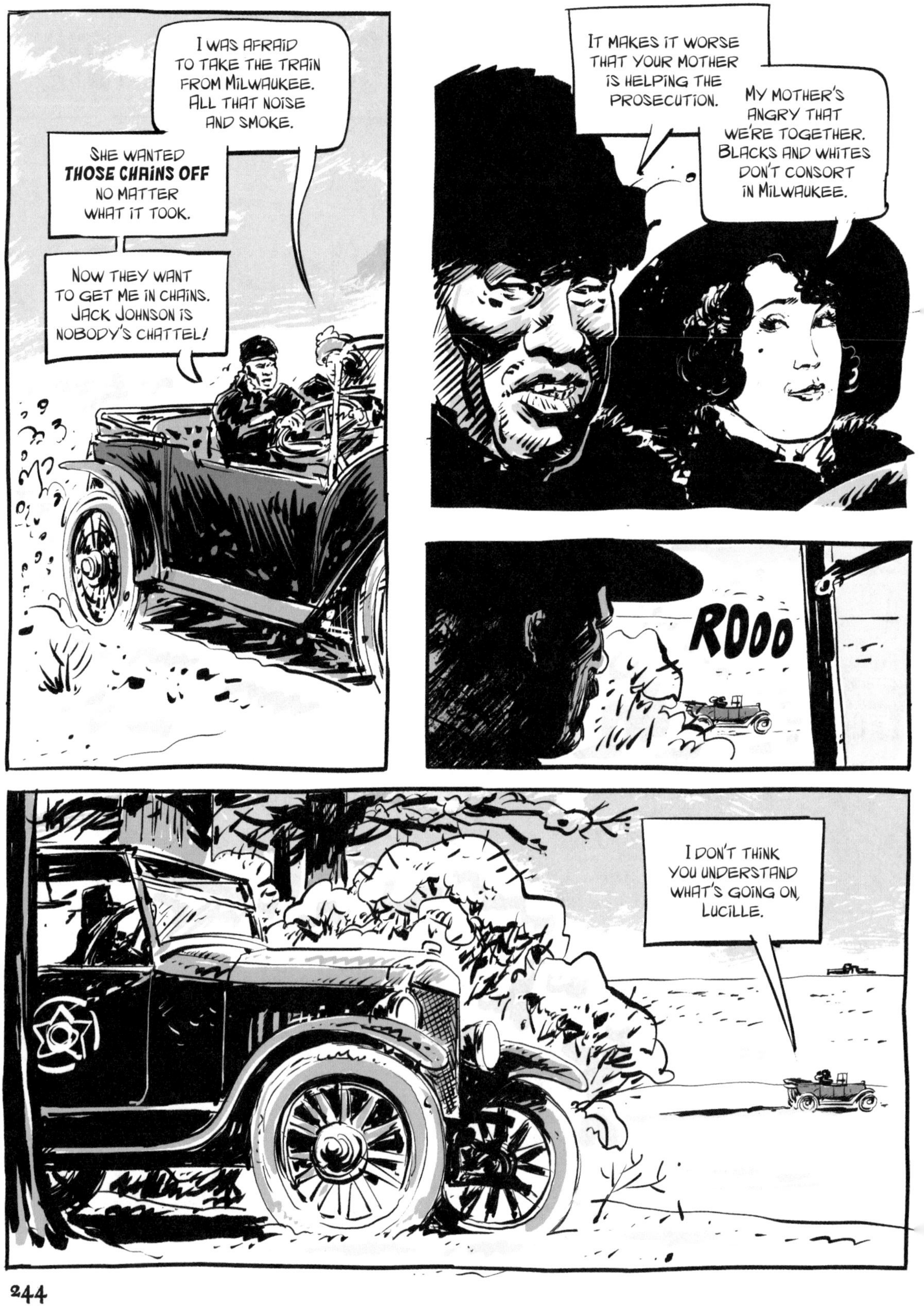

I WAS AFRAID TO TAKE THE TRAIN FROM MILWAUKEE. ALL THAT NOISE AND SMOKE.
SHE WANTED **THOSE CHAINS OFF** NO MATTER WHAT IT TOOK.
NOW THEY WANT TO GET ME IN CHAINS. JACK JOHNSON IS NOBODY'S CHATTEL!
IT MAKES IT WORSE THAT YOUR MOTHER IS HELPING THE PROSECUTION.
MY MOTHER'S ANGRY THAT WE'RE TOGETHER. BLACKS AND WHITES DON'T CONSORT IN MILWAUKEE.
ROOO
I DON'T THINK YOU UNDERSTAND WHAT'S GOING ON, LUCILLE.

NOW THAT THEY GOT ME

Some of my race have grand houses,
while others sleep under trees.
Some travel the world, while others
might never go farther from home
than they can walk. I've got a Lincoln
that's the fastest automobile around,
but some others can only get someplace
using their two feet.

We all share the common fear that
there's a white man with handcuffs
or a gun or a noose
waiting around the corner.

Always waiting.

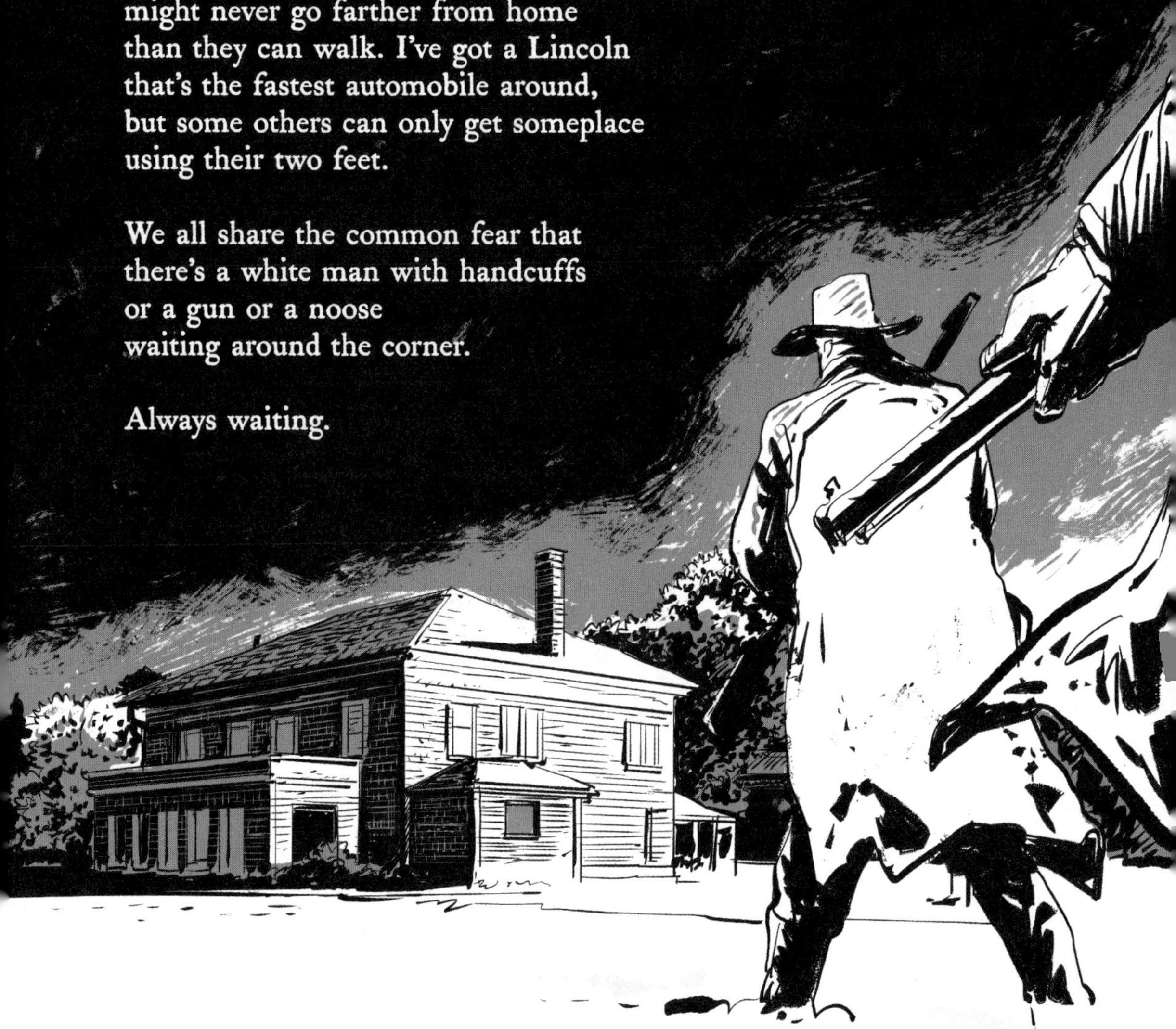

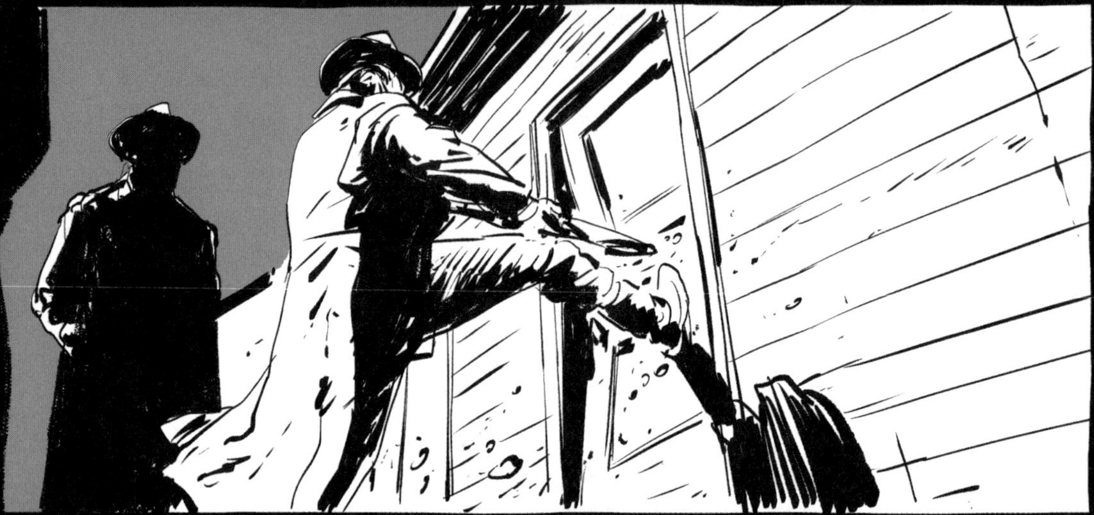

The marshals shouldered in the door
of my room without warning.
They must have expected a fight,
because there were at least ten of them.

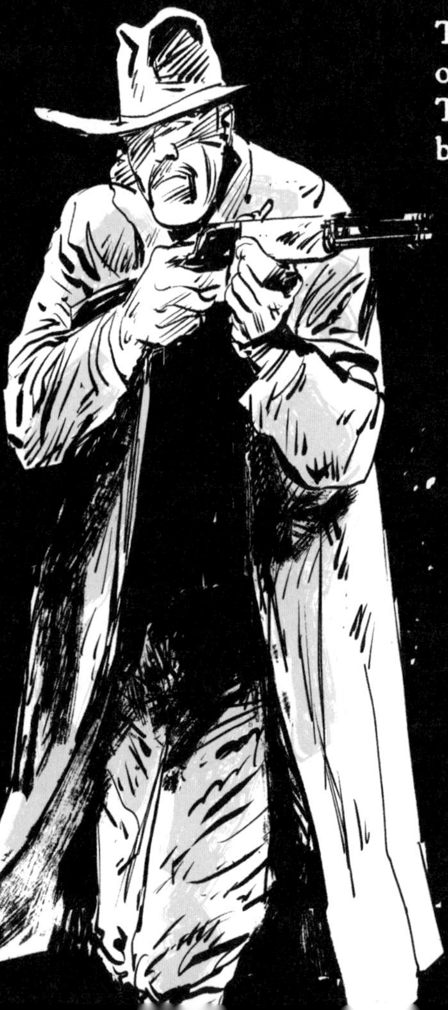

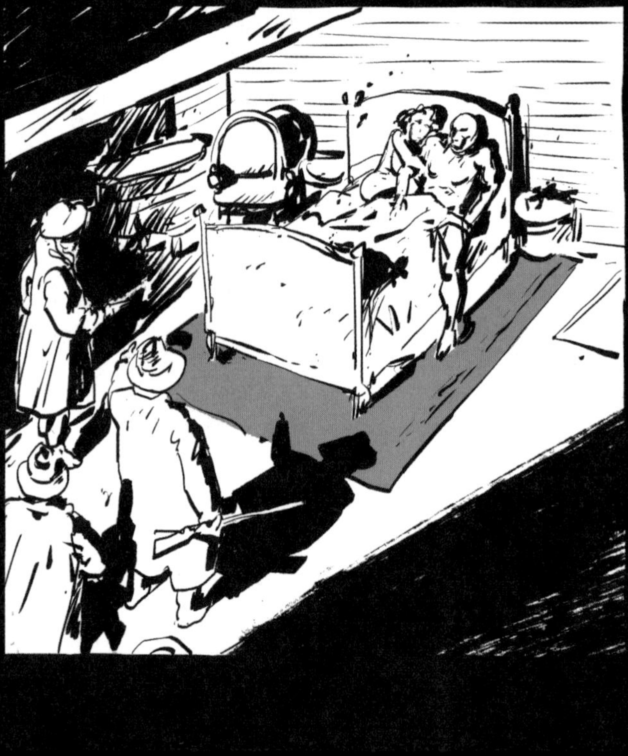

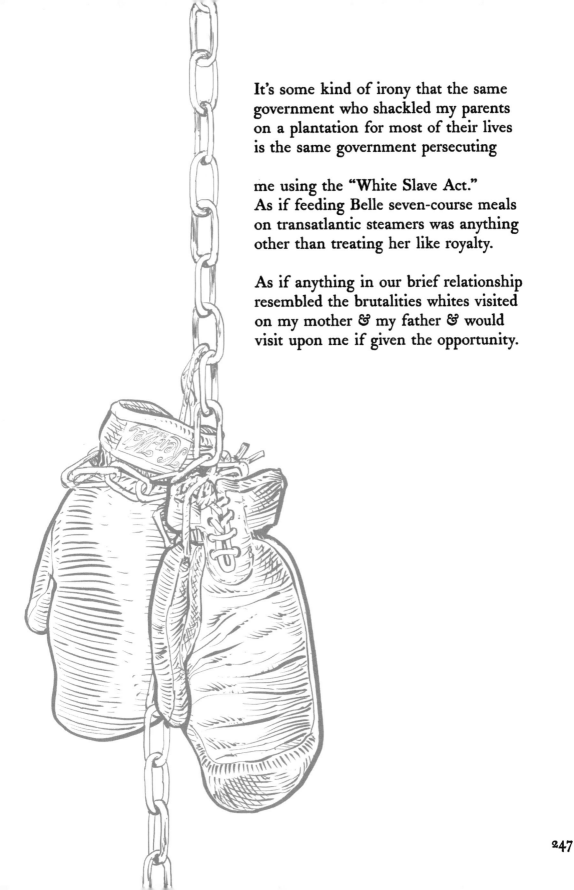

It's some kind of irony that the same
government who shackled my parents
on a plantation for most of their lives
is the same government persecuting

me using the "White Slave Act."
As if feeding Belle seven-course meals
on transatlantic steamers was anything
other than treating her like royalty.

As if anything in our brief relationship
resembled the brutalities whites visited
on my mother & my father & would
visit upon me if given the opportunity.

COURT BUILDING, CHICAGO, IL 1913

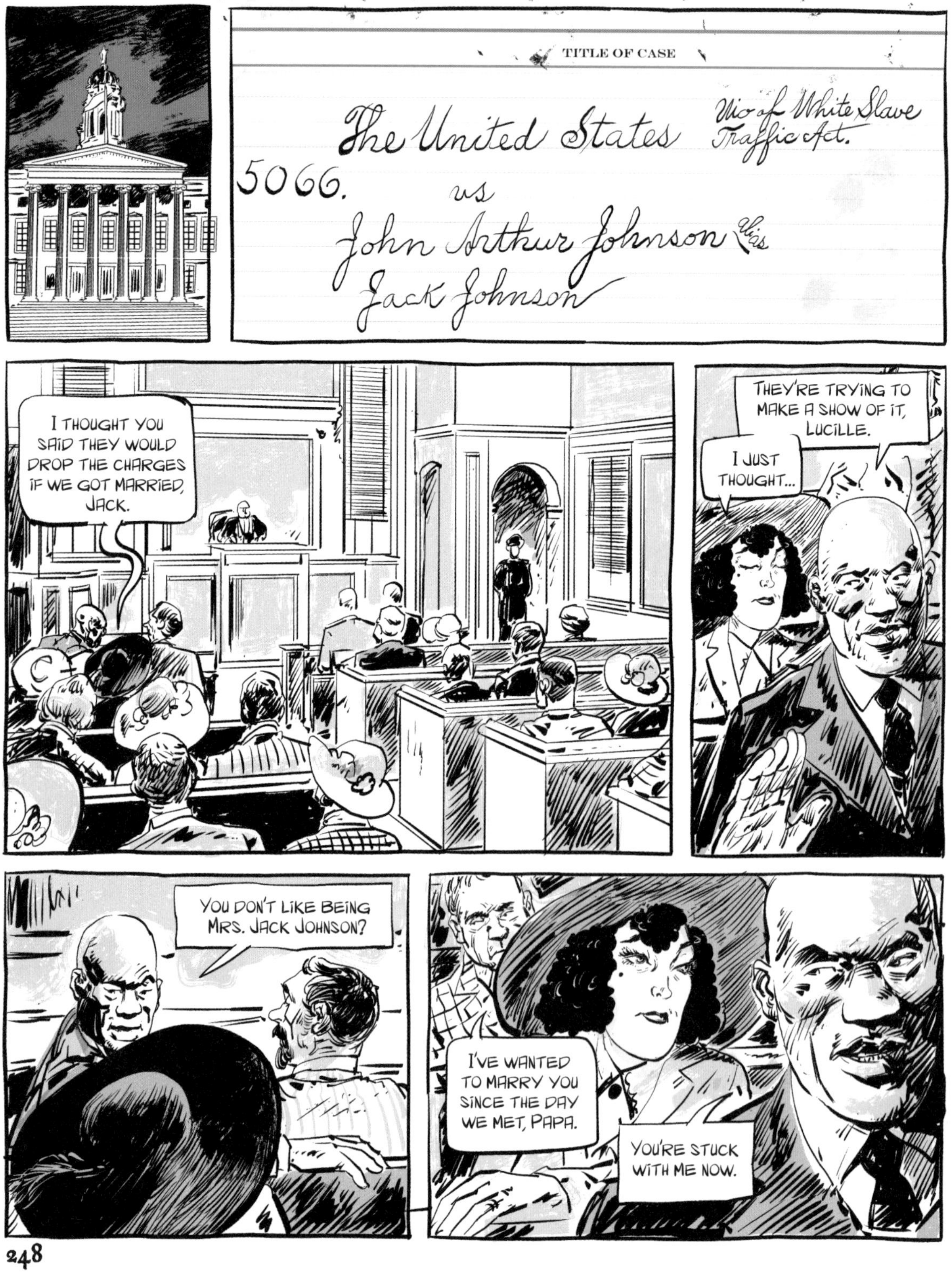

TITLE OF CASE
The United States
Vio of White Slave Traffic Act.
5066.
vs
John Arthur Johnson alias
Jack Johnson
I THOUGHT YOU SAID THEY WOULD DROP THE CHARGES IF WE GOT MARRIED, JACK.
THEY'RE TRYING TO MAKE A SHOW OF IT, LUCILLE.
I JUST THOUGHT...
YOU DON'T LIKE BEING MRS. JACK JOHNSON?
I'VE WANTED TO MARRY YOU SINCE THE DAY WE MET, PAPA.
YOU'RE STUCK WITH ME NOW.

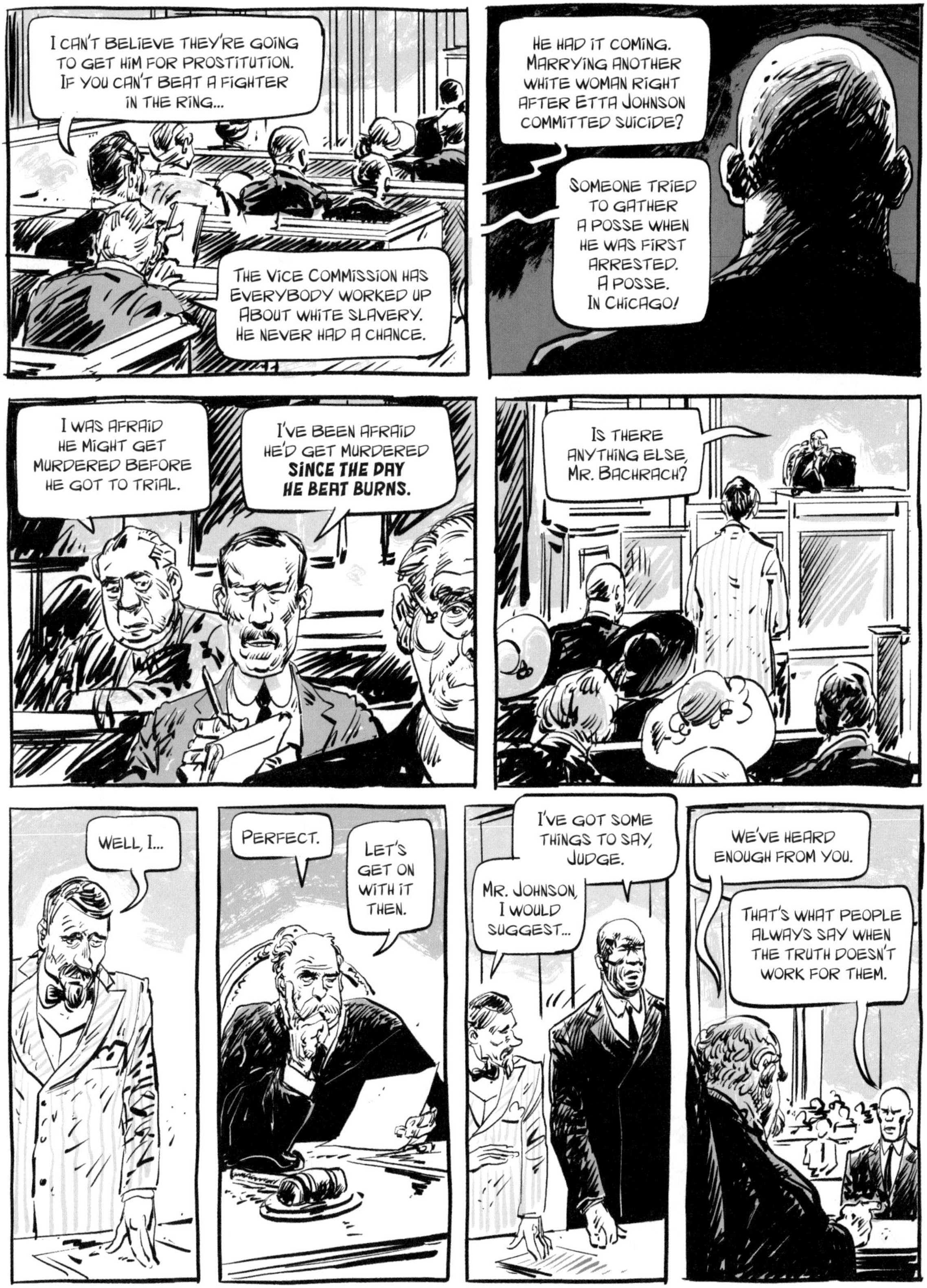
I CAN'T BELIEVE THEY'RE GOING TO GET HIM FOR PROSTITUTION. IF YOU CAN'T BEAT A FIGHTER IN THE RING...
THE VICE COMMISSION HAS EVERYBODY WORKED UP ABOUT WHITE SLAVERY. HE NEVER HAD A CHANCE.
HE HAD IT COMING. MARRYING ANOTHER WHITE WOMAN RIGHT AFTER ETTA JOHNSON COMMITTED SUICIDE?
SOMEONE TRIED TO GATHER A POSSE WHEN HE WAS FIRST ARRESTED. A POSSE. IN CHICAGO!
I WAS AFRAID HE MIGHT GET MURDERED BEFORE HE GOT TO TRIAL.
I'VE BEEN AFRAID HE'D GET MURDERED **SINCE THE DAY HE BEAT BURNS.**
IS THERE ANYTHING ELSE, MR. BACHRACH?
WELL, I...
PERFECT.
LET'S GET ON WITH IT THEN.
I'VE GOT SOME THINGS TO SAY, JUDGE.
MR. JOHNSON, I WOULD SUGGEST...
WE'VE HEARD ENOUGH FROM YOU.
THAT'S WHAT PEOPLE ALWAYS SAY WHEN THE TRUTH DOESN'T WORK FOR THEM.

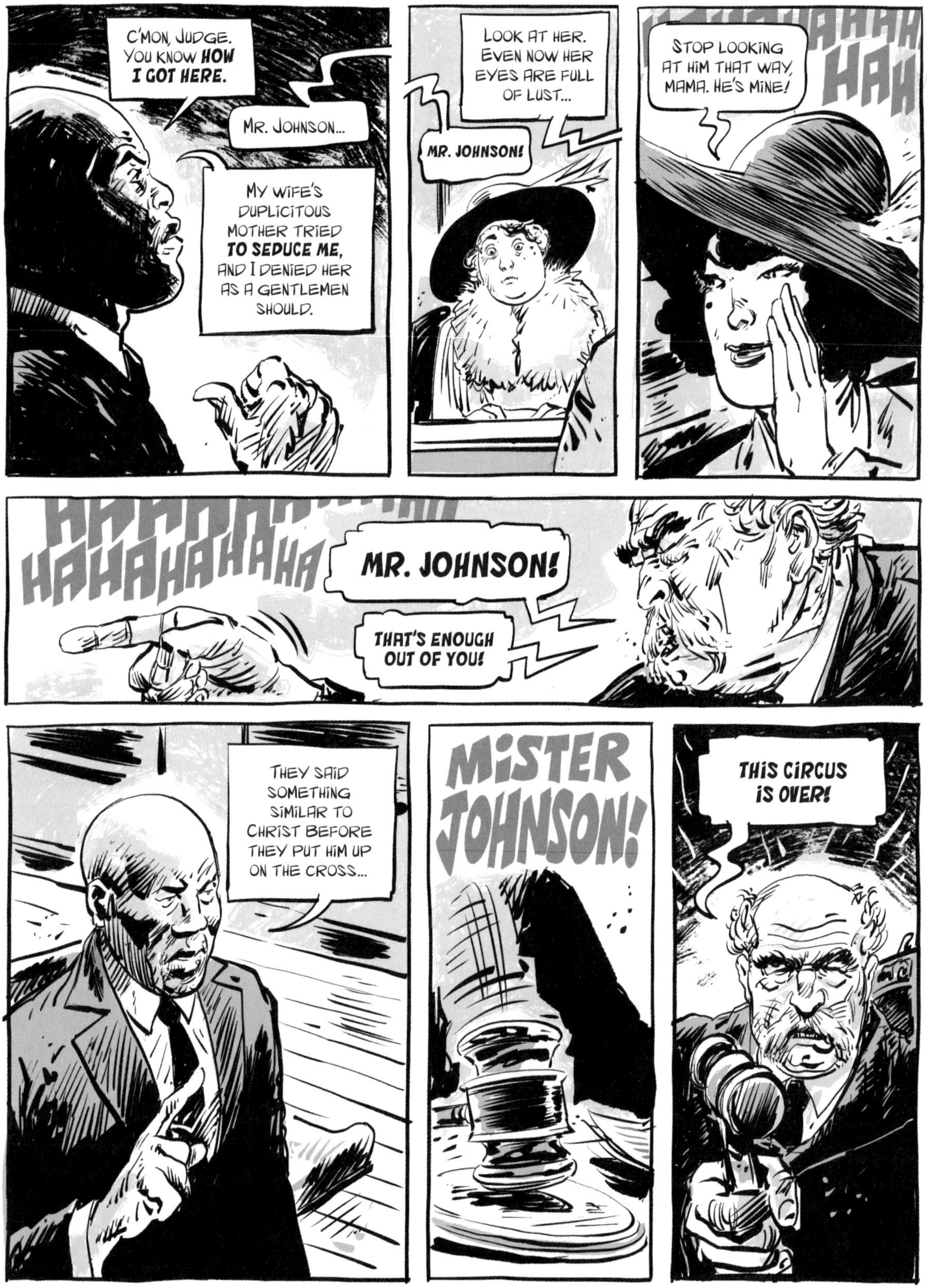
C'MON, JUDGE. YOU KNOW HOW I GOT HERE.
MR. JOHNSON...
MY WIFE'S DUPLICITOUS MOTHER TRIED TO SEDUCE ME, AND I DENIED HER AS A GENTLEMEN SHOULD.
LOOK AT HER. EVEN NOW HER EYES ARE FULL OF LUST...
MR. JOHNSON!
STOP LOOKING AT HIM THAT WAY, MAMA. HE'S MINE!
HAH
HAHAHAHAHAHA
MR. JOHNSON!
THAT'S ENOUGH OUT OF YOU!
THEY SAID SOMETHING SIMILAR TO CHRIST BEFORE THEY PUT HIM UP ON THE CROSS...
MISTER JOHNSON!
THIS CIRCUS IS OVER!

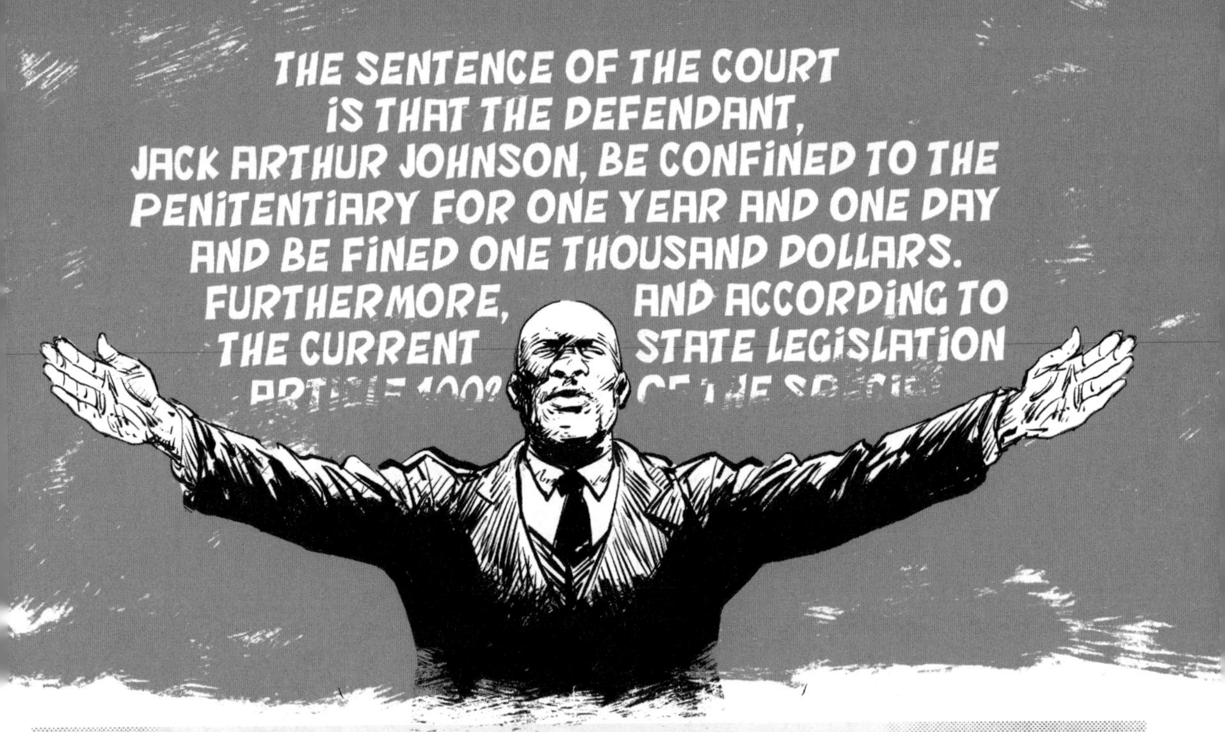

THE SENTENCE OF THE COURT
IS THAT THE DEFENDANT,
JACK ARTHUR JOHNSON, BE CONFINED TO THE
PENITENTIARY FOR ONE YEAR AND ONE DAY
AND BE FINED ONE THOUSAND DOLLARS.
FURTHERMORE,   AND ACCORDING TO
THE CURRENT   STATE LEGISLATION

Chicago THE Defender
WORLD'S ☆☆☆ GREATEST ☆☆☆ WEEKLY

JACK JOHNSON IS CRUCIFIED FOR HIS RACE

Famous fistic gladiator sails for France after being persecuted
in the United States. What has he done? If he chose a woman of
a different color for his companion and legally married her,
whose business is it? What has the white man done?
Jack Johnson has done no different from any other big sport.
For no other reason than whipping Jeffries and being a negro
is Jack Johnson persecuted. Consorting with white women
is no cause. Jack is one of that host that John couldn't number.

A Piece of Advice from Jack Johnson

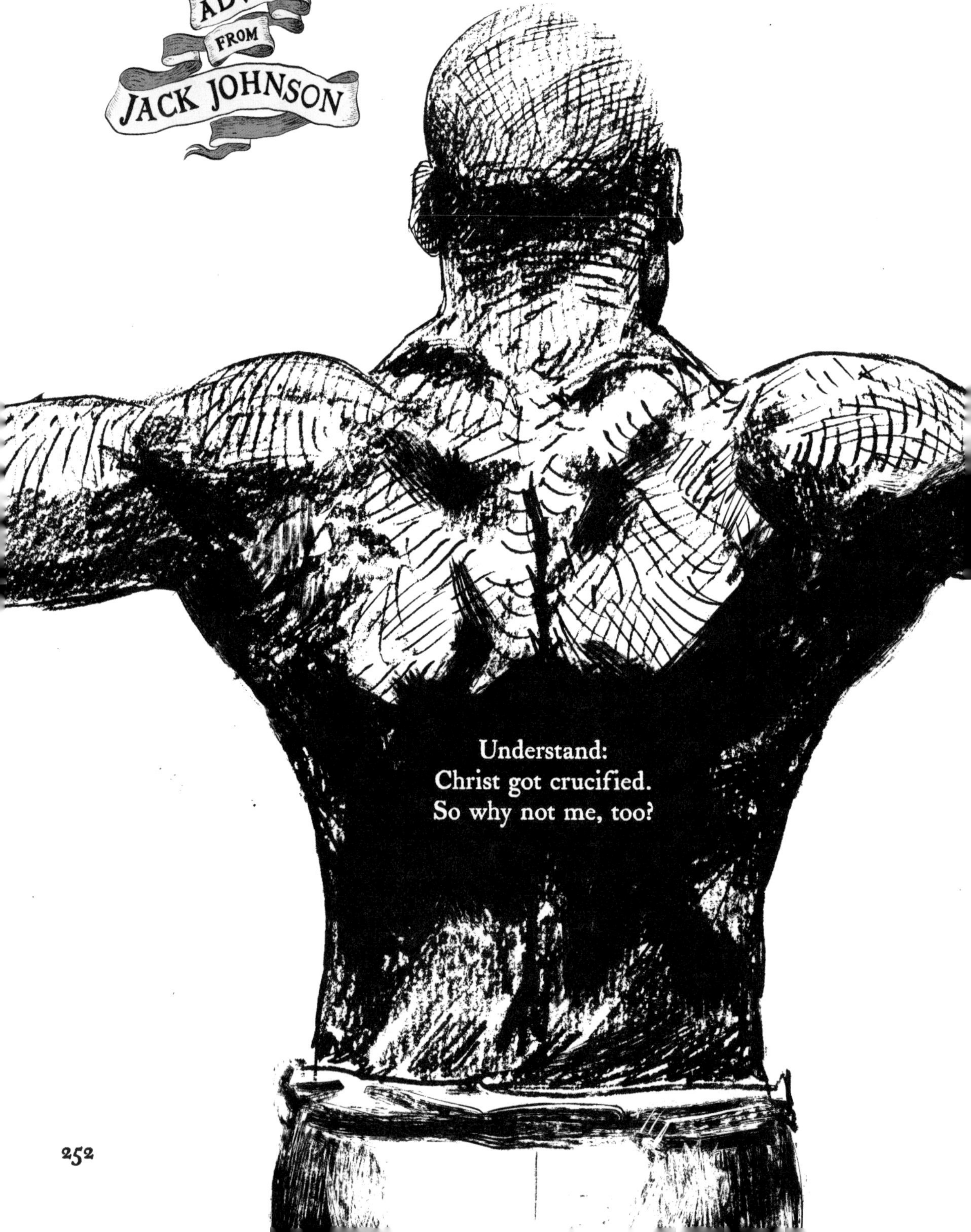
Understand:
Christ got crucified.
So why not me, too?

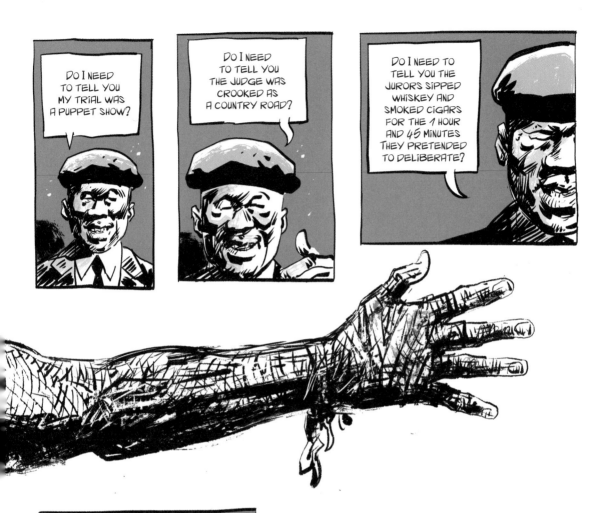

DO I NEED TO TELL YOU MY TRIAL WAS A PUPPET SHOW?

DO I NEED TO TELL YOU THE JUDGE WAS CROOKED AS A COUNTRY ROAD?

DO I NEED TO TELL YOU THE JURORS SIPPED WHISKEY AND SMOKED CIGARS FOR THE 1 HOUR AND 45 MINUTES THEY PRETENDED TO DELIBERATE?

DO I NEED TO TELL YOU I ALREADY HAD A PLAN FOR MY ESCAPE?

JACK JOHNSON IS NOBODY'S INMATE.

FROM THE DAY I WAS BORN

From the day I was born, I've been trying
to live my life like a man. I have eyes
& I have a heart & I make my choices
without the dictation of any other man.

That's how I wooed Etta.
That's how I became heavyweight champion.
That's how I made so much money
I had to get an extra safe just to have a place

to stash it. When they came to arrest me
on those trumped-up Mann Act charges,
I would have gone along easy, but they wanted
to make an example out of me.

After the trial the constables were
smiling when they came over & said,
"We've got a special set of bracelets
for you, Mr. Johnson."

I told them I wasn't going to fight,
but they insisted—laughing as each
cuff clicked around my wrist.
"You like jewelry, don't you, boy?"

& I could feel tears going down
my face even as I tried to find
a way to smile.

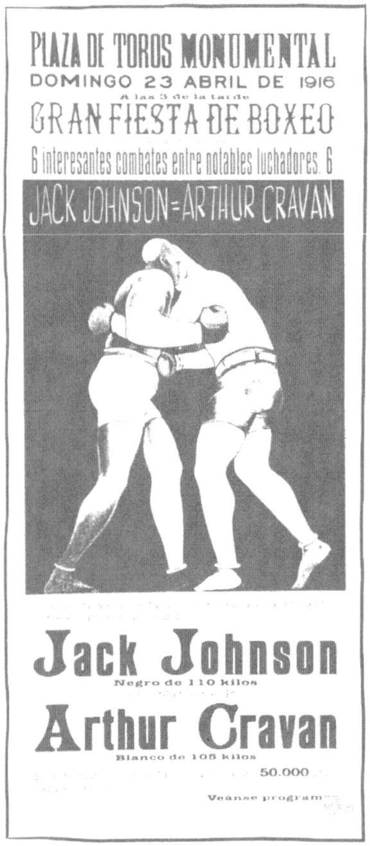
PLAZA DE TOROS MONUMENTAL
DOMINGO 23 ABRIL DE 1916
A las 3 de la tarde
GRAN FIESTA DE BOXEO
6 interesantes combates entre notables luchadores. 6
JACK JOHNSON = ARTHUR CRAVAN
Jack Johnson
Negro de 110 kilos
Arthur Cravan
Blanco de 105 kilos
50.000

I went from hero to exile the minute
Judge Carpenter dropped his gavel.
They closed down the Café de Champion
& padlocked my mother's house.
Promoters wouldn't schedule fights for me.
Friends & admirers turned their backs on me.
People acted like I had the Spanish Flu
when I walked to a restaurant.
I was an exile in my own city.
Etta warned me that my friends weren't
really friends, but I never understood
what she meant until I went on the run.
I'm still Jack Johnson, even in exile.

I fought bulls in front of Alphonso XIII.
I fought poets & actors for a quick buck,
then spent it all on furs for Lucille.
I played the clown, the savage,
& an African king on stage.
I tied horses to my biceps & flexed
& flexed as they tried to move.
I missed Etta & danced with Lucille
& sold my automobiles so we could
eat. I borrowed money, spent & borrowed
some more. I spent our last savings on train
tickets to St. Petersburg for a title fight
that would have gotten us out of debt,
only to find out the fight was canceled.

I always thought I'd be able to come back
to America, but things went from bad
to worse when Archduke Ferdinand got killed.
All the sudden there were soldiers & cannons
& explosions all over Europe.

The war didn't change
the way whites treated me.

I'm a man inside the ring
& out, but sometimes
it's difficult to remain a gentleman
while being called nigger or coon
or ape every time I make
an appearance. What would you
do if someone hated you
just because your skin
is a different hue? It's hard
to keep my composure when
the crowd is making
monkey sounds & throwing
watermelon rinds at me.

Words are only words
& most of those hecklers
were too afraid to put their fists
in front of them. But day after
day, year after year of that kind
of hatred wears on a man.

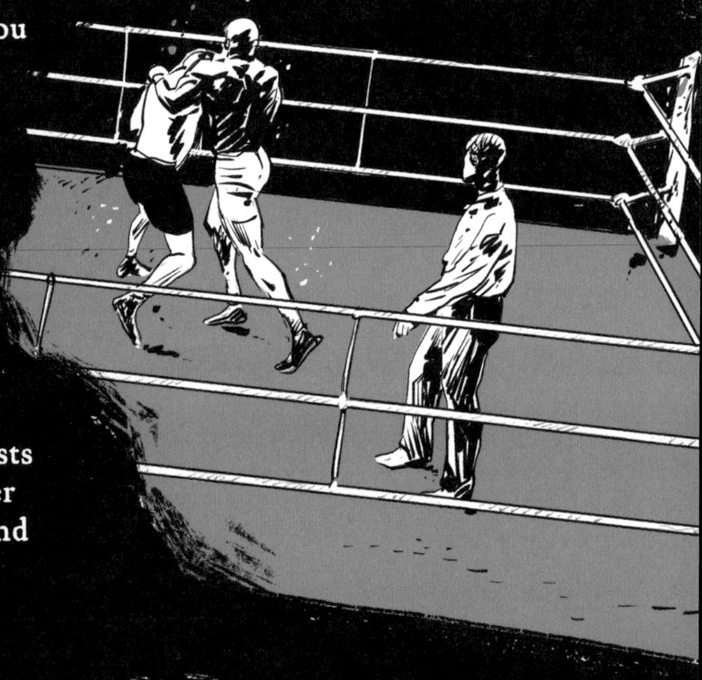

All that hate when men
are dying from bullets
& bombs & gas. I'll leave
it to the poets to tell
the stories of all the brave
soldiers who never came home.

Who could have imagined
such destruction & so many
lost lives because some royalty
couldn't get along?

PORTE DE VINCENNES, PARIS, FRANCE 1915

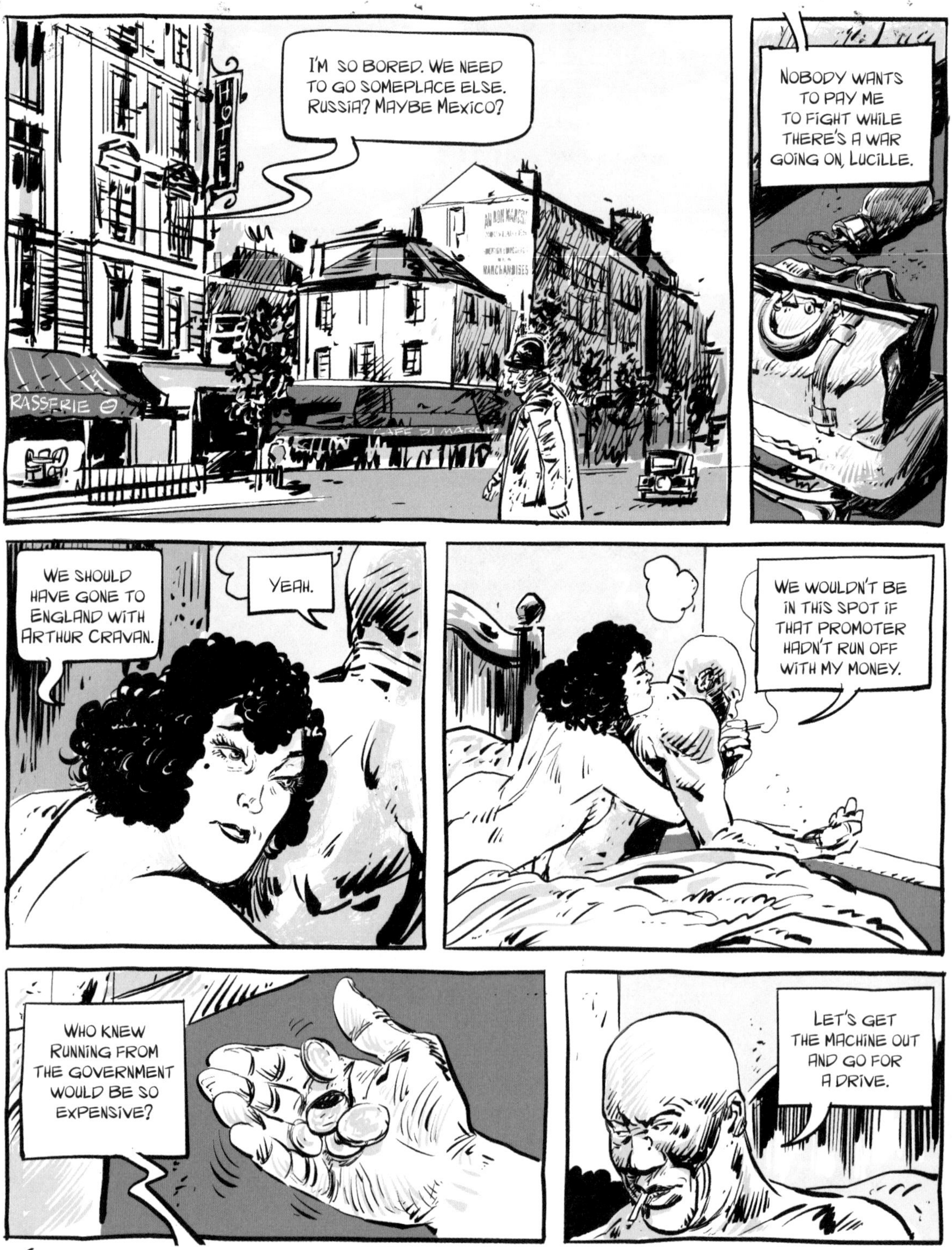
I'M SO BORED. WE NEED TO GO SOMEPLACE ELSE. RUSSIA? MAYBE MEXICO?
HOTEL
RASSERIE
CAFE DU MARCHE
NOBODY WANTS TO PAY ME TO FIGHT WHILE THERE'S A WAR GOING ON, LUCILLE.
WE SHOULD HAVE GONE TO ENGLAND WITH ARTHUR CRAVAN.
YEAH.
WE WOULDN'T BE IN THIS SPOT IF THAT PROMOTER HADN'T RUN OFF WITH MY MONEY.
WHO KNEW RUNNING FROM THE GOVERNMENT WOULD BE SO EXPENSIVE?
LET'S GET THE MACHINE OUT AND GO FOR A DRIVE.

METROPOLITAIN
DUBONNE
I DON'T KNOW. THIS MIGHT NOT BE THE BEST DAY FOR A PICNIC. I HEARD THE GERMANS ARE MARCHING TO PARIS.
DIDN'T YOU READ **LE PETIT JOURNAL**?
Le Petit Journal
SUPPLEMENT ILLUSTRE
THE WAR IS OUT IN THE COUNTRY STILL. WE'LL BE FINE.

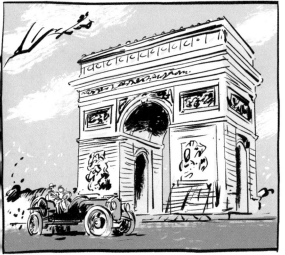

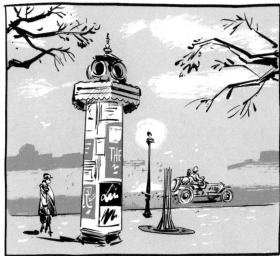

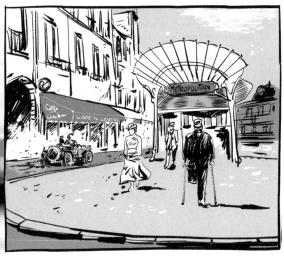

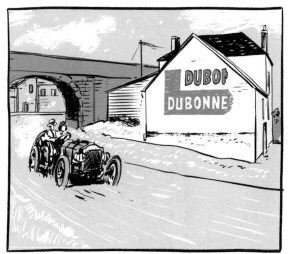

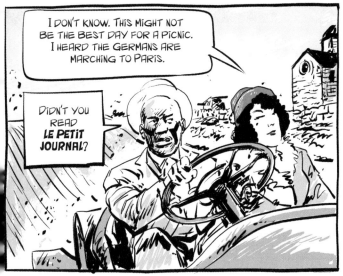

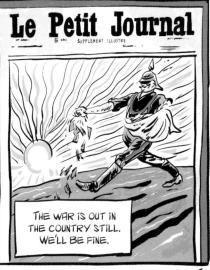

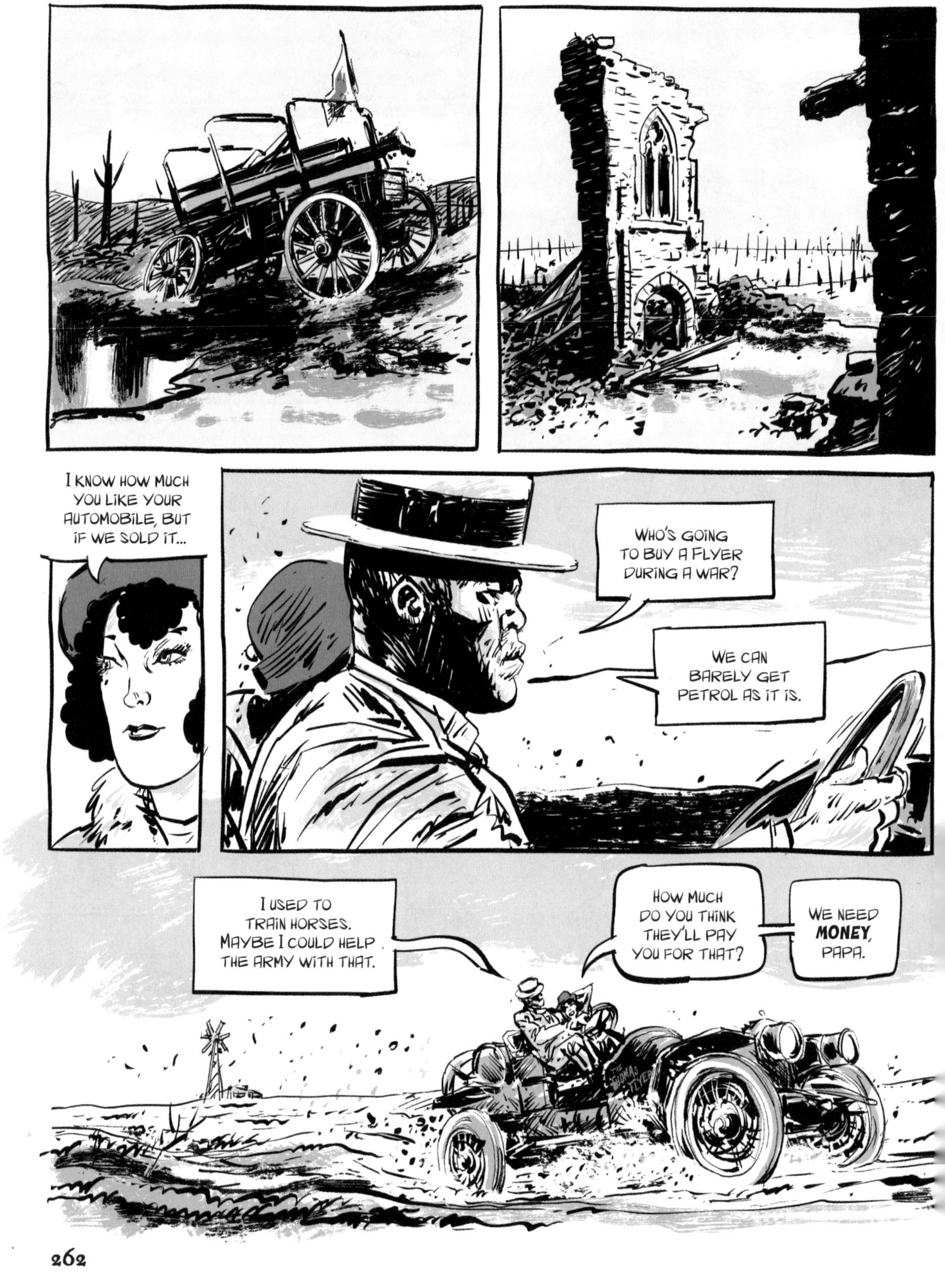
I KNOW HOW MUCH YOU LIKE YOUR AUTOMOBILE, BUT IF WE SOLD IT...
WHO'S GOING TO BUY A FLYER DURING A WAR?
WE CAN BARELY GET PETROL AS IT IS.
I USED TO TRAIN HORSES. MAYBE I COULD HELP THE ARMY WITH THAT.
HOW MUCH DO YOU THINK THEY'LL PAY YOU FOR THAT?
WE NEED **MONEY**, PAPA.

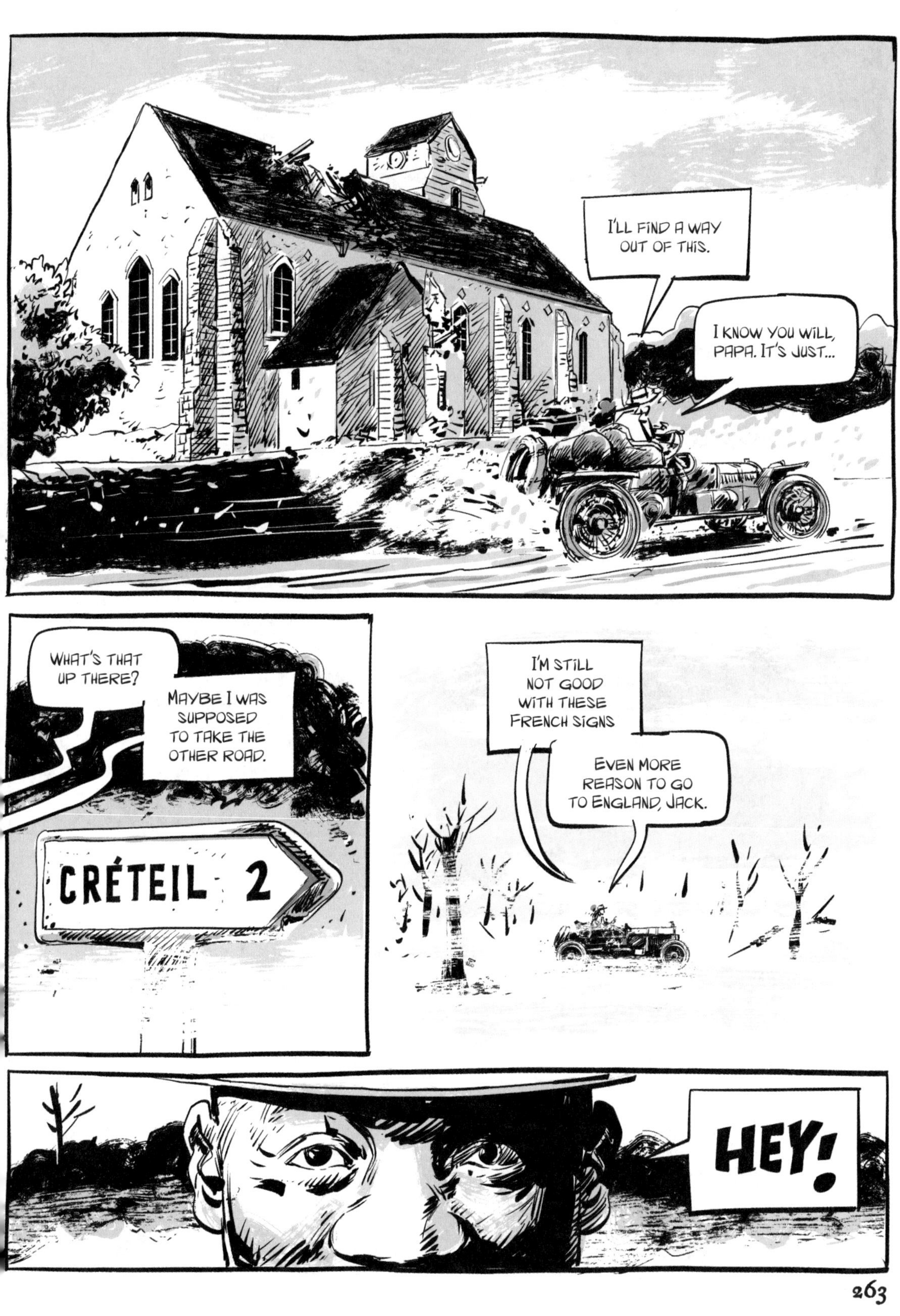

I'll find a way out of this.
I know you will, Papa. It's just...
What's that up there?
Maybe I was supposed to take the other road.
CRÉTEIL 2
I'm still not good with these French signs
Even more reason to go to England, Jack.
HEY!

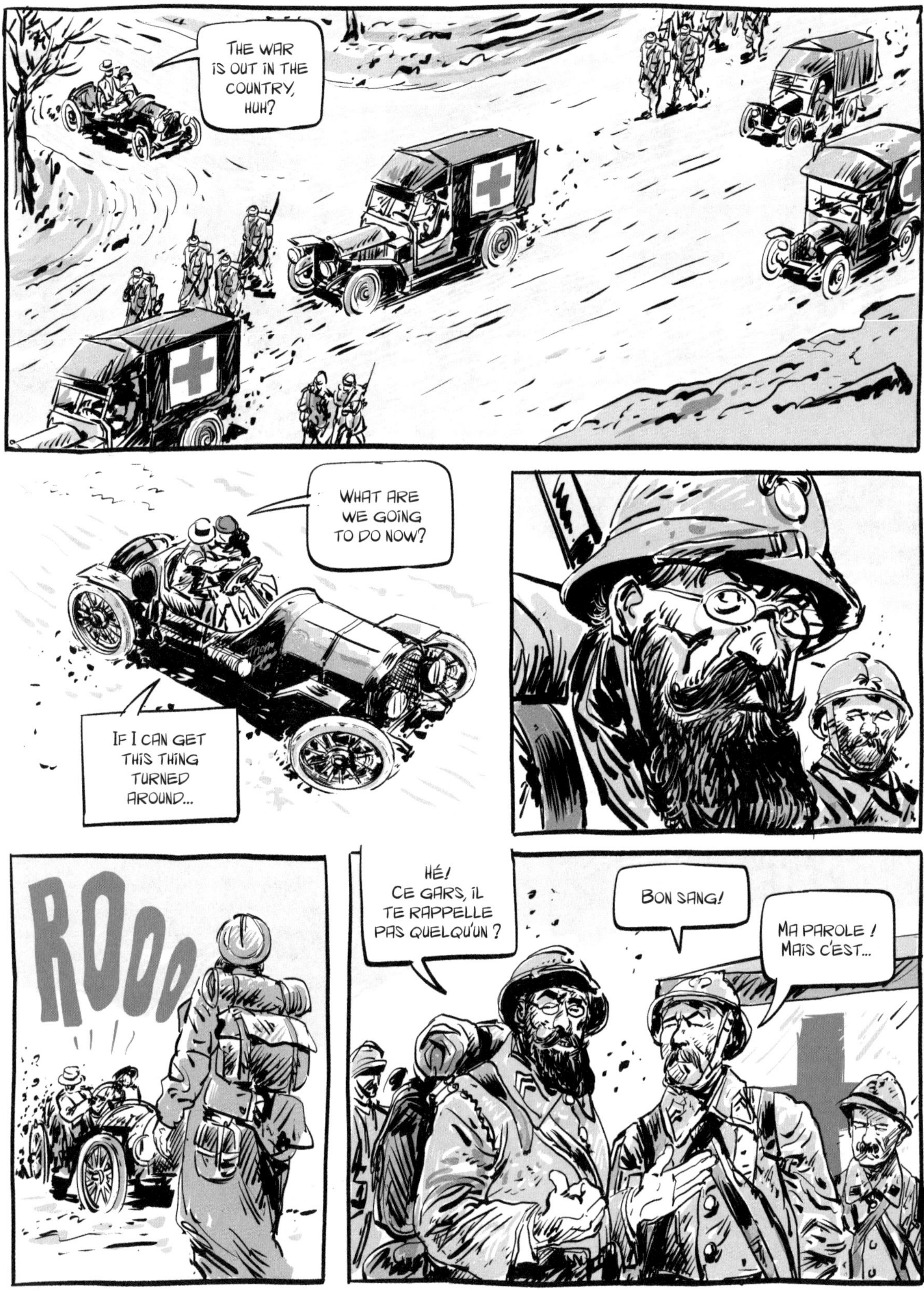
THE WAR IS OUT IN THE COUNTRY, HUH?
WHAT ARE WE GOING TO DO NOW?
IF I CAN GET THIS THING TURNED AROUND...
ROOO
HÉ! CE GARS, IL TE RAPPELLE PAS QUELQU'UN ?
BON SANG!
MA PAROLE ! MAIS C'EST...

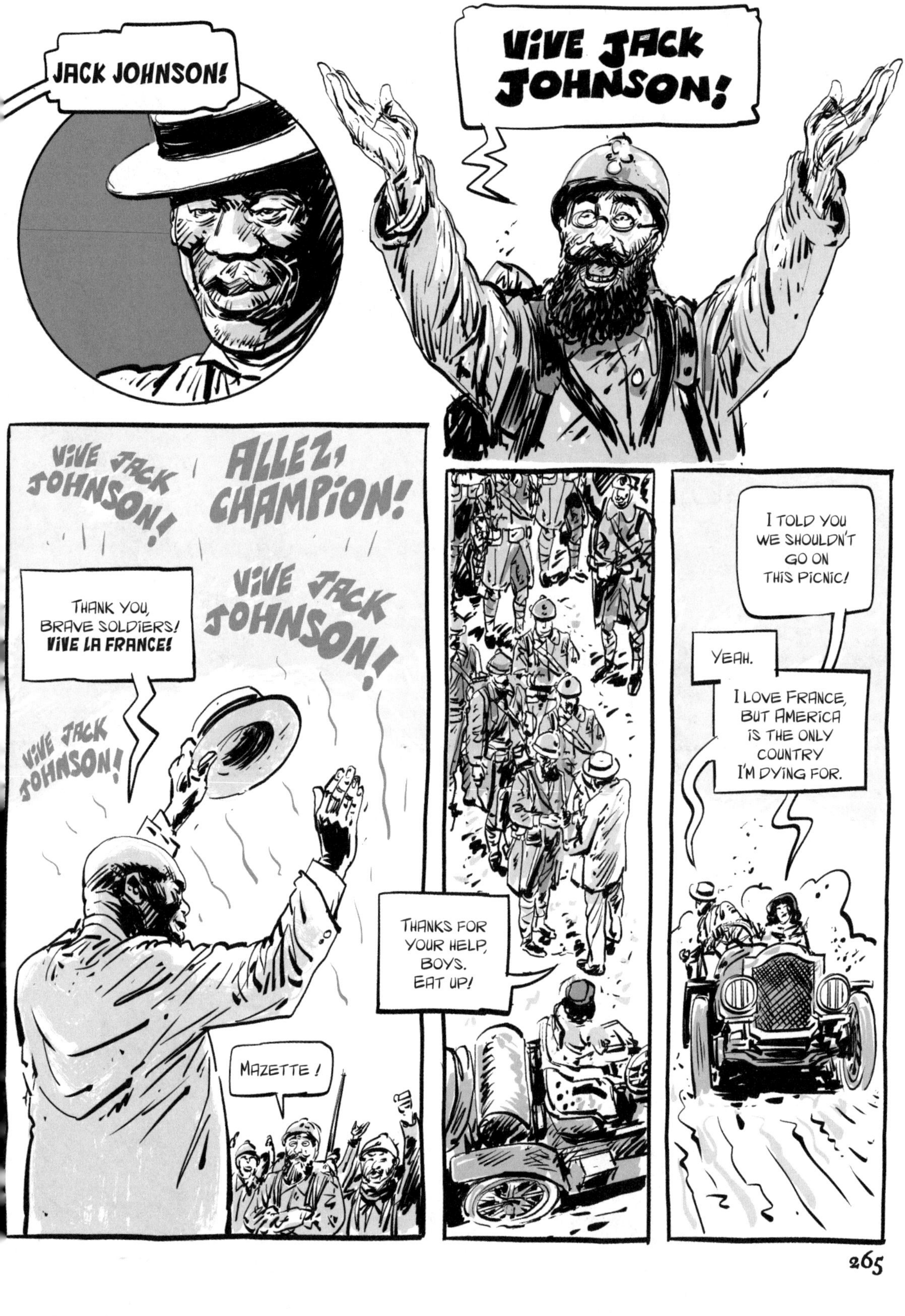
JACK JOHNSON!
VIVE JACK JOHNSON!
VIVE JACK JOHNSON!
ALLEZ, CHAMPION!
VIVE JACK JOHNSON!
THANK YOU, BRAVE SOLDIERS! VIVE LA FRANCE!
VIVE JACK JOHNSON!
MAZETTE !
THANKS FOR YOUR HELP, BOYS. EAT UP!
I TOLD YOU WE SHOULDN'T GO ON THIS PICNIC!
YEAH.
I LOVE FRANCE, BUT AMERICA IS THE ONLY COUNTRY I'M DYING FOR.

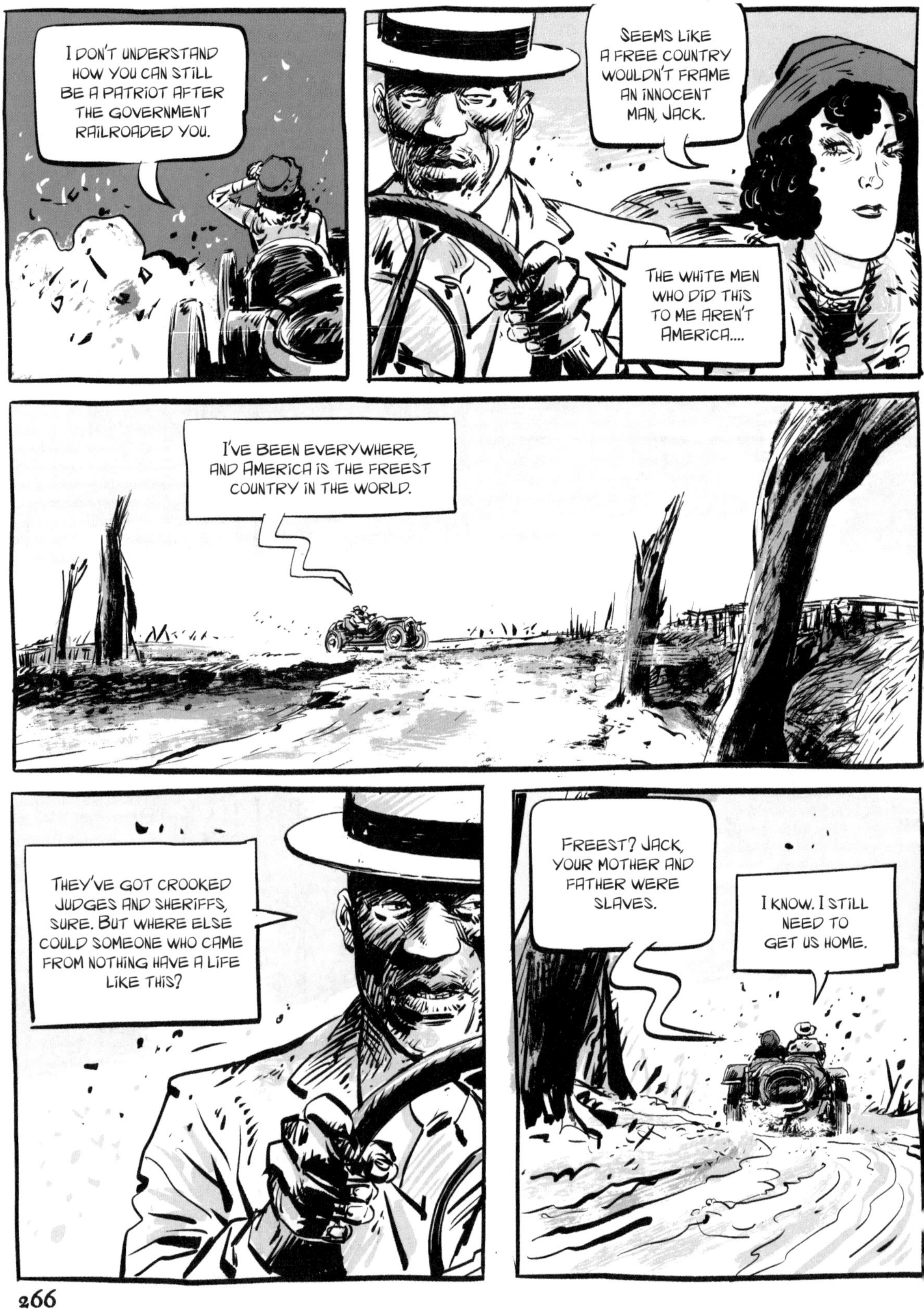
I DON'T UNDERSTAND HOW YOU CAN STILL BE A PATRIOT AFTER THE GOVERNMENT RAILROADED YOU.
SEEMS LIKE A FREE COUNTRY WOULDN'T FRAME AN INNOCENT MAN, JACK.
THE WHITE MEN WHO DID THIS TO ME AREN'T AMERICA....
I'VE BEEN EVERYWHERE, AND AMERICA IS THE FREEST COUNTRY IN THE WORLD.
THEY'VE GOT CROOKED JUDGES AND SHERIFFS, SURE. BUT WHERE ELSE COULD SOMEONE WHO CAME FROM NOTHING HAVE A LIFE LIKE THIS?
FREEST? JACK, YOUR MOTHER AND FATHER WERE SLAVES.
I KNOW. I STILL NEED TO GET US HOME.

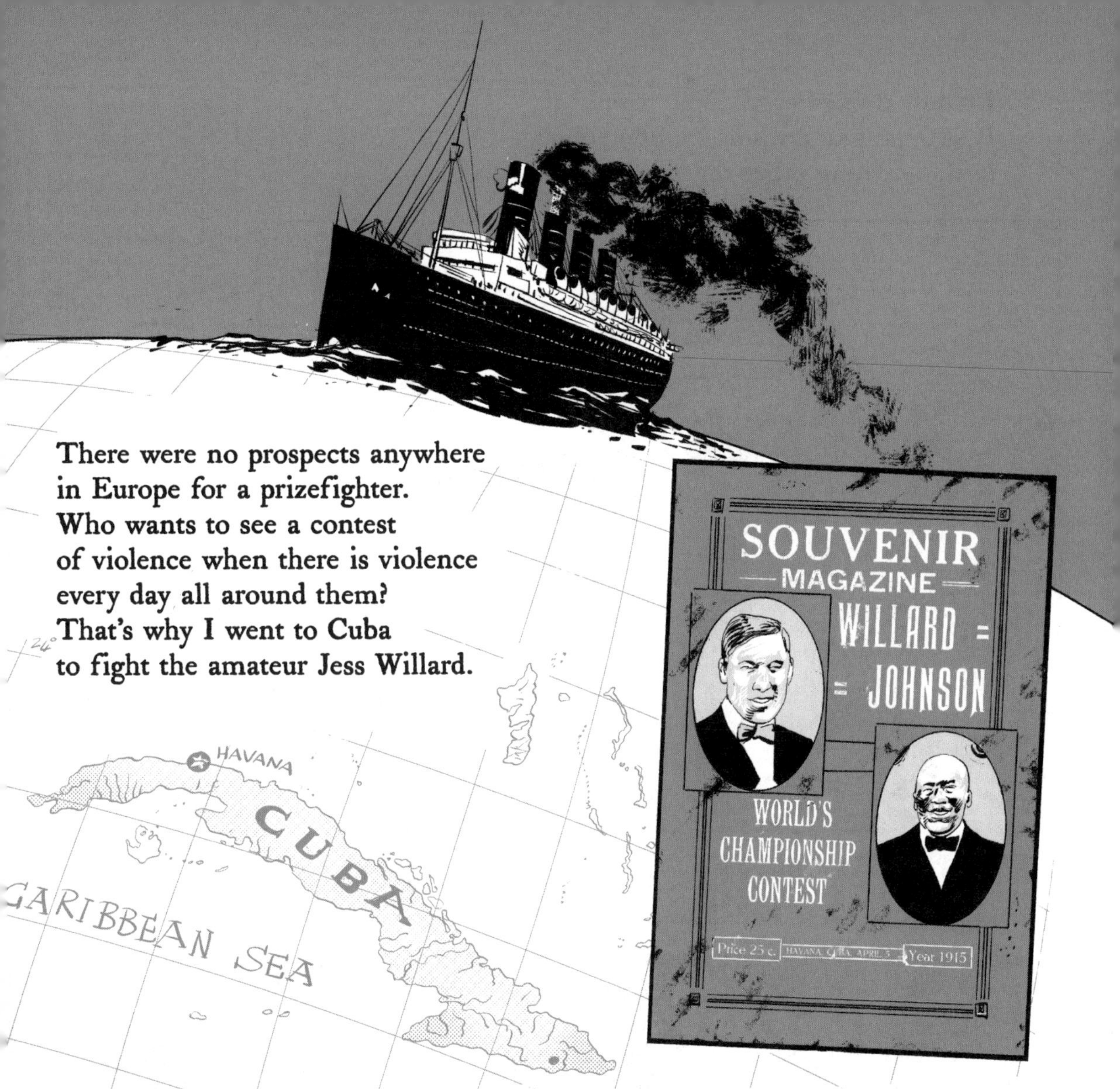
There were no prospects anywhere in Europe for a prizefighter. Who wants to see a contest of violence when there is violence every day all around them? That's why I went to Cuba to fight the amateur Jess Willard.
HAVANA
CUBA
CARIBBEAN SEA
SOUVENIR
MAGAZINE
WILLARD = = JOHNSON
WORLD'S CHAMPIONSHIP CONTEST
Price 25 c.
HAVANA, CUBA, APRIL 5
Year 1915

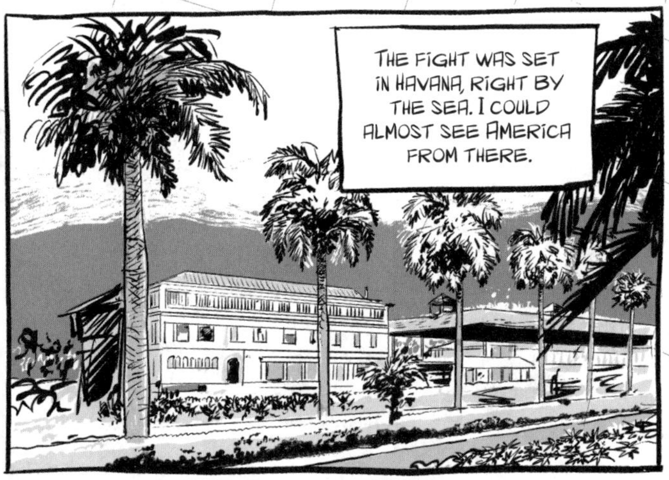
THE FIGHT WAS SET IN HAVANA, RIGHT BY THE SEA. I COULD ALMOST SEE AMERICA FROM THERE.

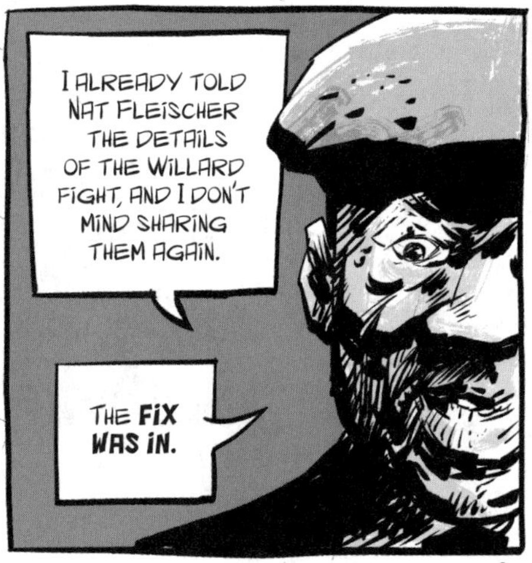
I ALREADY TOLD NAT FLEISCHER THE DETAILS OF THE WILLARD FIGHT, AND I DON'T MIND SHARING THEM AGAIN.
THE FIX WAS IN.

I barely trained at all. Why would I?
It seemed like a whole lot of hubbub
to do anything other than enjoy the sights.

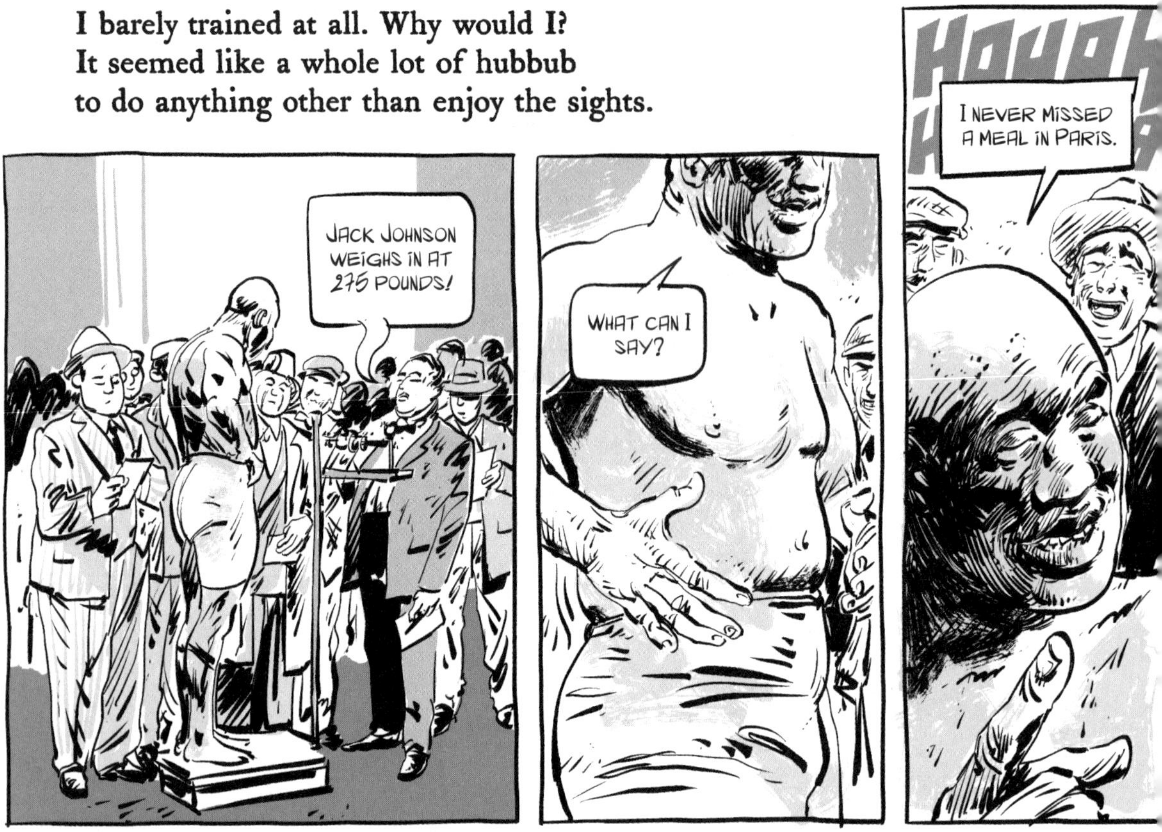

JACK JOHNSON WEIGHS IN AT 275 POUNDS!
WHAT CAN I SAY?
I NEVER MISSED A MEAL IN PARIS.

ORIENTAL PARK, HAVANA, CUBA APRIL 5, 1915

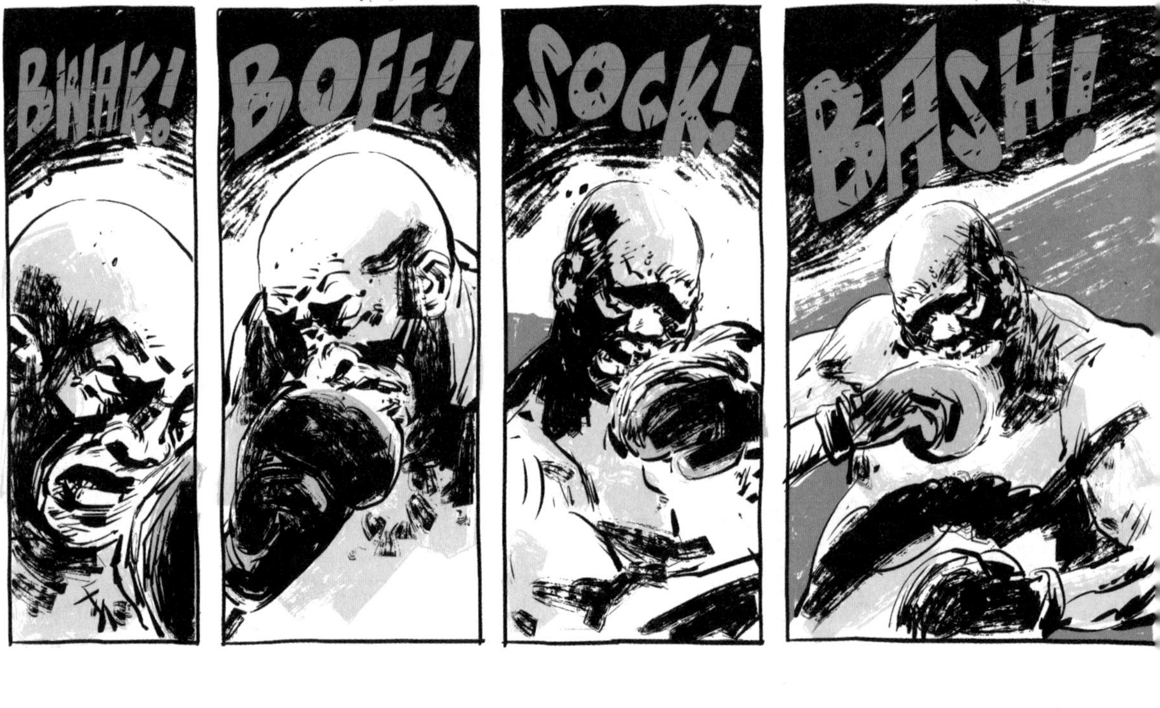

BWAK!
BOFF!
SOCK!
BASH!

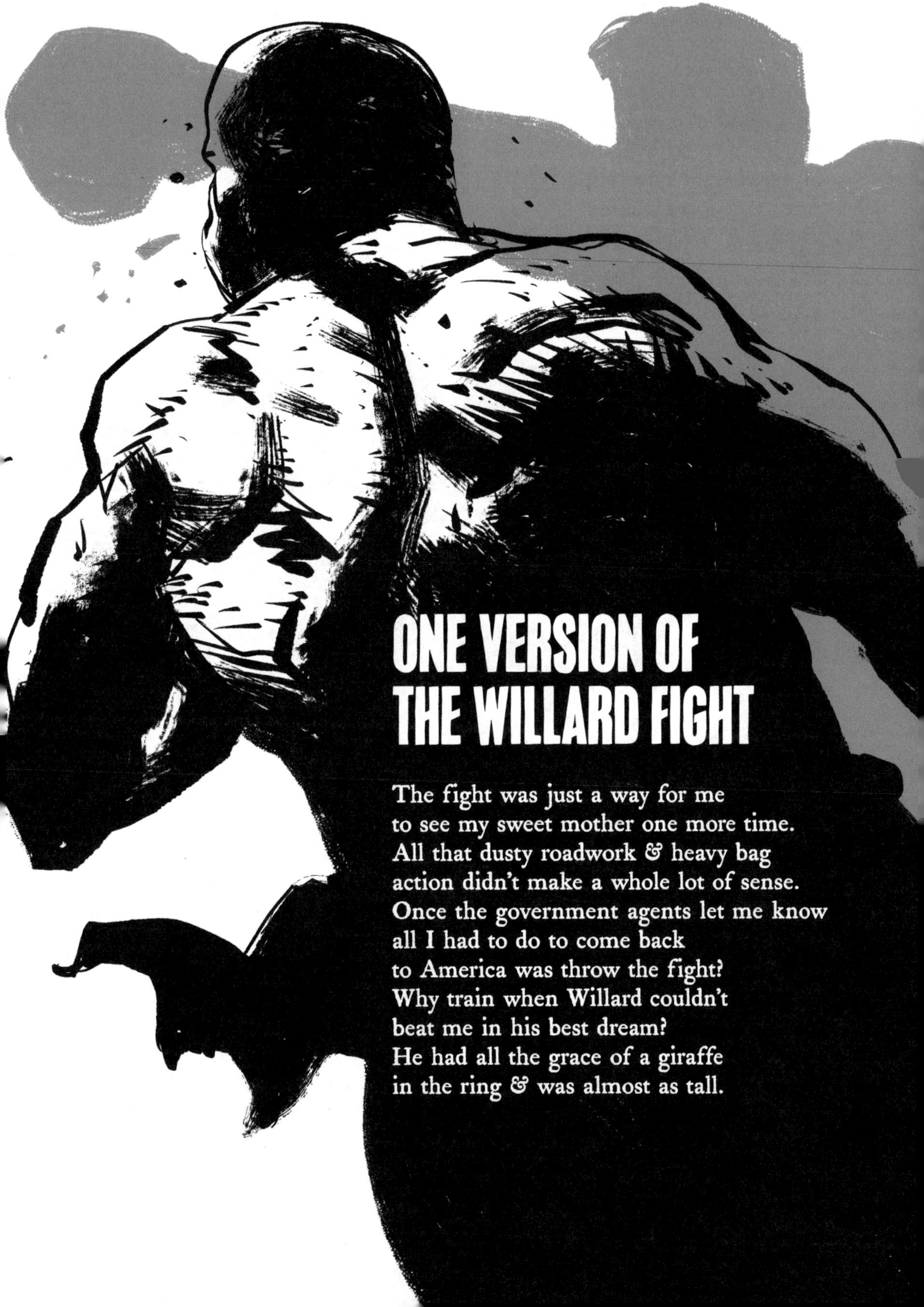

ONE VERSION OF THE WILLARD FIGHT

The fight was just a way for me
to see my sweet mother one more time.
All that dusty roadwork & heavy bag
action didn't make a whole lot of sense.
Once the government agents let me know
all I had to do to come back
to America was throw the fight?
Why train when Willard couldn't
beat me in his best dream?
He had all the grace of a giraffe
in the ring & was almost as tall.

So I spent my time in Havana on the town with Lucille. I met all manner of interesting people from that great island & abroad. We played music & danced & recited poetry. Kipling became my new favorite. His poem "If—" still inspires me every day:

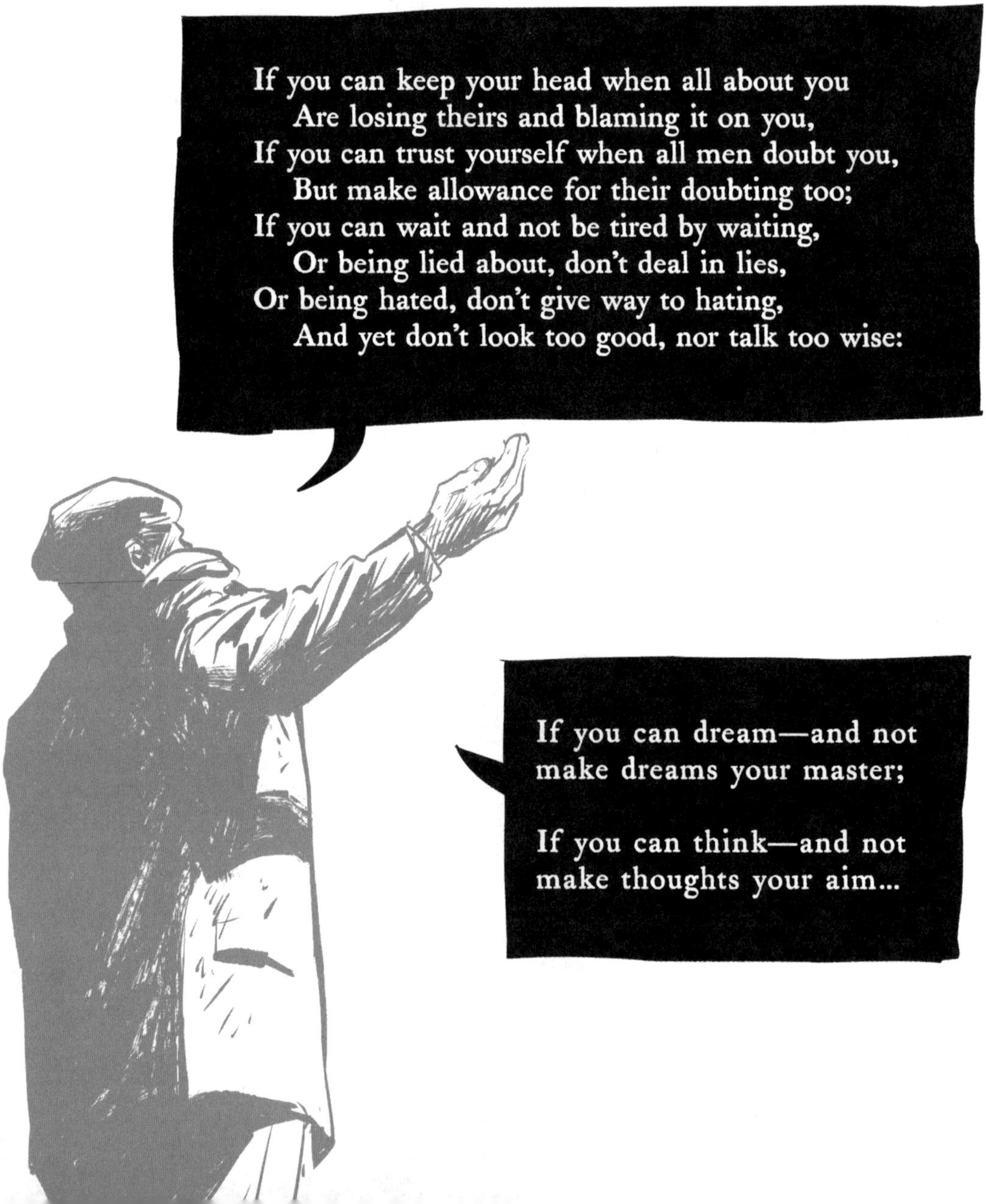
If you can keep your head when all about you
Are losing theirs and blaming it on you,
If you can trust yourself when all men doubt you,
But make allowance for their doubting too;
If you can wait and not be tired by waiting,
Or being lied about, don't deal in lies,
Or being hated, don't give way to hating,
And yet don't look too good, nor talk too wise:
If you can dream—and not make dreams your master;
If you can think—and not make thoughts your aim...

It ruined my pride
to let Willard become champion.
I believed Agent Wilson
because I wanted to see my mother.

If it had been a real fight, I would have
avoided his amateur clinches & dodged
his clumsy hooks while reading a book.

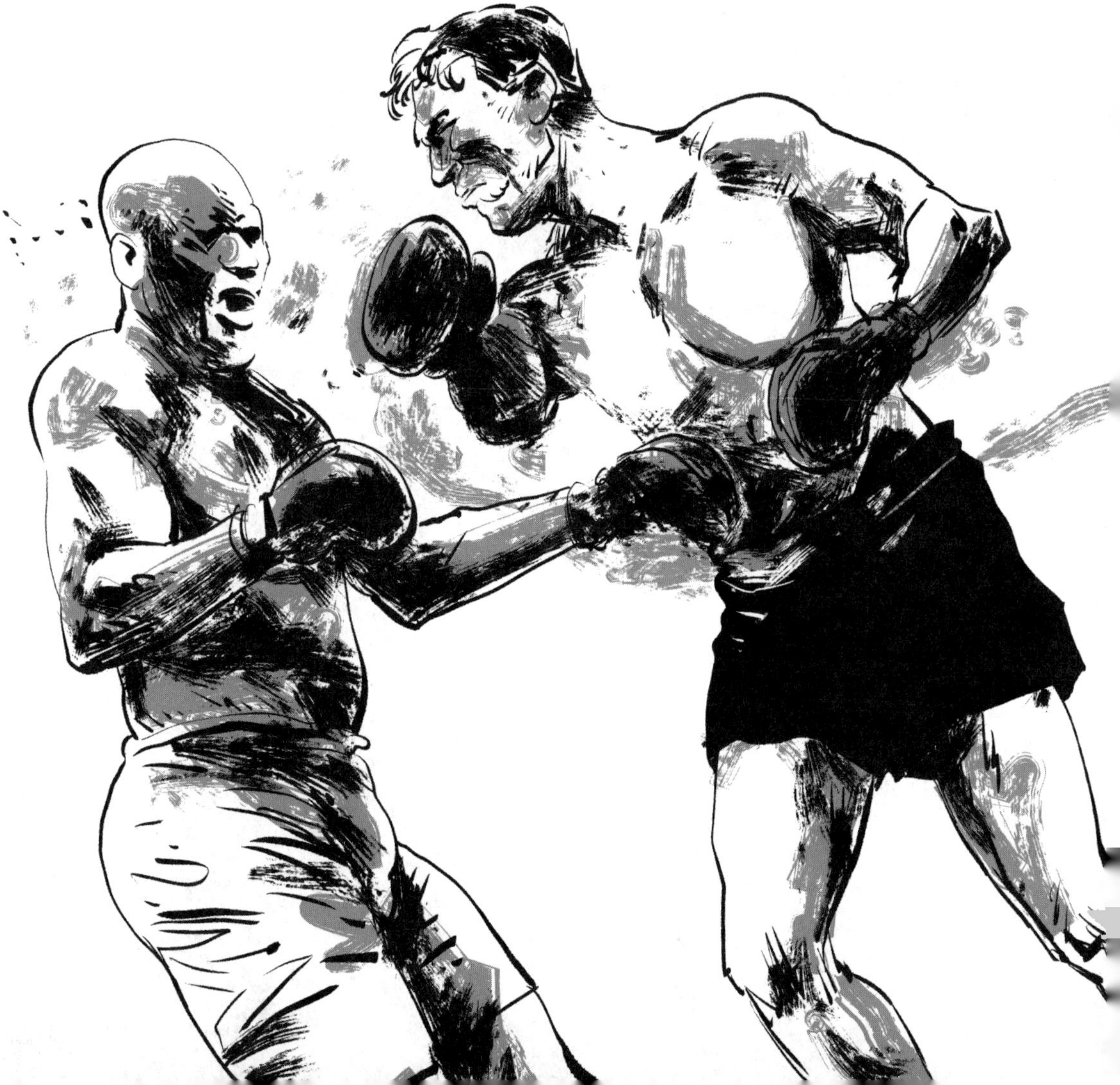

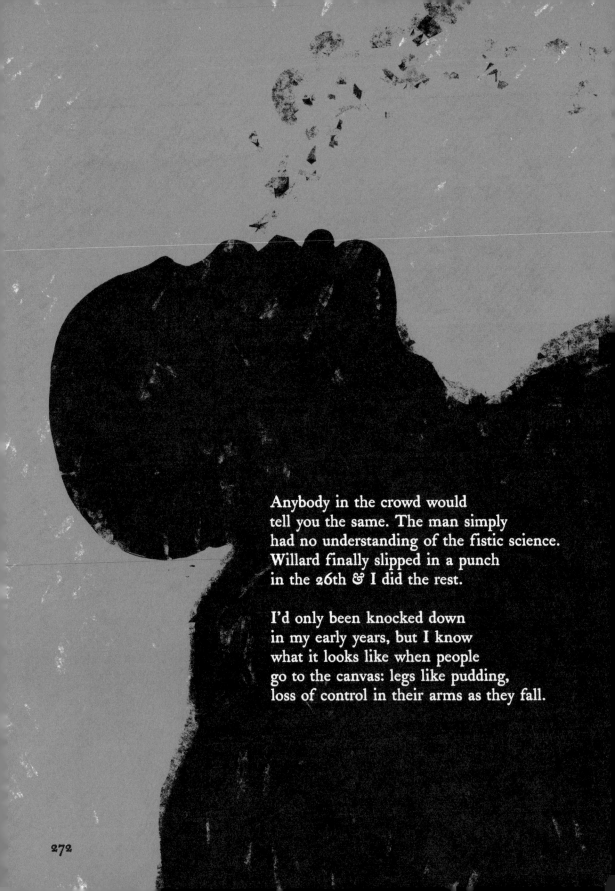

Anybody in the crowd would
tell you the same. The man simply
had no understanding of the fistic science.
Willard finally slipped in a punch
in the 26th & I did the rest.

I'd only been knocked down
in my early years, but I know
what it looks like when people
go to the canvas: legs like pudding,
loss of control in their arms as they fall.

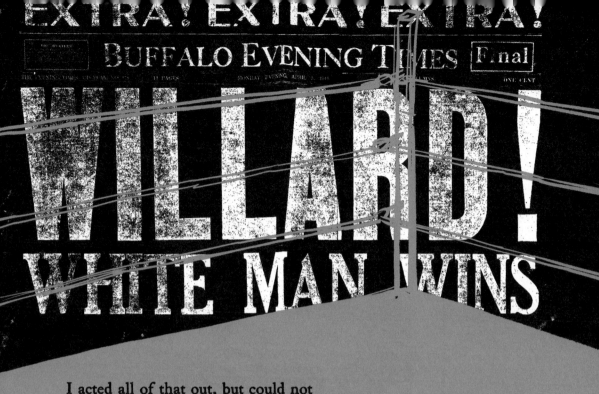

EXTRA! EXTRA! EXTRA!

BUFFALO EVENING TIMES Final

WILLARD!
WHITE MAN WINS

I acted all of that out, but could not resist shielding my eyes from the sun as the referee counted me out.

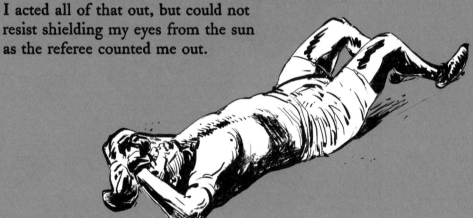

A few of those closer to the ring noticed I was smiling while I thought about finally being home.

273

OFF THE MAP

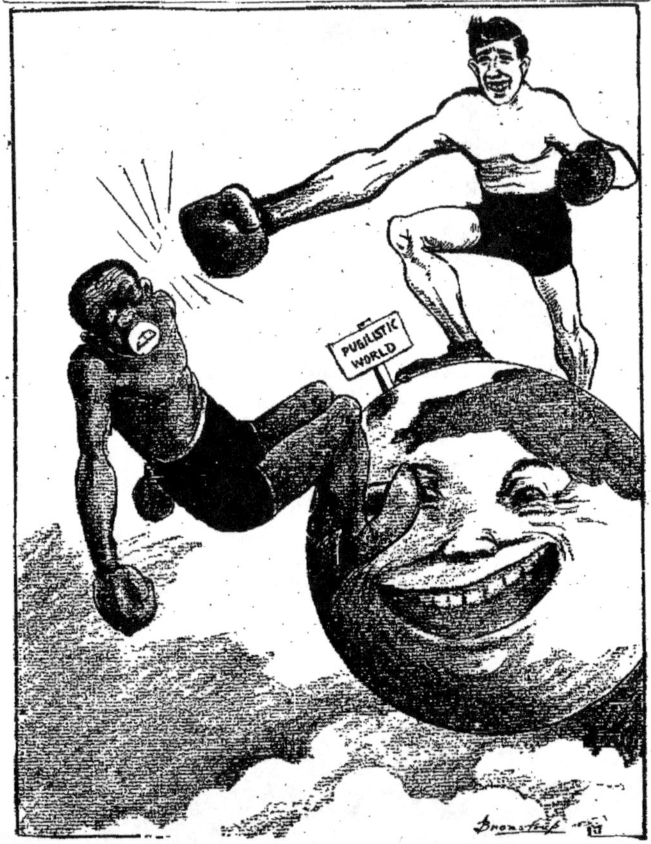
PUGILISTIC WORLD

MEXICO–UNITED STATES BORDER APRIL 1920

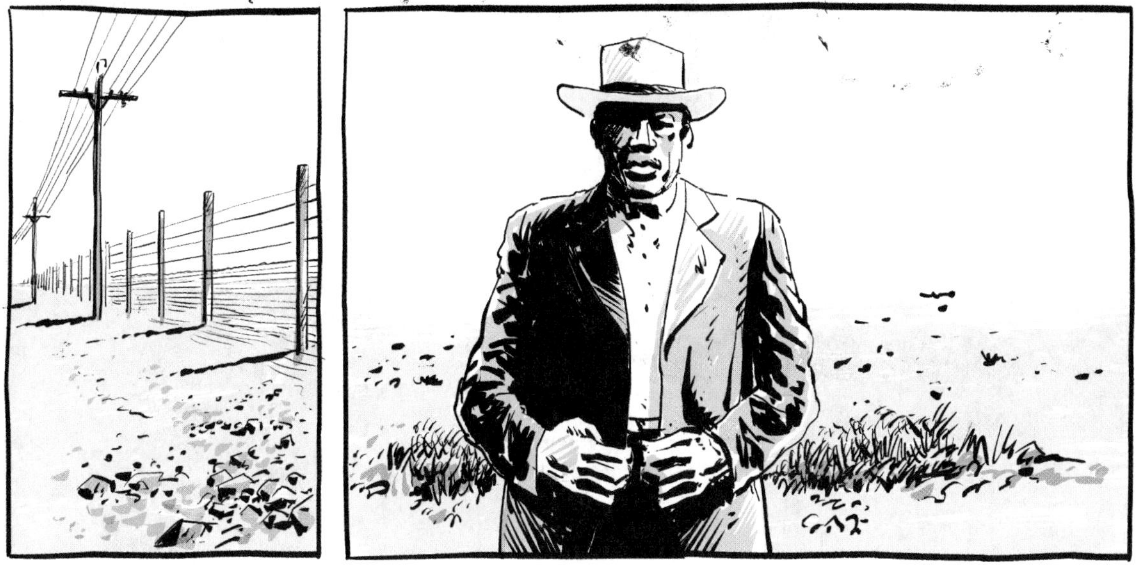

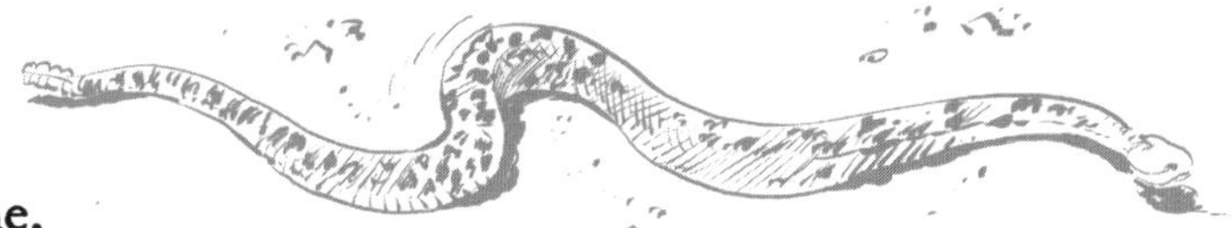

Almost home.
America double-crossed me.
I gave up the title & they still put me in prison.
The sheriff was waiting for me at the border, his smile as wide as Texas.

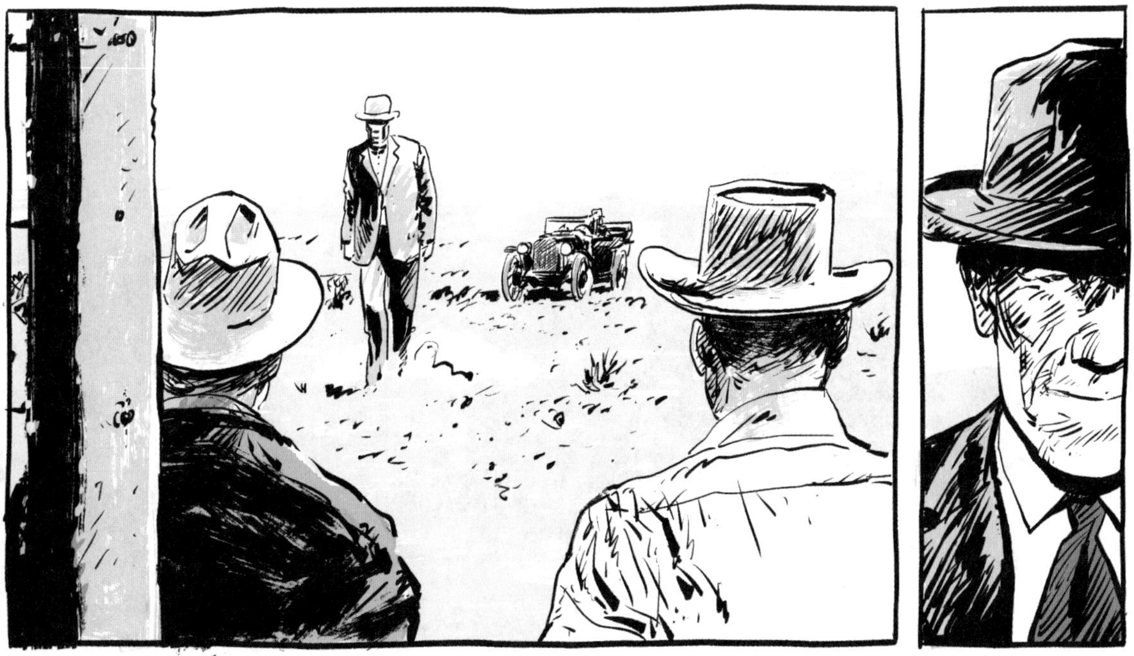

Almost home & it doesn't mean anything.

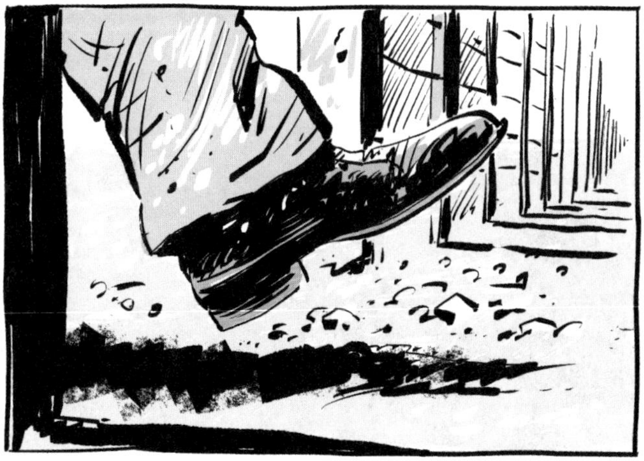

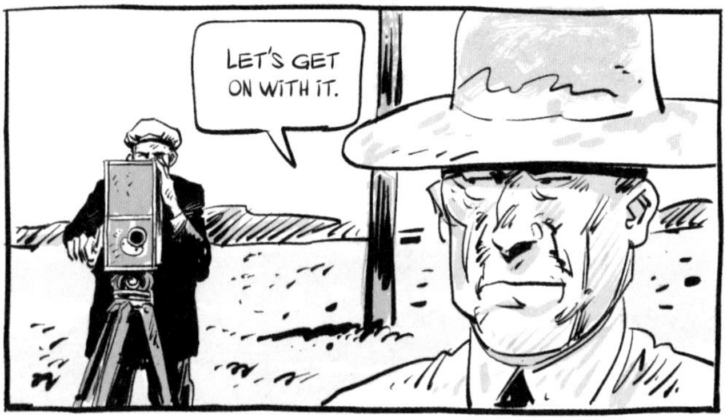
LET'S GET ON WITH IT.

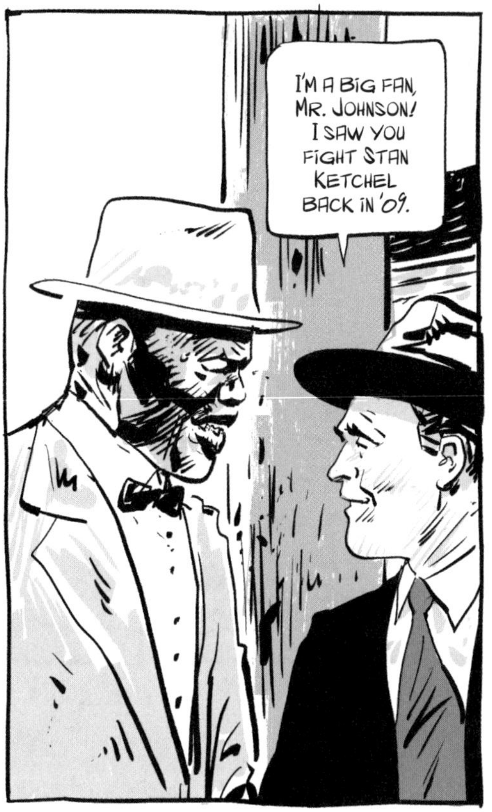
I'M A BIG FAN, MR. JOHNSON! I SAW YOU FIGHT STAN KETCHEL BACK IN '09.

They finally got me where they wanted me.

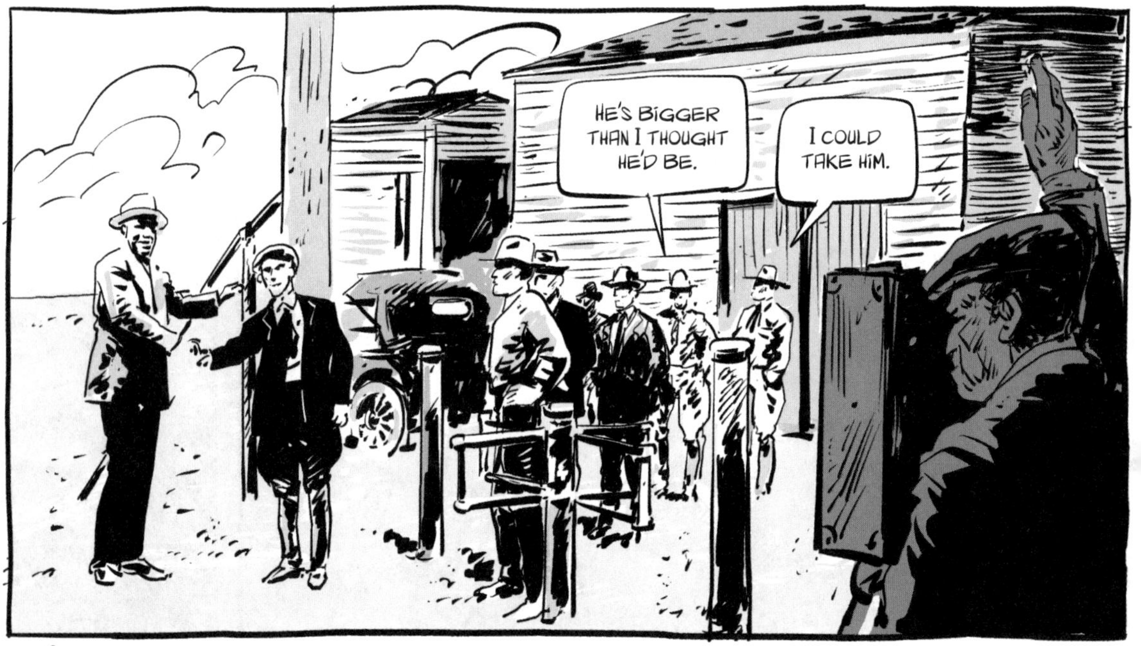
HE'S BIGGER THAN I THOUGHT HE'D BE.
I COULD TAKE HIM.

JACK JOHNSON ARRANGES SURRENDER

CALEXICO, Cal., April 3.—Jack Johnson, former world's heavyweight champion pugilist, sent for Sheriff Applestill of Imperial County yesterday and arranged to have the Sheriff take him personally into custody when Johnson crosses the international line to meet Federal charges pending against him in Chicago. Johnson said he hoped to be ready to surrender soon.

The purpose of prison is to take your time & your pride.
They got my time, but not even Leavenworth could get my pride.

15461, an indignant number if there ever was one.
I'm 1. As in the only one. As in the first & only
Black heavyweight champion of the world.

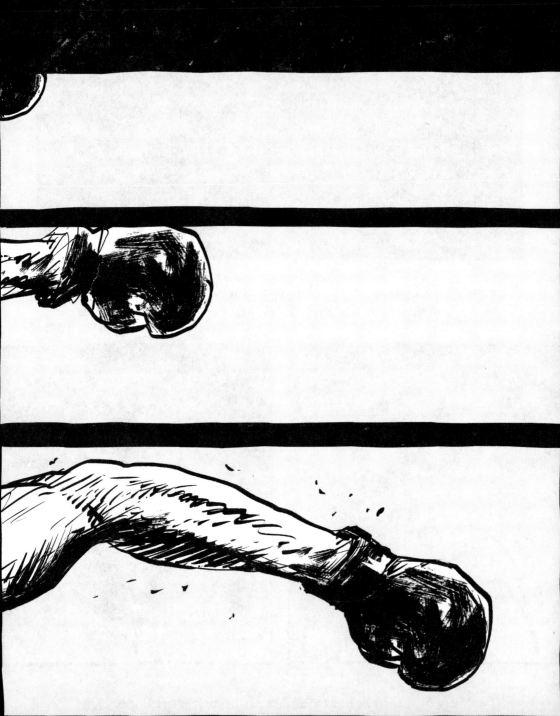

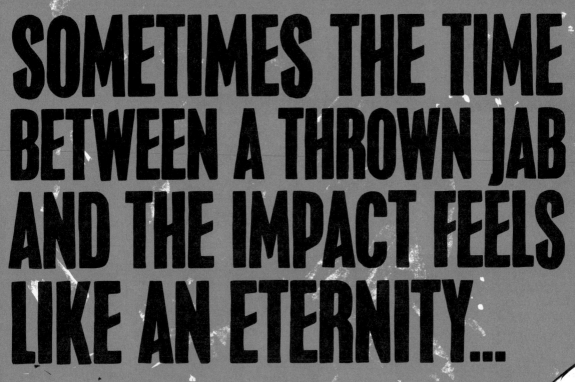

SOMETIMES THE TIME BETWEEN A THROWN JAB AND THE IMPACT FEELS LIKE AN ETERNITY...

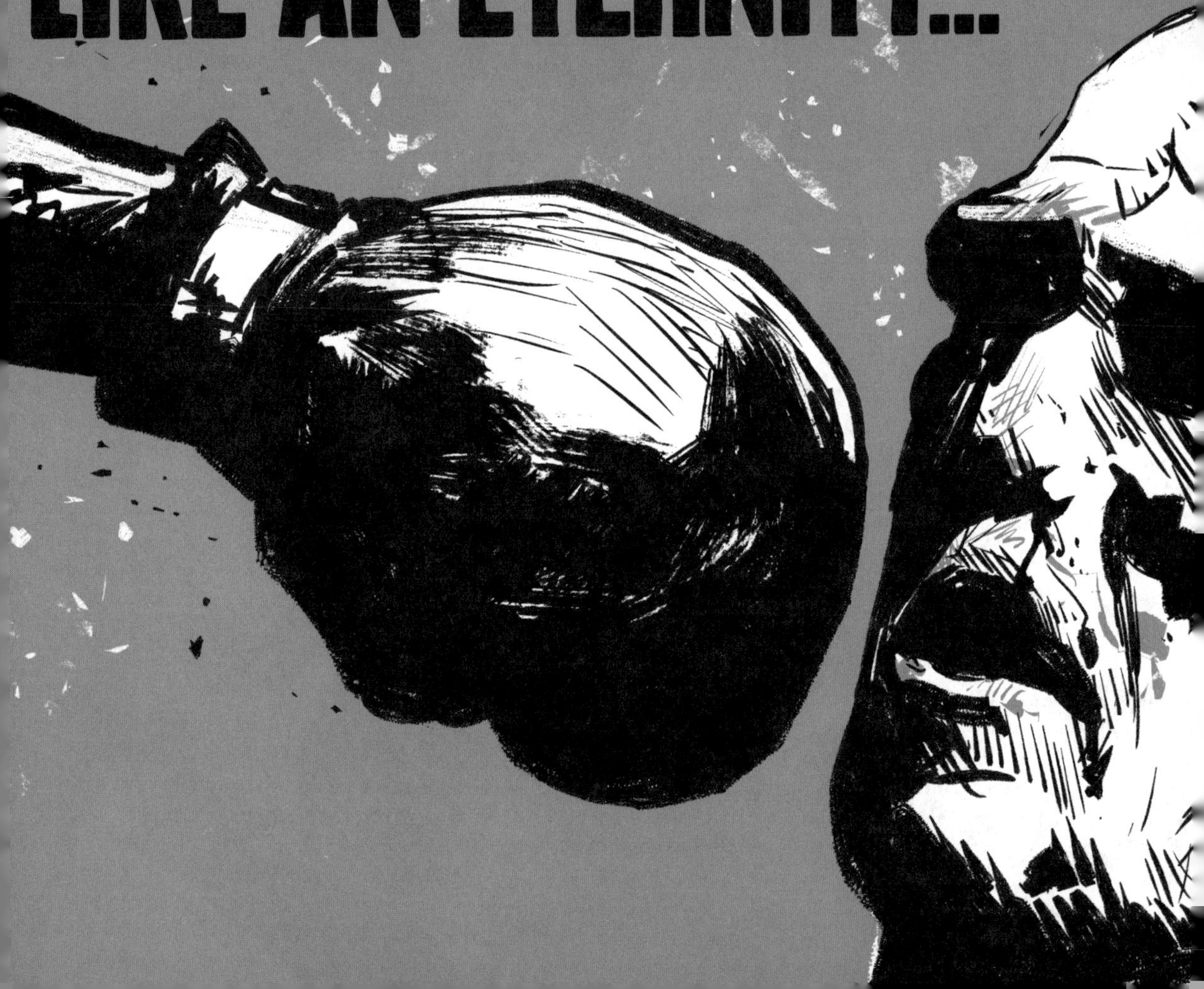

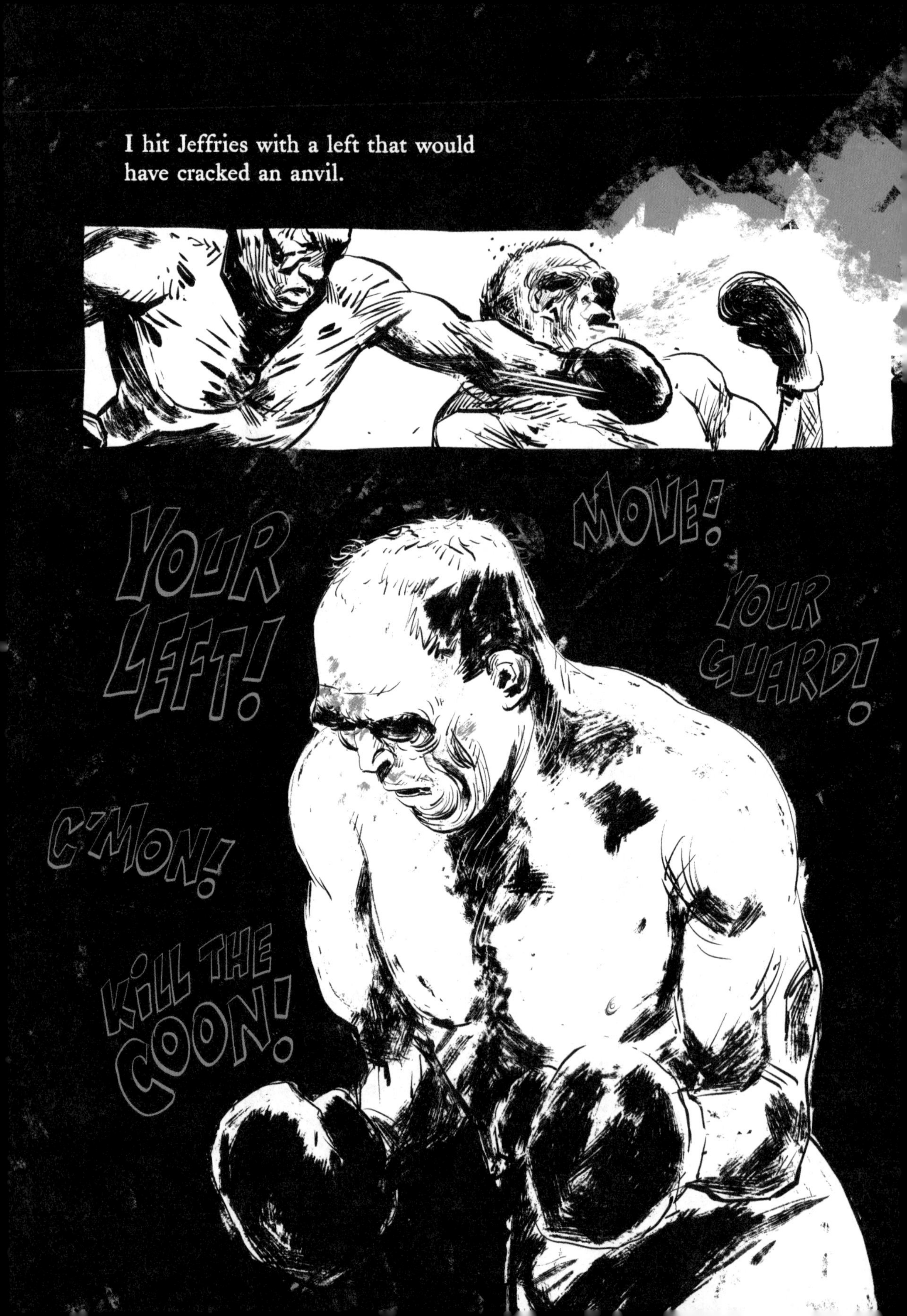
I hit Jeffries with a left that would have cracked an anvil.
YOUR LEFT!
MOVE!
YOUR GUARD!
C'MON!
KILL THE COON!

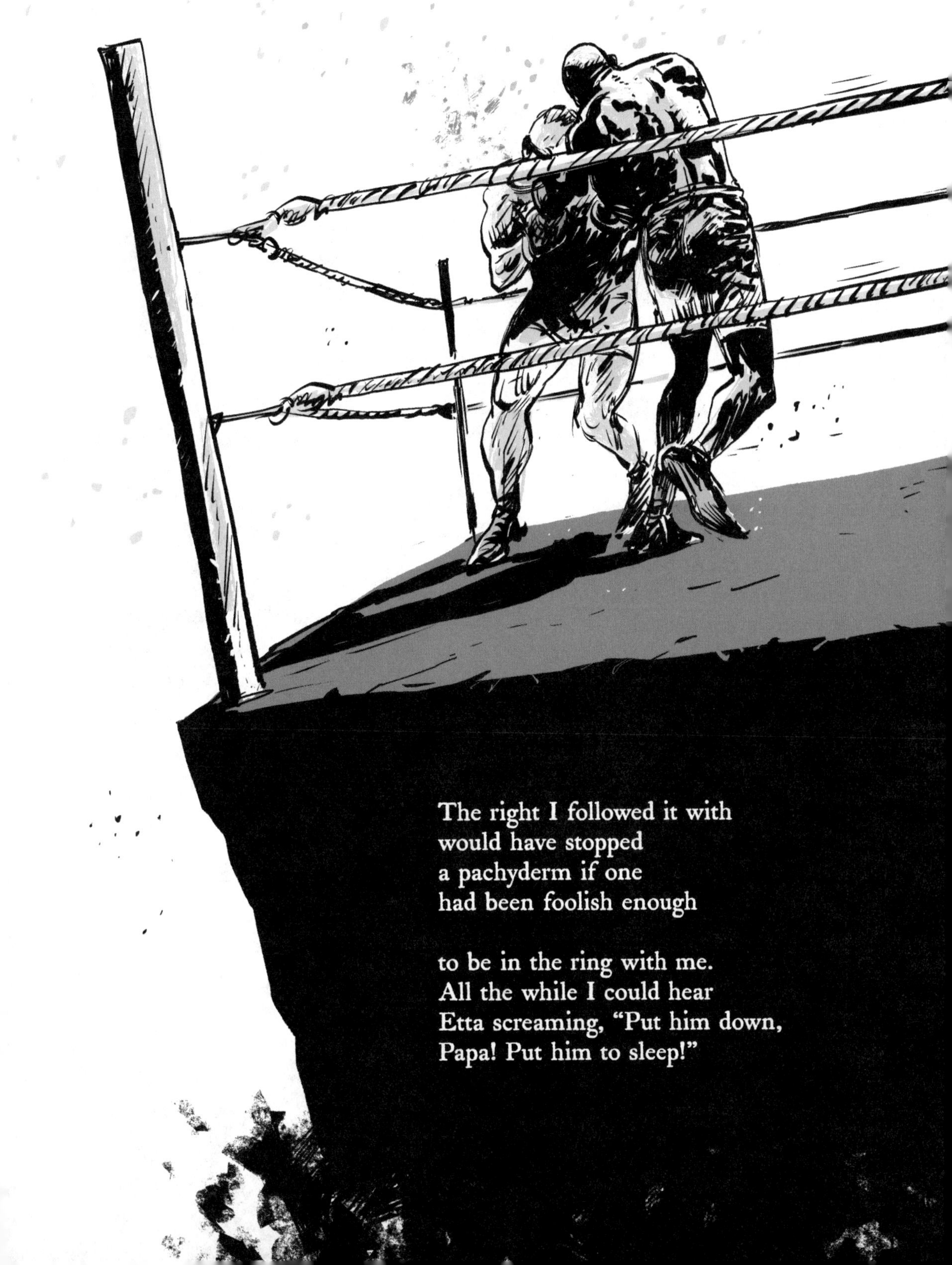
The right I followed it with
would have stopped
a pachyderm if one
had been foolish enough

to be in the ring with me.
All the while I could hear
Etta screaming, "Put him down,
Papa! Put him to sleep!"

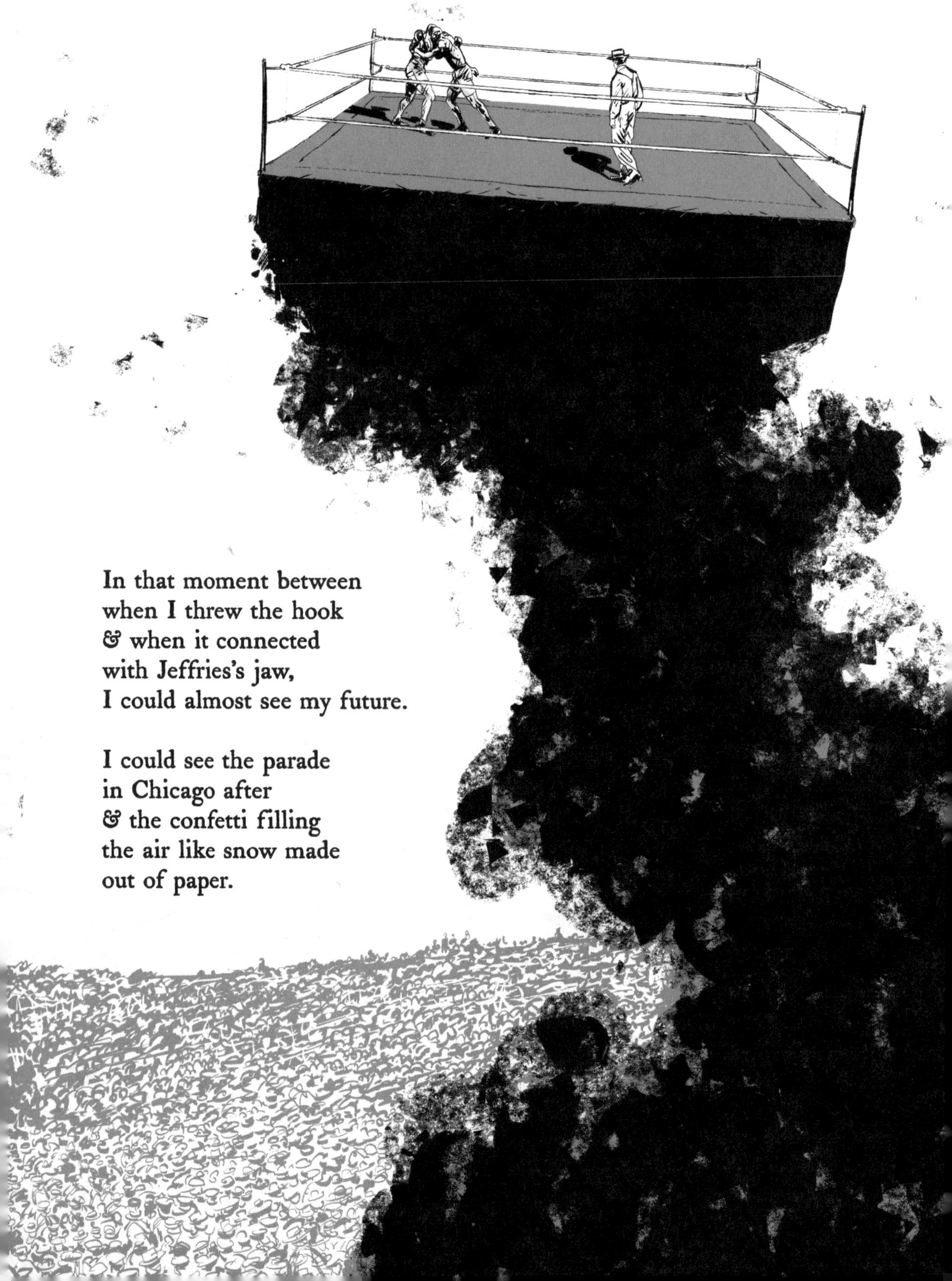

In that moment between
when I threw the hook
& when it connected
with Jeffries's jaw,
I could almost see my future.

I could see the parade
in Chicago after
& the confetti filling
the air like snow made
out of paper.

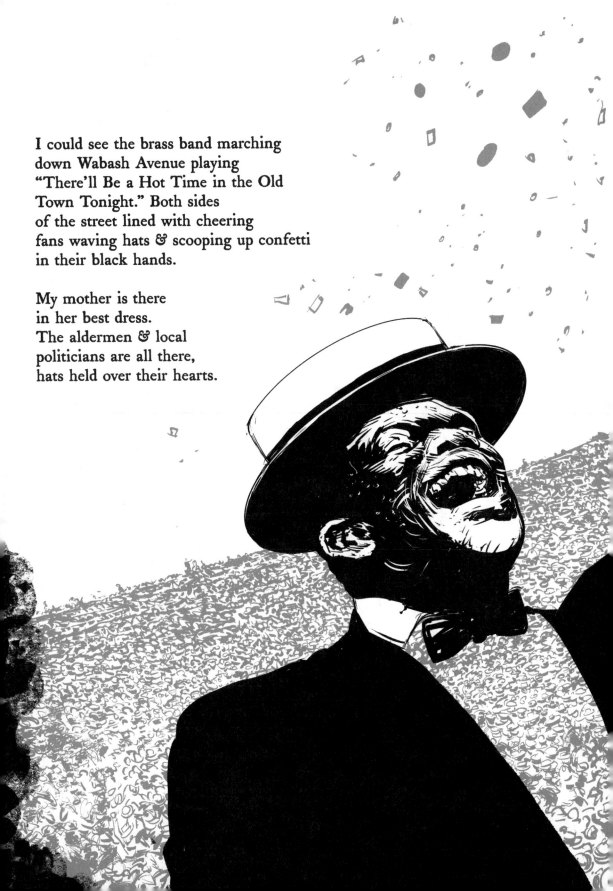

I could see the brass band marching
down Wabash Avenue playing
"There'll Be a Hot Time in the Old
Town Tonight." Both sides
of the street lined with cheering
fans waving hats & scooping up confetti
in their black hands.

My mother is there
in her best dress.
The aldermen & local
politicians are all there,
hats held over their hearts.

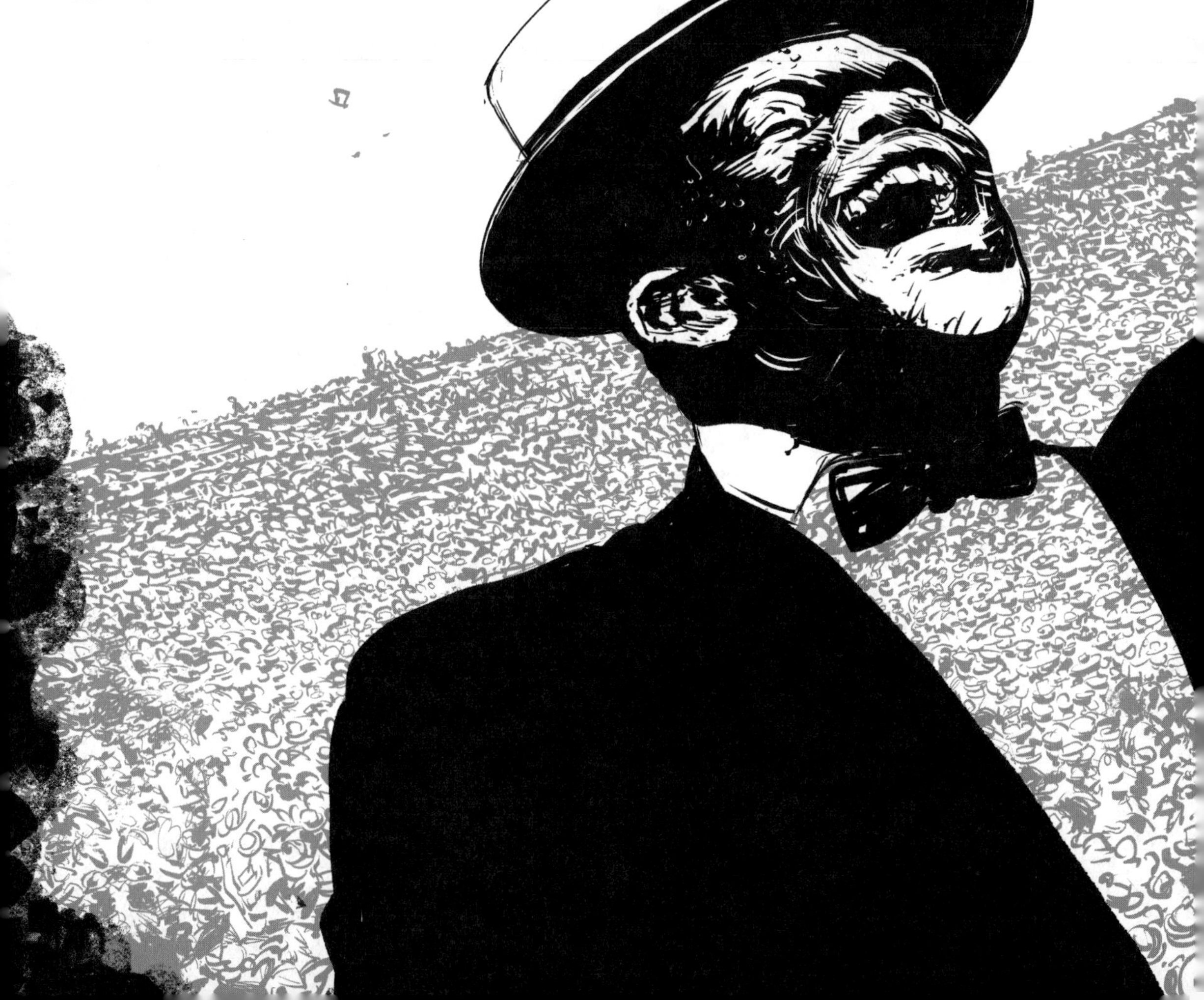

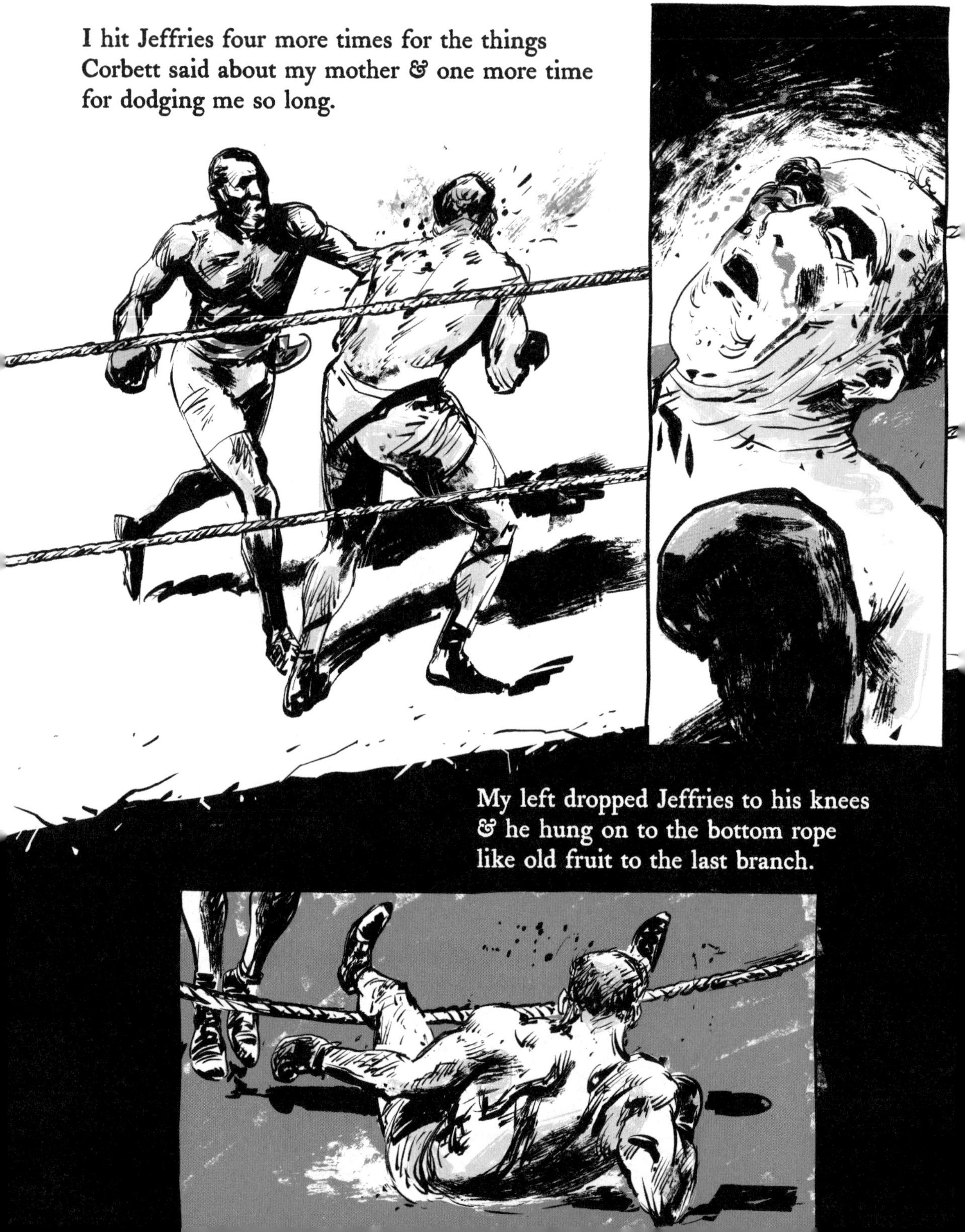
I hit Jeffries four more times for the things Corbett said about my mother & one more time for dodging me so long.
My left dropped Jeffries to his knees & he hung on to the bottom rope like old fruit to the last branch.

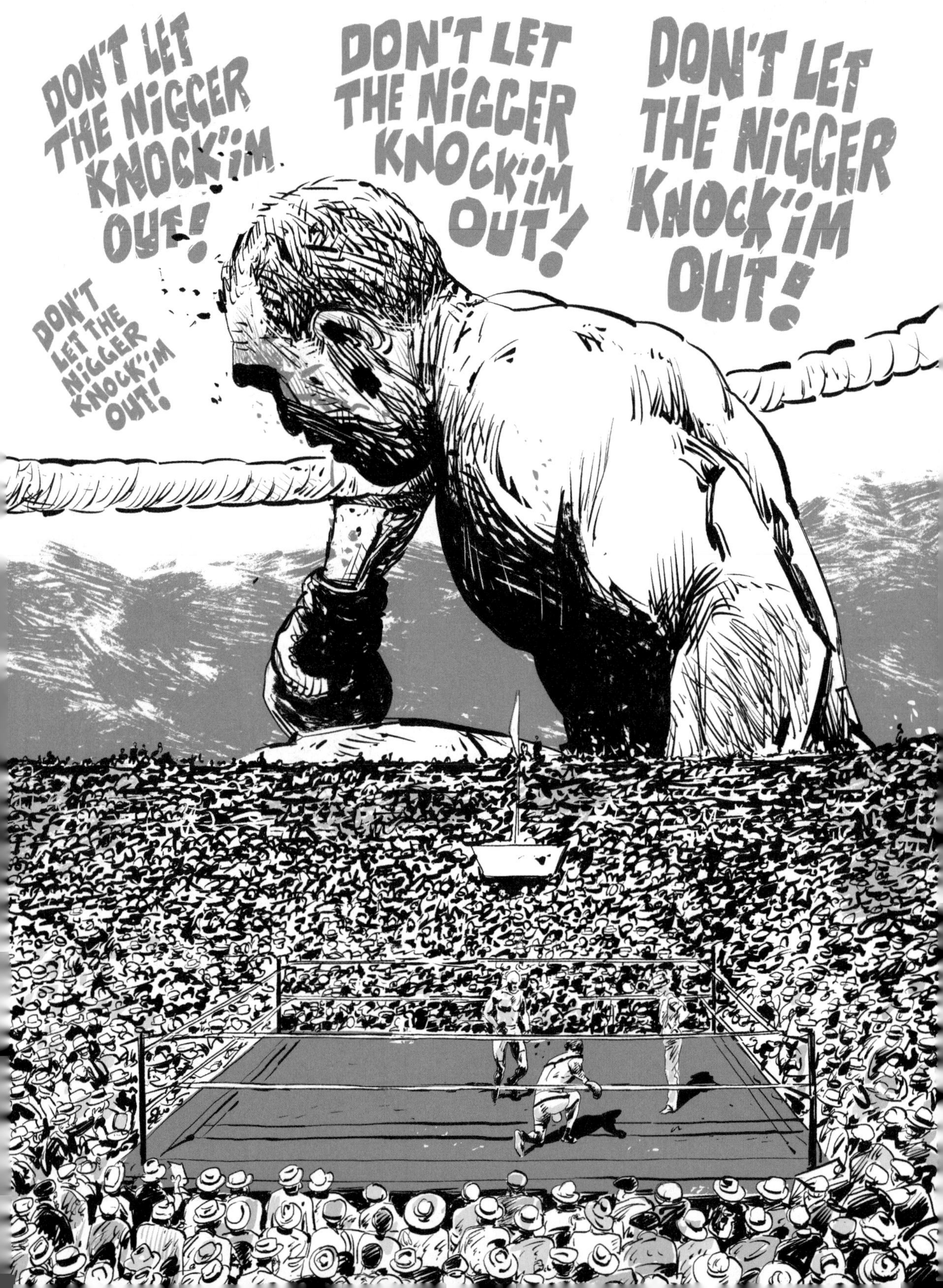
DON'T LET THE NIGGER KNOCK'IM OUT!
DON'T LET THE NIGGER KNOCK'IM OUT!
DON'T LET THE NIGGER KNOCK'IM OUT!
DON'T LET THE NIGGER KNOCK'IM OUT!

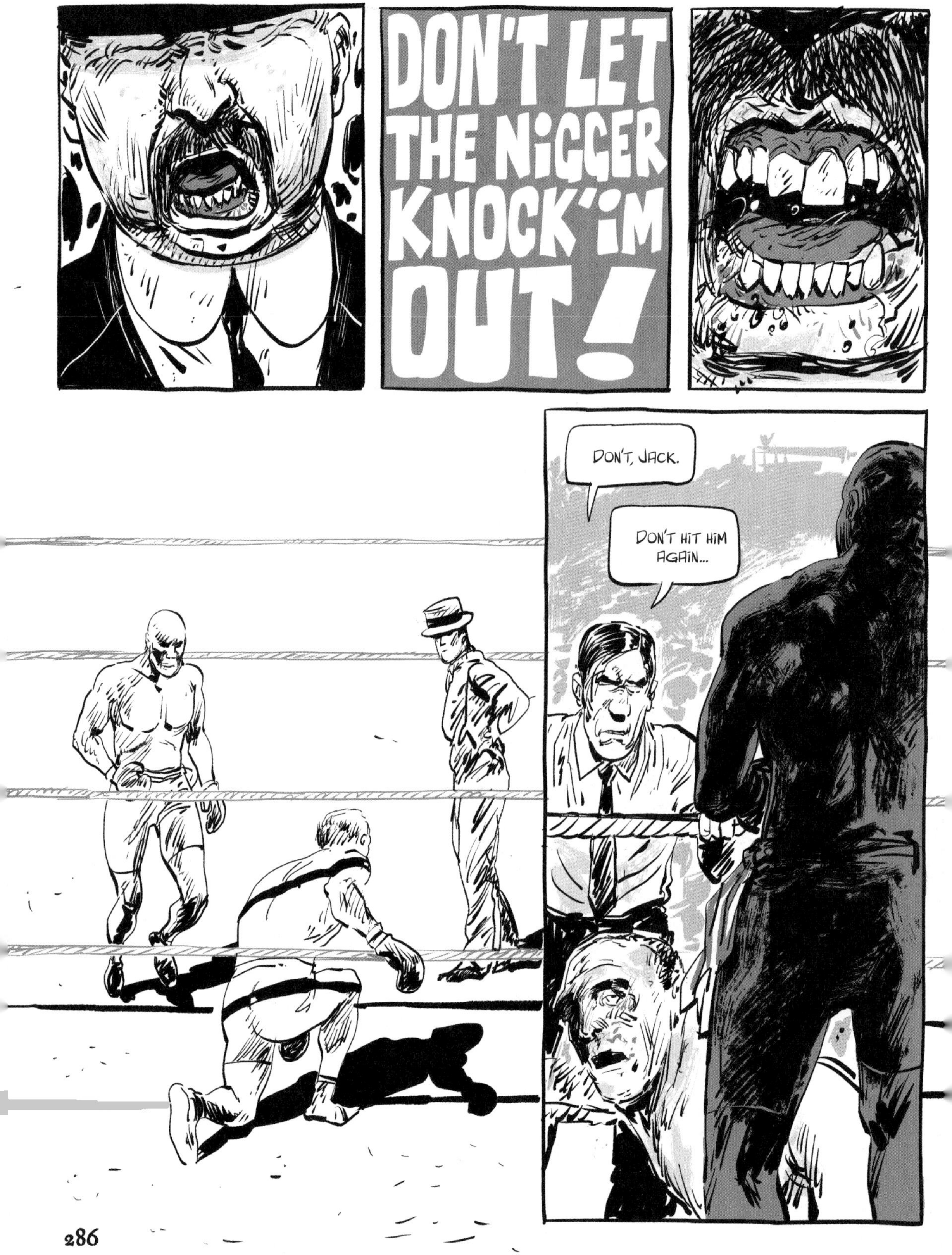

DON'T LET THE NIGGER KNOCK 'IM OUT!
DON'T, JACK.
DON'T HIT HIM AGAIN...

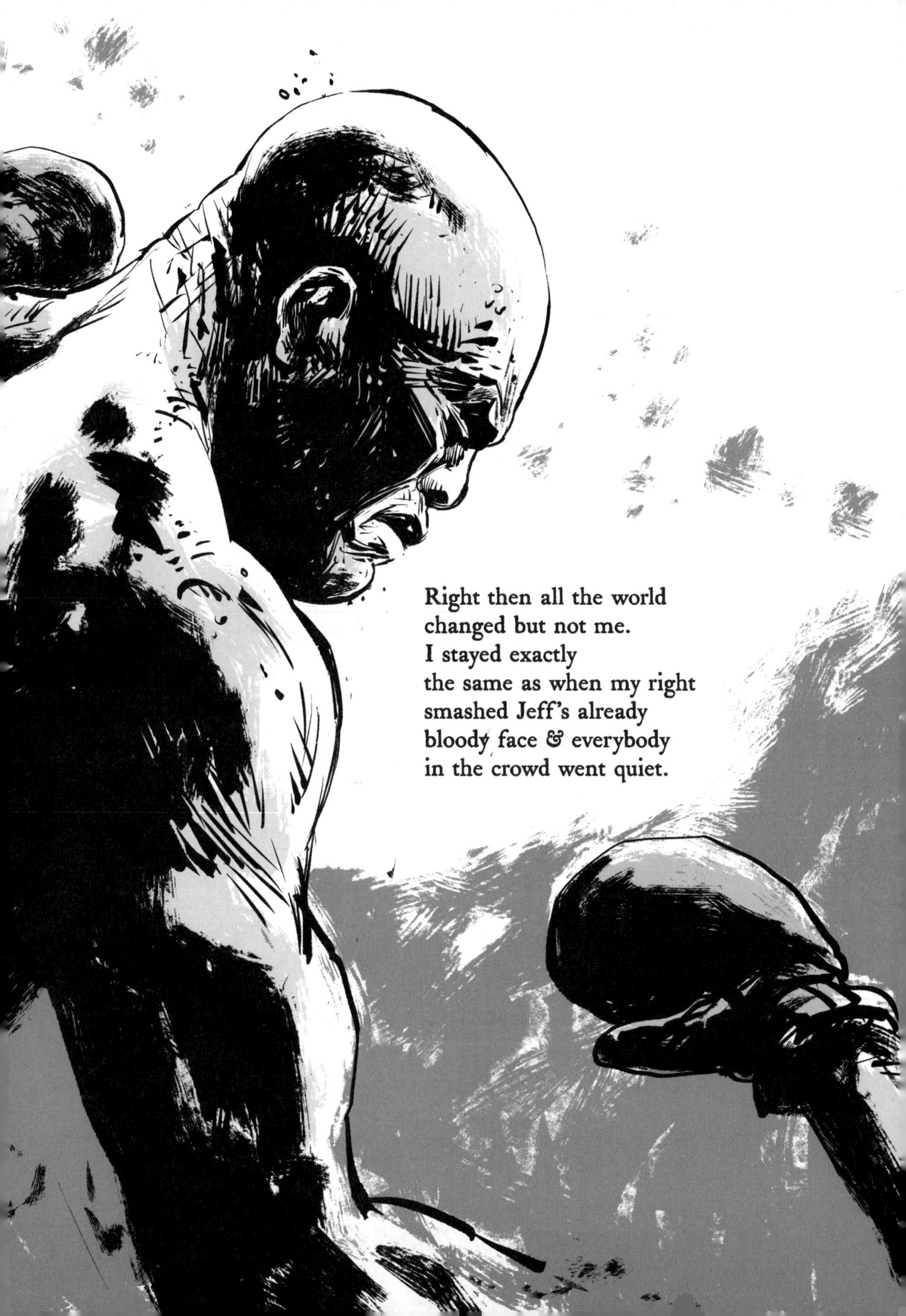

Right then all the world
changed but not me.
I stayed exactly
the same as when my right
smashed Jeff's already
bloody face & everybody
in the crowd went quiet.

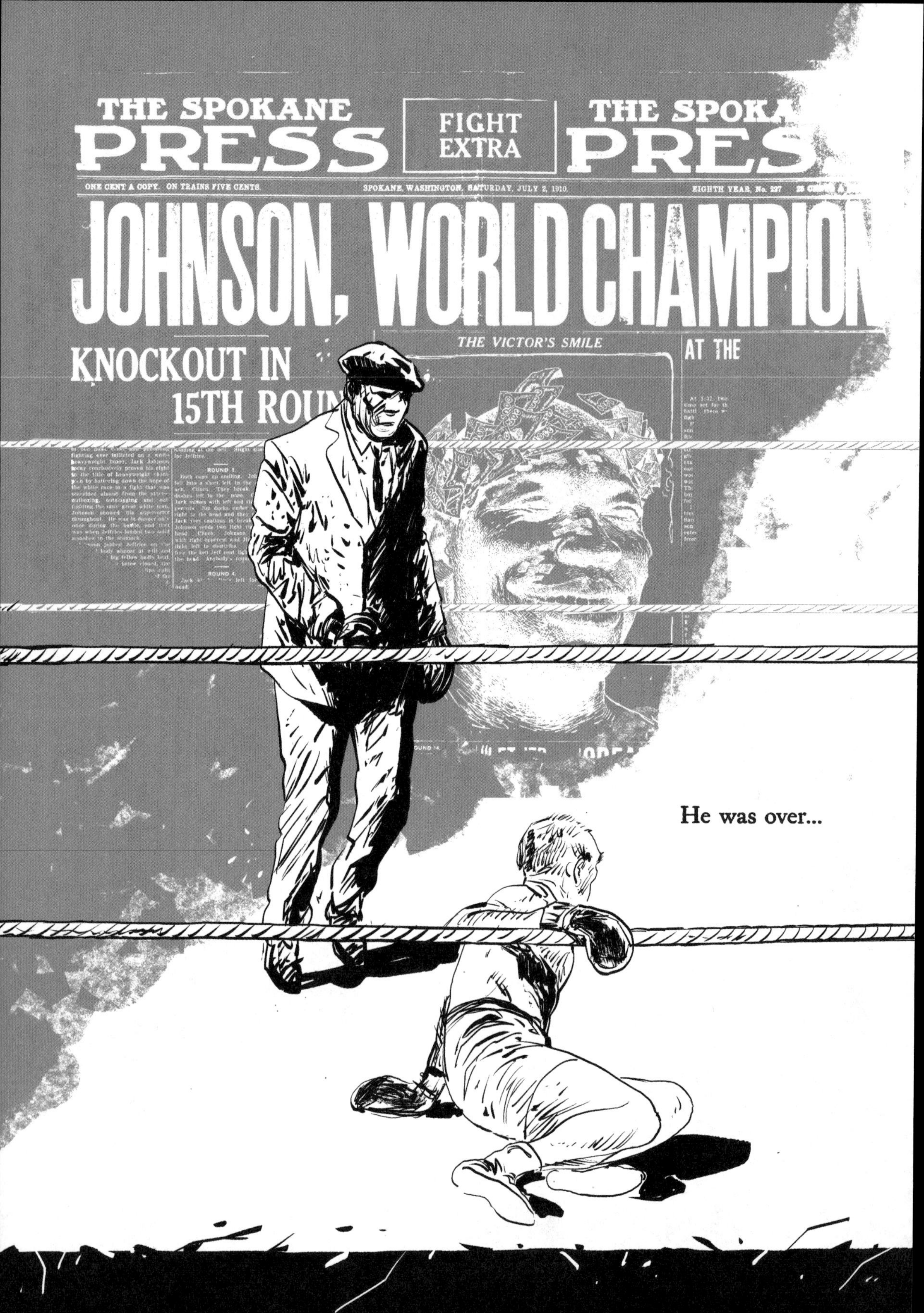
THE SPOKANE PRESS
FIGHT EXTRA
THE SPOKA PRES
ONE CENT A COPY. ON TRAINS FIVE CENTS.
SPOKANE, WASHINGTON, SATURDAY, JULY 2, 1910.
EIGHTH YEAR, No. 227
JOHNSON, WORLD CHAMPIO
THE VICTOR'S SMILE
AT THE
KNOCKOUT IN 15TH ROUN
He was over...

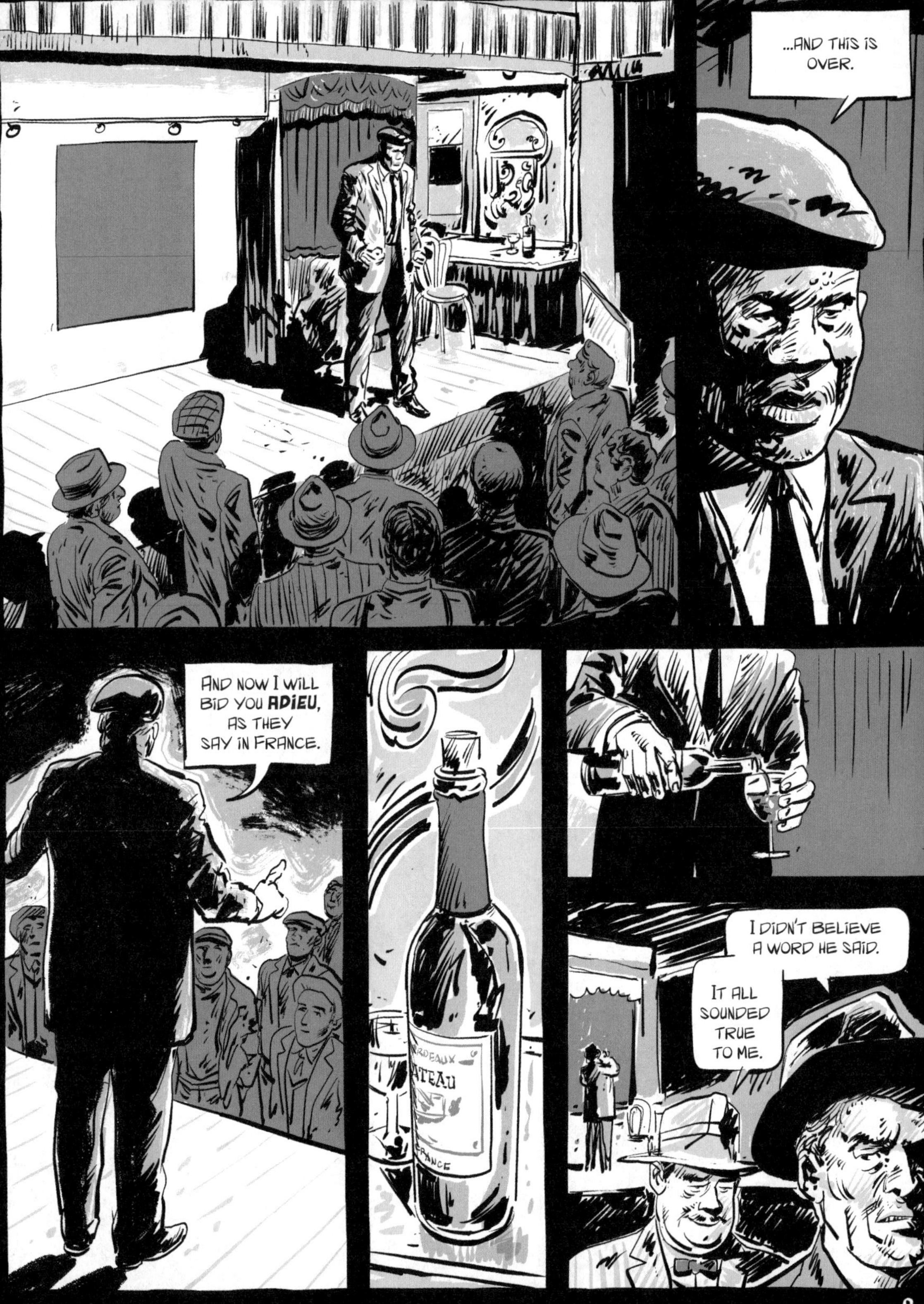
...AND THIS IS OVER.
AND NOW I WILL BID YOU **ADIEU**, AS THEY SAY IN FRANCE.
I DIDN'T BELIEVE A WORD HE SAID.
IT ALL SOUNDED TRUE TO ME.

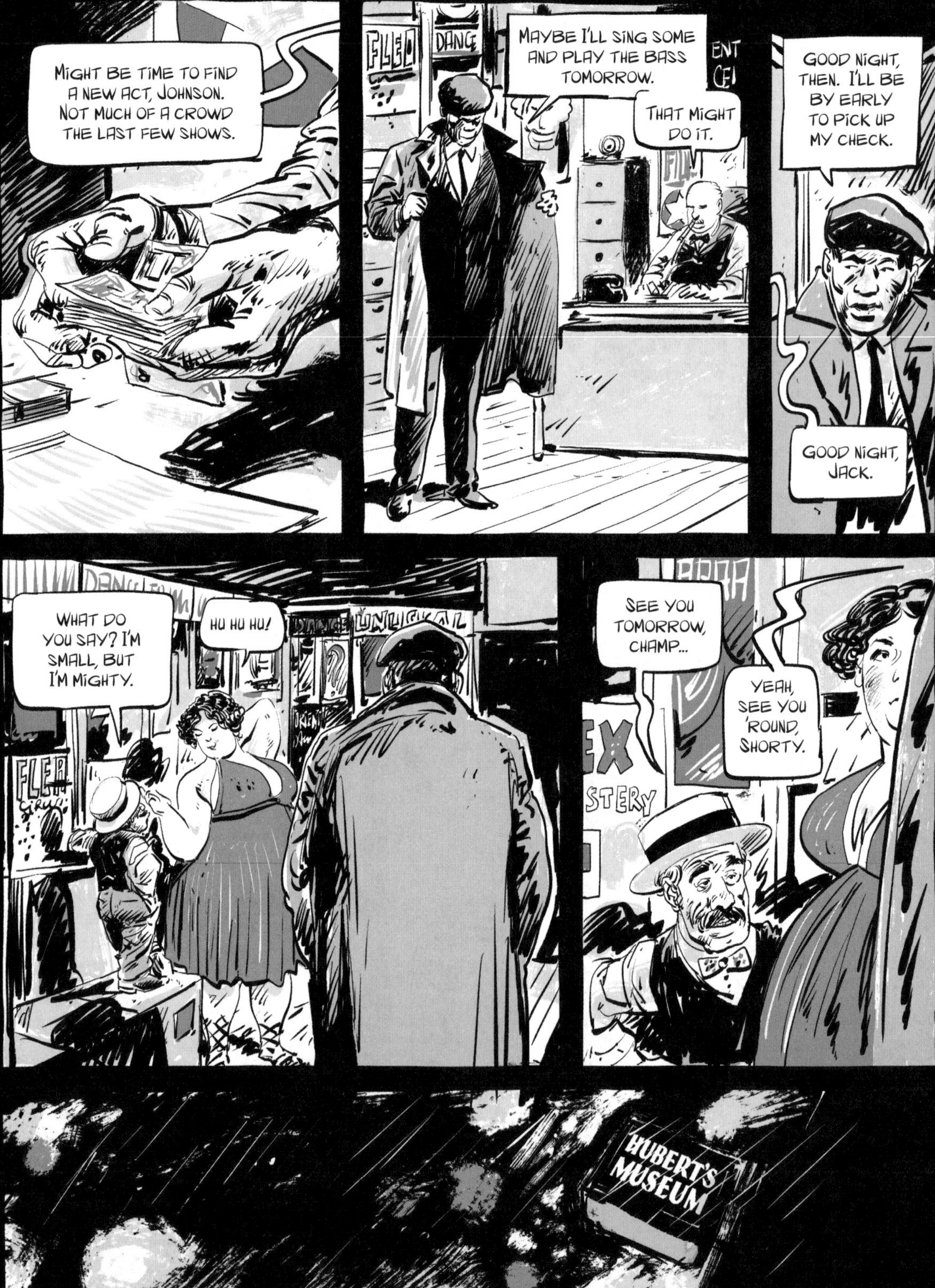
MIGHT BE TIME TO FIND A NEW ACT, JOHNSON. NOT MUCH OF A CROWD THE LAST FEW SHOWS.
MAYBE I'LL SING SOME AND PLAY THE BASS TOMORROW.
THAT MIGHT DO IT.
GOOD NIGHT, THEN. I'LL BE BY EARLY TO PICK UP MY CHECK.
GOOD NIGHT, JACK.
WHAT DO YOU SAY? I'M SMALL, BUT I'M MIGHTY.
HU HU HU!
SEE YOU TOMORROW, CHAMP...
YEAH, SEE YOU 'ROUND, SHORTY.
HUBERT'S MUSEUM

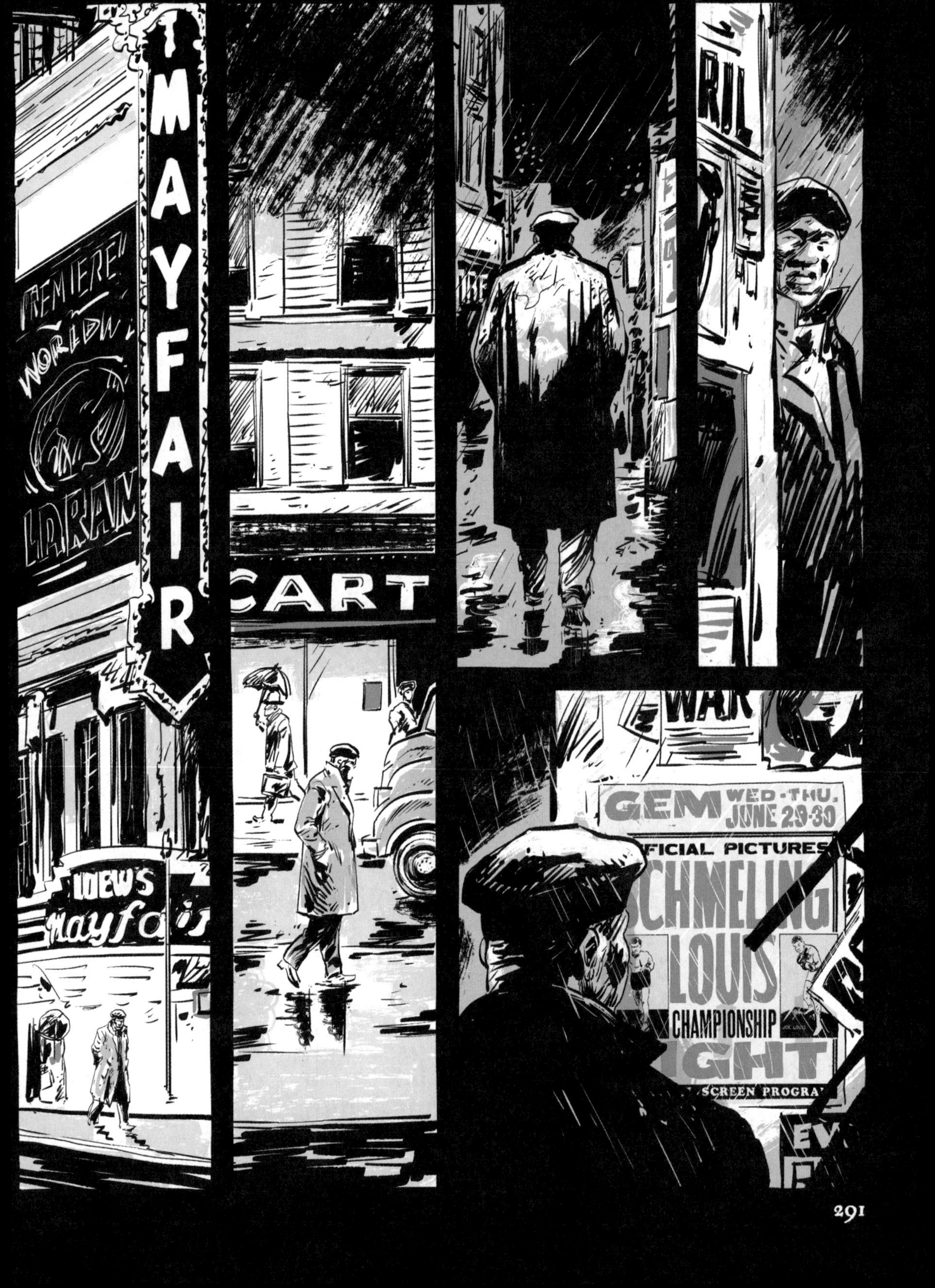
MAYFAIR
CART
WAR
GEM WED-THU. JUNE 29-30
LOUIS
CHAMPIONSHIP

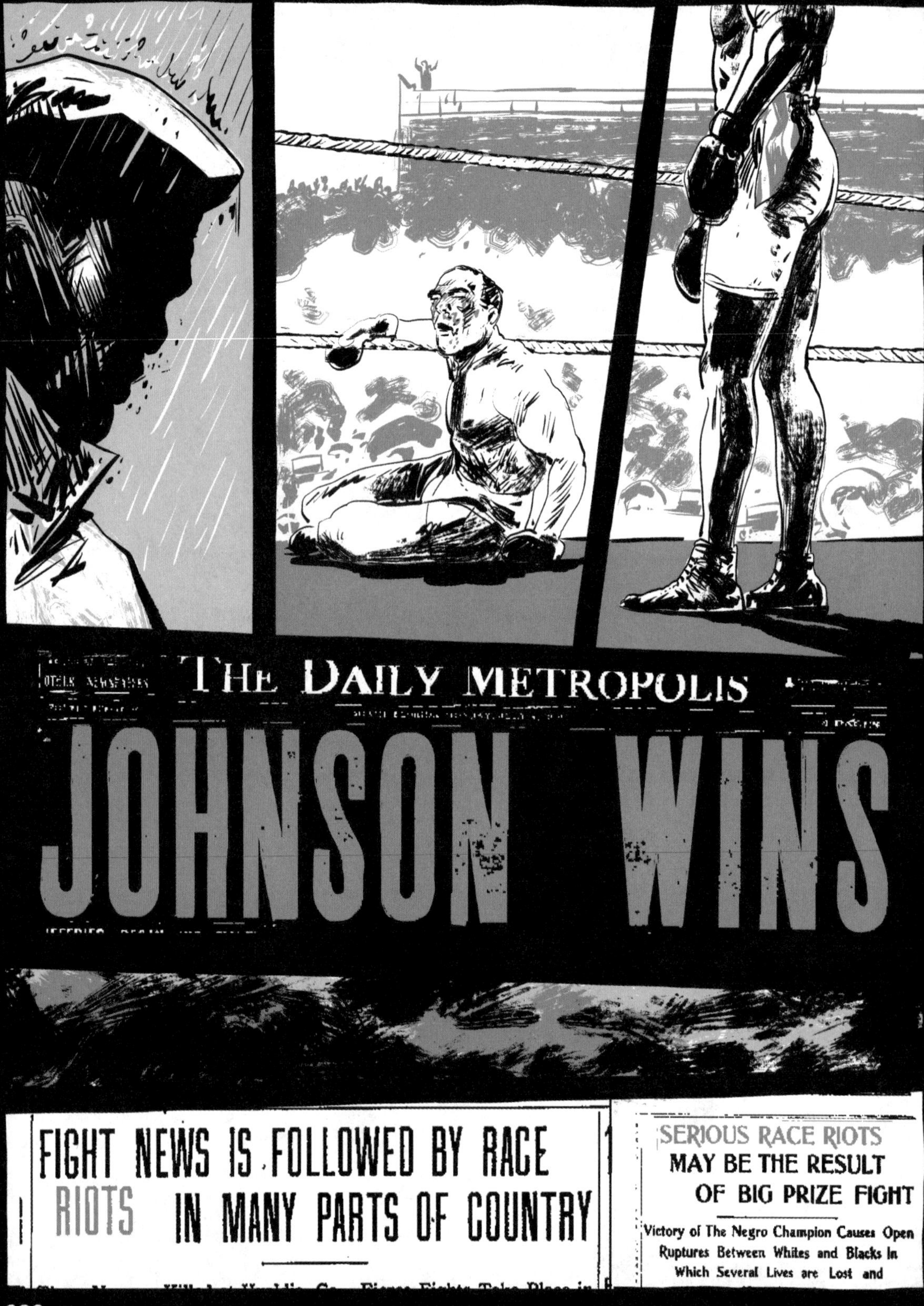
THE DAILY METROPOLIS
JOHNSON WINS
FIGHT NEWS IS FOLLOWED BY RACE RIOTS IN MANY PARTS OF COUNTRY
SERIOUS RACE RIOTS
MAY BE THE RESULT
OF BIG PRIZE FIGHT
Victory of The Negro Champion Causes Open Ruptures Between Whites and Blacks In Which Several Lives are Lost and

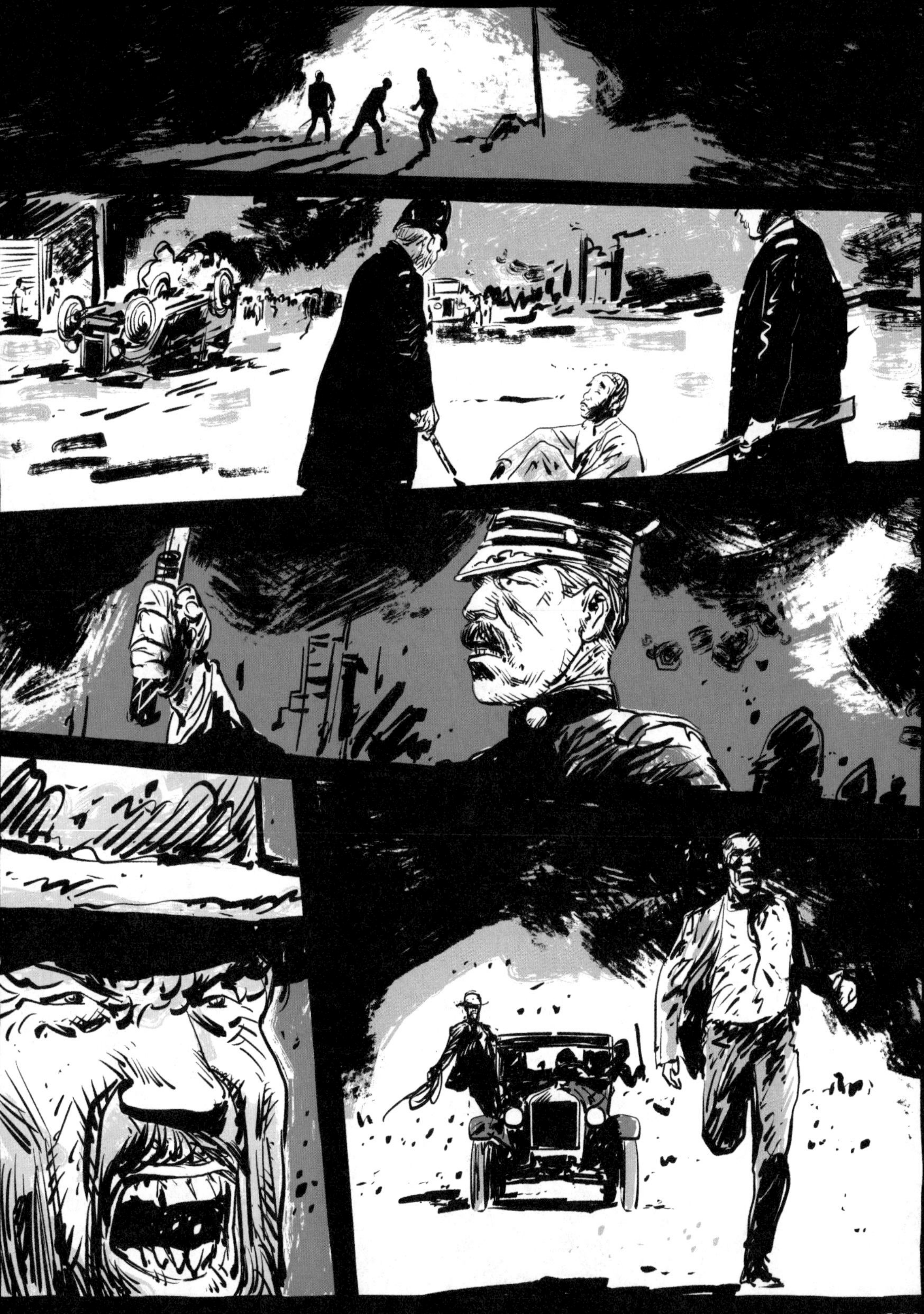

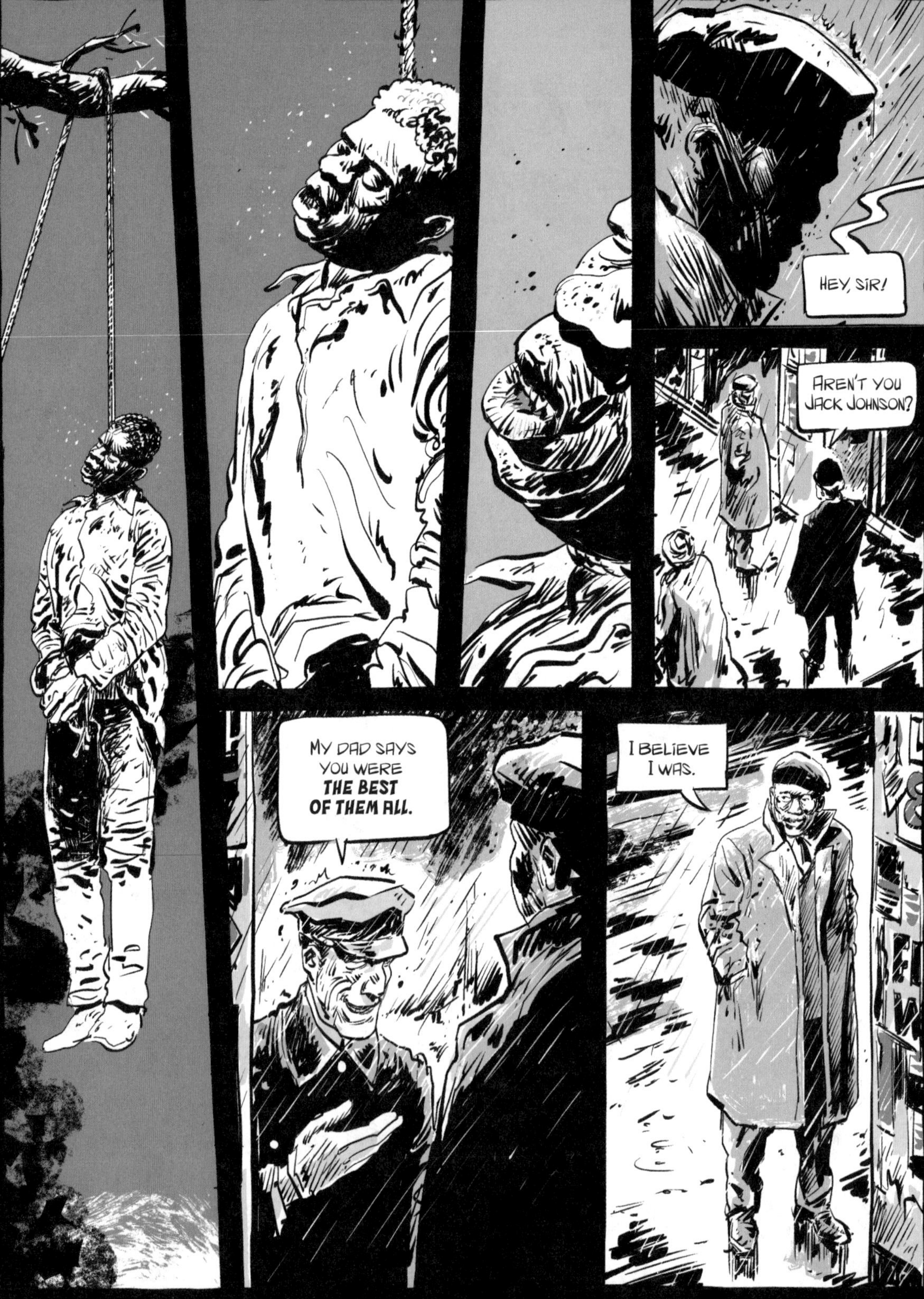
HEY, SIR!
AREN'T YOU JACK JOHNSON?
MY DAD SAYS YOU WERE **THE BEST OF THEM ALL.**
I BELIEVE I WAS.

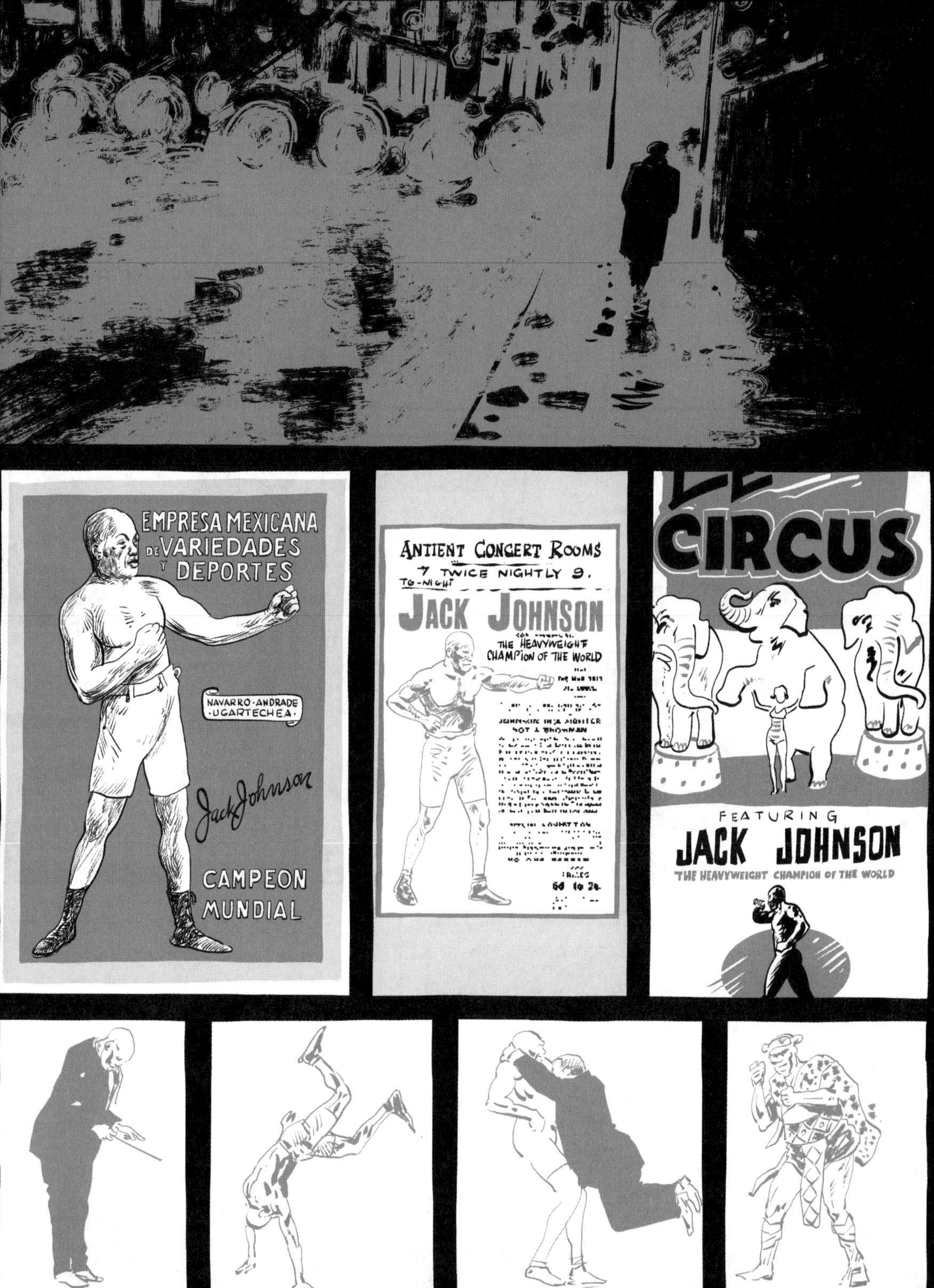
EMPRESA MEXICANA
DE VARIEDADES
Y DEPORTES
NAVARRO · ANDRADE · UGARTECHEA ·
Jack Johnson
CAMPEON
MUNDIAL
ANTIENT CONCERT ROOMS
7 TWICE NIGHTLY 9.
TO-NIGHT
JACK JOHNSON
THE HEAVYWEIGHT
CHAMPION OF THE WORLD
CIRCUS
FEATURING
JACK JOHNSON
THE HEAVYWEIGHT CHAMPION OF THE WORLD

NEAR FRANKLINTON, N. CAROLINA 1946

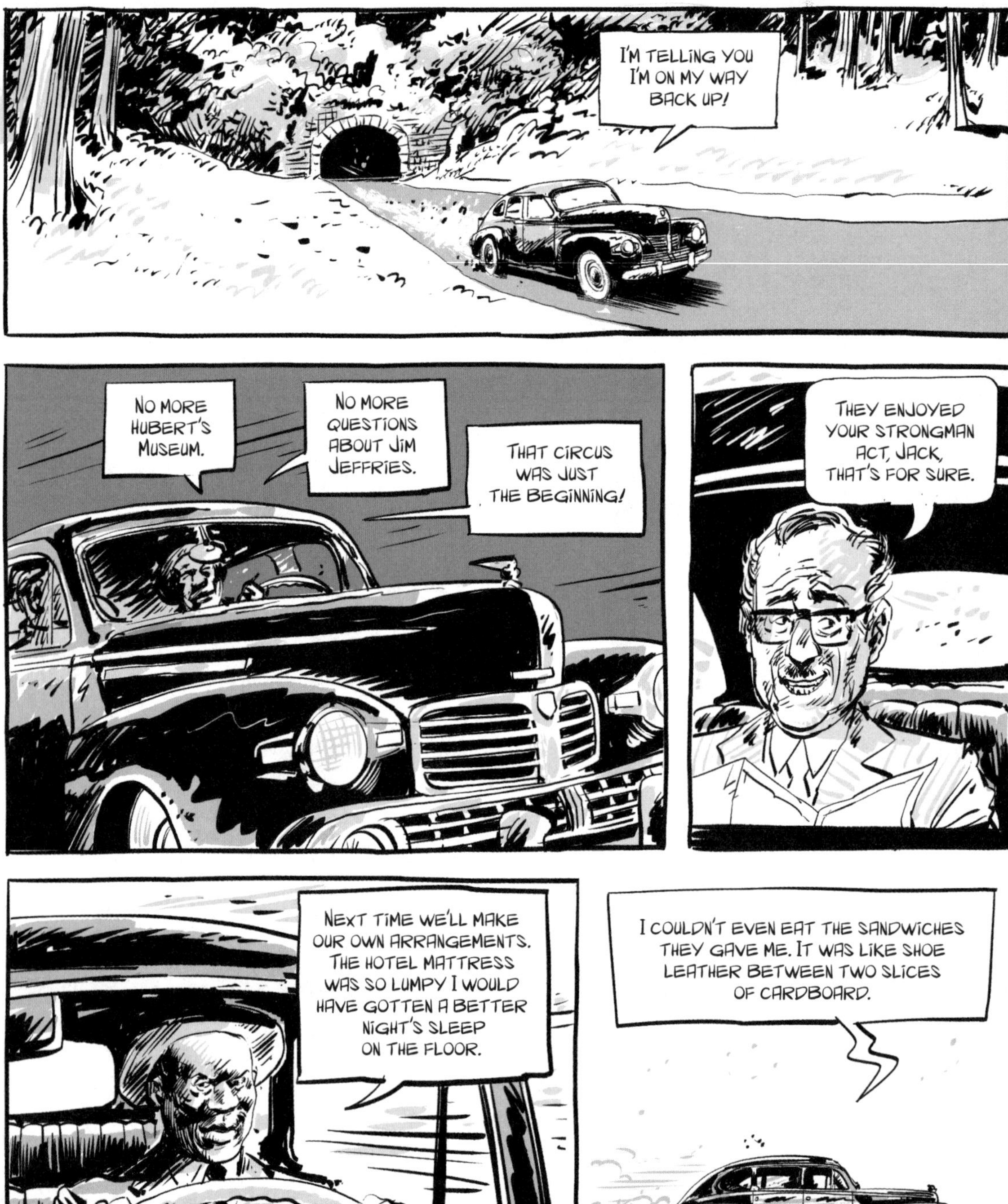

I'M TELLING YOU I'M ON MY WAY BACK UP!
NO MORE HUBERT'S MUSEUM.
NO MORE QUESTIONS ABOUT JIM JEFFRIES.
THAT CIRCUS WAS JUST THE BEGINNING!
THEY ENJOYED YOUR STRONGMAN ACT, JACK, THAT'S FOR SURE.
NEXT TIME WE'LL MAKE OUR OWN ARRANGEMENTS. THE HOTEL MATTRESS WAS SO LUMPY I WOULD HAVE GOTTEN A BETTER NIGHT'S SLEEP ON THE FLOOR.
I COULDN'T EVEN EAT THE SANDWICHES THEY GAVE ME. IT WAS LIKE SHOE LEATHER BETWEEN TWO SLICES OF CARDBOARD.

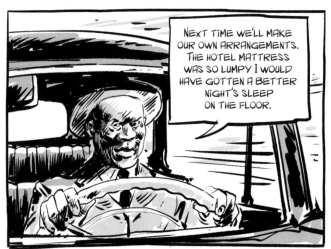

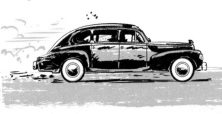

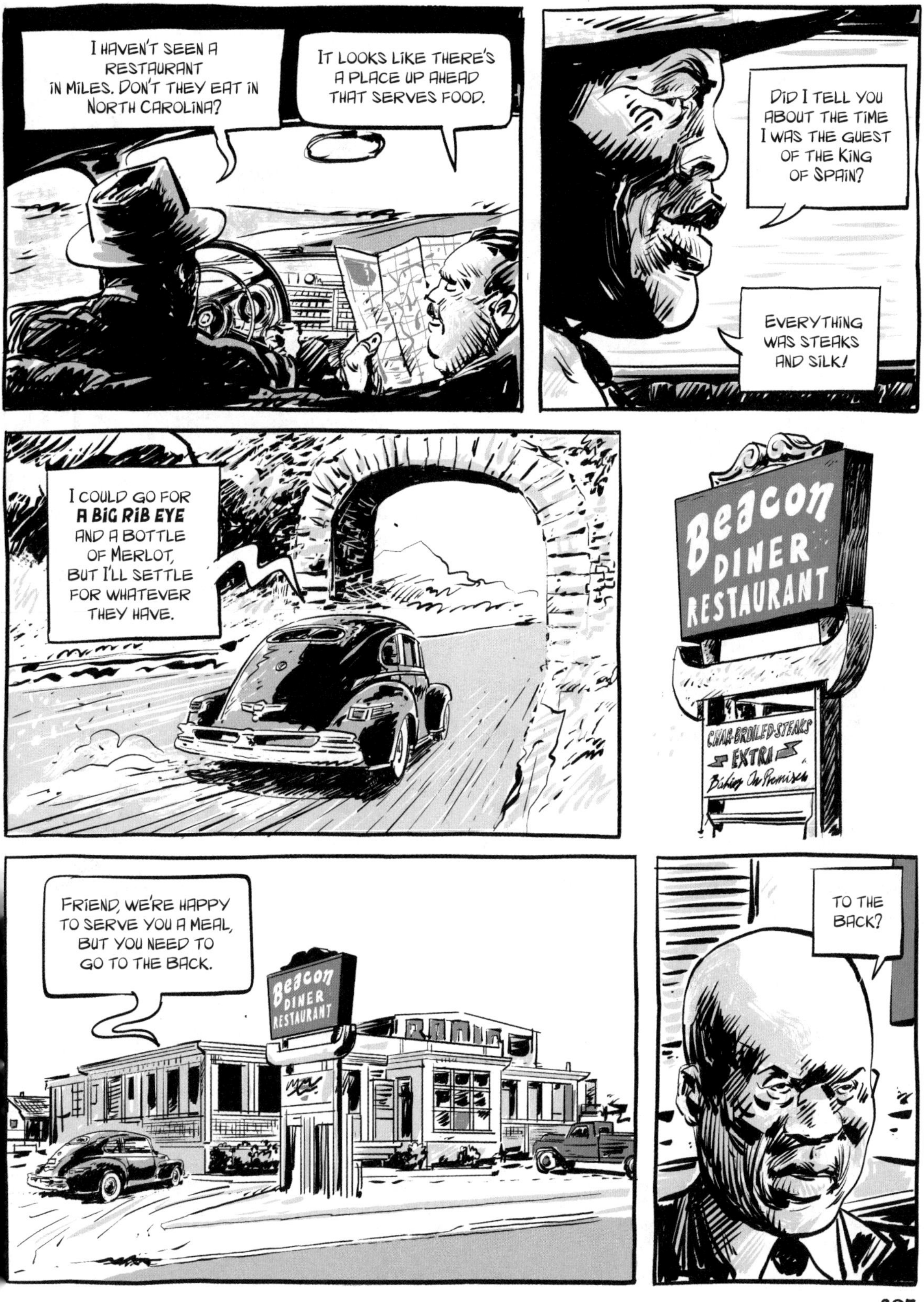
I HAVEN'T SEEN A RESTAURANT IN MILES. DON'T THEY EAT IN NORTH CAROLINA?
IT LOOKS LIKE THERE'S A PLACE UP AHEAD THAT SERVES FOOD.
DID I TELL YOU ABOUT THE TIME I WAS THE GUEST OF THE KING OF SPAIN?
EVERYTHING WAS STEAKS AND SILK!
I COULD GO FOR **A BIG RIB EYE** AND A BOTTLE OF MERLOT, BUT I'LL SETTLE FOR WHATEVER THEY HAVE.
Beacon
DINER
RESTAURANT
CHAR-BROILED STEAKS
EXTRA
Baking On Premises
FRIEND, WE'RE HAPPY TO SERVE YOU A MEAL, BUT YOU NEED TO GO TO THE BACK.
Beacon
DINER
RESTAURANT
TO THE BACK?

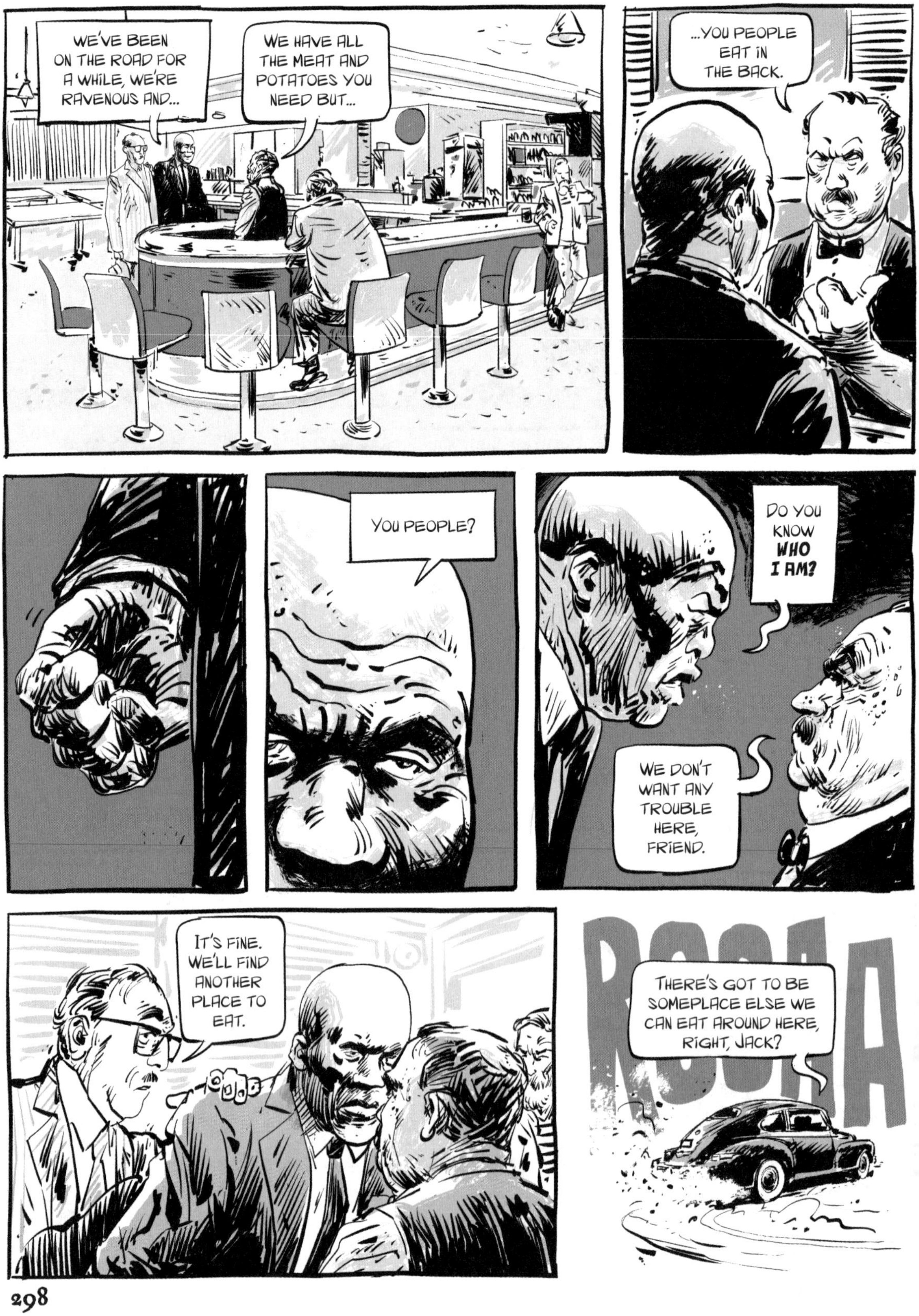
WE'VE BEEN ON THE ROAD FOR A WHILE, WE'RE RAVENOUS AND...
WE HAVE ALL THE MEAT AND POTATOES YOU NEED BUT...
...YOU PEOPLE EAT IN THE BACK.
YOU PEOPLE?
DO YOU KNOW **WHO I AM?**
WE DON'T WANT ANY TROUBLE HERE, FRIEND.
IT'S FINE. WE'LL FIND ANOTHER PLACE TO EAT.
THERE'S GOT TO BE SOMEPLACE ELSE WE CAN EAT AROUND HERE, RIGHT, JACK?

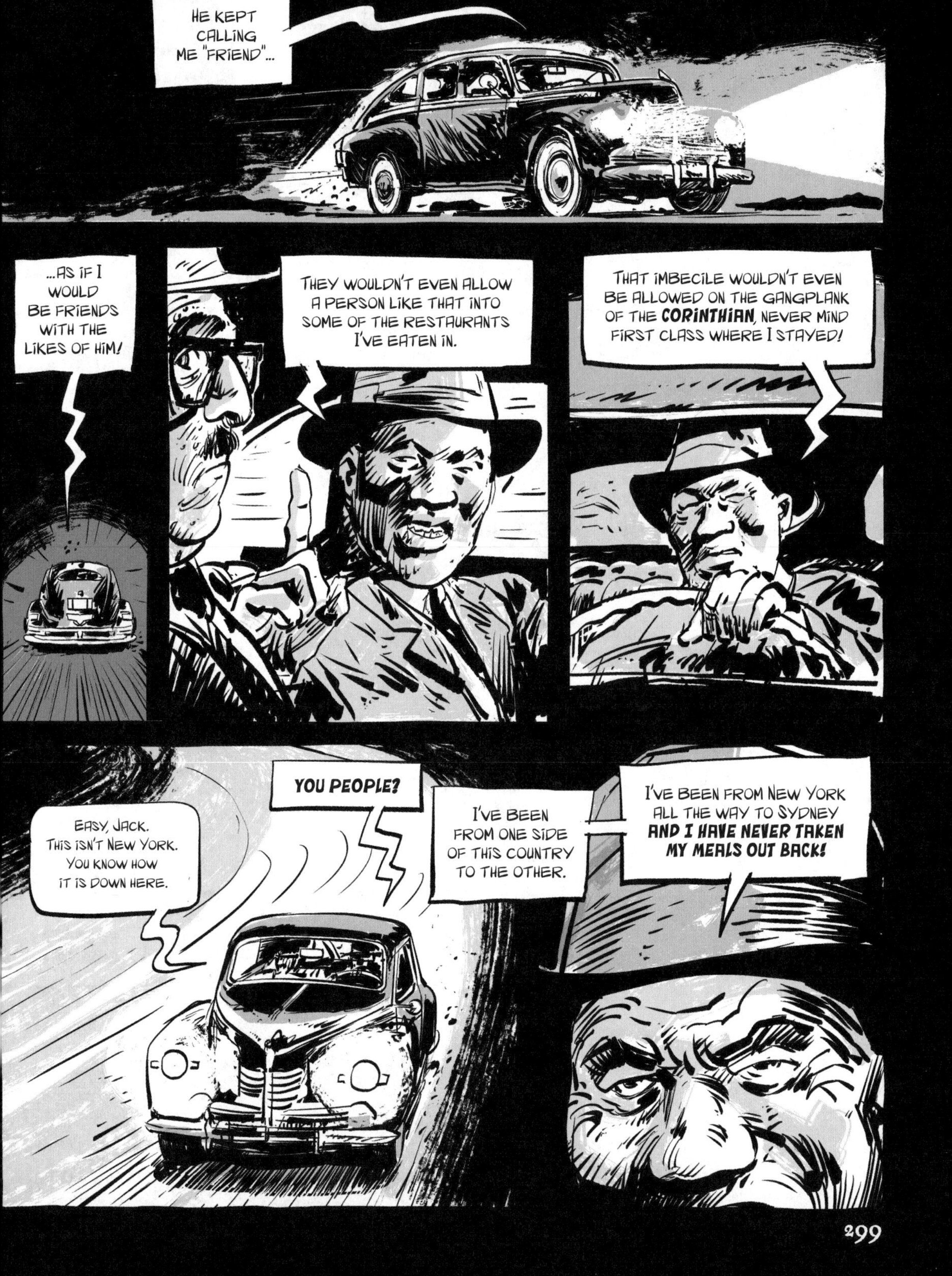
HE KEPT CALLING ME "FRIEND"...
...AS IF I WOULD BE FRIENDS WITH THE LIKES OF HIM!
THEY WOULDN'T EVEN ALLOW A PERSON LIKE THAT INTO SOME OF THE RESTAURANTS I'VE EATEN IN.
THAT IMBECILE WOULDN'T EVEN BE ALLOWED ON THE GANGPLANK OF THE **CORINTHIAN**, NEVER MIND FIRST CLASS WHERE I STAYED!
EASY, JACK. THIS ISN'T NEW YORK. YOU KNOW HOW IT IS DOWN HERE.
YOU PEOPLE?
I'VE BEEN FROM ONE SIDE OF THIS COUNTRY TO THE OTHER.
I'VE BEEN FROM NEW YORK ALL THE WAY TO SYDNEY **AND I HAVE NEVER TAKEN MY MEALS OUT BACK!**

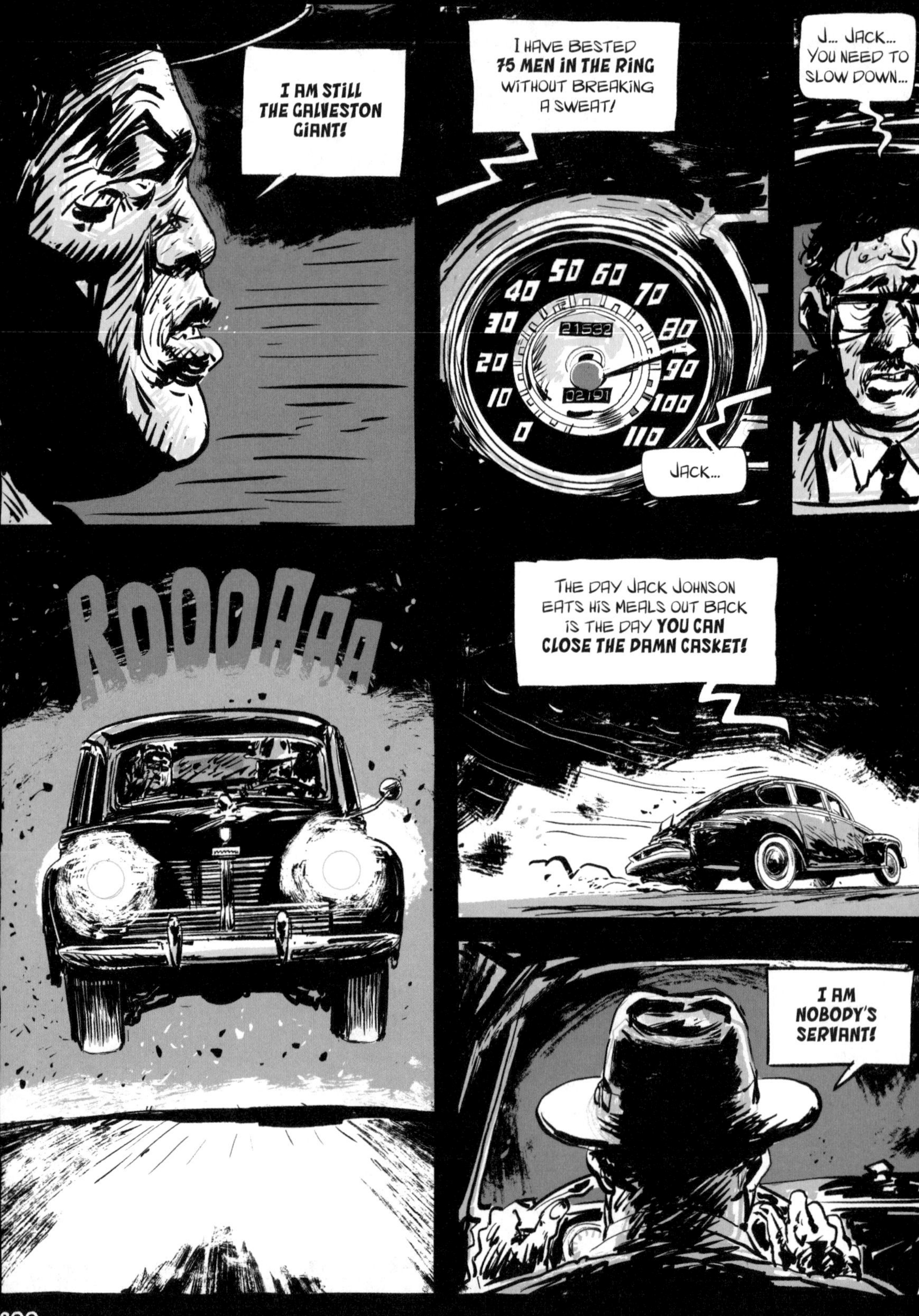
I AM STILL THE GALVESTON GIANT!
I HAVE BESTED 75 MEN IN THE RING WITHOUT BREAKING A SWEAT!
JACK...
J... JACK... YOU NEED TO SLOW DOWN...
ROOOAAA
THE DAY JACK JOHNSON EATS HIS MEALS OUT BACK IS THE DAY YOU CAN CLOSE THE DAMN CASKET!
I AM NOBODY'S SERVANT!

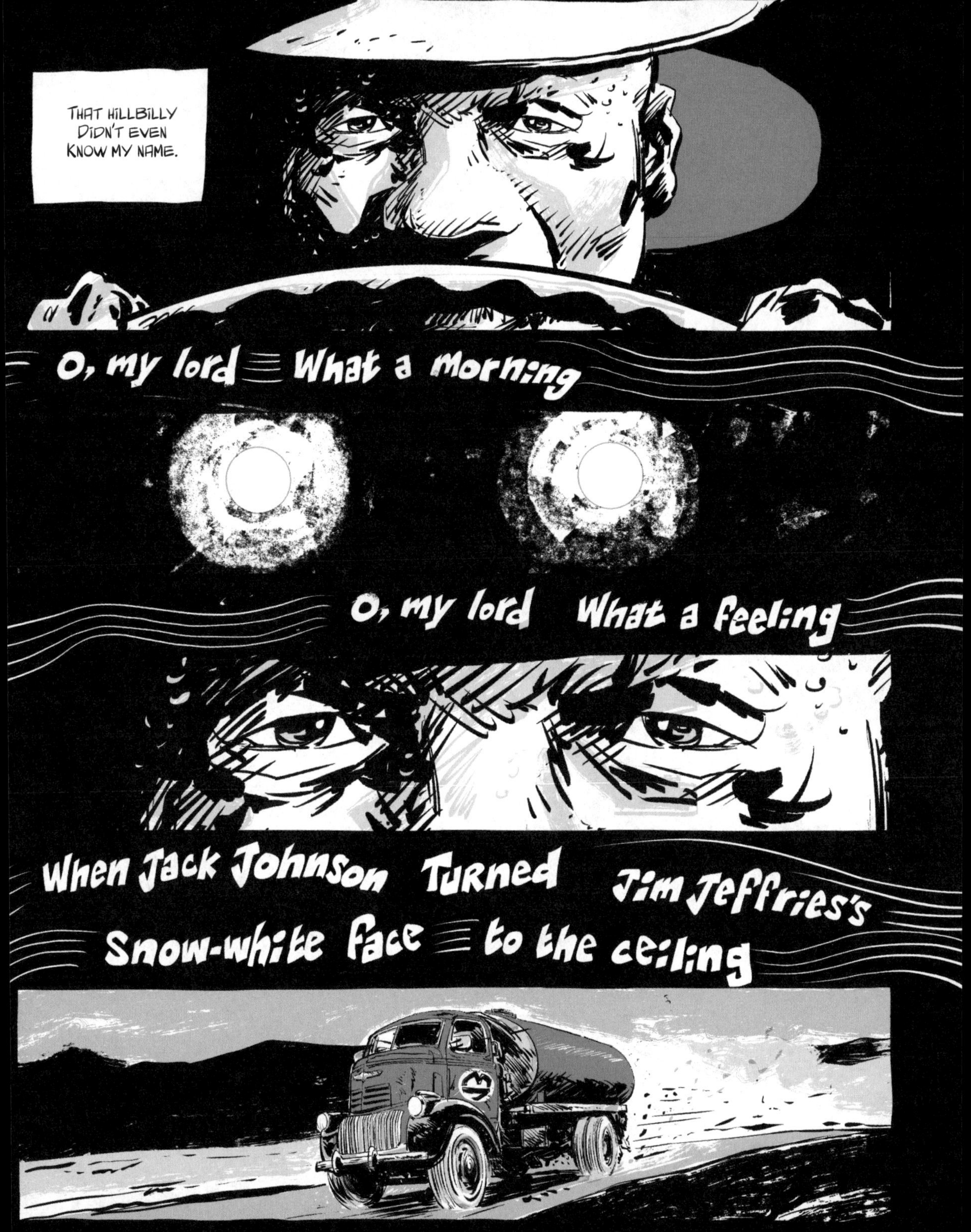
THAT HILLBILLY DIDN'T EVEN KNOW MY NAME.
O, my lord What a morning
O, my lord What a feeling
When Jack Johnson Turned Jim Jeffries's
Snow-white face to the ceiling

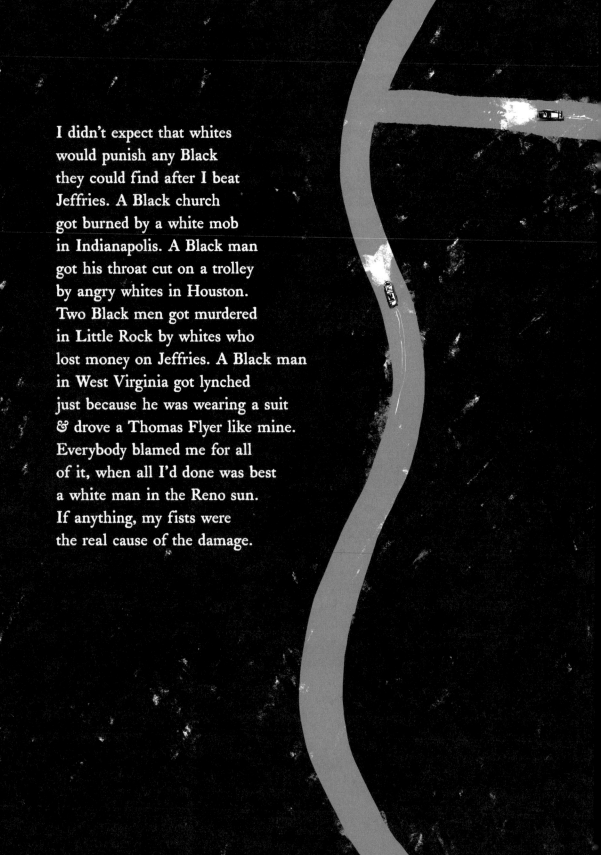

I didn't expect that whites
would punish any Black
they could find after I beat
Jeffries. A Black church
got burned by a white mob
in Indianapolis. A Black man
got his throat cut on a trolley
by angry whites in Houston.
Two Black men got murdered
in Little Rock by whites who
lost money on Jeffries. A Black man
in West Virginia got lynched
just because he was wearing a suit
& drove a Thomas Flyer like mine.
Everybody blamed me for all
of it, when all I'd done was best
a white man in the Reno sun.
If anything, my fists were
the real cause of the damage.

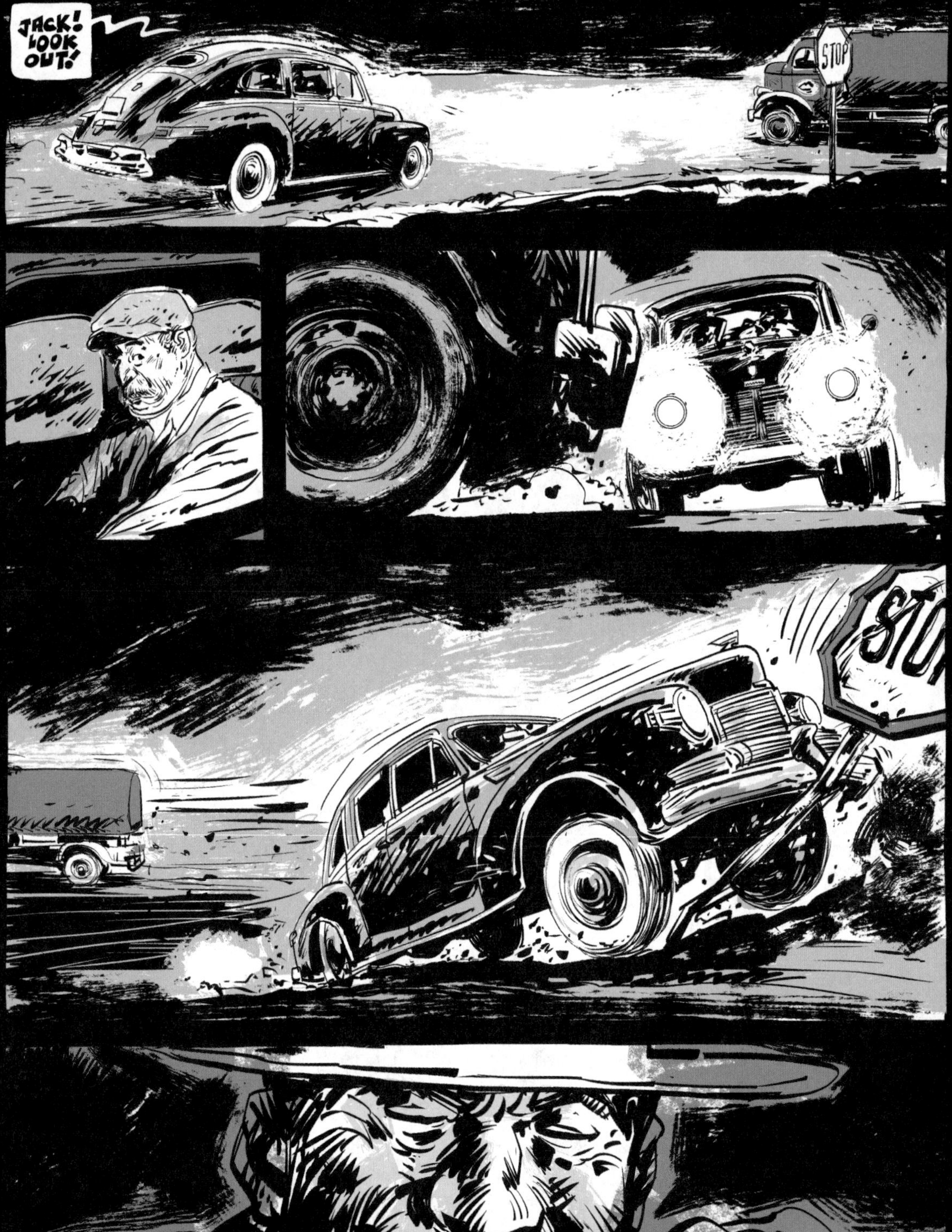
JACK! LOOK OUT!
STOP
STOP

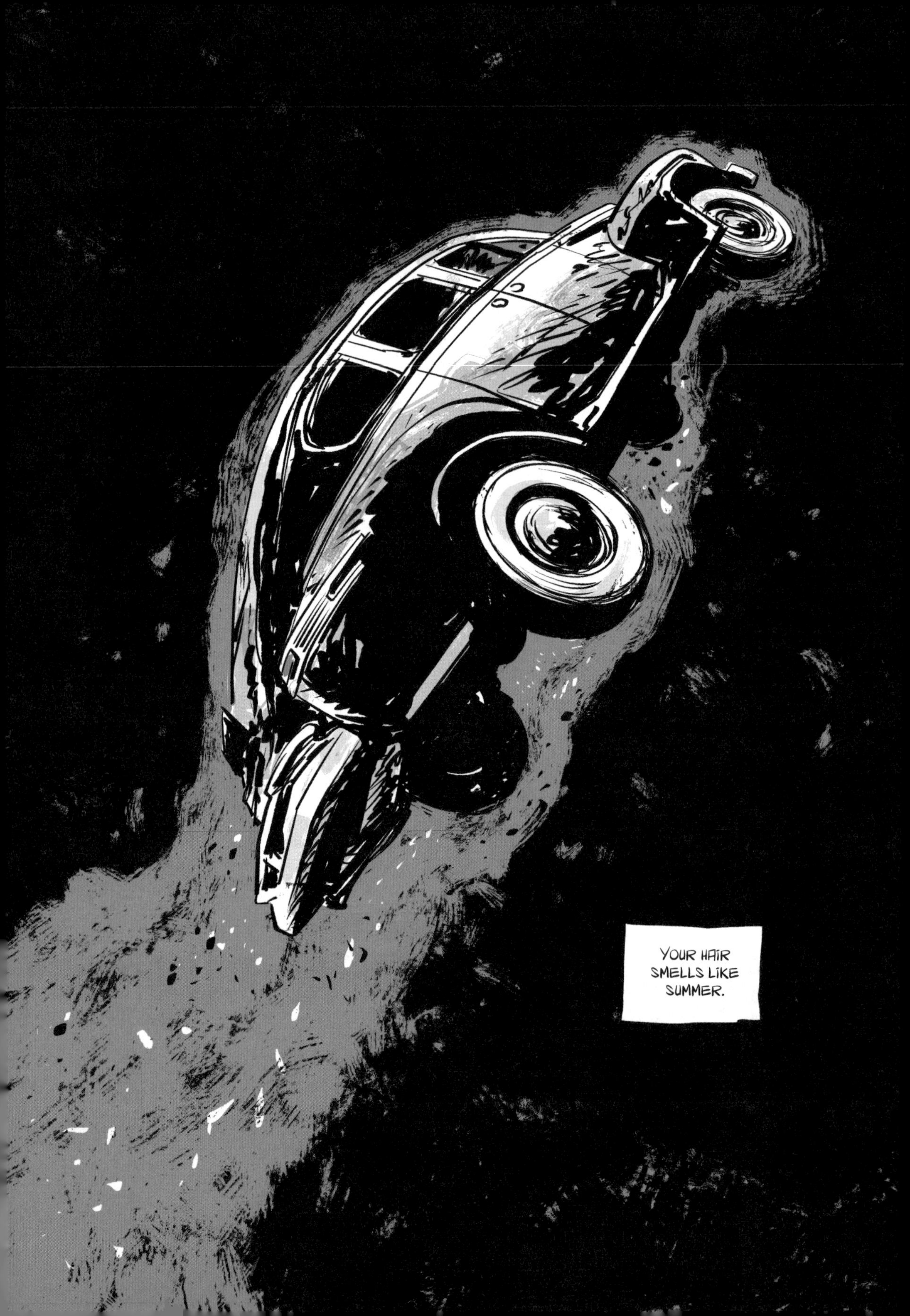
YOUR HAIR SMELLS LIKE SUMMER.

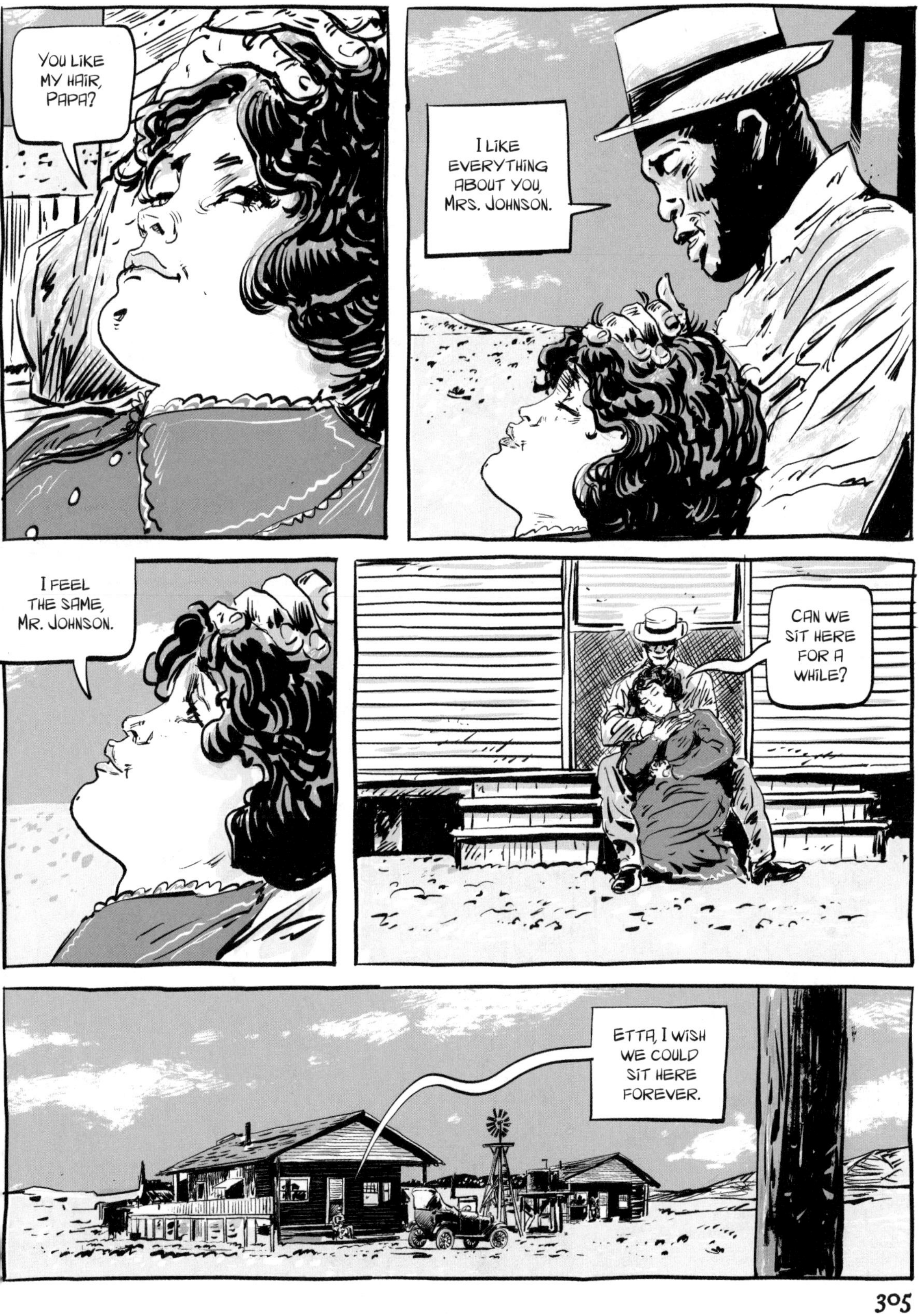
YOU LIKE MY HAIR, PAPA?
I LIKE EVERYTHING ABOUT YOU, MRS. JOHNSON.
I FEEL THE SAME, MR. JOHNSON.
CAN WE SIT HERE FOR A WHILE?
ETTA, I WISH WE COULD SIT HERE FOREVER.

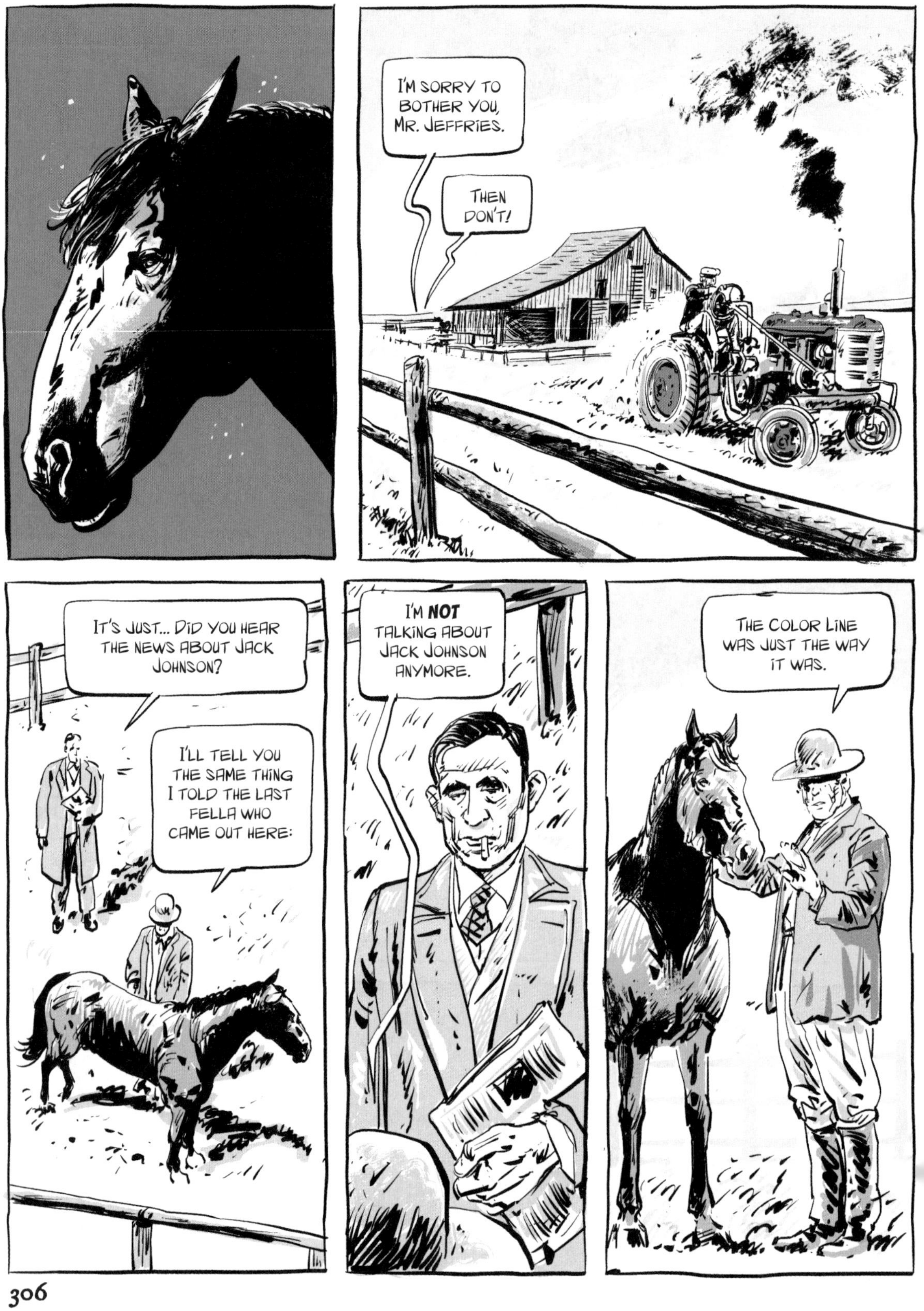

I'M SORRY TO BOTHER YOU, MR. JEFFRIES.
THEN DON'T!
IT'S JUST... DID YOU HEAR THE NEWS ABOUT JACK JOHNSON?
I'LL TELL YOU THE SAME THING I TOLD THE LAST FELLA WHO CAME OUT HERE:
I'M **NOT** TALKING ABOUT JACK JOHNSON ANYMORE.
THE COLOR LINE WAS JUST THE WAY IT WAS.

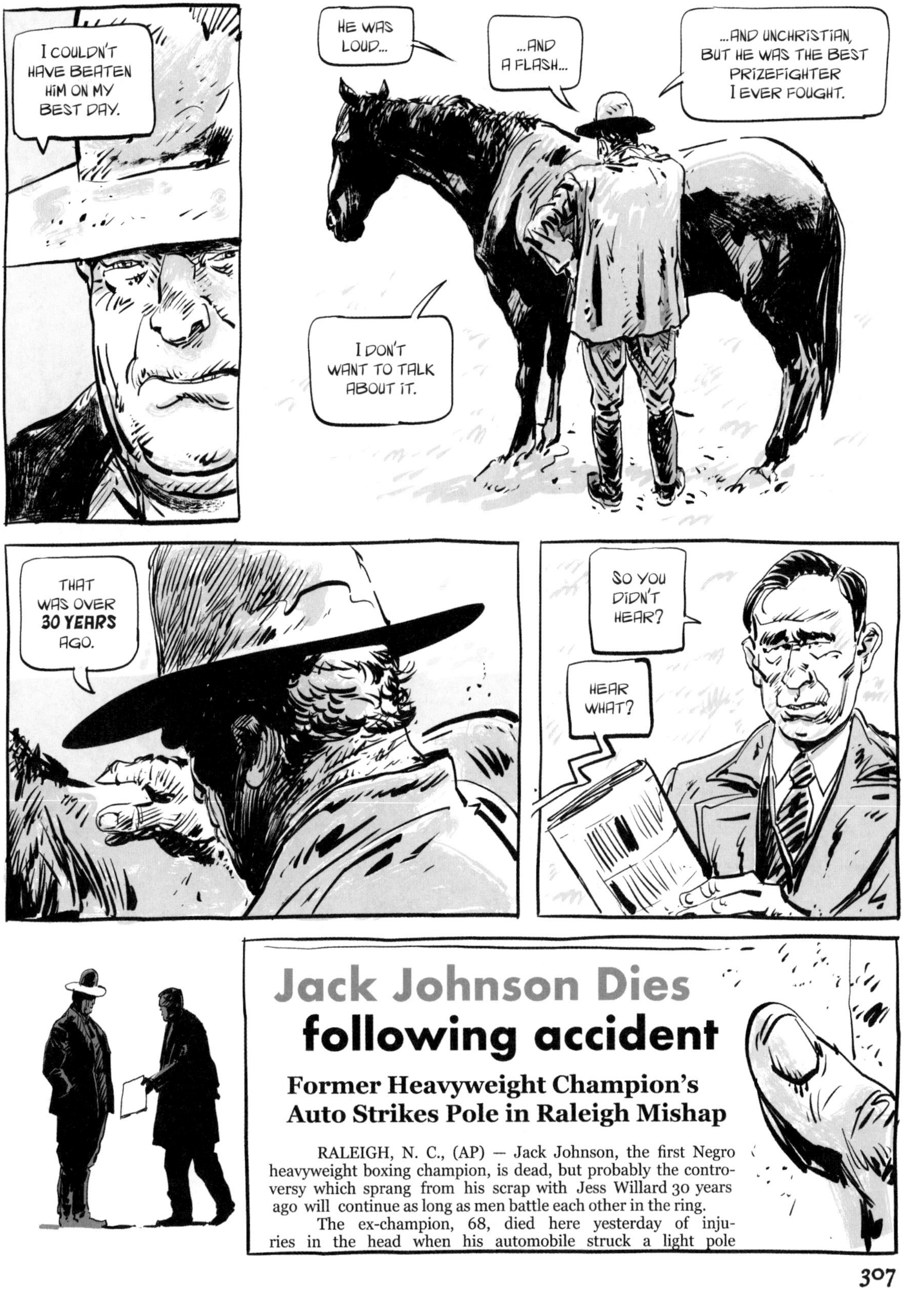

I COULDN'T HAVE BEATEN HIM ON MY BEST DAY.
HE WAS LOUD...
...AND A FLASH...
...AND UNCHRISTIAN, BUT HE WAS THE BEST PRIZEFIGHTER I EVER FOUGHT.
I DON'T WANT TO TALK ABOUT IT.
THAT WAS OVER 30 YEARS AGO.
SO YOU DIDN'T HEAR?
HEAR WHAT?
Jack Johnson Dies following accident
Former Heavyweight Champion's Auto Strikes Pole in Raleigh Mishap
RALEIGH, N. C., (AP) — Jack Johnson, the first Negro heavyweight boxing champion, is dead, but probably the controversy which sprang from his scrap with Jess Willard 30 years ago will continue as long as men battle each other in the ring.
The ex-champion, 68, died here yesterday of injuries in the head when his automobile struck a light pole

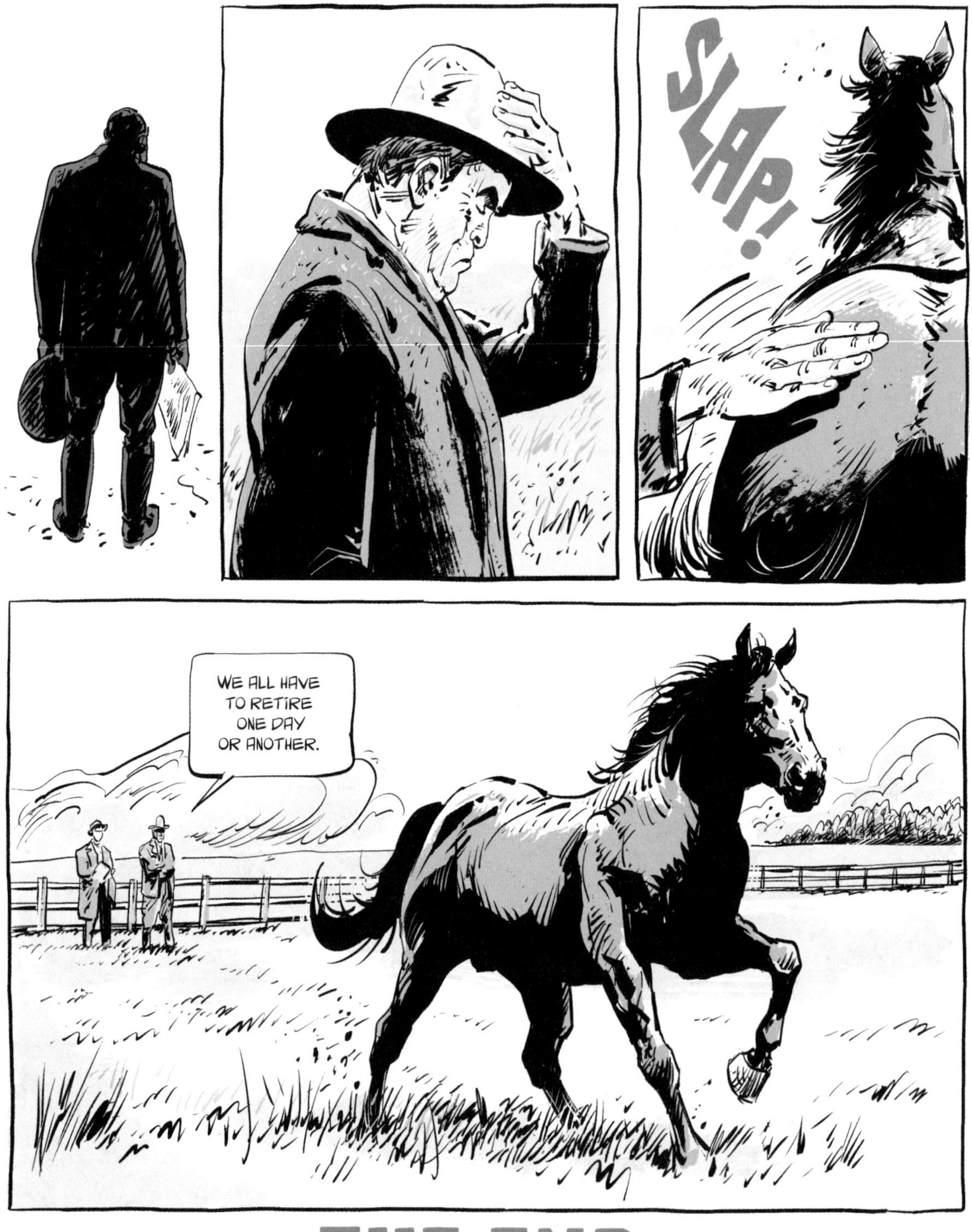
SLAP!
WE ALL HAVE TO RETIRE ONE DAY OR ANOTHER.

THE END

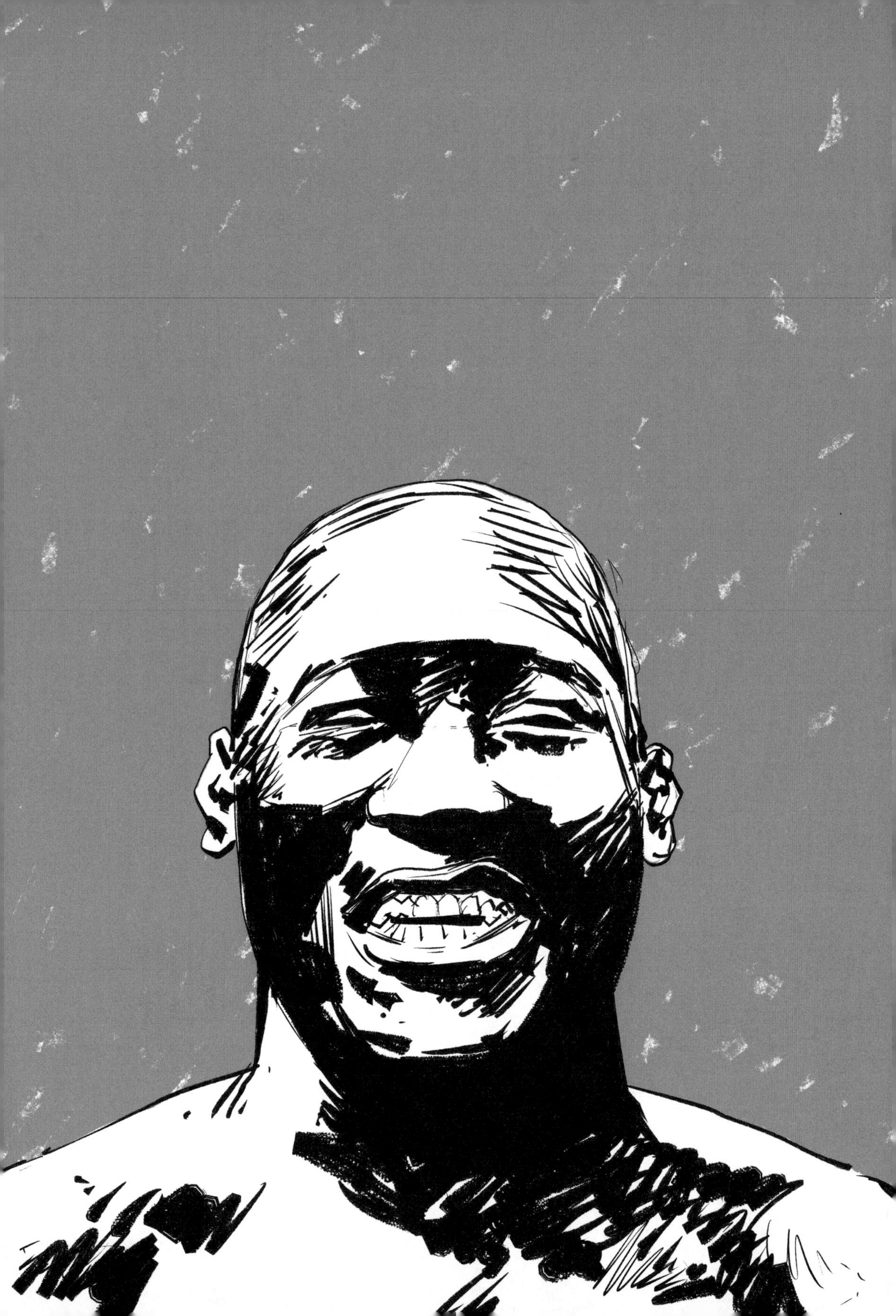

ACKNOWLEDGMENTS

The theory says that the comic artist's work is that of a graphic narrator. Graphic narrative uses frames and gutters to implement the pacing and rhythm of reading; it offers an intricately layered narrative language—the language of comics—that comprises the verbal, the visual, and the way these two representational modes interact on a page.

With *Last On His Feet*, I was compelled more than any time before to put the theory to the test, or rather, to always bear in mind its more critical assertions. I love words, and working with words—in this case, the striking poetics of Adrian Matejka—and the formidable momentum they can inject into art and page design. From the inception of the project, we were both completely conscious that the drawings should never be a simple set of illustrations but an integral part of the writing process, another thread that interacts with many others to form the very nature of this book. That work in unison and the intellectual collusion that arose from it was a great experience.

Telling the story of Jack Arthur Johnson in this form was no easy task, but it was a very special moment in my career, if only to know that such an individual stood out in the challenging and shifting times of the early twentieth century. It was a privilege and a rare opportunity.

For that, I would like to thank my agent, Holly McGhee, and Gina Iaquinta, Robert Weil, and the staff at Liveright for their trust and support.

—Youssef Daoudi

When I started this project about Jack Johnson in 2005, I couldn't have imagined that I would spend the next sixteen years researching, writing, researching more, and writing more about one of the first great boxing champions. I couldn't have imagined that there would be so much interest in Mr. Johnson's story, or that I would have the opportunity to share his tales in bookstores, boxing gyms, bars, and universities. I even got to read at the school Mr. Johnson attended as a child, which is now the Old Central Cultural Center in Galveston, complete with a statue and park in honor of the Galveston Giant.

What I did know very early in the process is that his story is too substantial for a single collection of poetry. I also knew that I didn't want to write two books of poetry, because for me, surprise is the main engine for poetics. And while I was startled, enlightened, frustrated, and overwhelmed during the eight-year process of writing *The Big Smoke*, I couldn't imagine an Emily Dickinson slant that might re-create those emotions for another traditional book of poems.

That's when the editor of *The Big Smoke*, Paul Slovak, and I came up with the idea of writing a graphic novel—something I'd never considered and had no idea how to do. I have been an avid reader and collector of comics and graphics since the 1970s, but the transition from reader to writer can be as rough as early morning roadwork. This is especially true for writing a graphic novel, with its particular balance of cinematography, wonder, and narrative—as well as dialogue, which is mostly absent from the world of poetry.

This is where my friend and fellow poet Holly McGhee came in. She helped me craft my idea for Jack's second act into a readable narrative and taught me how to avoid using exclamation points in dialogue like the old Marvel comics I read as a child. She was also the catalyst for connecting me with the transcendent artist of this book, Youssef Daoudi. Youssef collaborated with me to build out a narrative that wouldn't have been possible without his acumen and vision.

There are twenty primary and secondary resources included in this book's bibliography, and all are fascinating in different ways. I want to highlight Geoffrey C. Ward's excellent biography *Unforgivable Blackness* as well as the Ken Burns documentary of the same name as sources that were especially significant for the writing process. Also instrumental was Jack Johnson's unfinished, unpublished autobiography that was included in his Inmate Case File at Leavenworth Penitentiary. Johnson's other autobiographies, like *In the Ring and Out* and *My Life and Battles*, were ghostwritten or translated, so it is beautiful to read the man's actual words, even if they are written on prison stationery.

I want to express my gratitude to Gina Iaquinta, Robert Weil, and the staff at Liveright for believing in this book. Thanks, too, to Vaughan Ashlie Fielder, Nicholas Galanin, Walton Muyumba, Kevin Neireiter, Howard Rambsy II, and Dario Robleto for their insights. Gratitude to my wife, Kara, and the entire Carpenter/Gustin/Matejka family for supporting me during all the years I worked on this graphic novel. So many things happened on the page and in the world during that time, not the least of which was Jack Johnson's long overdue pardon in 2018 for the Mann Act offenses he didn't commit.

Lastly, my eternal thanks to Jack Johnson, Etta Duryea, Jim Jeffries, and the other humans in this book for trusting me with their stories. *Last On His Feet* might be a graphic novel, but many of the lives depicted in it were more real and difficult than I could ever find the words for.

—Adrian Matejka

TIMELINE OF ACTUAL EVENTS

January 1, 1863: Abraham Lincoln enacts Emancipation Proclamation, freeing all enslaved people in the Confederacy.

April 9, 1865: End of the Civil War.

March 31, 1878: John Arthur Johnson born in Galveston, Texas.

May 18, 1896: U.S. Supreme Court decides *Plessy v. Ferguson*, which legalizes "separate but equal" discrimination.

1899: Johnson participates in his first battle royal in Springfield, Illinois.

1899: Johnson lands his first professional fight in Chicago, against "Klondike" (John W. Haynes), a Black heavyweight, and loses.

June 9, 1899: James J. Jeffries becomes heavyweight champion of the world by defeating Bob Fitzsimmons.

September 8, 1900: The Great Storm hits Galveston, Texas, killing more than 6,000 people.

1901: Joe Choynski knocks Johnson out in the third round in Galveston. Both boxers are arrested because boxing is illegal, and Choynski spends their jail time teaching Johnson how to box. Choynski later serves as Jim Jeffries's trainer for the "Battle of the Century."

1903: Johnson beats "Denver" Ed Martin to become "Negro heavyweight champion."

December 17, 1903: Orville and Wilbur Wright pilot the *Wright Flyer* in first controlled, sustained flight.

1905: Jeffries retires, citing the lack of worthy opponents.

1908: Introduction of the Model T Ford.

December 26, 1908: Johnson defeats Tommy Burns in Sydney, Australia, to become the first Black heavyweight champion of the world.

1909: Johnson meets Belle Schreiber at Chicago's most exclusive brothel, the Everleigh Club.

October 1909: Johnson meets Etta Duryea at the Vanderbilt Cup car race on Long Island.

October 16, 1909: In Colma, California, Johnson defeats Stanley Ketchel in twelve rounds.

July 4, 1910: Jack Johnson defeats Jim Jeffries in the "Battle of the Century" in front of a crowd of 20,000 people in Reno, Nevada.

June 25, 1910: President William Howard Taft signs the Mann Act.

October 25, 1910: Johnson loses his only professional automobile race against champion automobilist Barney Oldfield in Brooklyn, New York.

November 20, 1910: Start of the Mexican Revolution.

January 18, 1911: Johnson and Etta Duryea marry in Pittsburgh.

1912: Johnson opens the Café de Champion, a mixed-race nightclub in Chicago.

April 15, 1912: The RMS *Titanic* sinks.

September 11, 1912: Etta Duryea Johnson commits suicide in the Café de Champion.

October 17, 1912: Johnson is arrested and charged with violating the Mann Act related to his white girlfriend, Lucille Cameron. Cameron refuses to cooperate, but the Department of Justice still pursues the charges.

December 4, 1912: Johnson marries Lucille Cameron.

May 17, 1913: Johnson's Mann Act trial begins in Chicago, with Judge George Albert Carpenter presiding. An all-white jury finds Johnson guilty in less than two hours.

June 4, 1913: Johnson is sentenced to one year and one day in federal prison. He skips bail and heads to Canada with Cameron.

1914: Johnson and Cameron travel to England, France, Spain, and finally Russia looking for opportunities to fight. Johnson is banned from entering some European countries including Belgium.

July 28, 1914: World War 1 begins

April 5, 1915: In Havana, Cuba, Jess Willard knocks out Johnson in the twenty-sixth round to become the new heavyweight champion.

1916: Johnson lives in Spain fighting exhibitions, including one against the poet Arthur Cravan. He also trains to be a matador.

March 17, 1918: Tiny Johnson dies in Chicago. Johnson hadn't seen his mother in almost five years.

June 28, 1919: The Treaty of Versailles is signed, ending World War I.

1919: Johnson and Cameron move to Mexico City and open Jack Johnson Land Company, catering to "the Colored People of the United States" who want to own land.

July 20, 1920: Broke and almost destitute, Johnson surrenders to U.S. authorities near the U.S.-Mexico border to begin serving his prison sentence.

July 9, 1921: Johnson is released from prison.

March 1924: Johnson and Cameron divorce.

June 9, 1946: Jack Johnson is killed in an automobile accident outside Raleigh, North Carolina.

BIBLIOGRAPHY

Abbott, Karen. *Sin in the Second City*. New York: Random House, 2007.

Bederman, Gail. *Manliness & Civilization: A Cultural History of Gender and Race in the United States, 1880–1917*. Chicago: University of Chicago Press, 1995.

Boxers: Jack Johnson. Dir. Marshall Cavendish. Marshall Cavendish Publishing, 1997. VHS.

Campbell, Eddie. *The Goat Getters: Jack Johnson, the Fight of the Century, and How a Bunch of Raucous Cartoonists Reinvented Comics*. San Diego, CA: IDW Publishing, 2018.

Farr, Finis. *Black Champion: The Life and Times of Jack Johnson*. New York: Charles Scribner's Sons, 1964.

Gilmore, Al-Tony. *Bad Nigger! The National Impact of Jack Johnson*. Port Washington, NY: National University Publications, 1975.

Greenwood, Robert. *The Prize Fight of the Century*. Reno, NV: Jack Bacon & Company, 2004.

Hietala, Thomas. *The Fight of the Century: Jack Johnson, Joe Louis, and the Struggle for Racial Equality*. Aramonk, NY: M. E. Sharpe, 2002.

Inmate Case Files; United States Penitentiary—Leavenworth: Records of the Federal Bureau of Prisons, Record Group 129 National Archives and Record Administration—Central Plains Region (Kansas City)

Johnson, Jack. *In the Ring and Out*. New York: Citadel Press, 1992.

Johnson, Jack. *Jack Johnson Is a Dandy*. New York: Chelsea House Publishers, 1968.

Johnson, Jack. *My Life and Battles*. Westport, CT: Praeger Publishers, 2007.

Kent, Graeme. *The Great White Hopes: The Quest to Defeat Jack Johnson*. Gloucestershire, UK: Sutton Publishing, 2005.

Levine, William W. *Black Culture and Black Consciousness: Afro-American Folk Thought from Slavery to Freedom*. New York: Oxford University Press, 1978.

Liebling, A. J. *The Sweet Science*. New York: North Point Press, 2004.

Roberts, Randy. *Papa Jack: Jack Johnson and the Era of White Hopes*. New York: Free Press, 1983.

Rozen, Wayne A. *America on the Ropes: A Pictorial History of the Johnson-Jeffries Fight*. Binghamton, NY: Casey Press, 2005.

Unforgivable Blackness: The Rise and Fall of Jack Johnson. Dir. Ken Burns. Florentine Films, 2004. DVD.

U.S. v. Johnson, General Records of the Department of Justice, File Number 16421, Record Group 60.

Ward, Geoffrey C. *Unforgivable Blackness: The Rise and Fall of Jack Johnson*. New York: Alfred A. Knopf, 2004.

© Frédéric Mangé

Youssef Daoudi is a comic artist and writer living in France. Before committing to writing and drawing graphic novels, he was an art director, producer, and director for multinational advertising firms for fifteen years. His books and short stories explore a great variety of styles and topics. His first English-language graphic, *Monk! Thelonious, Pannonica, and the Friendship Behind a Musical Revolution*, was an Eisner Award nominee.

Kara Matejka

Adrian Matejka is the author of six books, most recently a mixed media collection inspired by Funkadelic, *Standing on the Verge & Maggot Brain*, and a collection of poems, *Somebody Else Sold the World*, which was a finalist for the 2022 UNT Rilke Prize. His collection *The Big Smoke* was awarded the Anisfield-Wolf Book Award and was a finalist for the National Book Award and Pulitzer Prize in poetry. He served as Poet Laureate of the State of Indiana in 2018–19 and is the editor of *Poetry* magazine.